THE
BILL JAMES
BASEBALL
ABSTRACT
1984

THE BILL JAMES BASEBALL ABSTRACT 1984

Bill James

Ballantine Books • New York

Library of Congress Catalog Card Number: 83-91165
ISBN 0-345-31155-8

Manufactured in the United States of America

First Edition: April 1984

Book design by Gene Siegel

10 9 8 7 6 5 4

This book
is dedicated to
three men
that I don't know—
Bob Hentzen,
Jim Murray,
and
Leonard Koppett.

Contents

Acknowledgments

Sportswriters, not athletes, were the heroes of my adolescence. I have a feeling that Jim Murray, who is not young now and whose health comes and goes, probably hates my work. It doesn't matter if he does. Murray, a columnist for the L.A. *Times*, whose work is often shared with other papers around the country, was an important figure in my childhood, a man who wrote (and still does) with wit and intelligence and a great deal of fire. His work was carried three times a week in the *Topeka Journal*, and from reading it regularly I came to think it must be wonderful to be able to attack a subject with such weapons as words, images, humor and bald truth. I have taken a very different road as a sportswriter, but I may have learned just a little bit about how to use those weapons, and for giving me the opportunity to learn that, I want to credit Mr. Murray, and to bestow upon him such thanks as he will accept.

The road I chose, Leonard Koppett pointed to; for that he too is remembered, appreciated and thanked. Bob Hentzen is the editor of the sports pages of the *Topeka Capitol-Journal*, the constant reading of which left me with a strong faith that it was possible to do an ordinary thing well if you chose to do so. This book is dedicated to these three wonderful writers, for the part that they played in showing me what I wanted to do and teaching me how to do it.

Apart from them, an exponential number of people become thankable in the process of putting each year's edition together. My wife Susie (McCarthy) abandons her own work to help me on this project whenever she is asked to do so; for this as well as being the world's best wife she remains #1 on the acknowledgement list. Jim Baker now devotes more or less every waking hour to ensuring the continued growth and development of the book; that is more than I could or would ask. Randy Lakeman researches and figures stats (thanks, Randy). Peter Gethers edits, Roger Friedman arranges publicity and takes care of me when I am travelling around, and the Ballantine and Warner sales reps sell the book. When I was doing all those things myself it would sell about 2,000 copies and now it sells a whole bunch, so these people must be doing alright. Dan Okrent, Pete Palmer, and Liz Darhansoff have provided guidance, research, organization, contracts, contacts, encouragement, support, general assistance and diet soft drinks, respectively. Steven Copley, Paul Izzo, Perry Sailor, Alan and Randy Hendricks, Tom Reich, Craig Wright, Chuck Waseleski, Dick Krinsley, Audrey Simon; I don't know why, but your names all come when the word "Thanks" is mentioned. Larry Schwartz served as copy-editor (and when you do that for me, "servitude" is too kind a description) and somebody did a hell of a job on the cover design. Although they may not have played a direct role in the book, I would like to publicly thank Mike Lenehan, John Leon, Bob Costas, Chris Ketzel, Mike Myers, Vic Ziegal, George Will, Pete Axthelm, Barry Rubinowitz and Tom Evans for being super people and making this a better world for Bill James. I mention with pleasure the quiet people—D, T, I, LC, TB, B, C, the S and LF and SVC.

And most of all, I acknowledge an unending and unmeasurable debt to those who read.

INTRODUCTION

WELCOME

Has it been a year already? It's good to see you; lookin' good. Had a pretty good season, didn't we? A season most distinguished by the emergence of at least three players as stars of indeterminate but considerable magnitude. Looking forward to another one.

I've had a good year, too; I hope the book bears the marks of it. Several things are different this year than they have been in the past. I've hired an assistant, Jim Baker; you'll be seeing his name and initials throughout the book. I bought a small home computer; it can't write and it can't think, but it has its uses. Got a dog, too. A collie.

We'll have some new information in Section II, data on who hit what on turf and on natural grass. All of the breakdowns have been expanded to give you more information on walks, strike-outs and caught stealing. Of the three runs created formulas that were in use a year ago, two have been discarded and two new ones put in their place; this is explained in the major article in Section I. We also present with each team this year information on Victory-Important RBI.

These are explained in Section I (Introduction), detailed in Section II (Data and Team Comments) and commented upon in Section III (Player Ratings and Comments).

The method by which the players are rated has also been re-evaluated and tuned up in light of new knowledge that has been developed. The gray boxes discussing ballparks and talent analysis are gone; with each American League team this year we discuss the characteristics of the manager.

Section IV, which consists of general essays about the game, is longer and more diverse than it's ever been. *PROJECT SCORESHEET*, which is one of the biggest things in my life right now (all of the mail leaving my house is stamped "Support Project Scoresheet"), is alluded to throughout the book and finally explained in Section IV.

It's been a busy year. Who's your friend, there? Nice to meet you. I'm sort of a baseball agnostic; I make it a point never to believe anything just because it is widely known to be so. Let's go to the ballgame.

INSIDE-OUT PERSPECTIVE

Inside stuff is very big in sportswriting today. TV shows, newspaper columns and sometimes whole books are dubbed "Inside Baseball" and "Inside Football"; magazines run features called "Inside Pitch" and "Inside Corner" and promote "Inside Scouting Reports." A book appears called "High Inside," and months later, another follows called "High *and* Inside." The Society for American Baseball Research, an aggregation of dedicated outsiders outside of whom one can scarcely get, compiles a collection of research pieces into a book; this is called, of course, "Insiders Baseball."

Inside looks, inside glimpses, inside locker rooms and inside blimpses; within months we shall have seen the inside of everything that one can get inside of without a doctor's help, and now that I think about that I remember seeing a sample copy of a Las Vegas tout sheet that featured an "Inside Medical Report." In the collapse of the original "Inside Sports," perhaps the nickname shattered and the shards landed across the horizon.

What has really happened, of course, is that the walls between the public and the participants of sports are growing higher and higher and thicker and darker, and the media is developing a sense of desperation about the whole thing. It is easier to ape Steve Carlton's example in how to deal with a reporter than it is to effectively mimic his dedication to excellence, so every day more players become unapproachable; the sim-

ple expectation of being able to communicate with the inside is decaying.

Silence, though, is but the ultimate weapon, the last line of defense. The first line of defense is the cliché: How do you feel today Jim I'm optimistic I've always had good luck against Lefty Grove what did he throw you that you hit into the seats I think it was a breaking pitch that didn't break is this the biggest day of your life no this is just the first step we still have to win the series has Willie helped the team Willie has added a dimension to the team that we didn't have before and how about Frank Frank has adapted to his role well and hasn't complained at all about not being used more why did you fire Charlie I've the greatest respect for Charlie but sometimes a change just has to be made and we were just happy that Billy was available why did you sign this yoyo he's a winner and a gamer and you can throw away his batting average when the game is on the line.

Clichés are the soldiers of ignorance, and an army of sentries encircles the game, guarding every situation from which a glimmer of fresh truth might be allowed to escape. An occasional player—a George Hendrick here, an Amos Otis there—can never learn to command the cliché, thus is forced to keep silence, unless he chooses to see embarrassing revelations about himself splattered in ink. Players used to have public nicknames, wild things like Circus Solly and affectionate names like Sunny Jim and Unser Choe

(Our Joe) and media handles like the Commerce Comet and the Donora Greyhound. Now the big thing is to have *private* nicknames. The players invent them and use them and then the reporters make a game out of trying to overhear them and find out where they come from and reveal them to the public; once revealed, they evaporate, for their only purpose is to separate us from them, to designate in code the speaker and the one spoken to as true insiders.

This is *outside* baseball. This is a book about what baseball looks like if you step back from it and study it intensely and minutely, but from a distance.

You know the expression about not being able to see the forest for the trees? Let's use that. What are the differences between the way a forest looks when you are inside the forest and the way it looks from the outside?

The first thing is, the insider has a much better view of the details. He knows what the moss looks like, how high it grows around the base of an oak and how thickly it will cling to a sycamore. He knows the smells in the air and the tracks on the ground; he can guess the age of a redbud by peeling off a layer of bark. The outsider doesn't know any of that.

To a person who sees the image of anything as being only the sum of its details, to a person who can conceive of the whole of anything only by remembering this event and that event and piecing them together in a succession of images; such a person is likely to look at the *Baseball Abstract* and say, "What is this? This isn't BASEBALL. This guy James doesn't know anything about the chatter bouncing off of the dugout walls, nor about the glint in the eye of a superstar, nor about the routines and integral boredom of baseball's lifestyle, with which each player great and small must contend."

No sir, indeed I don't. There will be in this book no new tales about the things that happen on a team flight, no sudden revelations about the way that drugs and sex and money can ruin a championship team. I can't tell you what a locker room smells like, praise the Lord.

But perspective can be gained only when details are lost. A sense of the size of everything and the relationships between everything—this can never be put together from details. For the most essential fact of a forest is this: The forest itself is immensely larger than anything inside

of it. That is why, of course, you can't see the forest for the trees; each detail, in proportion to its size and your proximity to it, obscures a thousand or a million other details.

But is it not obvious that that is also the one most essential fact about a pennant race—the size of it, the enormity of it, the fact that no one, no matter how hard he tries, can take in an appreciable portion of the details of any one race? Consider a single moment in a pennant race, a July moment in a minor game against a meaningless team, but a moment in which a ball is hit very hard but caught by an outfielder who is standing in the right place, but before it is caught it must be hit, and before it is hit it must be thrown, and before it is thrown this pitch must be selected, and this pitcher must be selected, and this batter must be selected, and there are reasons why he was selected to throw and why he was selected to hit, and there are reasons why this pitch was selected and why it was thrown this way and why it was swung at and why it was hit and why, finally, the outfielder chanced to be in the right place, so that in this single moment, the simplest moment of a pennant race, there is a complexity that surpasses any understanding.

A game consists of dozens of batters and hundreds of pitches, and a season for one team consists of hundreds of games, and the league consists of a dozen or more teams. And how many details can you think about, to add up to a pennant race in your mind?

Is it not obvious, then, that it is only in stepping *away* from the pennant race that we can develop a vision of it? No one could remember at any one time a significant portion of the at-bats that Mike Fischlin has in a season—even Mike Fischlin's wife. How then, remember the season?

That is why statistics have such a place in baseball. Statistics look at games by the hundreds, and without the details. And that is why everyone who is a baseball fan—everyone, everyone, *everyone*—reads the statistics, studies the statistics and believes what he sees in the statistics. Without them, it is impossible to have any concept of the game, save for meaningless details floating in space.

Let's talk specifics. What, specifically, can you see from outside the forest that you could never see from inside of it?

For one thing, you can map the terrain. Let

us consider the players, the main component of the game, to be as the trees are to the forest. These are cognitive trees, able to see and think and answer questions if they take the notion. Suppose that there is a place in the forest where the ground is a little higher than it is in another place. Insiders, surely, would become aware of this as they trekked from one place to another.

But when it came time to measure the heights of the trees, how would they ever adjust for this? Can you tell the height of a tree by standing beside it and looking up? No, of course not; it's too big. And can you tell how good a hitter someone is by watching him hit? No, of course not; his season is too big. You could tell the biggest trees from the smallest; you could say in many cases that this tree was definitely bigger than that one. You could watch Dale Murphy and see quickly that he was a better hitter than Jerry Royster. But you couldn't guess the height of a tall tree when standing beside it within a 20-foot range, even if you stood and looked up at it for a year, and you couldn't guess the batting average of a hitter within a 20-point range by watching him hit, even if you watched him hit for a year.

To get an idea of how tall the tree is, you must stand back and look at it from a distance. And to get a clear notion of how good a hitter someone is, you must look at him from a distance—in the records.

So now you stand back from these trees, get out of the forest, and you see that one of them *appears* to be the tallest one. But then you remember: Isn't that where the high ground is? Maybe it only appears to be taller because the ground is higher over there.

Do you see where I'm heading? Let's talk Wade Boggs. Now he appears to be the best hitter in the league. But wait a minute—isn't that ground a little higher over there? Didn't Fred Lynn *appear* to be the best hitter in the league when he was playing over there? And when they traded him for Carney Lansford, didn't Lansford *appear* to be the best hitter in the league in 1981? How much higher is the ground? What *is* the tallest tree? Who *is* the best hitter?

Now if you are a dedicated student of inside baseball, what you do next is, you ask Wade Boggs about it. Or if you don't ask Wade Boggs, then you ask Rod Carew, or you ask Freddie Lynn, or you ask one of the other trees. And they naturally are going to give you different opinions on how much difference there is between the ground over here and the ground over there, depending to a large extent on where it is that they are positioned.

But if you are a student of *outside* baseball, you take a somewhat different approach. You say, "Damn, this doesn't seem to be that hard to figure out. The average height of a four-year-old walnut tree over here is this, and the average height of a four-year-old walnut over there is that. Do I really have to be a tree in order to figure this out?"

It is not only that the trees have a vested interest in the subject, and thus that they might lie to you or believe what it is in their best interests to believe. The trees really are not, when you think about it, in a very good position to evaluate the issue. I remember when Freddie Lynn went to California, he said he thought he'd hit better out there because he'd be close to his home. Now, he wasn't lying to us. He really thought that. The accommodation that he had made to Fenway Park was so subtle that it was subconscious. Remember this: All hitting takes place in the 4/10 of a second between the time the pitcher throws the ball and the time it reaches the plate. There isn't an awful lot of thinking going on there; it's mostly reflex.

As a tree grows its roots in one particular place in the forest, Freddie Lynn grew his roots in Fenway Park. And he learned something there. He learned that when they threw him a fastball on the outside part of the plate, he could slap it to leftfield and the result of that would often be something positive. Success. People would cheer for him.

To him, this has nothing to do with Fenway Park; it has to do with that pitch and that reflex. Only when you get him out of Fenway Park, you can throw him the same pitch and he can execute the same reflexive action (he has, by this time, no choice: he *must* execute that same reflexive action; he is conditioned to do it).

Only the result now is failure.

He was, you see, the ultimate insider of a forest, the tree itself. If he had looked at the question as an outsider, he could not possibly have been surprised by that failure. I mean, you take a guy who hits .380 in Fenway Park in some years and .260 on the road, you've got to figure that if you move him out of Fenway Park he's going to lose some points off the batting average.

If you take a 330-foot elm tree and you move it to where the ground is 40 foot lower, you've got to figure it's not going to stick up into the air quite as far—something more like 290 feet. But Freddie Lynn was surprised by it.

Another thing about forests is that they are awfully dark sometimes. There are shadows that reach halfway to the moon, there's a lot of underbrush, and there are many strange creatures who live in the forest, or who at the least are reported to live in the forest. Another important difference between inside and outside baseball is that baseball insiders see and report on lots of strange creatures there that we can't really see from out where we are. Clutch hitters are a big favorite.

Several people who have studied the issue from the outside have concluded—I hesitate to mention this—have concluded that clutch hitters don't exist. Dick Cramer was the first of those, and at the time I didn't think he had much of a point. What are they, then? We say, "The shadows of possums and squirrels, blown up to the size of a bear by poor light." They say, "You idiot; of course they exist. We see them all the time; see their tracks every day." I am much more modest than Cramer; I say merely that I have no idea whether they exist or not.

You do notice, though, that clutch hitters are *always* spotted briefly and in poor light. "There's really no way to measure clutch performance," insiders like to say; occasionally some statistics will leak out about batting averages with runners in scoring position, usually based on 100 or 150 at bats, and never systematically available for scrutiny. Brief film clips of clutch hitters blazing through crucial October games are much treasured by the advocates, but then the guy probably doesn't play 30 games in October in his career, or if he does he starts going 2-for-17 in the playoffs, and when you see these clutch hitters in clutch situations during the year, they never seem quite so terrifying. "Bring me the carcass of a single member of the species," we say. "Show me the evidence that there is a single player in all of baseball who consistently and predictably performs over his head in 'game' situations. Name in advance a single player who this year, 1984, will hit just 30 points over his average in the late innings of close games." But when no such evidence is forthcoming, they say, "The forest is dark and deep, and there are many places for a body to

decay without being found. We don't need that kind of evidence. We don't need to see statistics on them. We live in the forest with them; we know that they exist."

Ah well; when Project Scoresheet is in place, we will answer this once and for all. No need to judge the issue until then.

So I go to look at the trees, as close as I can get from the outside. I go to baseball games, and (unlike sportswriters, who are there under deadline and thus not free to enjoy the occasion) I love going to baseball games. I go with my wife and friends and stay sober and get as wrapped up in it as I can.

But this book is not about the things that I see at baseball games with my own eyes, at least not mostly. This book has a breadth and scope in its vision of the game that requires a perspective that comes only with distance. It has an honesty in facing certain questions that a reporter, that anyone who is inside the game or even near it, could never afford. It has a sense of balance about all the parts of the game that could not come from any point within the forest.

It also has blind spots the size of the World Trade Center with an oak tree growing in every window. There are a lot of things that you just can't see from out here, folks. Dedication and leadership and desire and commitment; I see glimpses of all that, but you just can't see those things clearly from the outside, and it's silly to pretend you can.

I've never said, never thought, that it was *better* to be an outsider than it was to be an insider, that my view of the game was better than anyone else's. It's different; better in some ways, worse in some ways. What I have said is, *since* we are outsiders, since the players are going to put up walls to keep us out here, let us use our position as outsiders to what advantage we can. Let us back off from the trees, look at the forest as a whole, and see what we can learn from that. Let us stop pretending to be insiders if we're not. Let us fly over the forest, you and I, and look down; let us measure every tract of land and map out all the groves, and draw in every path that connects each living thing. Let us drive around the edges and photograph each and every tree from a variety of angles and with a variety of lenses; and insiders will be amazed at what we can help them to see. Or maybe they won't; who knows. But anyway, we'll have some fun. Snake oil, $1.95.

LOGIC AND METHODS IN BASEBALL ANALYSIS

AXIOM I: *A ballplayer's purpose in playing baseball is to do those things which create wins for his team, while avoiding those things which create losses for his team.*

Ultimately, what we are trying to do here is to find the answers to questions, baseball questions. These are the same sorts of questions that every other baseball fan is interested in —they are, indeed, the same *questions* that every other baseball fan is interested in. Who is the best player in baseball? Who is the best second baseman in baseball? Is Cecil Cooper better than Eddie Murray? Why do some teams win and other teams lose? Is baseball 75% pitching? How are successful teams built? Are they mostly built through the farm system or through trades? What kinds of teams do well in a World Series? Who should have been the rookie of the year in the American League last year?

The way in which I have chosen to try to answer these questions could be loosely described as a science, the science of sabermetrics. I am, to tell the truth, something less than a world-class scientist; I am sloppy and hasty and inadequately trained in things like correlation methods, significance testing and computer science. My logic, though I am struggling here to make it less so, is largely intuitive. I probably could not define the term "axiom" to the satisfaction of a high school algebra teacher. On

top of that, I have to make a living, without government grants and without a university to support me. That means I have to get this book out every year, and all experiments then in progress have to go on the back burner.

I am, on the other hand, not a journalist, and thus my deadline is December 15th, not 10:45. If I want to spend a month of my life analyzing the role of an outfielder's throwing arm in preventing runs, I have that freedom. And that is the sort of thing that I am interested in, so that is the sort of thing that I do. I try to develop new knowledge about baseball.

The development of knowledge in any field waits upon two things: the development of methods and the availability of a compelling logic. Methods are the roads that one travels on in searching for the truth, and like all roads they can be constructed and abandoned as needed. The creation of a new method is basically a mental construction project; if you need the road, if you know where it is you want to go, then there is no doubt about one's ability to develop a method to get there. It's work, and the road that you develop might be a better road or a poorer road, but the job can always be done. As a road can be built out of many different kinds of materials and still take you where you want to go, methods in sabermetrics or in any other field of knowledge can be designed in different ways, one substantially as good as the other. Different men, analyzing the same questions with different methods, can and do reach the same conclusions.

A compelling logic, where it exists, is on the other hand a sun which shines on us all. Methods are the roads that take us to our conclusions; logic is the light that shows us the way. In its best form—compelling logic—it cannot be created; it simply *is*. In other areas, where there is no compelling logic, we must supply "headlights," the best answers we can give to the questions as best we can phrase them.

In the past two editions of *The Baseball Abstract*, I have in this section concentrated on explaining the methods that I have developed and will be using. This year, I thought I would try to give you a flashlight as well as a road map—that is, use this section as much to explain the reasoning process that a sabermetrician goes through in analyzing a question as the methods he travels on to get there.

It all begins with an assumption, the assumption that a player is on the field to create wins for his team, to avoid creating losses for his team. Everything that he does on a field—or off of it, I suppose—is "good" or is a benefit precisely in the degree to which it tends to create wins. Everything that he does is "bad" or is a detriment precisely in the degree to which it tends to create losses. In the world of sabermetrics, that is the great sun.

AXIOM II: *Wins result from runs scored. Losses result from runs allowed.*

First Corollary to AXIOM II: *An offensive player's job is to create runs for his team.*

The question of how it is that all of the things that a player does combine to form "wins" and "losses" is for the moment a bit more than we can chew. We will get back to it.

I take the truth of the first corollary to be self-evident; I take it to express a compelling logic. What I mean by that, for the moment, is that whenever I explain the idea to anybody, they usually don't say, "In your opinion"; they usually say, "Damn, that's right, isn't it?" People are in the habit of evaluating players by batting average; even the leagues are in the habit of listing team offensive statistics according to

batting average rather than in order of runs scored. But it is obvious, all the same, that the purpose of an offense is not to compile a high batting average. It is obvious that the term "the best hitting team in the American League" should not refer to the Toronto Blue Jays, the team with the highest batting average, but to the Chicago White Sox, the team which scored the most runs (although they finished eighth in the league in batting average). It is only habit; no one really thinks that the Blue Jays therefore have a better offense. A manager does not go out on an afternoon when he must face Mario Soto and say, "Gee, I sure hope we can hit .230 or .240 against this guy today." He says, "Gee, I hope we can score two or three runs, give our pitcher a chance."

Our goal now becomes to develop a formula which measures the number of runs that a player has created for his team—a formula that takes the numbers of hits and doubles and triples and home runs and whatever else and expresses them all as *runs*. Over the course of the last ten or twenty years, any number of people have seen that need, and for that reason the number of runs that a player has created for his team can be figured in a variety of ways. I myself have probably developed 30 or 40 runs created formulas, most of them now obsolete, surpassed by later, more accurate formulas. A year ago (in the *1983 Baseball Abstract*) I introduced three variations of my own runs created formula. Two of those are now obsolete.

The one which is not obsolete is the basic version of the formula:

$$\frac{(\text{Hits} + \text{Walks}) \times \text{Total Bases}}{\text{At-Bats} + \text{Walks}} = \text{Runs}$$

Basic it is, simple it is. It has only four elements and requires only two simple additions, one multiplication and one division. But it works.

What do I mean by "works"? I mean it predicts runs scored. I mean that if you take any team or any league, and you know how many hits they have had, how many walks, how many total bases and how many at-bats, you can tell how many runs they will have scored. You don't need to know how many stolen bases they had. You don't need to know what their batting average was with runners in scoring position. You don't need to know how many home runs they hit with men on base, and how many with the bases empty. You don't need to know how good a job they did of hitting behind the runner, moving him over with an out. You don't need to know how many errors their opposition made. All of those things might make marginal changes in the number of runs resulting from the four basic offensive elements, but only marginal changes. They might cause a team to score 680 runs rather than 650; they might, on rare occasion, cause a team to score 710 runs rather than 650. But that's all. A team that is expected to score 650 runs will *not* score 750 or 775, even if they steal 325 bases and hit .320 with runners in scoring position. It just does not happen.

Let's take a look at the extent to which this simplest form of the runs created equation accurately predicts runs scored. First we'll start with leagues.

CHART INTRO-I

LEAGUE	Hits	Walks	Total Bases	At-Bats	Runs Created	Actual Runs
1983 American	20,662	7,094	31,181	77,822	10,192	10,177
1983 National	16,781	6,424	24,696	65,717	7,944	7,993
1982 American	20,566	7,338	31,337	77,886	10,260	10,163
1982 National	17,085	5,964	24,695	66,263	7,881	7,947
1981 American	13,016	4,761	18,931	50,813	6,056	6,112
1981 National	11,141	4,107	15,887	43,654	5,072	5,035
1980 American	20,958	7,221	31,085	77,888	10,292	10,201
1980 National	17,186	5,969	24,817	66,272	7,954	7,852
1979 American	20,682	7,413	31,325	76,704	10,463	10,527
1979 National	17,229	6,188	25,432	66,088	8,240	8,186

Chart Intro-I above gives the necessary data (hits, walks, total bases and at-bats) to work the runs created formula for each league over the last five years. In 1983, for example, there were in the American league 20,662 hits, 7,094 walks, 31,181 total bases and 77,822 at-bats. Knowing that, one would expect that there would be about 10,192 runs scored in the league. There were actually 10,177 runs scored in the league, a difference of about one-seventh of one percent.

The formula doesn't usually work that well. But it is usually accurate, for a league, within one percent. Over the last five years, there has only been one time when it was not accurate, for a league, within 1%. That was in the National League in 1980, when the runs created estimate was too high by 1.3%.

The formula is that accurate for leagues because a league/season is a large collection of games (about a thousand of them), and during that period everything that is not in the formula

will even out. Some teams will exceed their run projection because they steal bases successfully, but other teams will try to steal bases and not be successful at it, and will lose as many runs as the other teams gain. Some teams will exceed their run projection because they hit well with runners in scoring position, others because they do a good job of avoiding the double-play ball. Other teams will negate those advantages. Some teams will be lucky; others will be unlucky. For the league as a whole, the formula will work.

It will also work, albeit not quite as well, for each team in the league. The chart identified as Intro-II on the next page presents the data for each major league team in 1983.

Of the 26 projections, 14 are within twenty of the team's actual run total. The Dodgers could have been expected to score 654 runs; they actually did score 654 runs.

Does the formula distinguish the good offenses from the bad offenses accurately? The teams which could have been expected to score the most runs were Toronto in the American League, which could have been expected to score 821 and actually scored 795, missing by five the league's highest total, and Atlanta, which could have been expected to score a league-leading 748 and actually did score a league-leading 746. The teams which could have been expected to score the fewest runs were Seattle, which had an expectation of scoring 577 and actually did score 558 (easily the lowest total in the league), and the Mets, who just about turned the Seattle figures around with an expectation of 558 and an actual runs scored total of 575. They could have been expected to be last in the league in runs scored by 40; they were actually last by 48.

On the other hand. . . .

The formula does not work equally well for every team. The Chicago White Sox could have been expected to score, ignoring baserunning and such like, only 740 runs, seventh-best total in the league (although still the highest in their division). They actually did score 800 runs—60 more than the projection. This is an error of 8.1%. Were the formula generally wrong by that amount, it would be nearly worthless, as that is near the standard deviation of runs scored. (In other words, in this particular case you could have done about as well by picking a number out of a hat.)

Why does it miss by so much? Everything doesn't even out for one team. Some of the rea-

	Hits	Walks	Total Bases	At-Bats	Runs Created	Actual Runs
AMERICAN LEAGUE						
East						
Baltimore	1,492	601	2,333	5,546	794	799
Detroit	1,530	508	2,387	5,592	797	789
New York	1,535	533	2,343	5,631	786	770
Toronto	1,546	510	2,431	5,581	821	795
Milwaukee	1,556	475	2,347	5,620	782	764
Boston	1,512	536	2,289	5,590	765	724
Cleveland	1,451	605	2,020	5,476	683	704
West						
Chicago	1,439	527	2,264	5,484	740	800
Kansas City	1,515	397	2,223	5,598	709	696
Texas	1,429	442	2,055	5,610	635	639
Oakland	1,447	524	2,103	5,516	686	708
California	1,467	509	2,214	5,640	711	722
Minnesota	1,463	467	2,248	5,601	715	709
Seattle	1,280	460	1,922	5,336	577	558
NATIONAL LEAGUE						
East						
Philadelphia	1,352	640	2,026	5,426	665	696
Pittsburgh	1,460	497	2,119	5,531	688	659
Montreal	1,482	509	2,167	5,611	705	677
St. Louis	1,496	543	2,133	5,550	714	679
Chicago	1,436	470	2,212	5,512	705	701
New York	1,314	436	1,874	5,444	558	575
West						
Los Angeles	1,358	541	2,061	5,440	654	654
Atlanta	1,489	582	2,187	5,472	748	746
Houston	1,412	517	2,062	5,502	661	643
San Diego	1,384	482	1,938	5,527	602	653
San Francisco	1,324	619	2,016	5,369	654	687
Cincinnati	1,274	588	1,901	5,333	598	623

sons for the White Sox "discrepancy" and for the other large discrepancies (San Diego 51, St. Louis 35) will be dealt with as we develop more complicated versions of the formula. Others will be addressed (hinted at, suggested, discussed) in the team comments concerning those teams.

This formula is of great use in trying to unravel the questions mentioned at the outset —who is more valuable than who, why do some teams score more runs than others. As we develop versions of it that are even more accurate, it becomes even more valuable. Before we get into those methods, though, there is another logical point that I would like to make.

It is this: The runs created formula could not possibly work as well as it does if it did not accurately describe how an offense functions. Two things which always move together may safely be said to be connected. If I see a car start up across the street, I do not know whether it will go left or go right. But I know this: If the front wheel goes one way, the back wheel will go in the same direction. I do not know whether

the American League's runs scored total next year will go up or down, but I know this: If the number of runs created by the players goes up, the number of runs scored by the teams will go up. If one goes down, both will go down.

THE KNOWN PRINCIPLES OF SABERMETRICS

ITEM I: *There are two essential elements of an offense: its ability to get people on base and its ability to advance runners.*

The formula works because it resembles so closely the offense which it describes. As it grows more complex, the runs created formula will retain its essential form. It has and will always have three parts. The relationship among those parts will remain the same. Those parts are:

● The A Factor, which represents the number of runners on base.

● The B Factor, which represents what is done to advance those runners.

● The C Factor, which measures the context in which A and B take place.

The relationship is (A multiplied by B) divided by C. Runs equal A multiplied by B, divided by C.

The A and B factors of the equation represent the two measured halves of a hitter's ability to produce runs. A player who has a high "A" Factor, a player who is *on base* a lot, will usually also have a high total of *runs scored*. A player who has a high "B" Factor, a player who has a lot of *total bases*, will also have a lot of *runs batted in*. A player who is high in both totals, like a Mike Schmidt, will have high totals in both runs scored and RBI. A player who is on base a lot but doesn't have many total bases, like a Rod Carew, will usually have a good total of runs scored, but not many RBI. A player who has a good many total bases but isn't on base a lot, like a George Foster, will usually have a good RBI total but not as many runs scored. A player who is low in both areas, like a Manny Trillo, will neither drive in nor score very many runs. A Factor, Runs Scored; B Factor, Runs Batted In.

Now then, we know more about an offense than we have made use of yet. The statistics tell us which teams are successful base stealers and which are not. The statistics tell us which teams ground into the most double plays. If we make use of that information, we can make the formula more accurate for teams and players.

We will begin by building the stolen base gamble into the formula. When a runner is caught stealing, that takes a man off base. The "A" Factor, the on-base element of the formula, is changed to reflect this:

A = Hits + Walks − Caught Stealing

If the gamble succeeds, then a base is gained by the baserunner. The "B" factor is changed to reflect this:

B = Total Bases + Stolen Bases

Now try A multiplied by B divided by C. For the American League (1983), with the subtraction of the 744 runners who were caught stealing, the A Factor becomes 27,012. The B Factor, with the addition of the 1,540 runners who stole successfully, becomes 32,721.

Oops. The American League's runs created total jumps to 10,409. That's 232 too high. The National League figure becomes 8,199, over the actual number of runs scored by 206.

Why? The stolen base advances only the baserunner and only one base; each base of a hit advances the batter and anyone else who is on base at the time, and often advances them more than one base. The advancement value of a stolen base is not equal to the advancement value of each base of a hit. The advancement value of a single is always at least one base, but it is often *three* bases and many times *five*. If a runner goes from first to third on a single, then how many bases are gained from the single? The situation before was that a runner was on first; now it's a runner on first and a runner on third. Three bases are gained. If the single is hit with runners on first and second, the runner on second will probably score and the runner from first may go to third—a gain of five bases on one base of a hit. But the base gained on the stolen base gets you only one, plus a second if an error is made on the play, which it will be 7% of the time.

So the formula will not work in this form; base-stealing teams will be projected to score far more runs than they will actually score. To make it work, you have to trim the value of the stolen base down to .55 of one total base.

A Factor: Hits + Walks − Caught Stealing
B Factor: Total Bases + 55% of Stolen Bases
C Factor: At-Bats + Walks

Now the formula works again. For the American League, it projects a runs scored total of 10,188, just eleven off the actual figure of 10,177. For the National League, it projects 7,950, moving the estimate six notches closer to the actual figure of 7,993.

This is what is called the stolen base version of the runs created formula. People who have read previous editions of the *Baseball Abstract* will remember that this is not the same stolen base version of the formula that I have used in the past, since 1979. In the past I weighted the stolen base gain at .70, and also added the number of runners caught stealing into the "C Factor," the opportunity factor, of the equation. I reasoned that when a runner is caught stealing, that eliminates a potential opportunity, and thus in effect expands the area in which the offense occurs.

Several people pointed out to me, and somebody finally got it through to me, that this does not quite make sense. When a player is removed from base by being caught stealing, when we subtract one from the "A" element of the formula, that in itself expands the offensive context; it expands the area of the nonproductive performance. Suppose that a player reaches base 100 times and has 100 total bases in 300 plate appearances.

$$\frac{100 \times 100}{300}$$

He will have created 33 and one-third runs. Suppose that that player now comes to bat again, and hits a single, after which he lights out for second base and returns unceremoniously to the dugout. Under the old version of the formula, his offense would now look like this:

$$\frac{(100 + 1 - 1) \times (100 + 1)}{(300 + 1 + 1)}$$

which is, of course

$$\frac{100 \times 101}{(302)}$$

which figures to 33.44 runs.

Suppose, however, that instead of hitting a single, he had simply grounded out to begin with. Then he would figure like this:

$$\frac{(100) \times (100)}{(301)}$$

The first player, who has hit a single and then been thrown out, is shown as having 202 nonproductive opportunities, 302–100. The second player is shown as having 201 nonproductive opportunities, 301–100. This doesn't quite make sense.

Besides making better sense, the new stolen base version of the formula has two other advantages. Number one, it is slightly more accurate than the old version; its run projections are slightly closer to the actual numbers of runs scored. And number two, it is simpler. It has fewer elements, as the caught stealing adjustment has been eliminated from the denominator. The simpler a formula is, the better. So the old stolen base version of the formula is now obsolete.

Finally, there is the "technical" version of the formula. The technical version of the formula tries to deal with *everything*—hit batsmen, double-play balls, sacrifice bunts and flies, intentional walks; when we have data on who hits what with runners in scoring position, we'll rebuild the technical version of the formula to accommodate that. The needed adjustments to the technical version of the formula can be described in three parts—adjustments to the A Factor, adjustments to the B Factor and adjustments to the C Factor.

A) *Adjustments to the "on base" or "A Factor" of the formula.*

The A Factor is adjusted in two ways; hit batsmen are added and double-play balls are subtracted. This creates a new "A Factor" which is (breaking into abbreviations):

$$H + W + HBP - CS - GIDP$$

B) *Adjustments to the "advancement" or "B Factor."*

The B Factor receives the most thorough overhaul in this version. First of all, sacrifice hits (SH) and sacrifice flies (SF) are added in, given the same weight as stolen bases. This weight is reduced from .55 to .52, because one of the advantages of the stolen base, which is that it helps to prevent double plays, is now being dealt with separately.

Second, we will now include a small adjustment for the advancement value of the walk. Initially, we assumed that a base on balls does nothing to help advance a baserunner. The B Fator, remember, represents a player's RBI potential (with the exception of the stolen base factor, which is something he does to advance himself, rather than someone else). How many RBI do you get a year by drawing walks? Not many. You're happy to have the walk when the bases are empty, or early in the inning. When there are men on base, or late in the inning, the walk is no longer as good as the hit.

Walks do, however, have some limited advancement value. The advancement value of a walk, as it turns out, is almost exactly one-half that of a stolen base. Intentional walks, for obvious reasons, have no advancement value. We weight hit batsmen (HBP) and nonintentional walks (TBB-IBB) at .26, and thus produce the new B Factor of the Runs Created Equation:

$$TB + .26 \times (TBB - IBB + HBP) + .52 \times (SB + SH + SF)$$

C) *Adjustments to the "opportunity" or "C Factor."*

All of the new things are thrown into the opportunity factor of the equation except double-play balls. Double-play balls are counted as at-bats; when you subtract one from the number of men on base, that (as in the caught stealing adjustment) automatically expands the nonproductive opportunity area. So the C Factor becomes:

$$AB + TBB + SH + SF + HBP$$

These are assembled as always: A multiplied by B, divided by C.

The technical version of the formula given in the 1983 *Baseball Abstract*, again, is obsolete.

I don't know that it is necessary to reexamine every offense with the more complex versions of the formula, but I will discuss briefly how the runs created estimates that don't work well in the basic version are changed in the later stages. The technical version of the method brings 17 of the 26 estimates to within twenty of the actual total; the basic method met that standard for 14 teams. The Chicago White Sox, you will recall, exceeded their expected total of runs scored by 60, scoring 800 with an expectation of 740. When you look at their base-stealing stats, part of the reason for this becomes clear. The White Sox stole 165 bases, the third-highest total in the league, and were caught stealing only 50 times. The White Sox have the type of base-stealing attack that you have to approve of: The two men who can steal bases successfully, do lots of it; the seven who can't don't try. Their 76.7% stolen base percentage was the second best in all of baseball, exceeded only by the Kansas City Royals.

When base stealing is taken into consideration, the White Sox runs created estimate moves up to 751, still 49 less than their actual total. The largest errors in any season occur not for any one reason but for several reasons, and thus will not be completely eliminated by any adjustment of which we are yet capable.

The White Sox also had the most hit batsmen

in the major leagues, 43, so when we make that adjustment, the Sox again will move forward. They grounded into only 113 double plays, tying Seattle for the lowest figure in the American League, so when that is included in the formula they will, again, move forward. Eventually, the White Sox runs created will be estimated in this way:

A Factor:
  1439 + 527 + 43 − 50 − 113 =   1846
B Factor:
  2264 + .26(527 + 43 − 50) + .52(53 + 56 + 165) =   2541.68
C Factor:
  5485 + 527 + 43 + 53 + 56 =   6164
Runs Created:
  (1846 × 2541.68) / 6164 =   761

So eventually, we bring the estimate up within 5% of the fact—not one of the method's finer hours, certainly, but still we can say accurately that the runs created estimate gives some hint as to why the White Sox scored the number of runs that they did.

The runs created estimates given in Section II and the player rankings given in section III are all based this year, for the first time, on the technical version of the formula. In the past, these figures were based on the stolen-base version of the formula, not the technical version. There are two reasons for the switch. Number 1, I now own—I did not, a year ago—a small personal computer, which makes it as easy to figure them one way as another. Number 2, the gains in accuracy with the technical version of the formula which was available a year ago were not all that substantial. The average error per team is about 23 runs with the basic version of the formula, 22 and a half with the stolen-base version. The old technical version of the formula eliminated only 5 to 7% of the error. The new technical version of the formula eliminates about 22% of the error of the stolen-base version, cutting the error to around 18 runs per team. That's a significant gain in accuracy. Further, whereas the old technical version was more accurate for teams but no more accurate for leagues, the new technical version is more accurate for both teams and leagues, and improves the accuracy of the estimates for teams in both the American and National Leagues. (Accuracy established by a test of 40 leagues, American and National, 1963–1982, and 200 teams.) So I felt it was worthwhile to make the change.

In what respects do the rankings change as a result of using the technical version of the formula? It does make a difference, although not a huge one. The largest difference in the rankings this year will be that the faster players will tend to rank a little higher, and the slower players a little lower. This is because of the use of the double-play totals, which is the one largest element of the technical version which is not dealt with in the stolen-base version.

In the past, I have declined to use GIDP (Grounded Into Double Play) totals. The basic reason for this is the argument that the runs created estimates in other respects were taken from a "clean" environment; that is, they were not influenced by who was batting ahead of the guy, as RBI totals are, or who was batting behind him, as runs scored totals are. A player in any game situation can draw a walk, hit a double or strike out. But only when there are runners on base can he ground into a double play. There is no way of knowing how many times he has batted with runners on first base, and thus no way of knowing whether he has grounded into a lot of double plays because he hits a lot of double-play type grounders, or merely because he batted a lot of times with men on first base. Using things like sac hits, sac flies and GIDP is drawing from a polluted well.

It is, but I decided to do it. Two principles collide:

1) *A "clean" measure of performance is always to be preferred to a "situation dependent" measure.*

2) *An accurate measure of performance is always to be preferred to a less accurate measure.*

In the past, I have gone with the first desire; this year, with the second. For three reasons. First of all, GIDP totals may be somewhat polluted by context, but they cannot possibly be so polluted that they tell you more about the context than about the player, as RBI counts and Runs Scored counts are on some occasions. The reason for that is the spread. Some players will ground into a double play about once every 20 at-bats. Tony Armas in 1983 grounded into a double play every 18.5 at-bats. Other players ground into double plays only once every one hundred at-bats. Kirk Gibson grounded into only

two double plays in 401 at-bats, one every 200.5 at-bats. Tony Armas might have batted with more runners on first base—conceivably as many as 30 or 40% per at-bat, though in truth it is *extremely* unlikely that it was 40%. He certainly did *not* bat with eleven times as many runners on first base. A possible 30 or 40% difference in their opportunities to ground into double plays does not provide a sufficient reason to ignore an 1100% difference in double plays grounded into. The possible 30 or 40% pollution factor, in my eyes, is not a sufficient reason to disallow the evidence.

Second, Craig Wright has pointed out to me that people generally hit better with runners on first base than they do with the bases empty. Not a lot better—just a few points. But still better. In that situation, the number of walks allowed goes down, but the number of hits allowed goes up, for the obvious reason that the pitcher does not want to risk the walk that would put the runner in scoring position, and thus will come in with a 2–0 or 3–1 pitch. Thus *IF* players are batting with an unusual number of runners on first base, they are deriving a hidden statistical advantage from it as well as acquiring a liability. Is it, then, unfair to charge them with the liability? When a business purchases the assets of another business, they also acquire their liabilities (or at least that's what Judge Wapner says).

A related sort of concern is this: stolen bases serve to prevent double-play balls (so, for that matter, do caught stealing). Rickey Henderson's 127 stolen-base attempts last year probably prevented 12 to 15 subsequent ground-ball double plays. They prevented them, however, not for Rickey Henderson but for Bill Almon or Dwayne Murphy or whoever would have been batting with Rickey on first. This might cause the formula to adjust correctly for *team* double-play totals, but incorrectly for *individual* double-play totals. Bill Almon (or whoever) reaps the rewards of Rickey Henderson's risk.

I might be more worried for this, except for one thing. Rickey Henderson is helped by the adjustment, not hurt. The players who steal the bases and the players who ground into the fewest double plays are, generally speaking, the same players. So if we are ignoring this factor to protect Rickey Henderson's "investment," we are doing a poor job of it. With the exception of an occasional player like John Wathan,

16

who both steals bases *and* grounds into double plays, the people who are helped by using the double-play totals are the base stealers.

Rickey Henderson is helped by the change for two reasons. His runs created figure is increased slightly be using the technical version of the formula, from 105 to 109 (104.6 to 109.1, actually). But the ratings are based not on runs created, but on runs created per game, or per out consumed. When you are not using double-play totals or sacrifice hits or flies, you base these on a 26-out game. The 27th out is the double play. Rickey Henderson figures at 104.6 runs on 382 outs (363 [at-bats minus hits], 19 caught stealing), which means 7.12 runs created per game (26 outs). With double-play adjustments, he has 109.1 runs created on 395 outs (add 11 double-play balls, one sacrifice hit and one sacrifice fly), which figures out to 7.46 runs created per (27-out) game. On the other hand, a player who grounds into a lot of double plays will figure by this method first of all to have created fewer runs, and second to have used more "games" in doing so.

This doesn't substantially alter my feelings about the running game, which are on record and will probably go on record again before this book is done. It's just a technical adjustment, a few small things that I've done to make the methods of measurement available to me a little bit more accurate. But it does improve the rankings of the base stealers.

The question could be asked, why do we need all these different types of runs created estimates? Wouldn't one of them do the job as well as all of them?

There are at least four major highways between Lawrence, Ks., and Kansas City—highways 10, 24, 40 and 70. Why is that? To hold the overflow when they drop the nukes on Kansas City?

No. It's because although you may still be in Lawrence, you can be in North Lawrence or South Lawrence. You may feel like paying the dollar to drive on the turnpike, or you may feel like driving through the beautiful country that surrounds highway 40. You might be driving a big truck, which they don't allow on highway 24. You might want to stop in Tonganoxie and pick up your Aunt Harriett, and there's only one of those roads that goes through Tonganoxie.

People who are interested in how many runs a player has created could be interested in that question in many different contexts. For some questions, the most detailed study of the issue that is possible might be the only one that is acceptable; for others, the amount of time invested just might not be worth it. If you're doing a study that mixes together a great many seasons authored by players of unlike abilities, the basic version of the formula might be all that's needed, because over a period of time, there is a strong likelihood that the other factors would tend to even out. The data set that you're dealing with is always limited in one way or another; data on double-play balls in the 1920s just doesn't exist. Different studies require different roads toward the same truth.

And while we are sort of on the subject, there is another road toward the same truth that I would like to say something about. That is the statistic called "Runs Produced," and it is figured by adding together runs scored and runs batted in, and subtracting home runs. This is what you might call the dirt road toward runs created; it's a convenient statistic, easy to figure at any point during the season, quick and available. It's not nearly as accurate as runs created, but the two are similar; that is, the number of runs that a player has scored and/or the number that he has driven in are going to be very close to the number that he has created most of the time. Dale Murphy last year had 131 runs scored and 131 runs created.

My problem with "Runs Produced" has to do with this bit about subtracting the number of home runs the player has hit. Why do you subtract the player's home run count? What you're figuring here isn't *whole* runs produced, it's *half* runs produced. One player provides the first half of the run—the on-base part of it; the A Factor; the run scored—and the other provides the second half of the run—the advancement part of it; the B Factor; the run batted in. Each is credited with one run produced. But when a player provides *both* the on-base act and the advancement act, he receives no more credit than if he had done only one. Does this make sense?

I believe that the practice of subtracting out the home runs is merely a manifestation of a prejudice against the home-run hitter. It is an unworthy continuation of an ancient, pre-Ruthian belief that the really good hitters were the people who hit for a high average, and that the home-run hitters really weren't doing that much to help their teams.

If, indeed, you were going to adjust for the home-run totals, it would make a lot more sense to adjust for them by *adding them back in again*, not by taking them out. One could accurately say that the player who hits the home run has provided for his team three things—the on-base portion of the run, the advancement portion of the run and THE ACT OF UNIFYING THE TWO. In many cases, if the run does not result from a homer, there is another, uncredited player who must supply this. With three straight singles, the first man gets a run produced, the third man gets a run produced, and the second man, though he gets nothing, has done the same thing as the other two. But the player who hits the home run has done the same thing as all three of them.

Consider this example. Player A hits .320 with 10 home runs, scores 100 runs and drives in 100 runs. Player B, for a different team, hits .320 with 100 runs scored and 100 RBI, but he hits 30 home runs. The two players have exactly the same totals of doubles, triples, stolen bases, walks and number of times gone first-to-third on a single. Who is really the better hitter?

Obviously, Player B. Because, he obviously plays in an inferior offensive context, with poorer hitters coming up behind him and ahead of him. He is required to do MORE to drive in and score the same number of runs—yet he is given arbitrarily a lower total of runs produced.

Don't like the theoretical example? OK, consider some real examples. I located, for the 1983 season, all of the pairs of players who had exactly the same runs scored and RBI totals (given a reasonable amount of playing time). Those pairs of players are listed below:

Player (HRs)	Runs	RBI
Larry Parrish (26)	76	88
Gary Ward (19)	76	88
Larry Bowa (2)	73	43
Jerry Remy (0)	73	43
Brian Downing (19)	68	53
Johnny Ray (5)	68	53
Terry Puhl (8)	66	44
Rod Carew (2)	66	44
Dan Driessen (12)	57	57
Mike Hargrove (3)	57	57
Luis Salazar (14)	52	45
Pete Rose (0)	52	45
Randy Bush (11)	43	56
Jeff Burroughs (10)	43	56

Player (HRs)	Runs	RBI
Cesar Cedeno (9)	40	39
Garth Iorg (2)	40	39
Bob Kearney (8)	33	32
Rick Dempsey (4)	33	32

Now look at those. Remember that, in every single case, the player listed on the bottom is given a higher total of runs produced because he hit fewer home runs. But did Gary Ward really have a better offensive season than Larry Parrish? Is Mike Hargrove really a better offensive player than Dan Driessen?

Here are the facts about the two groups of offensive players:

1) In all cases except two, the player who hit fewer home runs hit for a higher average than the other player. So there is a clear division between the two groups, a "power" group and a "high average" group. (The exceptions are that Salazar also hit for a higher average than Rose, and Kearney also hit for a higher average than Dempsey.)

2) In every case—every single case—the "power" player reached these runs scored and RBI totals in *fewer* at-bats than did the "high average" player. Every time. Also fewer plate appearances. In most cases, the differences in at-bat totals were quite substantial; the extremes are Downing (173 fewer at-bats than Ray) and Puhl (just 7 fewer at-bats than Carew). The "high average" players, as a group, used 4,348 at-bats to score their 508 runs and drive in their 457. The "power" group accomplished the same in 3,792 at-bats. In all cases except one, the "high average" players also made more outs than did the "power" group. The one exception is that Puhl did make more outs than Carew did.

3) In virtually every case, the "power" players reached those levels despite playing for inferior offensive teams—just as in my theoretical example. Ward's team scored 70 more runs than Parrish's team, Remy's team scored 23 more than Bowa's team, Carew's team scored 79 more runs than Driessen's team, Rose's team scored 43 more runs than Salazar's team, Iorg's team scored 172 more runs than Cedeno's team and Dempsey's team scored 91 more runs than Kearney's team. The one serious exception was that Downing's team did score 63 more runs than Ray's team; Bush's team also scored one more run (709–708) than Burroughs'.

So the "power" players scored and drove in

just as many runs, while batting *fewer* times, for *inferior* offensive teams. Doesn't that argue powerfully that they must have been *better* offensive players, not worse? There are two exceptions—Iorg in fact was a better hitter than Cedeno, and Carew better than Puhl. But otherwise, it is the "power" men, not the "high-average" men, who deserve a little extra credit.

Ah well; I didn't build that road. I'm probably not going to be allowed to repair it.

Which major league players, then, created the most runs for their teams in 1983? We'll figure that using the technical version of the formula. The players creating the most runs were Wade Boggs of Boston (130) and Dale Murphy of Atlanta (131). The top ten in each league are detailed below:

AMERICAN LEAGUE		NATIONAL LEAGUE	
Wade Boggs, Boston	130	Dale Murphy, Atlanta	131
Eddie Murray, Baltimore	127	Tim Raines, Montreal	120
Cal Ripken, Baltimore	120	Pedro Guerrero, LA	118
Robin Yount, Milwaukee	115	Mike Schmidt, Phila.	117
Lou Whitaker, Detroit	115	Andre Dawson, Montreal	113
Jim Rice, Boston	113	Jose Cruz, Houston	109
Willie Upshaw, Toronto	113	Darrell Evans, S.F.	104
Cecil Cooper, Mil.	110	Keith Hernandez, StL–NY	98
Rickey Henderson, Oak.	109	George Hendrick, StL	96
Lloyd Moseby, Toronto	104	Dickie Thon, Houston	95

Figures for the regulars and near-regulars on each team are given in Section II, along with breakdowns of what the player has done in various situations—during the first half of the season and during the second, against righthanded pitchers and against lefthanders, at home and on the road, on grass fields and on artificial turf.

Let us also, before leaving the field, take a quick look at who would be the leaders in what I will call "Half-Runs Produced." Half-Runs Produced, of course, is what runs produced should be, runs scored plus RBI, without the phony adjustment for home runs. The leaders are:

AMERICAN LEAGUE		NATIONAL LEAGUE	
Cecil Cooper, Milwaukee	232	Dale Murphy, Atlanta	252
Eddie Murray, Baltimore	226	Andre Dawson, Montreal	217
Cal Ripken, Baltimore	223	Mike Schmidt, Phila.	213
Jim Rice, Boston	216	Tim Raines, Montreal	204
Dave Winfield, New York	215	Pedro Guerrero, LA	190
Willie Upshaw, Toronto	203	Jose Cruz, Houston	177
Lance Parrish, Detroit	194	Darrell Evans, S.F.	176
Lloyd Moseby, Toronto	185	George Hendrick, StL	170
Tony Armas, Boston	184	George Foster, New York	164
Ted Simmons, Milwaukee	184	Ron Cey, Chicago	163

The two lists, as you can see, are substantially in agreement; the names "Dale Murphy" and "Andre Dawson" and "Eddie Murray" and "Cal Ripken" are prominent in both cases.

How can you measure the degree of agreement? Well, try this. The number one position on each list is valued at "10," the number ten position at one; if you're not on the list, that's zero. Multiply each player's value on one list by his value on the other, and add up the totals. If the two lists were identical, the sum would be 384 in each league (10 × 10, plus 9 × 9, plus 8 × 8...plus 1 × 1). If they were entirely different, the sum would be zero. Divide the actual sum by 384, and that is the "percentage of agreement" between the two leagues.

The National League lists are 96% in agreement; the players creating the most runs and the players producing the most half-runs are almost exactly the same players. The American League list of half-runs produced is notably missing the name of Wade Boggs, a phenomenon we must deal with somewhere in the book. The names of Robin Yount and Lou Whitaker are similarly, if less glaringly, absent, and so the agreement between the American League lists is only 61%.

AXIOM III: *All offense and all defense occurs within a context of outs.*

That probably sounds so simple as to be childish; it is. It is, at the same time, one of the least understood basic truths about an offense or about an offensive player.

Look, a team has got 27 outs a game to make its runs. If a player goes four-for-four, the other eight players still have 27 outs to split among them. He has, then, not used up any of the team's offensive opportunities.

And from that, this follows: Individual at-bat totals are an individual thing, and are of no significance whatsoever in understanding how a hitter fits into the context of his team. *At-bats are not the context in which offense occurs.*

Outs are the context in which offense occurs. A team has three outs an inning, 27 outs a game, 4,374 outs a year with which to win a pennant. They must score runs within those three outs in an inning, whether there are four at-bats there or fourteen. They must win games within those 27 outs, whether they can stretch 35 at-bats out of them or 55. They must win a pennant within those 4,374 outs, whether they use up those outs in 5,300 at-bats or can stretch them to 5,700. At-bats are irrelevant; outs are the context in which they are operating.

Consider two players, Willie Wilson of Kansas City and Tom Brunansky of Minnesota. Each player in 1983 went to the plate 611 times. Each player created 72 runs. Yet are they equivalent offensive players?

No, of course not. Because Brunansky consumed more outs. And because he made more outs, his teammates had fewer outs left in which to do their work. So Wilson is the more valuable offensive player.

I place the player's runs in an offensive context by figuring how many runs he has created per game that he has used. His team has 162 offensive games in a season, each consisting of 27 outs. So for every 27 outs that the player uses, he has used up one offensive game.

When figuring runs created by the "basic" runs created method, a game is considered to be 25.5 outs. Twenty-five and a half outs a game are made by hitters making outs, so if you figure a league by this method, the league's offensive won/lost percentage (which we will get to in a minute) will be .500, or very close to it. If you allow them 27 outs when they are only using 25.5, then the league will have an offensive won/lost percentage of something like .530.

When using the "stolen-base" version of the formula, a "game" is used up every 26 outs, as the caught stealing will add a half an out a game.

When using the "technical" version of the formula, which includes everything, then a game is used up every 27 outs.

The following are the players in each league who created the most runs per 27 outs used in 1983:

Player, Team	RPG	Player, Team	RPG
Boggs, Boston	8.80	Murphy, Atlanta	8.09
Brett, Kansas City	8.13	Schmidt, Philadelphia	7.55
Murray, Baltimore	8.00	Guerrero, Los Angeles	7.35
Henderson, Oakland	7.46	Horner, Atlanta	7.16
Yount, Milwaukee	7.37	Evans, San Francisco	7.15
Upshaw, Toronto	7.12	Lefebvre, San Diego-Phil.	7.01
Grich, California	7.11	Raines, Montreal	6.98
Moseby, Toronto	7.07	Cruz, Houston	6.84
Lowenstein, Balt.	7.07	Hendrick, St. Louis	6.69
Aikens, Kansas City	6.98	Hernandez, St. Louis-N.Y.	6.68

THE KNOWN PRINCIPLES OF SABERMETRICS

ITEM 2: *Batting and pitching statistics never represent pure accomplishments, but are heavily colored by all kinds of illusions and extraneous effects. One of the most important of these is park effects.*

A baseball player's statistics are going to be changed by the park in which he plays. Any baseball player; Babe Ruth hit home runs more often in some parks than in others. If two teams play 20 games in the Astrodome in Houston and 20 games in Fulton County Stadium in Atlanta, it is extremely likely that more runs will be scored in the 20 games in Atlanta.

The exact impact that each park has on run production is measurable, has been studied in great detail for a good many years. I have reported on the research extensively in the past; this year I'm not going to say much about it. But park effects will still have to be considered in certain issues.

I would present here the list of the most productive players with park adjustments taken into consideration, except that it is the same players and in the same order as the players having the highest offensive won/lost percentages. So we'll present the list when that method is explained.

THE KNOWN PRINCIPLES OF SABERMETRICS

ITEM 3: *There is a predictable relationship between the number of runs a team scores, the number they allow, and the number of games that they will win.*

That predictable relationship can be approximated in several ways. My choice is this: The ratio between a team's wins and its losses will be the ratio between the square of their runs scored and the square of their runs allowed.

This is called the Pythagorean approach to won/lost percentage. If you score three runs for every two scored by your opponent, you'll win nine games for each four that he wins. If you score four to his three, you'll win sixteen games to his nine.

There are many similar formulas that have been developed by other analysts of the game; Pete Palmer has one, Dallas Adams has one.

Another method that I have never tested but which I suspect would work as well as the others would be just to "double the edge"; that is, if a team scores 10% more runs than their opponents, then they should win 20% more games than their opponents. If they score 1% more runs, they should win 2% more games. That method would probably work as well or better than the Pythagorean approach. Again, it doesn't matter all that much what method you use. Methods are just roads. What matters is that you know where you're going.

Chart Intro-III below tells how many runs were scored in 1983 by each major league team, how many were allowed by each team, and what won/lost record might be expected to result from this combination. The chart also gives the actual won/lost record of each team.

As you can see if you'll take a minute to look at the chart, there are very few significant differences between how the teams could have been expected to finish based on their run and opposition run totals, and how they actually finished. In the American League Eastern division, there are no differences of any significance. The Orioles, with 799 runs scored and 652 allowed, could have been expected to finish about 97–65. They were actually 98–64. The other teams string out behind them exactly as would have been expected.

Before we discuss the rest of the chart, let us ask this question: What are the logical inferences that may be drawn from the knowledge that 2) there is a predictable relationship between runs scored, runs allowed and wins, and 1) virtually no teams vary from that relationship to a significant degree? The logical implication, to me, is clear: It isn't the *timing* of runs that determines who is a winner and who is a loser. Not over the course of a season, it isn't. It isn't an occasional clutch hit, a key run here and there, that distinguishes a contending team from a 75–87 team. It's a whole bunch of runs. With very rare exceptions—maybe the '69 Mets were the last exception—no one has ever been able to drag a championship won/lost record out of a

CHART INTRO–III

	Runs Scored	Runs Allowed	Projected W/L Pct.	Projected Wins	Projected Losses	Actual Wins	Actual Losses
AMERICAN LEAGUE							
East							
Baltimore	799	652	.600	97	65	98	64
Detroit	789	679	.575	93	69	92	70
New York	770	703	.545	88	74	91	71
Toronto	795	726	.545	88	74	89	73
Milwaukee	764	708	.538	87	75	87	75
Boston	724	775	.466	75	87	78	84
Cleveland	704	785	.446	72	90	70	92
West							
Chicago	800	650	.602	98	64	99	63
Kansas City	696	767	.452	73	89	79	83
Texas	639	609	.524	85	77	77	85
Oakland	708	782	.450	73	89	74	88
Minnesota	709	822	.427	69	93	70	92
California	722	779	.462	75	87	70	92
Seattle	558	740	.362	59	103	60	102
NATIONAL LEAGUE							
East							
Philadelphia	696	635	.546	88	74	90	72
Pittsburgh	659	648	.508	82	80	84	78
Montreal	677	646	.523	85	77	82	80
St. Louis	679	710	.478	77	85	79	83
Chicago	701	719	.487	79	83	71	91
New York	575	680	.417	68	94	68	94
West							
Los Angeles	654	609	.536	87	75	91	71
Atlanta	746	640	.576	93	69	88	74
Houston	643	646	.498	81	81	85	77
San Diego	653	653	.500	81	81	81	81
San Francisco	687	697	.493	80	82	79	83
Cincinnati	623	710	.435	70	92	74	88

team that doesn't score a lot more runs than they give up.

In the A.L. West, the White Sox have an expected winning record of 98–64 and an actual record of 99–63. Texas, which scored 30 more runs than its opponents, could have been expected to finish comfortably ahead of Kansas City, which allowed 71 more than they scored. But Texas, lacking an outstanding reliever, allowed more runs at key moments in the game than Kansas City, which has Quisenberry, and thus finished two games behind them. (Or maybe they just didn't get the breaks.)

The largest difference between expected wins and actual wins occurs in the National League East; the most significant occurs in the National League West. The Chicago Cubs scored enough runs in 1983 that they could have been expected to finish near .500—79–83, to be precise. They missed that projection by eight games; otherwise, the division finished up pretty much as expected. Montreal will be dealt with in the Montreal team comment.

The Western Division race, on the other hand, was truly decided not by the number of runs, but by the timing of the runs. The Atlanta Braves, who scored 92 runs more than the Dodgers did and allowed only 31 more, could have been expected to finish six full games in front of the Dodgers. I'm sure that many of you, looking at those two teams on paper, have been puzzled by how the Dodgers could possibly win it. The Braves' lineup is a lot more impressive.

But the Braves didn't win the close games, and in this particular case, the close games most certainly did decide the race. The two National League teams which had the worst records in one-run games were the Atlanta Braves (19–29) and the Chicago Cubs (18–27). That is exactly how you wind up with five or eight fewer wins than you should have. Next worst was Montreal (18–23). The Dodgers won the division by going 30–21 in one-run games.

But keep a close watch on what we are saying here. Winning close games can put you in first when you should be in second, while failing to win them can put you in second when you should be in first, or in third when you should be in second. It doesn't often do that; it just does that on a few occasions. But only on rare occasions would it do more than that.

I mention this because I know how strong the temptation is to think, sometimes, that it is only a run here and there, a tiny edge, which separates the winners from the losers. I grew up rooting for the Kansas City A's, and I know how tempting it is to delude yourself that you are really not that far away, that if you can just pick up a run here and there, you can make a big leap forward. I know that some of you, who are fans of let us say the New York Mets, are going to think from time to time, "You know, we're really not all that far away. I mean, I know we finished 68–94 this year, but all three of our outfielders had good years for us. We played an awful lot of close games, and I think that with just a little better luck next year and a run here and there, we could easily pick up 10, 12 games."

But that's just not the way it is. Yes, all three Met outfielders did have decent years with the bat. Yes, the Mets did play an awful lot of close games—57 one-run games, third-highest total in the league. They were 28–29 in those games. And you can fool yourself into saying that with just 24 additional runs, they have the opportunity to pick up a dozen victories by turning one-run losses into one-run wins. But what that would mean, of course, is that they would have to go 40–17 in their one-run decisions. That is just not going to happen. For a team to go 40–65 in other games, but pull itself up to near .500 by going 40–17 in one-run games simply is not going to happen. The Mets were *not* unlucky; they finished with exactly the record that they deserved. With the marginal exception of the Cubs, the same applies to every other team in the majors that won 72 games or less. The Mets can only move forward by making substantial improvements in their talent, and not by adding a run here and there at key moments.

While we are doing this, I thought it might be fun to phrase the question this way: Exactly how far away from contention *are* the New York Mets? How many runs are we talking about here? If they replace their second baseman who created 37 runs with a second baseman who creates 57 or 67, how far away will they be then?

Using this method, one can say with a fairly high degree of accuracy how many runs, offensively and defensively, are needed by the team to reach a given level of play. Let's define 90 games as "contention." Given that, and given normal luck:

The New York Mets would need to improve by 172 runs to move into contention.

Cincinnati would need to improve by 158 runs. The Cardinals would need to improve by 105 runs.

The Cubs would need to improve by 93 runs. The Giants would need to improve by 83 runs. The Astros would need to improve by 71 runs. The Padres would need to improve by 69 runs. The Pirates would need to improve by 58 runs. And the Expos would need to improve by 39 runs. Plus they would need to stop acting like that.

These runs in all cases are evenly split between offensive and defensive runs. In the American League, the totals are Seattle (251), Minnesota (194), Cleveland (160), Oakland (151), Kansas City (148), California (136), Boston (131), Texas (36), Milwaukee (22), and Toronto (12). The other teams are considered to be already in contention.

The Pythagorean method, and the similar methods employed by Palmer and other analysts of the game, act as a vital bridge linking *runs*, with which we deal most of the time, with *wins*, which are the goal which we are trying to reach. At other times, I have stated the relationship this way: In baseball's on-field economy, wins represent the "property" which each team is trying to acquire. Runs are the coin of the realm, the basic units of currency by which wins are acquired. Singles and doubles and triples are the game's equivalent to pocket change; a single is to a run exactly as a quarter is to a dollar. A run is to a win exactly as a dollar bill is to an item that might cost, on the average, eight or nine dollars.

Occasionally, of course, you will find a bargain. Occasionally, a single will change a loss into a win. You have purchased that win for a quarter. Congratulations.

But if you think you can purchase enough wins to make up a pennant at a quarter apiece, then you'd better find a way to start collecting them in February.

Stepping back, then, to the very first axiom: A ballplayer's purpose in playing baseball is to do those things which create wins for his team, while avoiding those things which create losses for his team.

We are in a position now to answer with some accuracy the question of how many wins and how many losses result from the player's singles, doubles, triples, outs made, etc. We do this by:

1) Figuring out how many runs the player has created for his team.

2) Expressing that as a number of runs per game.

3) Adjusting for the most important illusion, the park illusion.

4) Placing this in the context of the league in which the player performs.

We use the Pythagorean method to place the individual (park-adjusted) runs created per game figure in the context of the league. In the American League in 1983 there were 4.48 runs per game. A player who created exactly 4.48 runs per game, then, would have an offensive won/lost percentage of .500. This would be figured like this:

$$\frac{4.48^2}{4.48^2 + 4.48^2}$$

A player who created 4.00 runs per game would have an offensive won/lost percentage of .444:

$$\frac{4.00^2}{4.00^2 + 4.48^2}$$

A player who created six runs per game would have an offensive won/lost percentage of .642. Wade Boggs had a park-adjusted offensive won/lost percentage of .778.

Exactly what we are saying there is this: If every player on a team could hit the way Wade Boggs hits, and if the team had an average pitching staff and an average defense, then that team would win 77.8% of its games.

And we are not speculating about that. We can say with a high degree of accuracy how many runs per game a team full of Wade Boggses would score. We can say with a very high degree of accuracy how many games that team would win if it allowed an average number of runs.

There are many other methods which are in use throughout this book. I'll explain them when I use them. Some of these methods are new, some old. We will continue to search for more accurate methods and for better information on many elements of the game.

CHART IV
BEST OFFENSIVE PLAYERS, 1983
(Based on park-adjusted offensive totals.
Adjusts runs created for outs and park illusions.)

AMERICAN LEAGUE		NATIONAL LEAGUE	
Wade Boggs, Bos	.778	Dale Murphy, Atl	.778
Eddie Murray, Bal	.767	Pedro Guerrero, LA	.773
George Brett, KC	.762	Mike Schmidt, Phila	.767
Rickey Henderson, Oak	.753	Jose Cruz, Hou	.766
Robin Yount, Mil	.746	Darrell Evans, SF	.763
John Lowenstein, Bal	.722	Joe Lefebvre, SD-Phila	.740
Bobby Grich, Cal	.720	Tim Raines, Mon	.736
Willie Aikens, KC	.702	Bob Horner, Atl	.734
Alan Trammell, Det	.700	Keith Hernandez, StL-NY	.726
Cal Ripken, Bal	.696	George Hendrick, StL	.717

VICTORY IMPORTANT RBI

That which is commonly called clutch performance can exist on three levels: the run level, the game level and the season level. If a player's hits are "run clutch," then that would mean that his hits, because of the times at which they occurred, produced more runs than would normally be expected. If his hits were "game clutch," then that would mean that the runs that he created or produced, because of the times at which they occurred, yielded more wins than would normally be expected. If his performance was "season clutch," then that would mean that his contributions to wins increased at the time when the pennant race was most in doubt, and thus that his performance was such that, over the course of many pennant races, it would tend to yield more pennants than would normally be expected.

Victory Important RBI are one measure of one of those three elements. They pertain to game-clutch performance. What they measure, exactly, is this: Of all those runs that a player drives in, how many contribute to victories, and how vitally do they contribute?

The essential assumption of the VI-RBI is that all runs batted in are important in the degree to which they contribute to a win. If you drive in three runs and the team loses 7–3, that's not important because what is important is for the team to win. All RBI accumulated in defeats are counted at zero. If you drive in three runs in a game that the team wins 10–1, those runs are significant but not very significant; you receive credit for them but not a lot of credit. Since two of the ten runs in the win were essential to the victory, each RBI for the winning team is weighted at 2/10; three RBI in that game are worth 0.6 VI-RBI.

If, however, you win the game by one run, then every run is essential to victory, and every run is counted at one full VI-RBI. If you drive in four runs in a 4–3 win, then there are four big runs, and you get 4.00 VI-RBI.

VI-RBI are certainly an imperfect measure of game-clutch performance, but at the same time there can be no doubt that they will measure the extent to which a player drives in "big" runs. If two players on the same team drove in 100 runs each, but one player tended to drive in big bunches of runs in 8–0 and 14–3 games, while the other made a larger contribution to the 3–2 and 5–3 games, this measure of performance would unquestionably distinguish that difference. That is all that it tries to do, to distinguish among a player's RBI those which are contributions to victory, and those which are mere window-dressing.

The American League leaders in runs batted in in 1983 were:

Cecil Cooper, Milwaukee	126
Jim Rice, Boston	126
Dave Winfield, New York	116
Lance Parrish, Detroit	114
Eddie Murray, Baltimore	111
Ted Simmons, Milwaukee	108
Tony Armas, Boston	107
Willie Upshaw, Toronto	104
Cal Ripken, Baltimore	102
Ron Kittle, Chicago	100
Harold Baines, Chicago	99
Greg Luzinski, Chicago	95
George Brett, Kansas City	93
Larry Herndon, Detroit	92
Larry Parrish, Texas	88
Gary Ward, Minnesota	88

The leaders in Victory-Important RBI were:

Cecil Cooper, Milwaukee	63.16
Jim Rice, Boston	60.29
Harold Baines, Chicago	53.55
Dave Winfield, New York	52.32
Eddie Murray, Baltimore	51.97
Ron Kittle, Chicago	51.33
Ted Simmons, Milwaukee	50.62
Willie Upshaw, Toronto	47.20
Tony Armas, Boston	45.96
Cal Ripken, Baltimore	45.57
Lance Parrish, Detroit	44.28
Robin Yount, Milwaukee	42.54
Lloyd Moseby, Toronto	42.21
Greg Luzinski, Chicago	42.11
Larry Herndon, Detroit	40.29
Carlton Fisk, Chicago	39.42

The lists, as you can see, are basically similar; the players who drove in the most runs were also the players who drove in the most big runs. Using a method introduced in the last section, we could say that there is 93% agreement between the two lists. Cooper's pulling ahead of Rice is not surprising in view of the fact that Cooper played for a little better team, and thus a few more of his RBI would naturally contribute to victories. Larry Parrish and Gary Ward drop off the list, to be replaced by Lloyd Moseby and Carlton Fisk, who played for significantly better teams and drove in only a few less runs; again, that's not surprising.

But there are five player movements that seem to be significant:

(1) Harold Baines, with 99 RBI, drove in more meaningful runs than Ron Kittle (100 RBI), Cal Ripken (102), Willie Upshaw (104), Tony Armas (107), Ted Simmons (108), Eddie Murray (111), Lance Parrish (114) or Dave Winfield (116). Most of those people play for good teams, so that's not an explanation. Meanwhile his teammate, (2) Greg Luzinski, had almost as many RBI as Baines did, but isn't close to him in VI-RBI.

(3) Lance Parrish of Detroit, whom some considered to be an MVP candidate because he is a good defensive player who was fourth in the league in runs batted in, was just eleventh in the league in runs batted in contributing to victories.

(4) George Brett of Kansas City drove in 93 runs, (5) Robin Yount of Milwaukee drove in only 80 runs. There isn't a great difference in the performance of their teams; Brett's team won 79 games, Milwaukee won 87. Yet Brett drops entirely off the list of leaders in VI-RBI, while Yount, not even close to making the list of RBI leaders, is in the twelfth spot among the Victory-Important RBI leaders.

Let us then look more carefully at these players' years, and ask a few more questions about their RBI counts. How many game-winning RBI did they have? How many runs did they drive in when their teams were winning, and how many when they were losing? How many did they drive in when the team was winning 11–1, and how many when the team was winning 2–1 and 4–3?

1) Game-winning RBI.

Baines had 22 game-winning RBI, an American League record (you notice I didn't say an "All-Time American League record". Restrained myself.) His teammate Luzinski had ten game-winning RBI, the same as Yount. Parrish had 14 and Brett 12. So the two people who move up in VI-RBI had 32 GWRBI; the three people who move down had 36.

2) Runs driven in while winning and losing.

Baines drove in 85 of his 99 runs in games that his team was winning, easily the highest percentage in the group. The complete data for the five is given below:

Player	RBI	RBI in Wins	RBI in Losses	% of RBI In Wins
Harold Baines	99	85	14	85.9
Robin Yount	80	58	22	72.5
Greg Luzinski	95	68	27	71.6
Lance Parrish	114	81	33	71.1
George Brett	93	59	34	63.4

3) Runs driven in in one-run wins, and runs driven in in lopsided victories.

Harold Baines drove in 21 runs in one-run victories, his teammate Luzinski drove in 12. The White Sox won only 28 one-run games in 1983, so 21 RBI in these 28 games is an impressive total. Otherwise there is little difference in the RBI patterns of the two players; Baines drove in one more run (27–26) in 2- and 3-run victories, and one more (18–17) in wins with margins of seven or more. Luzinski, as the chart above shows, had nearly twice as many RBI (27–14) in games the White Sox lost.

Probably the most extreme contrast is between Lance Parrish of Detroit and Robin Yount of Milwaukee. Parrish drove in 114 runs, Yount only 80, yet their Victory Important RBI counts are about the same (Parrish 44.28, Yount 42.54). Looking closer at the runs that they drove in, I would be tempted to argue that Yount in fact drove in *more* important runs than Parrish did. There isn't much difference in the percentage of runs driven in in games that were lost; Yount drove in 28% of his runs in losses, Parrish 29%.

But there's a lot of difference in the runs driven in in victory. Yount drove in more in one-run victories than Parrish did, 17–14. Those runs are crucial; you take away any one of them and you could lose a ballgame. He also drove in more runs in games that were won by two or three runs (21–20), and more runs in games that were won by four or five runs (17–12).

But after that, Parrish takes over with a vengeance. Parrish drove in 16 runs in blowouts, in wins that were decided by eight or more runs. Yount drove in no runs, none at all, in games that his team won by eight or more. Parrish drove in 13 more runs in games that his team won by seven runs. Yount drove in only one run in games that Milwaukee won by seven. That is a 29–1 edge for Parrish in RBI that meant almost nothing. In games that were decided by six runs, he drove in six more; Yount drove in two. That makes it 35–3 in games decided by six or more. Add in the 33 runs that Parrish drove in when his team was losing, to 22 for Yount, and you've got a 68–25 differential in useless and largely useless RBI.

For the sake of clarity, I want to emphasize that I certainly am not saying that Parrish did not hit in the clutch, or that Yount is a great clutch performer. But I am saying, without reservations, that the difference of 34 RBI between Yount and Parrish is not a meaningful difference. It is wholly and entirely a matter of Parrish padding his statistics by driving in a huge number of runs that did nothing to change losses into wins. I think that when you're making out an MVP ballot, that's worth knowing.

George Brett's disappearance from the list of leaders in VI-RBI is attributable largely to the 34 runs that he drove in in games the Royals did not win. Brett drove in 17 runs in one-run wins, more than Parrish or Luzinski, and as many as Yount. He drove in only seven in lopsided (7-run) wins, more than Yount but less than half as many as Baines or Luzinski or Parrish. He finished with 37.19 VI-RBI, seventeenth in the league.

RBI IMPORTANCE

VI-RBI are but one of five categories of "RBI analysis" that are presented with the teams in Section II. The second category is "RBI Importance." RBI Importance is VI-RBI divided by total RBI. VI-RBI asks "how many important runs did the player drive in," without paying any attention to how many total runs he drove in. RBI Importance looks at all of the runs the player has driven in, and asks what share of them were contributions to the team's eventual victories.

Among players with 30 or more RBI, the American League leaders in RBI Importance were:

	RBI	VI-RBI	RBI-Importance
Dave Collins, Toronto	34	19.57	.576
Rick Dempsey, Baltimore	32	17.94	.561
Greg Walker, Chicago	55	30.36	.552
Juan Beniquez , California	34	18.73	.551
Gary Hancock, Oakland	30	16.34	.545
Harold Baines, Chicago	99	53.55	.541
Roy Smalley, New York	62	33.16	.535
Robin Yount, Milwaukee	80	42.54	.532
Lloyd Moseby, Toronto	81	42.21	.521
Ben Oglivie, Milwaukee	66	34.13	.517

Since that list is so heavily dominated by men with 33 RBI, let's move the qualification up to 60 RBI, run out some of the riff-raff:

	RBI	VI-RBI	RBI-Importance
Harold Baines, Chicago	99	53.55	.541
Roy Smalley, New York	62	33.16	.535
Robin Yount, Milwaukee	80	42.54	.532
Lloyd Moseby, Toronto	81	42.21	.521
Ben Oglivie, Milwaukee	66	34.13	.517

Tom Paciorek, Chicago	63	32.37	.514
Ron Kittle, Chicago	100	51.33	.513
Lou Whitaker, Detroit	72	36.70	.510
Cecil Cooper, Milwaukee	126	63.16	.501
Willie Aikens, Kansas City	72	35.66	.495

In the interests of presenting a balanced view of the issue, the following are the players who drove in the most meaningless runs in the league (left-most numbers indicate rank if 30 RBI is considered the cut-off; right numbers indicate rank with 60 RBI limit):

			RBI	VI-RBI	RBI-Importance
1		Rickey Nelson, Seattle	36	7.83	.218
2		Tom Brookens, Detroit	32	7.75	.242
3		Dave Hostetler, Texas	46	11.50	.250
4		Ron Hassey, Cleveland	42	10.94	.260
5		Carl Yastrzemski, Boston	56	16.56	.296
6	1	Bill Almon, Oakland	63	18.81	.299
7	2	Fred Lynn, California	74	23.02	.311
8		Dave Engel, Minnesota	43	16.50	.314
9		Randy Bush, Minnesota	56	17.90	.320
10		Tony Bernazard, two teams	56	18.03	.322
	3	Mike Davis, Oakland	62	20.01	.323
	4	Gorman Thomas, Mil/Cle	69	23.34	.338
	5	Andre Thornton, Cleveland	77	26.17	.340
	6	Dave Stapleton, Boston	66	22.73	.344
	7	George Wright, Texas	80	28.29	.354
	8	Gary Gaetti, Minnesota	78	27.90	.358
	9	Chet Lemon, Detroit	69	24.97	.362
	10	Dave Lopes, Oakland	67	24.56	.367

Most of you have probably noticed by now that the lists of the highest RBI Importance were dominated by players who played on good teams, and the list of the lowest RBI Importance is dominated by players from bad teams. RBI Importance is in the category of measurements of the game, like pitchers wins and won/lost percentage, batters runs scored and runs batted in and game-winning hits, which are to some degree team-dependent; it is easier to compile a good record in these areas when playing for a good team than it is when playing for a bad team. How much easier? The chart below gives the Victory-Important RBI, total RBI and RBI Importance for each American League team.

	VI-RBI	RBI	RBI-Importance
Baltimore	331.33	761	.435
Boston	296.07	691	.428
California	278.34	682	.408
Chicago	369.24	762	.485
Cleveland	241.98	659	.367
Detroit	313.85	749	.419
Kansas City	277.29	653	.425
Milwaukee	344.41	732	.470
Minnesota	268.70	671	.400
New York	333.08	728	.458
Oakland	256.69	662	.388
Seattle	198.36	536	.370
Texas	207.93	507	.354
Toronto	345.99	748	.463

The range of team performance is from .485 for Chicago to .354 for Texas.

We should not assume that this is totally an illusion; it is quite possible that the good teams have high figures and the poorer teams low figures not because of some sort of statistical illusion, but because the good teams have a superior ability to produce the big runs. If you believe in clutch ability, then you would argue that that is the basic reason for the difference; as a skeptic, I say that is only a small part of the difference. But the Texas Rangers scored 30 more runs than their opponents this year, yet finished 8 games under .500. That indicates that the Rangers, for whatever reason, did not produce the big runs that they needed at key moments in the game. Their RBI-Importance simply reflects that reality. The runs that are driven in by Rickey Nelson and Ron Hassey and Bill Almon are less important—they have a smaller impact on the win column—than the runs driven in by Rick Dempsey and Harold Baines and Roy Smalley. RBI-Importance simply recognizes that.

There are two more columns on the RBI analysis charts. One is called WBI (Wins Batted In) and the other is called RBI per win. This is another road which goes in the same direction; it measures the same thing a different way.

VI-RBI asks this question: How many of a player's *RBI* are contributions to *wins?* WBI asks this question: How many *wins* result from the player's *RBI?*

If a player drives in the only run of a 1–0 ballgame, as Harold Baines did on June 19th against Oakland, then that player is fully responsible, from an RBI standpoint, for that win. If he drives in four runs in a 4–3 game, same thing; no one else can claim a share of victory as far as the runs batted in are concerned. In each case, the player would receive 1.00 win batted in.

In all cases, the runs in a victory are divided evenly so as to create the win. If you drive in one run in a 12–0 game, that is .0833 WBI; one run in a 12–9 game, same thing.

VI-RBI take the position that driving in one run in a 2–1 game and driving in one run in a 7–6 game are equivalent accomplishments, each RBI separating victory from extra innings. I agree with that; they are equivalent. WBI does not measure them the same. When WBI measures evenly driving in one run in a 7–0 victory and driving in one run in a 7–6 victory, I can't agree with that; there is a difference.

Yet WBI says that there is a difference between driving in the only run of a 1–0 game three times (3.00 WBI), and driving in 3 runs in a 3–2 game once (1.00 WBI). I must agree with that; VI-RBI errs in weighting them equal at 3.00, as one accomplishment makes the difference in three games and the other in only one.

I don't know which measure I like better, so I present them both. The American League players batting in the most wins in 1983:

	WBI
Jim Rice, Boston	16.86
Cecil Cooper, Milwaukee	15.13
Harold Baines, Chicago	14.42
Eddie Murray, Baltimore	14.06
Dave Winfield, New York	13.78
Cal Ripken, Baltimore	13.77

Rice had a lot of big hits; you will notice that his VI-RBI count is also well above the Boston team average. Leading the league in WBI while playing for a sub-.500 team is a remarkable accomplishment. Rice, even leading the league in RBI, batted in only 18% of his team's runs. But he batted in 22% of their wins.

WBI are directly, one-to-one, comparable to Game-Winning RBI; the only difference is that Game-Winning RBI consider one of the runs in a win to be responsible for the whole thing, and WBI considers all of them to be equally responsible. Both systems are right and both wrong; all RBI in a win are not totally equal, yet no one of them can magically create the win without the others.

A final advantage of WBI is that it is automatically park-adjusted; there are no park illusions in WBI, since there are exactly as many wins in one park as there are in another.

The final column, RBI per win, asks how many runs the player has driven in for every win that he has accounted for. It is RBI/WBI; the lower the figure, the better. A normal figure is eight to ten; Baines drove in one win for every 6.9 runs, Gary Gaetti brought home a win with each 11.7 runs. Does this tell us more about the White Sox pitchers and Minnesota pitchers than about Baines and Gaetti? It tells us something about the pitchers, but Luzinski, also playing for the White Sox, had a ratio of 9.1/1, and Tom Brunansky, also with the Twins, had a ratio of 8.2/1. So it also tells us something about the player's performance.

About his performance; not necessarily about his ability. If I were a general manager considering the acquisition of a ballplayer, and I knew that that player had, the previous season, driven in astonishingly few VI-RBI, that fact would not greatly concern me. I doubt that it would deter me from going after him. If he had done this over a period of years, then that would certainly give me pause.

But if I were a sportswriter and making out an MVP ballot, and I knew that the player had driven in very few VI-RBI, then that certainly would be something that I would consider. He may have failed to drive in the big runs because he has no guts, or he may have failed to drive in the big runs simply because he wasn't lucky in the close games. It makes no difference; his value is the same either way.

No one doubts that over the course of a season, clutch performance exists. When the scoresheets are available and the issue can be studied for a year, we will most certainly find that some players have had an impact beyond what their numbers would suggest. What is subject to question is that this represents an ability. If there is such a thing as "clutch ability," then exactly what is it? We know what its signs would be, but what *is* it? How is it that a player who possesses the reflexes and the batting stroke and the knowledge and the experience to be a .260 hitter in other circumstances magically becomes a .300 hitter when the game is on the line? How does that happen? What is the process? What are the effects?

Until we can answer those questions, I see little point in talking about clutch ability.

WHERE DOES TALENT COME FROM

Where does a team's talent come from? Which major league organization has produced the most talent? Which has produced the least talent? Which teams are built basically by trade, and which are basically built through the farm system? Are the most successful teams the teams which are built through the system?

I will be discussing these issues in some depth throughout this book. What I wanted to do here is to set up a data bank from which we can draw during those discussions. First I need to explain the method that is being used.

The method is called the Value Approximation method. The Value Approximation method seeks to recognize what is obvious about the value of a ballplayer and state that in a convenient, useful form. It tries to make no fine judgments about who is better than whom, but simply to yield a quick assessment of who are the best players within a group, the worst players in a group and how the others string out between.

It does this by a series of "awards" based on the player's performance in various categories.

Batting average: Award one point if the player has hit .250 or better, 2 points if .275, 3 if .300 . . . 7 if .400 or higher.

Slugging percentage: Award one point if the player has a slugging percentage over .300, 2 if over .400, 3 if over .500 . . . 6 if over .800.

Other rules award points for drawing walks, hitting home runs, stealing bases, driving in runs, getting 200 hits in a season, havng a high fielding percentage or range factor, or various and sundry other offensive and defensive accomplishments. Pitchers' points are based largely on won/lost records, saves and ERAs, with a couple of other categories.

The system is set up so that a regular player will always accumulate a few points a year, even if the things that he does don't show up in impressive numbers. A player who plays 150 games, 550 or more at-bats, could not possibly have an Approximate Value of less than 4, and he would have to be incredibly bad to have an Approximate Value below 8. My feeling is that if a player can stay in the lineup, year after year, then he must be making a contribution to his ballclub, at least in the eyes of the manager or the general manager. I don't want to argue about that; I just want to register that value and go on with whatever issue I am studying. The Value Approximation method is not used to assess ballplayers. The Value Approximation method is used only to assign "weights" or "rough values" to seasons, so that groups of unlike seasons can be lumped together and evaluated.

The scale goes something like this: An exceptional MVP season might have a value of around 20. A 20-point season is Sandy Koufax in the mid-sixties, Mickey or Willy in the mid-fifties, Joe Morgan in the mid-seventies.

An ordinary MVP season would fall into the 16-to-18 point range.

A serious MVP candidate would usually fall into the 14-to-16 point range.

An All-Star season would usually fall into the 12-to-14 point range.

A "solid" or "above average" regular would fall into the 10-to-12 point range.

A "fair" or "below average" regular would fall into the 8-to-10 point range if he plays fulltime, 150 or more games. If he plays 130–150 games, the 7-to-9 range is more likely.

A productive platoon player might fall in the range of 6-to-10 points.

An unproductive platoon player might fall in the range of 3-to-6 points.

Any player below 5 points is either a player who hasn't played very much or a player who hasn't played very well.

To further establish these ranges in your mind, I'll discuss some particular AV (Approximate Values) from the 1983 season. Remember, the fact that one season is evaluated at "14" and another at "16" is not supposed to prove anything; it's just a way of getting the player into a group of players of comparable value.

The highest Approximate Value in the American League in 1983 belonged to Cal Ripken (17). The highest in the National League belonged to Dale Murphy (17).

The following were some players having 15-point seasons in 1983: Andre Dawson, Wade Boggs, Jack Morris, Carlton Fisk, Mike Schmidt, Richard Dotson, LaMarr Hoyt, Rickey Henderson, Tim Raines and Eddie Murray.

The following players were having 12-point seasons in 1983: Glenn Hubbard, Jody Davis, Mookie Wilson, Terry Kennedy, George Brett, Rich Gossage, Charlie Hough, Ryne Sandberg, Ozzie Smith and Jeff Leonard.

The following were having 9-point seasons in 1983: Gary Redus, Bo Diaz, Bobby Grich, Charlie Moore, Mike Davis, Jim Clancy, Phil Garner, Doug Sisk, Juan Bonilla and Storm Davis.

The following were having 6-point seasons

in 1983: Vern Ruhle, Cecilio Guante, Mike Krukow, Britt Burns, Steve Yeager, Joe Lefebvre, Dave Stapleton, Reggie Jackson, Bud Black and Steve Kemp.

The following were having 3-point seasons in 1983: Joe Beckwith, Jeff Lahti, Joe Nolan, George Vukovich, Ron Washington, Roy Thomas, Jerry Royster, Cesar Cedeno, Bob James and Richie Hebner.

Below that, you don't want to know.

These approximations become useful when you ask a question such as "which major league system has produced the largest share of its own talent," "which major league system has produced the smallest share of the team's talent," or "which system has produced the most talent for other organizations"?

You can answer those questions, if you want, just by counting ballplayers. But it doesn't seem quite right (nor should it), to give the Atlanta farm system equal credit for producing Dale Murphy and Paul Zuvella. Adding Approximate Value is the same as counting the players, except that it counts Dale Murphy 17 times, Brett Butler 11 times and Paul Zuvella no times.

The major league team which produced the largest share of its talent from its own system is the Cincinnati Reds. The following Reds players came from the Reds system: Mario Soto (Approximate Value: 12), Eddie Milner (11), Gary Redus (9), Dave Concepcion (8), Dan Driessen (8), Paul Householder (7), Ron Oester (7), Joe Price (7), Bill Scherrer (7), Bruce Berenyi (6), Johnny Bench (5), Frank Pastore (5), Nick Esasky (4), Ben Hayes (4), Tom Hume (4), Duane Walker (2), Jeff Russell (2), Tom Foley (1) and Jeff Jones (1). That's a total of 110 "units" of talent produced by their system.

Acquired from other organizations are Dann Bilardello (5), Ted Power (4), Cesar Cedeno (3), Charlie Puleo (3), Kelly Paris (2), Alex Trevino (2), Alan Knicely (1) and Rich Gale (1). That's a total of 21 points worth of talent acquired from other systems. 84% of the Reds' productive talent was produced by their own system.

On the other end of the scale, which established organization produced the smallest share of its own talent? Answer: Not surprisingly, the New York Yankees—14% of their own talent. The five teams producing the largest percentage of their own talent: Cincinnati (84%), Boston (80%), Montreal (71%), Los Angeles (71%)

and Atlanta (68%). The five teams producing the smallest percentages: New York (14%), Cleveland (15%), the Houston Astros (16%), the California Angels (17%) and the Chicago Cubs (21%).

The organization which has produced the most talent for everybody is, by far, the Los Angeles Dodgers. The Dodgers have produced some talent for 20 of the 26 major league teams, and have contributed significantly to most of the good ballclubs in the major leagues. A complete account of the 1983 talent they have produced:

INFIELD: Pedro Guerrero (15); Steve Sax (11); Greg Brock (9); Bill Russell (5); Dave Anderson (1); Rafael Landestoy (1); Dave Lopes, Oakland (13); Bill Buckner, Chicago (11); Ron Cey, Chicago (10); Ivan DeJesus, Philadelphia (10); Steve Garvey, San Diego (7); Ron Washington, Minnesota (3); Jerry Royster, Atlanta (3); Leo Hernandez, Baltimore (2). Infielders, 101 Total.

OUTFIELD: Mike Marshall (8); Ron Roenicke (4); Jeff Leonard, San Francisco (12); Rudy Law, Chicago (11); Tom Paciorek, Chicago (8); Mickey Hatcher, Minnesota (7); Lee Lacy, Pittsburgh (6); Bobby Mitchell, Minnesota (2); Mark Bradley, New York (1); Joe Simpson, Kansas City (1). Outfielders, 60 Total.

CATCHER: Steve Yeager (6); Mike Scioscia (1); Dann Bilardello, Cincinnati (5). Catchers, 12 Total.

PITCHER: Bob Welch (11); Fernando Valenzuela (10); Dave Stewart (10); Alejandro Pena (9); Steve Howe (9); Tom Niedenfuer (9); Joe Beckwith (3); Charlie Hough, Texas (12); Rick Rhoden, Pittsburgh (11); Rick Sutcliffe, Cleveland (10); Luis Sanchez, California (9); Geoff Zahn, California (8); Don Sutton, Milwaukee (7); Ted Power, Cincinnati (4); Doyle Alexander, Toronto (4); Bobby Castillo, Minnesota (3). Pitchers, 129 Total.

That's 302 points worth of talent, spread around the majors. An average figure is 154; the second-highest total is 227. (This is beginning to sound like a Midas advertisement. Can't you see Tommy Lasorda walking across the yard at Dodger Town, saying, "We've produced more outfielders than they have fielders; we've given away more pitchers than they have produced.")

Let's take a comprehensive look at who has produced talent for whom. First, let's look at where the talent is that has been produced by the National League teams:

	Atl	Chi	Cin	Hou	LA	Mon	NY	Phi	Pit	StL	SD	SF
Atl	113	3		3	3		1		13			6
Chi	6	32			21			41		23	1	
Cin			110	4	9		5			2		
Hou	3	11	20	25		1	15		6	16		7
LA	9	6	4	3	115					9		
Mon		5	5			112	10		10	1		4
NY	4			7	1	1	65		1	14		13
Phi	8	8	8	13	10		2	35	11	26		11
Pit	9		4	18	17		4	3	78			
StL		9	9				9	12		48	12	
SD			2		7		2	3	15	28	59	8
SF	13	6	7	12	2			4	10			57
Bal						2	7	14	1	5		
Bos									12			4
Cal			8	17	3	5	8	5				
Chi		12		10	19	2	8	11	7	1		
Cle	4			10				29		2	8	
Det			7					8	4	11	3	
KC		5		17	1	1		7	1	1		2
Mil					7			2		12	15	
Min		10		15	1							
NY		3	9				12		9	5	14	2
Oak				13	6			7	1		8	6
Tex	4			16	12	1			15	6		
Sea		15		5	3			6	3	2	2	2
Tor	9	3		9	4			6	8			6
Tot	182	113	217	106	302	163	164	169	200	212	122	128

The Cubs and Houston have produced the least talent of any National League team, and both have produced most what they have offered for other teams.

A directory of talent produced by American League teams is next:

	Bal	Bos	Cal	Chi	Cle	Det	KC	Mil	Min	NY	Oak	Tex	Sea	Tor	NL	Total
Atl				7	9						9				142	167
Chi		7	3	5			1		7		1				124	149
Cin							1								130	131
Hou			14	4	6		13				11				104	152
LA			12	2							3				146	163
Mon	8								1	1					147	157
NY	5						14				10				106	135
Phi	2	9		4					6						132	153
Pit			2		9	5					12				133	161
StL			1		4	1	27	2	12	11					99	157
SD			6	9		6	4	4							124	153
SF			2		29				6						111	148
Bal	92			3	7	2	6	26	7						29	172
Bos		128	13	3											16	160
Cal	16	21	24	7	7			13			6		1		46	141
Chi	15	21	47	8	3				15						70	179
Cle			20					15	5	10	4	22	4		53	133
Det	9					101	11				14	5			33	173
KC	2		10		3		88				1	1	6		35	146
Mil	30	3		5		5		83			2				36	164
Min	29	1			4				68	4	6	6			26	144
NY	12		12	2	6		7	14	22	3	26				54	158
Oak			12	4	15	3		6			69	5			41	155
Tex		8	6	6	11	3						64			54	152
Sea			3			6				9	2	8	51		42	121
Tor	9	15	3	9	5				31	1	9			49	45	176
Tot	146	227	174	91	106	155	157	155	129	151	149	170	62	49	2074	4000

If you read these charts across, then you are answering the question "where does this team's talent come from?" Two points of Baltimore's talent comes from the Los Angeles system, 7 points from Montreal . . . 26 points from the Yankee system, 7 from Oakland. The total 1983 talent possessed by the team is given in the right hand column of the American League chart.

The chart below breaks down the talent possessed by each team into three categories—talent produced by the system (S), talent acquired by trade (T) and talent purchased or signed from free agency (FA). The American League charts also have talent retained from expansion draft (EX).

Approximate Value possessed. This is very unusual, and to some degree deflates what we are trying to do with the bar graphs, which is show where one team pulls ahead of the others. There is still a strong positive correlation between Value Possessed and Wins (+.84), but it's not quite as strong as it usually is.

A final chart breaks down the talent possessed by each team into young talent (Y), players in their prime (P), players who are at an age where most players are past their prime (PP) and those who are old (O). The divisions:

YOUNG:	Up to Age 25 (as of July 1, 1983)
PRIME:	Ages 26 to 29
PAST-PRIME:	Ages 30 to 34
OLD:	Ages 35 and up

N.L. WEST

	S	T	FA	Total
L.A.	115	45	3	163
Atlanta	113	32	22	167
Houston	25	78	49	152
S.D.	59	72	22	153
San Fran.	57	82	9	148
Cincin.	110	12	9	131

N.L. EAST

	S	T	FA	Total
Phil.	35	108	10	153
Pittsburgh	78	73	10	161
Montreal	112	39	6	157
St. Louis	48	91	18	157
Chicago	32	90	27	149
New York	65	68	2	135

A.L. WEST

	S	T	FA	EX	Total
Chi.	47	92	40		179
K.C.	88	49	9		146
Tex.	64	61	27		152
Oak.	69	47	39		148
Minn.	68	56	20		144
Cal.	24	60	57		141
Seattle	51	42	23	5	121

A.L. EAST

	S	T	FA	EX	Total
Balt.	92	65	15		172
Det.	101	55	17		173
N.Y.	22	89	47		158
Tor.	49	75	15	37	176
Mil.	83	74	7		164
Bos.	128	32	0		160
Cleve.	20	113	0		133

N.L. WEST

	Y	P	PP	O	Total
L.A.	60	57	43	3	163
Atlanta	57	70	26	14	167
Houston	38	45	38	31	152
S. D.	37	93	21	2	153
San Fran.	37	54	40	17	148
Cin.	40	63	15	13	131

N.L. EAST

	Y	P	PP	O	Total
Phil.	16	22	77	38	153
Pit.	25	74	48	14	161
Mon.	36	84	27	10	157
StL.	49	62	44	2	157
Chi.	50	37	35	27	149
N. Y.	45	51	24	15	135

A.L. EAST

	Y	P	PP	O	Total
Balt.	43	52	51	26	172
Detroit	40	94	28	11	173
New York	22	45	79	12	158
Toronto	46	87	34	9	176
Mil.	17	72	68	7	164
Boston	40	73	36	11	160
Cleve.	27	37	69	1	133

A.L. WEST

	Y	P	PP	O	Total
Chi.	54	64	25	36	179
KC	14	43	58	31	146
Tex.	23	75	37	17	152
Oak.	62	54	20	19	148
Min.	59	82	3	0	144
Cal.	12	22	55	52	141
Sea.	42	50	27	2	121

At the end of the article, this same information is presented in bar graphs, thanks to Susie.

You will notice that in only one division was the champion the team with the highest total of

These numbers, too, will be rendered into bar graphs in the next few pages.

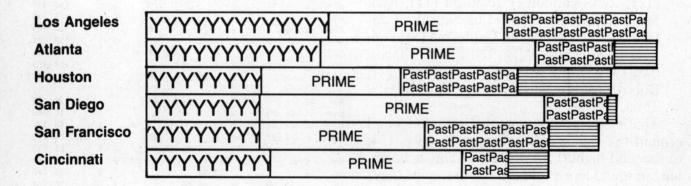

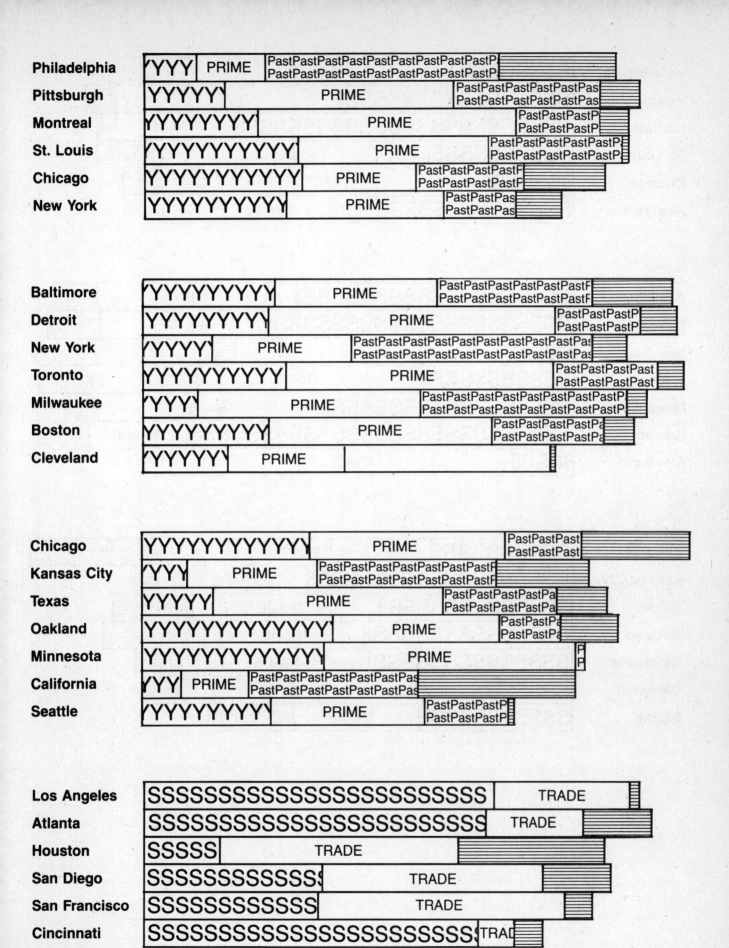

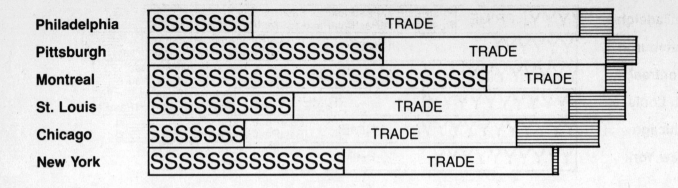

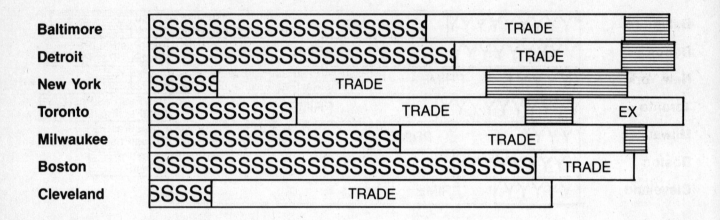

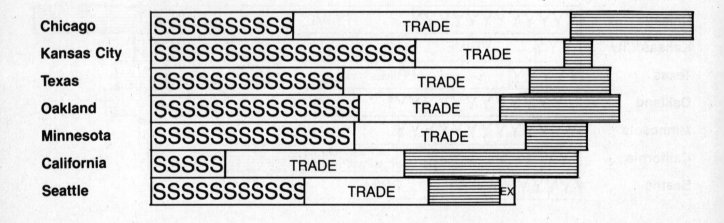

EXPLANATION OF DIVISION SHEETS

At the beginning of each section concerning the four divisions there is a Division Sheet like the one that follows. Each Division Sheet contains five charts.

FIRST CHART: Sets out the record of each team before the All-Star Game (includes games of July 4th) and after the All-Star Game; versus righthanded and lefthanded pitching; at home and on the road; on grass and AstroTurf; in the daytime and at night. This information is followed by season totals and winning percentage.

TURNAROUNDS: Gives the number of times each team has come from one run behind, two runs behind. . . eight runs behind. Conversely, "Blown Leads" show the number of times teams have lost after holding leads of one run, two runs. . .eight runs. The total lists the number of comebacks or blown leads. The point system gives a point for every run it took to come back or blow a lead. For instance, to come from four runs behind and win requires five runs and thus nets five points. Each game is counted only one time, even if a team comes back two or three times in the game, and is counted by the maximum difference between the two teams. If a team comes back, ties it up and then loses, that doesn't count.

DEFENSIVE RECORDS: This chart gives the number of bases stolen against the team (under OSB), the number of runners caught stealing (under OCS) and the opponents' success in stealing bases (as OSB%). The number of double plays turned by a team is next on the chart. OA/SFA gives the number of assists by the team's outfielders and sacrifice flies allowed by the team. The three remaining statistics are team fielding average, defensive efficiency record (percentage of balls put into play against a team that are turned into outs) and the number of runs allowed by a team.

OPPOSITION ERRORS: Here is listed the number of errors committed by each team's opponents position by position. "Un" is unidentified errors, which result when a player plays two positions in a game and commits an error at one of them. The uninformative box scores now in use do not give a clue as to which position it was.

LATE-INNING BALLCLUBS: Gives the record of each team when the team is ahead after seven innings, tied after seven or behind after seven. The "Net Change" is in half games.

EXPLANATION OF PLAYER BOXES

Accompanying each Team Comment are player and pitcher data boxes which contain the following information:

HITTERS: Boxes are given for all the team's regulars and reserves who could be considered semi-regular. The data given is
1) runs created by the player
2) the player's career record in seasonal notation
3) the player's 1983 record
4) his record before and after the All-Star Game
5) how he batted against right and lefthanded pitchers
6) what he did in his home park and on the road
7) his record on grass and on turf.

The breakdowns for performance against righthanded and lefthanded pitching are obtained from the teams, which means accuracy and availability, especially in the National League, are not always consistent.
means accuracy and availability, especially in the National League, are not always consistent.

The data which is presented for each player, and the order in which it is presented, is different this year. When I began the *Baseball Abstract*, I had no thought of making it anyone's baseball reference book. I'll tell you now: it's not a very good baseball reference book. If you're interested in a reference book, get *The Sporting News Guide* or *Register*, or both, or the *Sports Encyclopedia: Baseball*. What I thought I was doing was writing to a small subsection of the people who bought those books, those who wanted yet more information.

But funny things happen in the publishing business, and now a whole lot of people are reading this book who don't have any other access to some fairly basic information about the players, like how many times they walk, strikeout and are caught stealing. So I've been telling people they needed to pay more attention to how many times a player walks, but I wasn't giving them the data to pay attention to.

I hope the organization of the data doesn't throw you; it is more logical if less familiar. Next to at-bats comes hits; doubles, triples and home runs are together; runs and RBI are together; walks and strikeouts are together; stolen bases and caught stealing are together. We'll get used to it.

PITCHERS: Data is given for the 1982 and 1983 seasons for all pitchers who made 20 or more starts. The charts give, for each season, the pitcher's won/lost record, the number of games started, the number of runs scored by his team when he started, the average number of runs per start, the number of double plays turned behind him and the number of stolen bases by the opposition in games he started, plus the average. The pitcher's home and away record for the past two seasons follows. This year we also include grass/turf breakdowns for 1983. The categories are pretty obvious, but I'll list them just the same—games, innings pitched, wins and losses, won/lost percentage, earned runs allowed and earned run average.

NATIONAL LEAGUE EAST
DIVISION SHEET

Chart I

	1st	2nd	vs. RHP	vs. LHP	Home	Road	Grass	Turf	Day	Night	Total	Pct.
Philadelphia	38-36	52-36	73-54	17-18	50-31	40-41	16-26	74-46	29-19	61-53	90-72	.556
Pittsburgh	34-42	50-36	62-58	22-20	41-40	43-38	19-23	65-55	23-37	61-41	84-78	.519
Montreal	41-36	41-44	64-54	18-26	46-35	36-45	18-24	64-56	32-27	50-53	82-80	.506
St. Louis	40-39	39-44	57-62	22-21	44-37	35-46	18-24	61-59	31-24	48-59	79-83	.488
Chicago	38-41	33-50	49-63	22-28	43-38	28-53	58-56	13-35	51-55	20-36	71-91	.438
New York	30-50	38-44	51-70	17-24	41-41	27-53	54-60	14-34	23-28	45-66	68-94	.420

Chart II
COME FROM BEHIND WINS

Team	1	2	3	4	5	Total	Points
Philadelphia	22	13	7	1		43	116
Pittsburgh	18	8	7	1	1	35	99
Montreal	15	8	3			26	66
St. Louis	20	8	5	2		35	94
Chicago	18	6	5	1	1	31	85
New York	12	13	4	1	2	32	96

BLOWN LEADS

Team	1	2	3	4	5	6	Total	Points
Philadelphia	18	6	5				29	74
Pittsburgh	16	14	4	1	1		36	101
Montreal	22	8	4	0	0	1	35	91
St. Louis	13	6	6	2			27	78
Chicago	25	10	7	1	1		44	119
New York	21	5	5	3	2		36	104

Chart III
DEFENSIVE RECORDS

Team	OSB	OCS	OSB%	DP	OA/SFA	Fielding Avg.	DER	Opposition Runs
Philadelphia	167	79	.708	117	29/39	.976	.683	635
Pittsburgh	126	65	.660	165	19/	.982	.695	648
Montreal	115	88	.567	130	47/	.981	.705	646
St. Louis	110	64	.632	173	37/	.976	.697	710
Chicago	152	65	.700	164	27/	.982	.688	719
New York	194	72	.729	171	31/	.976	.707	680

Chart IV
OPPOSITION ERRORS

Team	C	1B	2B	3B	SS	LF	CF	RF	P	Un	Total
Philadelphia	10	11	20	29	24	4	16	8	5	6	133
Pittsburgh	30	25	20	16	17	11	7	5	21	1	153
Montreal	12	4	19	37	26	14	4	8	14	1	139
St. Louis	18	2	19	18	21	5	5	6	19	2	115
Chicago	15	9	19	19	34	7	5	10	14	2	134
New York	9	8	11	17	27	3	6	7	20	2	110

Chart V
LATE-INNING BALLCLUBS

Team	Ahead	Tied	Behind	Net Change
Philadelphia	69-6	12-11	9-55	+4
Pittsburgh	71-9	7-11	6-58	−7
Montreal	70-4	8-11	4-65	−3
St. Louis	56-5	12-12	11-66	+6
Chicago	58-4	8-15	5-72	−6
New York	45-6	17- 7	6-81	+10

PHILADELPHIA PHILLIES

I. AN UPDATE ON THE LEADOFF MEN

The Phillies' leadoff problems were discussed in the 1983 *Baseball Abstract*. Steps were taken to correct this problem in 1983, most of them positive. Runs scored increased, RBI production more than doubled and slugging percentage was up by 25%:

	G	AB	R	H	2B	3B	HR	RBI	Avg	Slug
1982	162	666	82	159	19	4	5	36	.237	.300
1983	162	659	97	177	30	4	11	83	.269	.376

In fact, substantial increases were made in every category save for triples. The difference, across the board, was Joe Morgan. The ghost of Morgan past got up and ran around when he was batted in the number one spot. Out of that position he slugged .513, as opposed to .335 elsewhere. He was especially nasty during the key September hot streak. With Joe leading off, the Phils averaged 5.16 runs per game; with Rose, 4.12; Dernier, 3.96; and Gross, 3.90.

1983 PHILLIE LEADOFF MEN (while hitting #1)

	G	AB	R	H	2B	3B	HR	RBI	Avg	BB	SB	Team Record When Starting W-L
Dernier	49	171	21	38	7	0	1	12	.222	11	14	26-19-1
Rose	44	164	20	44	7	1	0	17	.268	11	1	20-21
Morgan	42	156	31	44	12	0	8	28	.282	21	4	25-13
Gross	24	77	9	23	2	3	0	16	.299	7	1	12- 7
Samuel	15	56	11	15	1	0	1	4	.268	0	1	7- 6
Matthews	3	7	3	3	0	0	0	0	.429	3	3	0- 2
Hayes	3	6	1	1	0	0	0	0	.167	0	0	0- 1
Others (non-starters)	22	22	1	9	1	0	1	6	.409	4	0	---

A year ago it was also reported that Phillie second-place hitters scored only 88 runs. This year it was 91.

—Jim Baker

II. WHY THE PHILLIES PLAYED WELL IN SEPTEMBER

What I am about to say should be obvious, but obviously it is not. Mike Schmidt's early September rip at Paul Owens' lineup juggling, while it may have helped to clear the air heading into the pennant race, could not possibly have been more wrong in content. Schmidt said that the Phillies had no sense of direction and no stability. Players like Pete Rose, Garry Maddox and Joe Morgan, he said, were used to playing every day; they couldn't be expected to play their best playing four or five days a week. Because of that, he said, the Phillies were the least likely team to get hot in September.

Now wait a minute, Mr. Schmidt. The Phillies in 1982 used a set lineup. A very set lineup; at some spots it was set in concrete. Did they get hot in September? They had a strong sense of direction in September: straight down the toilet. Stability? Like a rock, they were.

Sure, Joe Morgan has played 150 games a year all his career. And he never hit a lick in September until he cut it out (see Morgan comment). Sure, Pete Rose has been playing 162 games a year for years, and he used to be a great September player. But he hit .234 in September of 1980 and .222 in September of 1982.

It is my belief that, in general, platoon teams play better in September than any other type of team. Weaver's teams did, and Stengel's did. But we're not talking about just any team here, but about an ancient team, a 1970s reliquary which has somehow, miraculously, survived into the mid-1980s. How on earth can you play them every day until they drop, and not expect them to drop?

The performance of the Phillies after Schmidt's outburst can be taken as proof that he was right or proof that he was wrong. I'll let you guess which way he took it. But remember what he said: He thought the Phillies were the *least* likely team to get hot in September.

III. WHY THE PHILLIES PLAY WELL ON ARTIFICIAL TURF

Why do the Phillies play so well on artificial turf? The Phillies last year had the very best record in the National League on artificial turf; they were 74-46. They had the very worst record in the league on grass surfaces, 16-26. This, you must admit, seems a little bit odd; ordinarily, you assume that if a team can play baseball, they can play baseball. Can a few weeds make that much difference?

Yet compounding that, the Phillies do not look, at a glance, to be what you would call a classic turf team. Their team speed is unexceptional, probably below average. They don't have the high-average, line-drive offense nor the aggressive baserunning that one associates with Whitey Herzog and his turf teams. They have an offense that has a lot of people on base because they draw four walks a game, and an offense that has above-average power—a 1950s offense, to exaggerate for illustrative purposes.

Further, their defense doesn't look like it should be hurt any by moving off artificial turf. If you had Pete Rose and Joe Morgan on the right side of your infield, wouldn't you welcome the chance to slow down the ground balls a little bit?

We can analyze this, as we can analyze most things in baseball, by details. We can look at the stats and see who hits well on turf and doesn't hit on grass. Pete Rose hit .157 on grass fields, .276 on turf; Garry Maddox hit .237 on grass, .333 on turf. We can break their offensive and defensive production per game out to grass and turf:

RUNS PER GAME

	Offense	Defense
Turf	4.50	3.72
Grass	3.71	4.50

Which tells us that the decline in performance on grass was half offense and half defense, and was not just a breakdown on one point or the other. If defensive statistics were properly conceived of and maintained, we could see with the same clarity who it was that did not perform well defensively on grass. We can break the turf/grass records into "home" and "road" to show that this is not just a matter of the Phillies playing best at home:

	WON	LOST	PCT.
Phillies at home (Turf)	50	31	.617
On road at turf parks	24	15	.615
On road at grass parks	16	26	.381

Even if you find some reason to ignore the 0–6 record in Los Angeles, that's still 16–20 on grass fields. In addition to which I will point out that there are five other N.L. teams which play on artificial turf in their home parks, and while they all played badly on grass, none of the others played as badly as the league champion Phillies.

But that is only details—a close-up examination of the issue. I'm trying to be an outsider here, step back from the issue. I submit that no one can really explain to me why the Philadelphia Phillies are such a good turf team, or such a poor grass team. The Dodgers are an exceptional artificial turf team; can anyone explain that? (Over the last three years they are 67–46 on artificial turf, and have been remarkably consistent from year to year. On the road in grass parks, they are 51–53 over the same three years.) Are the Dodgers your idea of a turf team? Is Bill Russell your idea of a fast-track shortstop?

I suggest, therefore, that there is a strong need for us all to do some thinking and maybe re-thinking about the whole issue of what it takes to play well on artificial turf.

I am presenting turf/grass records this year; I hope that gives you a couple of reference points while you are trying to sort it out. If we knew the answers to a few questions like "How many big innings occur on grass fields?" and "How many on artificial turf?" we could probably make use of that information.

Artificial turfs sprang onto the scene in our lifetime; there is no traditional, inherited wisdom here for us to be guided by. It is up to our generation, you and me, to figure it out. Apart from discovering the increased value of speed on the turf, I don't think we've done a very good job of it yet.

IV. DOUBLE PLAYS AND TURF TEAMS

The Phillies in 1983 turned 117 double plays, an exceedingly low total. They made 152 errors, which is a lot, and allowed 93 unearned runs to score, which is a lot. It could be argued that their inability to turn the double play hurt them more on grass than it did on turf.

That theory has a half-life of about twelve seconds. The National League divides neatly into teams which turned the double play and teams which didn't. There is a chasm between the two groups; the "Good DP" group ends at 164, the "Bad DP" group starts at 135. That should relieve you immediately of your concerns about double plays being influenced by the number of runners on base; the minimum difference between the two groups in dou-

ble plays is 21%, while the largest difference in the league in opposing baserunners allowed is just 9%.

By a second lucky coincidence, each group—good DPs, and bad DPs—consists of three "grass" teams and three "turf" teams.

The six teams which turned the double play well had a winning percentage of .490 on grass, .488 on turf. The poor double-play teams were at .510 on grass, .514 on turf. The difference, in a sample of this size, has no significance whatsoever.

V. MARGINALIA

The Phillies' team leader in hits last year was Mike Schmidt with 136. No other team has ever won a pennant without anybody on the team getting more than 136 hits.

VI. THE DEVIL AND JOE MORGAN

Do you remember the story of the Devil and Daniel Webster? It's a story about a man who sells his soul to the devil for earthly success, but when the time comes to face up to his responsibilities, pack a trunkful of Coppertone and prepare for a long, dry summer, instead of just saying "Well, OK, you're the Devil and a deal is a deal", he says "Nuts to you, I'm not going", and he calls in Daniel Webster to argue for him.

Well, the Phillies remind me of that story. The Phillies began to evolve into an old ballclub four or five years ago, and a lot of people (including yours truly) have been waiting for them to collapse ever since. What you're supposed to do when you begin to accumulate 35-year-olds on your roster is start to look to the future, begin breaking in some young talent, so as to cushion the decline phase—like the Dodgers have done.

What the Phillies did instead was to start bringing in more old ballplayers, beginning with Pete Rose in 1979. Ahah, we all said; you'll pay for this. Trying to stretch out your good times by a couple of years, when you could be going to church on Sunday and bringing along some younger talent; you'll burn in the second division for this, Philadelphia.

But when the moment of their reckoning arrived, and the aging of the talent became critical, the Phillies made a unique response: They sent for Joe Morgan. Instead of saying, "OK, you're right; we've got to start paying for this now," they brought in even more, even older ballplayers to prop up the team until the next generation of talent was assembled. They challenged their liability head-on.

One of the marvelous things about baseball is that, after all the years I've been a fan, everything that happens is still new and still surprising. I have never seen this before. I have never seen an organization, confronted with an aging roster, just decide that they would not yield to the problem, they would confront it.

And they got by with it. At the least, to this point they seem to have gotten by with it. The next generation of talent is here and ready to go. They've got Juan Samuel ready to go at second, and he looks great. Their backup outfield, not counting Greg Gross, is Von Hayes, Bob Dernier and Joe Lefebvre, and that is probably one of the better outfields in the division. They've got Matuszek at first, Virgil to catch. They could lose a lot of talent, and not lose a thing on the field.

VII. PETE ROSE AND RIGHTFIELD

I thought we would check to see how much of a defensive liability Pete Rose was in rightfield. Pete doesn't cover much ground at first base and his arm has always been suspect anyway, so you've got to wonder about the man's ability to cover rightfield. Well, the Phillies were not adversely affected by his presence there at all, or at least it doesn't show up in their record.

Phillies with:	W	L	Pct.	Opponents' Runs	Opp. Runs/ Game
Rose in Right	15	12	.556	105	3.89
Rose not in RF	75	60	.556	530	3.93

Pete, you done damn fine.

VIII. AND EVERYBODY CONTRIBUTED

Huge rosters are usually associated with such stalwart teams as the 1916 A's and 1969 Seattle Pilots, who both had over 50 players see action for them. Transience is often thought to be the mark of a directionless team headed nowhere. Trying out a lot of different ballplayers is a luxury a bad team has, since there are never any pressure moments and nothing is at stake. The '83 edition of the Phillies used 44 different players to capture the NL flag. Only one National League champion, the '47 Dodgers with 46, used more.

Pete ROSE, First Base
Runs Created: 46

	G	AB	Hit	2B	3B	HR	Run	RBI	BB	SO	SB	CS	Avg
20.06 Years	650	199	35	6	8	102	60	70	52	9	6	.306	
1983	151	493	121	14	3	0	52	45	52	28	7	7	.245
First Half	75	250	60	11	2	0	29	24			3		.240
Second Half	76	243	61	3	1	0	23	21			4		.251
vs. RHP		387	91			0		29					.235
vs. Lefties		106	30			0		16					.283
Home	76	241	63	8	3	0	26	22			2		.261
Road	75	252	58	6	0	0	26	23			5		.230
Grass	39	127	20	2	0	0	8	11			2		.157
Turf	112	366	101	12	3	0	44	34			5		.276

Ivan DeJESUS, Shortstop
Runs Created: 56

	G	AB	Hit	2B	3B	HR	Run	RBI	BB	SO	SB	CS	Avg
7.07 Years	575	146	22	6	3	77	40	59	80	25	11	.254	
1983	158	497	126	15	7	4	60	45	53	77	11	4	.254
First Half	75	226	56	6	4	1	22	21			6		.248
Second Half	83	271	70	9	3	3	38	24			5		.258
vs. RHP		377	90			4		36					.239
vs. Lefties		120	36			0		9					.300
Home	77	236	59	9	5	2	34	22			8		.250
Road	81	261	67	6	2	2	26	23			3		.257
Grass	42	125	35	3	2	1	14	10			3		.280
Turf	116	372	91	12	5	3	46	35			8		.245

Joe MORGAN, Second Base
Runs Created: 68

	G	AB	Hit	2B	3B	HR	Run	RBI	BB	SO	SB	CS	Avg
15.64 Years	570	155	27	6	17	102	70	115	62	44	10	.272	
1983	123	404	93	20	1	16	72	59	89	54	18	2	.230
First Half	59	196	42	9	0	6	37	23			5		.214
Second Half	64	208	51	11	1	10	35	36			13		.245
vs. RHP		336	79			15		50					.235
vs. LHP		68	14			1		9					.206
Home	54	160	41	8	0	9	34	29			10		.256
Road	69	244	52	12	1	7	38	30			8		.213
Grass	34	111	23	3	0	2	20	13			6		.207
Turf	89	293	70	17	1	14	52	46			12		.239

Gary MATTHEWS, Leftfield
Runs Created: 62

	G	AB	Hit	2B	3B	HR	Run	RBI	BB	SO	SB	CS	Avg
9.73 Years	599	171	27	5	19	90	81	72	90	17	6	.285	
1983	132	446	115	18	2	10	66	50	69	81	13	9	.258
First Half	70	260	64	10	1	8	37	27			6		.246
Second Half	62	186	51	8	1	2	29	23			7		.274
vs. RHP		318	79			8		37					.252
vs. Lefties		128	35			2		13					.273
Home	61	217	52	7	2	3	31	22			9		.240
Road	71	229	63	11	0	7	35	28			4		.275
Grass	39	126	36	6	0	4	18	17			2		.286
Turf	93	320	79	12	2	6	48	33			11		.247

Mike SCHMIDT, Third Base
Runs Created: 110

	G	AB	Hit	2B	3B	HR	Run	RBI	BB	SO	SB	CS	Avg
10.12 Years	560	148	27	5	38	106	106	107	141	16	8	.264	
1983	154	534	136	16	4	40	104	109	128	148	7	8	.255
First Half	73	253	62	10	2	15	44	47			5		.245
Second Half	81	281	74	6	2	25	60	62			2		.263
vs. RHP		419	107			33		91					.255
vs. Lefties		115	29			7		18					.252
Home	76	255	64	10	2	19	51	54			4		.251
Road	78	279	72	6	2	21	53	55			3		.258
Grass	41	140	35	1	1	12	22	28			1		.250
Turf	114	394	101	15	3	28	82	81			6		.256

Garry MADDOX, Centerfield
Runs Created: 34

	G	AB	Hit	2B	3B	HR	Run	RBI	BB	SO	SB	CS	Avg
9.64 Years	609	174	33	6	11	75	74	31	75	25	9	.286	
1983	97	324	89	14	2	4	27	32	17	31	7	6	.275
First Half	45	153	42	8	0	3	15	16			4		.275
Second Half	52	171	47	6	2	1	12	16			3		.275
vs. RHP		220	56			3		19					.255
vs. Lefties		104	33			1		13					.317
Home	50	160	48	11	2	2	15	20			2		.300
Road	47	164	41	3	0	2	12	12			5		.250
Grass	27	93	22	1	0	2	8	4			2		.237
Turf	70	231	77	13	2	2	19	28			5		.333

Von HAYES, Rightfield
Runs Created: 42

	G	AB	Hit	2B	3B	HR	Run	RBI	BB	SO	SB	CS	Avg
1.96 Years		504	129	21	5	11	67	67	47	65	31	13	.256
1983	124	351	93	9	5	6	45	32	36	55	20	12	.265
First Half	57	183	48	5	4	4	23	14			9		.262
Second Half	67	168	45	4	1	2	22	18			11		.268
vs. RHP		305	79			6		28					.259
vs. Lefties		46	14			0		4					.304
Home	65	198	43	3	3	3	21	13			7		.217
Road	59	153	50	6	2	3	24	19			13		.327
Grass	30	59	17	1	1	2	8	8			4		.288
Turf	94	292	76	8	4	4	37	24			16		.260

Bo DIAZ, Catcher
Runs Created: 49

	G	AB	Hit	2B	3B	HR	Run	RBI	BB	SO	SB	CS	Avg
2.96 Years		521	135	28	1	15	57	78	34	44	2	4	.260
1983	136	471	111	17	0	15	49	64	38	57	1	4	.236
First Half	62	214	50	10	0	7	27	29			0		.234
Second Half	74	257	61	7	0	8	22	35			1		.237
vs. RHP		357	85		0	13		55					.228
vs. Lefties		114	26		0	2		9					.228
Home	67	237	58	9	0	9	27	39			1		.245
Road	69	234	53	8	0	6	22	25			0		.226
Grass	37	122	25	5	0	6	14	14			0		.205
Turf	99	349	86	12	0	9	35	50			1		.246

Joe LEFEBVRE, Outfield
Runs Created: 54

	G	AB	Hit	2B	3B	HR	Run	RBI	BB	SO	SB	CS	Avg
2.35 Years		388	102	14	6	12	50	48	48	69	5	3	.262
1983	119	278	85	20	8	8	35	39	33	49	5	3	.306
First Half	43	65	21	33	2	3	9	9			1		.323
Second Half	76	213	64	17	6	5	26	30			4		.300
vs. RHP*		208	71			8		38					.341
vs. LHP		50	9			0		0					.180
Home	65	149	43	12	5	5	23	21			0		.289
Road	54	129	42	8	3	3	12	18			5		.326
Grass	38	79	22	5	0	2	6	12			2		.278
Turf	81	199	63	15	8	6	29	27			3		.317

*vs. RHP and LHP with Philadelphia only

Sixto LEZCANO, Outfield
Runs Created: 45

	G	AB	Hit	2B	3B	HR	Run	RBI	BB	SO	SB	CS	Avg
6.85 Years		549	150	26	5	19	74	79	73	103	5	4	.273
1983	115	356	85	12	2	8	49	56	52	75	1	0	.239
First Half	65	220	55	8	1	5	30	38			0		.250
Second Half	50	136	30	4	1	3	19	18			1		.221
vs. RHP		234	52			5		32					.222
vs. LHP		122	33			3		24					.270
Home	56	177	40	5	1	6	24	30			0	0	.226
Road	59	179	45	7	1	2	25	26			1	0	.251
Grass	78	246	57	8	1	6	35	39			1	0	.232
Turf	37	110	28	4	1	2	14	17			0	0	.255

Steve CARLTON

Year	(W–L)	GS	Run	Avg	DP	Avg	SB	Avg
1982	(23-11)	38	165	4.34	33	.87	22	.58
1983	(15-16)	37	138	3.73	25	.68	23	.62
1976-1983		277	1298	4.69	225	.81	168	.61

	G	IP	W	L	Pct	ER	ERA
1982 Home	18	148	13	4	.765	41	2.55
1983 Home	18	139.1	9	9	.500	57	3.68
1982 Road	20	147.2	10	7	.588	61	3.70
1983 Road	19	144.1	6	7	.462	41	2.56
1983 Grass	10	77.1	4	5	.444	18	2.10
1983 Turf	27	206.1	11	11	.500	80	3.49

John DENNY

Year	(W–L)	GS	Run	Avg	DP	Avg	SB	Avg
1982	(6-13)	25	109	4.36	16	.64	13	.52
1983	(19- 6)	36	165	4.58	32	.89	18	.50
1967-1983		216	976	4.52	234	1.08	127	.59

	G	IP	W	L	Pct	ER	ERA
1983 Home	19	142	11	2	.846	31	1.97
1983 Road	17	100.2	8	4	.667	33	2.95
1983 Grass	8	47.2	3	1	.750	13	2.46
1983 Turf	28	195	16	5	.762	51	2.35

Charles HUDSON

Year	(W–L)	GS	Run	Avg	DP	Avg	SB	Avg
1983	(8-8)	26	132	5.08	16	.62	33	1.27

	G	IP	W	L	Pct	ER	ERA
1983 Home	12	86.1	4	4	.500	32	3.34
1983 Road	14	83	4	4	.500	31	3.36
1983 Grass	6	30	0	3	.000	13	3.90
1983 Turf	20	139.1	8	5	.615	50	3.23

Marty BYSTROM

Year	(W–L)	GS	Run	Avg	DP	Avg	SB	Avg
1982	(5-6)	16	66	4.13	15	.94	21	1.31
1983	(6-9)	23	100	4.35	16	.70	31	1.35
1980-1983		53	241	4.55	39	.74	67	1.26

	G	IP	W	L	Pct	ER	ERA
1983 Home	12	62.1	2	2	.500	30	4.33
1983 Road	12	57	4	7	.364	31	4.90
1983 Grass	5	17	0	5	.000	21	11.12
1983 Turf	19	102.1	6	4	.600	40	3.52

1983 OTHERS

Pitcher	(W–L)	GS	Run	Avg	DP	Avg	SB	Avg
Gross	(4-6)	17	68	4.00	16	.94	26	1.53
Christenson	(2-4)	9	32	3.56	1	.11	16	1.78
Ruthven	(1-3)	7	33	4.71	7	1.00	8	1.14
Farmer	(0-6)	3	8	2.67	2	.67	5	1.67
Ghelfi	(1-1)	3	7	2.33	0	.00	2	.67
Comer	(1-0)	1	8	8.00	1	1.00	2	2.00
McGraw	(2-1)	1	5	5.00	0	.00	3	3.00

PHILADELPHIA PHILLIES
RUNS BATTED IN ANALYSIS

Player	RBI	RBI In Wins	Victory Important RBI	RBI Importance	Wins Batted In	RBI Per Win
Mike Schmidt	109	77	44.48	.408	10.07	10.8
Bo Diaz	64	51	34.31	.536	8.02	8.0
Joe Morgan	59	47	32.45	.550	8.75	6.7
Gary Matthews	50	47	23.84	.477	6.98	7.2
Ivan DeJesus	45	31	21.06	.468	5.15	8.7
Pete Rose	45	36	23.53	.523	5.46	8.2
Garry Maddox	32	27	13.09	.409	4.47	7.2
Von Hayes	32	19	13.40	.419	4.51	7.1
Joe Lefebvre	38	32	19.09	.502	5.41	7.0
Sixto Lezcano	7	5	4.33	.618	.68	10.3

PITTSBURGH PIRATES

I

One of the few people that I know of who expected the Pirates to have as good a year as they did in 1983 was Pete Palmer. Pete takes predictions very seriously (I don't), and he has a method for making them. What he does, as I dimly understand it, is to list the offensive and defensive elements of the team (1B, Offense; 1B, Defense; etc.), and pencil in numbers to represent a reasonable expectation of how the player who is there will perform.

The numbers that are penciled in are not runs created, but they are a similar thing, an estimate derived by linear weights of how many runs better or worse than the league average the player who occupies this position is likely to be. If the player over the last three years has been +5, +7, +4 (5 runs, then 7 runs, then 4 runs better than the league average), Pete would probably pencil in "+5." If the player was getting on in years, he might cut that to "+2" or something; if the player was acquired from another team, he would make a park adjustment before entering the figure.

You may not think too much of that method, and to be honest about it I don't either, but his predictions have been more accurate over a period of years than those of anyone else I know of. Anyway, when he was doing this a year ago, his basic reason for expecting the Pirates to have a good year was that he figured the loss of Omar Moreno had to help. When he doesn't know who is going to be playing a spot, he pencils in a below-average figure, a "−5" or "−8" or something. If a team loses a player who is, say, 12 runs better than average, that will knock them down by about 20 runs. But Omar Moreno is such a terrible offensive player that when you wipe him out and pencil in an unknown, he reasoned, then that will improve the team.

In retrospect, you've got to say that he had a point. The Pirates replaced Omar, their leadoff man and centerfielder, with a leadoff man and centerfielder chosen from baseball's grab bag, a "replacement level" centerfielder. That was Lee Mazzilli. When Mazzilli wasn't what they wanted, they found another replacement-level centerfielder, Marvell Wynne. Whereas Omar in 1982, playing almost every day (158 games, 645 at-bats), had scored 82 runs and driven in 44, Pirate leadoff men in 1983 (which was mostly their centerfielders) scored 114 runs and drove in 49. A little more complete data:

	Omar Moreno in 1982	Pirate Leadoff Men in '83
At-bats	645	657
Runs scored	82	114
Hits	158	185
Walks	44	71
On-base percentage	.293	.353
Doubles	18	29
Triples	9	5
Home runs	3	16
Runs batted in	44	49
Stolen bases	60	39
Caught stealing	26	(20)*
Batting average	.245	.282

	Omar Moreno in 1982	Pirate Leadoff Men in '83
Runs created	60	95
Outs consumed	513	492
Probable runs scored		
From first base	30.10	51.45
From second base	42.90	37.40
From third base	7.20	4.00
Home runs	3.00	16.00
Total expected runs	83.20	108.85
Actual runs	82	114
*Estimated		

So getting rid of Omar Moreno was worth about 30 runs offensively to the Pirates, as it turned out.

Pete Palmer has co-authored with John Thorn a new book, *The Hidden Game of Baseball*, from Doubleday in 1984. I recommend it to you whole-heartedly and without reservation. The work is informative, graceful, insightful and entertaining. It begins with a detailed account of the evolution of statistical information in baseball, from which I learned much; I promise to quit giving out mis-information on the subject. Thorn and Palmer do something that I have been wanting to do for years, which is to provide summaries and explanations of dozens of studies which have been done in sabermetrics. I will have a book on the history of the game out in a year or so, and at that time I will be able to make reference to and discuss many of those studies, because now I will have a place to send you if you want more information. They provide an alternative set of "tools" or "measures" which can be used to analyze questions; if you have a real strong desire to understand what I'm doing, then you should look at what Pete's doing so you understand better what the options are. A long set of charts applies Pete's measures to players throughout the history of the game. And best of all, John Thorn's writing is clear, careful and often delightful. He does not, unlike someone else I could name, feel entitled to make up his own rules of grammar, punctuation and usage; on this point and many others we disagree, but the book is a welcome addition to the field.

Anyway, the Pirates of 1982, with Moreno, were 21–25 against lefthanded pitchers, the ninth-best record in the league. Moreno can't hit lefthanders at all, and leading off against them he was a millstone. Without him in '83, they had the best record in the league against lefthanded pitching (22–20). Another thing that helped make them the best in the league in that regard was that the best two lefthanded starters in the league, at least by their won/lost records, were McWilliams and Candelaria, and the Pirates didn't have to face them.

The loss of Omar Moreno also further choked off Chuck Tanner's running game. Tanner, you may remember, converted to the stolen base in 1976, and like most converts he went through a phase of unrestrained ardor before he began to remember that there was more to life than stealing bases:

STOLEN BASES BY CHUCK TANNER'S TEAMS

Year	Team	Stolen Bases	Caught Stealing
1971	Chicago	83	65
1972	Chicago	100	52
1973	Chicago	83	73
1974	Chicago	64	53
1975	Chicago	101	54
1976	Oakland	341	123
1977	Pittsburgh	260	120
1978	Pittsburgh	213	90
1979	Pittsburgh	180	66
1980	Pittsburgh	209	102
1981	Pittsburgh	192*	82*
1982	Pittsburgh	161	75
1983	Pittsburgh	124	77

*Strike adjusted

He figures to be back down to pre-revelation totals in about two years. Which I am glad to see, because I have always admired Chuck Tanner, and I was tired of tagging onto the end of that an apology for all the pointless running.

The John Tudor trade is an interesting gamble, a move that seems to respond intelligently to the talent that was available, but has little to do with the needs of the team. Having lost Dave Parker to free agency, the Pirates were not in an ideal position to be dealing away an outfielder; with Candelaria and McWilliams, they did not have a real need for another lefthanded starter. But in terms of talent exchanged, how can you argue with it? When you trade a 33-year-old outfielder that you picked off the refuse pile five years ago for a fine starting pitcher like John Tudor, you're not risking much. Tudor has very good stuff and excellent command of it; he's had a winning record for four straight years even as a lefthander in Fenway Park, and the park was killing him for the last two years. I'd gladly have traded four Mike Easlers to acquire him.

Outfielders in line for more playing time in Pittsburgh:

1) Kevin Frobel. Frobel is 24, a lefthanded power hitter with some speed; strikes out a lot and is not a good outfielder at this time. But his power is such that if he hits .270, he's going to play, and he hit over .300 at Hawaii last year and .283 with the Pirates (17 for 60).

2) Brian Harper. You probably know more about him,

and it's a similar story. He's 24, righthanded, strikes out, but has power; a marginal outfielder. Probably has less potential as an outfielder than Frobel, but has hit 9 major-league home runs in 173 at-bats.

3) Lee Mazzilli, if and only if he cleans up his act, which seems unlikely.

4) Lee Lacy.

II

When the National League compressed from twelve teams to eight in 1900, the Louisville Colonels merged with the Pittsburgh Pirates. Or rather, the Colonels gave all of their best players to the Pirates and ceased to exist. That nucleus of talent included the likes of Fred Clarke, Chief Zimmer, Deacon Phillippe, Tommy Leach, Claude "Little All Right" Ritchey, Rube Waddell and Honus Wagner. When combined with the existing Pirates (who counted Sam Leever, Jesse Tannehill, Ginger Beaumont and Jack Chesbro among their number), they created the first great team of the 20th century. For their trouble, the city of Louisville has never hosted major league baseball again. They gave Pittsburgh three Hall of Famers, three pennants, an appearance in the first World Series and in return received absolutely squat.

Events of the past several years suggest that perhaps it's time to move the Pirates back to Louisville. Pirate fans do not seem to respond to major league baseball in major league numbers. Louisville Red Bird fans, however, respond in major league numbers to *minor* league baseball.

What purist could argue with the move? It is perhaps the most historically justified franchise transfer ever proposed. In fact, it is operating on three levels. The first, historical; the second, moral, to avenge the great loss suffered by a terrific baseball town; and third, financial, to take an underappreciated franchise and place it in a vibrant, burgeoning market. Any town that can draw a million people to Triple A ball is shouting big time to the world. And any town that does not support a solid, year in and year out contender to the fullest needs some years away from the big time to reexamine its attitudes about baseball.

1983 LOUISVILLE REDBIRDS 78–57 .578

POS	PLAYER	G	AB	H	2B	3B	HR	R	RBI	BB	SO	SB	CS	AVG	RC
1B	Greg Guin	58	203	45	9	1	3	23	23	7	29	3	2	.222	14
2B	Jeff Doyle	127	474	142	25	6	5	87	63	73	51	17	6	.300	81
3B	Bill Lyons	77	266	72	14	1	5	60	26	47	43	21	3	.271	59
SS	Jose Gonzalez	122	423	120	19	6	3	64	44	35	44	26	10	.284	55
RF	Jim Adduci	129	467	131	29	7	25	81	101	60	103	3	1	.281	92
LF	Gene Roof	114	450	139	23	5	3	74	60	65	53	15	15	.309	74
CF	Tito Landrum	111	431	126	23	12	19	79	77	38	88	15	6	.292	85
C	Thomas Nieto	115	383	104	17	1	5	44	51	41	78	0	2	.272	29
DH	Orlando Sanchez	116	424	125	27	2	16	70	89	30	54	4	2	.295	67
1B-3B	Andy Van Slyke	54	220	81	21	4	6	52	41	31	30	13	3	.368	58

Pitcher	G	IP	W-L	PCT	ER	ERA
Ricky Horton	30	157	10-6	.625	84	4.82
Kevin Hagen	21	131.1	6-9	.400	63	4.32
Rick Owenby	16	104	7-5	.583	42	3.63
Ralph Citarella	37	109.1	7-6	.538	58	4.77
Eric Rasmussen	11	71	8-1	.889	18	2.28
Kurt Kepshire	21	83.1	6-2	.750	34	3.67

—Jim Baker

Jason THOMPSON, First Base
Runs Created: 84

	G	AB	Hit	2B	3B	HR	Run	RBI	BB	SO	SB	CS	Avg
6.86		555	147	23	2	26	77	94	91	105	1	1	.265
1983	152	517	134	20	1	18	70	76	99	128	1	0	.259
First Half	75	257	70	11	1	11	31	38			1	0	.272
Second Half	77	260	64	9	0	7	39	38			0	0	.246
vs. RHP		394	104			16		65					.264
vs. LHP		123	30			2		11					.244
Home	78	255	67	5	1	10	36	34			0	0	.263
Road	74	262	67	15	0	8	34	42			1	0	.256
Grass	42	143	37	9	0	2	16	19			1	0	.259
Turf	110	374	97	11	1	16	54	57			0	0	.259

Marvell WYNNE, Centerfield
Runs Created: 43

	G	AB	Hit	2B	3B	HR	Run	RBI	BB	SO	SB	CS	Avg
.64 Years		576	140	25	3	11	104	41	60	82	19	16	.243
1983	103	366	89	16	2	7	66	26	38	52	12	10	.243
First Half	21	85	24	4	1	2	18	7			2		.282
Second Half	82	281	65	12	1	5	48	19			10		.231
vs. RHP		305	72			7		24					.236
vs. LHP		61	17			0		2					.279
Home	62	189	47	9	2	3	30	16			5		.249
Road	41	177	42	7	0	4	36	10			7		.237
Grass	18	95	25	5	1	2	18	7			4		.263
Turf	85	271	64	11	1	5	48	19			8		.236

Johnny RAY, Second Base
Runs Created: 73

	G	AB	Hit	2B	3B	HR	Run	RBI	BB	SO	SB	CS	Avg
2.12 Years		624	174	37	7	6	74	57	36	32	16	8	.279
1983	151	576	163	38	7	5	68	53	35	26	18	9	.283
First Half	74	279	82	20	1	1	30	20			7		.294
Second Half	77	297	81	18	6	4	38	23			11		.273
vs. RHP		478	140			5		47					.293
vs. LHP		98	23			0		6					.235
Home	74	276	81	13	4	3	31	31			8		.293
Road	77	300	82	17	2	2	37	22			10		.273
Grass	41	156	44	8	1	2	18	13			5		.282
Turf	110	420	119	30	6	3	50	40			13		.283

Dave PARKER, Rightfield
Runs Created: 67

	G	AB	Hit	2B	3B	HR	Run	RBI	BB	SO	SB	CS	Avg
8.03 Years		604	184	37	8	21	91	94	43	97	15	9	.305
1983	144	552	154	28	4	12	68	69	28	88	12	8	.279
First Half	61	231	56	13	1	3	26	21			3		.242
Second Half	83	321	98	15	3	9	42	48			9		.305
vs. RHP		412	118			5		43					.257
vs. LHP		140	36			7		26					.286
Home	71	269	79	18	4	6	39	38			7		.294
Road	73	283	75	7	0	6	29	31			5		.265
Grass	39	149	38	3	0	4	12	14			2		.255
Turf	105	403	116	25	4	8	56	55			10		.288

Bill MADLOCK, Third Base
Runs Created: 78

	G	AB	Hit	2B	3B	HR	Run	RBI	BB	SO	SB	CS	Avg
8.27 Years		594	188	33	4	15	86	78	56	41	19	10	.317
1983	130	473	153	21	0	12	68	68	49	24	3	4	.323
First Half	64	252	80	13	0	6	31	37			2		.317
Second Half	66	221	73	8	0	6	37	31			1		.330
vs. RHP		351	108			6		50					.308
vs. LHP		122	45			6		18					.369
Home	69	248	87	12	0	8	37	42			2		.351
Road	61	225	66	9	0	4	31	26			1		.293
Grass	32	116	34	3	0	2	18	9			1		.293
Turf	98	357	119	18	0	10	50	59			2		.333

Tony PENA, Catcher
Runs Created: 75

	G	AB	Hit	2B	3B	HR	Run	RBI	BB	SO	SB	CS	Avg
2.24 Years		567	170	27	4	12	54	67	25	70	4	7	.301
1983	151	542	163	22	3	15	68	70	31	73	6	7	.301
First Half	67	233	66	11	1	2	12	22			4		.283
Second Half	84	309	97	11	2	13	56	48			2		.314
vs. RHP		409	124			12		59					.303
vs. LHP		133	39			3		11					.293
Home	78	274	88	13	2	8	45	35			3		.321
Road	73	268	75	9	1	7	23	35			3		.280
Grass	36	136	38	4	0	3	11	15			1		.279
Turf	115	406	125	18	3	12	57	55			5		.308

Dale BERRA, Shortstop
Runs Created: 63

	G	AB	Hit	2B	3B	HR	Run	RBI	BB	SO	SB	CS	Avg
3.75 Years		491	119	21	2	10	49	54	41	79	8	3	.242
1983	161	537	135	25	1	10	51	52	61	84	8	5	.251
First Half	75	252	55	10	1	9	28	30			3		.218
Second Half	86	285	80	15	0	1	23	22			5		.281
vs. RHP		402	96			5		35					.239
vs. LHP		135	39			5		17					.289
Home	81	267	60	8	1	5	23	32			4		.225
Road	80	270	75	17	0	5	28	20			4		.278
Grass	41	141	39	8	0	1	11	6			3		.277
Turf	120	396	96	17	1	9	40	46			5		.242

Lee LACY, Designated Hitter
Runs Created: 42

	G	AB	Hit	2B	3B	HR	Run	RBI	BB	SO	SB	CS	Avg
6.44 Years		440	125	20	5	8	63	41	36	59	23	10	.283
1983	108	288	87	12	3	4	40	13	22	36	31	13	.302
First Half	55	179	53	6	2	3	27	8			20		.296
Second Half	53	109	34	6	1	1	13	5			11		.312
vs. RHP		139	37			1		4					.266
vs. LHP		149	50			3		9					.336
Home	58	139	49	10	1	0	21	6			16		.353
Road	50	149	38	2	2	3	19	7			15		.255
Grass	25	78	25	1	1	1	7	4			7		.321
Turf	83	210	62	11	2	3	33	9			24		.295

Mike EASLER, Leftfield
Runs Created: 57

	G	AB	Hit	2B	3B	HR	Run	RBI	BB	SO	SB	CS	Avg
3.68 Years		473	140	25	4	15	61	67	38	79	4	6	.296
1983	115	381	117	17	2	10	44	54	22	64	4	2	.307
First Half	59	195	65	6	1	4	21	20			3		.333
Second Half	56	186	52	11	1	6	23	34			1		.280
vs. RHP		334	104			10		52					.311
vs. LHP		47	13			0		2					.277
Home	56	176	60	9	1	2		21			3		.341
Road	59	205	57	8	1	8		33			1		.278
Grass	34	107	24	2	1	4	12	20			1		.224
Turf	81	274	93	15	1	6	32	34			3		.339

Lee MAZZILLI, Outfield
Runs Created: 34

	G	AB	Hit	2B	3B	HR	Run	RBI	BB	SO	SB	CS	Avg
5.58 Years		569	151	27	4	14	73	64	79	80	28	14	.266
1983	109	246	59	9	0	5	37	24	49	43	15	5	.240
First Half	65	188	50	8	0	5	31	22			13		.266
Second Half	44	58	9	1	0	0	6	2			2		.155
vs. RHP		188	49	0		5		18					.261
vs. LHP		58	10	0		0		6					.172
Home	53	110	21	7	0	1	13	11			8		.191
Road	56	136	38	2	0	4	24	13			7		.279
Grass	31	70	19	0	0	2	10	7			4		.271
Turf	78	176	40	9	0	3	27	17			11		.227

Rick RHODEN

Year	(W–L)	GS	Run	Avg	DP	Avg	SB	Avg
1982	(11-14)	35	147	4.20	23	.66	17	.49
1983	(13-13)	35	135	3.86	34	.97	28	.80
1976-1983		191	833	4.36	180	.94	126	.66

	G	IP	W	L	Pct	ER	ERA
1982 Home	17	118.2	7	6	.538	59	3.79
1983 Home	18	123.1	8	7	.533	41	2.99
1982 Road	18	111.2	4	8	.333	56	4.51
1983 Road	18	121	5	6	.455	43	3.20
1983 Grass	9	57.1	1	4	.200	26	4.08
1983 Turf	27	187	12	9	.571	58	2.79

Larry McWILLIAMS

Year	(W–L)	GS	Run	Avg	DP	Avg	SB	Avg
1982	(8-8)	20	76	3.80	14	.70	10	.50
1983	(15-8)	35	147	4.20	33	.94	21	.60
1978-1983		118	509	4.31	92	.78	74	.63

	G	IP	W	L	Pct	ER	ERA
1982 Home	22	83.4	4	4	.500	32	3.45
1983 Home	17	117	7	5	.583	46	3.54
1982 Road	24	75	4	3	.750	36	4.32
1983 Road	18	121	8	3	.727	40	2.98
1983 Grass	10	71	4	1	.800	23	2.92
1983 Turf	25	167	11	7	.611	63	3.40

John CANDELARIA

Year	(W–L)	GS	Run	Avg	DP	Avg	SB	Avg
1982	(12-7)	30	120	4.00	32	1.07	14	.47
1983	(15-8)	32	127	3.97	29	.91	22	.69
1976-1983		225	958	4.26	216	.96	90	.40

	G	IP	W	L	Pct	ER	ERA
1982 Home	17	97.1	6	5	.545	39	3.61
1983 Home	17	101.2	8	5	.615	33	2.92
1982 Road	14	77.1	6	2	.750	18	2.09
1983 Road	16	96	7	3	.700	38	3.56
1983 Grass	7	38.2	3	1	.750	14	3.26
1983 Turf	26	159	12	7	.632	57	3.23

Lee TUNNELL

Year	(W–L)	GS	Run	Avg	DP	Avg	SB	Avg
1982	(1-1)	3	16	5.33	0	.00	1	.33
1983	(11-6)	25	102	4.08	35	1.40	13	.52
1982-1983		28	118	4.21	35	1.25	14	.50

	G	IP	W	L	Pct	ER	ERA
1983 Home	18	86.2	4	5	.444	42	4.36
1983 Road	17	91	7	1	.875	30	2.97
1983 Grass	9	46	3	1	.750	21	4.11
1983 Turf	26	131.2	8	5	.615	51	3.49

1983 OTHERS

Pitcher	(W–L)	GS	Run	Avg	DP	Avg	SB	Avg
DeLeon	(7- 3)	15	65	4.33	15	1.00	21	1.40
Bibby	(5-12)	12	45	3.75	12	1.00	13	1.08
Robinson	(2- 2)	6	28	4.67	6	1.00	5	.83
Niemann	(0- 1)	1	4	4.00	1	1.00	1	1.00
Pulido	(0- 0)	1	6	6.00	1	1.00	2	2.00

PITTSBURGH PIRATES
RUNS BATTED IN ANALYSIS

Player	RBI	RBI In Wins	Victory Important RBI	RBI Importance	Wins Batted In	RBI Per Win
Jason Thompson	76	50	28.12	.370	8.83	8.6
Tony Pena	70	46	25.79	.368	8.16	8.6
Dave Parker	69	45	28.27	.410	8.87	7.8
Bill Madlock	68	42	25.45	.374	8.84	7.7
Mike Easler	54	41	22.86	.423	7.44	7.3
Johnny Ray	53	37	20.65	.390	6.34	8.4
Dale Berra	52	37	25.37	.488	5.87	8.6
Marvell Wynne	26	14	7.24	.278	2.67	9.7
Lee Mazzilli	24	18	12.22	.509	4.18	5.7
Lee Lacy	13	10	7.25	.557	1.80	7.2

MONTREAL EXPOS

I

A Canadian friend of mine, Bruce Dowbiggan, suggests that there are important similarities between the Montreal Expos of the last five years and the Milwaukee-Atlanta Braves in the 1959–66 period, which John McHale worked for and eventually presided over. In both cases the front-line talent was awesome. Both teams had a superstar outfielder (Dawson, Aaron) and another sure Hall of Famer (Carter, Mathews) in the lineup. Both had the kind of #1 starters that you dream of having to build a staff around (Rogers, Spahn). Both backed up the ace with other good starting pitchers (Gullickson, Burdette), and both brought along very talented young players to help (Wallach, Torre). The Braves had the best record in the league in 1959–60 combined, and nearly the best record in the league from 1959–64 combined, a phrase that has got to sound familiar to Expo fans. They were never out of contention. But they could never quite win it.

And why couldn't they win it? Their bench was always too thin. In one case the similarity is eerie. The 1959 race was lost when the second baseman, Red Schoendienst, fell ill, and the man ticketed to replace him, Felix Mantilla, was a wipeout (.215). They tried Johnny O'Brien. He hit .198. They tried Casey Wise. He hit .171. They tried Mel Roach. He hit .097. They tried Joe Morgan. Wrong Joe Morgan. They tried Chuck Cottier. He hit .125.

Finally, with two months to go, they acquired the 35-year-old Bobby Avila, and gave the job to him. He was nothing great, either. On balance they got no offense from the spot and were sixth in the league in double plays.

In 1960 the bench had a better year but the shortstop, Johnny Logan, collapsed, and now they had no double-play combination at all. They traded two young pitchers (Juan Pizarro and Joey Jay) and an outfielder to acquire a double-play combination, but lost the race in '61 because their pitching was too thin. Two pitchers went 39–24, the other twelve went 44–47. And on it went.

The Dodgers had Koufax, the Giants had Mays, the Braves had Aaron. But with Mathews, Spahn, Burdette, McMahon, Felipe Alou, Torre, Joe Adcock, Bob Buhl, Tony Cloninger and Lee Maye, the Braves would seem to have as much talent in that period as anyone in the league. But they could never quite get the right manager, plug up all the holes, and make a go of it.

II

The Montreal Expos of 1983 represent a challenge to the assumption that everything in baseball must be tangible, that there must be a specific, measurable reason why one team fails and another succeeds. Looking at the lineup of the Montreal Expos, with two outfielders (Andre Dawson and Tim Raines) having MVP-type years, with Al Oliver and Gary Carter and Tim Wallach and Steve Rogers, it is difficult to understand how this team could fail to annihilate the Philadelphia Phillies by the

first of August, blow away the Dodgers in three straight and go at it for the world championship against the Orioles. Their failure to do that is surely in some part attributable to a lack of leadership and direction, to a yielding of the team to the will and determination of the Phillies, but that doesn't really answer the question; it just removes it to a different level. With or without direction and leadership, Tim Raines still scored 133 runs, Andre Dawson still hit 32 home runs and drove in 113 runs, Al Oliver still hit .300, Gary Carter still drove in 79 runs and cut off the opponent's running game, and they still had three of the top five winners in the league in their starting rotation. Now that is an awful lot of tangible plus signs, and they still wound up the year with 82 tangible wins and 80 tangible losses, so there have got to be some large, looming negatives to offset all of those positives. What are they? Or, at the least, what are their tangible marks?

1) Al Oliver, although he hit .300, had no better offensive season than Greg Brock of Los Angeles, who hit .224.

Sound a little outrageous? Look at it: Offense consists of two things: getting runners on base and advancing baserunners. Does Oliver have a superior ability to get on base? Oliver hit .300, but he walked only 44 times and was hit by a pitch twice in 660 plate appearances, so his on-base percentage is .348, which is good but not great. Brock hit only .224, but he drew 83 walks and was hit by a pitch once in 539 plate appearances, so his on-base percentage was .345, virtually the same as Oliver's.

Does Oliver have a superior ability to advance runners? Oliver hit only 8 home runs, while Brock hit 20 in many fewer plate appearances. Ability in this regard is closely correlated with slugging percentage. A team which has a high slugging percentage will have a high percentage of its baserunners coming in to score; a team which has a low slugging percentage will have a low percentage of its baserunners scoring. Al Oliver's slugging percentage was .410; Brock's was .396. There is scarcely any difference.

In addition to those basic indicators of offensive ability, Oliver tried four stolen bases, and was caught three times, costing his team about .85 net runs. Brock tried six times and was successful five times, for a net gain for his team of about .65 runs. Oliver also grounded into double plays 32% more frequently than did Brock.

When you add all this together, Oliver created 81 runs while using 458 outs, which is 4.79 runs per game; Brock created 64 runs while using 371 outs, which is 4.69 per game. Further, Brock created his runs in Dodger Stadium in Los Angeles, where runs are scarcer and therefore more valuable than they are in Olympic Stadium in Montreal. When park adjustments are taken into account, Brock actually had a slightly better offensive season than did Al Oliver.

If you find the methodology difficult to swallow, then just look at the number of runs the players drove in and the number they scored. Oliver, who had 81 runs created, drove in 84 runs and scored only 70. Brock, who created 64 runs, drove in 66 and scored 64. So Oliver, while using 23% more outs than Brock, scored only 9% more runs and drove in 27% more. Can you even pretend to attribute that difference to the situations in which they were hitting? Of course not; Al Oliver was hitting cleanup after Andre Dawson or fifth after Gary Carter. That's hardly a weak offensive context. Oliver hit .300; he just did not do the things that put runs on the scoreboard.

2) The Expos lineup has conspicuous, measurable strengths, but it also has conspicuous, measurable weaknesses. Tim Raines, the Expos' best offensive player, created 6.98 runs per game, but Doug Flynn created only 2.46, the worst of any regular player in the league except for the ridiculous Jose Oquendo. Raines' productivity was the best in the league at his position, but it is only a little bit better than that of players like Jose Cruz and Lonnie Smith, while Flynn's production at second is a lot worse than that of most of the league's second basemen. So if you balance the two:

	LF Runs Per Game	2B Runs Per Game	Total
St. Louis	6.25	5.96	12.21
Houston	6.84	4.94	11.78
Philadelphia	4.70	5.50	10.20
Pittsburgh	5.49	4.40	9.89
Cincinnati	5.59	4.06	9.65
Montreal	6.98	2.46	9.44

To put this in plain, unmistakable English, Doug Flynn does just as much to destroy the Montreal offense as Tim Raines can do to build it. If you give him the opportunity to do it, Doug Flynn can do just as much to lose games with his bat as Tim Raines can do to win them. And Bill Virdon chose to give him that opportunity.

3) The Expos do not have enough power in the middle of their lineup to win a pennant. Despite Dawson and Carter, the Expos hit only 102 home runs, the ninth-best figure in the league. And they most obviously lack power where they most need it, in the 4–5 spots in the lineup. Oliver hit only 8 home runs; Carter hit 17, which is a lot for a catcher but not very many for a cleanup hitter. I haven't checked, but I would bet that the Montreal Expos were outhomered by their opponents in the 4–5 spots in their lineup last year by a ratio of about 2–1. They were seriously outhomered as a team, 120–102.

4) The Expos second-line pitching is terrible. The Expos' top three starters in 1983 (Rogers, 36 starts; Gullickson, 34 starts; Lea, 33 starts) had a combined record of 50 wins and 35 losses, easily the best record in the league for a big three. The Braves and Pirates had slightly better percentages from their big three, but nobody else had close to as many wins. But the rest of their staff was the worst in the league—worse even than the Mets, the Reds, and the Cubbies. Complete records:

3 PITCHERS WITH MOST STARTS	W	L	Pct	REST OF THE STAFF	W	L	Pct
1. Atlanta	41	27	.603	Los Angeles	49	38	.563
2. Pittsburgh	43	29	.597	Houston	50	41	.549
3. Montreal	50	35	.588	Philadelphia	48	42	.533
4. Philadelphia	42	30	.583	Atlanta	47	47	.500
5. Los Angeles	42	33	.560	San Diego	45	47	.489
6. San Francisco	35	33	.515	St. Louis	51	54	.486
7. San Diego	36	34	.514	San Francisco	44	50	.468
8. Houston	35	36	.493	Pittsburgh	41	49	.456
9. Cincinnati	35	39	.473	Cincinnati	39	49	.443
10. Chicago	30	36	.455	Chicago	41	55	.427
11. St. Louis	28	39	.418	New York	39	53	.424
12. New York	29	41	.414	Montreal	32	45	.416

The Expos experienced a dropoff of 172 percentage points when they were not pitching one of their big three. No other team in the league experienced a similar dropoff; only Pittsburgh (−.141) and Atlanta (−.103) suffered declines even half as large. The Expos' big three accounted for 61% of their team's wins; of the other eleven teams, only Pittsburgh (51%) had over half of their wins accounted for by their big three. And the Pirates have reacted to that problem by adding DeLeon and Tudor.

There are other strengths on the team (the Expos stole 138 bases in 182 attempts, a brilliant 76%, while their opponents stole only 115 in 203 tries, or 57%) and other weaknesses (the bullpen). It is not my intention to make a full accounting of these; I don't bother to say things that are obvious. My point is that the Expos' problems, while they may very well have their origin in some distant, aloof intangible, do not find their way into the loss column by some mystical route. The Expos lose games because specific ballplayers fail to do specific things. The Expos have the core of a great team, but they are not ever going to win as long as they surround that core with Doug Flynns and Ray Burrises.

Al OLIVER, First Base
Runs Created: 81

	G	AB	Hit	2B	3B	HR	Run	RBI	BB	SO	SB	CS	Avg
13.29 Years		628	192	37	6	16	85	94	37	52	6	5	.305
1983	157	614	184	38	3	8	70	84	44	44	1	3	.300
First Half	77	308	99	20	2	5	37	35			0		.321
Second Half	80	306	85	18	1	3	33	49			1		.278
vs. RHP		440	147										.334
vs. LHP		174	37										.213
Home	80	311	97	21	2	6	34	50			0		.312
Road	77	303	87	17	1	2	36	34			1		.287
Grass	37	150	42	7	0	2	17	19			1		.280
Turf	120	464	142	31	3	6	53	65			0		.306

Manny TRILLO, Second Base
Runs Created: 49

	G	AB	Hit	2B	3B	HR	Run	RBI	BB	SO	SB	CS	Avg
7.87 Years		575	153	23	4	6	57	57	43	69	7	7	.265
1983	119	441	119	21	1	3	49	45	31	64	1	3	.270
First Half	68	259	70	8	1	0	28	19	20	36	1	1	.270
Second Half	51	182	49	13	1	3	21	26	11	28	0	2	.269
vs. RHP		343	93										.271
vs. LHP		98	26										.265
Home													
Road													
Grass	84	305	82	11	1	1	30	28			1		.269
Turf	35	136	37	10	0	2	19	17			0		.272

Tim WALLACH, Third Base
Runs Created: 85

	G	AB	Hit	2B	3B	HR	Run	RBI	BB	SO	SB	CS	Avg
2.41 Years		582	153	30	3	22	68	76	44	91	2	3	.263
1983	156	581	156	33	3	19	54	70	55	97	0	3	.269
First Half	77	296	83	19	3	8	23	32			0		.280
Second half	79	285	73	14	0	11	31	38			0		.256
vs. RHP		437	117										.268
vs. LHP		144	39										.271
Home	78	289	76	19	2	9	24	39			0		.263
Road	78	292	80	14	1	10	30	31			0		.274
Grass	41	154	44	6	1	5	16	17			0		.286
Turf	115	427	112	27	2	14	38	53			0		.262

Doug FLYNN, Shortstop
Runs Created: 33

	G	AB	Hit	2B	3B	HR	Run	RBI	BB	SO	SB	CS	Avg
6.51 Years		485	116	15	5	1	38	38	19	39	2	3	.240
1983	143	452	107	18	4	0	44	26	19	38	2	1	.237
First Half	64	209	42	5	3	0	18	7			0		.201
Second Half	79	243	65	13	1	0	26	19			2		.267
vs. RHP		311	74										.238
vs. LHP		141	33										.234
Home	75	233	58	12	2	0	24	17			1		.249
Road	68	219	49	6	2	0	20	9			1		.224
Grass	34	112	23	2	0	0	10	5			1		.205
Turf	109	340	84	16	4	0	34	21			1		.247

Tim RAINES, Leftfield
Runs Created: 120

	G	AB	Hit	2B	3B	HR	Run	RBI	BB	SO	SB	CS	Avg
2.60 Years		614	176	30	9	8	112	58	86	72	95	16	.287
1983	156	615	183	32	8	11	133	71	97	70	90	14	.298
First Half	75	302	87	12	6	5	60	36			34		.288
Second Half	81	313	96	20	2	6	73	35			56		.307
vs. RHP		451	135										.299
vs. LHP		164	48										.293
Home	81	311	96	19	6	5	71	38			51		.309
Road	75	304	87	13	2	6	62	33			39		.286
Grass	37	153	44	3	1	2	31	15			20		.288
Turf	119	462	139	29	7	9	102	56			70		.301

Andre DAWSON, Centerfield
Runs Created: 113

	G	AB	Hit	2B	3B	HR	Run	RBI	BB	SO	SB	CS	Avg
6.40 Years		636	182	33	9	26	98	91	39	101	33	10	.287
1983	159	633	189	36	10	32	104	113	38	81	25	11	.299
First Half	75	308	99	20	6	17	48	65			12		.321
Second Half	84	325	90	16	4	15	56	48			13		.277
vs. RHP		474	134										.283
vs. LHP		159	55										.346
Home	78	298	80	18	4	10	44	43			12		.268
Road	81	335	109	18	6	22	60	70			13		.325
Grass	42	171	58	11	5	9	32	36			3		.339
Turf	117	462	131	25	5	23	72	77			22		.284

Warren CROMARTIE, Rightfield
Runs Created: 49

	G	AB	Hit	2B	3B	HR	Run	RBI	BB	SO	SB	CS	Avg
6.41 Years		592	166	35	5	9	70	58	48	60	8	5	.280
1983	120	360	100	26	2	3	37	43	43	48	8	3	.278
First Half	67	214	61	14	1	2	20	21			6		.285
Second Half	53	146	39	12	1	1	17	22			2		.267
vs. RHP		311	89										.286
vs. LHP		49	11										.224
Home	59	169	57	20	1	0	20	21			3		.337
Road	61	191	43	6	1	3	17	22			5		.225
Grass	31	104	26	3	1	1	12	10			4		.250
Turf	89	256	74	23	1	2	25	33			4		.289

Gary CARTER, Catcher
Runs Created: 80

	G	AB	Hit	2B	3B	HR	Run	RBI	BB	SO	SB	CS	Avg
7.71 Years		574	154	29	3	24	79	89	63	78	4	4	.269
1983	145	541	146	37	3	17	63	79	51	57	1	1	.270
First Half	69	263	70	15	1	10	31	34			0		.266
Second Half	76	278	76	22	2	7	32	45			1		.273
vs. RHP		390	104										.267
vs. LHP		151	42										.278
Home	67	237	66	22	1	6	31	40			0		.278
Road	78	304	80	15	2	11	32	39			1		.263
Grass	40	158	43	8	1	5	16	20			1		.272
Turf	105	383	103	29	2	12	47	59			0		.269

Bryan LITTLE, Infield
Runs Created: 42

	G	AB	Hit	2B	3B	HR	Run	RBI	BB	SO	SB	CS	Avg
.83 Years		470	120	18	4	1	65	47	65	34	7	7	.255
1983	106	350	91	15	3	1	48	36	50	22	4	5	.260
First Half	60	211	53	8	3	1	29	24			4		.251
Second Half	46	139	38	7	0	0	19	12			0		.273
vs. RHP		309	84										.272
vs. LHP		41	7										.171
Home	45	143	30	7	3	0	19	14			2		.210
Road	61	207	61	8	0	1	29	22			2		.295
Grass	35	123	37	6	0	1	19	18			2		.301
Turf	71	227	54	9	3	0	29	18			2		.238

Chris SPEIER, Infield
Runs Created: 31

	G	AB	Hit	2B	3B	HR	Run	RBI	BB	SO	SB	CS	Avg
10.88 Years		557	138	23	4	8	60	56	67	73	3	4	.248
1983	88	261	67	12	2	2	31	22	29	37	2	1	.257
First Half	49	159	38	9	1	1	16	13			1		.239
Second Half	39	102	29	3	1	1	15	9			1		.284
vs. RHP		167	46										.275
vs. LHP		94	21										.223
Home	50	145	42	11	1	1	21	9			1		.290
Road	38	116	25	1	1	1	10	13			1		.216
Grass	14	37	7	0	0	1	3	5			0		.189
Turf	74	224	60	12	2	1	28	17			2		.268

Steve ROGERS

Year	(W–L)	GS	Run	Avg	DP	Avg	SB	Avg
1982	(19-8)	35	149	4.26	29	.83	25	.71
1983	(17-12)	36	141	3.92	27	.75	25	.69
1976-1983		268	1026	3.83	225	.84	172	.64

	G	IP	W	L	Pct	ER	ERA
1982 Home	19	146.1	6	7	.462	49	3.01
1983 Home	16	126.2	9	5	.643	45	3.20
1982 Road	16	131.1	13	1	.929	25	1.71
1983 Road	20	146.1	8	7	.533	53	3.26
1983 Grass	10	68.1	4	5	.444	31	4.08
1983 Turf	26	204.2	13	7	.650	67	2.95

Bill GULLICKSON

Year	(W–L)	GS	Run	Avg	DP	Avg	SB	Avg
1982	(12-14)	34	153	4.50	21	.62	23	.68
1983	(17-12)	34	158	4.65	24	.71	22	.65
1980-1983		109	474	4.35	77	.71	79	.72

	G	IP	W	L	Pct	ER	ERA
1982 Home	14	99.2	5	5	.500	46	4.15
1983 Home	19	138.2	13	3	.813	59	3.83
1982 Road	20	137	7	9	.438	48	3.15
1983 Road	15	103.2	4	9	.308	42	3.65
1983 Grass	6	41.1	2	4	.333	23	5.01
1983 Turf	28	201	15	8	.652	78	3.49

Charlie LEA

Year	(W–L)	GS	Run	Avg	DP	Avg	SB	Avg
1982	(12-10)	27	120	4.44	18	.67	17	.63
1983	(16-11)	33	144	4.36	25	.76	29	.88
1980-1983		90	392	4.35	69	.77	66	.73

	G	IP	W	L	Pct	ER	ERA
1982 Home	11	73.2	3	6	.333	28	3.42
1983 Home	17	124.1	10	5	.667	40	2.90
1982 Road	16	104	9	4	.692	36	3.12
1983 Road	16	97.2	6	6	.500	37	3.41
1983 Grass	8	53	3	3	.500	17	2.89
1983 Turf	25	169	13	8	.619	60	3.20

1983 OTHERS

Pitcher	(W–L)	GS	Run	Avg	DP	Avg	SB	Avg
Burris	(4- 7)	17	58	3.41	12	.71	10	1.55
Sanderson	(6- 7)	16	61	3.81	12	.75	7	.44
Smith	(6-11)	12	41	3.42	18	1.50	3	.25
Welsh	(0- 1)	5	29	5.80	3	.60	7	1.40
Lerch	(1- 3)	5	23	4.60	8	1.60	6	1.20
Bargar	(2- 0)	3	17	5.67	0	.00	2	.67
Schatzedar	(5- 2)	2	5	2.50	1	.50	4	2.00

MONTREAL EXPOS
RUNS BATTED IN ANALYSIS

Player	RBI	RBI In Wins	Victory Important RBI	RBI Importance	Wins Batted In	RBI Per Win
Andre Dawson	113	75	47.72	.422	12.59	9.0
Tim Raines	71	53	30.52	.430	9.30	7.6
Al Oliver	84	57	31.00	.369	10.13	8.3
Tim Wallach	70	47	30.76	.439	8.13	8.6
Gary Carter	79	63	37.58	.476	10.31	7.7
Doug Flynn	26	17	10.09	.388	3.32	7.8
Warren Cromartie	43	35	19.77	.460	5.43	7.9
Chris Speier	22	12	7.11	.323	2.25	9.8
Manny Trillo	16	12	5.00	.313	1.63	9.9
Brian Little	36	20	15.15	.421	4.72	7.6

ST. LOUIS CARDINALS

I. Support Bowie Kuhn

I think Peter O'Malley is on to something here, I really do. The Dodgers are refusing to sell Busch beer in Dodger Stadium this year because it was that mean old August Busch Jr. who wouldn't let Bowie Kuhn stay on as commissioner of baseball. Susie and I have talked this over and decided that we, too, want to do our part to support Bowie, and we have been discussing what our options are to hit Gussie Busch right where it hurts, right in the old pocketbook. We have decided on the following, unprecedented actions:

1) We're going to drink more wine and less beer, and we're going to sample some of Busch's competitors' products if he hasn't driven them all out of business.

2) If or when we go to spring training this year, we are not going to make a side trip to Busch Gardens' Dark Continent, or if we do go we are not going to put any money into any of those machines that make those neat little plastic monkeys.

3) We're going to go take the tour of the Budweiser plant four or five times next summer, and every time we do we're going to gulp down as much free Michelob as we can at the end, even though it might make us sick, because we know that it costs them money to provide this service. Also, we plan to stuff our pockets full of those funny little pretzels before we leave.

4) When we go to see the Cardinals play, we're not going to park in their parking garage.

5) We are not going to buy any souvenir batting helmets or anything that has "St. Louis Cardinals" on it.

6) Whenever we see a parade and the Clydesdales are in it, we're not going to watch. We're going to turn off the television set until they're past. Also, we don't plan to laugh at any of Ed McMahon's jokes or buy any of Leon Redbone's records.

7) Finally, we plan to get a can of spray paint and make up a little stencil that says "Welcome to Miller Time" and spray it on our sidewalks, just so that our neighbors know where we stand on this issue.

It might take a while, but in time these actions, if followed by hundreds of people, will constitute an effective boycott, drive Busch to his knees and make him plead for Bowie Kuhn to quit playing darts and come back to lead baseball to greater and greater heights of prosperity. Support Bowie Kuhn. The next time you see a Budweiser truck parked at a liquor store, go let the air out of the tires.

II

It was not a good year to be a Whitey Herzog fan. As the 1982 season, like a soft light on the face of an aging woman, brought out all of Whitey Herzog's strong points as a manager, the 1983 light glared down from over his head, and pointed accusingly to all of his shortcomings. The temptation is to say that he was not as good a manager as he appeared to be in 1982, and is not as bad as he appeared in 1983; the truth is more likely that he is every bit as good as he appeared in 1982, and better, and he is every bit as bad as he appeared in 1983, and worse.

The watershed of the season seems to be the Keith Hernandez trade, so let's talk about that a moment. If you look at the Keith Hernandez trade on the basis of the talents exchanged—Hernandez for Allen—then the trade doesn't seem to make a lot of sense. Allen is certainly a better pitcher than he seemed to be at the moment of the trade, but he doesn't look like MVP material, either. But if you look at the move as being representative of the things that Whitey Herzog believes in, as all moves present an image of the philosophy that guides them, then the trade makes perfect sense. Hernandez lacks the speed that Herzog values so highly, at least in Busch Stadium. Hernandez is a 30-year-old ballplayer whose reputation was made four or five years ago; Whitey Herzog has always preferred to rest his fate with hungry ballplayers, with aggressive young men who play as if they had something to prove. Hernandez is a patient hitter whose strongest point is his ability to get on base, which has never been something that Whitey placed a high premium on. Hernandez may be on the decline; his batting averages over the last five years are .344, .321, .306, .299, and .297, and his runs scored and RBI counts, with an adjustment for the strike in 1981, are 116/105 in 1979, 111/99 in 1980, 103/76 in 1981, 79/94 in 1982 and 77/63 in 1983. But at any stage in his career, Hernandez simply never was one of the hustling, aggressive types of players that Herzog has always preferred to have. He doesn't challenge the defense on balls hit down the line; he won't run out ground balls if his manager doesn't insist on it. Most fans, many sportswriters and a few managers can successfully turn a blind eye to that. Losing managers often insist that their teams are hustling when they very clearly are not. But Herzog just isn't made that way.

If you were to sum up Whitey Herzog as a manager and as a man in one word, that word would have to be "aggressiveness." When he was rebuilding this ballclub at the winter meetings in 1980 and 1981, his aggressiveness in making deals stunned a baseball community that had become so cautious that many had concluded that it was no longer possible to make big-name player deals. Most of the agents that I deal with can't stand Herzog because he is so aggressive in contract negotiations. When things stall, he won't hesitate to call up the player himself and lay it out for him, put pressure on him to make a decision. He can't stand for people to waste his time warming up; he wants them to get to the bottom line. He doesn't get involved in the negotiations to negotiate; he gets involved to settle things. He has no use for anyone or anything who is tentative, indecisive.

And on the field, he's exactly the same in every area. The 1982 Cardinals played their average 9-inning game in 2 hours, 22 minutes, the fastest in the majors. Whitey does not want his pitchers out there nibbling at corners; he wants them to be aggressive, go after the hitters. His baserunners are noted for their aggressiveness in asking for an additional base from time to time. In his first year as a manager, in 1973, he had Jeff Burroughs on the roster, whom Ted Williams had been trying to teach to be selective at the plate. Whitey didn't want that; he wanted Burroughs to be more aggressive at the plate. He made a wager with Burroughs, in which if Burroughs swung at a strike and missed he would pay him a dollar—but if Burroughs took a pitch in the strike zone, he owed Whitey a dollar. Burroughs had his first good year that year, hitting 30 home runs.

I have mixed feelings about all of that aggression; 1982 shows the good side of it, 1983 the bad side. Aggressiveness puts the pressure on the opposing defense—but it takes the pressure off the opposing pitching staff. The sequence begins with the ball in the pitcher's hand, and the pressure on him to throw a strike; an aggressive hitter sometimes too willingly takes that pressure on himself in an attempt to pass it on to the defense. Whitey will stay for a long time with a hitter whose aggressiveness at the plate is costing him runs; Willie McGee is one example, Frank White another. At the same time, Jeff Burroughs' walks might be valuable, but his career would almost certainly have been better than it has been if he had stayed a little more aggressive at the plate, instead of sitting back on his heels waiting for a pitch he liked. Whitey's baserunners often make very poor percentage gambles, but over a period of time they learn what they can do and what they cannot do, who they can take advantage of and who they can't. They wind up being able to do more than they otherwise would have. A poor percentage move can still have positive psychological consequences, and Whitey's teams can get awfully hot in September.

III

Toward the end of the 1983 season, Whitey Herzog was discussing the problems of his starting pitchers. "I don't have the figures," he said, "I do know the scores. I would venture to say there were 25 or 30 ballgames that we were down five runs by the fourth inning." Whitey was pretty close. There were only eleven games that fit the exact description he gave, but another 21 in which the Cardinals fell behind early. Of those 32 games, they won only two, an April 23rd contest in which they overcame an early 4–0 deficit to win 9–5, and a June 15 game that they won 5–4 after trailing 3–0 in the 4th. There were long periods during the year in which they did not have this problem at all (they were blown out early only three times in forty days between April 23 and June 3), but other periods when it was almost a daily thing (they were blown out early nine times in seventeen days between June 10 and June 26).

To what extent this is unusual, I couldn't say. My memory tells me that the same thing happened to the Royals in 1979, Whitey's last year there. Jim checked the log of the other National League team that had the same won/lost record as the Cardinals, 79–83, and found that their totals were similar. The Giants were three runs behind in the first four innings of the game 29 times in 1983, and were 1–28 in those games. The Giants were five behind in the first four ten times.

IV

There were two other things I wanted to say about the Hernandez trade.

1) Herzog has made virtually the same move one time before. It was controversial then, and it didn't work particularly well then, but that didn't stop Whitey from doing it again. He traded, or actually gave away, John Mayberry in Kansas City, or perhaps the organization gave him away at Whitey's insistence. Mayberry was one of the organization's big stars, a lefthanded-hitting first baseman of about Hernandez's age at the time Herzog decided he didn't want him any more. Although Mayberry was a power hitter and Hernandez is a high average hitter, they embody most of the same virtues on the field. Mayberry, like Hernandez, was a patient, selective hitter with a high on-base percentage. Mayberry, like Hernandez, was not an aggressive or speedy baserunner. Mayberry, like Hernandez, was an excellent defensive first baseman, with large soft hands. That trade, like this Hernandez trade, was made in part because Herzog wanted to play a rookie —Clint Hurdle in that case, Andy Van Slyke in this one. In both cases, there were rumors.

2) This is a very odd type of trade for a team to make after they have just won their division, let alone the World. That fact seems emphasized, rather than mitigated, by the fact that the Milwaukee Brewers made a similar move in unloading Gorman Thomas in midseason. Ordinarily, a team that wins its division freezes up, resists making any move that is not powerfully dictated by necessity, and waits to be drawn toward the center of the league.

To me, then, the Hernandez trade shows very clearly that Whitey is not looking at the Cardinals as a team that has arrived where they are going. Even though they won a World's Championship, Whitey is still looking at the team that they could be. The Hernandez trade was made in part because Whitey was so overwhelmed by the young talent available to him that he wanted to play it all—he wanted to get David Green in the lineup, and Van Slyke, and he didn't want to move Willie McGee out of center.

If the gamble works, he winds up with a great team. After the Cincinnati Reds had their first outstanding year in 1970, they turned in a season exactly like this one, a 79–83 campaign. Whitey is still working here with an excellent talent base; by the method given in the comment on the California Angels, it measures at 755 units. It's going to be interesting to see what he does with it over the next four or five years.

ST. LOUIS CARDINALS

Player	Record in Lineup	Record Without
Lonnie Smith	64-57	15-26
Ozzie Smith	74-80	5- 3
George Hendrick	69-69	10-14
Willie McGee	67-72	12-11
Ken Oberkfell	62-66	17-17
Darrell Porter	58-63	21-20
David Green	46-51	33-32
Andy Van Slyke	35-46	44-37
Tom Herr	39-44	40-39
Mike Ramsey	24-23	55-60
Keith Hernandez	28-25	51-58
Glen Brummer	15-10	64-73
Floyd Rayford	15-10	64-73
Dane Iorg	18-10	61-73
Jamie Quirk	6-10	73-73
Steve Braun	3- 9	76-74
Bill Lyons	8- 5	71-78
Jeff Doyle	2- 7	77-76
Jim Adduci	1- 4	78-79
Jim Sexton	0- 1	79-82
Rafael Santana	0- 1	79-82

George HENDRICK, First Base
Runs Created: 96

	G	AB	Hit	2B	3B	HR	Run	RBI	BB	SO	SB	CS	Avg
9.92 Years		587	166	28	3	23	79	93	47	83	6	4	.283
1983	144	529	168	33	3	18	73	97	51	76	3	4	.318
First Half	73	268	93	19	0	11	40	58			1		.347
Second Half	71	261	75	14	3	7	33	39			2		.287
vs. RHP		367	111			12		74					.302
vs. LHP		162	57			6		23					.352
Home	73	262	80	14	3	10	33	46			2		.305
Road	71	267	88	19	0	8	40	51			1		.330
Grass	35	129	40	9	0	4	21	20	15		1		.310
Turf	109	400	128	24	3	14	52	77	36		2		.320

Tom HERR, Second Base
Runs Created: 53

	G	AB	Hit	2B	3B	HR	Run	RBI	BB	SO	SB	CS	Avg
2.57 Years		563	155	23	9	1	81	50	61	53	25	11	.275
1983	89	313	101	14	4	2	43	31	43	27	6	8	.323
First Half	62	214	61	10	2	2	28	17			4		.285
Second Half	27	99	40	4	2	0	15	14			2		.404
vs. RHP		225	75			2		26					.333
vs. LHP		88	26			0		5					.295
Home	41	137	55	7	2	1	20	16			2		.401
Road	48	176	46	7	2	1	23	15			4		.261
Grass	29	102	28	6	1	1	12	7	15		2		.275
Turf	60	211	73	8	3	1	31	24	28		4		.346

Ken OBERKFELL, Third Base
Runs Created: 71

	G	AB	Hit	2B	3B	HR	Run	RBI	BB	SO	SB	CS	Avg
4.07 Years		536	156	26	7	3	8	49	61	36	11	6	.291
1983	151	488	143	26	5	3	62	38	61	27	12	6	.293
First Half	75	272	78	13	3	0	40	18			6		.287
Second Half	76	216	65	13	2	3	22	20			6		.301
vs. RHP		391	124			3		27					.317
vs. LHP		97	19			0		11					.196
Home	77	225	69	9	4	0	35	18			9		.307
Road	74	263	74	17	1	3	27	20			3		.281
Grass	40	138	34	3	0	2	15	10	14		2		.246
Turf	111	350	109	23	5	1	47	28	47		10		.311

Ozzie SMITH, Shortstop
Runs Created: 65

	G	AB	Hit	2B	3B	HR	Run	RBI	BB	SO	SB	CS	Avg
5.44 Years		602	142	22	5	1	72	41	60	43	38	11	.235
1983	159	552	134	30	6	3	69	50	64	36	34	7	.243
First Half	79	273	56	10	3	0	26	23			15		.205
Second Half	80	279	78	20	3	3	43	27			19		.280
vs. RHP		399	99			0		32					.248
vs. LHP		153	35			3		18					.229
Home	79	256	58	15	3	1	43	25			20		.227
Road	80	296	76	15	3	2	26	25			14		.257
Grass	41	147	40	8	3	2	12	11	16		8		.272
Turf	118	405	94	22	3	1	57	39	48		26		.232

Lonnie SMITH, Leftfield
Runs Created: 85

	G	AB	Hit	2B	3B	HR	Run	RBI	BB	SO	SB	CS	Avg
2.98 Years		535	169	32	7	7	108	50	52	68	57	23	.316
1983	130	492	158	31	5	8	83	45	41	55	43	18	.321
First Half	50	196	61	10	2	3	28	19			11		.311
Second Half	80	296	97	21	3	5	55	26			32		.328
vs. RHP		346	112			6		35					.324
vs. LHP		146	46			2		10					.315
Home	64	243	83	19	5	4	42	27			27		.342
Road	66	249	75	12	0	4	41	18			16		.301
Grass	34	129	43	6	0	3	23	11	10		7		.333
Turf	96	363	115	25	5	5	60	34	31		36		.317

Willie McGEE, Centerfield
Runs Created: 73

	G	AB	Hit	2B	3B	HR	Run	RBI	BB	SO	SB	CS	Avg
1.67 Years		614	178	20	10	5	72	79	23	94	38	12	.290
1983	147	601	172	22	8	5	75	75	26	98	39	8	.286
First Half	65	265	84	10	1	3	34	30			13		.317
Second Half	82	336	88	12	7	2	41	45			26		.262
vs. RHP		442	127			3		51					.287
vs. LHP		159	45			2		24					.283
Home	73	276	69	11	5	4	38	40			20		.250
Road	74	325	103	11	3	1	37	35			19		.317
Grass	40	178	55	6	0	1	20	17	4		10		.309
Turf	107	423	117	16	8	4	55	58	22		29		.277

David GREEN, Rightfield
Runs Created: 53

	G	AB	Hit	2B	3B	HR	Run	RBI	BB	SO	SB	CS	Avg
1.50 Years		415	115	15	7	7	53	63	27	73	30	13	.277
1983	146	422	120	14	10	8	52	69	26	76	34	16	.284
First Half	69	187	56	7	5	2	20	29			13		.299
Second Half	77	235	64	7	5	6	32	40			21		.272
vs. RHP		256	75			3		38					.293
vs. LHP		166	45			5		31					.271
Home	77	225	64	5	8	5	29	34			23		.284
Road	69	197	56	9	2	3	23	35			11		.284
Grass	36	106	35	4	0	3	16	24	7		7		.330
Turf	110	316	85	10	10	5	36	45	19		27		.269

Darrell PORTER, Catcher
Runs Created: 71

	G	AB	Hit	2B	3B	HR	Run	RBI	BB	SO	SB	CS	Avg
8.75 Years		525	131	23	5	17	73	77	86	92	3	4	.250
1983	145	443	116	24	3	15	57	66	68	94	1	3	.262
First Half	73	227	53	7	3	10	32	39			1		.233
Second Half	72	216	63	17	0	5	25	27			0		.292
vs. RHP		337	91			14		58					.270
vs. LHP		106	25			1		8					.236
Home	71	210	54	11	2	5	28	25			0		.257
Road	74	233	62	13	1	10	29	41			1		.266
Grass	39	121	34	9	0	6	20	23	13		1		.281
Turf	106	322	82	15	3	9	37	43	55		0		.255

Andy VAN SLYKE, Utility
Runs Created: 50

	G	AB	Hit	2B	3B	HR	Run	RBI	BB	SO	SB	CS	Avg
.62 Years		496	130	24	8	13	82	61	74	103	34	11	.262
1983	101	309	81	15	5	8	51	38	46	64	21	7	.262
First Half	22	75	15	3	1	4	16	13			6		.200
Second Half	79	234	66	12	4	4	35	25			15		.282
vs. RHP		255	68			6		31					.267
vs. LHP		54	13			2		7					.241
Home	49	145	36	6	5	3	22	18			11		.248
Road	52	164	45	9	0	5	29	20			10		.274
Grass	26	83	25	4	0	4	16	13	10		5		.301
Turf	75	226	56	11	5	4	35	25	36		16		.248

Mike RAMSEY, Infield
Runs Created: 18

	G	AB	Hit	2B	3B	HR	Run	RBI	BB	SO	SB	CS	Avg
2.02 Years		340	85	11	3	1	38	27	22	45	7	3	.249
1983	97	175	46	4	3	1	25	16	12	23	4	2	.263
First Half	50	100	27	3	2	0	16	9			3		.270
Second Half	47	75	19	1	1	1	9	7			1		.253
vs. RHP		108	34			1		10					.315
vs. LHP		67	12			0		6					.179
Home	39	70	18	1	2	0	14	6	8		2		.257
Road	58	105	28	3	1	1	11	10	4		2		.267
Grass	31	52	16	2	0	1	5	4	2		1		.308
Turf	66	123	30	2	3	0	20	12	10		3		.244

Joacquin ANDUJAR

Year	(W–L)	GS	Run	Avg	DP	Avg	SB	Avg
1982	(15-10)	37	147	3.94	30	.81	27	.73
1983	(6-16)	34	136	4.00	29	.85	23	.68
1976-1983		182	683	3.75	154	.85	158	.87

	G	IP	W	L	Pct	ER	ERA
1982 Home	19	140	8	5	.615	38	2.44
1983 Home	17	97.2	4	7	.364	48	4.42
1982 Road	19	125.2	7	5	.583	35	2.51
1983 Road	22	126	2	9	.182	56	4.00
1983 Grass	11	61.1	2	5	.286	24	3.52
1983 Turf	28	161.2	4	11	.267	80	4.45

Bob FORSCH

Year	(W–L)	GS	Run	Avg	DP	Avg	SB	Avg
1982	(15-9)	34	148	4.35	33	.97	26	.76
1983	(10-12)	30	122	4.07	22	.73	24	.80
1976-1983		248	1097	4.42	250	1.01	179	.72

	G	IP	W	L	Pct	ER	ERA
1982 Home	18	133.2	11	2	.846	47	3.16
1983 Home	16	103.2	6	5	.546	41	3.56
1982 Road	18	99.1	4	7	.364	43	3.90
1983 Road	18	83.1	4	7	.364	48	5.18
1983 Grass	11	49.1	1	5	.167	35	6.39
1983 Turf	23	137.2	9	7	.563	54	3.53

John STUPER

Year	(W–L)	GS	Run	Avg	DP	Avg	SB	Avg
1982	(9-7)	21	73	3.48	19	.90	8	.36
1983	(12-11)	30	135	4.50	32	1.07	21	.70
1982-1983		51	208	4.08	51	1.00	29	.57

	G	IP	W	L	Pct	ER	ERA
1982 Home	13	80.1	4	4	.500	35	3.92
1983 Home	15	117.2	7	6	.539	49	3.75
1982 Road	10	56.1	5	3	.625	16	2.56
1983 Road	20	79.2	5	5	.500	33	3.73
1983 Grass	13	46.1	3	4	.429	27	5.24
1983 Turf	2	151	9	7	.529	55	3.28

Dave LaPOINT

Year	(W–L)	GS	Run	Avg	DP	Avg	SB	Avg
1982	(9-3)	21	1100	4.76	31	1.48	33	1.57
1983	(12-9)	29	132	4.55	37	1.28	15	.52
1980-1983		55	274		74		53	

	G	IP	W	L	Pct	ER	ERA
1982 Home	21	66.2	3	3	.500	29	3.91
1983 Home	18	102.2	6	6	.455	38	3.34
1982 Road	21	86	6	0	1.000	29	3.03
1983 Road	19	89	6	3	.667	42	4.24
1983 Grass	8	38.1	3	1	.750	22	5.16
1983 Turf	29	153	9	8	.500	58	3.41

Neil ALLEN

Year	(W–L)	GS	Run	Avg	DP	Avg	SB	Avg
1983	(12-13)	22	94	4.27	28	1.27	16	.73
1979-1983		27	105	3.89	34	1.26	21	.78

	G	IP	W	L	Pct	ER	ERA
1983 Home	23	95.1	8	4	.667	33	3.12
1983 Road	23	79.1	4	9	.308	43	4.88
1983 Grass	22	85	6	4	.600	30	3.18
1983 Turf	24	89.2	6	9	.400	46	4.62

1983 OTHERS

Pitcher	(W–L)	GS	Run	Avg	DP	Avg	SB	Avg
Cox	(3-2)	12	34	2.83	18	1.50	8	.67
Martin	(3-1)	5	30	6.00	6	1.20	3	.60
Hagen	(2-2)	4	12	3.00	7	1.75	4	1.00

ST. LOUIS CARDINALS
RUNS BATTED IN ANALYSIS

Player	RBI	RBI In Wins	Victory Important RBI	RBI Importance	Wins Batted In	RBI Per Win
George Hendrick	97	73	47.66	.491	12.01	8.1
Willie McGee	75	52	35.12	.468	9.47	7.9
Darrell Porter	66	41	27.23	.413	6.97	9.5
David Green	69	46	25.16	.365	7.94	8.7
Ken Oberkfell	38	27	19.03	.501	4.86	7.8
Ozzie Smith	50	35	18.54	.371	4.91	10.2
Lonnie Smith	45	28	16.34	.363	4.38	10.3
Keith Hernandez	26	19	13.12	.505	3.54	7.3
Tom Herr	31	20	12.72	.410	3.22	9.6
Andy Van Slyke	38	19	10.88	.286	3.57	10.6
Mike Ramsey	16	13	5.86	.366	1.78	9.0

CHICAGO CUBS

If anybody offers you 100 odds against the Chicago Cubs winning the National League East in 1984, take him up on it. Every spring I see odds printed in the paper listing one or two teams at 200–1 to win their division, and others at 100–1. I have serious doubts that any team should even be considered a 200–1 shot to win a division. If you take a bad team that is a long way away from the pennant, like, say, the Minnesota Twins, and you ask "What has to go right for this team to win the pennant?" you'll get a substantial list. In the Twins' case they'll have to come up with a leadoff man who can magnify the value of their middle-of-the lineup punch. They'll have to replace Gary Ward in left field with somebody who contributes a little bit. Ken Schrom will have to stay where he was a year ago, and Smithson and Butcher will have to come through and stabilize the rotation. The White Sox will have to drop off by about ten games, and the Twins will have to be lucky in the close games.

That's a long list, and the chance that all of those things will happen certainly does make for long odds. On the other hand, it is extremely difficult to gauge exactly how long the odds are. Our memories are not long enough to teach us distinctions that fine; a tiny sliver of a chance looks pretty much the same whether it is a 1/50th sliver or a 1/200th sliver. But my perception is that a lot of these teams, like the Twins, which come out listed at 100–1 or 150–1 or 200–1 should, in fact, be listed at 30–1 or 40–1 or 60–1. I think that if you go over that list of all the things that have to happen, and you assign probabilities to each of these things (this has about a 40% chance of happening, this only 20%, this 60%) and multiply them in sequence (.40 × .20 × .60) to figure the chance that all of them will happen, you're much more likely to come out with a figure of .032 to .015 (30–1 to 60–1) than of .010 to .005 (100–1 to 200–1). I also think that if you look at the history of the game, you'll find that miracle teams happen more like one time in 40 than one time in 200.

In the last 25 years, there have been two recognized miracle teams—the Red Sox of 1967 and the Mets of 1969—and a third team whose qualifications as a Miracle team are just as good, the Reds of 1961.

Anyway, to get back to the Chicago Cubs . . . if I have ever seen a dead giveaway set-up for a miracle, this is it. There are several reasons for saying that:

1) A substantial portion of the 19-game difference between the Cubs and the top of the division is not a real difference in talent. It might be called an illusion, it might be called a difference in luck, it might be called a difference in the ability to play one-run baseball. But whatever it is, it isn't a difference in the ability to score runs or the ability to prevent the opposition from scoring runs. The Cubs scored five more runs than the Phillies did, and they allowed only 84 more runs than the Phillies did. A difference of 79 runs between two teams will not ordinarily mean a difference of 19 games in the win column.

As was discussed in Section I, a normal record for a team which scored 701 runs and allowed 719 would be 79 wins, 83 losses, not 71–91. This is an unusually large disparity—8 games—between projected performance and actual performance. And as was discussed a year ago in the comment on the Toronto Blue Jays, these disparities do not hold up from year to year; a team which wins more games than they could expect to in one year will usually decline in performance the next year, while a team like the Cubs which has eight games of slack in its record is fairly certain to improve in the following year.

2) The Shotton Syndrome (see Milwaukee comment). It's not a classic Shotton Syndrome because the Cubs are not an established contender, but Elia is definitely a high-pressure manager, and Jim Frey is definitely a low-pressure manager, an optimist. When that happens, the team usually has a good year.

3) Miracles usually happen in compressed leagues, in leagues where the difference between the best teams and the worst teams is not too wide. A miracle is unlikely to happen in the American League West because it is 39 games from the top of the division to Seattle, and the standard deviation of wins in the division is 12.04. In the N.L. East the distance from top to bottom is only 22 games and the standard deviation is just 8.25.

Compressed leagues come and go, and at the moment both divisions in the National League are very compressed. Some people have taken that as a sign that there are not going to be any great teams any more. I don't see it that way. I think that the basic reason that there are not great teams at the moment is that the two teams which should be there, Montreal and Atlanta, have made some silly mistakes and have not at least yet arrived at that pinnacle. But looking at the Cardinals and the Dodgers, the White Sox in the American League, I see the potential for teams that are just as great as the 1976 Reds or the 1973 A's.

That's a digression; the relevant point ended with "compressed leagues come and go"; there have been many moments in the history of baseball when there was no great team, no dominant team. It is in those times that miracle teams come forward. The National League in 1968, the year before the Miracle of Flushing Meadow, was only 25 games from top to bottom and had a standard deviation of 7.56 wins; the expansion spread that out artificially in 1969. The American League in 1966 was 26½ games top to bottom; the 1966 Red Sox finished ninth at 72–90, and the standard deviation was 8.96 wins. The American League, as I said in the Tigers' comment, had no dominant team between the collapse of the Yankees after 1964 and the rise of the Orioles in 1969.

The National League in 1960, from which the Reds arose to win in 1961, was not a compressed league, but it was, like the American League in 1966, in the middle of a five-year period with no dominant team. Starting with the gradual decline of the Braves following the 1958 season, and ending with the rise of the Koufax/Drysdale Dodgers in 1963, the National League, then as now, lacked an outstanding team. The Reds in 1960 had a 67–87 record, a worse record than the Mets in '68, the Red Sox in '66 or the Cubs in '83. They had not finished over .500 for several years. But in a power vacuum, they put it together and reigned for one year.

Basing their strengths on Ron Cey, Bill Buckner and Larry Bowa, I certainly don't see the Cubs as having the potential to be a great team, a dominant team over a period of time. But that's not really germane; miracle teams are never great teams. They're teams that have a moment, teams that slip through a window of dominance.

4) The incumbent champion in the division, the Phillies, has obvious problems that it must overcome in order to stay around the 90-win level.

5) The Cubs have taken steps this winter to solidify their pitching, something that almost all miracle teams do.

6) The Cubs have a specific, correctable weakness, action on which can have a huge impact on the won/lost record. I speak of their ability on artificial turf. The Cubs last year were a winning team on grass fields (58–56; 43–38 at home and 15–18 on road grass), but were the worst team in baseball on artificial turf (13–35) by a wide margin. The reasons for this are not hard to understand. They have a power-hitting offense without much speed, and their defense has three players (Bowa, Cey and Moreland), who don't move so much as sort of melt toward the ball. Their staff is composed heavily of ground-ball pitchers —the staff unquestionably had more ground balls hit off of them than any other staff in the major leagues—and ground-ball pitchers get killed on artificial turf.

Jim Frey cut his manager's teeth on a fast carpet in KC, and he should be able to deal with this problem if he has any material to work with. What should he do? Probably the most pressing thing is to rest Bowa on artificial turf. Bowa had a pretty decent year at short in '83, but at 38 he is not nearly quick enough to play a shallow shortstop on artificial turf, nor is his arm good enough to back up and play deep. Besides, he hit only .214 on turf (.290 on grass), so you're not exactly making an offensive sacrifice. The Cubs likely will keep a young shortstop (Dan Rohn or Dave Owen), and Frey ought to play him on artificial turf.

Ron Cey, who has outgrown diving for baseballs, does hit well on turf and has no obvious replacement, so he

represents a trickier problem. Between these two is Keith Moreland.

The Cubs have a young outfielder named Joe Carter who is in the same class as Mel Hall—possibly, if you can believe this, even better than Hall, although a year behind. He is 24, and was in the opinion of many the best all-around player in the American Association last year. He has nothing left to prove in the minor leagues, but unless they make a trade there is no place for him in the majors; the outfield is too good. He could, however, replace Moreland in right field on artificial turf. Moreland hit fairly well on turf (.281; he hit .311 on grass), but it is still questionable whether his offense on turf justifies his defense.

Ryne Sandberg hit only .208 on turf last year; you'll probably just have to let him outgrow that.

But more importantly than that, Lee Elia (and other Cub managers) gave Steve Trout 13 starts on artificial turf (41% of his starts; the Cubs played only 30% of their games on artificial turf), while starting Ferguson Jenkins only 5 times on turf (17% of his starts). This seems to have been a deliberate choice—start the ground-ball pitcher on turf and the fly-ball pitcher on grass—but if it was, it was a stupid deliberate choice. Elia seems to have been mixed up about what type of pitcher pitches well on artificial turf. Trout was 6–6 on grass but 3–8 on artificial turf; Chuck Rainey, the other extreme ground-ball type pitcher on the staff, was 13–5 on grass but 1–8 on turf. Between the two, they were 19–11 on grass but 4–16 on artificial turf, a breakdown that has got to be statistically significant.

So all Frey has got to do to improve the team's performance on artificial turf is stop pitching the ground-ball pitchers. I don't care how good his options are; I don't care if he has to start a middle-inning reliever. Anything is better than throwing games out the window.

I am certainly not saying here that the Chicago Cubs will be a miracle team, that they will win the division. Pittsburgh's starting rotation is terrific, and the Cardinals are a better team than they seemed to be last year. I am saying that the true odds against the Cubs winning this division are not all that long, that they are probably about 6–1 or 8–1. I expect the Cubs to play about .500 baseball. In this division at this moment, that puts them in the race.

The Cubs hit 140 home runs in 1983 to their opponents' 117. Only one other N.L. team (the Dodgers, 146–97) had as good a ratio.

Bill BUCKNER, First Base
Runs Created: 83

	G	AB	Hit	2B	3B	HR	Run	RBI	BB	SO	SB	CS	Avg
10.65 Years		623	185	33	4	11	74	74	29	28	14	6	.296
1983	153	626	175	38	6	16	79	66	25	30	12	4	.280
First Half	79	323	86	21	3	10	38	38			3		.266
Second Half	74	303	89	17	3	6	41	28			9		.294
vs. RHP		433	123	26	6	14	59	51	20	16	6		.284
vs. LHP		193	52	12	0	2	20	15	5	14	6		.269
Home	78	315	89	21	4	6	44	31			5		.283
Road	75	311	86	17	2	10	35	35			7		.277
Grass	109	452	126	29	5	11	61	50	17		11		.279
Turf	44	174	49	9	1	5	18	16	8		1		.282

Mel HALL, Centerfield
Runs Created: 71

	G	AB	Hit	2B	3B	HR	Run	RBI	BB	SO	SB	CS	Avg
.90 Years		556	153	29	6	21	74	69	53	135	7	8	.275
1983	112	410	116	23	5	17	60	56	42	101	6	6	.283
First Half	35	137	40	8	1	2	19	8			2		.292
Second Half	77	273	76	15	4	15	41	48			4		.278
vs. RHP		340	108	23	5	17	55	51	33	69	5		.318
vs. LHP		70	8	0	0	0	5	5	9	32	1		.114
Home	58	206	57	11	3	7	29	25			3		.277
Road	54	204	59	12	2	10	31	31			3		.289
Grass	78	284	82	15	3	13	43	40	33		4		.289
Turf	34	126	34	8	2	4	17	16	9		2		.270

Ryne SANDBERG, Second Base
Runs Created: 75

	G	AB	Hit	2B	3B	HR	Run	RBI	BB	SO	SB	CS	Avg
2.02 Years		631	167	29	4	7	99	51	43	84	34	11	.265
1983	158	633	165	25	4	8	94	48	51	79	37	11	.261
First Half	76	299	84	17	3	5	43	25			17		.281
Second Half	82	334	81	8	1	3	51	23			20		.243
vs. RHP		458	121	17	2	6	69	35	36	59	30		.264
vs. LHP		175	44	8	2	2	25	13	15	20	7		.251
Home	80	308	89	17	2	4	58	29			22		.289
Road		325	76	8	2	4	36	19			15		.234
Grass	110	441	125	17	2	7	77	39	44		29		.283
Turf	48	192	40	8	2	1	17	9	7		8		.208

Keith MORELAND, Rightfield
Runs Created: 93

	G	AB	Hit	2B	3B	HR	Run	RBI	BB	SO	SB	CS	Avg
2.65 Years		533	152	24	3	15	60	80	53	66	2	5	.285
1983	154	533	161	30	3	16	76	70	68	73	0	3	.302
First Half	76	271	82	10	3	12	45	44			0		.303
Second Half	78	262	79	20	0	4	31	26			0		.302
vs. RHP		398	109	23	1	9	49	48	47	55	0		.274
vs. LHP		135	52	7	2	7	27	22	21	18	0		.385
Home	77	263	83	19	1	8	42	35			0		.316
Road	77	270	78	17	2	8	34	35			0		.289
Grass	110	380	118	25	2	11	56	53	46		0		.311
Turf	44	153	43	5	1	5	20	17	22		0		.281

Ron CEY, Third Base
Runs Created: 90

	G	AB	Hit	2B	3B	HR	Run	RBI	BB	SO	SB	CS	Avg
10.12 Years		573	152	25	2	25	78	92	82	91	2	3	.265
1983	159	581	160	33	1	24	73	90	62	85	0	0	.275
First Half	77	286	73	14	0	9	34	38			0	0	.255
Second Half	82	295	87	19	1	15	39	52			0	0	.295
vs. RHP		425	124	26	1	14	53	65	42	58	0	0	.292
vs. LHP		156	36	7	0	10	20	25	20	27	0	0	.231
Home	81	284	74	17	1	11	36	48			0	0	.261
Road	78	297	86	17	0	13	37	42			0	0	.290
Grass	113	408	112	25	1	15	52	66	46		0	0	.275
Turf	46	173	48	8	0	9	21	24	16		0	0	.277

Jody DAVIS, Catcher
Runs Created: 72

	G	AB	Hit	2B	3B	HR	Run	RBI	BB	SO	SB	CS	Avg
2.08 Years		533	141	27	2	19	53	75	43	102	0	2	.264
1983	151	510	138	31	2	24	56	84	33	93	0	2	.271
First Half	71	228	57	13	1	13	21	45			0		.250
Second Half	80	282	81	18	1	11	35	39			0		.287
vs. RHP		382	102	25	1	19	44	58	24	72	0		.267
vs. LHP		128	36	6	1	5	12	26	9	21	0		.281
Home	75	241	69	19	2	15	35	54			0		.286
Road		269	69	12	0	9	21	30			0		.257
Grass	107	355	101	25	2	19	46	69	24		0		.285
Turf	44	155	37	6	0	5	10	15	9		0		.239

Larry BOWA, Shortstop
Runs Created: 56

	G	AB	Hit	2B	3B	HR	Run	RBI	BB	SO	SB	CS	Avg
12.52 Years		624	164	19	7	1	75	39	35	42	24	7	.263
1983	147	499	133	20	5	2	73	43	35	30	7	3	.267
First Half	76	268	67	7	5	2	42	26			2		.250
Second Half	71	231	66	13	0	0	31	17			5		.286
vs. RHP		367	92	10	3	0	55	23	29	21	6		.251
vs. LHP		132	41	10	2	2	18	20	6	9	1		.311
Home	74	239	64	11	3	1	41	33			1		.268
Road		260	69	9	2	1	32	10			6		.265
Grass	103	345	100	14	4	2	62	41	26		2		.290
Turf	44	154	33	6	1	0	11	2	9		5		.214

Jay JOHNSTONE, Outfield
Runs Created: 22

	G	AB	Hit	2B	3B	HR	Run	RBI	BB	SO	SB	CS	Avg
10.36 Years		445	119	20	3	10	55	51	41	59	5	4	.267
1983	86	140	36	7	0	6	16	22	20	24	1	1	.257
First Half	44	90	25	5	0	4	10	14			1		.278
Second Half	42	50	11	2	0	2	6	8			0		.220
vs. RHP		127	33	6	0	6	16	21	20	21	1		.260
vs. LHP		13	3	1	0	0	0	1	0	3	0		.231
Home	40	58	18	2	0	4	9	11	13		1		.310
Road	46	82	18	5	0	2	7	11	7		0		.220
Grass	60	94	30	5	0	5	14	18	15		1		.319
Turf	26	46	6	2	0	1	2	4	5		0		.130

Leon DURHAM, Leftfield
Runs Created: 64

	G	AB	Hit	2B	3B	HR	Run	RBI	BB	SO	SB	CS	Avg
2.66 Years		566	162	30	9	20	85	83	67	101	27	14	.286
1983	100	337	87	18	8	12	58	55	66	83	12	6	.258
First Half	54	184	57	12	3	10	36	34			9		.310
Second Half	46	153	30	6	5	2	22	21			3		.196
vs. RHP		250	59	13	6	10	40	40	48	57	10		.236
vs. LHP		87	28	5	2	2	18	15	18	26	2		.322
Home	55	181	49	9	4	9	35	39			3		.271
Road	45	156	38	9	4	3	23	16			9		.244
Grass	79	272	69	14	6	10	48	49	51		6		.254
Turf	21	65	18	4	2	2	10	6	15		6		.277

Gary WOODS, Outfield
Runs Created: 18

	G	AB	Hit	2B	3B	HR	Run	RBI	BB	SO	SB	CS	Avg
2.20 Years		387	94	20	1	5	42	44	26	67	8	5	.244
1983	93	190	46	9	0	4	25	22	15	27	5	3	.242
First Half	45	109	29	5	0	2	16	13			5		.266
Second Half	48	81	17	4	0	2	9	9			0		.210
vs. RHP		62	14	4	0	3	10	7	5	10	0		.226
vs. LHP		128	32	5	0	1	15	15	10	17	5		.250
Home	49	102	27	4	0	3	12	13	9		3		.265
Road	44	88	19	5	0	1	13	9	6		2		.216
Grass	65	133	34	6	0	3	15	15	11		3		.256
Turf	28	57	12	3	0	1	10	7	4		2		.211

Chuck RAINEY

Year	(W–L)	GS	Run	Avg	DP	Avg	SB	Avg
1982	(7- 5)	25	123	4.92	28	1.12	22	.88
1983	(14-13)	34	154	4.53	41	1.21	24	.71
1979-1983		90	432	4.80	121	1.34	58	.64

	G	IP	W	L	Pct	ER	ERA
1982 Home	14	65.2	2	1	.667	41	5.62
1983 Home	18	114	10	3	.769	44	3.47
1982 Road	13	63.1	5	4	.556	31	4.41
1983 Road	16	77	4	10	.286	51	5.96
1983 Grass	24	142.1	13	5	.722	68	4.30
1983 Turf	10	48.2	1	8	.111	27	4.99

Dick RUTHVEN

Year	(W–L)	GS	Run	Avg	DP	Avg	SB	Avg
1982	(11-11)	31	122	3.94	20	.65	36	1.16
1983	(13-12)	32	159	4.97	29	.91	27	.84
1976-1983		230	988	4.30	208	.90	246	1.07

	G	IP	W	L	Pct	ER	ERA
1982 Home	18	112.2	7	4	.636	39	3.12
1983 Home	16	95.1	7	6	.539	46	4.34
1982 Road	15	91.2	4	7	.364	47	4.61
1983 Road	16	87.2	6	6	.500	43	4.42
1983 Grass	21	123.1	9	7	.563	57	4.16
1983 Turf	11	59.2	4	5	.444	32	4.83

Steve TROUT

Year	(W–L)	GS	Run	Avg	DP	Avg	SB	Avg
1982	(6- 9)	19	80	4.21	22	1.16	11	.58
1983	(10-14)	32	134	4.19	31	.97	33	1.03
1978-1983		101	436	4.32	114	1.13	60	.59

	G	IP	W	L	Pct	ER	ERA
1983 Home	14	85.2	6	4	.600	35	3.68
1983 Road	20	94.1	4	10	.286	58	5.53
1983 Grass	20	112.1	7	6	.538	55	4.41
1983 Turf	14	67.2	3	8	.273	38	5.05

1983 OTHERS

Pitcher	(W–L)	GS	Run	Avg	DP	Avg	SB	Avg
Noles	(5-10)	18	69	8.62	13	.72	22	1.22
Moskau	(3- 2)	8	40	5.00	8	1.00	5	.62
Lefferts	(3- 4)	5	14	2.80	4	.80	5	1.00
Reuschel	(1- 1)	4	13	3.25	3	.75	1	.25
Schulze	(0- 1)	3	15	5.00	2	.67	5	1.67
Patterson	(1- 2)	2	13	6.50	3	1.50	3	1.50
Bordi	(0- 2)	1	1	1.00	1	1.00	3	3.00
Hernandez	(1- 0)	1	6	6.00	0	.00	2	2.00

Ferguson JENKINS

Year	(W–L)	GS	Run	Avg	DP	Avg	SB	Avg
1982	(14-15)	34	152	4.47	22	.65	40	1.18
1983	(6- 9)	29	117	4.03	34	1.17	30	1.03
1976-1983		232	1082	4.66	219	.94	176	.76

	G	IP	W	L	Pct	ER	ERA
1982 Home	19	118.1	8	7	.533	43	3.27
1983 Home	20	112	6	5	.545	43	3.46
1982 Road	15	98.2	6	8	.429	33	3.01
1983 Road	13	55.1	0	4	.000	37	6.02
1983 Grass	27	137.2	6	8	.429	69	4.51
1983 Turf	6	29.2	0	1	.000	11	3.34

CHICAGO CUBS
RUNS BATTED IN ANALYSIS

Player	RBI	RBI In Wins	Victory Important RBI	RBI Importance	Wins Batted In	RBI Per Win
Jody Davis	84	65	39.09	.465	11.26	7.5
Ron Cey	90	53	35.25	.392	8.70	10.3
Keith Moreland	70	46	27.64	.395	8.49	8.2
Mel Hall	56	35	21.81	.389	5.51	10.2
Bill Buckner	66	36	21.60	.327	6.34	10.4
Larry Bowa	43	28	19.64	.457	4.52	9.5
Ryne Sandberg	48	26	16.19	.337	4.93	9.7
Leon Durham	55	25	15.64	.284	3.99	13.8
Jay Johnstone	22	11	6.85	.311	2.02	10.9
Gary Woods	22	10	6.06	.275	1.62	13.6

NEW YORK METS

I have always been attracted to lost causes. Irrevocably lost causes. My favorite car, for instance, is the Packard. Packard went out of business before I was born, yet I'm still pulling for them to make a comeback. I am fascinated by those hopeless cause historical movies, like "The Alamo" or "Khartoum" (with Charlton Heston as Gordon) where a small group of men fights desperately against all odds and . . . loses. Unrequited love is another topic near to my heart. It should come as no surprise, then, to find out that I am a Mets fan.

It's a chicken-and-egg thing with me. I'm not sure that I'm attracted to lost causes because I'm a Mets fan or being a Mets fan is a smaller part of the whole syndrome. I have a feeling it's the former since Met fandome came before all these other interests. I hope I don't start actualizing these fascinations, you know— putting my money in failed banks or falling in love with married women.

There is something misshapenly noble about losing or rooting for a losing team. A kind of honor permeates the deed. In April I (and 4,040 other misshapen, noble beings) attended a Mets doubleheader against the Pirates. It was 35° at game time and dropped steadily after that. I guess it didn't drop too far because the cold rain that fell for the entire five hours we were there never turned to snow. What was I doing there? I think I was trying to prove a point. I wanted to make a statement about how far I could go for my team. "Look how I suffer." There is glory in martyrdom. (Pouring Amoco Premium on your head and torching it is a bit extreme, though. Better to ally yourself with a bad ballclub.)

There is something called "losers' chic," too. The operative logic in loser's chic is that if you can't have the best team, or even a good one, you might as well have the worst. At least being the worst is notable—more notable than being second or third worst anyway. It also evokes a sympathy that the decent or mediocre cannot hope to conjure. "What a burden it must be for him to shoulder. Every second, knowing, that no matter what else happens, no matter how good other things may be going, his baseball team is still the worst."

Part of "losers' chic" is "defending" your team on these grounds. Have you ever heard two fans of different bad teams arguing that theirs is more pathetic. I have. I've done it. "My team is so bad, they traded away a pennant's worth of talent" . . . "Oh yeah, well my team is so bad they didn't have a pennant's worth of talent to trade away." Well, what else are you going to talk about? Whose 15-a-year home run slugger strikes out less?

Many mistake these attitudes for a kind of cynicism. I disagree. I call it realism. Logic dictates that any defense of this team on qualitative grounds is futile, so why swim against the tide? Don't have illusions of grandeur about this team, go with the flow. And if the flow has a wicked undertoe, ride down with it. Most people perceive the losing fan as a loser anyway. But if you want to cross that line from being somebody who has made a bad-team choice to being recognized as somebody with loose rivets, try to convince them your bad team is actually good.

Belittling your bad team is also a "first strike" mechanism. It prevents some smug bastard who roots for a good team from doing it first. "Hey, your team stinks," he says, as if I don't know. I read the boxscores, I go to the games—I know. I'll confess it. I'll brag about it rather than give someone the satisfaction that they could bother me with their astute, demeaning observations. Confession feels good: "I stole the collection plate"—"The Mets are about as unproductive as a team can be." There, I've said it. I feel better. The good team fan is usually taken aback by this, but then, they have a different set of values and expectations than I have developed. They want their appliances to work and their spouses to remain faithful and for it not to rain on the day of the company picnic. They want their car keys to be in the first pants pocket they check. The fan of a loser knows that no matter where he starts or what pattern of search he chooses, the keys will be in the fourth out of four pockets. And should he find them earlier, well, that's a nice surprise. It's the small things in life, isn't it? A complete game. A two-run homer. A three-run inning. A month of .500 ball. I never take these things for granted.

Then there's the crowd that wants you to stop being a fan of your team. "What do you want to root for them for?" they ask. "I can't help it any more. It's been so long I can't remember why I started," you answer. "Why not go with a winner?" Do they really expect to convert you? Fandom is a very, very deep thing. I know people who have changed religions and remained Mets fans. I'm not sure which is the bigger step.

But losing, above all, is not fun. Mets fans, remember, have been to the mountain and back, and it was much more enjoyable on top. Requited love beats all; I think the Mets will be requiting some love soon. First of all, Dave Johnson seems to have his head screwed on right. His comments since taking over the club have seemed pretty insightful. More importantly, they have been *concrete*. He doesn't seem to push any of this "these boys can be taught to win" nonsense. His approach is more of a "these boys stink and they'll be shown the gate" kind of thing.

Secondly, the minor league system is for real. *Baseball America*, the well-respected minor league newspaper, named the Mets Organization of the Year. The Mets now have in their possession the Class A Player of the Year (Dwight Gooden), the Class AA Player of the Year (Sid Fernandez, acquired from Los Angeles) and the Class AAA championship team in Tidewater. Met farm teams had the best combined record in baseball in 1983. Granted, this does not guarantee future success, but it is indicative that the Mets have turned an important corner. They are at last rebounding from the disastrous reign of the de Roulets.

What is also pleasing is the type of talent they seem to be producing. Both Gooden and Fernandez are power pitchers who should excel at Shea Stadium, which has been shown in *Abstracts* past to favor power pitching. Now Gooden and Fernandez may never pan out. Talent has a way of vaporizing on its way to the majors. I wish I had a dollar for every failed strikeout king from the low minors. But what Gooden and Fernandez represent goes beyond their chances of making it. They represent another important turning point for the Mets, and that is, they have at least begun to identify and confront the problems that have beset them for years. Diagnosis seems so simple, so rudimentary, yet the bottom of the standings* are littered with teams that failed to make that first step: the correct analysis of what is wrong. That the Mets have begun to work on their problems by developing and acquiring talent that is, above all, appropriate to their needs is, at least, a very good sign.

—Jim Baker

II

A couple of miscellaneous notes on the team . . . . Did you ever see such a bad team with such a good bench? The lineup was terrible but their punch off the bench was terrific. They had a fine offensive outfielder in Danny Heep, an exceptional pinch hitter in Rusty Staub, a man who drove in 99 runs just one year ago in Dave Kingman, and (at the beginning of the year) another quality pinch hitter/defensive sub in Mike Jorgensen. For infield help they had Bob Bailor who, as bad as he is, is a far better offensive player than either the starting second baseman or shortstop and about as good as the third baseman. Out of the bullpen, of course, they had one of the best in Orosco. But in the modern game "bench" and "bullpen" are entirely separate discussions.

This bench and bullpen between them explain one of the season's odder statistical footnotes: The Mets were the best late-inning ballclub in the league. The Mets were tied after seven innings in 24 games last year and won 17 of them.

As you get further down in the organization, the same principle seems to apply. The Mets Triple-A team at the start of the year had to be better than their major league team; they had an outfield of Strawberry, Wynne and Hurdle, Terrell and Darling and others on the mound, Wally Backman at second base. Even without most of

*Now there is an ideal spot to use the phrase "second division," but it seems to have gone out of baseball jargon. I guess divisional play rendered the notion of a "first" and "second" division rather useless. The seven team divisions of the American League really iced the cake though. Is a fourth-place team first division? Second? . . .

these people, they won the Little World Series. And when you get on down to the low minors, that's where you get the Dwight Goodens and the Lenny Dykstras, the people who are really exciting.

So in some sense, Davey Johnson's job this year shouldn't be all that tough. The Mets' organization is a pyramid standing on its head, and all he has to do is put it right side up. If he just lets Clint Hurdle and Hubie Brooks compete for the third base job, Hurdle will eat Brooks' lunch.

Conceptually easy; not all that easy to execute. Danny Heep is a better offensive player than George Foster, but it's not going to be easy to bench a man who makes a million dollars a week or whatever it is and play an "unproven" leftfielder. Mookie Wilson is a terrible lead-off man, but he is strongly entrenched in that position, buttressed by a public that evaluates a leadoff man by batting average and stolen bases, and it's not going to be easy for Johnson to move him to seventh and lead off with Hernandez or Backman or somebody who can get on base. Backman can make an offensive contribution but the press is going to be on him for his defense. But the potential for a large improvement is there.

III

EX-MET PITCHERS, 1983

	All-Star Break			Final			
	W	L	Pct.	W	L	Pct.	−/+
Andy Hassler	0	3	.000	0	5	.000	*
Jerry Koosman	6	1	.857	11	7	.611	−.246
Juan Berenguer	4	1	.800	9	5	.643	−.157
Jon Matlack	2	2	.500	2	4	.333	−.167
Roy Lee Jackson	6	1	.857	8	3	.727	−.130
Pete Falcone	7	1	.875	9	4	.692	−.183
Charlie Puleo	3	4	.429	6	12	.333	−.096
Nolan Ryan	7	1	.875	14	9	.609	−.266
Mike Scott	4	3	.571	10	6	.625	+.054
Pat Zachry	2	0	1.000	6	1	.857	−.143
Ray Burris	3	3	.500	4	7	.364	−.136
Jeff Reardon	3	4	.429	7	9	.438	+.009
Tug McGraw	1	0	1.000	2	1	.667	−.333
Neil Allen	3	1	.750	10	6	.625	−.125
Dale Murray	1	1	.500	2	4	.333	−.167
Ex-Met totals	52	26	.667	95	79	.546	−.121
1983 Mets	31	52	.373	68	74	.420	+.047

Former Met pitchers outdistanced current Mets by 11 games in 1983. Their combined record at the All-Star break was even more fantastic, but the second half proved to be their undoing. Perhaps they remembered their heritage, and a sort of mass reversion to losing ways resulted. "Hey, we used to be Mets, we shouldn't be doing this well." Only two of the fifteen managed to improve their records in the second half. Group destiny?

—J.B.

Keith HERNANDEZ, First Base
Runs Created: 98

	G	AB	Hit	2B	3B	HR	Run	RBI	BB	SO	SB	CS	Avg
7.78 Years		565	169	35	7	12	91	81	83	74	11	6	.299
1983	150	538	160	23	7	12	77	63	88	72	9	5	.297
First Half	77	301	91	17	5	5	45	37			3		.302
Second Half	73	237	69	6	2	7	32	26			6		.291
vs. RHP		370	117	14	4	9			66	45			.316
vs. LHP		168	43	9	3	3			22	27			.256
Home	78	279	88	10	3	10	39	38			6		.315
Road	72	259	72	13	4	2	38	25			3		.278
Grass	80	277	82	8	1	9	37	34			5		.296
Turf	70	261	78	15	6	3	40	29			4		.299

Mookie WILSON, Centerfield
Runs Created: 71

	G	AB	Hit	2B	3B	HR	Run	RBI	BB	SO	SB	CS	Avg
2.65 Years		644	177	24	10	6	93	47	31	107	54	19	.274
1983	152	638	176	25	6	7	91	51	18	103	54	16	.276
First Half	78	329	82	14	4	2	51	27			30		.249
Second Half	74	309	94	11	2	5	40	24			24		.304
vs. RHP		463	131	19	6	4			15	69			.283
vs. LHP		175	45	6	0	3			3	34			.257
Home	78	335	100	13	1	4	48	30			31		.299
Road	74	303	76	12	5	3	43	21			23		.251
Grass	105	447	131	15	3	5	65	42			39		.293
Turf	47	191	45	10	3	2	26	9			15		.236

Brian GILES, Second Base
Runs Created: 37

	G	AB	Hit	2B	3B	HR	Run	RBI	BB	SO	SB	CS	Avg
1.23 Years		444	103	16	0	4	43	30	39	89	19	9	.233
1983	145	400	98	15	0	2	39	27	36	77	17	10	.245
First Half	73	219	53	10	0	0	19	10			10		.242
Second Half	72	181	45	5	0	2	20	17			7		.249
vs. RHP		301	68	7	0	2			25	63			.226
vs. LHP		99	30	8	0	0			11	14			.303
Home	76	190	41	6	0	1	16	12			10		.216
Road	69	210	57	9	0	1	23	15			7		.271
Grass	103	276	61	8	0	2	27	18			13		.221
Turf	42	124	37	7	0	0	12	9			4		.298

Darryl STRAWBERRY, Rightfield
Runs Created: 74

	G	AB	Hit	2B	3B	HR	Run	RBI	BB	SO	SB	CS	Avg
.75 Years		558	143	20	9	35	84	98	62	170	25	8	.257
1983	122	420	108	15	7	26	63	74	47	128	19	6	.257
First Half	48	168	34	5	2	8	18	28			7		.202
Second Half	74	252	74	10	5	18	45	46			12		.294
vs. RHP		321	85	9	7	22			39	90			.265
vs. LHP		99	23	6	0	4			8	38			.232
Home	65	222	56	8	4	10	33	38			11		.252
Road	57	198	52	7	3	16	30	36			8		.263
Grass	88	301	72	10	4	16	42	49			15		.239
Turf	34	119	36	5	3	10	21	25			4		.303

Hubie BROOKS, Third Base
Runs Created: 51

	G	AB	Hit	2B	3B	HR	Run	RBI	BB	SO	SB	CS	Avg
2.46 Years		603	161	25	4	5	55	59	33	100	9	5	.267
1983	150	586	147	18	4	5	53	58	24	96	6	4	.251
First Half	79	308	86	9	3	5	30	34			4		.279
Second Half	71	278	61	9	1	0	23	24			2		.219
vs. RHP		439	107	14	2	4			16	76			.244
vs. LHP		147	40	4	2	1			8	20			.272
Home	77	299	76	9	3	4	34	31			1		.254
Road	73	287	71	9	1	1	19	27			5		.247
Grass	105	411	102	15	3	4	40	42			4		.248
Turf	45	175	45	3	1	1	13	16			2		.257

Ron HODGES, Catcher
Runs Created: 31

	G	AB	Hit	2B	3B	HR	Run	RBI	BB	SO	SB	CS	Avg
3.72 Years		355	86	14	1	5	31	37	54	54	2	3	.242
1983	110	250	65	12	0	0	20	21	49	42	0	3	.260
First Half	61	150	33	2	0	0	10	10			0		.220
Second Half	49	100	32	10	0	0	10	11			0		.320
vs. RHP		222	59	12	0	0			41	36			.266
vs. LHP		28	6	0	0	0			8	6			.214
Home	57	122	33	6	0	0	11	9			0		.270
Road	53	128	32	6	0	0	9	12			0		.250
Grass	77	176	44	9	0	0	14	12			0		.250
Turf	33	74	21	3	0	0	6	9			0		.284

Jose OQUENDO, Shortstop
Runs Created: 19

	G	AB	Hit	2B	3B	HR	Run	RBI	BB	SO	SB	CS	Avg
.74 Years		443	95	9	0	1	39	23	26	81	11	12	.213
1983	120	328	70	7	0	1	29	17	18	60	8	9	.213
First Half	57	165	41	6	0	0	14	14			5		.248
Second Half	63	163	29	1	0	1	15	3			3		.178
vs. RHP		236	46	6	0	0			11	40			.195
vs. LHP		92	24	1	0	1			7	20			.261
Home	66	167	36	6	0	0	16	7			3		.216
Road	54	161	34	1	0	1	13	10			5		.211
Grass	90	239	51	7	0	1	21	9			4		.213
Turf	30	89	19	0	0	0	8	8			4		.213

Bob BAILOR, Utility
Runs Created: 28

	G	AB	Hit	2B	3B	HR	Run	RBI	BB	SO	SB	CS	Avg
5.04 Years		534	141	20	4	2	64	44	35	31	17	7	.264
1983	118	340	85	8	0	1	33	30	20	23	18	3	.250
First Half	51	140	34	5	0	1	16	11			7		.243
Second Half	67	200	51	3	0	0	17	19			11		.255
vs. RHP		243	57	6	0	0			15	20			.235
vs. LHP		97	28	2	0	1			5	3			.289
Home	61	173	42	1	0	0	16	13			10		.243
Road	57	167	43	7	0	1	17	17			8		.257
Grass	87	250	61	3	0	0	25	23			16		.244
Turf	31	90	24	5	0	1	8	7			2		.267

George FOSTER, Leftfield
Runs Created: 68

	G	AB	Hit	2B	3B	HR	Run	RBI	BB	SO	SB	CS	Avg
9.97 Years		575	160	26	4	29	83	104	57	115	5	3	.278
1983	157	601	145	19	2	28	74	90	38	111	1	1	.241
First Half	77	283	70	8	1	14	34	43			0		.247
Second Half	80	318	75	11	1	14	40	47			1		.236
vs. RHP		440	103	16	1	16			27	85			.234
vs. LHP		161	42	3	1	12			11	26			.261
Home	80	296	73	10	2	18	39	50			1		.247
Road	77	305	72	9	0	10	35	40			0		.236
Grass	110	416	114	11	2	25	59	74			1		.274
Turf	47	185	31	8	0	3	15	16			0		.168

Danny HEEP, Outfield
Runs Created: 33

	G	AB	Hit	2B	3B	HR	Run	RBI	BB	SO	SB	CS	Avg
1.73 Years		375	93	21	1	7	34	36	40	55	2	3	.248
1983	115	253	64	12	0	8	30	21	29	40	3	3	.253
First Half	53	130	37	5	0	4	17	12			3		.285
Second Half	62	123	27	7	0	4	13	9			0		.220
vs. RHP		222	58	10	0	8			27	31			.261
vs. LHP		31	6	2	0	0			2	9			.065
Home	63	127	36	7	0	6	15	9			0		.283
Road	52	126	28	5	0	2	15	12			3		.222
Grass	81	180	47	9	0	6	22	12			1		.261
Turf	34	73	17	3	0	2	8	9			2		.233

Tom SEAVER

Year	(W–L)	GS	Run	Avg	DP	Avg	SB	Avg
1982	(5-13)	21	69	3.29	17	.81	18	.86
1983	(9-14)	34	123	3.62	31	.91	56	1.65
1976-1983		239	994	4.16	183	.77	237	.99

	G	IP	W	L	Pct	ER	ERA
1982 Home	9	44	3	6	.333	29	5.93
1983 Home	19	131.2	6	7	.462	48	3.28
1982 Road	12	67.1	2	7	.222	39	5.21
1983 Road	15	99.1	3	7	.300	43	3.90
1983 Grass	26	174.2	7	10	.412	66	3.40
1983 Turf	8	56.1	2	4	.333	25	3.99

Mike TORREZ

Year	(W–L)	GS	Run	Avg	DP	Avg	SB	Avg
1982	(9-9)	31	178	5.74	33	1.06	21	.68
1983	(10-17)	34	113	3.32	27	.79	44	1.29
1976-1983		265	1302	4.91	277	1.04	204	.77

	G	IP	W	L	Pct	ER	ERA
1982 Home	15	80	3	4	.429	43	4.84
1983 Home	18	111.2	6	7	.462	43	3.47
1982 Road	16	95.2	6	5	.545	59	5.55
1983 Road	21	110.2	4	10	.286	65	5.29
1983 Grass	25	149	7	9	.438	65	3.93
1983 Turf	14	73.1	3	8	.273	43	5.28

Ed LYNCH

Year	(W–L)	GS	Run	Avg	DP	Avg	SB	Avg
1982	(4-8)	12	43	3.58	10	.83	0	.00
1983	(10-10)	27	119	4.41	37	1.37	12	.44
1980-1983		56	218	3.89	64	1.14	25	.45

	G	IP	W	L	Pct	ER	ERA
1983 Home	16	88	3	6	.333	41	4.19
1983 Road	14	86.2	7	4	.636	42	4.36
1983 Grass	21	125.1	7	6	.538	51	3.66
1983 Turf	9	49.1	3	4	.429	32	5.84

Walt TERRELL

Year	(W–L)	GS	Run	Avg	DP	Avg	SB	Avg
1982	(0-3)	3	4	1.33	4	1.33	6	2.00
1983	(8-8)	20	64	3.20	19	.95	21	1.05
1982-1983		23	68	2.96	23	1.00	27	1.17

	G	IP	W	L	Pct	ER	ERA
1983 Home	12	68.1	4	4	.500	33	4.35
1983 Road	9	65.1	4	4	.500	20	2.76
1983 Grass	16	98.2	6	6	.500	44	4.01
1983 Turf	5	35	2	2	.500	9	2.31

1983 OTHERS

Pitcher	(W–L)	GS	Run	Avg	DP	Avg	SB	Avg
Swan	(2-8)	18	67	3.72	19	1.05	20	1.11
Holman	(1-7)	10	29	2.90	12	1.20	13	1.30
Darling	(1-3)	5	13	2.60	11	2.20	7	1.40
Allen	(2-7)	4	16	4.00	6	1.50	6	1.50
Gorman	(1-4)	4	8	2.00	3	.75	4	1.00
Ownby	(1-3)	4	11	2.75	5	1.25	6	1.50
Leary	(1-1)	2	12	6.00	1	.50	4	2.00

NEW YORK METS
RUNS BATTED IN ANALYSIS

Player	RBI	RBI In Wins	Victory Important RBI	RBI Importance	Wins Batted In	RBI Per Win
George Foster	90	57	35.43	.394	10.84	8.3
Darryl Strawberry	74	53	33.02	.446	9.46	7.8
Mookie Wilson	51	31	21.69	.425	6.07	8.4
Hubie Brooks	58	29	19.60	.338	6.25	9.3
Brian Giles	27	21	18.10	.670	4.61	5.9
Keith Hernandez	37	22	17.58	.475	4.09	9.0
Bob Bailor	30	19	13.86	.462	3.80	7.9
Ron Hodges	21	12	8.74	.416	2.46	8.5
Dan Heep	21	8	6.35	.302	2.87	7.3
Jose Oquendo	17	10	5.94	.349	1.56	10.9

NATIONAL LEAGUE WEST
DIVISION SHEET

Chart I

	1st	2nd	VS. RHP	VS. LHP	Home	Road	Grass	Turf	Day	Night	Total	Pct.
Los Angeles	47-31	34-40	82-50	9-21	48-32	43-39	66-54	25-17	20-26	71-45	91-71	.562
Atlanta	49-31	39-43	66-49	22-25	46-34	42-40	63-56	25-18	30-17	58-57	88-74	.543
Houston	40-40	45-37	60-54	25-23	46-36	39-41	22-25	63-52	17-20	68-57	85-77	.525
San Diego	41-38	40-43	59-60	22-21	47-34	34-47	67-53	14-28	22-28	59-52	81-81	.500
San Francisco	39-40	40-43	56-59	23-24	43-38	36-45	62-58	17-25	35-32	44-51	79-83	.488
Cincinnati	34-47	40-41	57-65	17-23	36-45	38-43	22-26	52-62	26-25	48-63	74-88	.457

Chart II
COME FROM BEHIND WINS

Team	1	2	3	4	5	6	7	Total	Points
Los Angeles	17	8	4	2				31	84
Atlanta	14	11	4	3	2			34	104
Houston	23	5	3	3	0	1		35	95
San Diego	30	7	7	1	0	0	1	46	122
San Francisco	14	13	0	1	1			29	78
Cincinnati	24	8	5	2				39	102

BLOWN LEADS

Team	1	2	3	4	5	6	7	Total	Points
Los Angeles	16	10	2	1	1			30	81
Atlanta	13	13	4	3				33	96
Houston	16	12	5	1	1	0	1	36	107
San Diego	21	9	4	2				36	95
San Francisco	19	9	3	2				33	87
Cincinnati	27	6	5	2	1			41	108

Chart III
DEFENSIVE RECORDS

Team	OSB	OCS	OSB%	DP	OA/SFA	Fielding Avg.	DER	Opposition Runs
Los Angeles	114	87	.567	132	18/	.974	.698	609
Atlanta	172	68	.717	176	37/	.978	.696	640
Houston	182	53	.774	165	26/	.977	.718	646
San Diego	152	75	.670	135	37/	.979	.713	653
San Francisco	167	73	.696	109	49/	.973	.693	697
Cincinnati	135	81	.625	121	36/	.981	.707	710

Chart IV
OPPOSITION ERRORS

Team	C	1B	2B	3B	SS	LF	CF	RF	P	Un	Total
Los Angeles	23	12	9	24	35	8	5	7	11	3	127
Atlanta	24	19	19	27	26	6	11	7	17	7	163
Houston	10	18	19	11	27	5	3	7	18	3	121
San Diego	21	17	32	34	40	9	8	7	21	1	190
San Francisco	23	17	18	20	21	11	9	8	14	5	136
Cincinnati	14	10	21	23	19	7	5	5	14	4	122

Chart V
LATE-INNING BALLCLUBS

Team	Ahead	Tied	Behind	Net Change
Los Angeles	71-5	16-14	4-52	+1
Atlanta	68-9	12-10	8-55	+1
Houston	69-6	11-11	5-60	−1
San Diego	64-4	14-15	3-62	−2
San Francisco	65-7	8-13	6-63	−6
Cincinnati	55-8	13- 8	6-72	+3

LOS ANGELES DODGERS

I

I picked the Los Angeles Dodgers to win the NL West in 1983, and a month into the season I could neither remember nor reconstruct the reasoning behind this selection. I remember thinking that the loss of Steve Garvey had to help the team, and I suppose it did. That is hardly an explanation of how the Dodgers won 91 games. By the middle of the summer, the Atlanta Braves were playing like the best team in baseball, in command of the race and talking about having eight .300 hitters in the lineup. I was prematurely embarrassed.

How the Dodgers could win in 1983 is a puzzle, much as how the Expos could lose; stand everything that I said about the Expos on its head, and you have a pretty good explanation of the Dodgers' success:

a) The Expos are not able to win their division even when their talent seems overpowering because of organizational indecisiveness and lack of direction. The Dodgers seem to be able to win at any moment, even when their talent is unimpressive, out of sheer organizational weight and presence. The Expos seem unable to overcome inertia and win; the Dodgers seem able to win out of unaided momentum.

b) The Expos have overpowering talent but glaring weaknesses; the Dodgers don't have overpowering talent but have no glaring weaknesses. They receive at least respectable offensive production from all eight spots.

Let's talk specifics:

c) The Expos' power looks impressive but they were outhomered by their opponents 120–102. The Dodgers don't seem to have impressive power but outhomered their opponents 146–97. The Dodgers' power advantage is, in fact, the one most basic reason for their success in 1983. The Dodgers hit 51 home runs more than their opponents, which probably means that they scored about 80 runs more than their opponents did on home runs. Overall, they outscored their opponents by only 45 runs. So in all phases of the game except hitting home runs and preventing home runs, the Dodgers were less than an impressive club.

The Expos have power (15 or more home runs) at only three spots—centerfield, catcher and third base. The Dodgers have power at six spots—catcher, first base, third base, leftfield, centerfield and rightfield. That's a big difference.

d) One of the Expos' perceived strengths is at catcher, Gary Carter. For the Dodgers, this is a perceived weakness. But though Carter hit in the middle of the lineup and the Dodger catchers usually hit about seventh, their offensive production is not all that different:

	AB	R	H	2B	3B	HR	RBI	Avg
Carter	541	63	146	37	3	17	79	.270
Ramos	61	2	14	3	1	0	5	.230
Blackwell	15	0	3	1	0	0	2	.200
Montreal	617	65	163	41	4	17	86	.264

	AB	R	H	2B	3B	HR	RBI	Avg
Yeager	335	31	68	8	3	15	41	.203
Fimple	148	16	37	8	1	2	22	.250
Sciosia	35	3	11	3	0	1	7	.314
Los Angeles	518	50	116	19	4	18	70	.224

e) Brock and Oliver, discussed before.

f) One of the more precise contrasts is at shortstop. The Dodgers have stayed for over a decade with a shortstop who has probably taken as much unwarranted criticism as any player of our time, Bill Russell. Russell does not do many things that a shortstop is supposed to do —make flashy diving plays behind second base, fire the ball out of the hole. He was always less than spectacular on the spectacular plays, and at times he was less than ordinary on the ordinary plays. But the Dodgers stayed with him all these years, and continued to stay with him even after getting rid of their other three infielders, because he did give them some specific, tangible benefits. He could hit .260, steal a base now and then, hit 25 or 30 doubles in a year.

The Expos, on the other hand, chose the "intangible" virtues of Doug Flynn. The reason that the things that Doug Flynn does are intangible is that they don't exist. Most things which don't exist are intangible. Nobody wins a pennant on intangible runs (we have a late score here for you from the West Coast . . . the Montreal Expos have edged the Dodgers 7 to 6. The Expos had only three tangible runs in the game, but added a grand slam intangible by Doug Flynn in the top of the ninth to stun the Dodgers. The Dodgers had five tangible runs and had gone ahead 6–3 on an intangible of their own when third baseman Pedro Guerrero showed a lot of heart and a lot of guts and determination in chasing down a foul ball hit by Al Oliver. "These intangibles are just killing us," said Dodger manager Tommy Lasorda after the game. "That's the fourth intangible ballgame we have lost in the last week.") Flynn is a fielder, but the number of tangible opposition runs that he prevents does not justify a spot on a major league roster.

Pedro Guerrero now seems to be suffering from a somewhat similar recognition problem, at a higher level. It seems to me that people are talking an awful lot about what he doesn't do as a third baseman, and some pin-brained scout described him last summer as "a Latin Butch Hobson." Gimme a break, fella. Sure, he's got some defensive problems, but he didn't field .899 and he is, after all, probably the best hitter in baseball. Surely that counts for something.

g) The Dodgers should have won 87 games with the number of runs they scored and allowed, but actually won 91. The Expos should have won 85 but actually won 82.

h) The root of the Expos' malaise is that they have been, ever since firing Dick Williams, afraid to try to solve their problems with their own talent. They have a second-base problem, but they have had second base prospects coming out of their ears—Bryan Little, Tony Bernazard, Wallace Johnson, Mike Gates. They have potential solutions to the right field problem on their roster in Francona, Roy Johnson and Mike Stenhouse. But they can't bring themselves to put their fate in the hands of those players, because that would mean relying on their own judgment, and if it didn't work they would have no good excuse for it. They compulsively import "proven" outsiders like Manny Trillo, Al Oliver and Doug Flynn to try to solve their problems, because that way they have a good answer if a news reporter asks them why they are playing this guy.

The Dodgers, on the other hand, are not at all reluctant to rest their case with the players coming out of the system; indeed, they are anxious for the opportunity, so anxious that they will get rid of established, entrenched players who are still playing well to get the next generation in place. Do you suppose Jim Campanis cares this much if some newspaper columnist thinks that Greg Brock can't handle a major league curve?

While we're on the subject, why do people keep saying that a lot of the Dodger's Triple A players really aren't all that good, they're just minor league hitters? The Dodgers won 91 games last year with players who were mostly minor leaguers three years ago. Mickey Hatcher hit .317 with Minnesota, Jeff Leonard drove in 87 runs for San Francisco, Rudy Law stole 77 bases and hit well and fielded well for the White Sox, and Rick Sutcliffe won 17 games for Cleveland, and every time you mention the Dodgers' minor league system to anybody they say, "Oh, a lot of those guys really aren't all that good." When exactly do they intend to stop saying this?

If you just say that minor league batting statistics are meaningless, then of course you don't have to figure out what they mean. It's a popular belief because it makes life so much simpler; some of them are misleading, so you just throw them all out the window. But it's not true. Minor league hitting stats are not meaningless. They are extremely meaningful; they just don't always mean exactly what you might, at first, think that they mean. More on this subject next year.

II

The Dodgers won the National League West last year despite having a record of 9–21 against lefthanded pitching, which is truly a remarkable thing. I doubt seriously that any team has ever won a division while playing that badly against lefthanders; the chart below gives the record against lefthanders of the last 8 division champion teams:

	Won	Lost	Pct
1982 Brewers	34	18	.654
1983 White Sox	37	20	.649
1982 Braves	26	15	.634
1983 Orioles	25	19	.568
1982 Cardinals	30	24	.556
1982 Angels	30	29	.508
1983 Phillies	17	18	.486
1983 Dodgers	9	21	.300

This, like the Phillies' record on grass fields, is symptomatic of the strange, compressed nature of the National League at this time, the complete lack of anything that could even pose as a great team. Generally, you figure that if a team can play baseball, they can play baseball, that a good team is a good team and a bad team is a bad team regardless of where they are playing or when they are playing. The "percentages" just shade things up and down a little, they don't reverse the positives and negatives.

But in the National League in 1983, any team that could do one thing well probably could not do another. The Dodgers were the best team in the league against righthanders and the worst team against lefthanders. The Phillies were the best team on artificial turf, the worst on grass. The Padres were the best team in the league on grass, and one of the worst on artificial turf; indeed, almost every team in the league which was good on grass was bad on turf, and vice versa. Only the Dodgers and Braves were good on both. Only one team in the league was over .500 against both lefthanded and righthanded pitching. The Cardinals were the best team in the league in one-run decisions (29–18), but were putrid (50–65) the rest of the time. The best team in the league when the game was *ot* decided by one run, Atlanta, was the worst team in the league when it was decided by one (69–45 otherwise, 19–29 in one-run games). The Reds were almost the worst team in the league when the game was not decided by one run (46–67), but one of the best when it was (28–21). The Mets were the worst team in the league in games that were decided in nine innings (56–90), the best when the game went into extra innings (12–4) and the best when the game was tied up after seven (17–7). The Dodgers were the best team in the league in night games (71–45) and the third-worst in day games (20–26); the Pirates were second-best in night games (61–41) and the very worst in day games (23–37). The Phillies had the best record of any team against the Eastern Division (60–30) but the third worst against the West (30–42). The National League in 1983 was a gambler's paradise in which 5th-place teams could be expected to destroy 1st-place teams if the circumstances were right.

But, again, we are at a moment in history, a moment in which there are no great teams. That doesn't even suggest, to me, that there will be no more. I think the Dodgers of the '80s are shaping up as a better team than either the Dodgers of the '70s or the Dodgers of the '60s. And they're going to have to be pretty good, to keep beating the Braves.

III

The Dodgers had the third best record in the National League in one-run games (30–21). What were the Dodgers doing right in these games?

Their pitching, which is extraordinary anyway, really outdid itself in close shaves. Dodger pitchers, with the exception of Steve Howe and Jerry Reuss, all had lower ERAs in these games, and while overall ERAs and batting averages are lower in one-run games, that didn't seem to mean much to the Braves (see page 72). Tom Niedenfeur was especially effective in one-run games posting seven of his eight victories in them and making 24 scoreless appearances.

Below is a chart of all key Dodger players and pitchers and their records in one-run games.

	G	AB	R	H	2B	3B	HR	RBI	SB	Avg
Sax	48	199	34	62	5	1	2	9	19	.312
Landreaux	45	136	18	35	6	1	7	22	4	.257
Baker	48	156	16	41	7	1	5	22	1	.263
Guerrero	49	173	23	50	9	0	10	26	6	.289
Marshall	44	144	9	30	5	0	2	8	0	.208
Brock	46	136	13	31	4	0	5	18	2	.228
Russell	40	137	10	36	3	0	1	11	4	.263
Yeager	35	104	7	16	1	1	2	6	0	.154
Monday	34	50	6	10	2	1	0	3	0	.200
Thomas	38	69	9	15	2	1	0	2	3	.217

	G	IP	W	L	ERA	Sv
Valenzuela	14	106	6	3	2.72	—
Pena	12	57.1	3	1	2.67	0
Welch	9	58.2	4	2	2.01	0
Reuss	9	56.1	0	2	3.03	0
Hooton	8	44.1	2	0	2.84	0
Howe	23	30.1	2	7	2.08	6
Niedenfeur	28	36	7	3	1.25	3
Stewart	17	22.2	2	1	2.78	5
Beckwith	7	14.2	2	0	1.23	0
Zachry	6	11	2	1	1.64	0
Others	7	26	0	1	3.46	1

Sax, Baker, Brock and Russell all hit for a higher average in one-run games; Sax, Landreaux, Baker and Russell had better slugging averages. No Braves' regular had a better batting average in one-run games and only Claudell Washington and Dale Murphy slugged better, and then only by a few points. (Murphy did account for 39% of his home runs in Braves one-run games, which comprised only 30% of their schedule.)

—Jim Baker

Greg BROCK, First Base
Runs Created: 64

	G	AB	Hit	2B	3B	HR	Run	RBI	BB	SO	SB	CS	Avg
1.01 Years		466	103	15	2	20	64	66	83	85	5	1	.220
1983	146	455	102	14	2	20	64	66	83	81	5	1	.224
First Half	75	251	55	8	2	11	36	36			5		.219
Second Half	71	204	47	6	0	9	28	30			0		.230
vs. RHP		382	86			18		53					.225
vs. LHP		73	16			2		11					.219
Home	69	215	49	5	0	14	38	37			2		.228
Road	77	240	53	9	2	6	26	29			3		.221
Grass	105	317	72	8	0	17	49	46			4		.227
Turf	41	138	30	6	2	3	15	20			1		.217

Steve SAX, Second Base
Runs Created: 76

	G	AB	Hit	2B	3B	HR	Run	RBI	BB	SO	SB	CS	Avg
2.07 Years		665	187	21	6	5	95	47	55	68	53	27	.281
1983	155	623	175	18	5	5	94	41	58	73	56	30	.281
First Half	71	284	77	10	5	4	45	20			29		.271
Second Half	84	339	98	8	0	1	49	21			27		.290
vs. RHP		500	140			4		33					.280
vs. LHP		123	35			1		8					.285
Home	78	304	90	6	3	3	44	20			28		.296
Road	77	319	85	12	2	2	50	21			28		.267
Grass	119	476	135	12	3	3	65	24			43		.284
Turf	36	147	40	6	2	2	29	17			13		.272

Pedro GUERRERO, Third Base
Runs Created: 118

	G	AB	Hit	2B	3B	HR	Run	RBI	BB	SO	SB	CS	Avg
3.17 Years		555	168	26	5	27	81	92	58	95	17	7	.302
1983	160	584	174	28	6	32	87	103	72	110	23	7	.298
First Half	78	286	86	10	2	17	47	50			12		.301
Second Half	82	298	88	18	4	15	40	53			11		.295
vs. RHP		472	142			25		86					.301
vs. LHP		112	32			7		17					.286
Home	79	283	82	10	4	13	38	40			14		.290
Road	81	301	92	18	2	19	49	63			9		.306
Grass	120	455	134	20	4	24	61	65			17		.295
Turf	40	129	40	8	2	8	26	38			6		.310

Bill RUSSELL, Shortstop
Runs Created: 40

	G	AB	Hit	2B	3B	HR	Run	RBI	BB	SO	SB	CS	Avg
11.80 Years		566	149	22	5	4	62	49	36	52	13	6	.264
1983	131	451	111	13	1	1	47	30	33	31	13	9	.246
First Half	58	185	47	3	1	1	22	12			4		.254
Second Half	73	266	64	10	0	0	25	18			9		.241
vs. RHP		342	86			1		29					.252
vs. LHP		109	24			0		1					.220
Home	64	216	53	7	0	0	23	16			4		.245
Road	67	235	58	6	1	1	24	14			9		.247
Grass	95	322	74	7	0	0	29	19			5		.230
Turf	36	129	37	6	1	1	18	11			8		.287

Dusty BAKER, Leftfield
Runs Created: 78

	G	AB	Hit	2B	3B	HR	Run	RBI	BB	SO	SB	CS	Avg
10.77 Years		584	163	27	2	21	80	84	60	76	12	6	.280
1983	149	531	138	25	1	15	71	73	72	59	7	1	.260
First Half	74	273	63	14	0	8	30	38			3		.231
Second Half	75	258	75	11	1	7	41	35			4		.291
vs. RHP		432	114			13		62					.264
vs. LHP		99	24			2		11					.242
Home	77	276	71	11	1	8	39	39			2		.257
Road	72	255	67	14	0	7	32	34			5		.263
Grass	114	406	104	14	1	12	56	54			3		.256
Turf	35	125	34	11	0	3	15	19			4		.272

Ken LANDREAUX, Centerfield
Runs Created: 70

	G	AB	Hit	2B	3B	HR	Run	RBI	BB	SO	SB	CS	Avg
4.72 Years		575	159	27	8	12	77	70	42	60	22	8	.276
1983	141	481	135	25	3	17	63	66	34	52	30	11	.281
First Half	67	232	62	11	2	7	33	27			17		.267
Second Half	74	249	73	14	1	10	30	39			13		.293
vs. RHP		438	129			17		62					.295
vs. LHP		43	6			0		4					.140
Home	66	213	63	7	1	10	32	25			13		.296
Road	75	268	72	18	2	7	31	41			17		.269
Grass	104	347	93	16	1	16	45	44			21		.268
Turf	37	134	42	9	2	1	18	22			9		.313

Mike MARSHALL, Rightfield
Runs Created: 72

	G	AB	Hit	2B	3B	HR	Run	RBI	BB	SO	SB	CS	Avg
1.25 Years		467	128	18	1	18	47	60	45	123	7	2	.274
1983	140	465	132	17	1	17	47	65	43	127	7	3	.284
First Half	62	182	44	8	0	7	16	22			1		.242
Second Half	78	283	88	9	1	10	31	43			6		.311
vs. RHP		366	107			15		60					.292
vs. LHP		99	25			2		5					.253
Home	69	225	69	9	0	9	26	35			3		.307
Road	71	240	63	8	1	8	21	30			4		.263
Grass	103	337	101	12	1	13	37	50			5		.300
Turf	37	128	31	5	0	4	10	15			2		.242

Steve YEAGER, Catcher
Runs Created: 28

	G	AB	Hit	2B	3B	HR	Run	RBI	BB	SO	SB	CS	Avg
6.74 Years	465	107	16	2	14	49	53	45	95	2	1		.229
1983	113	335	68	8	3	15	31	41	23	57	1	1	.203
First Half	70	223	52	5	3	13	25	33			1		.233
Second Half	43	112	16	3	0	2	6	8			0		.143
vs. RHP		249	49			9		27					.197
vs. LHP		86	19			6		14					.221
Home	53	157	30	4	0	7	11	15			1		.191
Road	60	178	38	4	3	8	20	26			0		.213
Grass	81	235	48	6	1	11	18	29			1		.204
Turf	32	100	20	2	2	4	13	12			0		.200

Rick MONDAY, Outfield
Runs Created: 26

	G	AB	Hit	2B	3B	HR	Run	RBI	BB	SO	SB	CS	Avg
12.07 Years	505	133	20	5	20	78	64	76	124	8	8		.264
1983	99	178	44	7	1	6	21	20	29	42	0	0	.247
First Half	47	72	13	3	0	4	11	9			0	0	.181
Second Half	52	106	31	4	1	2	10	11			0	0	.292
vs. RHP		174	44	7	1	6		19			0	0	.253
vs. LHP		4	0	0	0	0		1			0	0	.000
Home	48	76	14	2	1	4	8	9			0	0	.184
Road	51	102	30	5	0	2	13	11			0	0	.294
Grass	72	127	31	7	1	5	13	11			0	0	.244
Turf	27	51	13	0	0	1	8	9			0	0	.255

Derrel THOMAS, Utility
Runs Created: 27

	G	AB	Hit	2B	3B	HR	Run	RBI	BB	SO	SB	CS	Avg
8.72 Years	494	124	16	6	4	62	7	42	50	16	10		.250
1983	118	192	48	6	6	2	38	8	27	36	9	3	.250
First Half	46	99	30	5	3	0	20	5			6		.303
Second Half	72	93	18	1	3	2	18	3			3		.194
vs. RHP		132	32			2		5					.242
vs. LHP		60	16			0		3					.267
Home	54	89	23	3	2	0	19	2			6		.258
Road	64	103	25	3	4	2	19	6			3		.243
Grass	84	131	33	6	3	2	27	7			6		.252
Turf	34	61	15	0	3	0	11	1			3		.246

Fernando VALENZUELA

Year	(W–L)	GS	Run	Avg	DP	Avg	SB	Avg
1982	(19-13)	37	145	3.92	33	.89	26	.70
1983	(15-10)	35	169	4.83	28	.80	31	.89
1981-1983		97	404	4.27	74	.76	83	.86

	G	IP	W	L	Pct	ER	ERA
1982 Home	20	151	10	7	.588	50	2.98
1983 Home	15	112	8	3	.727	37	2.97
1982 Road	17	134	9	6	.600	41	2.75
1983 Road	20	145	7	7	.500	70	4.35
1983 Grass	25	184.2	12	9	.571	79	3.85
1983 Turf	10	72.1	3	1	.750	28	3.48

Jerry REUSS

Year	(W–L)	GS	Run	Avg	DP	Avg	SB	Avg
1982	(18-11)	37	165	4.46	29	.78	21	.57
1983	(12-11)	31	117	3.77	31	1.00	15	.48
1976-1983		214	925	4.32	217	1.01	123	.57

	G	IP	W	L	Pct	ER	ERA
1982 Home	19	126.2	9	5	.643	37	2.63
1983 Home	15	112	5	5	.500	34	2.73
1982 Road	20	128	9	6	.600	51	3.59
1983 Road	17	111.1	7	6	.538	39	3.15
1983 Grass	22	153.1	7	8	.467	52	3.05
1983 Turf	10	70	5	3	.625	21	2.70

Bob WELCH

Year	(W–L)	GS	Run	Avg	DP	Avg	SB	Avg
1982	(16-11)	36	163	4.53	23	.64	22	.61
1983	(15-12)	31	99	3.19	26	.84	13	.42
1978-1983		147	592	4.03	101	.69	88	.60

	G	IP	W	L	Pct	ER	ERA
1982 Home	18	124.1	7	6	.538	36	2.61
1983 Home	15	102.1	7	7	.500	30	2.64
1982 Road	18	111.1	9	5	.643	52	4.20
1983 Road	16	101.2	8	5	.615	30	2.66
1983 Grass	25	166.1	12	9	.571	45	2.44
1983 Turf	6	37.2	3	3	.500	15	3.58

Burt HOOTON

Year	(W–L)	GS	Run	Avg	DP	Avg	SB	Avg
1982	(4-7)	21	81	3.86	20	.95	26	1.24
1983	(9-8)	27	123	4.56	17	.63	22	.81
1976-1983		229	961	4.20	185	.81	205	.89

	G	IP	W	L	Pct	ER	ERA
1982 Home	13	77	4	4	.500	32	3.74
1983 Home	17	92	6	4	.600	39	3.82
1982 Road	8	43.2	0	3	.000	22	4.53
1983 Road	16	68	3	4	.429	36	4.76
1983 Grass	26	132	7	6	.538	61	4.16
1983 Turf	7	28	2	2	.500	14	4.50

Alejandro PENA

Year	(W–L)	GS	Run	Avg	DP	Avg	SB	Avg
1983	(12-9)	26	95	3.65	20	.77	21	.81

	G	IP	W	L	Pct	ER	ERA
1983 Home	16	90.2	7	5	.583	29	2.88
1983 Road	18	86.1	5	4	.556	25	2.61
1983 Grass	22	120	8	8	.500	43	3.22
1983 Turf	12	57	4	1	.800	11	1.74

1983 OTHERS

Pitcher	(W–L)	GS	Run	Avg	DP	Avg	SB	Avg
Honeycutt	(2-3)	7	33	4.71	6	.86	7	1.00
Beckwith	(3-4)	3	6	2.00	2	.67	4	1.33
Fernandez	(0-1)	1	3	3.00	1	1.00	0	.00
Stewart	(5-2)	1	7	7.00	0	.00	0	.00
Zachry	(6-1)	1	2	2.00	1	1.00	0	.00

LOS ANGELES DODGERS
RUNS BATTED IN ANALYSIS

Player	RBI	RBI In Wins	Victory Important RBI	RBI Importance	Wins Batted In	RBI Per Win
Pedro Guerrero	103	76	49.12	.477	14.71	7.0
Ken Landreaux	66	54	36.64	.555	9.98	6.6
Mike Marshall	65	57	35.22	.542	9.57	6.8
Greg Brock	66	55	33.89	.514	10.38	6.4
Dusty Baker	73	53	32.19	.441	9.28	7.9
Steve Yeager	41	34	21.10	.514	5.88	7.0
Steve Sax	41	31	18.11	.442	5.91	6.9
Bill Russell	30	19	10.91	.364	4.15	7.3
Rick Monday	20	12	6.76	.338	2.00	10.0
Derrel Thomas	8	2	1.25	.156	.29	27.6

ATLANTA BRAVES

I. MOVING BASERUNNERS

Despite what is generally perceived as a power-hitting lineup, the Braves were outhomered by their opponents in 1983, 130–132. On a head-to-head comparison, they probably got killed at catcher (Benedict hit two; opposition catchers probably hit over 15) and left field (Butler hit only 5). Despite having pretty good team speed, they also got murdered in the stolen-base matchups, stealing 146 to their opponents' 172 and being caught 88 times to their opponents' 68. The Braves base stealing was a break-even gesture (actually, they probably scored 1 or 2 fewer runs than they would have had they not attempted to steal any bases), while their opponents picked up about ten runs on their stolen-base attempts.

II. DEAR BILL

10/3/83

Dear Bill,

While doing a little research on the Cubs' late-season fadeouts, I noticed the following pattern in Joe Torre-managed teams:

Year	Record through July 31	Aug. 1 to end of season
77 NY	43–59* (.422)	21–39 (.350)
78 NY	45–62 (.421)	21–34 (.382)
79 NY	44–56 (.440)	19–43 (.306)
80 NY	48–51 (.485)	19–44 (.302)
82 Atl	61–40 (.604)	28–33 (.459)
83 Atl	64–41 (.610)	24–33 (.421)

*15–29 under Frazier
28–30 under Torre

The Mets did do better in the second half of the wacky '81 season, but it certainly appears that there's a noticeable pattern here. Was it "late-season injuries" every year? I think Joe would make a good America's Cup skipper.

Best wishes,

Don Zminda
Evanston, Il

III. BUT IF THEY DIDN'T PINCH-HIT FOR HIM IN KEY SITUATIONS, HE'D BE DOWN TO .350 IN NO TIME

With 4 hits in 8 at-bats in 1983, Terry Forster lifted his lifetime batting average to .408 (29 for 71). It was the fourth time in Forster's career that he had hit over .400; the only time that he has ever hit under .400 with more than 2 at-bats was in 1977, when he hit .346 (9 for 26).

IV. BRAD KOMMINSK WILL PUT AN END TO THIS

All three Atlanta outfielders in 1983 stole 30 bases; so did all three St. Louis Cardinals' outfielders. Before 1983, no team had had three outfielders stealing 30 bases each since the New York Giants of 1912. (The 1976 Oakland A's had two outfielders with over 30, one of them also Claudell Washington, and a DH-outfielder with 52. But he was primarily a DH; Joe Rudi was the third outfielder on the team.)

V. NOW IF HE COULD JUST TEACH THEM THE INTENTIONAL STRIKEOUT

In his playing days, Braves' pitching coach Bob Gibson was one to eschew the intentional walk. He especially despised giving it to the number eight hitter. He figured, and rightly so, if he couldn't get the number eight hitter out, he shouldn't be pitching in the major leagues. I wanted to see if Bob Gibson the pitching coach still thinks like Bob Gibson the player. Well, he does. The Braves gave out the fewest intentional walks of any NL team (46).

—Jim Baker

VI. DEAR BILL

Nov. 21, 1983

Dear Bill,

Now that it is the "day after" we have decided what will happen to Lawrence, Kansas, let's talk about a real problem: What will happen to the Atlanta Braves?

No need to beat a dead horse. All we had to do was go .500 for the last ⅓ of the season and we had it won, even with the Dodgers' great finish.

The management blamed it on:
  a) Bob Horner's injury
  b) collapse of the relief pitching.

I blame it on:
  a) Bob Horner's injury.
  b) the management.

Horner first. It's fairly obvious. Braves starting 3rd basemen drove in ten runs after Horner got hurt. Horner, depending on whether you project his career or season stats, could reasonably have been expected to drive in 28–34 over the same period. Using your Pythagorean projection, what's that? Looks like a solid 2–3 wins offensively. On defense, Randy Johnson played well, Jerry Royster played Jerry Royster (better than Horner, but . . .).

Yes, it's also obvious that the relief pitching failed us late in the year (almost as obvious as the fact that it is easier to protect a 2-run lead than a 1-run lead).

Still, we did score 746 runs. My point is this (and I hope you can help me prove it): Torre plays offensive baseball as if he had studied Earl Weaver and decided that Earl didn't know how to win. Torre is forever playing for one run; bunting up and down the lineup; stealing with guys who can't outrun Nancy Reagan (Chambliss 2 SB of 9 tries, Hubbard 3 of 11). Check the SB/CS stats. We were 6th in the league in steals, but I'll bet we led the league in caught stealing. Our SB success rate was under 60%, I recall. Torre seems to think that he has a no-talent offensive team that has to scratch and claw for every run. He seems to be afraid that any minute he'll wake up and discover that Hubie Brooks, not Bob Horner, is still his 3rd baseman.

(One last offensive note: As you know, last winter the Braves management decided to raise the fences from 6 to 10 feet to cut down on the "cheap" homers. I said at the time it was as if Herzog had asked the Cardinals to slow down the Busch Stadium turf a little to cut down on the "cheap" doubles and triples. Insane. You've got a team that's built around the home run and then you penalize them for doing what they're supposed to do. Well, anyway, my friend Ed Jelks and I (he was at 65–70 games, I was at about 50), counted the balls that hit the fence between 6 and 10 feet up. The Braves hit 11; the opposition hit 4. There's another win or two, right there.)

Now the defense.

Your comment last year on managers' constructing their teams on the basis of images acquired over the years, really tells the story of the Braves' pitching philosophy. The Honeycutt-Barker fiasco is the best example.

Torre-Gibson are wedded to the Power Pitcher. Of course, I would be also, if I had a staff of Bob Gibsons.

The Braves apparently had a shot at getting Honeycutt (a lefty sinkerballer) in August, blew it, settled for Barker (a righty power pitcher), then claimed that they really wanted Barker all along. Let me see if I can make sense of this in retrospect. We have no reliable lefty starter; sinkerballers are what you need in Atlanta Stadium; Honeycutt is leading the AL in wins and ERA . . . and we'd rather have Barker!?!

And, of course, thanks to the *Abstract*, we know that the difference between Honeycutt and Barker is hardly subtle. Indeed, each is almost the extreme of each type, with Honeycutt getting the most double-play support in the league and Barker getting the least. (See the "fence" comment above; once again we penalize our strength, there HRs, here DPs.)

Torre-Gibson could not have picked two guys that better demonstrate that Torre-Gibson are the captives of images past.

Well, enough about the Winter of My Discontent. The Braves will continue to contend. They have too much talent not to (thanks to Paul Snyder and Pat Nugent). But I am afraid that, like Detroit and Montreal, we are in for several more such winters.

I hope I'm wrong, but I suspect that this version, at least of Ted Turner's "dynasty," ended last August when Horner broke his wrist.

Looking forward to March,

Larry Taylor
Atlanta, Georgia

P.S.—Death before DH!

Dear Larry,
Thanks for the letter; hope you don't mind reading it in the *Abstract*, but I thought that the reflections of an on-the-scenes, involved analytical thinker might make a nice change of pace from the detached, distant analysis for which I am infamous. A few facts concerning your letter:

a) The Braves' record after 108 games was 66–42. If they had split from there on, they would, indeed, have won the division at 93–69. This reminds me of two things: 1) Earl Weaver's rhetorical question "Do you know how hard it can be to play .500 ball in September?" and 2) Earl Weaver's teams never had any trouble doing it.

b) Hmmm. I had assumed all those times Chambliss was caught stealing were busted hit and run plays.

The Braves did not lead the league in runners caught stealing, but they were third. Their percentage, 62.4, was better than Pittsburgh's, worse than anyone else's.

Sometimes I combine "sacrifice hits" and "caught stealing" into something called "outs invested by the manager in first-run strategies," or "first-run outs" for short. The Braves invested 166 outs in first-run strategies, the second highest total of any major league team. I've got to say that I do find that more than a little bit strange for this lineup. Despite this, they were third-high in the league in grounding into double plays, making you wonder what he was using the bunt for. On the other hand (see Houston comments), the Braves did have 79 big innings, as many as any National League team. It could be argued that with the offense they had, they should have had more big innings than Philadelphia, and not just as many, but that's just an argument.

c) It seems likely that what raising the fences did was turn home runs into doubles and triples, which is what it could have been expected to do. Your estimate of the size of the effect seems reasonable, if a little conservative. However, Bob Horner, who always benefited the most from the Launching Pad, increased his home-run frequency in home games in 1983 by only 18% (it has generally been over 100%), but set a career high in doubles (25) in just 104 games. Chris Chambliss, who never increased his home-run output here greatly, hit 9 homers in Atlanta, 11 on the road but had 15 doubles in Atlanta, 9 on the road. Dale Murphy, having his greatest year, hit 17 home runs at home, 19 on the road but had the same doubles breakdown as Chambliss. Compared to 1982, the team as a whole hit 16 fewer home runs, but 3 more doubles and 23 more triples. Part of the increase in triples was created by having Brett Butler in the lineup. Opposition home runs increased from 126 to 132; according to a study by Bill Carr, Atlanta opponents in 1983 also hit nine more doubles, but 10 fewer triples than in 1982.

So I can't really agree with that point, either. It didn't really take the home runs away from them, and besides that, as I said, I don't think the Braves' power is all that impressive. I think stabilizing the pitching staff was as important. The Braves' record in Fulton County Stadium actually improved by four games; it was their road record which was off by five games.

Thanks for writing.

—Bill James

VII. IN ONE-RUN GAMES

At 19–29, the Braves had the worst one-run game record in the National League. If the Braves could have only managed to finish two games below .500 in their one-run games the West would have been theirs.

What went wrong? What happened? Not one Braves' regular managed to rise to the occasion. Averages in one-run games do tend to be lower. Horner, Hubbard and Chambliss were all way under their established 1983 norms in these close contests. The pitching, with few exceptions, was poor. Seven of the most active Braves' pitchers had ERAs higher than their season's mark—exactly the opposite of what you would expect in one-run games. The Dodgers only had one hurler do the unexpected.

The chart below details the performances of key Braves personnel in one-run ballgames.

	G	AB	R	H	2B	3B	HR	RBI	SB	Avg
Butler	45	144	17	39	5	1	2	9	15	.271
Ramirez	45	182	24	52	3	0	11	8	6	.286
Washington	40	134	19	32	6	2	5	13	13	.239
Murphy	48	177	29	47	5	1	14	37	5	.266
Horner	27	108	16	25	5	0	4	14	1	.231
Chambliss	42	140	17	32	7	0	7	17	0	.299
Hubbard	41	137	13	32	7	1	3	11	2	.234
Benedict	42	123	11	34	3	0	1	5	0	.276
Royster	28	90	6	17	2	0	0	8	5	.189
Harper	25	68	4	16	0	1	1	3	6	.235
Watson	24	42	5	19	2	0	4	19	0	.452

	G	IP	W	L	ERA	Sv
Perez	10	72.2	4	3	1.98	—
McMurtry	11	66	3	3	2.86	0
Niekro	12	62	1	1	5.37	0
Falcone	8	24.2	2	2	3.65	0
Bedrosian	26	43.1	1	6	3.32	5
Garber	16	19.2	3	4	6.41	1
Forster	20	27.2	2	1	2.28	4
Moore	10	11.1	0	3	3.97	0
Dayley	6	26	1	1	4.85	0
Camp	9	34.2	1	2	3.64	0
Others	13	34.2	1	1	4.41	1

The bench contained some obvious extremes. Royster was all but useless in these games. Seven of Harper's hits came in just two games. For the other 23 he hit a whole .150. I absolutely despise the term "gamer," but if I had to use it, I would use it on Bob Watson. The record shown above includes 8 for 14 as a pinch-hitter with 11 RBI. That's right—eleven.

—J.B.

Glenn HUBBARD, Second Base
Runs Created: 68

	G	AB	Hit	2B	3B	HR	Run	RBI	BB	SO	SB	CS	Avg
4.01 Years		580	144	25	4	10	71	62	58	81	5	6	.248
1983	148	517	136	24	6	12	65	70	55	71	3	9	.263
First Half	73	260	78	13	3	5	34	37	28	32	2		.300
Second Half	75	257	58	11	3	7	31	33	27	39	1		.226
vs. RHP		382	100	17	3	6		54	41	52			.262
vs. LHP		135	36	7	3	6		16	14	18			.267
Home	75	261	68	9	3	6	33	37	27	34	3		.261
Road	73	256	68	15	3	6	32	33	28	36	0		.266
Grass	108	361	98	12	5	9	47	52			3		.271
Turf	40	156	48	12	1	3	18	18			0		.308

Bob HORNER, Third Base
Runs Created: 76

	G	AB	Hit	2B	3B	HR	Run	RBI	BB	SO	SB	CS	Avg
4.06 Years		606	171	26	1	39	98	113	54	85	3	3	.282
1983	104	386	117	25	1	20	75	68	50	63	4	2	.303
First Half	67	244	71	14	1	13	45	44	34	38	3		.291
Second Half	37	142	46	11	0	7	30	24	16	25	1		.324
vs. RHP		282	84	16	1	14		48	44	42			.298
vs. LHP		104	33	9	0	6		20	6	21			.317
Home	58	216	71	16	1	12	46	40	27	30	1		.329
Road	46	170	46	9	0	8	29	28	23	33	3		.271
Grass	75	292	91	21	1	14	56	47			1		.312
Turf	29	94	26	4	0	6	19	21			3		.277

Rafael RAMIREZ, Shortstop
Runs Created: 76

	G	AB	Hit	2B	3B	HR	Run	RBI	BB	SO	SB	CS	Avg
2.80 Years		608	166	21	4	7	72	50	35	63	19	11	.273
1983	152	622	185	13	5	7	82	58	36	48	16	12	.297
First Half	73	297	87	6	2	2	42	17	19	24	10		.293
Second Half	79	325	98	7	3	5	40	41	17	24	6		.302
vs. RHP		463	128	6	3	4		41	26	39			.276
vs.LHP		159	57	7	2	3		18	10	9			.358
Home	73	294	84	6	2	2	40	32	15	20	4		.286
Road	79	328	101	7	3	5	42	26	21	28	12		.308
Grass	110	452	132	9	5	3	59	46			7		.292
Turf	42	170	53	4	0	4	23	12			9		.312

Brett BUTLER, Leftfield
Runs Created: 76

	G	AB	Hit	2B	3B	HR	Run	RBI	BB	SO	SB	CS	Avg
1.73 Years		529	138	14	9	3	79	28	57	62	40	18	.260
1983	151	549	154	21	13	5	84	37	54	56	39	22	.281
First Half	70	248	67	9	7	2	36	17			20		.270
Second Half	81	301	87	12	6	3	48	20			19		.289
vs. RHP													
vs. LHP						Not Available							
Home	73	265	88	10	5	4	43	17			12		.332
Road	78	284	66	11	8	1	41	20			27		.232
Grass	111	394	120	17	7	4	60	28			25		.305
Turf	40	155	34	4	6	1	24	9			14		.219

Chris CHAMBLISS, First Base
Runs Created: 78

	G	AB	Hit	2B	3B	HR	Run	RBI	BB	SO	SB	CS	Avg
11.36 Years		606	170	32	4	15	74	79	48	73	3	3	.280
1983	131	447	125	24	3	20	59	78	63	68	2	7	.280
First Half	73	242	68	11	2	8	25	47	33	31	2		.281
Second Half	58	205	57	13	1	12	34	31	30	37	0		.278
vs. RHP		369	109	21	2	18		72	54	46			.295
vs. LHP		78	16	3	1	2		6	9	22			.205
Home	65	212	65	15	2	9	31	46	33	29	1		.307
Road	66	235	60	9	1	11	28	32	30	39	1		.255
Grass	104	313	90	17	2	14	44	59			1		.288
Turf	27	134	35	7	1	6	15	19			1		.261

Dale MURPHY, Centerfield
Runs Created: 131

	G	AB	Hit	2B	3B	HR	Run	RBI	BB	SO	SB	CS	Avg
5.41 Years		588	160	22	3	30	95	98	69	125	17	6	.272
1983	162	589	178	24	4	36	131	121	90	110	30	4	.302
First Half	80	287	93	12	4	19	76	58	47	54	14		.324
Second Half	82	302	85	12	0	17	55	63	43	56	16		.281
vs. RHP		426	137	16	1	31		100	73	73			.322
vs. LHP		163	41	8	3	5		21	17	37			.252
Home	80	285	97	15	3	17	73	61	46	49	11		.340
Road	82	304	81	9	1	19	58	60	44	61	19		.266
Grass	119	435	136	19	4	30	105	97			15		.313
Turf	43	154	42	5	0	6	26	24			15		.273

Claudell WASHINGTON, Rightfield
Runs Created: 67

	G	AB	Hit	2B	3B	HR	Run	RBI	BB	SO	SB	CS	Avg
7.36 Years		598	166	30	7	12	82	72	37	112	31	13	.279
1983	134	496	138	24	8	9	75	44	35	103	31	9	.278
First Half	70	266	78	16	5	3	43	23	16	58	18		.293
Second Half	64	230	60	8	3	6	32	21	19	45	13		.261
vs. RHP		418	121	20	8	9		40	30	75			.289
vs. LHP		78	17	4	0	0		4	5	28			.218
Home	69	246	81	10	7	4	47	29	19	47	17		.329
Road	65	248	57	14	1	5	28	15	16	56	14		.230
Grass	101	367	104	14	7	8	59	34			23		.283
Turf	33	129	34	10	1	1	16	10			8		.264

Bruce BENEDICT, Catcher
Runs Created: 57

	G	AB	Hit	2B	3B	HR	Run	RBI	BB	SO	SB	CS	Avg
3.46 Years		497	130	18	1	3	40	50	57	42	3	4	.261
1983	134	423	126	13	1	2	43	43	61	24	1	3	.298
First Half	71	229	64	7	1	1	23	20	30	15	1		.279
Second Half	63	194	62	6	0	1	20	23	31	9	0		.320
vs. RHP		320	88	9	1	1		32	53	18			.291
vs. LHP		121	38	4	0	1		11	8	6			.314
Home	69	207	70	9	0	1	23	27	36	9	0		.338
Road	65	216	56	4	1	1	20	16	25	15	1		.259
Grass	101	309	94	10	1	2	33	37			1		.304
Turf	33	114	32	3	0	0	10	6			0		.281

Terry HARPER, Outfield
Runs Created: 24

	G	AB	Hit	2B	3B	HR	Run	RBI	BB	SO	SB	CS	Avg
1.17 Years		410	107	16	2	6	40	45	44	80	17	9	.262
1983	80	201	53	13	1	3	19	26	20	43	6	5	.264
First Half	48	133	37	7	1	3	12	21	15	31	3		.278
Second Half	32	68	16	6	0	0	7	5	5	12	3		.235
vs. RHP		87	25	6	0	1		10	6	17			.287
vs. LHP		114	28	7	1	2		16	14	26			.246
Home	35	85	18	4	0	2	9	11	10	17	1		.212
Road	45	116	35	9	1	1	10	15	10	26	5		.302
Grass	57	138	34	6	1	2	12	14			5		.246
Turf	23	71	19	7	0	1	7	12			1		.268

Jerry ROYSTER, Utility
Runs Created: 25

	G	AB	Hit	2B	3B	HR	Run	RBI	BB	SO	SB	CS	Avg
6.16 Years		516	129	18	5	4	70	40	49	60	28	11	.251
1983	91	268	63	10	3	3	32	30	28	35	11	7	.235
First Half	48	124	32	5	1	1	16	12	15	19	5		.258
Second Half	43	144	31	5	2	2	16	18	13	16	6		.215
vs. RHP		167	41	6	1	2		19	21	27			.246
vs. LHP		101	22	4	2	1		11	7	8			.218
Home	42	124	28	5	1	2	12	16	9	13	4		.226
Road	49	144	35	5	2	1	20	14	19	22	7		.243
Grass	61	196	47	10	1	2	21	23			10		.240
Turf	30	72	16	0	2	1	11	7			1		.222

Craig McMURTRY

Year	(W–L)	GS	Run	Avg	DP	Avg	SB	Avg
1983	(15–9)	35	167	4.77	43	1.23	31	.89

	G	IP	W	L	Pct	ER	ERA
1983 Home	19	119.2	8	3	.727	35	2.6
1983 Road	17	105	7	6	.539	42	3.60
1983 Grass	28	168.1	10	8	.556	61	3.26
1983 Turf	8	56.1	5	1	.833	16	2.56

Phil NIEKRO

Year	(W–L)	GS	Run	Avg	DP	Avg	SB	Avg
1982	(17–4)	35	189	5.40	28	.80	28	.80
1983	(11–10)	33	145	4.39	36	1.09	37	1.12
1976–1983		293	1235	4.21	217	.74	283	.97

	G	IP	W	L	Pct	ER	ERA
1982 Home	14	91	3	3	.500	51	5.04
1983 Home	17	95.1	4	5	.444	48	4.53
1982 Road	21	143.1	14	1	.933	43	2.61
1983 Road	17	106.1	7	5	.583	41	3.47
1983 Grass	24	142.2	8	7	.533	62	3.91
1983 Turf	10	59	3	3	.500	27	4.12

Pascual PEREZ

Year	(W–L)	GS	Run	Avg	DP	Avg	SB	Avg
1982	(4–4)	11	44	4.00	9	.82	8	.73
1983	(15–8)	33	149	4.52	36	1.09	32	.97
1982–1983		44	193	4.39	45	1.02	40	.91

	G	IP	W	L	Pct	ER	ERA
1983 Home	14	91.2	8	2	.800	39	3.83
1983 Road	19	123.2	7	6	.539	43	3.19
1983 Grass	21	133	10	6	.625	60	4.06
1983 Turf	12	82.1	5	2	.714	22	2.41

1983 Others

Pitcher	(W–L)	GS	Run	Avg	DP	Avg	SB	Avg
Camp	(10–9)	16	71	4.44	21	1.31	17	1.06
Dayley	(5–8)	16	81	5.06	15	.94	15	.94
Falcone	(9–4)	15	79	5.27	19	1.27	16	1.07
Barker	(1–3)	6	21	3.50	2	.33	13	2.17
Behenna	(3–3)	6	24	4.00	4	.67	5	.83
Bedrosian	(9–10)	1	3	3.00	0		5	5.00
Walk	(0–0)	1	6	6.00	0		4	4.00

ATLANTA BRAVES
RUNS BATTED IN ANALYSIS

Player	RBI	RBI In Wins	Victory Important RBI	RBI Importance	Wins Batted In	RBI Per Win
Dale Murphy	121	77	51.96	.429	13.13	9.2
Bob Horner	68	54	30.89	.454	9.75	7.0
Chris Chambliss	78	50	29.82	.382	7.30	10.7
Glenn Hubbard	70	52	29.50	.421	8.96	7.8
Rafael Ramirez	58	45	27.68	.477	7.18	8.1
Brett Butler	37	30	19.56	.529	5.23	7.1
Bruce Benedict	43	36	18.54	.431	5.90	7.3
Jerry Royster	30	25	17.14	.571	4.60	6.5
Claudell Washington	44	28	17.05	.388	4.33	10.2
Terry Harper	26	21	11.85	.456	3.35	7.8

HOUSTON ASTROS

I. THE BIG BING THEORY

Let us begin with a question: Are the Houston Astros a big-inning ballclub? The answer seems to be "yes." The Astros, who scored 643 runs in 1983 (8th best in the league, but a pretty good figure for a team in the Astrodome), scored 39% of those runs in innings of three or larger. Only one N.L. team, the Phillies, exceeded that figure. That is the one major surprise that can be drawn from the following chart, which presents the number of times that each National League team scored 1 run, 2 runs . . . 9 runs in an inning in 1983:

NUMBER OF TIMES SCORED X RUNS IN INNING

	1	2	3	4	5	6	7	8	9	Total
Philadelphia	219	95	51	16	8	1	1	1	1	696
Pittsburgh	221	103	50	15	2	2				659
Montreal	254	95	39	18	5	2	1			677
St. Louis	266	92	33	17	7	2	1	1		679
Chicago	233	105	33	23	4	3	3	1		701
New York	199	87	34	15	3	3	1			575
Los Angeles	222	96	42	18	3	2	1	1		654
Atlanta	257	105	48	25	2	3	1			746
Houston	228	83	42	15	10	1	1			643
San Diego	250	86	43	16	3		1	2		635
San Francisco	210	118	43	17	6	1		1		687
Cincinnati	246	89	27	8	10	2	1	1	1	623

The Astros had 69 innings in which they scored three or more runs—more than the Dodgers, the Cubs or the Expos.

A year ago I presented the same data (and also the same data as in the chart below) for the American League teams. The reason for doing it then, and repeating it now, is that this information is useful in trying to sort out how it is that strategic decisions impact on runs scored . . . if you bunt 20 times, how many one-run innings will that create and how many 5-run innings will it mess up, that sort of thing. These questions we cannot answer now; we will be able to answer them within a few years.

Other things, comparing this chart and the one for the American League a year ago, can be seen now. The American League, as you might expect, is much more of a big-inning league. Half of the teams in the American League scored 42% or more of their runs in big innings; no National League team in 1983 did that. There is more bunting in the NL, there are more stolen base attempts, and there is less hitting. One would expect that to lead to fewer big innings. Philadelphia is the only team in the National League which could be considered a big-inning team by American League standards.

In the American League data, there was a sharp division between the big-inning teams and the others; in the N.L. in '83, there is no clear division, and in fact it is very difficult to say which National League teams were big-inning teams and which were not, beyond saying that Philadelphia was a big-inning outfit, and St. Louis and Cincinnati were not. Whereas in the American League there are teams which invest 160 outs a year in first-run strate-

gies but also many teams which invest considerably fewer than 100, there is little spread in the National League; the Astros invested the most, 176, and the Cubs the least, 111. Everybody bunts, and everybody runs.

I think that this points up something that I have written before, which is that the designated hitter rule, far from draining strategy out of the game, simply removes from the game the most trite, predictable, nonstrategic part of it. Strategy exists only in making choices, only in the face of options. The National League game confronts the NL manager with frequent no-option situations, situations in which he *must* bunt or he *must* pinch-hit. The American League game allows a true option, and thus true strategy. That is clearly reflected in the fact that the American League has clear groups of big-inning teams and one-run teams, while the National League does not.

The chart below gives, in order, the number of runs scored by each team, the number of innings in which they scored, the average number of runs per inning that they scored when they scored, and the percentage of their runs that they scored in bunches of three or more:

	Runs	Innings	R/I	Big Innings Pct.
Philadelphia	696	393	1.77	.412
Pittsburgh	659	393	1.68	.352
Montreal	677	414	1.64	.344
St. Louis	679	419	1.62	.337
Chicago	701	405	1.73	.368
New York	575	342	1.68	.351
Los Angeles	654	385	1.70	.367
Atlanta	746	441	1.69	.374
Houston	643	380	1.69	.387
San Diego	653	401	1.63	.354
San Francisco	687	396	1.73	.351
Cincinnati	623	385	1.62	.319

It appears that in a general way, the number of big innings a team will have can be approximated by the formula (extra bases on hits times the square of on-base percentage), which will make perfect sense if you think about it for a while. It also appears that teams which bunt a lot or sacrifice a lot of bases to the running game tend to fall short of that estimate.

Then we come to the question, why are the Astros a good big-inning team, in view of the fact that they invested 176 outs in first-run strategies? There is a lucid answer to that on one level, and a not-so-clear answer on another. The Astros grounded into only 76 double plays in 1983, which (without checking) seems to me to be the lowest figure I have seen in years. That, obviously, contributed heavily to the cause of keeping the big-inning alive. If a manager invests 30 outs in first-run strategies, but invests them in such a way that it eliminates 30 double-play balls, then there is no effective cost to the first-run strategy.

What is not clear is to what extent this resulted from Lillis' choices (stealing bases early in the inning prevents double plays, hitting-and-running a lot prevents double plays), to what extent it resulted from his talent, to what extent it resulted from good luck. I could discuss these issues at great length, but frankly my interest in the subject would not warrant it.

II. ON A RELATED NOTE

To the extent that the Astros are perceived as a team with little power, it is largely a park illusion. The Astros hit only 26 home runs in the Astrodome (their opponents hit 28), but they hit 71 home runs in neutral parks. Only the Dodgers hit more.

III. SMART-ASS COMMENTS

I just wish the Astros had asked me whether they should sign Omar Moreno. I could have saved them a hell of a lot of money.

IV. IDENTITY CRISIS

What I try to do with each team is to pick up something that has been said about the team, preferably some-

thing that has been said several times, and examine it, shine all the light on it that I can.

It is hard to think of anything about the Astros that has been said in the last two years. They are a team whose group identity was lost three years ago, and is only now beginning to recrystallize. In some parts they are an old team, but the brilliant young double-play combination certainly does not reinforce that image. At times they seem to be one of those organizations which lacks confidence in its own talent, and can easily be mesmerized by an Omar Moreno or a Bob Knepper as long as someone else has him; at other times they have moved to solve problems from their own system. They don't have great power, but they do have power; they run a lot, but they really do not have good team speed. The organization has been incongruously slow to react to some obvious problems (Ashby, Pujols, Knepper). At season's end the Atlanta Braves' roster contained 804 units of trade value, the Dodgers 758, the Padres 663, the Astros 554. Neither the organization nor the talent on hand would justify any expectation that the Astros will be able to keep up with the brisk pace that is going to be set in this division over the next three to five years by the Dodgers and Braves.

Ray KNIGHT, First Base
Runs Created: 77

	G	AB	Hit	2B	3B	HR	Run	RBI	BB	SO	SB	CS	Avg
5.54 Years		512	146	32	4	8	56	63	38	58	2	3	.285
1983	145	507	154	36	4	9	43	70	42	62	0	3	.304
First Half	73	256	86	21	1	5	20	38			0		.336
Second Half	72	251	68	15	3	4	23	32			0		.271
vs. RHP		339	104			6		51			0		.307
vs. LHP		168	50			3		19			0		.298
Home	81	243	63	20	3	3	18	31			0		.259
Road	64	264	91	16	1	6	25	39			0		.345
Grass	45	160	60	8	1	5	18	27			0		.375
Turf	100	347	94	28	3	4	25	43			0		.271

Phil GARNER, Third Base
Runs Created: 68

	G	AB	Hit	2B	3B	HR	Run	RBI	BB	SO	SB	CS	Avg
8.41 Years		563	147	28	7	10	69	69	51	73	24	11	.260
1983	154	567	135	24	2	14	76	79	63	84	18	12	.238
First Half	79	293	72	12	1	9	37	45			10		.246
Second Half	75	274	63	12	1	5	39	34			8		.230
vs. RHP		390	93			9		58					.238
vs. LHP		177	42			5		21					.237
Home	77	283	70	16	2	4	42	41			14		.247
Road	77	284	65	8	0	10	34	38			4		.229
Grass	45	167	39	5	0	5	18	21			3		.234
Turf	109	400	96	19	2	9	58	58			15		.240

Bill DORAN, Second Base
Runs Created: 76

	G	AB	Hit	2B	3B	HR	Run	RBI	BB	SO	SB	CS	Avg
1.11 Years		569	155	14	6	7	73	41	81	70	15	11	.272
1983	154	535	145	12	7	8	70	39	86	67	12	12	.271
First Half	77	248	60	7	4	3	30	17			4		.242
Second Half	77	287	85	5	3	5	40	22			8		.296
vs. RHP		353	105			5		26					.297
vs. LHP		182	40			3		13					.220
Home	78	264	66	6	4	1	27	11			6		.250
Road	76	271	79	6	3	7	43	28			6		.292
Grass	44	158	46	2	2	6	24	19			6		.291
Turf	110	377	99	10	5	2	46	20			6		.263

Dickie THON, Shortstop
Runs Created: 95

	G	AB	Hit	2B	3B	HR	Run	RBI	BB	SO	SB	CS	Avg
2.80 Years		547	152	29	7	8	73	50	41	61	30	11	.279
1983	154	619	177	28	9	20	81	79	54	73	34	16	.286
First Half	79	322	99	13	4	10	44	43			19		.307
Second Half	75	297	78	15	5	10	37	36			15		.263
vs. RHP		430	116			17		64					.270
vs. LHP		189	61			3		15					.323
Home	77	305	89	15	6	4	38	31			14		.292
Road	77	314	88	13	3	16	43	48			20		.280
Grass	46	186	54	6	1	12	28	28			14		.290
Turf	108	433	119	22	8	8	53	51			20		.275

Jose CRUZ, Leftfield
Runs Created: 109

	G	AB	Hit	2B	3B	HR	Run	RBI	BB	SO	SB	CS	Avg
10.78 Years		542	154	27	6	11	71	73	63	68	25	11	.284
1983	160	594	189	28	8	14	85	92	65	86	30	16	.318
First Half	77	289	86	18	3	6	38	37			13		.298
Second Half	81	305	103	10	5	8	47	45			17		.338
vs. RHP		414	134			12		67					.324
vs. LHP		180	55			2		25					.306
Home	80	288	90	13	6	3	37	45			17		.313
Road	80	306	99	15	2	11	48	47			13		.324
Grass	47	185	59	9	2	5	27	28			6		.319
Turf	113	409	130	19	6	9	48	64			24		.318

Jerry MUMPHREY, Centerfield
Runs Created: 64

	G	AB	Hit	2B	3B	HR	Run	RBI	BB	SO	SB	CS	Avg
6.25 Years		535	154	22	7	6	74	55	51	71	24	10	.288
1983	127	410	118	21	6	8	58	53	50	56	7	3	.288
First Half	53	170	39	7	3	5	29	22	15	18	2	2	.229
Second Half	74	240	79	14	3	3	29	31	35	38	5	1	.329
vs. RHP		271	80			6		38					.295
vs. LHP		139	38			2		15					.273
Home	61	189	59	10	4	2	29	24			5	2	.312
Road	66	221	59	11	2	6	34	29			2	1	.267
Grass	76	245	71	13	4	7	41	36			3	3	.290
Turf	51	165	47	8	2	1	17	17			4	0	.285

Terry PUHL, Rightfield
Runs Created: 70

	G	AB	Hit	2B	3B	HR	Run	RBI	BB	SO	SB	CS	Avg
5.46 Years		599	168	27	7	8	85	50	57	59	30	13	.281
1983	137	465	136	25	7	8	66	44	36	48	24	11	.292
First Half	61	176	49	6	3	2	14	15			9		.278
Second Half	76	289	87	19	4	6	47	29			15		.301
vs. RHP		368	120			8		40					.326
vs. LHP		97	16			0		4					.165
Home	72	225	65	10	3	1	27	15			10		.284
Road	65	240	72	15	4	7	39	29			14		.300
Grass	37	134	36	6	2	4	22	13			7		.264
Turf	100	331	100	19	5	4	44	31			17		.302

Alan ASHBY, Catcher
Runs Created: 31

	G	AB	Hit	2B	3B	HR	Run	RBI	BB	SO	SB	CS	Avg
5.55 Years		496	117	23	2	9	47	58	53	76	1	2	.236
1983	87	275	63	18	1	8	31	34	31	38	0	0	.229
First Half	52	169	45	14	1	6	22	22					.266
Second Half	35	106	18	4	0	2	9	12					.170
vs. RHP		208	43			7		29					.207
vs. LHP		67	20			1		5					.299
Home	45	125	27	9	0	2	9	12					.216
Road	42	150	36	9	1	6	22	22					.240
Grass	27	96	23	5	0	1	11	11					.240
Turf	60	179	40	13	1	7	20	23					.223

Tony SCOTT, Outfield
Runs Created: 216

	G	AB	Hit	2B	3B	HR	Run	RBI	BB	SO	SB	CS	Avg
5.69 Years		477	119	19	5	3	56	44	31	77	22	12	.250
1983	80	186	42	6	1	2	20	17	11	39	5	4	.226
First Half	47	127	28	33	0	2	14	13			2		.220
Second Half	33	59	14	3	1	0	6	4			3		.237
vs. RHP		85	16			1		10					.188
vs. LHP		101	26			1		7					.257
Home	36	83	17	2	1	1	5	5			4		.205
Road	44	103	25	4	0	1	15	12			1		.243
Grass	24	59	15	3	0	1	9	10			0		.254
Turf	56	127	27	33	1	1	11	7			5		.213

Kevin BASS, Utility
Runs Created: 16

	G	AB	Hit	2B	3B	HR	Run	RBI	BB	SO	SB	CS	Avg
.62 Years		355	76	11	5	3	44	31	10	57	3	5	.215
1983	88	195	46	7	3	2	25	18	6	27	2	2	.236
First Half	42	103	25	4	2	1	13	9			2		.243
Second Half	46	92	21	3	1	1	12	9			0		.228
vs. RHP		77	21			1		12					.273
vs. LHP		118	25			1		6					.212
Home	52	118	30	4	3	2	18	15			2		.254
Road	36	77	16	3	0	0	7	3			0		.208
Grass	23	57	10	1	0	0	3	1			0		.175
Turf	45	142	36	6	3	2	22	17			2		.254

Joe NIEKRO

Year	(W–L)	GS	Run	Avg	DP	Avg	SB	Avg
1982	(17-12)	35	119	3.40	34	.97	37	1.06
1983	(15-14)	38	156	4.11	28	.74	51	1.34
1977-1983		214	858	4.01	190	.89	238	1.11

	G	IP	W	L	Pct	ER	ERA
1982 Home	18	143	10	5	.667	38	2.39
1983 Home	20	146	10	6	.625	40	2.47
1982 Road	17	127	7	7	.500	36	2.55
1982 Road	18	117.2	5	8	.385	62	4.74
1983 Grass	10	70.1	3	6	.333	46	5.89
1983 Turf	28	193.1	12	8	.600	56	2.61

Nolan RYAN

Year	(W–L)	GS	Run	Avg	DP	Avg	SB	Avg
1982	(16-12)	35	134	3.83	26	.74	41	1.17
1983	(14- 9)	29	108	3.72	31	1.07	24	.83
1976-1983		261	1003	3.84	215	.82	303	1.16

	G	IP	W	L	Pct	ER	ERA
1982 Home	15	111.1	5	6	.455	42	3.50
1983 Home	16	103.1	6	6	.500	33	2.87
1982 Road	20	139	11	6	.647	46	2.98
1983 Road	13	93	8	3	.727	32	3.10
1983 Grass	9	69.2	7	1	.875	19	2.46
1983 Turf	20	126.2	7	8	.467	46	3.27

Bob KNEPPER

Year	(W–L)	GS	Run	Avg	DP	Avg	SB	Avg
1982	(5-15)	29	93	3.21	30	1.03	40	1.38
1983	(6-13)	29	101	3.48	32	1.10	35	1.21
1977-1983		209	589	2.82	191	.91	212	1.01

	G	IP	W	L	Pct	ER	ERA
1982 Home	19	94.2	3	5	.375	46	4.37
1983 Home	15	91.2	3	4	.429	23	2.26
1982 Road	14	85.1	2	10	.167	43	4.54
1983 Road	20	111.1	3	9	.250	49	3.96
1983 Grass	12	65.2	0	4	.000	32	4.39
1983 Turf	23	137.1	6	9	.400	40	2.62

Mike SCOTT

Year	(W–L)	GS	Run	Avg	DP	Avg	SB	Avg
1982	(7-13)	22	89	4.05	12	.55	20	.91
1983	(10- 6)	24	115	4.79	26	1.08	26	1.08
1979-1983		84	344	4.09	78	.93	69	.82

	G	IP	W	L	Pct	ER	ERA
1982 Home	18	71.1	4	3	.571	31	3.91
1983 Home	13	81	5	5	.500	32	3.56
1982 Road	19	52.2	3	10	.231	53	6.88
1983 Road	11	64	5	1	.833	28	3.94
1983 Grass	5	24.2	2	0	1.000	10	3.65
1983 Turf	19	120.1	8	6	.571	50	3.74

1983 OTHERS

Pitcher	(W–L)	GS	Run	Avg	DP	Avg	SB	Avg
LaCoss	(5-7)	17	69	4.06	17	1.00	23	1.35
Madden	(9-5)	13	3	3.31	21	1.61	11	.85
Ruhle	(8-5)	9	37	4.11	7	.78	9	1.00
Heathcock	(2-1)	3	14	4.67	1	.33	2	.67

HOUSTON ASTROS
RUNS BATTED IN ANALYSIS

Player	RBI	RBI In Wins	Victory Important RBI	RBI Importance	Wins Batted In	RBI Per Win
Dickie Thon	79	58	43.73	.554	12.73	6.2
Phil Garner	79	57	39.56	.501	10.91	7.2
Jose Cruz	92	66	37.05	.403	12.96	7.1
Ray Knight	70	44	32.03	.458	8.52	8.2
Terry Puhl	44	32	19.80	.450	5.50	8.0
Bill Doran	39	19	12.58	.323	4.49	8.7
Omar Moreno	25	19	10.06	.402	2.75	9.1
Tony Scott	17	12	9.88	.581	2.25	7.6
Alan Ashby	34	18	8.20	.241	2.68	12.7
Jerry Mumphrey	17	12	8.20	.482	1.97	8.6
Kevin Bass	18	9	5.83	.324	2.31	7.8

SAN DIEGO PADRES

I. CRUISE CONTROL

Did you ever know one of those people who could drive for hundreds of miles at exactly 58 miles per hour? The Padres of 1982–1983 have become the first National League team ever to play exactly .500 ball for two years; they were 81–81 in 1982 and again in 1983. One American League team, a Twins team, also did this. This is old stuff to the Padres though. They once played .379 baseball for two straight years (61–100 in 1971, 58–95 in 1972), then followed that up with two straight records of 60 wins, 102 losses.

II. A SHORT CIRCUIT

The Padres led the majors last year in odd-looking runs scored and RBI totals. Their leadoff man, Alan Wiggins, scored 83 runs and drove in only 22, which is not a record but is not your normal everyday leadoff man's ratio, either. I don't think that any regular player has had that kind of a ratio since Richie Ashburn in 1959 (86 runs scored, 20 RBI). Matty Alou was fairly close.

The Padres' cleanup man, Terry Kennedy, scored 47 runs and drove in 98, an even weirder ratio. You ever see anybody drive in 98 runs and score only 47 before?

Steve Garvey's runs scored total, while not an oddity, is almost as surprising. Garvey has never scored 100 runs in a season. In 1982, playing 162 games with the Dodgers, he scored only 66 runs, and in 1980, having his last big year, he scored only 78. Before his injury last year, he scored 76 runs in just 100 games; he was certain to score 100 and in danger of leading the league.

What this says about the Padres, of course, is that they had a 1-to-4 offense. Their offense began with Wiggins, and it ended with Kennedy. They got no offensive production from three infield positions, and distinctly less than championship-calibre production from two outfield spots. And you cannot win a pennant with a four-man offense.

III. WHY THE PADRES SCORED 653 RUNS

The Padres scored 653 runs last year although the runs created formula would have projected their total at only 602. Why did this happen?

The one largest reason is probably the Padre infield. Not the players, the infield. Padre opponents last year made 190 errors, the highest total in the major leagues by a comfortable margin. The Padres scored 106 unearned runs (an average figure would be 63). That accounts for the lion's share of the difference between the estimated and actual runs.

A probable contributory cause is the effect discussed before, the 1-to-4 offense. A "bunched" offense is much more efficient than a spread-out offense; you receive a higher return on your opportunities.

The way in which offensive units are put together is not the major nor even *a* major influence on the number of runs resulting, but it can have an impact. Remember the A, B, and C factors of an offense from the Introduction—A is getting on base, B is advancing baserunners, C is context. Suppose that you take two players who get on base 400 times and have 500 total bases in 1,000 plate appearance between them. If you split that evenly, their runs created will be:

	A	B	C	Runs
#1 son	200	250	500	100
#2 son	200	250	500	100
TOTAL	400	500	1,000	200

But if they are not split evenly, if one player is far better than the others, the runs created total will increase:

	A	B	C	Runs
#1 son	250	300	500	150
#10 son	150	200	500	60
TOTAL	400	500	1,000	210

The more offense is bunched together, the more efficient. Within normal ranges of internal deviation, this doesn't measurably change the number of runs resulting. In a few extreme cases, it does.

This is just speculation, but a formless offense often seems to be inefficient. The Red Sox offense is inefficient because they lack a leadoff man who can get on base. The Expo offense is inefficient because they lack power in the middle of the lineup. The Cardinal offense is inefficient because they have so many people who all do the same thing that it is hard to form the offense; it has no locus of danger. Whitey aggravated this problem by batting McGee and Green in the middle of the lineup. The White Sox offense is very efficient because they have people at the top of the order who can get on base and people in the middle of the order who can drive them around. They, like the Padres, do have a couple of non-productive spots near the bottom of the order.

IV. WHY THE PADRES SHOULD SCORE EVEN MORE RUNS NEXT YEAR

We know (it has been established) that teams which exceed their Pythagorean projection for wins have a strong tendency to decline in the following year; that is, if a team scores 650 runs and allows 650, but wins 88 games anyway, then the odds strongly favor their failing to win 88 the next year. It is possible (it has not been established) that there could be a similar effect in the runs created method, that teams which could be expected to score 600 but actually score 650 then decline offensively in the following year.

Whether that is true or not, the Padres are likely to score more runs in 1984 than they did last year, maybe a lot more. They have taken two actions over the last two years to improve the hitting characteristics of the park.

The first, moving in the fences and getting rid of the 17-foot high walls, had comparatively little effect. The second was to install a "batter's eye," a new background for the hitters. This, according to people who have looked at the issue (Bill Carr and Craig Wright), seems to have had a large impact, such a large impact that we might expect the batting statistics of the Padre players to move significantly forward next year.

Besides that, Dick Williams ain't stupid. He knows he's got a 4-man offense. Two rookies of considerable offensive potential (Kevin McReynolds and Carmello Martinez) will move into the lineup; Dick Williams's record in working with young hitters is spectacular. It should be at least a six-man offense next season.

The batter's eye probably also helped to concentrate more of the Padres' hits into the second half of the season, further "bunching" the offense and causing more runs than expected to result.

V. THEY'RE MORE COMFORTABLE PLAYING IN MUD

You remember the comments concerning Philadelphia on grass teams and turf teams, how we really don't understand what it takes to play well on artificial surfaces. The Padres were the best team in the National League last year on grass (67–53), but were 14–28 on artificial turf:

Home (grass):	47-34	.580
Road grass:	20-19	.513
Road turf:	14-28	.333

Would you have guessed that? Don't the Padres look like the kind of team that should do well on turf? They have tremendously quick, wide-ranging infielders, plus excellent speed in the outfield. They're a line-drive hitting, aggressive base-running team. Why wouldn't they play well on turf?

It was the pitching or defense that did it (see breakdowns). All four starters had terrible records on turf.

Kennedy's arm or lack thereof probably contributed, but the turf must have exposed some gigantic weaknesses in the Padre defense.

VI. TURF 2

The Philadelphia comments also included some unsupported speculation about how double-play ability changed how a team played on turf. The Padres must have the only double-play combination in history that is in danger of grounding into more double plays than they complete. Templeton grounded into 16 double plays in 126 games, Bonilla grounded into 19. Only two other middle infielders in the league grounded into 15 or more (Cincinnati's two, Oester and Concepcion). Garvey would have led the league in GIDP if he hadn't been hurt.

If the Padres could have exchanged double-play combinations with the Astros, the Padres would have won the division and the Astros would have finished last:

Doran and Thon scored 151 runs; Bonilla and Templeton scored 94.

Doran and Thon drove in 188 runs; Bonilla and Templeton drove in 85.

Bill and Dickie grounded into 18 double plays; Juan and Garry grounded into 35.

The Astros turned 165 double plays; the Padres turned 135.

VII. WE'LL GET 'EM NEXT DECADE

My respect for Ballard Smith and his orderly, effective administration of this team continues to grow. The Padres are going to be one of the most exciting teams to watch in 1984; if McReynolds and Martinez come through, they could be tough to beat. The Padres don't sit on the problems; they attack them.

Smith took over an organization that was 50 years behind the Dodgers, and in just three years he has cut that to 40 years behind. The Padres are like an aggressive intelligent spider monkey, preparing to do battle with a gorilla.

Steve GARVEY, First Base
Runs Created: 57

	G	AB	Hit	2B	3B	HR	Run	RBI	BB	SO	SB	CS	Avg
11.28 Years		615	185	31	3	20	82	93	35	70	7	5	.300
1983	100	388	114	22	0	14	76	59	29	39	4	1	.294
First Half	79	313	93	19	0	14	64	49			3		.297
Second Half	21	75	21	3	0	0	12	10			1		.280
vs. RHP		288	79										.274
vs. LHP		100	35										.350
Home	51	192	56	11	0	8	38	36			2		.292
Road	49	196	58	11	0	6	38	23			2		.296
Grass	77	300	88	19	0	11	56	49	22		2		.293
Turf	23	88	26	3	0	3	20	10	7		2		.295

Ruppert JONES, Centerfield
Runs Created: 37

	G	AB	Hit	2B	3B	HR	Run	RBI	BB	SO	SB	CS	Avg
5.65 Years		571	144	28	5	16	80	70	66	100	22	13	.253
1983	133	335	78	12	3	12	42	49	35	58	11	11	.233
First Half	62	149	30	5	0	4	19	17			3		.201
Second Half	71	186	48	7	3	8	23	32			8		.258
vs. RHP		272	70										.257
vs. LHP		63	8										.127
Home	72	153	29	5	1	5	22	16			6		.190
Road	61	182	49	7	2	7	20	33			5		.269
Grass	100	240	49	7	1	8	29	31	25		8		.204
Turf	33	95	29	5	2	4	13	18	10		3		.305

Juan BONILLA, Second Base
Runs Created: 50

	G	AB	Hit	2B	3B	HR	Run	RBI	BB	SO	SB	CS	Avg
1.83 Years		606	159	20	4	3	58	43	47	43	4	5	.262
1983	152	556	132	17	4	4	55	45	50	40	3	0	.237
First Half	77	298	76	8	3	1	32	26			0		.255
Second Half	75	258	56	9	1	3	23	19			3		.217
vs. RHP		400	90										.225
vs. LHP		156	42										.269
Home	75	268	55	7	4	3	31	24			3		.205
Road	77	288	77	10	0	1	24	21			0		.267
Grass	114	418	104	11	4	4	48	34	41		3		.249
Turf	38	138	28	6	0	0	7	11	9		0		.203

Tony GWYNN, Rightfield
Runs Created: 42

	G	AB	Hit	2B	3B	HR	Run	RBI	BB	SO	SB	CS	Avg
.86 Years		572	172	28	5	2	78	62	43	43	17	8	.302
1983	86	304	94	12	2	1	34	37	23	21	7	4	.309
First Half	11	39	11	3	0	0	4	4			1		.282
Second Half	75	265	83	9	2	1	30	33			6		.313
vs. RHP		239	79										.331
vs. LHP		65	15										.231
Home	46	164	50	8	2	0	18	20			1		.305
Road	40	140	44	4	0	1	16	17			6		.314
Grass	65	231	74	12	2	0	26	31	17		5		.320
Turf	21	73	20	0	0	1	8	6	6		2		.274

Luis SALAZAR, Third Base
Runs Created: 53

	G	AB	Hit	2B	3B	HR	Run	RBI	BB	SO	SB	CS	Avg
2.67 Years		590	161	20	8	10	65	64	24	96	29	11	.273
1983	134	481	124	16	2	14	52	45	17	80	24	9	.258
First Half	65	231	66	8	0	3	20	15			12		.286
Second Half	69	250	58	8	2	11	32	30			12		.232
vs. RHP		328	78										.238
vs. LHP		153	46										.301
Home	67	239	61	6	0	10	30	26			12		.255
Road	67	242	63	10	2	4	22	19			12		.260
Grass	101	365	93	11	1	11	38	34	11		18		.255
Turf	33	116	31	5	1	3	14	11	6		6		.267

Bobby BROWN, Outfield
Runs Created: 31

	G	AB	Hit	2B	3B	HR	Run	RBI	BB	SO	SB	CS	Avg
2.09 Years		490	123	13	5	11	70	46	37	89	42	12	.251
1983	57	225	60	5	3	5	40	22	23	38	27	9	.267
First Half													
Second Half	57	225	60	5	3	5	40	22	23	38	27	9	.267
vs. RHP		175	44										.251
vs. LHP		50	16										.320
Home	27	102	34	5	0	4	22	16	12		15		.333
Road	30	123	26	0	3	1	18	6	11		12		.211
Grass	39	151	44	5	0	4	28	17	16		22		.291
Turf	18	74	16	0	3	1	12	5	7		5		.216

Garry TEMPLETON, Shortstop
Runs Created: 42

	G	AB	Hit	2B	3B	HR	Run	RBI	BB	SO	SB	CS	Avg
6.05 Years		663	194	28	13	6	92	64	23	86	30	17	.292
1983	126	460	121	20	2	3	39	40	21	57	16	6	.263
First Half	46	161	39	9	0	2	16	17			2		.242
Second Half	80	299	82	11	2	1	23	23			14		.274
vs. RHP		334	86										.257
vs. LHP		126	35										.278
Home	58	202	50	6	1	1	19	14			11		.248
Road	68	258	71	14	1	2	20	26			5		.275
Grass	95	348	90	11	2	3	32	31	15		12		.259
Turf	31	112	31	9	0	0	7	9	6		4		.277

Terry KENNEDY, Catcher
Runs Created: 81

	G	AB	Hit	2B	3B	HR	Run	RBI	BB	SO	SB	CS	Avg
3.27 Years		574	164	34	2	14	59	88	42	89	1	2	.285
1983	149	549	156	27	2	17	47	98	51	89	1	3	.284
First Half	74	276	83	14	1	6	21	49			0		.301
Second Half	75	273	73	13	1	11	26	49			1		.267
vs. RHP		404	116										.287
vs. LHP		145	40										.276
Home	78	275	79	11	2	8	22	51			1		.287
Road	71	274	77	16	0	9	25	47			0		.281
Grass	111	405	120	18	2	15	37	79	43		1		.296
Turf	38	144	36	9	0	2	10	19	8		0		.250

Alan WIGGINS, Leftfield
Runs Created: 72

	G	AB	Hit	2B	3B	HR	Run	RBI	BB	SO	SB	CS	Avg
1.43 Years		541	147	16	4	1	89	26	55	43	71	13	.271
1983	144	503	139	20	2	0	83	22	65	43	66	13	.276
First Half	66	212	59	8	1	0	36	10			19		.278
Second Half	78	291	80	12	1	0	47	12			47		.275
vs. RHP		360	97										.269
vs. LHP		143	42										.294
Home	74	258	69	7	2	0	49	12			29		.267
Road	70	245	70	13	0	0	34	10			37		.286
Grass	108	362	101	15	2	0	65	17	55		46		.279
Turf	36	141	38	5	0	0	18	5	10		20		.270

Gene RICHARDS, Outfield
Runs Created: 28

	G	AB	Hit	2B	3B	HR	Run	RBI	BB	SO	SB	CS	Avg
5.80 Years		589	171	21	11	4	84	43	58	70	42	15	.291
1983	95	233	64	11	3	3	37	22	17	17	14	5	.275
First Half	58	180	50	9	3	3	29	18			12		.278
Second Half	37	53	14	2	0	0	8	4			2		.264
vs. RHP		190	51										.268
vs. LHP		43	13										.302
Home	48	102	30	4	2	2	17	15	7		9		.294
Road	47	131	34	7	1	1	20	7	10		5		.260
Grass	68	159	47	9	3	3	30	20	13		11		.296
Turf	27	74	17	2	0	0	7	2	4		3		.230

Eric SHOW

Year	(W–L)	GS	Run	Avg	DP	Avg	SB	Avg
1982	(10-6)	14	56	4.00	13	.93	17	1.21
1983	(15-12)	33	131	3.97	22	.67	23	.70
1982–1983		47	187	3.98	35	.74	40	.85

	G	IP	W	L	Pct	ER	ERA
1983 Home	20	116.2	10	3	.769	49	3.78
1983 Road	15	84	5	9	.357	44	4.71
1983 Grass	28	163	14	6	.700	66	3.64
1983 Turf	7	37.2	1	6	.143	27	6.45

Ed WHITSON

Year	(W–L)	GS	Run	Avg	DP	Avg	SB	Avg
1982	(4-2)	9	29	3.22	5	.56	8	.89
1983	(5-7)	21	84	4.00	14	.67	18	.86
1977-1983		112	415	3.71	85	.76	103	.92

	G	IP	W	L	Pct	ER	ERA
1983 Home	12	62.2	1	2	.333	26	3.73
1983 Road	19	81.2	4	5	.444	43	4.74
1983 Grass	20	103.1	4	4	.500	42	3.65
1983 turf	11	39.2	1	3	.250	27	6.13

Tim LOLLAR

Year	(W–L)	GS	Run	Avg	DP	Avg	SB	Avg
1982	(16-9)	34	143	4.21	21	.62	18	.53
1983	(7-12)	30	113	3.77	19	.63	28	.93
1980-1983		76	300	3.95	52	.68	51	.67

	G	IP	W	L	Pct	ER	ERA
1983 Home	18	124.2	8	6	.571	41	2.97
1983 Home	13	84	4	5	.444	30	3.21
1982 Road	18	108.1	8	3	.727	40	3.32
1983 Road	17	91.2	3	7	.300	60	5.89
1983 Grass	23	141	6	10	.375	62	3.96
1983 Turf	7	34.2	1	1	.333	28	7.27

1983 Others

Pitcher	(W–L)	GS	Run	Avg	DP	Avg	SB	Avg
Hawkins	(5-7)	19	65	3.42	20	1.05	19	1.00
Thurmond	(7-3)	18	81	4.50	18	1.00	22	1.22
Montefusco	(9-4)	10	45	4.50	13	1.30	13	1.30
Booker	(0-1)	1	3	3.00	0	.00	1	1.00
Rasmussen	(0-0)	1	4	4.00	1	1.00	0	.00
Sosa	(1-4)	1	6	6.00	1	1.00	0	.00
Welsh	(0-1)	1	1	1.00	0		0	

Dave DRAVECKY

Year	(W–L)	GS	Run	Avg	DP	Avg	SB	Avg
1982	(5-3)	10	36	3.60	12	1.20	9	.90
1983	(14-10)	28	111	3.96	27	.96	27	.96
1982-1983		38	147	3.87	39	1.03	36	.95

	G	IP	W	L	Pct	ER	ERA
1983 Home	14	93.2	8	5	.615	37	3.56
1983 Road	14	90	6	5	.546	36	3.60
1983 Grass	20	139.2	12	6	.667	51	3.29
1983 Turf	8	44	2	4	.333	22	4.50

SAN DIEGO PADRES
RUNS BATTED IN ANALYSIS

Player	RBI	RBI In Wins	Victory Important RBI	RBI Importance	Wins Batted In	RBI Per Win
Terry Kennedy	98	66	47.20	.482	11.75	8.3
Sixto Lezcano	49	40	32.12	.656	7.03	7.0
Steve Garvey	59	43	29.07	.493	8.29	7.1
Luis Salazar	45	34	22.86	.508	6.50	6.9
Ruppert Jones	49	30	21.67	.442	5.91	8.3
Anthony Gwynn	37	29	20.02	.541	5.42	7.8
Juan Bonilla	45	26	19.98	.444	4.41	10.2
Garry Templeton	31	27	19.96	.644	5.24	5.9
Alan Wiggins	22	15	10.88	.495	2.37	9.3
Gene Richards	22	15	10.57	.480	2.52	8.7
Bobby Brown	22	18	9.86	.448	2.00	11.0
Joe Lefebvre	1	1	.50	.500	.25	4.0

SAN FRANCISCO GIANTS

I. RAISING THE ROOF

The desire to build a domed stadium for the Giants has given birth to an odd, bass-ackwards advertising campaign for the Giants, a campaign that accentuates the negatives. It is an appropriate advertising campaign for a team that leads off a .240 hitter, plays an outfielder at second base and seems hell-bent on trading their best ballplayer when he is coming off his poorest season in several years. With respect to the team, all it seems necessary to say is that I realize now that my impression a year ago that the organization had gained a degree of purpose seems obviously over-optimistic. With respect to domed stadiums, a few thoughts.

1) We have moved into a distinctly different era of stadium construction, out of the time of Veterans and Riverfront and Royals Stadium—the stadiums called by some the sterile ashtray stadiums—and into an era in which stadiums are a) very difficult to get built, and b) most dreamed of and sought after in the domed condition. Seattle, New Orleans, Minnesota and a couple of other places have succeeded in convincing the bankers; Cleveland, San Francisco, Buffalo and many others are desirous but lackin' the backin'.

2) What is it, exactly, that attracts people so to the idea of putting a roof over a park? I know people who have lived in Minneapolis and gone to a good many baseball games there, and what they remember most is the weather, the wonderful warm evenings, sitting there at maybe 75, 80 degrees on a June evening, feeling in your face the same wind that carries the ball in from the track.

And yet, incongruously, it was the weather that they wanted to keep out. Sometimes people become so problem-oriented, so focused on the worst part of a thing, that they fail even to see that in shutting out the bad weather, they are also shutting out the good weather, and that there is at least as much good weather as bad. An odd psychological mechanism at work here, the perception of weather as inherently negative, something to be avoided.

Somehow, I always thought people moved to San Francisco because they *liked* the climate. Why don't the Giants try to deal with it—play more day games, put up wind breaks to cut the chill, sell large mugs of hot chocolate along with the cold beer? Why do they want to spend $100 million to play baseball in a warehouse?

3) Getting back to the first point, I think that many people fear that the stadiums are losing their individuality, becoming more and more alike. I understand that fear, and I don't want to see the stadiums all wind up looking alike, either. But I think it's a fault of perception; I don't really think that stadium architecture is collapsing toward a center. It is certainly true that the stadiums opened in the eight years 1966–1974 all look quite a bit alike; it is probably true that the stadiums built in any ten-year period have important similarities. If evolution in stadium design stopped at any moment, they would all bear the stamp of that moment.

But ask this question for yourself: Is the difference between all the stadiums less now than it was twenty years ago? I think there is far more variety in stadiums now than there was then. We still have a few of the gracious parks of the 1910–25 era, mixed in with quite a few postwar, "relocation era" parks, a couple of converted minor league facilities, more than enough sterile ashtrays; now we are past that era and building domes. Something can be said for domes: It's almost impossible to standardize their dimensions. But only if time stands still or if 26 stadiums are thrown up in a period of five years can we wind up with 26 identical parks. I don't think there's a tremendous danger of that.

Further, stadiums acquire an individuality more than they are built with it. When the stadiums of the 1966–74 era are redesigned a time or two to accommodate larger crowds, to provide better seating, to get rid of the turf and put in grass like the stadiums of the 1990s will have, or just to repair the ravages of time, then they'll stop looking alike. Neighborhoods and trees will grow up around them. So let's not just focus on the negatives of the new stadiums. For a baseball purist to focus on the negatives of modern stadiums and fail to see the positives is really no different than for the Giants to focus on the negatives of the weather, and fail to catch the scent of salt water in the breeze.

II. THE FUTURE OF CHILI DAVIS

Did you ever sit down with the records of a ballplayer and try to pencil in what the rest of his career is going to look like? After I got my computer last July I wasted about two weeks trying to put into it a set of formulas that would do that—that is, here's the first three years of Frank Robinson's career, computer, what is the rest of it going to look like? At the top of the next page is the way my formulas would answer that question (computer projection at left; Frank's real career record on the right).

It is tempting to call this a "computer projection" because it is done on a computer, but that's a misleading description. I made up all the rules that caused the career to project that way; I will have to change the rules to make it do any differently. The fascination with the "computer" part of it, as I explained in the comment across the bay, is a short-term thing that will pass out of your vocabulary three months after you buy a computer. I do confess, however, that it would be very difficult without a computer. (I suppose to some of you, this is beginning to sound like a "guns don't kill people, people kill people" argument. I'd say it's more on the level of "guns don't hold up liquor stores; people hold up liquor stores." It is very difficult for a computer to discharge acciden-

	G	AB	R	H	2B	3B	HR	RBI	BB	Avg
1956	152	572	122	166	27	6	38	83	64	.290
1957	150	611	97	197	29	5	29	75	44	.322
1958	148	554	90	149	25	6	31	83	62	.269
1959	156	604	109	186	29	6	34	105	59	.308
1960	156	588	111	181	29	6	37	107	66	.308
1961	156	590	102	162	25	5	33	95	66	.275
1962	156	583	111	174	27	5	41	107	65	.298
1963	151	563	112	176	28	5	44	111	63	.312
1964	150	553	100	159	25	4	37	97	62	.287
1965	148	543	92	145	23	4	33	88	61	.267
1966	145	529	93	153	24	3	33	91	59	.289
1967	143	518	94	158	24	3	33	93	58	.305
1968	141	507	76	124	19	2	25	72	57	.244
1969	104	372	59	100	15	2	20	57	42	.269
1970	94	334	57	101	15	2	19	57	37	.302
1971	110	387	59	103	16	2	19	57	43	.266
1972	100	349	52	93	14	1	17	51	39	.267
1973	98	341	48	85	13	1	15	46	38	.249
1974	75	258	40	73	11	1	12	39	29	.283
1975	66	227	29	52	8	1	8	28	25	.229
1976	39	132	18	33	5	0	5	17	15	.251
1977	14	49	6	12	2	0	2	6	5	.244
	2652	9765	1677	2782	433	72	565	1564	1058	.285

	G	AB	R	H	2B	3B	HR	RBI	BB	Avg
1956	152	572	122	166	27	6	38	83	64	.290
1957	150	611	97	197	29	5	29	75	44	.322
1958	148	554	90	149	25	6	31	83	62	.269
1959	146	540	106	168	31	4	36	125	69	.311
1960	139	464	86	138	33	6	31	83	82	.297
1961	153	545	117	176	32	7	37	124	71	.323
1962	162	609	134	208	51	2	39	136	76	.342
1963	140	482	79	125	19	3	21	91	81	.259
1964	156	568	103	174	38	6	29	96	79	.306
1965	156	582	109	172	33	5	33	113	70	.296
1966	155	576	122	182	34	2	49	122	87	.316
1967	129	479	83	149	23	7	30	94	71	.311
1968	130	421	69	113	27	1	15	52	73	.268
1969	148	539	111	166	19	5	32	100	88	.308
1970	132	471	88	144	24	1	25	78	69	.306
1971	133	455	82	128	16	2	28	99	72	.281
1972	103	342	41	86	6	1	19	59	55	.251
1973	147	534	85	142	29	0	30	97	82	.266
1974	144	477	81	117	27	3	22	68	85	.245
1975	49	118	19	28	5	0	9	24	29	.237
1976	36	67	5	15	0	0	3	10	11	.224
1977	0	0	0	0	0	0	0	0	0	0
	2808	10006	1829	2943	528	72	586	1812	1420	.294

tally and forecast with any accuracy how Darrell Evans is going to hit next year.)

Anyway, what the projection is is a mess of interlocking formulas, hundreds of them, that create a series of numbers that look something like a baseball player's record. The formulas are designed to increase a player's batting average irregularly until he is 27 years old and decrease it after that, to reduce his playing time gradually as he gets older and to decrease it sharply when he loses his effectiveness, and to adjust all of the other totals according to fixed rules. This is the career that these formulas project for Chili Davis:

Year	G	AB	R	H	2B	3B	HR	RBI	BB	Avg
1981	8	15	1	2	0	0	0	0	1	.133
1982	154	641	86	167	27	6	19	76	45	.261
1983	137	486	54	113	21	2	11	59	55	.233
1984	156	598	85	152	26	4	17	76	57	.254
1985	149	546	75	125	22	3	14	62	60	.229
1986	156	579	82	139	24	3	18	71	59	.240
1987	149	544	82	142	25	3	20	74	58	.261
1988	147	535	73	126	22	3	16	64	56	.235
1989	146	528	66	112	19	2	14	57	56	.212
1990	107	385	51	91	16	2	11	46	40	.236
1991	97	346	48	87	15	1	10	43	36	.251
1992	113	402	44	76	13	1	9	37	42	.189
1993	51	181	21	39	7	1	4	19	19	.216
1994	21	74	10	18	3	0	2	9	8	.243
1995	45	157	17	31	5	0	3	15	16	.198
1996	19	66	7	13	2	0	1	6	7	.198
16 yr	1656	6083	803	1433	246	31	169	715	615	.236

The formulas' view of Johnnie LeMaster is that he's not really good enough to be playing major league baseball, and thus that the rest of his career will look like this:

	G	AB	R	H	2B	3B	HR	RBI	BB	Avg
1984	30	107	13	25	3	0	1	10	10	.233
1985	49	181	24	46	6	0	2	18	20	.255
1986	36	128	14	26	3	0	1	10	13	.203
1987	9	34	4	7	1	0	0	3	4	.208
1988	8	27	3	7	1	0	0	3	3	.259
1989	8	30	3	6	1	0	0	3	3	.198
1990	2	7	1	2	0	0	0	1	1	.277

While the projected career totals for the other '83 Giant regulars look like this:

JACK CLARK

	G	AB	H	HR	RBI	Avg
Current record	987	3528	969	152	551	.275
Career totals	1726	6137	1608	242	883	.262

JEFF LEONARD

	G	AB	H	HR	RBI	Avg
Current record	504	1602	436	37	238	.272
Career totals	950	3196	835	88	439	.261

JOEL YOUNGBLOOD

	G	AB	H	HR	RBI	Avg
Current record	854	2444	662	55	279	.279
Career totals	1313	3721	993	94	445	.267

DARRELL EVANS

	G	AB	H	HR	RBI	Avg
Current record	1853	6348	1607	249	910	.253
Career totals	2487	8550	2155	354	1213	.252

Now then, does the system work?

Oh, hell no. I didn't say the formulas *worked*. Did anybody hear me say that these formulas worked? I said I had a lot of fun playing around with them, wasting time. Sometimes they work; a lot of times they don't.

They work well for Frank Robinson, for a couple reasons. For one thing, Frank's career was one of the ones I was using when I was trying to construct the model. More than that, predicting the career totals of great ballplayers is easy. If you start projecting the future of Robin Yount, you can safely figure that he's going to play regularly most of the time from now until he's 40, and he's not going to hit 11 home runs a year, and he's not going to hit 40 home runs a year, and he's not going to hit .260, and he's not going to hit .340. How far can you miss?

It's Chili Davis that's tough; it's Davis and Johnnie LeMaster and Jeff Leonard who are tough to project.

To give you an idea of what the accuracy of the projections are, I thought I'd give you the projections of the final career totals of the Giant regulars of 1963:

WILLIE McCOVEY

	G	AB	H	HR	RBI	Avg
Totals thru '63	502	1573	444	108	295	.282
Projected career	2106	6977	1889	528	1246	.271
Actual career	2588	8197	2211	521	1555	.270

Pretty good start, huh? Let's not get carried away;

ORLANDO CEPEDA

	G	AB	H	HR	RBI	Avg
Totals thru '63	900	3566	1105	191	650	.310
Projected career	2620	9969	3017	555	1722	.303
Actual career	2124	7927	2351	379	1365	.297

Didn't anticipate an injury or two, there. Chuck Hiller and Jose Pagan, the method prematurely retired:

CHUCK HILLER

	G	AB	H	HR	RBI	Avg
Totals thru '63	342	1259	316	11	93	.251
Projected career	370	1362	341	12	103	.250
Actual career	704	2121	516	20	152	.243

JOSE PAGAN

	G	AB	H	HR	RBI	Avg
Totals thru '63	495	1591	395	18	145	.248
Projected career	557	1800	441	20	164	.245
Actual career	1326	3689	922	52	372	.250

Which is probably what will happen to Johnnie LeMaster, too—the system's judgment of how long he will stay in the league is too harsh. It was a little hard on Felipe Alou:

FELIPE ALOU

	G	AB	H	HR	RBI	Avg
Totals thru '63	719	2292	631	85	325	.275
Projected career	1326	4437	1231	152	620	.277
Actual career	2082	7339	2101	206	852	.286

Just as it probably undercuts Jack Clark some. And Jim Davenport:

JIM DAVENPORT

	G	AB	H	HR	RBI	Avg
Totals thru '63	797	2647	704	54	276	.266
Projected career	1092	3573	944	66	381	.264
Actual career	1501	4427	1142	77	456	.258

On the other hand, it is far too optimistic about the remaining future of Ed Bailey:

ED BAILEY

	G	AB	H	HR	RBI	Avg
Totals thru '63	1022	3129	803	145	480	.257
Projected career	1834	5357	1345	268	792	.251
Actual career	1213	3584	915	155	540	.255

Just as it probably is now about Darrell Evans. It does a good job with Willie Mays:

WILLIE MAYS

	G	AB	H	HR	RBI	Avg
Totals thru '63	1691	6458	2033	406	1179	.315
Projected career	2997	11264	3483	678	2006	.309
Actual career	2992	10881	3283	660	1903	.302

At this time, the system is a little more than a formatted copy of my feeling about how players' careers change over time; it almost certainly is not as accurate in projecting actual careers as my own judgment would be, or your judgment would be. No superstitious respect should rightfully be attributed to the phrase "computer projection."

Why do it, then? Because formulas are much more capable of refinement and improvement than is human judgment. I have my judgment, you have yours, and the people of the last generation had theirs, which was probably just as good. Science always begins at a point of knowledge which is below the level of common understanding; when Newton got up and pointed at the apple tree and said, "Ahah, that thing fell down" this was not a revelation to the passing tradesman.

When we project future careers by formulas, we can step back in history and see what has to be done to make them more accurate. We can say, "Well, if I increase this factor by .003, does that make the projections more accurate or less accurate?" If the formulas overreact to a bad year or a good year (and they do, as of now), we can find that out and adjust it. If the projections are too conservative for light hitting middle infielders, we can change that. In the process, we can learn a lot about what it takes to stay in the major leagues, a lot about how careers change over time. There is no expectation that we will ever be able to make a full accounting of the differences among individuals.

But don't take this thing too seriously. It's just the first step up a long, dark stairway.

Darrell EVANS, First Base
Runs Created: 104

	G	AB	Hit	2B	3B	HR	Run	RBI	BB	SO	SB	CS	Avg
11.44 Years		555	140	22	3	23	84	80	99	81	8	4	.253
1983	142	523	145	29	3	30	94	82	84	80	6	6	.277
First Half		281	82	14	1	19	56	49	45	35	5	1	.292
Second Half		242	3	15	2	11	38	33	39	45	1	5	.250
vs. RHP		357	107	23	2	24		64	69	47			.300
vs. LHP		166	38	6	1	6		18	15	38			.229
Home		254	65	11	2	16	49	41	42	37	4	2	.256
Road		269	80	18	1	14	45	41	42	48	2	4	.297
Grass		394	108	17	2	24	68	65	59	56	5	4	.274
Turf		129	37	12	1	6	26	17	25	24	1	2	.287

Chili DAVIS, Centerfield
Runs Created: 52

	G	AB	Hit	2B	3B	HR	Run	RBI	BB	SO	SB	CS	Avg
1.85 Years		619	153	26	4	16	76	73	55	122	20	14	.247
1983		486	113	21	2	11	54	59	55	108	10	12	.233
First Half		243	54	10	1	9	25	32	31	58	7	6	.222
Second Half		243	59	11	1	2	27	27	24	50	3	5	.243
vs. RHP		327	79	13	0	4		32	41	71			.242
vs. LHP		159	34	8	2	7		27	14	37			.214
Home		256	60	8	2	7	30	32	31	57	7	6	.234
Road		230	53	13	0	4	22	27	24	51	3	5	.230
Grass		349	86	14	2	11	40	46	39	79	3	9	.246
Turf		137	27	7	0	0	12	13	16	29	2	2	.197

Brad WELLMAN, Second Base
Runs Created: 14

	G	AB	Hit	2B	3B	HR	Run	RBI	BB	SO	SB	CS	Avg
.54 Years		342	74	6	0	2	29	29	41	74	9	6	.215
1983	82	182	39	3	0	1	15	16	22	39	5	3	.214
First Half		102	23	2	0	1	9	9	13	18	5	1	.225
Second Half		80	16	1	0	0	5	7	9	21	0	2	.200
vs. RHP		103	21	2	0	1		9	12	21			.204
vs. LHP		79	18	1	0	0		7	10	18			.228
Home		107	20	0	0	1	10	12	12	21	4	2	.187
Road		75	19	3	0	0	4	4	10	18	1	1	.253
Grass		143	31	1	0	1	12	14	16	31	5	2	.217
Turf		39	8	2	0	0	2	2	6	8	0	1	.205

Jack CLARK, Rightfield
Runs Created: 80

	G	AB	Hit	2B	3B	HR	Run	RBI	BB	SO	SB	CS	Avg
6.09 Years		579	159	31	5	25	93	90	75	88	10	7	.275
1983	135	492	132	25	0	20	82	66	74	79	5	3	.268
First Half	282	282	73	14	0	13	43	40	44	50	2	3	.259
Second Half		211	59	11	0	7	40	27	30	30	3	2	.280
vs. RHP		351	94	18	0	12		48	49	62			.268
vs. LHP		142	38	7	0	8		19	25	18			.268
Home		250	65	15	0	11	41	39	40	37	4	1	.260
Road		243	67	10	0	9	42	28	34	43	1	2	.276
Grass		375	101	19	0	17	62	49	56	59	4	2	.269
Turf		118	31	6	0	3	21	18	18	21	1	1	.263

Tom O'MALLEY, Third Base
Runs Created: 45

	G	AB	Hit	2B	3B	HR	Run	RBI	BB	SO	SB	CS	Avg
1.40 Years		500	133	20	4	5	47	51	61	61	1	5	.265
1983	135	410	106	16	1	5	40	45	52	47	2	4	.259
First Half		230	63	11	0	3	23	19	24	25	2	3	.274
Second Half		180	43	5	1	2	20	26	28	22	1	1	.239
vs. RHP		302	78	12	1	4		35	41	34			.258
vs. LHP		108	28	4	0	1		10	11	13			.259
Home		198	54	8	0	3	23	19	31	23	1	2	.273
Road		212	52	8	1	2	20	26	21	24	2	2	.245
Grass		294	76	10	0	4	30	28	42	34	3	3	.259
Turf		116	30	6	1	1	13	17	10	13	0	1	.259

Bob BRENLY, Catcher
Runs Created: 30

	G	AB	Hit	2B	3B	HR	Run	RBI	BB	SO	SB	CS	Avg
1.16 Years		436	111	16	3	10	58	46	53	67	14	9	.255
1983	104	281	63	12	2	7	36	34	37	48	10	7	.224
First Half		139	26	5	2	4	15	15	18	25	2	1	.187
Second Half		142	37	7	0	3	21	19	19	23	7	5	.261
vs. RHP		143	36	8	1	2		16	25	23			.252
vs. LHP		138	27	4	1	5		18	12	25			.196
Home		131	26	5	1	5	19	21	15	22	1	2	.198
Road		150	37	7	1	2	17	13	22	26	8	4	.247
Grass		196	44	5	1	6	26	26	23	31	6	3	.224
Turf		85	19	7	1	1	10	8	14	17	3	3	.224

Johnnie LeMASTER, Shortstop
Runs Created: 57

	G	AB	Hit	2B	3B	HR	Run	RBI	BB	SO	SB	CS	Avg
4.58 Years		572	130	21	4	4	58	41	48	96	17	10	.228
1983	141	534	128	16	1	6	81	30	59	96	39	19	.240
First Half		272	70	10	1	4	43	19	42	42	27	8	.257
Second Half		262	58	6	0	2	39	11	17	54	12	11	.221
vs. RHP		369	86	9	1	4		22	36	66			.233
vs. LHP		165	42	7	0	2		8	23	30			.255
Home		264	66	8	0	4	48	15	35	43	20	8	.250
Road		270	62	8	1	2	34	15	24	53	19	11	.230
Grass		407	102	12	0	6	69	24	46	70	31	14	.251
Turf		127	26	4	1	0	13	6	13	26	8	5	.205

Joel YOUNGBLOOD, Utility
Runs Created: 64

	G	AB	Hit	2B	3B	HR	Run	RBI	BB	SO	SB	CS	Avg
5.27 Years		464	126	25	4	10	62	53	39	72	10	8	.271
1983	124	373	109	20	3	17	59	53	33	59	7	4	.292
First Half		133	33	3	1	8	19	16	7	25	2	0	.248
Second Half		240	76	17	2	9	40	37	26	34	5	4	.317
vs. RHP		229	61	11	2	9		28	17	33			.256
vs. LHP		144	48	9	1	8		25	16	26			.333
Home		177	54	10	1	6	27	23	22	26	7	2	.305
Road		196	55	10	2	11	32	30	11	33	0	2	.281
Grass		277	81	16	2	14	48	41	29	46	7	4	.292
Turf		96	28	4	1	3	11	12	4	13	0	0	.292

Jeff LEONARD, Leftfield
Runs Created: 77

	G	AB	Hit	2B	3B	HR	Run	RBI	BB	SO	SB	CS	Avg
3.11 Years		515	140	22	7	12	66	77	45	105	24	8	.272
1983	139	516	144	17	7	21	74	87	35	116	26	7	.279
First Half		234	65	10	2	7	34	32	17	48	12	5	.278
Second Half		282	79	7	5	14	39	55	18	68	14	2	.280
vs. RHP		355	92	12	7	10		57	21	87			.259
vs. LHP		161	52	5	0	11		30	14	29			.323
Home		261	69	12	2	9	39	41	21	67	16	3	.264
Road		255	75	5	5	12	34	46	14	49	10	4	.294
Grass		394	107	13	3	17	58	63	26	93	20	4	.272
Turf		122	37	4	4	4	15	24	9	23	6	3	.303

Max VENABLE, Outfield
Runs Created: 27

	G	AB	Hit	2B	3B	HR	Run	RBI	BB	SO	SB	CS	Avg
1.86 Years		326	72	8	4	4	39	26	31	50	20	6	.222
1983	94	228	50	7	4	6	28	27	22	34	15	2	.220
First Half		116	23	4	2	4	14	18	8	13	6	2	.198
Second Half		111	27	3	2	2	12	8	14	21	9	0	.243
vs. RHP		200	47	7	4	6		25	20	29			.235
vs. LHP		27	3	0	0	0		1	2	5			.111
Home		82	23	3	1	3	9	10	8	11	6	1	.280
Road		145	27	4	3	3	17	16	14	23	9	1	.186
Grass		160	39	4	1	6	18	21	12	24	12	2	.244
Turf		67	11	3	3	0	5	5	10	10	3	0	.164

Fred BREINING

Year	(W–L)	GS	Run	Avg	DP	Avg	SB	Avg
1982	(11- 6)	9	40	4.44	5	.56	5	.56
1983	(11-12)	32	139	4.34	17	.53	27	.84
1982-1983		42	183	4.36	23	.55	34	.81

	G	IP	W	L	Pct	ER	ERA
1983 Home	17	116.2	6	7	.462	40	3.09
1983 Road	15	86	5	5	.500	46	4.81
1983 Grass	23	154	9	7	.563	55	3.21
1983 Turf	9	48.2	2	5	.286	31	5.73

Mike KRUKOW

Year	(W–L)	GS	Run	Avg	DP	Avg	SB	Avg
1982	(13-11)	33	136	4.12	29	.88	38	1.14
1983	(11-11)	31	147	4.74	11	.35	37	1.19
1982-1983		204	883	4.33	169	.83	232	1.14

	G	IP	W	L	Pct	ER	ERA
1982 Home	15	92.1	6	7	.462	34	3.31
1983 Home	15	91.1	7	3	.700	35	3.45
1982 Road	18	115.2	7	4	.636	38	2.96
1983 Road	16	93	4	8	.333	46	4.45
1983 Grass	21	127.1	8	5	.615	50	3.53
1983 Turf	10	57	3	6	.333	31	4.90

Bill LASKEY

Year	(W–L)	GS	Run	Avg	DP	Avg	SB	Avg
1982	(13-12)	31	134	4.32	23	.74	32	1.03
1983	(13-10)	25	109	4.36	20	.80	27	1.08
1982-1983		56	243	4.34	43	.77	59	1.05

	G	IP	W	L	Pct	ER	ERA
1982 Home	18	110.2	5	8	.385	38	3.09
1983 Home	15	98.1	8	6	.571	38	3.48
1982 Road	14	78.2	8	4	.667	29	3.20
1983 Road	10	50	5	4	.556	31	5.58
1983 Grass	21	129	10	10	.500	61	4.26
1983 Turf	4	19.1	3	0	1.000	8	3.72

Atlee HAMMAKER

Year	(W–L)	GS	Run	Avg	DP	Avg	SB	Avg
1982	(12-8)	27	105	3.89	19	.70	33	1.22
1983	(10-9)	23	81	3.52	20	.87	14	.61
1981-1983		56	209	3.75	45	.80	52	.93

	G	IP	W	L	Pct	ER	ERA
1982 Home	15	94.1	8	3	.727	41	3.91
1983 Home	11	81.2	6	2	.750	14	1.54
1982 Road	14	80.2	4	5	.444	39	4.35
1983 Road	12	90.2	4	7	.364	29	2.88
1983 Grass	18	136.1	9	6	.600	33	2.18
1983 Turf	5	36	1	3	.250	10	2.50

Mark DAVIS

Year	(W–L)	GS	Run	Avg	DP	Avg	SB	Avg
1983	(6-4)	20	100	5.00	19	.95	10	.50
1981-1983		29	134	5.62	21	.72	22	.76

	G	IP	W	L	Pct	ER	ERA
1983 Home	10	57.2	2	3	.400	24	3.75
1983 Road	10	52.1	4	1	.800	19	3.27
1983 Grass	15	85.1	4	4	.500	35	3.69
1983 Turf	5	25.2	2	0	1.000	8	2.81

1983 OTHERS

Pitcher	(W–L)	GS	Run	Avg	DP	Avg	SB	Avg
McGaffigan	(3-9)	16	48	3.00	9	.56	19	1.19
Martin	(2-4)	6	26	4.33	6	1.00	16	2.67
Garrelts	(2-2)	5	13	2.60	5	1.00	10	2.00
Calvert	(1-4)	4	24	6.00	3	.75	2	.50

SAN FRANCISCO GIANTS
RUNS BATTED IN ANALYSIS

Player	RBI	RBI In Wins	Victory Important RBI	RBI Importance	Wins Batted In	RBI Per Win
Darrell Evans	82	58	38.61	.471	9.76	8.4
Jeff Leonard	87	55	35.24	.405	10.56	8.2
Jack Clark	66	46	28.22	.428	8.89	7.4
Chili Davis	59	35	23.60	.400	6.38	9.2
Joel Youngblood	53	34	19.93	.338	5.16	10.3
Tom O'Malley	45	29	17.90	.398	4.65	9.7
Bob Brenly	34	20	14.20	.418	3.93	8.7
Max Venable	27	18	12.75	.472	2.98	9.1
Johnny LeMaster	30	17	11.64	.388	2.57	11.7
Brad Wellman	16	6	3.93	.246	1.26	12.7

CINCINNATI REDS

I. AND THAT MEANS *EVERYBODY*

The Cincinnati Reds now allow their minor league teams to employ the designated hitter. They have signed their first large free agent. They appear, in brief, to have abandoned all hope that Dick Wagner's adolescence will return, and have committed themselves to living in a world not of their own construction. Since the Reds are so conscious of symbols, so determined to maintain intact the integrity of their fifties image that they would rip the organization to shreds fighting internal battles over beards, shoes, stocking stirrups and other details of proper 1956 fashion and attire, we here have been wondering how they could mark the transition forward in time with appropriate symbolic gestures. If you raise the fashions of 1984 to the level of a moral imperative, what do you get?

1) Any player reporting for a team flight without properly coiffed and styled hair will not be allowed to make the trip. A list of approved hair-fashion consultants will be maintained on a bulletin board in the clubhouse.

2) The wearing of earrings is an absoute must. $50 fine for any player appearing before the public without his earrings.

3) If glasses are to be worn, they must be those ones that turn brown when you go out in the sun. This is a major league organization.

4) Proper on-field foot attire means either designer shoes, or else some kind of shoe with the name printed on it large enough to be read from the third deck. For travel and other team events, only Thom McAnn's can be considered appropriate.

5) The uniform that is issued to you will include chains; you have your choice of a crucifix or a little gold spoon, or you may wear both if you prefer. Contact the equipment manager *immediately* if your chain is misplaced. (These chains do not need to be removed during showering or other intimate times.)

6) If the temperature drops below 60 during the game, you will be allowed to button the top two buttons on your shirt.

7) Computer classes are available; the club will assist you in selecting one that fits your needs. Contact Jamie Lynn for details.

8) Wives are cordially invited to join us each morning for our special *Cincinnati Reds aerobic workout*. Selected wives might become eleigible for valuable bonuses for cooperating in our community-wide aerobic program.

—Jim Baker and
Bill James

II.

Here's a Baseball Abstract Kwik-Kwiz: What does the following line of data represent?

AB	R	H	2B	3B	HR	RBI	Ave.
612	63	140	23	2	6	69	.229

Is it:

a) Horace Clarke's best season.
b) Totals for the Minnesota Twins' eighth-place hitters.
c) The Seattle Mariners' shortstop totals.
d) Stats for the best player on the 1899 Cleveland Spiders.
e) None of the above.

The answer is "e," none of the above. The line of data is the totals for all Reds *third*-place hitters for 1983. I swear it.
Scary, huh?

—Jim Baker

III. THE RETURN OF VERNON (HIGHWAY) RAPP

Among many baseball people, the name of Vernon Rapp had come to stand for "minor league manager," for the total experience of failure as a manager by one so dedicated to The Dream that he would pay for it in decades. I know a man who works in the front office of a National League team which recently interviewed a group of potential managers. A leading candidate came in and gave one of the ringing My-way-or-the-highway speeches, making a great impression on the owner and sending a chill down the spine of everyone else. "He really scared me," the guy said, "I thought we had another Vern Rapp situation on our hands." A couple of years ago I asked a player whether a coach who had been with the team the year before had potential as a major league manager. "He's got potential as a Vern Rapp," he sneered.

The return of Rapp to a major league dugout, then, was a bit of a shock, and was greeted with predictable derisive chatter from the nation's pressboxes. It was, so they said, a sign that nothing had really changed except the name plate on the GM's desk. Let's deal with the Rapp decision on two levels, first as to what it says about the organizaton, and second as to Rapp himself.

I beg to differ. It is certainly true that Bob Howsam has a taste for strict "disciplinarian" managers; he always has had. But that was not the defining characteristic of the Reds' organization under Dick Wagner. The defining characteristic of the Reds' organization under Dick Wagner was inflexibility. The fact that this rigidity was allied to old-line "disciplinarian" policies is certainly not incidental, but my point is that there have been any number of successful hard-line managers and organizations. If you keep the hard-line policies but get rid of the inflexibility, then you are dealing with a totally different situation.

When Dick Wagner made a decision, he wrote it down and closed the book. Wagner was concerned not with whether a decision was "working" or was "not working," but with whether it was "right" or "wrong." And if he made a decision, then it was therefore the right decision, and he was *not* going to review it. When the policy was adopted that the Reds would not use the designated hitter in the minor leagues, that was a reasonable decision. But what happened was, the costs of the decision escalated and escalated and escalated, while the policy was yielding returns that were not even visible; no one could see that the Reds' hitters were hitting any better than anybody else's were. But Wagner refused to review the decision; it was the right decision, and therefore whether its benefits outweighed its costs was not a matter for discussion. To refuse to meet the salary expectations of established ballplayers was a right decision; whether or not it ruined the ballclub was not important. The decision was made that Dan Driessen was going to play first base for the Reds, and Johnny Bench was going to catch—a reasonable decision at the time. But when Driessen didn't develop and Bench didn't want to catch, he wouldn't adjust; he would not review the decision.

Wagner could not understand that the contexts in which decisions were made was changing, and that therefore there was a need to review those decisions. He was concerned not with what came out of a decision, but with what went into it.

There is a word for people who think this way. It's a common word, something you always have on your person. Dick Wagner was like a man driving down a road who is stopped and informed that a section of the bridge over the river has collapsed, and who responds to this by saying, "Goddammit, the county is supposed to maintain that bridge. I pay taxes, I've been driving over that bridge for 30 years, and I feel that I have a right to drive over that bridge." And so he does.

So the relevant question about Bob Howsam is not whether he too drives on that road, or whether he too pays taxes, or whether he too expects the county to maintain the bridges. The relevant question is whether or not he is flexible enough to choose an alternate route when a bridge goes out. Which, as he has demonstrated consistently throughout his long and distinguished career, he is.

Second point. I see no reason to expect here a repeat of the Rapp fiasco in St. Louis. Very few of the critical factors which created that mess are present here.

a) *Rapp now has major league exposure.*

Rapp was hired to manage a major league team without having spent any time on a major league roster, either as a player or a coach. That, to me, was a serious error. He had all of these ideas about how he was going to do this and how he wanted to do that and how that ought to be done and by whom, but he had no real idea of how things *were* done at the major league level. He didn't know which of his ideas were realistic and which were not. He had no way of gauging how much resistance any proposal would meet with, no way of knowing what the costs would be. He just was not ready for the job; he needed to spend a couple of years on the scene watching. He has done that now.

b) *Ted Simmons is not on this ballclub.*

We now are in a position to understand about the St.

Louis situation something which at that time he had no way of knowing: Rapp was dealing with a deadly collection of talent. Since then, three other managers (Ken Boyer, Whitey Herzog and Bob Rodgers) have found out that Ted Simmons is not exactly Eddie Murray, a keep-your-mouth-shut-and-do-your-job kind of a guy. He had Garry Templeton on that ballclub, he had Hrabosky; he had John Denny and Joel Youngblood before the Lord took an interest in them. Certainly Rapp made some mistakes, but it was not all his fault.

c) *Look at the record.*

Despite all of the squabbling, the Cardinals won eleven more games for Vern Rapp in 1977 than they did for Red Schoendienst the year before, and 14 more than they did for Ken Boyer the year after.

d) *The personnel is different.*

The Cardinals had on their team a number of established ballplayers who responded to Ted Simmons' leadership and resisted anyone else's attempt to take control of the club. The Reds are mostly a bunch of kids, a year or two out of the minors and (hopefully) looking for leadership. The only star of any magnitude is Mario Soto, a decent and coachable gentleman whose major interest is winning ballgames.

So speaking just for myself, I am glad to see Vern Rapp get a second chance to manage in the major leagues. I think he's worked hard for that chance, and he deserves it. I trust Bob Howsam's judgment. The Reds, like the Padres, are a long way from being on an equal footing with the Braves or the Dodgers. But they're about five years closer than they were in the middle of last summer.

CINCINNATI REDS

	Record in the Lineup	Record Without
Ron Oester	70-82	4- 6
Dave Concepcion	61-76	13-12
Eddie Milner	59-70	15-18
Gary Redus	56-62	18-26
Dan Driessen	53-57	21-31
Paul Householder	44-51	30-37
Dann Bilardello	43-47	31-41
Nick Esasky	39-44	35-44
Cesar Cedeno	37-48	37-40
Johnny Bench	29-44	45-44
Alex Trevino	24-29	50-59
Duane Walker	16-31	58-57
Kelly Paris	13-16	61-72
Tom Foley	12-12	62-76
Alan Knicely	10-13	64-75
Wayne Krenchicki	9- 8	65-80
Jeff Jones	8- 5	66-83
Bill Barnes	5- 3	69-85
Dallas Williams	4- 3	70-85
Steve Christmas	0- 4	74-84

Dan DRIESSEN, First Base
Runs Created: 66

	G	AB	Hit	2B	3B	HR	Run	RBI	BB	SO	SB	CS	Avg
8.64 Years		521	141	26	3	15	73	74	74	71	17	7	.270
1983	122	386	107	17	1	12	57	57	75	51	6	4	.277
First Half	48	148	39	2	0	5	23	24			3		.264
Second Half	74	238	68	15	1	7	34	33			3		.286
vs. RHP		312	93	16	0	10		49					.298
vs. LHP		74	14	1	1	2		8					.189
Home	62	185	51	8	1	3	25	23			3		.276
Road	60	201	56	9	0	9	32	34			3		.279
Grass	32	105	31	4	0	4	16	22			2		.295
Turf	90	281	76	13	1	8	41	35			4		.270

Eddie MILNER, Centerfield
Runs Created: 67

	G	AB	Hit	2B	3B	HR	Run	RBI	BB	SO	SB	CS	Avg
1.69 Years		544	115	79	18	8	48	39	65	60	35	14	.210
1983	146	502	131	23	6	9	77	33	68	60	41	12	.261
First Half	78	268	64	14	1	3	34	18			17		.239
Second Half	68	234	67	9	5	6	43	15			24		.286
vs. RHP		408	116	18	6	8		26					.284
vs. LHP		94	15	5	0	1		7					.160
Home	73	254	68	15	4	3	39	14			25		.268
Road	73	248	63	8	2	6	38	19			16		.254
Grass	44	153	41	5	2	3	26	11			9		.268
Turf	102	349	90	18	4	6	51	22			32		.258

Ron OESTER, Second Base
Runs Created: 66

	G	AB	Hit	2B	3B	HR	Run	RBI	BB	SO	SB	CS	Avg
3.24 Years		545	145	23	6	8	65	52	47	88	5	5	.267
1983	157	549	145	23	5	11	63	58	49	106	2	2	.264
First Half	80	294	85	12	4	6	32	30			1		.289
Second Half	77	255	60	11	1	5	31	28			1		.235
vs. RHP		406	111	19	4	10		45					.273
vs. LHP		143	34	4	1	1		13					.238
Home	80	272	80	17	4	6	39	31			0		.294
Road	77	277	65	6	1	5	24	27			2		.235
Grass	46	169	45	3	0	4	12	20			1		.266
Turf	111	380	100	20	5	7	51	38			1		.263

Paul HOUSEHOLDER, Rightfield
Runs Created: 48

	G	AB	Hit	2B	3B	HR	Run	RBI	BB	SO	SB	CS	Avg
1.88 Years		485	115	21	5	9	51	50	45	88	18	13	.236
1983	123	380	97	24	4	6	40	43	44	60	12	12	.255
First Half	54	168	46	6	3	3	13	19			3		.274
Second Half	69	212	51	18	1	3	27	24			9		.241
vs. RHP		249	62	13	3	4		26					.249
vs. LHP		131	35	11	1	2		17					.267
Home	60	182	49	11	3	5	21	22			5		.269
Road	63	198	48	13	1	1	19	21			7		.242
Grass	38	124	31	7	1	1	13	13			4		.250
Turf	85	256	66	17	3	5	27	30			8		.258

Nick ESASKY, Third Base
Runs Created: 46

	G	AB	Hit	2B	3B	HR	Run	RBI	BB	SO	SB	CS	Avg
.52 Years		576	152	19	10	23	78	88	51	189	11	4	.265
1983	85	302	80	10	5	12	41	46	27	99	6	2	.265
First Half	16	58	19	3	1	3	11	9			2		.328
Second Half	69	244	61	7	4	9	30	37			4		.250
vs. RHP		231	54	7	2	10		35					.234
vs. LHP		71	26	3	3	2		11					.366
Home	42	140	32	4	2	6	22	18			2		.229
Road	43	162	48	6	3	6	19	28			4		.296
Grass	28	111	33	4	1	4	13	19			2		.297
Turf	57	191	47	6	4	8	28	27			4		.246

Dann BILARDELLO, Catcher
Runs Created: 30

	G	AB	Hit	2B	3B	HR	Run	RBI	BB	SO	SB	CS	Avg
.67 Years		443	106	27	0	13	40	56	22	73	3	1	.238
1983	109	298	71	18	0	9	27	38	15	49	2	1	.238
First Half	52	144	32	11	0	2	14	11			1		.222
Second Half	57	154	39	7	0	7	13	27			1		.253
vs. RHP		205	46	12	0	7		27					.224
vs. LHP		93	25	6	0	2		11					.269
Home	61	164	40	12	0	7	15	26			2		.244
Road	48	134	31	6	0	2	12	12			0		.231
Grass	31	86	20	3	0	2	7	8			0		.233
Turf	78	212	51	15	0	7	20	30			2		.241

Dave CONCEPCION, Shortstop
Runs Created: 43

	G	AB	Hit	2B	3B	HR	Run	RBI	BB	SO	SB	CS	Avg
11.73 Years		583	157	26	4	7	68	66	48	82	22	7	.269
1983	143	528	123	22	0	1	54	47	56	81	14	9	.233
First Half	74	275	61	12	0	1	29	24			7		.222
Second Half	69	253	62	10	0	0	25	23			7		.245
vs. RHP		394	91	14	0	0		31					.231
vs. LHP		134	32	8	0	1		16					.239
Home	74	269	66	12	0	0	29	31			12		.245
Road	69	259	57	10	0	1	25	16			2		.220
Grass	42	159	37	5	0	1	16	10			2		.233
Turf	101	369	86	17	0	0	38	37			12		.233

Cesar CEDENO, Outfield
Runs Created: 38

	G	AB	Hit	2B	3B	HR	Run	RBI	BB	SO	SB	CS	Avg
10.79 Years		608	174	37	5	17	91	64	56	77	48	16	.286
1983	98	332	77	16	0	9	40	39	33	53	13	9	.232
First Half	50	177	41	9	0	4	20	20			5		.232
Second Half	48	155	36	7	0	5	20	19			8		.232
vs. RHP		230	53	11	0	4		27					.230
vs. LHP		102	24	5	0	5		12					.235
Home	46	151	37	9	0	7	19	23			7		.245
Road	52	181	40	7	0	2	21	16			6		.221
Grass	31	112	24	3	0	1	13	9			1		.214
Turf	67	220	53	13	0	8	27	30			12		.241

Gary REDUS, Leftfield
Runs Created: 76

	G	AB	Hit	2B	3B	HR	Run	RBI	BB	SO	SB	CS	Avg
.90 Years		599	145	26	12	20	114	65	85	147	56	18	.243
1983	125	453	112	20	9	17	90	51	71	111	39	14	.247
First Half	60	223	56	9	3	13	48	29			23		.251
Second Half	65	230	56	11	6	4	42	22			16		.243
vs. RHP		324	75	12	6	14		37					.231
vs. LHP		129	37	8	3	3		14					.287
Home	69	249	56	12	5	7	51	29			20		.225
Road	56	204	56	8	4	10	39	22			19		.275
Grass	37	133	33	5	2	5	26	14			13		.248
Turf	88	320	79	15	7	12	64	37			26		.247

Johnny BENCH, Infield
Runs Created: 37

	G	AB	Hit	2B	3B	HR	Run	RBI	BB	SO	SB	CS	Avg
13.32 Year		575	154	29	2	29	82	103	67	96	5	3	.267
1983	110	310	79	15	2	12	32	54	24	38	0	1	.255
First Half	67	243	61	14	1	7	25	35			0		.251
Second Half	43	67	18	1	1	5	7	19			0		.269
vs. RHP		205	46	12	0	7		27					.224
vs. LHP		105	33	3	2	5		27					.314
Home	58	170	43	10	0	5	16	30			0		.253
Road	52	140	36	5	2	7	16	24			0		.257
Grass	31	80	15	1	1	2	5	8			0		.188
Turf	79	230	64	14	1	10	27	46			0		.278

Mario SOTO

Year	(W–L)	GS	Run	Avg	DP	Avg	SB	Avg
1982	(14-13)	34	130	3.82	20	.59	27	.79
1983	(17-13)	34	122	3.59	17	.50	26	.76
1977-1983		116	456	3.93	71	.61	106	.91

	G	IP	W	L	Pct	ER	ERA
1982 Home	17	137	9	5	.643	41	2.69
1983 Home	17	138	9	6	.600	41	2.67
1982 Road	17	120.2	5	8	.385	39	2.91
1983 Road	17	135.2	8	7	.533	41	2.72
1983 Grass	10	78	3	5	.375	25	2.89
1983 Turf	24	195.2	14	8	.636	57	2.62

Charlie PULEO

Year	(W–L)	GS	Run	Avg	DP	Avg	SB	Avg
1982	(9- 9)	24	101	4.21	22	.92	32	1.33
1983	(6-12)	24	94	3.92	22	.92	35	1.46
1981-1983		49	197	4.02	45	.92	69	1.41

	G	IP	W	L	Pct	ER	ERA
1982 Home	19	94	7	4	.636	40	3.83
1983 Home	14	79.1	5	5	.500	39	4.42
1982 Road	17	77	2	5	.286	45	5.26
1983 Road	13	64.1	1	7	.125	39	5.46
1983 Grass	9	44	0	6	.000	29	5.93
1983 Turf	18	99.2	6	6	.500	49	4.42

Bruce BERENYI

Year	(W–L)	GS	Run	Avg	DP	Avg	SB	Avg
1982	(9-18)	34	88	2.59	39	1.15	45	1.32
1983	(9-14)	31	132	4.26	30	.97	26	.84
1980-1983		91	340	3.74	94	1.03	110	1.21

	G	IP	W	L	Pct	ER	ERA
1982 Home	17	119.2	4	10	.286	45	3.38
1983 Home	18	114.2	7	7	.500	48	3.78
1982 Road	17	102.2	5	8	.385	38	3.33
1983 Road	14	71.2	2	7	.222	32	4.02
1983 Grass	7	35.1	2	2	.500	17	4.33
1983 Turf	25	151	7	12	.368	63	3.75

Joe PRICE

Year	(W–L)	GS	Run	Avg	DP	Avg	SB	Avg
1982	(3-4)	1	4	4.00	0	.00	0	.00
1983	(10-6)	21	60	2.90	12	.57	16	.76
1980-1983		35	119	3.40	27	.77	27	.77

	G	IP	W	L	Pct	ER	ERA
1983 Home	11	82	5	4	.556	26	2.85
1983 Road	10	62	5	2	.714	20	2.90
1983 Grass	5	32	3	1	.750	8	2.25
1983 Turf	16	112	7	5	.583	38	3.05

Frank PASTORE

Year	(W–L)	GS	Run	Avg	DP	Avg	SB	Avg
1982	(8-13)	29	114	3.93	31	1.07	25	.86
1983	(9-12)	29	129	4.45	25	.86	18	.62
1979-1983		116	494	4.26	102	.88	91	.78

	G	IP	W	L	Pct	ER	ERA
1982 Home	16	115.1	5	7	.417	44	3.43
1983 Home	17	81	3	5	.375	48	5.33
1982 Road	13	73	3	6	.333	39	4.81
1983 Road	19	103.1	6	7	.462	52	4.53
1983 Grass	13	68	3	5	.375	34	4.50
1983 Turf	23	116.1	6	7	.462	66	5.11

1983 OTHERS

Pitcher	(W–L)	GS	Run	Avg	DP	Avg	SB	Avg
Russell	(4-5)	10	37	3.70	6	.60	7	.70
Gale	(4-6)	7	29	4.14	6	.86	3	.43
Power	(5-6)	6	20	3.33	3	.50	5	.83

CINCINNATI REDS
RUNS BATTED IN ANALYSIS

Player	RBI	RBI In Wins	Victory Important RBI	RBI Importance	Wins Batted In	RBI Per Win
Gary Redus	51	40	27.65	.542	7.51	6.8
Ron Oester	57	34	25.17	.442	6.65	8.6
Dan Driessen	58	36	23.27	.408	6.98	8.3
Dave Concepcion	47	31	22.46	.478	6.11	7.7
Johnny Bench	54	28	19.89	.368	5.31	10.2
Nick Esasky	46	30	19.26	.419	6.24	7.4
Dann Bilardello	38	32	18.11	.477	6.56	5.7
Paul Householder	43	27	17.21	.400	4.65	10.1
Eddie Milner	33	22	12.00	.364	3.97	8.3
Cesar Cedeno	39	18	11.81	.328	3.31	11.8

AMERICAN LEAGUE EAST
DIVISION SHEET

Chart I

	1st	2nd	VS. RHP	VS. LHP	HOME	ROAD	GRASS	TURF	DAY	NIGHT	TOTAL	PCT.
Baltimore	42-34	56-30	73-45	25-19	50-31	48-33	82-56	16-8	30-19	68-45	98-64	.605
Detroit	41-35	51-35	69-52	23-18	48-33	44-37	79-58	13-12	23-27	64-43	92-70	.568
New York	41-35	50-36	54-38	37-34	51-30	40-41	79-59	12-12	26-15	65-56	91-71	.562
Toronto	43-33	46-40	59-42	30-31	48-33	41-40	30-33	59-40	35-23	54-50	89-73	.549
Milwaukee	38-37	51-38	60-42	27-33	52-29	35-46	76-71	11-14	32-19	55-56	87-75	.537
Boston	39-38	39-46	46-65	32-19	38-43	40-41	66-71	12-13	23-32	55-52	78-84	.481
Cleveland	34-44	36-48	51-65	19-27	36-45	34-47	58-80	12-12	21-30	49-62	70-92	.432

Chart II
COME FROM BEHIND WINS

Team	1	2	3	4	5	6	7	8	Total	Points
Baltimore	21	8	3	2	1	0	1	1	37	111
Detroit	18	18	4	1	0	0	1		42	119
Milwaukee	12	13	4	2	1	0	1		33	103
Toronto	26	10	3	4	2	2			47	140
New York	21	9	5						35	89
Boston	15	11	6	1	0	1			34	99
Cleveland	11	9	5	1					26	74

BLOWN LEADS

Team	1	2	3	4	5	6	7	8	Total	Points
Baltimore	14	9	4						27	71
Detroit	15	6	7	2	1				31	92
Milwaukee	18	10	8	1	0	0	1	1	39	120
Toronto	14	10	7						31	86
New York	21	8	2	4	0	1			36	101
Boston	14	13	5	2	0	1	1		36	112
Cleveland	15	9	6	2	1	0	1		34	105

Chart III
DEFENSIVE RECORDS

Team	OSB	OCS	OSB%	DP	OA/SFA	Fielding Avg.	DER	Opposition Runs
Baltimore	98	47	.676	159	31/46	.981	.703	652
Detroit	80	63	.559	142	29/39	.980	.724	679
New York	111	51	.685	157	28/59	.978	.694	703
Toronto	82	46	.641	148	43/50	.981	.704	726
Milwaukee	157	47	.770	162	28/57	.982	.701	708
Boston	153	53	.743	166	41/57	.979	.687	775
Cleveland	102	55	.650	174	30/54	.980	.685	782

Chart IV
OPPOSITION ERRORS

Team	C	1B	2B	3B	SS	LF	CF	RF	P	UN	Total
Baltimore	8	11	12	18	26	6	9	5	9	4	108
Detroit	11	17	12	25	34	14	4	11	13	2	141
New York	11	10	18	17	25	9	10	11	13	2	116
Toronto	11	13	17	22	25	8	5	13	20	0	134
Milwaukee	12	15	15	17	22	10	6	8	9	0	104
Boston	12	8	11	22	35	7	11	2	5	2	115
Cleveland	18	12	8	32	32	9	5	6	13	6	141

Team	Ahead	Tied	Behind	Net Change
Baltimore	76- 8	16- 4	6-52	+10
Detroit	73- 7	10- 7	9-56	+ 5
New York	71- 6	10- 6	10-59	+ 8
Toronto	65-11	15- 7	9-55	+ 6
Milwaukee	63- 8	12- 8	12-60	+ 8
Boston	61- 6	9-12	8-66	− 1
Cleveland	56-10	8-10	6-72	− 6

BALTIMORE ORIOLES

I

I am about to violate here two of my own policies. Number one, I don't reconsider a prediction that I have made before it is absolutely proven true or false. I don't do this because a) it just gives you a chance to be wrong twice and b) I can't stand those people who issue seven sets of predictions between February and August 15, and then try to tell you in October that they were right about everything.

Number two, I don't discuss in one *Abstract* the prediction I made the year before, because predictions are basically an ego thing that have very little to do with knowledge or understanding. Once in a while I can't resist making predictions, but I try to draw the line at reviewing them a year or so later. Besides, you just get caught in a I-was-right No-you-weren't Yes-I-was No-you-weren't Well-I-was-right-about-that-then Who-cares argument.

But several people have asked me how I feel now about my comments a year ago on the Orioles post-Weaver, and so I suppose there is some remaining interest among us in those comments. Let me see if I can prod them in such a way as to learn something.

In retrospect, the Orioles in the first year post-Weaver remind me a great deal of two other teams, the Yankees in the first year post-Stengel, and the Giants in the first year post-McGraw. Casey Stengel managed the Yankees through the period of their greatest and most utter domination of the American League, and the talent with which he accomplished this seemed to grow less and less impressive as the years rode by. He won the American League in 1960 with a roster that had a lot of people asking "Who are these guys?" lost the World Series and was axed. There were many people within the press corps of the time who predicted the demise of the Yankees in Stengel's wake, and as you may recall it didn't happen.

It didn't happen here, either, and some of the reasons why it didn't happen are probably the same. In both cases, we're talking about managers who received from the press an inordinate share of the credit for the team's success. By "inordinate," I mean not that it was more than they deserved, but that it was more than a manager usually receives. With the departure of that manager, the team tended to gather together and say, "Let's show them. Let's show them that it was us, not him, that's been winning these things."

Which, of course, it was, at least on the simplest level; it wasn't Earl who was hitting those 3-run homers. I think that any time you get ballplayers to gather together and say, "Let's show them" then you've probably got a good thing going (unless, of course, they're saying "Let's show them that they made a mistake in trading Charlie." When "them" means your own front office, you've always got a problem. When "them" means the press or the opposition, that's good.)

Anyway, they showed us. The next parallel was that Stengel and Weaver were both, in their own way, high-pressure managers. Earl was a high-pressure manager because he's so intense that it drives him crazy to lose. Stengel also had every intention of winning, and while he may not have displayed his intensity quite as openly as Weaver, he got the message through. He tended to communicate it through working on the player's insecurity. He liked to make changes. He was known, on occasion, to pinch-hit for the pitcher when he was behind 4–1 in the third inning. Virtually no one on his roster had a regular position—he holds the world's record for hyphenated second-base-third base-shortstop-outfield semi-regulars. And if you were a pitcher, you could have a great year for him one year, make about four bad starts the next April and find yourself pitching for the Athletics.

I think that one of the key factors in the Yankees' 1961 season was that the players were reacting to the release from the pressure of that insecurity, just as the Orioles in 1983 reacted positively to escaping the pressure of life with Earl. Rich Dauer put it well—"Weaver taught us to win; Altobelli lets us win."

There are other similarities, perhaps trivial but odd, between the '61 Yanks and the '83 Orioles. Both teams had substantially rebuilt pitching staffs. The '61 Yankees had 40 victories out of pitchers who had spent at least part of the 1960 season in the minor leagues, including two of their top starters, Bill Stafford (14–9) and Rollie Sheldon (11–5). Stafford was only 21, Sheldon 24, and the number 2 starter, Ralph Terry, was 25 and having his first good season. I trust you can see the parallels there without my help. Both new managers, Altobelli and Houk, inherited bullpens featuring a righthanded flame thrower (Ryne Duren, Tim Stoddard) and a lefthander with better control (a Latin lefthander, as it happens). Both managers made the lefthander the bullpen ace, deemphasized the role of the righthander and then traded him. Both teams had the MVP *and* the runner-up in the voting.

Going back even further in history, before the memory of anyone living except Howard Cosell, Ronald Reagan and Bob Hope, we come to another team of a similar nature, the New York Giants of the first full season after John McGraw. The Giants stumbled away from the gate in 1932; McGraw was ill, quit in May and the team went nowhere. In 1933, with substantially the same talent, they were a consensus sixth-place team. But they regrouped for the new manager, Bill Terry, and they, too, won the World's Championship. Terry, again, substantially and successfully rebuilt his pitching staff, featuring young, unproven pitchers.

McGraw, Stengel and Weaver may be the three most highly-praised managers of all time; the fact that all three teams took over the world when their man left is a pretty fair coincidence. Could it, then, have been anticipated?

Well, I'll say this. I have joined together in print the names of Casey Stengel and Earl Weaver and the term "complex platooning" so many times that whenever I would write the first half of that sentence, Peter (Gethers, my editor) would automatically strike the second half. In view of that, the notion that what happened to the Yankees after Stengel *might* happen to the Orioles after

Weaver should at least have grazed my brow. If I was half as smart as I'm supposed to be, I'd have caught it.

From which we learn, what? To recognize this effect the next time we see it? That might be twenty years from now, and whose memory is that good? One thing that we might think about is that perhaps we underestimate the extent to which a great manager makes his contribution to his team not just as a leader and tactician, but as a teacher. I have read in the last few months autobiographies by both Stengel and Weaver, plus *Pitching In A Pinch*, in which McGraw figures massively. One thing which struck me was that all three men were very proud of their ability as teachers; all felt that it was something the public didn't understand about them. Perhaps they were right. I would also like to say that the latter two of those books are two of the five best baseball books that I have ever read. *Pitching In A Pinch* is a delightful accounting of the game as played in 1912, precise and evocative by detail. As to Weaver's book, done with Berry Stainback . . . well, it's so much *baseball*; I've never read a book that had so much *baseball* in it. He writes about strategies and tactics, about philosophies and theories of the game, but drawn through personalities and drawn through game experiences. The book is actually exciting to read. Consider this brief selection:

> *Rick Dempsey is another guy who always thinks I'm picking on him. "If Weaver picks on anyone else," Rick has said . . . "I sure haven't noticed it." He's been saying that since 1976 when he joined us, and he's too stubborn to ever change his views.*
>
> *In our system, for example, the pitchers call their own games. But Dempsey kept trying to call the pitchers . . . I tried to point out to Rick some fundamental truths. A manager manages. A pitcher pitches. And a catcher receives. We had a big fight on this subject. "Rick, a catcher catches the ball," I said. "When you're given more responsibility, then we'll change the title. We'll call you an executive receiving engineer or something."*

Look at what has been accomplished in those two paragraphs. He's made important strides toward developing 1) an honest portrait of Rick Dempsey as a person, and of 2) the relationship between the two of them, and 3) how that impacts on the ballgame. He has told you something important about how the Orioles' system is different from the way most other teams operate. And it's funny; not hilarious, but fun to read. I've read whole books on baseball that didn't accomplish as much.

There is no doubt that I particularly enjoy Weaver's book because I agree with him on virtually everything. Although the ways in which we have developed our ideas are radically different, I don't think that there is any substantive point of disagreement between Earl Weaver and myself on how it is that baseball games are won and lost, how successful teams are built and how they differ from unsuccessful teams. And his ideas on these subjects spill off of every page, because, like me, he is obsessed by those issues. It's fun to see my own ideas and my own convictions pour out, page after page, but coming from such a different perspective. A reporter asks him after a game why he didn't bunt, and he says, "Why don't you take the sacrifice bunt and stuff it up somebody's ass and leave it there." That's not exactly the way I would have phrased it, Earl, but I pretty much have to agree with the sentiments.

Anyway, to return to the present Orioles . . . no, I no longer see any reason to anticipate a significant decline in the Orioles' performance over the next three or four years. The Giants after 1933 remained over 90 victories a year for four more years, and then entered a period of sharp and progressive declines. The Yankees after 1961 remained strong for three more years, and then degenerated suddenly. Both teams lasted as long as the core of talent that the master had assembled was strong, and then fell apart. I wouldn't begin to predict what would happen to the Orioles in three or four years. But between now and then, they look solid.

II

A year ago, in the 1983 *Abstract*, I presented in the Baltimore Orioles' team comment a chart that gives the month-by-month won/lost records and percentages of 13 major league teams for the years 1971 to 1980. (That is, during those ten years, Milwaukee's won/lost percentage in July was .460, etc.) I was intently studying something else at the time, and did not notice what might be the most interesting thing about the chart.

What the chart shows is that there is a strong decentralization effect that takes place in September. The good teams, the .570 teams, move up to .590 or .600; the .450 teams drop to .430 or .400. Look:

Team	Overall W/L%	W/L% after Sept. 1
Baltimore	.585	.646
Cincinnati	.584	.594
Los Angeles	.567	.589
New York	.561	.603
Boston	.554	.543
Houston	.501	.493
Detroit	.493	.451
San Francisco	.486	.454
Milwaukee	.471	.434
Cleveland	.462	.426
Atlanta	.454	.436
San Diego	.421	.417
Toronto	.361	.303

The four best teams all improve in September; the other nine all decline.

I have long speculated that this "September decentralization" effect should exist; I commented upon it in the 1978 *Baseball Abstract*. The reasons why it exists are fairly obvious; Thomas Boswell's comments on "Summer Baseball" and "Autumn Baseball" apply. But the ways in which I had tried to prove that it existed were in some ways defective, because I had not been able to show that it actually happens.

But it does.

INTRODUCTION TO MANAGER'S BOXES

With each American League team this year, there is a box discussing the characteristics of the manager. These boxes should be seen as an attempt to force ourselves to see things that we were not seeing before. What I am trying to do is ask a series of questions about how one manager differs from another, and then study records, boxscores, game sheets or whatever in order to answer those questions as best I can.

In many cases, I have no clear evidence on the issue, no way of answering the question. You do have that—for your own team. If you are a Red Sox fan, you should know more than I do about how much Ralph Houk uses the hit and run. If you do have that kind of knowledge and would take a minute to share it with me, that would be appreciated.

I guess what I am saying is that if we start *trying* to answer these questions now, we'll be able to answer them in a few years. An unfortunate side effect is that I'm probably going to get some of the answers wrong now; not only some of the answers but some of the questions. Is there a clear difference between managers who are "emotional leaders" and those who are "decision makers"? Probably not; I'm just trying to see things that I wasn't seeing otherwise.

A few things may need further explanation. Each manager's season is compared to a record that would be "Par" for this team in view of the team's record over the previous two seasons. The "Par Percentage" for a team in 1984 is figured by (1982 Wins + 1983 Wins + 81) divided by (Same + 1982 Losses + 1983 Losses + 81). If a team finished 84–78 in 1982 and 90–72 in 1983, their "Par" for 1984 would be 85 wins. If they were 60–102 in 1982 and 57–105 in '83, their "par" in 1984 would be 66 wins. If the team were to win 70 games, that would be 15 games below par for the first team, but four games over par for the second team.

This formula is used because it is the most accurate single way of projecting how a team will do in 1984, adjusting for the quality of the team that the man has inherited, but also for the Law of Competition Balance, which moves all teams toward .500. A manager who takes over a .400 team and fails to advance them is not achieving success, while a man who takes over a .600 team and keeps them there is doing a hell of a job.

Obviously, there are other factors involved; the retrogression of the Red Sox under Ralph Houk is not necessarily attributible to Ralph Houk. But the fact remains that the Red Sox's performance under Ralph Houk has been a disappointment; it has been below a normal continuation of the success the team was having. In that sense, it has been below par.

The distinction between an "optimist" and a "problem solver" is not entirely clear in my mind, so I'm not going to be able to make it clear in yours. What I was aiming for is something about how a manager reacts to a problem, to a weakness in a player or in the organization. Let's say that you have a player who is maybe a .260-hitting second baseman, but he has a huge hitch in his swing that keeps him from being the hitter he might be. Does the manager say, "Well, he's hitting well enough to help the team. If we start fooling around with his stroke he's liable to wind up hitting .220." That's an optimist; let things take their course. The problem-solver will go to the hitter and try to get him to take corrective action, smooth out his swing. Both approaches have problems. The optimists are mostly nice people—Sparky Anderson, Chuck Tanner —whereas the problem-solvers are thick-skinned, tough-as-leather types. It's a black-and-white description of a gray world, but it is still worth the effort to ask yourself how gray is it?

THE MANAGER

NAME: Joe Altobelli

AGE: 51 (turns 52 in May)

MANAGERS FOR WHOM PLAYED IN MAJORS: Al Lopez, Kerby Farrell, Cookie Lavagetto, Sam Mele.

CHARACTERISTICS AS A PLAYER: Excellent defensive first baseman; didn't hit with any power until he was 24, some power after that, but .250 hitter in the minors.

MANAGERIAL RECORD:

Team	Year	Par	Wins	Losses	Pct.	+ or −
SF	1977	78	75	87	.463	− 3
SF	1978	82	89	73	.549	+ 7
SF	1979	75	61	79	.436	−14
Balt	1983	88	98	64	.605	+10
4 Years		323	323	303	.516	0

WHAT HE BRINGS TO THE BALLCLUB

IS HE AN INTENSE MANAGER OR MORE OF AN EASY-TO-GET-ALONG-WITH TYPE? Compared to Weaver, at least, he's a relaxed manager, easy to get along with. Projects the image of a strong manager, though.

IS HE MORE OF AN EMOTIONAL LEADER OR A DECISION-MAKER? I wouldn't say that either label describes him particularly well on the basis of what I know about him. But given the choice, I'd say he's more of a decision-maker. He did not try simply to carry on with what Weaver had done here; he reviewed everything and changed quite a number of things. In San Francisco, too, he made some personnel moves that were decisive, even unusual. They didn't work out as well there, but he's certainly not somebody who is afraid to face a decision.

IS HE MORE OF AN OPTIMIST OR MORE OF A PROBLEM SOLVER? I'm not sure, but he certainly goes after problems vigorously. An "optimist," as I am using the term here, would probably have tried to work with Leo Hernandez at third base, keep telling him he was going to get his defensive problems worked out. Altobelli decided to try somebody else.

HOW HE USES HIS PERSONNEL

DOES HE FAVOR A SET LINEUP OR A ROTATION SYSTEM? Definitely the latter. In his first year in San Francisco, he had people moving all over the place. No one played more than 136 games at any position for him that year. He keeps trying combinations until he finds something that he likes. However, his best year in San Francisco was the year that he was able to get through with pretty much the lineup he made up in April.

DOES HE LIKE TO PLATOON? He platooned here even more than Weaver did. In San Francisco, he platooned McCovey and Ivie at first base, Whitfield and Herndon in leftfield, and also part of the time at shortstop. I'm sure he'd like to have eight Cal Ripkens, but short of that he probably is going to platoon.

DOES HE TRY TO SOLVE HIS PROBLEMS WITH PROVEN PLAYERS OR WITH YOUNGSTERS WHO STILL HAVE SOMETHING TO PROVE? HOW MANY PLAYERS HAS HE MADE REGULARS OUT OF WHO WERE NOT REGULARS BEFORE, AND WHO WERE THEY? In his first year in San Francisco, he made a full-time regular out of one player, Jack Clark, and gave considerable playing time to four other players who had not had much or as much before: Rob Andrews, Gary Thomasson, Terry Whitfield and Marc Hill. Here, he gave quite a bit of playing time to the rookie Shelby in centerfield, and he opened the year with a rookie as his regular third baseman. Later on in SF, he made a regular out of Johnnie LeMaster. Same with pitchers; in his first year in San Francisco, he made a rotation starter out of the rookie Bob Knepper; here, he did the same with Mike Boddicker. So he is not at all reluctant to go with a player who has neither proven major league credentials nor overpowering talent.

DOES HE PREFER TO GO WITH GOOD OFFENSIVE PLAYERS OR DOES HE LIKE THE GLOVE MEN? Uncertain. The switch at third base to Cruz, a glove man but a proven non-hitter, when Hernandez really was hitting reasonably well, might indicate the latter. But in San Francisco, he tried to play Bill Madlock at second base to get an extra bat in the lineup. No clear preference shown.

DOES HE LIKE AN OFFENSE BASED ON POWER, SPEED OR HIGH AVERAGES? The Giants hit 84 and 85 home runs in the two years before he took them over, and 80 the year after he left. Under Altobelli, they were well over 100 every year. Stolen bases were level (didn't increase or decrease) except for his third year there, when he had Bill North in the lineup. Batting averages dropped and walks increased. I'd say he was in the Oriole tradition of the offense based on the three-run homer.

DOES HE USE THE ENTIRE ROSTER OR DOES HE KEEP PEOPLE AROUND SITTING ON THE BENCH? He uses everybody. Complete involvement of the roster.

DOES HE BUILD HIS BENCH AROUND YOUNG PLAYERS WHO CAN STEP INTO A BREACH IF NEED BE OR AROUND VETERAN ROLE-PLAYERS WHO HAVE THEIR OWN FUNCTIONS WITHIN A GAME? Well, sometimes it's hard to say who his bench is and who his regulars are, so that question is not easy to answer. But as I mentioned, he does like to bring along the youngsters.

GAME MANAGING AND USE OF STRATEGIES

DOES HE GO FOR THE BIG INNING OFFENSE OR DOES HE LIKE TO USE THE ONE-RUN STRATEGIES? Big-inning offense.

DOES HE PINCH HIT MUCH, AND IF SO WHEN? He makes platoon switches within a game, which give him an average or above average number of pinch-hitters used, but he rarely pinch hits just to get a better hitter up there at one particular moment. His peculiar roster of 1983, with just one backup infielder for three positions, two of which were staffed by non-hitters, shows that clearly. Without a designated hitter in the World Series, he had a five-man offense and a bench that was packed to the rafters with .285 hitters, but he couldn't use them because he had no one to send in to play the infield.

You should understand that in general, a manager who platoons extensively is not going to have many situations in which he calls one man back just to send a better bat up to the plate. If you platoon two shortstops and two leftfielders and two catchers, and if a righthanded pitcher is on the mound, then you probably are not going to send the spare leftfielder up to bat for the shortstop, since that would mean calling back a lefthander, sending up a righthander to hit against a righthander, and then sending a righthanded hitting shortstop in to play defense. Generally speaking, a manager does one or the other; he keeps people on the bench who can pinch-hit and defensive substitutes to replace them, or he platoons.

DOES HE USE THE SAC BUNT OFTEN? With San Francisco in '78, he led the N.L. in sac hits; with Baltimore last year, he bunted even less than Weaver did. No clear pattern.

DOES HE LIKE TO USE THE RUNNING GAME? His teams have never run a lot. The '79 team, with Bill North, was third in the league in stolen bases. Stolen base percentages have been pretty good.

DOES HE DRAW THE INFIELD IN MUCH? In a bunt situation, he will have the infield charging in with the pitch quite often. As to just playing them in, I don't think he does much.

IN WHAT CIRCUMSTANCES WILL HE ISSUE AN INTENTIONAL WALK? I've never seen him use it to set up a double play. I have at least 30 scoresheets of Oriole games from 1983, and the only three cases I can find of his using an intentional walk were places where there was a runner on third and he could get a platoon advantage on the hitter. I suspect that mostly he instructs his pitchers to nibble, rather than giving an out-and-out walk, and that his intentional walks result when they get behind 2-0. There was a semi-intentional walk to DeJesus during the series (sixth inning, game 3). But in game one, he declined to walk Schmidt with first base open, one out and a lefthander on the mound. In game two, he again pitched to Schmidt with first base open and one out, although this time with a righthander on the mound.

DOES HE HIT AND RUN VERY OFTEN? Not that I have seen.

ARE THERE ANY UNIQUE OR IDIOSYN-CRATIC STRATEGIES THAT HE PARTICU-LARLY LIKES? The closest thing that I have noticed would be the charging of the infielders. A lot of people don't like to do that, but I wouldn't really say that it was idiosyncratic. Having eight outfielders and only one backup infielder on his club in '83 was certainly odd.

HANDLING THE PITCHING STAFF

DOES HE LIKE POWER PITCHERS OR PRE-FER TO GO WITH THE PEOPLE WHO PUT THE BALL IN PLAY? He likes the people who can throw the ball. In San Francisco he deemphasized the role of Jim Barr (finesse pitcher), and he (or the Giants while he was there) never gave much of a shot to Rob Dressler and gave up on Mike Caldwell. He based his staff there around Halicki and Montefusco, brought up Knepper and brought in Vida Blue. Baltimore strikeouts were up significantly in 1983.

DOES HE STAY WITH THE STARTER OR GO TO THE BULLPEN QUICKLY? He keeps a four- or five-man bullpen busy. He'll go to the bullpen in the fourth, fifth inning more often than an average manager. (Removed his starter in the first five innings 39 times in 1983.) He lifted his starting pitcher before the pitcher had either pitched seven innings or allowed four runs 38 times in 1983, easily the highest total in the division:

Number of Times Removed Starter
Before Seven Innings Pitched
or Four Runs Allowed

Joe Altobelli, Baltimore	38
Harvey Kuenn, Milwaukee	30
Billy Martin, New York	29
Ralph Houk, Boston	28
Bobby Cox, Toronto	26
Sparky Anderson, Detroit	24
Ferraro and Corrales, Cleveland	23

DOES HE LIKE THE FOUR-MAN OR THE FIVE-MAN ROTATION? Last year he was just determined to go to a five-man rotation. It was really an odd thing. The Orioles had been successful for years with four starters, Flanagan and Palmer and (briefly) McGregor were hurting, Martinez was getting pounded, and he just insisted that he would not go back to a four-man rotation. He got by with it.

DOES HE USE THE ENTIRE STAFF OR DOES HE TRY TO GET FIVE OR SIX PEOPLE TO DO MOST OF THE WORK? The entire staff is very much involved. With SF in '77, he had Gary Lavelle (73 appearances), Randy Moffitt (64), Dave Heaverlo (56), Charlie Williams (55) and John Curtis (43). That's a lot of bullpen.

HOW LONG WILL HE STAY WITH A STARTER WHO IS STRUGGLING? Until the bullpen is ready.

ARE THERE ANY PARTICULAR TYPES OF PITCHERS OF WHOM HE IS FOND? His last staff in San Francisco had over a hundred starts by left-handed pitchers, which is unusual but might not mean anything.

IS THERE ANYTHING UNIQUE ABOUT HIS HANDLING OF HIS PITCHERS? He let Boddicker throw an exceptional number of pitches, and in particular breaking pitches, during the playoffs and World Series. This was unusual but it was, after all, a World Series. I don't want to make him sound like Captain Hook; if a pitcher has his stuff, Altobelli will live or die with him. It's just that he reacts very quickly when things start going downhill.

WHAT IS HIS STRONGEST POINT AS A MANA-GER? I have to be honest with you: I'm not exceptionally impressed by Altobelli as an in-game manager. I keep looking at the ninth inning of Game 3, when he let Sammy Stewart hit in the top of the ninth, and then replaced him as soon as Joe Lefebvre was announced as a pinch-hitter. What was the point in that? Everybody knew Lefebvre was on the bench. Did he want that badly for him to be announced? Did he let Stewart, a non-hitter if there ever was one, swing a bat when he had a one-run lead in the ninth inning, just so that Paul Owens would have to use Rose, rather than Diaz, to lead off the inning? That seems to me to be a very strange trade, and it seems to me that Altobelli makes more than a few of them.

And all that sort of stuff doesn't sway three games a year from the loss column to the win or vice versa. Altobelli does do some things well. Probably his strongest point is the aggressiveness with which he attacks the problems of his team. He is not at all reluctant to make a change that he thinks needs to be made, whether it is in a game or in the regular lineup. He projects an image of strength. He has confidence in his own judgment, particularly talent judgment.

IF THERE WERE NO PROFESSIONAL BASE-BALL, WHAT WOULD THIS MANAGER PROB-ABLY BE DOING? Working as the genial Italian heavy in commercials for Godfathers Pizza.

Eddie MURRAY, First Base
Runs Created: 126

	G	AB	Hit	2B	3B	HR	Run	RBI	BB	SO	SB	CS	Avg
6.44 Years		614	182	32	2	31	95	108	68	88	6	2	.297
1983	156	582	178	30	3	33	115	111	86	90	5	1	.306
First Half	76	286	88	13	0	13	51	48	39	49	2	1	.308
Second Half	80	296	90	17	3	20	64	63	26	14	1	1	.304
vs. RHP		378	119	22	3	21	79	80	56	60	3	1	.315
vs. LHP		204	59	8	0	12	36	31	30	30	2	0	.289
Home	75	272	83	9	2	16	53	56	36	46	3	0	.305
Road	81	310	95	21	1	17	62	55	50	44	2	1	.306
Grass	132	483	149	24	2	27	97	91	77	81	5	1	.308
Turf	24	99	29	6	1	6	18	20	9	9	0	0	.293

Al BUMBRY, Centerfield
Runs Created: 47

	G	AB	Hit	2B	3B	HR	Run	RBI	BB	SO	SB	CS	Avg
8.08 Years		571	162	25	6	6	90	46	54	82	30	11	.284
1983	124	378	104	14	4	3	63	31	31	33	12	5	.275
First Half	58	178	48	5	1	3	27	15	16	18	7	5	.270
Second Half	66	200	56	9	3	0	36	16	15	15	5	0	.280
vs. RHP		365	102	14	4	3	56	28	29	32	12	4	.279
vs. LHP		13	2	0	0	0	7	3	2	1	0	1	.154
Home	64	197	62	5	3	2	35	22	16	20	7	4	.315
Road	60	181	42	9	1	1	28	9	15	13	5	1	.232
Grass	106	322	89	11	3	3	50	30	24	31	11	5	.276
Turf	18	56	15	3	1	0	13	1	7	2	1	0	.268

Rich DAUER, Second Base
Runs Created: 42

	G	AB	Hit	2B	3B	HR	Run	RBI	BB	SO	SB	CS	Avg
5.73 Years		563	147	28	1	7	69	58	44	33	1	2	.261
1983	140	459	108	19	0	5	49	41	47	29	1	1	.235
First Half	64	224	46	7	0	3	18	19	21	15	0	0	.205
Second Half	76	235	62	12	0	2	31	22	26	14	1	1	.264
vs. RHP		296	66	13	0	3	33	31	28	21	1	1	.223
vs. LHP		163	42	6	0	2	16	10	19	8	0	0	.258
Home	70	226	57	13	0	2	30	18	28	13	0	1	.252
Road	70	233	51	6	0	3	19	23	19	16	1	0	.219
Grass	118	382	92	19	0	4	44	34	42	19	1	1	.241
Turf	22	77	16	0	0	1	5	7	5	10	0	0	.208

Dan FORD, Rightfield
Runs Created: 59

	G	AB	Hit	2B	3B	HR	Run	RBI	BB	SO	SB	CS	Avg
6.79 Years		589	160	31	6	18	86	82	43	102	9	5	.272
1983	103	407	114	30	4	9	63	55	29	55	9	2	.280
First Half	52	217	61	18	2	5	35	31	16	35	6	2	.281
Second Half	51	190	53	12	2	4	28	24	13	30	3	0	.279
vs. RHP		257	71	15	3	5	40	35	18	33	5	1	.276
vs. LHP		150	43	15	1	4	23	20	11	22	4	1	.287
Home	47	180	54	14	1	3	27	26	12	27	5	1	.300
Road	56	227	60	16	3	6	36	29	17	28	4	1	.264
Grass	84	326	90	28	2	3	50	41	27	44	6	2	.276
Turf	19	81	24	2	2	6	13	14	2	11	3	0	.296

Todd CRUZ, Third Base
Runs Created: 29

	G	AB	Hit	2B	3B	HR	Run	RBI	BB	SO	SB	CS	Avg
2.77 Years		500	110	20	2	11	43	52	18	103	3	7	.220
1983	146	437	87	13	3	10	37	48	22	108	4	7	.199
First Half	68	225	43	5	2	8	23	27	9	58	1	3	.191
Second Half	78	212	44	8	1	2	14	21	13	50	3	4	.208
vs. RHP		258	53	10	1	8	24	36	9	74	2	3	.205
vs. LHP		179	34	3	2	2	13	12	13	34	2	4	.190
Home	73	219	43	6	2	6	18	20	8	54	3	2	.196
Road	73	218	44	7	1	4	19	28	14	54	1	5	.202
Grass	96	264	52	10	2	3	20	26	19	64	3	5	.197
Turf	50	173	35	3	1	7	17	22	3	44	1	2	.202

Rick DEMPSEY, Catcher
Runs Created: 36

	G	AB	Hit	2B	3B	HR	Run	RBI	BB	SO	SB	CS	Avg
6.51 Years		450	108	21	2	6	47	41	51	54	2	5	.240
1983	127	347	80	16	2	4	33	32	40	55	1	1	.231
First Half	61	173	42	7	0	2	17	13	22	33	1	1	.243
Second Half	66	174	38	9	2	2	16	19	18	22	0	0	.218
vs. RHP		184	44	10	0	2	15	22	23	31	1	1	.239
vs. LHP		163	36	6	2	2	18	10	17	24	0	0	.221
Home	64	163	36	8	2	3	14	14	23	26	0	0	.221
Road	63	184	44	8	0	1	19	18	17	29	1	1	.239
Grass	109	292	71	15	2	4	27	29	35	47	1	1	.243
Turf	18	55	9	1	0	0	6	3	5	8	0	0	.164

Cal RIPKEN, Shortstop
Runs Created: 120

	G	AB	Hit	2B	3B	HR	Run	RBI	BB	SO	SB	CS	Avg
2.13 Years		610	176	37	3	26	100	92	49	94	1	3	.289
1983	162	663	211	47	2	27	121	102	58	97	0	4	.318
First Half	76	302	84	17	2	13	52	46	36	52	0	2	.278
Second Half	86	361	127	30	0	14	69	56	22	45	0	2	.352
vs. RHP		444	143	30	2	19	81	71	36	69	0	1	.322
vs. LHP		219	68	17	0	8	40	31	22	28	0	3	.311
Home	81	321	101	23	1	12	53	50	29	44	0	1	.315
Road	81	342	110	24	1	15	68	52	29	53	0	3	.322
Grass	138	566	178	40	2	21	99	84	47	79	0	4	.314
Turf	24	97	33	7	0	6	22	18	11	18	0	0	.340

Ken SINGLETON, Designated Hitter
Runs Created: 86

	G	AB	Hit	2B	3B	HR	Run	RBI	BB	SO	SB	CS	Avg
12.17 Years		561	160	25	2	20	79	85	101	97	2	1	.286
1983	151	507	140	21	3	18	52	84	99	83	0	2	.276
First Half	68	218	60	14	2	9	21	32	42	40	0	0	.275
Second Half	83	289	80	7	1	9	31	52	57	43	0	2	.277
vs. RHP		335	95	15	1	13	40	60	69	53	0	0	.284
vs. LHP		172	45	6	2	5	12	24	30	30	0	2	.262
Home	72	236	52	7	1	8	24	40	51	41	0	0	.220
Road	79	271	88	14	2	10	28	44	48	42	0	2	.325
Grass	129	432	110	15	3	13	40	63	86	73	0	2	.255
Turf	22	75	30	6	0	5	12	21	13	10	0	0	.400

John LOWENSTEIN, Leftfield
Runs Created: 61

	G	AB	Hit	2B	3B	HR	Run	RBI	BB	SO	SB	CS	Avg
7.72 Years		412	106	16	2	14	62	53	53	70	16	9	.257
1983	122	310	87	13	2	15	52	60	49	55	2	1	.281
First Half	60	158	44	7	1	8	26	32	26	32	2	1	.278
Second Half	62	152	43	6	1	7	26	28	23	23	0	0	.283
vs. RHP		309	87	13	2	15	52	60	48	54	2	1	.282
vs. LHP		1	0	0	0	0	0	0	1	1	0	0	.000
Home	62	160	39	4	0	7	23	24	24	29	0	1	.244
Road	60	150	48	9	2	8	29	36	25	26	2	0	.320
Grass	102	255	68	10	1	14	43	52	40	45	1	1	.267
Turf	20	55	19	3	1	1	9	8	9	10	1	0	.345

Gary ROENICKE, Outfield
Runs Created: 49

	G	AB	Hit	2B	3B	HR	Run	RBI	BB	SO	SB	CS	Avg
3.98 Years		442	114	22	1	21	62	68	60	71	3	4	.258
1983	115	323	84	13	0	19	45	64	30	35	2	2	.260
First Half	54	151	41	8	0	9	25	33	12	16	1	1	.272
Second Half	61	172	43	5	0	10	20	31	18	19	1	1	.250
vs. RHP		116	25	4	0	1	12	16	9	17	1	0	.216
vs. LHP		207	59	9	0	18	33	48	21	18	1	2	.285
Home	60	169	43	7	0	10	23	34	13	23	1	2	.254
Road	55	154	41	6	0	9	22	30	17	12	1	0	.266
Grass	104	297	74	13	0	17	42	59	25	32	2	2	.249
Turf	11	26	10	0	0	2	3	5	5	3	0	0	.385

Scott McGREGOR

Year	(W–L)	GS	Run	Avg	DP	Avg	SB	Avg
1982	(14-12)	37	175	4.73	28	.76	17	.46
1983	(18- 7)	36	195	5.42	35	.97	16	.44
1977-1983		191	810	4.24	182	.95	77	.40

	G	IP	W	L	Pct	ER	ERA
1982 Home	20	120	7	6	.538	60	4.50
1983 Home	15	98.1	4	6	.400	46	4.21
1982 Road	17	106.1	7	6	.538	56	4.74
1983 Road	21	161.2	14	1	.933	46	2.56
1983 Grass	29	200.1	11	7	.611	84	3.77
1983 Turf	7	59.2	7	0	1.000	8	1.21

Mike FLANAGAN

Year	(W–L)	GS	Run	Avg	DP	Avg	SB	Avg
1982	(15-11)	35	164	4.69	33	.94	17	.49
1983	(12- 4)	20	104	5.20	24	1.20	4	.20
1977-1983		223	1022	4.58	254	1.14	86	.39

	G	IP	W	L	Pct	ER	ERA
1982 Home	18	120	9	4	.692	50	3.75
1983 Home	12	74.2	8	3	.727	29	3.50
1982 Road	18	116	6	7	.462	54	4.19
1983 Road	8	50.2	4	1	.800	17	3.02
1983 Grass	19	117	11	4	.733	46	3.54
1983 Turf	1	8.1	1	0	1.000	0	0.00

Storm DAVIS

Year	(W–L)	GS	Run	Avg	DP	Avg	SB	Avg
1982	(8-4)	8	43	5.38	7	.88	6	.75
1983	(13-7)	29	154	5.31	26	.90	11	.38
1982-1983		37	197	5.32	33	.89	17	.46

	G	IP	W	L	Pct	ER	ERA
1982 Home	15	55.1	5	2	.714	18	2.93
1983 Home	16	91.2	2	5	.286	34	3.34
1982 Road	14	45.1	3	2	.600	21	4.17
1983 Road	18	108.2	11	2	.846	46	3.81
1983 Grass	28	160.1	8	6	.571	58	3.26
1983 Turf	6	40	5	1	.833	22	4.95

1983 Others

Pitcher	(W–L)	GS	Run	Avg	DP	Avg	SB	Avg
Palmer	(5-4)	11	49	4.45	12	1.09	9	.82
Ramirez	(4-4)	10	50	5.00	13	1.30	11	1.10
Mirabella	(0-0)	2	12	6.00	3	1.50	0	.00
Swaggerty	(1-1)	2	12	6.00	1	.50	1	.50
Stewart	(9-4)	1	0	.00	1	1.00	1	1.00

Mike BODDICKER

Year	(W–L)	GS	Run	Avg	DP	Avg	SB	Avg
1983	(16-8)	26	119	4.58	19	.73	21	.81
1980-1983		27	123	4.56	20	.74	22	.81

	G	IP	W	L	Pct	ER	ERA
1983 Home	16	115	11	3	.786	27	2.11
1983 Road	11	64	5	5	.500	28	3.94
1983 Grass	22	151	14	6	.700	42	2.50
1983 Turf	5	28	2	2	.500	13	4.18

EARL WEAVER'S MANAGERIAL RECORD

Team	Year	Par	Wins	Losses	Pct	+ or –
Balt	1968	43	48	34	.585	+ 5
Balt	1969	83	109	53	.673	+26
Balt	1970	94	108	54	.667	+14
Balt	1971	97	101	57	.639	+ 4
Balt	1972	93	80	74	.519	−13
Balt	1973	90	97	65	.599	+ 7
Balt	1974	87	91	71	.562	+ 4
Balt	1975	88	90	69	.556	+ 2
Balt	1976	88	88	74	.543	0
Balt	1977	86	97	64	.602	+11
Balt	1978	88	90	71	.559	+ 2
Balt	1979	88	102	57	.642	+14
Balt	1980	92	100	62	.617	+ 8
Balt	1981	62	59	46	.562	− 3
Balt	1982	91	94	68	.580	+ 3
15 Years		1270	1354	919	.596	+84

Dennis MARTINEZ

Year	(W–L)	GS	Run	Avg	DP	Avg	SB	Avg
1982	(16-12)	39	184	4.72	34	.87	35	.90
1983	(7-16)	25	104	4.16	26	1.04	25	1.00
1977-1983		190	852	4.48	186	.98	161	.85

	G	IP	W	L	Pct	ER	ERA
1982 Home	23	135.1	10	4	.714	74	4.92
1983 Home	17	81	4	8	.333	50	5.56
1982 Road	17	116.2	6	8	.429	44	3.39
1983 Road	15	72	3	8	.273	44	5.50
1983 Grass	29	138	7	13	.350	82	5.48
1983 Turf	3	15	0	3	.000	10	6.00

BALTIMORE ORIOLES
RUNS BATTED IN ANALYSIS

Player	RBI	RBI In Wins	Victory Important RBI	RBI Importance	Wins Batted In	RBI Per Win
Eddie Murray	111	85	51.97	.468	14.06	7.9
Cal Ripkin	102	83	45.57	.447	13.77	7.4
Ken Singleton	84	62	35.69	.425	9.38	9.0
John Lowenstein	60	48	26.32	.439	6.78	8.8
Gary Roenicke	64	52	26.27	.410	8.20	7.8
Dan Ford	55	40	24.78	.451	7.76	7.1
Rick Dempsey	32	31	17.94	.561	4.68	6.8
Rich Dauer	41	36	17.00	.415	5.45	7.5
Al Bumbry	31	25	12.93	.417	3.40	9.1
Todd Cruz	27	23	11.84	.439	2.84	9.5

DETROIT TIGERS

I wrote an article last summer for the *Detroit Free Press* (for which, by the way, they never paid me. So *that's* what that means; I'd been wondering since I was a kid how they could stay in business giving their paper away). No, I didn't write it for the money, I wrote it because they happened to contact me at a moment when I had been thinking about the Tigers, and I had some things that I wanted to say to the Tiger fans. What I had to say about the Tigers then is more interesting than anything else I have to say about them now, so I am just going to reprint the article here exactly the way I wrote it. I'll add a few retrospective comments at the end. The rest of the article won't be new to you Detroit readers, for which I apologize, but on the other hand the other 99 and a half percent of the book is new, so write to me and I'll send you your four pennies back. Just as soon as I get a check from your damn newspaper.

One thing you can say about the Detroit Tigers: The team has never lacked for stars. There is an odd consistency in the history of many franchises, an odd way that patterns have of repeating themselves in different times and with different characters, but in the same cities and wearing the same uniforms.

Ty Cobb played for the Tigers for seventeen years after they last won a pennant with him, a fact that would seem to have little enough to do with the current ambitions of Lou Whitaker, Lance Parrish and their talented if un-Cobbian colleagues. Cobb hit .377 during those seventeen years, casting a shadow over even such distinguished teammates as Sam Crawford, the Roberto Clemente of his time, and Harry Heilmann, whose statistics make George Brett look like a wimp. These magnificent soldiers played in frustration as the Athletics, the Red Sox, the White Sox, the Yankees and even the Senators took turns dominating the league for a few years at a time. The Tiger management, at every moment when the league title became vacant, was not ready or willing or able to seize that moment and make an all-out, let-'er-rip bid for the championship. In 1911, when Cobb and Crawford hit a combined .798 (Cobb .420, Crawford .378), the Tigers finished a distant second because the team had only one quality starter, George Mullin, and a third baseman, George Moriarty, who had escaped from a Sherlock Holmes story and spent six mysterious years as a Tiger regular, never hitting higher than .254 or swatting more than two home runs. He could be described, perhaps, as the Tom Brookens of his day.

In 1915 the American League throne room became open when Connie Mack dismantled his powerhouse Philadelphia Athletics. By then Moriarty had been replaced by another third baseman, Ossie Vitt, whose career highs were to be, believe it or not, exactly the same—a .254 average, 2 home runs. The Tigers finished second, and the Red Sox began a mini-dynasty. Six years later the championship was thrown up for grabs again when the

Red Sox were divided up by another hard-pressed owner, and the White Sox—the Black Sox—destroyed by scandal. In 1921 Cobb hit .389, second in the league to Heilmann's .394, but it was the Yankees who stepped into the breech. Cobb went on hitting, and Heilmann went on hitting, and the Tigers went on finishing second and third and occasionally worse.

I thought of those Tigers the other day, while pondering the extraordinary patience for which the modern Tigers, the Kaline and post-Kaline Tigers, have become known. Patience is a wonderful thing for a ballclub. Patience with a player allows the player to work through his weaknesses and develop his skills, so that you avoid the San Francisco Giants' problem of seeing all your babies grown up and winning pennants for somebody else. Patience allows the fans to develop a sense of unity with the players. The Tiger fans have never suffered the Cleveland fans' problem of adjusting to four or five new faces in the lineup every year. Patience allows the players to form into a team, in the deepest sense of the word, people who know each other and care about each other and play with a common purpose. The Cleveland Indians will never be a team; Gabe Paul wouldn't stand for it. Patience is the one thing that an organization most needs to develop stars—patience, and scouts.

High on history's mountain, it is easy to see how the Tigers of Ty Cobb's era lost the edge following the World Series debacles of 1907 to 1909. But you know, I haven't figured out yet how the Tigers lost the pennant in 1967. For the four years between the collapse of the Yankees in 1965 and the rise of the Orioles in '69, a void existed in the American League's power structure, and the Tigers were the obvious team to move into it. Over those years the Tigers had Al Kaline in rightfield, and the best starting pitcher in the league in Denny McLain, and one of the best lefthanded starting pitchers in Mickey Lolich. To say that Bill Freehan was the best catcher in the league is understating it; the man was third in the Most Valuable Player voting one year, second the next. They had the best leadoff man in the league in Dick McAuliffe. They had a 100-RBI man in Willie Horton. They had a first baseman who would hit 377 home runs in his career.

And yet, in 1965 they finished fourth behind three most unmemorable teams, and in '66 they moved up to third, and in '67 they tied for second behind a team that had only two regulars who were older than 24, a team whose three catchers hit .199, .203 and .147, a team whose number 2, 3, and 4 starters had a combined record of 25 wins and 29 losses. Why? Because with those stars, there were some other players, some people who were fan favorites, who . . . well, they weren't really good but they were *part of the team*. They were "we" ballplayers, as Sparky Anderson would say.

And eventually, they did all come together and win a pennant, if only one. And eventually, the current Tigers will win something. An article in the *Free Press* earlier this year might have given the idea that I was down on the Tigers, that I don't care much for Lou Whitaker or Lance Parrish or Chet Lemon or Jack Morris. Nothing could be further from the truth. I may have commented on certain things that those players do not do, but that is done with a recognition that every player, like every writer, every manager, every friend and every janitor, is a unique blend of positives and negatives, things you love and things you could live without. Lou Whitaker is on the border of being a great ballplayer, the finest second baseman in a period of fine second basemen. Lance Parrish is one of a half-dozen catchers in history to combine multi-dimensional offensive skills with an arm coveted by the military as an artillery weapon. Wilson and Trammell and Petry —these guys are super; Chet Lemon is better than people give him credit for. Sparky Anderson has never been my favorite manager, but he's been in the World Series before, and there is no reason he couldn't be there again.

But if ever there was a moment for patience, buddy, this is *not* the time. The history of baseball in all eras has been that it is dominated by mini-dynasties lasting three to six years. The Yankee franchise from 1921 to 1964 is different in that they put a series of mini-dynasties together, rebuilding quickly and effectively each time decline seemed near. It could be that free agency will change that somehow, but I doubt it. I take the origins of the pattern to be psychological, and summarized by two statements:

Team A: Hey, we beat these guys last year, didn't we?

Team B: I don't know; they beat us last year.

We sit right now, at the All-Star break in 1983, at a key moment in the history of the American League East. After the collapse of the Oriole Dynasty from 1969–1974, there was a transition season in which the Red Sox snaked in a pennant. After the collapse of the Yankee dynasty of 1976–1981, there was a transition season in which the Brewers sneaked in a pennant. The Brewers can't get anything going; the Orioles are in their first season post-Weaver, playing well but their pitching looks weaker than it has in years.

The Tigers have a long history of missing these moments. One more I should mention: when the leagues began to sort themselves out, after World War II, the Tigers were in a perfect position to take over the league for a few years. They had an offense built around Hank Greenberg and George Kell, and they had a superb starting rotation of Hal Newhouser, Virgil Trucks, Dizzy Trout and Fred Hutchinson. Instead the Tigers played a waiting game, sold off Greenberg and went into hiding. The team failed to dominate the league in the mid-sixties, when there is no reason they shouldn't have, and they weren't ready to move in in the mid-seventies. That leaves the Detroit fans with one lousy pennant to show for 37 star-studded years.

Well, this is the mid-eighties. The next dynasty begins *right now.* The history of the Detroit Tigers in twenty-two words: When patience was needed, they have always had patience. When a sense of urgency was needed, they have always had patience instead.

The Tigers have the best eight-man lineup in the league; they have three good starters and a good bullpen. But if you look around the division, it is not hard to find somebody who is going to win it if the Tigers don't. As they have so often in the past, the Yankees have rebuilt overnight. That is a brand new team you see in New York, the Kemp/Winfield/Righetti/Robertson Yankees, and it is a *good* team. It is a very good team. And if they beat the Tigers this year, then they're going to beat them again next year, and the next year, and the next year. If there's a button that you can push to get a team out of "building" and into "winning," somebody had better push it. Now.

Postseason Addition: I blew a detail on Moriarty. He did hit higher than .254 once. He hit .273 in 1909.

I still believe absolutely the thesis of the article. The middle of last summer will be, from the standpoint of the 1990s, a pivotal moment in the history of this division. It wasn't the Yankees who seized that moment; it was the Orioles. But the point still holds: They have marched into a power void and established order. That order is likely to hold for three or four years.

I also think that I see something now that I didn't see then about these mini-dynasties of which I was writing. They almost always commence within a year or two after a new manager has come on the scene. The Oriole dynasty began in 1969, Earl's first year there; the late-seventies Yankee period began in 1976, Billy's first full year there. The Reds' dynasty began in 1970, Sparky's first year in Cincinnati; the Dodgers didn't supplant them until Walter retired and Lasorda was hired. The Royals' dominion over the West began in the first full year under Herzog. However, the 1983 White Sox team, which is the beginning of a dynasty if I've ever seen one, didn't come until LaRussa's fifth season.

A new manager brings to a team a fresh insight on their needs. He brings a new beginning and a new enthusiasm; he escapes the emotional commitment that every manager has to last year's decisions and last year's talent. Altobelli brought that to Baltimore at the moment when they needed it. Sparky tried very hard to push all those buttons, but they just didn't quite make it. Maybe he was hired too soon.

For reasons that I'm not entirely sure of (probably something that a Detroit reader said in a letter), I decided last summer to have Jim keep track of what kind of production the Tigers were getting out of the #3 spot in their lineup. The data sorted itself out quickly and did not move appreciably. On May 13th, Larry Herndon was batting .322 and slugging .508 as a #3 hitter; Kirk Gibson, the other primary #3 hitter, was hitting .157 while batting third. The final data is given below:

RECORDS WHILE BATTING THIRD

	G	AB	R	H	2B	3B	HR	RBI	Avg	Slugging Pct
Herndon	93	389	58	126	18	6	11	69	.324	.532
Gibson	56	212	28	39	7	4	5	24	.184	.325
Grubb	12	37	3	10	0	0	1	3	.270	.351
Cabell	7	34	2	7	2	0	0	2	.206	.265
Others	10	19	3	6	1	0	0	3	.316	.368
Total	162	681	94	188	28	10	17	100	.276	.421

The Tigers' production there was decent; that it was below the standards expected of a championship team (and it is, clearly) is largely due to the number of games Gibson spent there.

Herndon hit .353 and slugged .597 against lefthanded pitching last year; his production in the #3 spot probably reflects the fact that he was there mostly against left-handers. On the other hand, that means that Gibson must have been there mostly against righthanders, and Gibson is supposed to be able to hit righthanders. His batting record again, compared to what it was when he was not hitting in the third spot in the order:

KIRK GIBSON

	G	AB	R	H	2B	3B	HR	RBI	Avg	Slugging Pct
Third	56	212	28	39	7	4	5	24	.184	.325
Other spots	72	189	32	52	5	5	10	27	.275	.513

It does make you wonder if part of Gibson's problems don't stem from putting pressure on himself, a fear of letting the team down.

It would be easy to point a finger of blame about something like this, but to be fair about it, Sparky probably doesn't know these statistics now; it wouldn't have been reasonable to expect him to have anticipated them a year ago. That might be an argument for employing a sabermetrician, employing somebody who would recognize these patterns before they reach this size; on the other hand, it might not. The Tigers desperately need a big, strong lefthanded hitter in the middle of their lineup. Gibson is the biggest and strongest lefthander they've got, and the temptation to ask him to be a #3 or #4 hitter would not be easy for any manager to resist.

THE MANAGER

NAME: Sparky Anderson.

AGE: 50 (That's right, 50)

MANAGERS FOR WHOM PLAYED IN MAJORS: Eddie Sawyer

CHARACTERISTICS AS A PLAYER: As a minor league second baseman he was highly enough thought of that the Phillies traded three players to get him. One of those three, Jim Golden, was a legitimate pitching prospect, and another, Rip Repulski, was an outfielder who was just 30 and had had some good years. His minor league defensive stats were super, and he hit in the .270 to .295 range although he had no power. But he got one full year to try to earn a place in the majors, and he just didn't do enough with the bat to stick around.

MANAGERIAL RECORD:

Team	Year	Par	Wins	Losses	Pct.	+ or −
Cin	1970	84	102	60	.630	+18
Cin	1971	91	79	83	.488	−12
Cin	1972	83	95	59	.617	+12
Cin	1973	86	99	63	.611	+13
Cin	1974	93	98	64	.605	+ 5
Cin	1975	93	108	54	.667	+15
Cin	1976	96	102	60	.630	+ 6
Cin	1977	97	88	74	.543	− 9
Cin	1978	90	92	69	.571	+ 2
Det	1979	52	56	49	.533	+ 4
Det	1980	84	84	78	.519	0
Det	1981	56	60	49	.550	+ 4
Det	1982	84	83	79	.512	− 1
Det	1983	84	92	70	.568	+ 8
14 Years		1173	1238	911	.576	+65

WHAT HE BRINGS TO THE BALLCLUB

IS HE AN INTENSE MANAGER OR MORE OF ANY EASY-TO-GET-ALONG-WITH TYPE? He has expectations of a player. He might be easy to get along with if you're Pete Rose or Joe Morgan or Johnny Bench, but I would hesitate to put him in that class. He certainly doesn't belong in the "intense" group with Martin and Weaver, either.

IS HE MORE OF AN EMOTIONAL LEADER OR A DECISION-MAKER? More of an emotional leader. The contribution that he tries to make, I believe, is in demanding of the players that they do what they are capable of doing. I don't think he's ever seen himself as a chess player.

IS HE MORE OF AN OPTIMIST OR MORE OF A PROBLEM SOLVER? He's an optimist, a sales-man. He's always trying to build up his players, make them see what they are capable of. He doesn't make a big deal out of trying to correct their weaknesses; he's much more interested in trying to build up their strengths.

HOW HE USES HIS PERSONNEL

DOES HE FAVOR A SET LINEUP OR A ROTA-TION SYSTEM? A set lineup; he doesn't like to deal with "partial ballplayers," with players who can hit but not field, players who can field but not hit, players who can hit lefthanders but not righthanders. What he is trying to do most of the time is to find the eight best players that he can get and let them win the pennant.

DOES HE LIKE TO PLATOON? Not at all; he won't platoon unless he absolutely has to.

The effect of this can be seen by looking at the number of at-bats the Tigers have when their batter has a platoon advantage, and the number they have when they do not have a platoon advantage. If you go down the roster, for example, Brookens had 145 at bats against lefthanders, when he did have the platoon advantage, and 187 at-bats against right-handers, against whom he did not have the advantage. Gibson had 361 at-bats against righthanders, when he did have the advantage, and 40 against lefthanders, when he did not. The data for all Tiger players is given below:

At-bats with the platoon advantage: Brookens, 145; Butera, 2; Cabell, 171; Castillo, 59; Fahey, 21; Gibson, 361; Gonzalez, 7; Grubb, 134;

Herndon, 201; Ivie, 21; Johnson, 66; Jones, 44; Krenchicki, 131; Laga, 21; Leach, 233; Lemon, 149; Molinaro, 2; Nahorodny, 1; Parrish, 185; Trammell, 169; Whitaker, 438; Wilson, 182; Wockenfuss, 172. TEAM TOTAL, 2,915.

At-bats without the platoon advantage: Brookens, 187; Butera, 3; Cabell, 221; Castillo, 60; Fahey, 1; Gibson, 40; Gonzalez, 14; Grubb, 0; Herndon, 402; Ivie, 21; Johnson, 0; Jones, 20; Krenchicki, 2; Laga, 0; Leach, 9; Lemon, 342; Molinaro, 0; Nahorodny, 0; Parrish, 420; Trammel, 336; Whitaker, 205; Wilson, 321; Wockenfuss, 73. TEAM TOTAL, 2,677.

By contrast, a platoon manager such as Altobelli may have a 2-1 or better ratio of at-bats with the platoon advantage; the Orioles had 3,792 at-bats in 1983 going with the percentage, and 1,754 going against it. Bobby Cox's Toronto Blue Jays had 4,047 at-bats with the platoon advantage, 1,534 against it. So Sparky is passing up maybe 750, 800 at-bats a year of having the platoon advantage with him (about five a game) in order to have a set lineup (which, of course, does have its own advantages. I'm not commenting on the value of the move; just trying to outline its dimensions). And he is platooning more now than he used to. In 1982 the Tigers actually had more at-bats against the edge than with it.

DOES HE TRY TO SOLVE HIS PROBLEMS WITH PROVEN PLAYERS OR WITH YOUNGSTERS WHO STILL HAVE SOMETHING TO PROVE? HOW MANY PLAYERS HAS HE MADE REGULARS OUT OF WHO WERE NOT REGULARS BEFORE, AND WHO WERE THEY? In his first year in Cincinnati, he went with the lineup he inherited except that whereas Bristol had split shortstop between Woody Woodward and Darrell Chaney, he split it between Woodward and Dave Concepcion (eventually, of course, he made Concepcion the regular), and in leftfield he replaced Alex Johnson, who had been traded, with a platoon combination of the rookies Bernie Carbo and Hal McRae. He did move another rookie, Wayne Simpson, into the starting rotation until Simpson's arm blew out halfway through the year. Later on he gave regular jobs to George Foster, Ken Griffey, Cesar Geronimo and Dan Driessen. The players that he has made first-time regulars or near-regulars in Detroit are Tom Brookens, Kirk Gibson and Rick Peters; otherwise, again, he is working with players who a) were already here or b) were already established major leaguers.

He could and probably should be given some credit for bringing Champ Summers out of the minor leagues and getting a couple of outstanding platoon seasons from him. Summers' conflict with him over wanting more playing time may have tended to cloud the fact that Summers was a 30-year-old minor leaguer before Sparky brought him along and gave him some playing time, and he's never done anything for any-

body else. Champ probably would have been a lot better off if he'd kept his mouth shut and continued to make a living off of righthanded pitchers, rather than taking the route he did.

In a sense, this question is irrelevant to Sparky's career because he has inherited so much talent that he was not called upon to build up the lineup. His assignment has always been to take a team that was in place and try to win with it.

DOES HE PREFER TO GO WITH GOOD OFFENSIVE PLAYERS OR DOES HE LIKE THE GLOVE MEN? Again, Sparky likes whole ballplayers; he's not one to try to take a player who does one thing or two things well and try to make some use of him, as Weaver would. But I don't think that he has ever had a strong offensive player in his lineup who was a liability with the glove, whereas he has used some players who didn't hit too much but were strong defensively, like Geronimo and (arguably) Brookens. So in this category, I'd have to say the latter. For a manager who was a no-hit, good field player himself to make much use of the opposite type of player would be very unusual.

DOES HE LIKE AN OFFENSE BASED ON POWER, SPEED OR HIGH AVERAGES? Again, he likes the complete players. His 1976 Reds team led the league in everything you can name. What *type* of player you look for is a question that you deal with when you are building a platoon lineup or a ballclub composed of role players; it really doesn't enter into the discussion much when you're building around an eight-man lineup.

DOES HE USE THE ENTIRE ROSTER OR DOES HE KEEP PEOPLE AROUND SITTING ON THE BENCH? I don't know; ask Bill Fahey.

DOES HE BUILD HIS BENCH AROUND YOUNG PLAYERS WHO CAN STEP INTO A BREACH IF NEED BE OR AROUND VETERAN ROLE-PLAYERS WHO HAVE THEIR OWN FUNCTIONS WITHIN A GAME? Maybe I didn't phrase this question right. It's definitely not the former, and it's not quite the latter. He mostly keeps players who are 28 or older—Fahey, Lynn Jones, Wockenfuss—on his bench. Some of them have a role on the team, and some of them have very little role on the team. But he doesn't seem to like to keep people on the bench who are itching for a chance to play.

GAME MANAGING AND USE OF STRATEGIES

DOES HE GO FOR THE BIG-INNING OFFENSE OR DOES HE LIKE TO USE THE ONE-RUN STRATEGIES? He's not a "big bang" manager; he will use the one-run weapons. Fairly balanced in this respect, I would say.

DOES HE PINCH-HIT MUCH, AND IF SO

WHEN? His top pinch-hitter, Wockenfuss, had 24 at bats in that role in 1983. He uses more pinch-hitters than you might expect in view of 1) his lack of platooning, and 2) the strength of his lineups. He definitely is not going to let a Tom Brookens or a Marty Castillo bat in a game situation.

ANYTHING UNUSUAL ABOUT HIS LINEUP SELECTION? Not really; see comment in major article on team.

DOES HE USE THE SAC BUNT OFTEN? Average amount; no pronounced tendency.

DOES HE LIKE TO USE THE RUNNING GAME? Again, he uses a balanced offense. His teams stole a lot of bases in Cincinnati, but it's never been a matter of changing the lineup to get more speed in there. It's just that he had some players who could also run.

DOES HE DRAW THE INFIELD IN MUCH? In a bunting situation, yes, he will have his infield in. He doesn't like to concede a run even early in the game, and he's never had a Graig Nettles at third base, so he has to keep the infield tight.

IN WHAT CIRCUMSTANCES WILL HE ISSUE AN INTENTIONAL WALK? He'll rarely pass up a chance to use an intentional walk if it puts the double play back in order. In the sixth inning of Game One of the 1975 Series, the Red Sox had runners at second and third, one out and Rick Burleson up. Left-hander on the mound, Cecil Cooper on deck, pitcher up behind him. Scoreless tie.

He walked Burleson intentionally to pitch to Cooper, setting up a possible double play. It worked; Cooper hit a fly ball and the runner from third was doubled out at the plate. It still seems a little extreme. Wouldn't you rather pitch to Rick Burleson without the double play in order, and then if you get him walk Cooper and makes the inning come to rest on the pitcher? Of course, Cecil Cooper wasn't very Cooperish then, but he did hit .311 and slug .544 that year.

He is very cautious about using an intentional walk when he is ahead; about the same situation occurred in Game 3 of that Series (top of the fifth) with Lynn at the plate and Petrocelli up behind him. Same situation, plus you've got the MVP at the plate and a .239 hitter on deck. Yet he did not walk Lynn, and you have to figure that the key was that he now had a 2–1 lead.

That's what got him in trouble last April 20 when he let Brett beat him with a base open and George on a tear. He had a 7–6 lead in the ninth inning, and he just couldn't bring himself to put the lead run on base. Brett hit his third home run of the game, and the fans really got on Sparky's case about it. But the precept that he was following—never put the lead run on base—exists for good reasons.

DOES HE HIT AND RUN VERY OFTEN? Yes,

he likes to hit and run; he'll hit and run with Trammell, Cabell, Wockenfuss, sometimes Chet Lemon and Whitaker. For the same reason as before—he's very big on the role of double plays. He's said at times that the key to success in baseball is to keep the double play in order on defense, and stay away from it on offense. So he'll hit and run with nobody or one out whenever he has to stay away from the DP.

ARE THERE ANY UNIQUE OR IDIOSYN-CRATIC STRATEGIES THAT HE PARTICU-LARLY LIKES? Along the same line, Sparky was one of the pioneers of the field-the-bunt-and-make-the-play-to-second generation. As percentage moves go, this is closely allied to suicide.

HANDLING THE PITCHING STAFF

DOES HE LIKE POWER PITCHERS OR PRE-FER TO GO WITH THE PEOPLE WHO PUT THE BALL IN PLAY? Staffs have always been built around power pitchers, with the exception of a few years in the mid-seventies when his teams were so overpowering that he just asked his pitchers not to lose it for him.

DOES HE STAY WITH THE STARTER OR GO TO THE BULLPEN QUICKLY? You know this story already; used to be known for going to the pen immediately, now stays with his starters. He did not take Jack Morris out of a game unless Morris had pitched seven innings or allowed four runs to score one time last year; Morris lasted at least seven 33 times in 37 starts last year (for comparison, McGregor lasted seven 23 times in 36 starts, Dave Stieb 28 in 36, Rick Sutcliffe 19 times in 35 starts. Only pitcher in the division who was comparable was Guidry, who went seven 27 times in 31 starts.)

DOES HE LIKE THE FOUR-MAN OR THE FIVE-MAN ROTATION? Has used a four-man rotation here since 1980; used a four-man rotation most of the time in Cincinnati 1970–74; five man rotation from '75–'78.

DOES HE USE THE ENTIRE STAFF OR DOES HE TRY TO GET FIVE OR SIX PEOPLE TO DO MOST OF THE WORK? For the moment, at least, he's trying to get all he can out of Petry and Morris, and the rest of the staff is sort of "I'll let you know when I need you." He's had trouble finding a decent lefthander or long man.

HOW LONG WILL HE STAY WITH A STARTER WHO IS STRUGGLING? He had eleven games last year in which he let a starting pitcher start an inning after he had already surrendered five runs. That's the most in the division.

ARE THERE ANY PARTICULAR TYPES OF PITCHERS OF WHOM HE IS FOND? He's always willing to take a look at a Bob James, a Juan

Berenguer, a Doug Capilla. You get the feeling that when a pitcher shows up in spring training he says, "Let me hear your fastball."

IS THERE ANYTHING UNIQUE ABOUT HIS HANDLING OF HIS PITCHERS? Nothing consistent; different things at different times.

WHAT IS HIS STRONGEST POINT AS A MANAGER? His record.

IF THERE WERE NO PROFESSIONAL BASEBALL, WHAT WOULD THIS MANAGER PROBABLY BE DOING? Painting houses.

Enos CABELL, First Base
Runs Created: 51

	G	AB	Hit	2B	3B	HR	Run	RBI	BB	SO	SB	CS	Avg
8.25 Years		594	164	26	6	6	77	59	24	71	26	13	.275
1983	121	392	122	23	5	5	62	46	16	41	4	8	.311
First Half	55	161	54	10	1	3	28	17	7	22	2	5	.335
Second Half	66	231	68	13	4	2	34	29	9	19	2	3	.294
vs. RHP		221	65	14	4	2	32	30	9	27	3	3	.294
vs. LHP		171	57	9	1	3	30	16	7	14	1	5	.333
Home	62	198	64	12	4	1	35	17	10	21	2	5	.323
Road	59	194	58	11	1	4	27	29	6	20	2	3	.299
Grass	101	326	100	18	4	4	52	35	12	31	3	7	.307
Turf	20	66	22	5	1	1	10	11	4	10	1	1	.333

Alan TRAMMELL, Shortstop
Runs Created: 96

	G	AB	Hit	2B	3B	HR	Run	RBI	BB	SO	SB	CS	Avg
5.25 Years		552	155	24	4	8	82	58	61	63	17	9	.280
1983	142	505	161	31	2	14	83	66	57	64	30	10	.319
First Half	61	194	54	13	1	3	27	22	23	27	4	4	.278
Second Half	81	311	107	18	1	11	56	44	34	37	26	6	.344
vs. RHP		336	103	20	2	11	54	44	38	50	25	7	.307
vs. LHP		169	58	11	0	3	29	22	19	14	5	3	.343
Home	70	238	72	8	0	8	33	32	25	31	15	4	.303
Road	72	267	89	23	2	6	50	34	32	33	15	6	.333
Grass	119	421	126	19	1	11	64	52	44	53	23	10	.299
Turf	23	84	35	12	1	3	19	14	13	11	7	0	.417

Lou WHITAKER, Second Base
Runs Created: 114

	G	AB	Hit	2B	3B	HR	Run	RBI	BB	SO	SB	CS	Avg
5.21 Years		567	160	23	7	7	84	61	71	74	13	7	.282
1983	161	643	206	39	6	12	94	72	67	70	17	10	.320
First Half	76	313	97	20	5	5	46	31	29	34	8	5	.310
Second Half	85	330	109	19	1	7	48	41	38	36	9	5	.330
vs. RHP		438	143	29	6	8	64	44	45	49	15	6	.326
vs. LHP		205	63	10	0	4	30	28	22	21	2	4	.307
Home	81	315	99	18	3	7	45	34	28	35	4	4	.314
Road	80	328	107	21	3	5	49	38	39	35	13	6	.326
Grass	137	545	178	35	6	11	82	60	54	63	13	9	.327
Turf	24	98	28	4	0	1	12	12	13	7	4	1	.286

Larry HERNDON, Left Field
Runs Created: 97

	G	AB	Hit	2B	3B	HR	Run	RBI	BB	SO	SB	CS	Avg
6.20 Years		540	150	20	10	11	69	59	35	87	13	8	.278
1983	153	603	182	28	9	20	88	92	46	95	9	3	.302
First Half	71	280	74	15	6	7	39	38	19	50	3	0	.264
Second Half	82	323	108	13	3	13	49	54	27	45	6	3	.334
vs. RHP		402	111	16	7	9	51	49	33	73	5	3	.276
vs. LHP		201	71	12	2	11	37	43	13	22	4	0	.353
Home	78	288	81	15	6	7	45	39	31	49	6	1	.281
Road	75	315	101	13	3	13	43	53	15	46	3	2	.321
Grass	131	510	153	24	7	16	77	72	38	78	9	2	.300
Turf	22	93	29	4	2	4	11	20	8	17	0	1	.312

Tom BROOKENS, Third Base
Runs Created: 32

	G	AB	Hit	2B	3B	HR	Run	RBI	BB	SO	SB	CS	Avg
3.46 Years		483	119	20	5	10	57	58	33	76	12	9	.246
1983	138	332	71	13	3	6	50	32	29	46	10	4	.214
First Half	71	204	46	8	1	4	25	19	20	25	6	3	.225
Second Half	67	128	25	5	2	2	25	13	9	21	4	1	.195
vs. RHP		187	36	9	2	2	23	10	12	32	6	3	.193
vs. LHP		145	35	4	1	4	27	22	17	14	4	1	.241
Home	73	164	39	6	2	5	28	13	12	19	4	2	.238
Road	65	168	32	7	1	1	22	19	17	27	6	2	.190
Grass	118	281	61	9	2	6	42	26	23	38	10	4	.217
Turf	20	51	10	4	1	0	8	6	6	8	0	0	.196

Chet LEMON, Centerfield
Runs Created: 79

	G	AB	Hit	2B	3B	HR	Run	RBI	BB	SO	SB	CS	Avg
6.51 Years		572	161	34	5	18	85	72	60	79	7	9	.281
1983	145	491	125	21	5	24	78	69	54	70	0	7	.255
First Half	69	232	58	9	1	11	40	27	32	40	0	4	.250
Second Half	76	259	67	12	4	13	38	42	22	30	0	3	.259
vs. RHP		342	90	15	4	18	54	54	32	52	0	4	.263
vs. LHP		149	35	6	1	6	24	15	22	18	0	3	.235
Home	71	234	56	9	2	14	37	35	21	29	0	2	.239
Road	74	257	69	12	3	10	41	34	33	41	0	5	.268
Grass	120	404	99	17	4	20	60	58	39	54	0	4	.245
Turf	25	87	26	4	1	4	18	11	15	16	0	3	.299

Glenn WILSON, Rightfield
Runs Created: 62

	G	AB	Hit	2B	3B	HR	Run	RBI	BB	SO	SB	CS	Avg
1.41 Years		586	163	28	5	16	67	70	28	92	2	3	.278
1983	144	503	135	25	6	11	55	65	25	79	1	1	.268
First Half	71	260	73	10	6	9	36	44	11	31	0	1	.281
Second Half	73	243	62	15	0	2	19	21	14	48	1	0	.255
vs. RHP		321	81	13	4	9	36	41	15	53	1	1	.252
vs. LHP		182	54	12	2	2	19	24	10	26	0	0	.297
Home	73	251	71	11	3	9	26	39	14	44	0	1	.283
Road	71	252	64	14	3	2	29	26	11	35	1	0	.254
Grass	123	423	119	18	5	10	48	59	22	64	1	1	.281
Turf	21	80	16	7	1	1	7	6	3	15	0	0	.200

Lance PARRISH, Catcher
Runs Created: 86

	G	AB	Hit	2B	3B	HR	Run	RBI	BB	SO	SB	CS	Avg
4.74 Years		595	159	32	4	27	81	93	45	117	4	4	.267
1983	155	605	163	42	3	27	80	114	44	106	1	3	.269
First Half	70	280	85	25	1	8	38	49	17	54	1	1	.304
Second Half	85	325	78	17	2	19	42	65	27	52	0	2	.240
vs. RHP		420	117	36	2	18	54	82	26	82	1	2	.279
vs. LHP		185	46	6	1	9	26	32	18	24	0	1	.249
Home	74	283	80	21	1	12	39	56	22	42	0	1	.283
Road	81	322	83	21	2	15	41	58	22	64	1	2	.258
Grass	130	497	135	34	2	21	66	97	38	83	1	2	.272
Turf	25	108	28	8	1	6	14	17	6	23	0	1	.259

Kirk GIBSON, Designated Hitter
Runs Created: 59

	G	AB	Hit	2B	3B	HR	Run	RBI	BB	SO	SB	CS	Avg
2.12 Years		553	149	21	7	20	76	69	51	118	22	12	.269
1983	128	401	91	12	9	15	60	51	53	96	14	3	.227
First Half	59	199	44	8	5	6	32	32	20	50	3	2	.221
Second Half	69	202	47	4	4	9	28	19	33	46	11	1	.233
vs. RHP		361	85	12	8	14	55	49	51	76	13	3	.235
vs. LHP		40	6	0	1	1	5	2	2	20	1	0	.150
Home	63	193	42	5	7	5	26	19	25	52	4	2	.218
Road	65	208	49	7	2	10	34	32	28	44	10	1	.236
Grass	106	338	77	11	9	12	52	40	46	86	12	3	.228
Turf	22	63	14	1	0	3	8	11	7	10	2	0	.222

John WOCKENFUSS, Catcher-Designated Hitter
Runs Created: 37

	G	AB	Hit	2B	3B	HR	Run	RBI	BB	SO	SB	CS	Avg
4.18 Years		444	116	17	2	19	59	68	57	59	1	3	.261
1983	92	245	66	8	1	9	32	44	31	37	1	1	.269
First Half	37	97	24	3	0	4	11	19	7	17	0	1	.247
Second Half	55	148	42	5	1	5	21	25	24	20	1	0	.284
vs. RHP		73	18	1	1	2	7	9	11	13	0	0	.247
vs. LHP		172	48	7	0	7	25	35	20	24	1	1	.279
Home	46	117	32	2	0	8	16	29	21	18	0	0	.274
Road	46	128	34	6	1	1	16	15	10	19	1	1	.266
Grass	77	199	52	6	1	9	25	37	26	28	1	0	.261
Turf	15	46	14	2	0	0	7	7	5	9	0	1	.304

Dan PETRY

Year	(W–L)	GS	Run	Avg	DP	Avg	SB	Avg
1982	(15- 9)	35	176	5.03	38	1.09	16	.46
1983	(19-11)	38	205	5.39	53	1.39	24	.63
1979-1983		135	637	4.72	164	1.21	72	.53

	G	IP	W	L	Pct	ER	ERA
1982 Home	16	122.2	8	2	.800	33	2.42
1983 Home	17	114.1	6	6	.500	56	4.41
1982 Road	19	123.1	7	7	.500	55	4.01
1983 Road	21	152	13	5	.722	60	3.55
1983 Grass	33	229.2	15	11	.577	101	3.96
1983 Turf	5	36.2	4	0	1.000	15	3.68

Jack MORRIS

Year	(W–L)	GS	Run	Avg	DP	Avg	SB	Avg
1982	(17-16)	37	151	4.08	32	.86	15	.41
1983	(20-13)	37	173	4.68	24	.65	24	.65
1977-1983		175	815	4.66	167	.95	108	.62

	G	IP	W	L	Pct	ER	ERA
1982 Home	19	138.1	9	6	.600	53	3.51
1983 Home	17	131	10	4	.714	50	3.44
1982 Road	18	128	8	10	.444	67	4.71
1983 Road	20	162.2	10	9	.526	59	3.26
1983 Grass	32	254.1	17	11	.607	94	3.33
1983 Turf	5	39.1	3	2	.600	15	3.43

Milt WILCOX

Year	(W–L)	GS	Run	Avg	DP	Avg	SB	Avg
1982	(12-10)	29	144	4.97	34	1.17	13	.45
1983	(11-10)	26	124	4.77	20	.77	8	.31
1977-1983		117	524	4.48	127	1.08	53	.45

	G	IP	W	L	Pct	ER	ERA
1982 Home	13	93	6	5	.545	31	3.00
1983 Home	13	100.1	6	4	.600	36	3.23
1982 Road	16	100.2	6	5	.545	47	4.20
1983 Road	13	85.2	5	6	.454	46	4.83
1983 Grass	22	161.1	11	8	.579	68	3.79
1983 Turf	4	24.2	0	2	.000	14	5.11

Glenn ABBOTT

Year	(W–L)	GS	Run	Avg	DP	Avg	SB	Avg
1983	(7-4)	21	90	4.29	16	.76	14	.67
1977-1983		153	635	4.15	165	1.08	118	.77

	G	IP	W	L	Pct	ER	ERA
1983 Home	13	75	3	4	.429	33	3.96
1983 Road	8	54	4	0	1.000	19	3.17
1983 Grass	9	56.2	3	1	.750	16	2.54
1983 Turf	12	72.1	4	3	.571	36	4.48

1983 OTHERS

Pitcher	(W–L)	GS	Run	Avg	DP	Avg	SB	Avg
Berenguer	(9-5)	19	98	5.16	13	.68	12	.63
Rozema	(8-3)	16	97	6.06	11	.69	3	.19
Pashnick	(1-3)	6	21	3.50	5	.83	3	.50
Ujdur	(0-4)	6	21	3.50	5	.83	2	.33
Bailey	(5-5)	3	13	4.33	3	1.00	0	.00
Rucker	(1-2)	3	19	6.33	2	.67	2	.67
Bair	(7-3)	1	2	2.00	0	.00	1	1.00

DETROIT TIGERS
RUNS BATTED IN ANALYSIS

Player	RBI	RBI In Wins	Victory Important RBI	RBI Importance	Wins Batted In	RBI Per Win
Lance Parrish	114	81	44.28	.388	13.35	8.5
Larry Herndon	92	69	40.29	.438	10.64	8.6
Lou Whitaker	72	61	36.70	.510	9.45	7.6
Alan Trammell	66	50	32.53	.493	7.38	8.9
Glen Wilson	.446 65	51	28.96		8.26	7.9
Chet Lemon	69	54	24.97	.362	8.88	7.8
Kirk Gibson	51	35	22.37	.439	6.07	8.4
Enos Cabell	46	41	19.85	.432	5.34	8.6
John Wockenfuss	44	35	19.68	.447	5.48	8.0
Tom Brookens	32	22	7.75	.242	2.80	11.4

NEW YORK YANKEES

I

A friend of mine who teaches a class in baseball literature at the University of Kansas has recommended that I resolve to have the only publication in the field which does not mention That Game. There is a wisdom in this, but on the other hand there were three major points about the issue which were almost totally missed in the noise surrounding it (two were totally missed and the third was largely obscured), and I want to point them out:

1) <u>There is no interpretation of 1.10(b) under which the umpire did not err.</u> Tim McClelland and the Yankees have made maximum use of the after-the-fact confusion of the rule book; one rule says that he should have thrown out the bat, the other that he should have disallowed the home run which was hit. And they're right; *after the fact*, McClelland's ruling is technically as correct as any other. But what that fails to address is that rule 1.10(b) clearly and unmistakably says that if a player comes to the plate with too much pine tar on his bat, the umpire is supposed to remove that bat from the game. This is not an umpire's option; it is his responsibility. That is what he is supposed to do when a batter comes up with too much pine tar on the bat. It is not an appeal play.

So if McClelland's action after the home run was hit is correct, then his failure to act before the home run was hit was in error. If he was correct before the play, then he was in error after it. But any conceivable way you look at it, McClelland blew it. He did not enforce the rule.

2) <u>There is no such thing in sports as selective enforcement of the rules by one team.</u> McClelland's failure to enforce the rule while the offending bat was in use placed the Yankees, according to the Yankees, in the position of calling for enforcement of the rule in such a way and at such a time that it did their team the most good. *No team, in any sport, at any time, is ever in that position.* Get the scenario: One team allows a rule infraction to become an ongoing thing, and then, at the moment when it does the other team the greatest damage, calls the rule into effect. It's preposterous. No rule has ever been enforced on that basis.

3) <u>Baseball is the one major sport in which what you see is what you get.</u> In basketball, the official is constantly hovering over the play, making sure that every little thing is done by the rules. Bodies crunch, a shot flies and clips the net, a whistle blows—and *then* you find out whether the shot counts or not, whether it was all done according to the rules. When a touchdown pass is called back in football, that's no big thing; happens every week. But in baseball, when somebody hits a double, that's a double.

Of course, baseball umpires have many decisions to make; they are the eyes on the scene. They make safe/out calls because somebody has to make them; that's like a football referee's job in looking down the goal line and deciding whether the ball was over the line, or spotting the ball any other time. A basketball referee has to decide whether you were in-bounds or out-of-bounds.

But in those sports, the officials have a second, separate responsibility in distinguishing what has been done legally from what has been done illegally. Baseball officials, with minor exceptions, do not perform that function; they throw no flags and blow no whistles. The losing fans rarely leave a baseball game saying, "We were robbed." MacPhail took the action that he took in a conscious effort to protect that virtue.

II

In all of American League history, the two best performances ever by a team that had lost 100 games the year before are by the Texas Rangers in 1974 (84–76) and the Oakland A's in 1980 (83–79). What happened in both cases was the same thing: Billy Martin took over.

III

In the May 9th issue of *The Sporting News*, Murray Chass wrote an article on the salary structure of the Yankees called "George Plays to Win." Included with the piece was a chart giving the lengths of contracts, guaranteed value and average salary per year for some 27 Yankee players. (Bonuses were not included.) I thought it would be fun to see what kind of value Mr. George is getting for his money. Using approximate value (squared, to keep the figures constant, and give more weight to the players with the higher AVs) and the chart provided by Chass, we can figure a rough dollar value for the '83 Yankees.

Category	Player	1983 salary	AV	Salary/AV²
Easy Streeters	John Mayberry	$ 500,000	−30	$ ∞
	Rudy May	687,500	0	∞
	Doyle Alexander	550,000	0	∞
	Bobby Murcer	375,000	0	∞
	Roger Erickson	180,000	0	∞
Leisure Class	Bob Shirley	$ 683,333	2	$170,833.25
	Rick Cerone	625,000	2	156,250.00
	Lou Pinella	375,000	2	93,750.00
Upwardly Immobile	Dale Murray	$ 160,000	2	$ 40,000.00
	Oscar Gamble	350,000	3	38,888.89
	Steve Kemp	1,090,000	6	30,277.78
	Jerry Mumphrey	661,667	5	26,466.68
	Ken Griffey	1,041,667	8	16,276.05
Blue Chips	Butch Wynegar	$ 444,000	6	$ 12,333.33
	Dave Winfield	1,531,600	12	10,636.11
	Willie Randolph	468,973	7	9,570.88
	Don Baylor	918,750	10	9,187.50
	Graig Nettles	506,250	8	7,910.15
Workin' Joes	Shane Rawley	$ 697,500	10	$ 6,975.00
	Dave Righetti	566,250	10	5,662.50
	Roy Smalley	612,500	11	5,061.98
	Ron Guidry	987,500	14	5,038.27
	Andre Robertson	45,000	3	5,000.00
Bargain Basement	Rich Gossage	$ 458,000	12	$ 3,180.56
	George Frazier	125,000	7	2,551.02
	Don Mattingly	35,000	4	2,187.50

Ironically, it was Lou Pinella, who we can see was not one of the better Yankee investments of 1983, who was quoted in Chass's article as saying, "If you want a good team in today's market, you certainly have to pay for it. It just depends on how much return on your investment you want."

Apart from his infamous and well-documented qualities, Mr. George has a sort of wide charitable streak running through him. Whether it is fueled by guilt or a desire to be liked—or *well* liked as Willy Loman would emphasize—I don't know. But it is from this mercy streak that come many strange transactions; players given bonuses to be demoted to the minor leagues, managers promised jobs years in advance—really weird stuff, unprecedented as far as I know, in baseball history. George seems to think that cash eases all pain. Whether it's being sent to the minors, losing a manager's job or being demoted in the front office, if enough money is thrown at the problem, it will go away. Yankee dollars, it seems, can soften any blow. It's very odd; the aging, incompetent and non-productive are all rewarded. And should a player outlive his usefulness on the field, Mr. George can always make room for him in the broadcast booth. It is this tactic that has inflicted Fran Healy* and Bobby Murcer on the ears of New York fans in the past few years. But that's Steinbrenner, putting men where they don't belong because he thinks he owes them something.

—Jim Baker

IV

I did a study several years ago which I keep intending to repeat but never get the time to do. The study was done in a way vaguely similar to Jim's bit, putting together the money that had been paid to free agents with their production as measured by approximate value. The idea was to try to assess not only free-agent investments, but free-agent investment strategies.

I think this study was done in 1979, so I only had about three years worth of information to deal with. The conclusion, I am trying to say, is highly speculative; God knows what the same study would show today. But what it suggested then was that the best free-agent strategy was probably what we might call the early Steinbrenner approach: ignore the needs of your team, ignore the strengths and weaknesses of the players available. Just identify the best player out there, and go after him.

Why does that work? Because there is a security in it. What has happened several times with minor investments is that adjustment factors of some sort throw a monkey wrench into them. A team sees that a first baseman is available and says, "Hey, we need a first baseman. Let's go after him." This first baseman creates, let's say, 5.5 runs per game, which is 80 runs a year, which is a productive player.

Only you sign him, and you realize that he doesn't create 5.5 runs a game in your park. He creates about 4.8. And you know what that is? That's useless. Because Pat Putnam creates 5.0 runs a game. You don't need to

*My editor insists that Healy does not deserve this comment.

pay somebody free-agent money to do that. You've wasted your money.

Suppose, however, that you sign a Dave Winfield, and you find out that *he* doesn't hit well in your park. (Winfield doesn't hit well in Yankee Stadium, you know.) But it doesn't really matter, because *he's Dave Winfield.* If he'd create 8 runs a game somewhere else, he creates 7.3 for you. So what? Big deal.

Or suppose that you sign a 29-year-old rightfielder to a five-year contract. This rightfielder has been driving in 80 runs a year in other parks, but you figure he can drive in 90 for you because he'll have more people on in front of him.

And he does. He drives in 90 runs. But what you forget is, by the time he's in the middle of the contract, he's going to be 31 or 32. And most players will drop off sharply in performance when they get to about 31 or 32.

So your player drives in 90 runs one year and then drops to 65. And you know what you've done? You've wasted your money.

Suppose, however, you'd shelled out the extra potatoes to get the rightfielder who drives in 110 runs a year, which you figure will be 120 in your park. We'll call this guy Reggie Jackson. And he does have a big year or two for you, and then he does decline a little. But it doesn't matter, because *he's Reggie Jackson.* So he drops from 120 RBI to 95. So what? He's still going to help you.

What I'm saying is this: Great players' careers are relatively much less vulnerable to fluctuations in value than are ordinary players' careers. That's why great players hang around until they're 40; if they have a bad year, they still have value. There is a security in them.

When George signed Reggie, some very smart baseball people said: "What'd he do that for? They've already got lefthanded power on that team. They've got Nettles and Chambliss and Gamble. What do they need Reggie for?" When he signed Goose Gossage, some people said that it had nothing to do with the needs of the Yankee team. They already had a relief pitcher who had just won the Cy Young Award. What more could Goassage do? When he signed Tommy John people said, "Look at all the lefthanded starters that he's already got."

Another thing that I think people often underestimate is how difficult it can be to accurately assess your needs. A lot of the free-agent signings that have been made in response to needs, it seems to me, have worked out badly. The Padres signed Oscar Gamble because they thought they needed power. The Yankees signed Dave Collins because they thought they needed speed.

Whenever you talk yourself into thinking that you *need* a player that's when you pay too much for him. And that's what George has been doing in the last few years. Or perhaps he's been forced into that because the superstars just are not getting into the free-agent market anymore.

I should hasten to point out now 1) that I'm not talking about Steve Kemp, and 2) that I'm mostly propounding a theory here, not asserting that that theory is valid. But I think it has some validity.

THE MANAGER

NAME: Billy Martin (Since replaced by Yogi).

AGE: 55 (56 in May)

MANAGERS FOR WHOM PLAYED IN MAJORS:
Casey Stengel, Lou Boudreau, Harry Craft, Jack
Tighe, Bill Norman, Joe Gordon, Fred Hutchinson,
Charlie Dressen, Cookie Lavagetto, Sam Mele. (In
1961 Billy was a teammate of Joe Altobelli and
Billy Gardner; I wonder if all three of them were
ever in the infield at the same time. An outfielder on
the team, Jim Lemon, also managed in the majors;
another teammate, Jim Kaat, just retired.)

CHARACTERISTICS AS A PLAYER: Had surprising power, a good arm, terrific range and could turn
the DP. If he hadn't been drafted after his best season at the age of 25, if he could have stayed out of
trouble and stayed with the Yankees, his career could
easily have been an impressive one. Got into a lot of
fights.

MANAGERIAL RECORD:

Team	Year	Par	Wins	Losses	Pct.	+ or −
Minn	1969	84	97	65	.599	+ 13
Det	1971	83	91	71	.562	+ 8
Det	1972	81	86	70	.551	+ 5
Det	1973	77	76	67	.531	− 1
Tex	1973	9	9	14	.391	0
Tex	1974	64	84	76	.525	+ 20
Tex	1975	44	44	51	.463	0
NY	1975	29	30	26	.536	1
NY	1976	83	97	62	.610	+ 14
NY	1977	88	100	62	.617	+ 12
NY	1978	54	52	42	.553	− 2
NY	1979	55	55	41	.573	0
Oak	1980	68	83	79	.512	+ 15
Oak	1981	49	64	45	.587	+ 15
Oak	1982	85	68	94	.420	− 17
NY	1983	82	91	71	.562	+ 9
16 Years		1035	1127	936	.546	+ 92

WHAT HE BRINGS TO THE BALLCLUB

IS HE AN INTENSE MANAGER OR MORE OF
AN EASY-TO-GET-ALONG-WITH TYPE? Oh,
he's a sweetheart. Super-intense.

IS HE MORE OF AN EMOTIONAL LEADER OR
A DECISION-MAKER? He's both. Like Weaver.

IS HE MORE OF AN OPTIMIST OR MORE OF
A PROBLEM SOLVER? He expects the players to
work on the things that they can't do; in that way,
he's a problem solver, going after weaknesses. You
may remember that he had some problems with
Mickey Rivers at one time because he felt that some
of Mickey's throwing problems could be corrected if
he would stride forward as he threw or something. It
wasn't natural to Mickey, and it caused some friction.

HOW HE USES HIS PERSONNEL

DOES HE FAVOR A SET LINEUP OR A ROTA-
TION SYSTEM? Well, until 1983 that would have
been an easy question to answer. He always has used
a set lineup, maybe not an 8-player set lineup but six
or seven set positions and well-defined jobs for the
other people. But in 1983, he didn't make many in-
roads against the shufflin' around the Yankees have
been doing since 1981. Smalley is still a shortstop-
third baseman-first baseman, there is still no number
1 catcher and the outfield mess is still a mess.

DOES HE LIKE TO PLATOON? Some, but not a
lot. He'll platoon at the left end of the defensive spectrum a bit, platoon first basemen or leftfielders or
designated hitters. But if he does any shifting at
catcher or shortstop or second base, it has usually
not been platooning but just experimentation.

DOES HE TRY TO SOLVE HIS PROBLEMS
WITH PROVEN PLAYERS OR WITH YOUNG-
STERS WHO STILL HAVE SOMETHING TO
PROVE? HOW MANY PLAYERS HAS HE MADE
REGULARS OUT OF WHO WERE NOT REGU-
LARS BEFORE, AND WHO WERE THEY? Has
given regular jobs to 12 players who had not had them
before: Rich Reese, Mike Hargrove, Joe Lovitto, Jim
Sundberg, Lenny Randle, Roy Howell, Willie Ran-
dolph, Fred Stanley, Mario Guerrero, Tony Armas,
Mike Heath and Andre Robertson.

In all of his jobs, he basically has worked with
the talent that he has inherited. He has in some cases
pulled players out of the minors to fill a slot, and he
has on several cases helped to orchestrate trades to
strengthen a middle-of-the-field position. But mostly,
he has taken over the talent that was there and won
with it.

DOES HE PREFER TO GO WITH GOOD OF-
FENSIVE PLAYERS OR DOES HE LIKE THE
GLOVE MEN? He won't keep a nonhitter in the
lineup. I remember a year ago, when he was talking
about even such a brilliant defensive player as Andre
Robertson, he said something to the effect that "I'd
sure like to have his glove in the lineup, but I can't
keep him in there if he doesn't hit." In his battle
between two catchers last spring, some people thought
he might lean toward Cerone because Cerone was
stronger defensively. But Cerone didn't hit, and by
the end of the year Wynegar was doing most of the
catching.

Billy's improvement of his teams is both offensive and defensive, and about balanced between the
two. The Yankees in 1983 improved by 61 runs
offensively (709 to 770), but only 13 defensively
(716 to 703).

DOES HE LIKE AN OFFENSIVE BASED ON
POWER, SPEED, OR HIGH AVERAGES? Muscle.
Muscle and intimidation. He works with the talent
he's got, but don't give me any stories about "Billy
Ball" winning the division in Oakland. The 1983 Oakland A's hit more home runs than any other team in
baseball that year.

I can't over-stress the point that Martin works with the talent that he inherits, whatever their strengths are. If he takes over a 20-homer man, the man tends, for reasons I couldn't really explain, to hit 30 home runs. If he inherits a .300 hitter, the guy tends to hit .330. He works hard at picking up "edges," a little thing he can see that could help this guy, a pitch that this pitcher needs to throw or stop throwing. He probably does that more successfully for more different types of players than anybody else around.

DOES HE USE THE ENTIRE ROSTER OR DOES HE KEEP PEOPLE AROUND SITTING ON THE BENCH? Everybody has a job, and you can always figure out what that job is, but sometimes it's not a major role. He will have a player sitting there all year and batting 75 times if that's all the role he has for the player.

Again, the 1983 Yankees were not entirely typical in this respect because 1) the team was so unsettled —whose role was what was never very clear, and Billy to my surprise did not make it much clearer, and 2) there were a lot of injuries that kept redefining jobs.

DOES HE BUILD HIS BENCH AROUND YOUNG PLAYERS WHO CAN STEP INTO A BREACH IF NEED BE OR AROUND VETERAN ROLE-PLAYERS WHO HAVE THEIR OWN FUNCTIONS WITHIN A GAME? Both; I would say more of the former. He always seems to have around at least a couple of those Dan Mattingly, Steve Balboni and Mike Davis types, just sitting there waiting for a chance to get into the lineup. He also, of course, makes some use of the veterans who used to be regulars, like Campy or Milbourne or Pinella.

GAME MANAGING AND USE OF STRATEGIES

DOES HE GO FOR THE BIG-INNING OFFENSE OR DOES HE LIKE TO USE THE ONE-RUN STRATEGIES? He's very much a big-inning manager. The Yankees used only 37 sac bunts in 1983 (Casey would turn over in his grave if Billy decided to be Gene Mauch), and tried only 124 stolen base attempts. Only three teams bunted less often, and only four ran less often. He does react to the talent that he has, as any intelligent manager does, and he did bunt more in Oakland and Texas, where he did not have the talent to blow people away.

DOES HE PINCH-HIT MUCH, AND IF SO WHEN? Well, I don't believe that he's ever had on any of his teams a specialty pinch-hitter, a guy like Hairston in Chicago or Manny Mota or Smokey Burgess or Jose Morales; even Gates Brown, who pinch-hit 40, 50 times a year before and after Billy managed Detroit, was cut down to less than 30 tries a year while Martin was there.

He often platoons at two or three positions, and he usually draws his pinch-hitters from those positions.

He seems to feel that a hitter won't stay sharp without some playing time.

ANYTHING UNUSUAL ABOUT HIS LINEUP SELECTION? It's brilliant; I don't know if you'd say that was unusual.

A central theme in understanding Billy Martin as a manager would have to be his understanding and command of diverse types of players, and how it is that they are ALL needed to add up to a ballclub. If you look at his teams, you always find that he has a leadoff man, or he has two or three leadoff types, and that they are good at what they do. He's managed several of the greatest leadoff men of our time —Henderson, Carew, Randolph. The first two or three spots of the lineup will always be filled by people who get on base.

And after that, you always find power hitters. You never find Billy Martin managing one of those Cleveland Indian-type wishy-washy offenses where everybody does a little bit of everything. On his bench, he'll have outfielders who can hit but not play defense well enough and infielders or outfielders who can play defense but not hit. But you'll never see him with one of these Joe Fergusons or Rick Leaches that you don't know exactly what it is that they're supposed to be doing or why they're there. He is able to knit unlike talents into a coherent whole.

DOES HE USE THE SAC BUNT OFTEN? Not usually, no.

DOES HE LIKE TO USE THE RUNNING GAME? He'll use it when he has the talent for it; he won't force it if he doesn't. He's never had a team that ran much as a group except in Oakland.

IN WHAT CIRCUMSTANCES WILL HE ISSUE AN INTENTIONAL WALK? Very, very rarely. Mostly out of respect to the big gun, the Johnny Bench or Jim Rice or George Brett. Looking over his World Series games, you don't find him using the walk much as a strategic thing, to fill up a base or get a platoon advantage. I doubt that you could find five times a year when he walks a number 8 hitter to set up a force play and try to use the number 9 hitter as an escape hatch. The Yankees issued only 24 intentional walks last year. The only team in the majors to issue less was Kansas City, with 23. In 1976 the Yankees gave away only 16 intentional passes, which may be (I haven't checked) the lowest total in many years.

DOES HE HIT AND RUN VERY OFTEN? Quite a bit, yes. One of the reasons he wasn't thrilled when the Yankees first got Reggie was that he had wanted them to get somebody he could hit and run with a little more. I've read that as a player he was a terrific hit-and-run man himself.

ARE THERE ANY UNIQUE OR IDIOSYN-CRATIC STRATEGIES THAT HE PARTICU-LARLY LIKES? He likes to try to deke the opposition once in awhile, keep the threat in their mind that he is going to try something funny, hence creating a second of hesitation at a key moment. I guess you probably know that.

HANDLING THE PITCHING STAFF

DOES HE LIKE POWER PITCHERS OR PREFER TO GO WITH THE PEOPLE WHO PUT THE BALL IN PLAY? An awful lot of Billy Martin's success as a manager is directly attributable to his ability to convince power pitchers to throw strikes. Or maybe it's Art Foweler's ability; who knows. Anyway, one thing you can absolutely, positively say about Billy Martin is that he will not use a pitcher who doesn't throw strikes. He cannot and will not abide a pitcher who goes out there and nibbles, tries to throw three or four pitches that he doesn't have command of, and loses the ball game with the fielders standing there watching. In that sense, they're putting the ball in play.

But it's not finesse pitchers who are doing this; it's mostly people who can throw pretty hard. He's had a lot of success working with pitchers like Jim Bibby, Dave Righetti, Mike Norris and Ron Guidry who could always throw hard, but who for some reason were not winning ballgames. He gets them to throw strikes, puts a defense behind them and an offense in front of them, and they win. A tremendous number of pitchers have won 20 games for him.

New York pitchers in 1982 walked 491 men, sixth-lowest total in the league. In 1983 they cut in to 455, third in the league. Oakland pitchers in 1979 walked 654 men, most in the league. Under Billy in 1980, they cut it to 521, eighth in the league. Yankee pitchers in 1975 walked 502 men; under Billy in 1976, they cut it to 448. Ranger pitchers in 1973 walked 680 men; under Billy, they cut that to 449 (!). Tiger pitchers in 1970 walked 623 men; under Billy, they cut that to 609 in 1971 and 465 in 1972.

DOES HE STAY WITH THE STARTER OR GO TO THE BULLPEN QUICKLY? He goes with the starter as long as possible. He doesn't work them as hard here as he did in Oakland because he has a good bullpen behind them, but the Yankees still led the league in complete games in 1983. Most of Billy's teams have.

DOES HE LIKE THE FOUR-MAN OR THE FIVE-MAN ROTATION? Last year what he was using might be called a four-man, five-day rotation, with Guidry, Rawley, Righetti and later Fontenot being used every fifth day if it was at all possible, and Shirley, Howell, Keough *et al* being shuffled in and out to accommodate them. Early in his career he used not only a four-man rotation, but a four-day rotation for his ace starter.

DOES HE USE THE ENTIRE STAFF OR DOES HE TRY TO GET FIVE OR SIX PEOPLE TO DO MOST OF THE WORK? He works the front end of the staff; the other three or four guys are not going to see much work or any work in a game situation.

HOW LONG WILL HE STAY WITH A STARTER WHO IS STRUGGLING? He expects his ace pitchers to get out of their own jams.

ARE THERE ANY PARTICULAR TYPES OF PITCHERS OF WHOM HE IS FOND? We've covered this.

IS THERE ANYTHING UNIQUE ABOUT HIS HANDLING OF HIS PITCHERS? He has worked more pitchers harder than anyone else in the modern history of baseball—that is, since the lively ball was introduced. You look back to the fifties, the forties, the twenties even, and you won't find any manager asking his starting pitchers to do as much as Martin has asked them to do.

WHAT IS HIS STRONGEST POINT AS MANAGER? Intense desire to win; intolerance of sloppiness, complete understanding of the game, ability to form unlike and unrelated talents into a comprehensive whole.

IF THERE WERE NO PROFESSIONAL BASEBALL, WHAT WOULD THIS MANAGER PROBABLY BE DOING? Fifteen to life.

Ken GRIFFEY, First Base
Runs Created: 74

	G	AB	Hit	2B	3B	HR	Run	RBI	BB	SO	SB	CS	Avg
7.98 Years		602	183	31	8	10	101	66	62	75	21	7	.304
1983	118	458	140	21	3	11	60	46	34	45	5	1	.306
First Half	62	240	80	11	2	5	36	21	19	26	3	0	.333
Second Half	56	218	60	10	1	6	24	25	15	19	2	1	.275
vs. RHP		275	89	14	3	6	38	27	23	25	5	1	.324
vs. LHP		183	51	7	0	5	22	19	11	20	0	0	.279
Home	60	223	68	11	0	8	31	33	18	21	0	0	.305
Road	58	235	72	10	3	3	29	13	16	24	5	1	.306
Grass	102	399	118	20	2	11	53	43	28	35	5	1	.296
Turf	16	59	22	1	1	0	7	3	6	10	0	0	.373

Omar MORENO, Centerfield
Runs Created: 52

	G	AB	Hit	2B	3B	HR	Run	RBI	BB	SO	SB	CS	Avg
6.72 Years		616	156	20	11	4	89	45	51	109	67	23	.272
1983	145	557	136	21	12	1	65	42	30	103	37	16	.244
First Half	75	320	79	9	8	0	37	18			26		.247
Second Half	70	237	57	12	4	1	28	24			11		.241
vs. RHP		388	108			0	28						.278
vs. LHP		169	28			1	14						.166
Home	72	272	77	16	7	1	39	23			20		.283
Road	73	285	59	5	5	0	26	19			17		.207
Grass	77	273	65	12	3	1	28	23			20		.238
Turf	68	284	71	9	9	0	37	19			17		.250

Willie RANDOLPH, Second Base
Runs Created: 55

	G	AB	Hit	2B	3B	HR	Run	RBI	BB	SO	SB	CS	Avg
6.59 Years		600	163	24	7	4	100	50	93	49	29	9	.272
1983	104	420	117	21	1	2	73	38	53	32	12	4	.279
First Half	49	191	49	6	1	1	29	17	23	14	9	2	.257
Second Half	55	229	68	15	0	1	44	21	30	18	3	2	.297
vs. RHP		248	70	10	1	2	44	24	29	23	11	2	.282
vs. LHP		172	47	11	0	0	29	14	24	9	1	2	.273
Home	55	221	64	8	0	1	39	22	28	18	6	2	.290
Road	49	199	53	13	1	1	34	16	25	14	6	2	.266
Grass	95	384	108	18	1	2	68	37	46	28	12	4	.281
Turf	9	36	9	3	0	0	5	1	7	4	0	0	.250

Steve KEMP, Rightfield
Runs Created: 45

	G	AB	Hit	2B	3B	HR	Run	RBI	BB	SO	SB	CS	Avg
5.88 Years		588	164	26	4	20	89	97	86	82	5	4	.280
1983	109	373	90	17	3	12	53	49	41	37	1	0	.241
First Half	66	235	64	12	2	9	30	39	23	21	1	0	.272
Second Half	43	138	26	5	1	3	23	10	18	16	0	0	.188
vs. RHP		246	60	14	2	11	37	36	28	26	0	0	.244
vs. LHP		127	30	3	1	1	16	13	13	11	1	0	.236
Home	52	178	37	8	0	3	23	15	17	14	0	0	.208
Road	57	195	53	9	3	9	30	34	24	23	1	0	.272
Grass	89	299	72	14	2	8	43	35	34	29	0	0	.241
Turf	20	74	18	3	1	4	10	14	7	8	1	0	.243

Graig NETTLES, Third Base
Runs Created: 71

	G	AB	Hit	2B	3B	HR	Run	RBI	BB	SO	SB	CS	Avg
13.09 Years		575	144	21	2	25	77	83	68	76	2	3	.251
1983	129	462	123	17	3	20	56	75	51	65	0	1	.266
First Half	64	222	60	7	1	12	26	37	29	29	0	0	.270
Second Half	65	240	63	10	2	8	30	38	10	9	0	0	.263
vs. RHP		297	78	9	3	15	34	53	35	38	0	1	.263
vs. LHP		165	45	8	0	5	22	22	16	27	0	0	.273
Home	61	209	65	11	1	11	25	46	21	32	0	0	.311
Road	68	253	58	6	2	9	31	29	30	33	0	1	.229
Grass	110	388	105	14	2	18	50	71	41	56	0	1	.271
Turf	19	74	18	3	1	2	6	4	10	9	0	0	.243

Butch WYNEGAR, Catcher
Runs Created: 54

	G	AB	Hit	2B	3B	HR	Run	RBI	BB	SO	SB	CS	Avg
5.87 Years		552	143	24	2	8	67	66	77	53	2	2	.260
1983	94	301	89	18	2	6	40	42	52	29	1	1	.296
First Half	46	153	46	11	0	5	19	19	21	14	0	1	.301
Second Half	48	148	43	7	2	1	21	23	31	15	1	0	.291
vs. RHP		200	63	13	2	4	28	29	39	21	1	1	.315
vs. LHP		101	26	5	0	2	12	13	13	8	0	0	.257
Home	56	182	49	11	0	4	29	19	29	17	0	1	.269
Road	38	119	40	7	2	2	11	23	23	12	1	0	.336
Grass	80	253	73	16	0	5	35	31	46	25	0	1	.289
Turf	14	48	16	2	2	1	5	11	6	4	1	0	.333

Roy SMALLEY, Shortstop
Runs Created: 74

	G	AB	Hit	2B	3B	HR	Run	RBI	BB	SO	SB	CS	Avg
7.14 Years		582	152	25	3	16	79	73	80	90	3	4	.261
1983	130	451	124	24	1	18	70	62	58	68	3	3	.275
First Half	70	247	69	11	0	10	38	31	35	37	3	3	.279
Second Half	60	204	55	13	1	8	32	31	23	31	0	0	.270
vs. RHP		255	70	10	1	12	41	39	39	52	2	1	.275
vs. LHP		196	54	14	0	6	29	23	19	16	1	2	.276
Home	67	209	57	11	0	7	32	27	35	23	3	2	.273
Road	63	242	67	13	1	11	38	35	23	45	0	1	.277
Grass	110	367	101	18	1	14	56	49	56	49	3	3	.275
Turf	20	84	23	6	0	4	14	13	2	19	0	0	.274

Don BAYLOR, Designated Hitter
Runs Created: 96

	G	AB	Hit	2B	3B	HR	Run	RBI	BB	SO	SB	CS	Avg
10.10 Years		593	159	27	2	23	89	90	57	67	27	10	.268
1983	144	534	162	33	3	21	82	85	40	53	17	7	.303
First Half	69	251	75	14	2	9	37	33	21	21	11	4	.299
Second Half	75	283	87	19	1	12	45	52	19	32	6	3	.307
vs. RHP		285	73	15	1	8	43	38	15	37	10	5	.256
vs. LHP		249	89	18	2	13	39	47	25	16	7	2	.357
Home	72	261	79	14	3	10	41	41	19	29	8	2	.303
Road	72	273	83	19	0	11	41	44	21	24	9	5	.304
Grass	121	450	141	24	3	19	71	76	33	43	13	5	.313
Turf	23	84	21	9	0	2	11	9	7	10	4	2	.250

Dave WINFIELD, Leftfield
Runs Created: 99

	G	AB	Hit	2B	3B	HR	Run	RBI	BB	SO	SB	CS	Avg
9.35 Years		591	168	27	6	25	89	98	65	82	18	6	.284
1983	152	598	169	26	8	32	99	116	58	77	15	6	.283
First Half	73	282	69	9	5	13	38	46	31	38	10	2	.245
Second Half	79	316	100	17	3	19	61	70	27	39	5	4	.316
vs. RHP		345	94	16	6	18	58	69	35	52	11	3	.272
vs. LHP		253	75	10	2	14	41	47	23	25	4	3	.296
Home	75	284	74	15	6	13	44	62	26	40	6	1	.261
Road	77	314	95	11	2	19	55	54	32	37	9	5	.303
Grass	129	503	138	24	8	24	82	96	47	70	11	2	.274
Turf	23	95	31	2	0	8	17	20	11	7	4	4	.326

Andre ROBERTSON, Shortstop
Runs Created: 26

	G	AB	Hit	2B	3B	HR	Run	RBI	BB	SO	SB	CS	Avg
0.94 Years		489	118	23	3	3	58	33	17	81	2	5	.242
1983	98	322	80	16	3	1	37	22	8	54	2	4	.248
First Half	59	186	50	9	2	1	19	14	5	30	2	2	.269
Second Half	39	136	30	7	1	0	18	8	3	24	0	2	.221
vs. RHP		181	41	9	3	0	21	13	2	29	1	3	.227
vs. LHP		141	39	7	0	1	16	9	6	25	1	1	.277
Home	52	171	38	8	3	1	19	16	4	30	2	2	.222
Road	46	151	42	8	0	0	18	6	4	24	0	2	.278
Grass	82	276	67	13	3	1	32	21	5	48	2	3	.243
Turf	16	46	13	3	0	0	5	1	3	6	0	1	.283

Shane RAWLEY

Year	(W–L)	GS	Run	Avg	DP	Avg	SB	Avg
1982	(11-10)	17	78	4.29	18	1.06	9	.53
1983	(14-14)	33	137	4.15	31	.94	9	.27
1978-1983		55	239	4.34	53	.96	24	.44

	G	IP	W	L	Pct	ER	ERA
1982 Home	23	83.1	5	5	.500	31	3.35
1983 Home	17	118.1	5	8	.385	54	4.11
1982 Road	24	80.2	6	5	.545	43	4.80
1983 Road	17	120	9	6	.600	46	3.45
1983 Grass	30	202.1	10	14	.417	96	4.27
1983 Turf	4	36	4	0	1.000	4	1.00

Dave RIGHETTI

Year	(W–L)	GS	Run	Avg	DP	Avg	SB	Avg
1982	(11-10)	27	112	4.15	20	.74	23	.85
1983	(14- 8)	31	160	5.16	38	1.23	26	.84
1979-1983		76	340	4.47	68	.89	65	.85

	G	IP	W	L	Pct	ER	ERA
1982 Home	19	103	7	4	.636	37	3.23
1983 Home	16	115.1	9	3	.750	39	3.04
1982 Road	14	80	4	6	.400	40	4.50
1983 Road	15	101.2	5	5	.500	44	3.90
1983 Grass	28	196	13	8	.619	78	3.58
1983 Turf	3	21	1	0	1.000	5	2.14

Ron GUIDRY

Year	(W–L)	GS	Run	Avg	DP	Avg	SB	Avg
1982	(14-8)	33	181	5.48	29	.88	19	.58
1983	(21-9)	31	141	4.55	25	.81	21	.68
1977-1983		204	977	4.79	182	.89	79	.39

	G	IP	W	L	Pct	ER	ERA
1982 Home	17	113.1	6	5	.545	45	3.57
1983 Home	16	138.1	14	2	.875	36	2.34
1982 Road	17	108.1	8	3	.727	49	4.06
1983 Road	15	112	7	7	.500	59	4.74
1983 Grass	26	216.1	19	7	.731	21	3.00
1983 Turf	5	34	2	2	.500	5	6.09

1983 OTHERS

Pitcher	(W–L)	GS	Run	Avg	DP	Avg	SB	Avg
Shirley	(5-8)	17	78	4.59	18	1.06	11	.65
Fontenot	(8-2)	15	86	5.73	16	1.07	12	.80
Keough	(5-7)	12	65	5.42	14	1.17	9	.75
Howell	(1-5)	12	51	4.25	9	.75	12	1.00
Montefusco	(5-0)	6	28	4.67	4	.67	5	.83
Alexander	(7-8)	5	24	4.80	1	.20	5	1.00

NEW YORK YANKEES
RUNS BATTED IN ANALYSIS

Player	RBI	RBI In Wins	Victory-Important RBI	RBI Importance	Wins Batted In	RBI Per Win
Dave Winfield	116	78	52.32	.451	13.78	8.4
Don Baylor	85	55	36.50	.429	8.64	9.8
Graig Nettles	75	51	33.92	.452	7.99	9.4
Roy Smalley	62	51	33.16	.535	7.63	8.1
Ken Griffey	46	30	19.77	.430	6.40	7.2
Steve Kemp	49	33	18.21	.372	5.58	8.8
Willie Randolph	38	28	17.98	.473	4.62	8.2
Butch Wynegar	42	30	15.86	.378	4.48	9.4
Omar Moreno	17	15	10.51	.618	2.44	7.0
Andre Robertson	22	15	8.18	.372	2.37	9.3

TORONTO BLUE JAYS

Talent in baseball is not normally distributed. This is a fundamental fact of baseball life, and if you have any analytical interest in the game it is terrifically important to understand that. For that reason, I should spend more time than I do talking about baseball's unique talent distributions. I don't, because I'm always afraid of turning off readers who are not familiar with things like distribution curves and standard deviations, and can't see what they have to do with baseball. They have everything to do with baseball, but baseball is not at its best when seen through a fog of methodology.

O.K., I can explain these things crudely and risk offending the mathematicians in the audience, or I can explain them carefully and risk annoying the baseball fans. Easy choice.

The normal distribution curve is a bell-shaped graph which describes the distribution curve of things in an enormous variety of unlike areas. It describes, for example, the distribution of most measurable talents among human beings. If you pick a hundred people off the street, ask them to run a foot race, do a series of math problems, fix lunch, sing "The Star Spangled Banner," sell hot dogs door-to-door, play a dozen games of darts and make an obscene phone call, and you measure their individual abilities to do all of these things, and you graph what you have measured, you probably will wind up with a bell-shaped curve in every instance.

A bell-shaped curve looks like this:

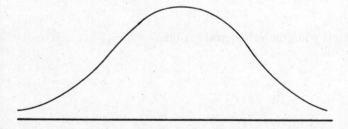

It looks like a bell. What that means is, the largest number of people are always going to be right in the middle. If the average time in which those hundred people can run a hundred yards each is 17.1, the largest number of people are probably going to run the hundred yards in 16 to 18 seconds, and there are going to be about as many people who run it in 22 seconds or more as there are who run it in 12 or less. If the average number of math problems solved is 30, then there are going to be a whole lot of people who solve somewhere between 25 and 35, and there are going to be about as many who solve 10 as there are who solve 50. If the average number of hot dogs sold is 75, there are probably going to be about as many people who sell 50 as there are who sell 100.

Sort of. A major problem here is that in these examples, as in most measures of anything you can think of, the measurement itself is closed on one end. If your

average time for the hundred yard dash in this group is 17 seconds, it is much more likely that you will have somebody who requires 27 seconds to accomplish the task than it is that you will have somebody who can do the 100 yards in 7 flat. The easiest way to deal with this problem, mathematically speaking, is to round up all of the people in your group who run the hundred in more than 24 seconds and shoot them. If you don't shoot them, then you've got to take a whole lot of math classes, and we don't have time for that here.

Anyway, once you have established that you have a normal distribution of talent, all kinds of predictable relationships occur. Suppose that you have one fellow in your group who is just dead average in every respect. We'll call this fellow "Siebern." In any normally distributed population, 15.87% of the population is going to be one standard deviation better than the norm, Siebern, and 15.87% is going to be one standard deviation worse than the norm, Siebern. In baseball terms, suppose that your league average is .272, and your standard deviation (the standard deviation can be described as "about what your average deviant would hit") is .024. There are 200 players in the league. Knowing that, you could predict with a fair degree of certainty how many players in the league would hit .300 (about 24 players would hit .300 or better), how many would hit .330 (one or two would hit .330) and how many would hit .370 (ain't no way in hell anybody's going to hit .370).

To have those predictable relationships among the things you are studying is very convenient in many types of analysis, and for that reason people often assume that talent in baseball is normally distributed. Only it isn't. I could show you places in print where people assured us that batting averages were normally distributed, earned run averages were normally distributed, wins by teams were normally distributed, runs per game were normally distributed and several other things were normally distributed.

And they are all, in scientific parlance, chock full of it. Because none of those things is normally distributed in major league baseball, and indeed I don't know of anything that is.

The reason they aren't normally distributed is because major league baseball players are chosen from the far righthand part of the normal distribution curve. The curve which describes the baseball abilities of the entire population looks like this:

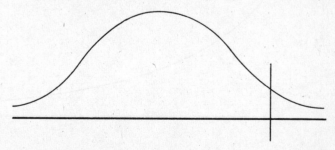

The righthand edge of it represents the people who are really, really good at playing baseball. That part of it looks like this:

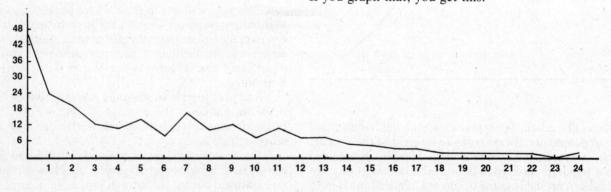

And that is how talent in the major leagues is distributed.

Whereas in the general population, the most common level is the average or norm, in major league baseball the more common level of talent is the bottom, the worst fellow out there.

This is, when you think about it from a baseball perspective rather than a social sciences perspective, pretty obvious, and extremely difficult to argue about. The American League batting average last year was .266. How many players are there who are capable of hitting 95 points better than that? One, Wade Boggs. How many are there who are capable of hitting 95 points less than that? Hundreds.

There are hundreds, or there are none, depending on how you look at it. There are hundreds who are capable of hitting .171; there are none around who can get by with it. There are only about 125 regular American League jobs available, and once you get about 25 points below that .266 average, the jobs are all filled up. To put that same statement the other way, the league average is going to be only about 25 points above the league's replacement level. (You can, of course, stay around if you are

below that figure in batting average, but only if you are better-than-average in some other aspect of the game.)

This same distribution can be drawn from a graph of actual data, rather than derived theoretically, in any number of ways. If you look at the American League in 1983, and you count the number of pitchers winning 0 games, 1 game, 2 games, 3 games, 4 games . . . 24 games:

0 wins	....	46 pitchers
1 win	....	25 pitchers
2 wins	....	20 pitchers
3 wins	....	12 pitchers
4 wins	....	10 pitchers
5 wins	....	14 pitchers
6 wins	....	8 pitchers
7 wins	....	16 pitchers
8 wins	....	8 pitchers
9 wins	....	11 pitchers
10 wins	....	6 pitchers
11 wins	....	9 pitchers
12 wins	....	6 pitchers
13 wins	....	6 pitchers
14 wins	....	4 pitchers
15 wins	....	3 pitchers
16 wins	....	2 pitchers
17 wins	....	2 pitchers
18 wins	....	1 pitcher
19 wins	....	1 pitcher
20 wins	....	1 pitcher
21 wins	....	1 pitcher
22 wins	....	1 pitcher
23 wins	....	0 pitchers
24 wins	....	1 pitcher

If you graph that, you get this:

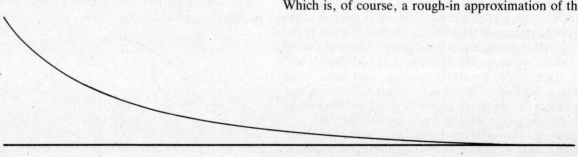

Which is, of course, a rough-in approximation of this

the far right end of a normal distribution curve.

Of course, if you draw the graph based on a percentage measure—won/lost percentage, ERA, offensive won/lost percentage—you don't get such a neat curve. You will, however, always find that far more players are below average than are above average. You will always find that those who are above average are further from the average in absolute terms than those who are below average. (Richard Dotson was fifteen games over .500, LaMarr Hoyt fourteen games over, Guidry twelve over, McGregor eleven and Moose Haas ten. But no pitcher in the league was ten games under .500.)

I may have explained this in such a direct, logical fashion that it seems obvious. It *is* obvious. It is, nonetheless (I am sure that I am exaggerating now, but I believe it as I am writing it), exactly this understanding which most clearly and most consistently separates the good baseball organizations from the poor organizations. It is the knowledge that talent is available, the confidence that problems can be solved from the pool of common resources. That is what the Toronto Blue Jays have now that they did not have three years ago.

Let me try to phrase the difference clearly. Poor organizations virtually always act as if they believed that talent was in short supply. They believe that there is a magic in "proven" major league talent. Why do teams keep playing people like Rick Manning, like Charlie Moore, like Hubie Brooks? Why do they give those players regular jobs, and suffer with them for years and years after they have shown themselves to be below-average players?

Because they believe talent to be in short supply. Why do the Angels keep throwing away money on people like Ellis Valentine? Because they believe talent to be in short supply.

What the Blue Jays have proven clearly with their experience in the post-Bavasi era is that it is *not* in short supply, that there are any number of players around who can help you win ballgames if you will give them the chance to do it. Rance Mulliniks two years ago was available. Randy Moffittt was available. Buck Martinez was available. They were cheap, unwanted, marginal players.

But all players play better in some conditions than they do in others. All players either can hit lefthanders better or righthanders better, or else they can hit better on turf or they can hit better on grass, or else they can pull the ball and be useful in a power park or they can spray it and be useful in a singles-hitters park. Marginal players can always do *something* to help a team win.

The Blue Jays simply recognized that, took advantage of those talents, and pieced together a ballclub.

Of course that's not all there is to it. They wouldn't have done what they have done without some whole talents as well, without Lloyd Moseby and Dave Stieb and Willie Upshaw. Those players, from the far right part of the graph, are anything but available; they are precious.

But all the same, I would say this. I would say that if you look at any successful manager, with very few exceptions you'll find a manager who is not afraid to make changes. You'll find a manager who is not afraid to look at a kid who has not proven what he can do in the major leagues, and say, "This kid can help me."

Unsuccessful organizations have good excuses for their timidity; they say things like "minor league batting records don't mean anything" and "young pitchers will break

your heart." But what it comes down to is, they have no confidence in their own judgment, their ability to solve a problem. They look at their lineup and when they consider the possibility of making a change, they see themselves as teetering on the brink of an abyss.

A Whitney Herzog, a Billy Martin, a Dick Williams, a Bobby Cox or an Earl Weaver doesn't see it that way. Consider the following quotes from the writing of Earl Weaver:

I firmly believe that I could put together a group of scouts—people I've worked with—who in two years could put together an expansion team that would play well over .500 ball in its first season as a major league ballclub.

And also, writing about George Bamberger.

"Well, if you don't want to win twenty, it's all right," he'd say. "If you do, that's all right, too. There are a number of guys here who do want to win twenty, though."

(Emphasis mine, quotes from *It's What You Learn After You Know It All That Counts*.)

The confidence that a good manager has in his ability to draw useful talent from alternative sources puts him in a position of strength when dealing with a player. He can say, "If you don't want to do this the way we need to have it done, we'll try somebody else." He can say that, and mean it. The lack of confidence in his options places a John McNamara or a Bill Virdon in a position of weakness, which he must cover with an autocratic veneer.

I'm oversimplifying, of course. Dick Wagner had enormous confidence in his judgment of his talent, and look where it got him.

Two things to wrap up. To get back to the Blue Jays; a year ago, they had a DH problem. They recognized the problem, they dipped into the pool of available talent, and they found Cliff Johnson, a man who can certifiably hit a baseball, sitting on the bench for Oakland, and Jorge Orta to swing from the other side. Results:

Toronto Designated Hitters

	G	AB	R	H	2B	3B	HR	RBI	SB	Avg
1982	162	596	52	142	18	3	8	56	7	.238
1983	162	601	86	151	29	3	34	113	0	.251

They went from having clearly the worst DH production in the league to having arguably the best—their DHs led the league in home runs and RBIs—and they did it without giving up anything.

Getting back to the issue of how talent is distributed ... the same thing that applies to batting averages and won/lost percentages applies, in one way or another, to every other individual player statistic. Many of these statistics might look like they're normally distributed at a casual glance, but if you really look, you're going to find that they're not. So no more questions about why don't I use stanine scores or something to rank the players by; I don't use them because they're not pertinent.

As to team wins, if you think they're normally distributed, look again. The distribution of team wins is abnormal in at least two respects. Over a period of years, more teams are going to be over .500 than are going to be under .500. (I did a count last summer of how many teams in this century have been over .500 and how many under, but I've lost the damn thing. As I recall, there were more .500+ than .500- teams in every decade.) And two, distinctly fewer teams than the normal distribution curve would predict will win 105 or 110 games in a year. The key to both abnormalities is the Law of Competitive Balance. A team is trying to compose itself so as to win 90 or 95 games a year. As it drops further below that goal, it increases its tendency to take risks in an attempt to move into that area,

which will sometimes cause it either to move back into the race or to drop even further off the pace. As a team moves closer to that 90-to-95 win range, it decreases its tendency to take risks, and thus rarely rises significantly above that level. This causes more teams than you would "normally" expect to settle in the 82-to-100 wins range, and causes a slight bulge in the normal distribution curve.

Which doesn't have a lot to do with baseball. But seeing clearly the distribution of talent: that has everything to do with baseball.

THE MANAGER

NAME: Bobby Cox

AGE: 42 (43 in May)

MANAGERS FOR WHOM PLAYED IN MAJORS: Ralph Houk

CHARACTERISTICS AS A PLAYER: A good-hitting infielder in the minor leagues, he made very slow upward progress, for reasons that are not easy to see at this point.

MANAGERIAL RECORD

Team	Year	Par	Wins	Losses	Pct.	+ or −
Atl	1978	71	69	93	.426	− 2
Atl	1979	69	66	94	.413	− 3
Atl	1980	72	81	80	.503	+ 9
Atl	1981	50	50	56	.472	0
Tor	1982	70	78	84	.481	+ 8
Tor	1983	74	89	73	.549	+15

WHAT HE BRINGS TO THE BALLCLUB

IS HE AN INTENSE MANAGER OR MORE OF AN EASY-TO-GET-ALONG WITH TYPE? It's hard to remember any widely publicized conflicts he has had with his players, either here or in Atlanta.

IS HE MORE OF AN EMOTIONAL LEADER OR A DECISION-MAKER? Both; he's a leader, but his actions are decisive rather than predictable.

IS HE MORE OF AN OPTIMIST OR MORE OF A PROBLEM SOLVER? Well, he's definitely an optimist. He was talking pennant all year in 1980 with a team nobody expected to be in the race. But he doesn't have the acceptance of weaknesses that some "optimist" managers have, either.

HOW HE USES HIS PERSONNEL

DOES HE FAVOR A SET LINEUP OR A ROTATION SYSTEM? In Atlanta he went with a set lineup except at one or two spots; here, he did all kinds of switching. It's hard to know which is the real Bobby Cox.

DOES HE LIKE TO PLATOON? He does here. This was, of course, the most extensive platoon system in the major leagues in 1983.

DOES HE TRY TO SOLVE HIS PROBLEMS WITH PROVEN PLAYERS OR WITH YOUNGSTERS WHO STILL HAVE SOMETHING TO PROVE? HOW MANY PLAYERS HAS HE MADE REGULARS OUT OF WHO WERE NOT REGULARS BEFORE, AND WHO WERE THEY? Very much the latter. He has made first-time regulars out of ten players—Dale Murphy, Glenn Hubbard, Bob Horner, Pepe Frias, Bruce Benedict, Rafael Ramirez, Rufino Linares, Willie Upshaw, Rance Mulliniks and Jesse Barfield.

DOES HE PREFER TO GO WITH GOOD OFFENSIVE PLAYERS OR DOES HE LIKE THE GLOVE MEN? I'd say he puts a priority on getting some runs on the scoreboard.

DOES HE LIKE AN OFFENSE BASED ON POWER, SPEED OR HIGH AVERAGES? Power. The Blue Jays led the league in average last year, but they also missed by only one of leading in home runs. In 1981 they were eleventh in the league in home runs. The Braves in 1980 under Cox just missed leading the NL in home runs. He gets a lot of power production from people like Ernie Whitt, who aren't expected to hit much.

DOES HE USE THE ENTIRE ROSTER OR DOES HE KEEP PEOPLE AROUND SITTING ON THE BENCH? He gets the whole roster involved, and that was true even in Atlanta, where he was not platooning.

DOES HE BUILD HIS BENCH AROUND YOUNG PLAYERS WHO CAN STEP INTO A BREACH IF NEED BE OR AROUND VETERAN ROLE-PLAYERS WHO HAVE THEIR OWN FUNCTIONS WITHIN A GAME? He doesn't seem to like to have youngsters on the bench. If there's a 23-year-old kid on a Bobby Cox team, it's a safe bet that he'll be in the lineup.

GAME MANAGING AND USE OF STRATEGIES

DOES HE GO FOR THE BIG-INNING OFFENSE OR DOES HE LIKE TO USE THE ONE-RUN STRATEGIES? Low-to-moderate use of the one-run strategies.

DOES HE PINCH-HIT MUCH, AND IF SO WHEN? A lot, yes. The Blue Jays are a terrific late-inning ballclub (15–7 in games that were tied after seven innings) and a terrific come-from-behind ballclub (47 comeback wins, see Division Sheet). One of the reasons for that is that with the productive platoon combinations that he has, it is dangerous to switch from a lefthander to a righthander in the middle of a game, or vice versa, against him. He'll wait until he gets a runner on and then he'll start stacking the deck. If you've got a righthander, he'll find four straight lefthanders who can put the ball in the seats. I can't prove this, but my feeling is, if you start a righthander against him, you'd better just stay with a righthander. Don't give him a chance to start pulling Barfield and Bonnell and Martinez and Cliff Johnson off the bench when there are two runners on base.

ANYTHING UNUSUAL ABOUT HIS LINEUP SELECTION? It's traditional but effective. Credit him with the good sense to get Alfredo Griffin out of the top part of the lineup.

DOES HE USE THE SAC BUNT OFTEN? The Braves in 1980 used the fewest bunts in the National League; the Blue Jays last year were 12th in the league in bunts used. When he hasn't had as much power on the roster, he has bunted more.

DOES HE LIKE TO USE THE RUNNING GAME? The Blue Jays were fifth in AL in stolen bases last year; Braves were last in league one year he was there.

IN WHAT CIRCUMSTANCES WILL HE ISSUE AN INTENTIONAL WALK? He will use it sometimes to get a platoon advantage, sometimes to get away from a big hitter. But I think—I'm not sure—that he rarely uses it early in an inning (with none out or one out) to set up a double play.

DOES HE HIT AND RUN VERY OFTEN? Doesn't have real good hit-and-run talent here; he'll try it when he has a chance, and he'll force it sometimes. I have seen him hit and run with Cliff Johnson at the plate.

ARE THERE ANY UNIQUE OR IDIOSYNCRATIC STRATEGIES THAT HE PARTICULARLY LIKES? Can't think of any.

HANDLING THE PITCHING STAFF

DOES HE LIKE POWER PITCHERS OR PREFER TO GO WITH THE PEOPLE WHO PUT THE BALL IN PLAY? Again, what he's doing here is not what he did in Atlanta. In Atlanta, he shifted more and more to control pitchers over his time there; here, it's been Power pitchers with a capital P. Team strikeout and walk totals in Atlanta (1977 was the year before Cox came):

	K	W
1977	915	701
1978	848	624
1979	779	494
1980	696	454

DOES HE STAY WITH THE STARTER OR GO TO THE BULLPEN QUICKLY? That depends on whether his starter is named Dave Stieb or Jim Gott. He took out his starter in the first five innings 40 times last year, a high number; Stieb came out early only twice, but Clancy 9 times, Leal 9 times and Gott 10. Most of those times they were getting hit hard, but he has always kept three or four relief pitchers busy.

DOES HE LIKE THE FOUR-MAN OR THE FIVE-MAN ROTATION? Has always used a four-man rotation; went to five late last year when Alexander was pitching well and Stieb was in and out. Will be interesting to see what he does this year.

DOES HE USE THE ENTIRE STAFF OR DOES HE TRY TO GET FIVE OR SIX PEOPLE TO DO MOST OF THE WORK? Well, he'll use five pitchers in a game sometimes. You do get the staff involved that way.

HOW LONG WILL HE STAY WITH A STARTER WHO IS STRUGGLING? He'll stay with Stieb a long time; otherwise he'll get the pitcher out.

ARE THERE ANY PARTICULAR TYPES OF PITCHERS OF WHOM HE IS FOND? Don't see any.

IS THERE ANYTHING UNIQUE ABOUT HIS HANDLING OF HIS PITCHERS? He likes his pitchers to be aggressive, go after the hitter. That's hardly unique, I suppose.

WHAT IS HIS STRONGEST POINT AS A MANAGER? His ability to work with young players, help them develop their skills.

IF THERE WERE NO PROFESSIONAL BASEBALL, WHAT WOULD THIS MANAGER PROBABLY BE DOING? Running his own construction company (four crews, mostly roads and industrial concrete).

Willie UPSHAW, First Base
Runs Created: 113

	G	AB	Hit	2B	3B	HR	Run	RBI	BB	SO	SB	CS	Avg
3.15 Years		494	132	21	6	17	72	67	48	81	8	7	.268
1983	160	579	177	26	7	27	99	104	61	98	10	7	.306
First Half	76	272	81	10	4	15	52	48	31	44	6	3	.298
Second Half	84	307	96	16	3	12	47	56	30	54	4	4	.313
vs. RHP		372	113	16	5	20	60	78	41	53	7	4	.304
vs. LHP		207	64	10	2	7	39	26	20	45	3	3	.309
Home	80	286	97	16	3	16	46	55	31	47	4	1	.339
Road	80	293	80	10	4	11	53	49	30	51	6	6	.273
Grass	62	226	58	6	3	7	36	30	22	40	5	5	.257
Turf	98	353	119	20	4	20	63	74	39	58	5	2	.337

Lloyd MOSEBY, Centerfield
Runs Created: 104

	G	AB	Hit	2B	3B	HR	Run	RBI	BB	SO	SB	CS	Avg
3.16 Years		567	146	29	6	14	74	70	42	115	17	9	.258
1983	151	539	170	31	7	18	104	81	51	85	27	8	.315
First Half	71	241	69	13	3	9	39	34	22	46	15	6	.286
Second Half	80	298	101	18	4	9	65	47	29	39	12	2	.339
vs. RHP		353	115	20	4	14	71	55	38	52	25	3	.326
vs. LHP		186	55	11	3	4	33	26	13	33	1	5	.296
Home	78	267	88	14	3	13	60	45	32	48	16	2	.330
Road	73	272	82	13	3	5	44	36	19	37	10	6	.301
Grass	59	220	62	7	3	5	32	30	15	30	8	5	.282
Turf	92	319	108	24	4	13	72	51	36	55	18	3	.339

Damaso GARCIA, Second Base
Runs Created: 66

	G	AB	Hit	2B	3B	HR	Run	RBI	BB	SO	SB	CS	Avg
3.15 years		632	183	30	5	4	81	46	22	55	36	17	.290
1983	131	525	161	23	6	3	84	38	24	34	31	17	.307
First Half	65	263	76	10	2	2	37	18	9	20	16	11	.289
Second Half	66	262	85	13	4	1	47	20	15	14	15	6	.324
vs. RHP		300	95	13	2	2	48	25	19	14	16	9	.317
vs. LHP		225	66	10	4	1	36	13	5	20	15	8	.293
Home	67	261	85	13	6	1	39	23	15	12	17	6	.326
Road	64	264	76	10	0	2	45	15	9	22	14	11	.288
Grass	46	183	44	3	0	2	31	12	7	18	8	6	.240
Turf	85	342	117	20	6	1	53	26	17	16	23	11	.342

Jesse BARFIELD, Rightfield
Runs Created: 55

	G	AB	Hit	2B	3B	HR	Run	RBI	BB	SO	SB	CS	Avg
1.80 Years		487	120	16	4	26	66	75	38	115	3	7	.247
1983	128	388	98	13	3	27	58	68	22	110	2	5	.253
First Half	62	180	38	7	0	10	25	26	6	57	1	1	.211
Second Half	66	208	60	6	3	17	33	42	16	53	1	4	.288
vs. RHP		174	43	5	1	14	26	31	10	50	1	4	.247
vs. LHP		214	55	8	2	13	32	37	12	60	1	1	.257
Home	67	207	63	9	3	22	41	49	11	61	2	3	.304
Road	61	181	35	4	0	5	17	19	11	49	0	2	.193
Grass	48	141	27	3	0	3	11	12	7	35	0	1	.191
Turf	80	247	71	10	3	24	47	56	15	75	2	4	.287

Rance MULLINIKS, Third Base
Runs Created: 62

	G	AB	Hit	2B	3B	HR	Run	RBI	BB	SO	SB	CS	Avg
2.78 Years		445	110	29	2	7	54	46	50	65	2	2	.246
1983	129	364	100	35	3	10	54	48	57	43	0	2	.275
First Half	59	168	49	19	2	3	23	19	24	24	0	1	.292
Second Half	70	196	51	16	1	7	31	29	33	19	0	1	.260
vs. RHP		336	94	32	3	8	51	44	53	38	0	1	.280
vs. LHP		28	6	3	0	2	3	4	4	5	0	1	.214
Home	65	182	57	22	3	4	28	23	25	21	0	0	.313
Road	64	182	43	13	0	6	26	25	32	22	0	2	.236
Grass	50	138	35	9	0	4	18	22	23	14	0	2	.254
Turf	79	226	65	26	3	6	36	26	34	29	0	0	.288

Ernie WHITT, Catcher
Runs Created: 55

	G	AB	Hit	2B	3B	HR	Run	RBI	BB	SO	SB	CS	Avg
2.72 Years		434	106	20	2	13	47	58	45	60	4	3	.245
1983	123	344	88	15	2	17	53	56	50	55	1	1	.256
First Half	58	170	44	7	1	8	27	27	24	27	0	1	.259
Second Half	65	174	44	8	1	9	26	29	26	28	1	0	.253
vs. RHP		310	84	15	2	17	49	55	41	40	1	1	.271
vs. LHP		34	4	0	0	0	4	1	9	15	0	0	.118
Home	62	168	51	11	2	11	38	33	23	32	0	0	.304
Road	61	176	37	4	0	6	15	23	27	23	1	1	.210
Grass	45	120	29	3	0	4	10	19	20	18	1	1	.223
Turf	78	214	59	12	2	13	43	37	30	37	0	0	.276

Alfredo GRIFFIN, Shortstop
Runs Created: 52

	G	AB	Hit	2B	3B	HR	Run	RBI	BB	SO	SB	CS	Avg
4.72 Years		590	148	24	10	2	63	41	29	54	14	15	.251
1983	162	528	132	22	9	4	62	47	27	44	8	10	.250
First Half	76	252	63	11	6	2	29	22	8	18	6	6	.250
Second Half	86	276	69	11	3	2	33	25	19	26	2	4	.250
vs. RHP		326	74	11	9	3	38	32	22	26	5	5	.227
vs. LHP		202	58	11	0	1	24	15	5	18	3	5	.287
Home	81	258	70	11	6	2	31	30	14	21	3	5	.271
Road	81	270	62	11	3	2	31	17	13	23	5	5	.230
Grass	63	212	47	9	3	1	20	10	9	20	4	5	.222
Turf	99	316	85	13	6	3	42	37	18	24	4	5	.269

Cliff JOHNSON, Designated Hitter
Runs Created: 76

	G	AB	Hit	2B	3B	HR	Run	RBI	BB	SO	SB	CS	Avg
6.35 Years		454	114	21	1	24	64	81	67	85	1	2	.252
1983	142	407	108	21	1	22	59	76	67	69	0	1	.265
First Half	67	194	54	12	1	14	33	45	38	37	0	1	.278
Second Half	75	213	54	11	0	8	26	31	29	32	0	0	.254
vs. RHP		194	51	11	0	8	22	38	30	38	0	1	.263
vs. LHP		213	57	12	1	14	37	38	36	31	0	0	.268
Home	72	193	48	13	1	10	31	30	37	33	0	1	.249
Road	70	214	60	10	0	12	28	46	29	36	0	0	.280
Grass	54	161	41	9	0	11	22	32	24	26	0	0	.255
Turf	88	246	67	14	1	11	37	44	42	43	0	1	.272

Dave COLLINS, Leftfield
Runs Created: 50

	G	AB	Hit	2B	3B	HR	Run	RBI	BB	SO	SB	CS	Avg
6.20 Years		524	143	18	5	4	74	39	51	75	41	16	.273
1983	118	402	109	12	4	1	55	34	43	67	31	7	.271
First Half	46	176	38	4	1	0	19	11	17	29	9	3	.216
Second Half	72	226	71	8	3	1	36	23	26	38	22	4	.314
vs. RHP		321	84	12	3	1	46	25	32	57	19	4	.262
vs. LHP		81	25	0	1	0	9	9	11	10	12	3	.309
Home	62	199	44	6	3	0	30	11	28	34	19	3	.221
Road	56	203	65	6	1	1	25	23	15	33	12	4	.320
Grass	42	148	43	4	0	0	17	10	12	24	10	3	.291
Turf	76	254	66	8	4	1	38	24	31	43	21	4	.260

Barry BONNELL, Outfield
Runs Created: 64

	G	AB	Hit	2B	3B	HR	Run	RBI	BB	SO	SB	CS	Avg
4.94 Years		514	142	24	4	10	62	59	40	61	12	7	.275
1983	121	377	120	21	3	10	49	54	33	52	9	7	.318
First Half	66	184	58	9	2	4	23	30	15	25	5	3	.315
Second Half	55	193	62	12	1	6	26	24	18	27	4	4	.321
vs. RHP		191	54	9	1	4	25	32	15	31	6	4	.283
vs. LHP		186	66	12	2	6	24	22	18	21	3	3	.355
Home	55	174	59	11	2	6	29	29	14	28	6	1	.339
Road	66	203	61	10	1	4	20	25	19	24	3	6	.300
Grass	54	167	53	9	1	2	16	21	15	22	2	6	.317
Turf	67	210	67	12	2	8	33	33	18	30	7	1	.319

Dave STIEB

Year	(W–L)	GS	Run	Avg	DP	Avg	SB	Avg
1982	(17-14)	38	149	3.92	32	.84	11	.29
1983	(17-12)	36	163	4.53	31	.86	18	.50
1979-1983		139	588	4.23	161	1.16	69	.50

	G	IP	W	L	Pct	ER	ERA
1982 Home	17	129.1	8	6	.571	46	3.20
1983 Home	20	157.1	11	7	.611	52	2.97
1982 Road	21	159	9	8	.529	58	3.32
1983 Road	16	120.2	6	5	.545	42	3.13
1983 Grass	14	106.2	6	3	.667	31	2.62
1983 Turf	22	171.1	11	9	.550	63	3.31

Jim GOTT

Year	(W–L)	GS	Run	Avg	DP	Avg	SB	Avg
1982	(5-10)	23	73	3.17	20	.87	15	.65
1983	(9-14)	30	140	4.67	26	.87	23	.77
1982-1983		53	213	4.02	46	.87	38	.72

	G	IP	W	L	Pct	ER	ERA
1982 Home	15	72.2	3	5	.375	33	4.09
1983 Home	19	91	7	6	.538	51	5.04
1982 Road	15	63.1	2	5	.286	34	4.83
1983 Road	15	85.2	2	8	.200	42	4.41
1983 Grass	11	68.2	2	5	.286	26	3.41
1983 Turf	23	108	7	9	.437	67	5.58

Luis LEAL

Year	(W–L)	GS	Run	Avg	DP	Avg	SB	Avg
1982	(17-14)	38	149	3.92	32	.84	11	.29
1983	(13-12)	35	179	5.11	32	.91	19	.54
1979-1983		102	453	4.44	89	.87	65	.64

	G	IP	W	L	Pct	ER	ERA
1982 Home	17	129.1	8	6	.571	46	3.20
1983 Home	14	82.2	4	4	.500	48	5.23
1982 Road	21	159	9	8	.529	58	3.32
1983 Road	21	134.2	9	8	.529	56	3.74
1983 Grass	16	98	5	8	.385	42	3.86
1983 Turf	19	119.1	8	4	.667	62	4.68

Doyle ALEXANDER

Year	(W–L)	GS	Run	Avg	DP	Avg	SB	Avg
1982	(1-7)	11	34	3.09	11	1.00	9	.82
1983	(7-8)	20	85	4.25	20	1.00	12	.60
1976-1983		195	837	4.29	173	.88	141	.72

	G	IP	W	L	Pct	ER	ERA
1982 Home	8	37.2	0	3	.000	24	5.73
1983 Home	12	72.2	4	4	.500	42	5.20
1982 Road	8	29	1	4	.200	21	6.70
1983 Road	13	72.1	3	4	.429	29	3.61
1983 Grass	13	66.1	2	4	.333	33	4.48
1983 Turf	12	78.2	5	4	.556	38	4.35

Jim CLANCY

Year	(W–L)	GS	Run	Avg	DP	Avg	SB	Avg
1982	(16-14)	40	172	4.30	42	1.05	13	.33
1983	(15-11)	34	164	4.82	26	.76	11	.32
1977-1983		184	717	3.90	174	.95	81	.44

	G	IP	W	L	Pct	ER	ERA
1982 Home	21	118.1	7	8	.467	63	4.79
1983 Home	17	114.2	9	4	.692	52	4.08
1982 Road	19	148.1	9	6	.600	47	2.85
1983 Road	17	108.1	6	7	.461	45	3.74
1983 Grass	13	81.1	4	6	.400	35	3.87
1983 Turf	21	141.2	11	5	.687	62	3.94

1983 OTHERS

Pitcher	(W–L)	GS	Run	Avg	DP	Avg	SB	Avg
Acker	(5-1)	5	49	9.80	9	1.80	1	.20
Morgan	(0-3)	4	14	3.50	7	1.75	2	.50
Williams	(1-1)	3	25	8.33	1	.33	2	.67

TORONTO BLUE JAYS
RUNS BATTED IN ANALYSIS

Player	RBI	RBI In Wins	Victory-Important RBI	RBI Importance	Wins Batted In	RBI Per Win
Willie Upshaw	104	77	47.20	.454	11.14	9.3
Lloyd Moseby	81	61	42.21	.521	10.10	8.0
Jesse Barfield	68	48	31.12	.458	6.93	9.8
Cliff Johnson	76	50	29.29	.385	7.74	9.8
Ernie Whitt	56	39	27.42	.490	6.71	8.3
Rance Mulliniks	49	41	24.09	.492	5.90	8.3
Barry Bonnell	54	42	23.32	.432	6.00	9.0
Alfredo Griffin	47	35	19.93	.424	5.24	9.0
Dave Collins	34	30	19.57	.576	4.36	7.8
Damaso Garcia	38	27	13.87	.365	3.64	10.4

MILWAUKEE BREWERS

One way of assessing what Victory-Important RBI and their related RBI "sorters" mean and do not mean is to look at them over a period of years, to select a stable group of players—a league would be best, but that would take forever—and break down those players' RBI production over a period of years. The Milwaukee Brewers have had probably the most stable personnel in the American League over the last five years, and for that reason they are a suitable team with which to study RBI Importance. If you study the Seattle Mariners, you're looking at a different group of players every year.

I'm going to look at this year-by-year, beginning in 1979:

1979

In 1979 I figured Victory-Important RBI and RBI Importance for the entire American League, and ran the data in the *1980 Baseball Abstract*. The Brewers that year were a 95-66 ballclub, one of the best in baseball. One member of the Brewers, Paul Molitor, led the league in RBI Importance (.554); another, Gorman Thomas, in Victory-Important RBI. With a figure of 66.89.

Since Cecil Cooper almost matched it last year, you may not get the full import of that figure. That is the highest VI-RBI count that I have ever seen. Thomas had nine more Victory-Important Runs Batted In that year than anyone else in the American League.

He was third in the league in the total number of runs batted in (123), but he was also second in the league in the importance of those runs. That's a lot of big runs.

I think that on that basis, a strong argument can be made that Thomas should have been the American League's Most Valuable Player in 1979. He was seventh in the voting; Don Baylor won it.

And why did Don Baylor win it? Because he drove in 139 runs, and anybody who drives in 139 runs is going to win an MVP award. The last player to drive in 139 runs and not win an MVP award was Tommy Davis in 1962, and that year they gave it to the man that he was driving in.

But look at the two players. Baylor was a leftfielder-designated hitter, a man with no defensive value at all. Thomas was a centerfielder, a man who played a key defensive position, and at that time played it a lot better than he does now. Both men played for teams that were awful good but weren't about to beat the Baltimore Orioles.

So must Baylor win the award, because he has driven in 16 more runs? Perhaps, except. Except that Baylor was driving in largely meaningless runs—8 runs in a 24–2 shellacking of the hapless Blue Jays, four runs in an 11–2 defeat of the Minnesota Twins, four more in a 13–1 rout of Oakland, four more in a 9–1 win over Chicago, four more in a 14–2 drubbing of Kansas City, five in another (17–6) pasting of the Oakland A's, three in a 8–1 squeaker over Oakland, three in an 11–5 loss to Chicago.

Of course Baylor drove in some meaningful runs. But Thomas drove in more meaningful runs. The question is, must a player be given an MVP award if he runs his numbers up to an impressive enough level by driving in meaningless runs?

Anyway, the Brewers' regulars, in order of RBI Importance for 1979: Molitor (.554), Thomas (.544), Oglivie (.523), Sixto Lezcano (.437), Robin Yount (.431), Cecil Cooper (.417), Dick Davis (.396) and Sal Bando (.375). RBI Importance for players with 20-40 RBI: Don Money (.593), Jim Gantner (.548), Charlie Moore (.457) and Buck Martinez (.456).

I have no 1979 data on Wins Batted In or RBI per win.

1980

The Brewers, despite terrific seasons from Oglivie (41 homers, 118 RBI, .304 average), Cooper (.352, 122 RBI) and Yount (49 doubles, 10 triples, 23 homers) slipped to 86-76, 17 games off the mark.

What happened? They drove in too many meaningless runs and too few key runs. Their ratio of RBI Importance reflects this. They scored 811 runs and allowed only 682; they should have gone about 95-67. But their 12–22 record in one-run games was the worst in baseball.

No regular on the team had an RBI Importance of higher than .416. Oglivie was there; he was followed by Yount (.403), Cooper (.374), Molitor (.366) and Lezcano (.356). Thomas drove in 105 runs, but in 1980 he didn't drive in the big runs; he drove in only 36.80 runs that were essential to victory (.350).

Ben Oglivie in 1980 drove in the runs that were responsible for 15.07 wins; that is an impressive figure. No Brewer topped it until Cecil Cooper in 1983, and that just barely. But Molitor, Yount, Thomas and Moore produced less than one win for every 10 runs that they drove in, and you just can't win doing that. If it takes you 1,000 runs to post 100 wins, then you're not going to get to 100 wins.

1981

1981 was the year that they split the season and the Brewers won half of it; they finished 62-47, the best combined record in the division. And this time they won four more games than they could have expected to.

Ben Oglivie, again, was the most productive player on the team in terms of producing the runs that meant ball games. Oglivie had a remarkable 1981 season. He hit just .243, and he had only 15 doubles and 14 homers, a .395 slugging percentage, his worst figure with the Brewers by far. Yet he drove in a team-leading 72 runs, well over a 100-RBI pace, and those 72 runs produced 10.47 wins. He was accounting for one win with each 6.9 runs driven in, again the best figure among the Brewer regulars. Whenever the Brewers that year were winning games 8–1 and 11–1 and 12–1, Oglivie was nowhere to be found in the RBI lists. But when they were winning 5–3 and 3–0, it was Benji who was driving home the runs.

The newly acquired Ted Simmons was second on the Brewers in RBI, and also second in the ratio of wins produced per RBI (1/6.91). Cecil Cooper was third in the number of runs driven in (60) and also third in win rate (1/7.4 RBI). In the other measures of RBI Importance, though, it was Cooper who came to the front, with a team-leading 35.28 Victory-Important RBI and an RBI Importance of .588. Three Brewer regulars (Cooper, Simmons and Yount) had an RBI Importance over .500 in 1981.

1982

1982 was the Brewers' championship season. Four Brewer regulars drove in 100 runs; Simmons was at 97.

Cecil Cooper in 1982 led the team in Victory-Important RBI (51.18) and Wins Batted In (13.35). The only man close to him in either category was Gorman Thomas (50.78 and 13.03). The MVP, Robin Yount, did not drive in a large number of runs that were essential to victory; his RBI Importance (.398) was the lowest among the regulars except for Oglivie. (Remember, however, that Yount did drive in a terrific number of runs against the Baltimore Orioles, the team Milwaukee had to beat, and also against New York and Detroit. Remember, clutch performance exists on three levels: run clutch, game clutch and pennant clutch. We are focusing only on one of those levels, the game level.)

1983

Cecil Cooper led the league in Victory-Important RBI with 62.84, and led the team in Wins Batted In, with 14.81. Robin Yount, as noted in the introduction, drove in only 80 runs but a lot of big runs. Ben Oglivie drove in not too many runs, but was second to Yount in both RBI Importance (.517) and the rate of wins produced per run batted in (1/8.02). Gorman Thomas drove in virtually no runs that meant anything before being traded early in the year. Rick Manning and Charlie Moore didn't drive in too many runs, but did drive in some that counted.

More complete data for each player is detailed in Chart Brewer-I. For the four years as a whole, Ben Oglivie has produced easily more wins per run batted in than any other player on the team; he has 43.22 Wins Batted In on the basis of 358 runs batted in. For the five years as a whole, Charlie Moore had the highest RBI Importance on the team (.484).

The charts suggest that over a period of time there is little difference in the importance of the runs driven in by different players, at least with this group. Over the last five years, 44.8% of the Runs Batted In of Cecil Cooper were essential to victories, 44.7% of those driven by Paul Molitor were essential to victories, 44.6% of those driven in by Robin Yount, 44.9% of those driven in by Oglivie, 48.4% of those driven in by Charlie Moore, 43.7% of those by Gantner, and 47.0% of those by Simmons. Thomas had his up years and his down years and came in at 44.5%.

If one of these players has an ability to produce big runs, as opposed merely to an ability to produce runs, then all of them have it to roughly the same extent; if one of them does not have that ability, then they all lack that ability. But let us assume, for the moment, that it is an ability. How important are the differences in that ability with this group of players?

The strongest case for "big RBI" value could be made on behalf of Oglivie, who produced more than 43 wins with just over 350 RBI. The players with the poorest ratio in this respect produced one win for each 9.6 RBI. If there was a predictable difference between two players of this extent, and if one of those players drove in 100 runs and the other drove in 86, then they would be of equal value to their teams as run producers. In other words, if one player drives in few runs but tends to drive in big runs, and the other drives in many runs but tends not to drive in big runs, then it is reasonable to speculate that the player who drives in fewer runs might be more valuable because of his ability in this regard so long as the difference between the two of them as RBI producers does not exceed 14%. But if one player drives in 80 runs and the other drives in 40, then you'd better leave "but he drove in some large runs for us" out of the conversation.

But the charts honestly would not tend to support the notion that an "ability" was being measured; there is variable performance in driving in big runs, but is there a variable ability to drive in big runs?

A friend of mine, whom we will call Beelzebub because he's about to get me in a lot of trouble, makes the following argument:

a) It is stupid to talk about clutch ability if you don't even know whether or not it exists.

b) No one has ever offered any proof at all that it does exist (or even a definition of exactly what it is, if it does).

c) People talk about clutch performance constantly. ergo

d) People

Well, OK, we're stupid. No, no one has proven that clutch ability exists, and no one will ever prove that it doesn't exist. Why? Can you prove that dodo birds are extinct? We only *believe* that dodo birds and dinosaurs are extinct; we can't prove it. The subject requires an honest search, and I'll keep looking.

THE MANAGER

NAME: Bob Rodgers (1980–82), Harvey Kuenn (1982–83) and Rene Lachemann (1984).

AGE: Rodgers is 45, Kuenn 52, Lachemann 38 (39 in May).

MANAGERS FOR WHOM PLAYED IN MAJORS: Rodgers played for Bill Rigney for his entire 9-year major league career; Kuenn played for Fred Hutchinson, Bucky Harris, Jack Tighe, Bill Norman, Jimmy Dykes, Joe Gordon, Alvin Dark, Herman Franks, Bob Kennedy, Lou Klein, Leo Durocher and Gene Mauch. Lachemann played for Mel McGaha, Haywood Sullivan, Alvin Dark and Bob Kennedy.

CHARACTERISTICS AS A PLAYER: Rodgers was a well-respected defensive catcher who didn't hit much; Kuenn was a terrific singles-and-doubles hitter who started out as shortstop and didn't field much. Lachemann was a bonus boy who spent the entire year in the majors when he was 20 years old. A catcher, he had some power but was slow, struck out too much and did not have an outstanding arm, and never made it back to the majors.

MANAGERIAL RECORD:

Team	Year	Par	Wins	Losses	Pct.	+ or −
RODGERS						
Mil	1980	38	39	31	.557	+ 1
Mil	1981	59	62	47	.569	+ 3
Mil	1982	25	23	24	.489	− 2
3 Years		122	124	102	.549	+ 2
KUENN						
Mil	1975	0	1	0	1.000	+ 1
Mil	1982	61	72	43	.626	+11
Mil	1983	89	87	75	.537	− 2
3 Years		150	160	118	.576	+10
LACHEMANN						
Sea	1981	36	38	47	.447	+ 2
Sea	1982	69	76	86	.469	+ 7
Sea	1983	37	26	47	.356	−11
3 Years		142	140	180	.438	− 2

WHAT HE BRINGS TO THE BALLCLUB

IS HE AN INTENSE MANAGER OR MORE OF AN EASY-TO-GET-ALONG-WITH TYPE? IS HE MORE OF AN EMOTIONAL LEADER OR A DECISION-MAKER? IS HE MORE OF AN OPTIMIST OR MORE OF A PROBLEM SOLVER?

There is a common scenario that is being replayed here with unusual perfection. It is what we might call the Burt Shotton Syndrome.

Rodgers is an intense manager, a man with an interest in details who can be rather demanding to work for. Kuenn is a low-key, low-pressure guy who takes things in stride, whose attitude says, "Let's have some fun and play good baseball." When a low-pressure manager replaces an intense manager with

a good ballclub, the ballclub will very often have a sustained period, a period of a year or more, in which the talent simply seems to gush out of them. These teams frequently win a pennant—one pennant—in this period; other examples of the same thing happening are Jim Frey following Whitey Herzog in Kansas City, Bob Lemon following Billy Martin in New York and (of course) Burt Shotton following Leo Durocher in Brooklyn. To some degree, Joe Altobelli following Earl Weaver is the Shotton Syndrome, and to some some degree, Sparky Anderson following Dave Bristol in 1970 is the Shotton Syndrome. Sparky isn't exactly a low-key manager, but compared to Dave Bristol, anybody seems like a low-key manager.

What happens, I think, is that the demands that the "intense" manager makes on his players creates a resistance, a deodorant shield that locks in talent and locks out advice. The Martins and the Durochers and the Rodgereses are teachers, among other things, but sometimes they try so hard to teach the players that they seem threatening and overbearing; they trigger a defense mechanism in the players, and it seems like they're just not getting through anymore.

The low-key manager takes over, the resistance melts, and suddenly all of the things that the high-pressure manager has been trying to say sink in. And the talent seems simply to ooze forth.

Seems, I say. This is not simply a "honeymoon" period, such as any manager might have, which lasts for maybe two weeks. The new manager clears the air, and what does he clear the air of? Tension. But whereas most managers would immediately begin putting tension back in the air, the low-key manager just keeps it clear.

The problem with low-key managers is that most of the time they don't have a very good command of details, nor indeed a very strong command of anything. Kuenn certainly didn't; he had no judgment at all about talent and very little about strategy. Eventually, the team begins to lose confidence in him; they begin to wonder who is steering the ship.

That is a very bad thing to have your team wondering. So who do you replace the low-key manager with?

A tactician, a strategist. You don't need a teacher now; this team is a proven winner. You get a student of the game. That's what the Brewers did in replacing Kuenn with Lachemann, it's what the Dodgers did in replacing Shotton with Dressen; Dick Howser, in the strategist class of managers, followed Frey in Kansas City and also managed the Yankees after Lemon, although with Martin as a detour.

This creates a most interesting question, which is: "What usually happens when the tactician takes over a team like this?"

Howser in Kansas City went 90-72 and finished second; Dressen in Brooklyn went 97-60 and finished second. Both teams were in command of their pennant races, but lost them.

That, generally, is about what I would expect of the Brewers in 1984. They should win more than 87 games because they're a better team than that. But they've got to jump over four good teams to win, and that's not going to be easy.

HOW HE USES HIS PERSONNEL

DOES HE FAVOR A SET LINEUP OR A ROTATION SYSTEM? Rodgers and Kuenn each inherited a set lineup and largely went with it; Lachemann in Seattle inherited a chaotic situation and stabilized it.

DOES HE LIKE TO PLATOON? Neither Rodgers nor Kuenn likes to platoon; Lachemann platooned some in Seattle, and my guess would be that he will here, too.

DOES HE TRY TO SOLVE HIS PROBLEMS WITH PROVEN PLAYERS OR WITH YOUNGSTERS WHO STILL HAVE SOMETHING TO PROVE? HOW MANY PLAYERS HAS HE MADE REGULARS OUT OF WHO WERE NOT REGULARS BEFORE, AND WHO WERE THEY? None of them has a long enough or varied enough career to answer this question very well. Lachemann introduced some new talent (Dave Henderson, Manny Castillo, Rick Sweet) into the lineup in Seattle, and will have that opportunity here.

DOES HE PREFER TO GO WITH GOOD OFFENSIVE PLAYERS OR DOES HE LIKE THE GLOVE MEN? Both Rodgers and Kuenn would have to be said to lean toward the offensive on the basis of the decisions they have made—Kuenn, oddly, with more reservations. The Brewers under Kuenn made an offense-for-defense switch in the Thomas/Manning trade, and also moved Simmons to DH in an attempt to gain defense behind the plate.

DOES HE LIKE AN OFFENSE BASED ON POWER, SPEED, OF HIGH AVERAGES? Rodgers and Kuenn inherited a power offense; Kuenn reduced its power to no visible purpose. Lachemann has never had an offense to work with.

DOES HE USE THE ENTIRE ROSTER OR DOES HE KEEP PEOPLE AROUND SITTING ON THE BENCH? A player can sit on the bench for Bob Rodgers for a long time; Kuenn, too, had people he didn't use. Lachemann probably will get the rest of the roster more involved in the effort. There is some talent on that bench.

DOES HE BUILD HIS BENCH AROUND YOUNG PLAYERS WHO CAN STEP INTO A BREACH IF NEED BE OR AROUND VETERAN ROLE-PLAYERS WHO HAVE THEIR OWN FUNCTIONS WITHIN A GAME? Lachemann's bench in Seattle was a young bench, but then he wasn't managing a contending team, either.

GAME MANAGING AND USE OF STRATEGIES

DOES HE GO FOR THE BIG-INNING OFFENSE OR DOES HE LIKE TO USE THE ONE-RUN STRATEGIES? At times, Kuenn managed this team as if he were managing the '64 Dodgers. They were second in the league in bunts, which with a lineup like this is simply unbelievable; Rodgers has made moderate use and Lachemann limited use of first-run strategies.

DOES HE PINCH-HIT MUCH, AND IF SO WHEN? Lachemann used a lot of pinch-hitters in Seattle in '81; otherwise none of the three has used many.

ANYTHING UNUSUAL ABOUT HIS LINEUP SELECTION? Well, as much as I like Lachemann, I wouldn't be honest with you if I didn't point out that his lineup selection in Seattle was very strange and very ineffective. He probably didn't have anyone in that lineup batting where they should have been batting; he led off with people who didn't get on base, and he followed them up with the wrong talent in the wrong order.

DOES HE USE THE SAC BUNT OFTEN? The Brewers lost 127 runs last year, down from 891 to 764. They'll get about 30 back because Lachemann will cut out a lot of the bunting and hit and run instead.

DOES HE LIKE TO USE THE RUNNING GAME? Lachemann ran some in '82; of course, that's what he had the talent to do. The Brewers under Kuenn ran a lot more than they did under Rodgers.

IN WHAT CIRCUMSTANCES WILL HE ISSUE AN INTENTIONAL WALK? Lachemann uses notably few intentional walks; Rodgers used more than Kuenn did.

DOES HE HIT AND RUN VERY OFTEN? Lachemann uses the hit and run, and Rodgers loved to hit and run. Kuenn didn't use it as much, and I think it really hurt the team. Their GIDP (grounded into double play) totals were way up last year.

ARE THERE ANY UNIQUE OR IDIOSYNCRATIC STRATEGIES THAT HE PARTICULARLY LIKES? Can't think of any.

HANDLING THE PITCHING STAFF

DOES HE LIKE POWER PITCHERS OR PREFER TO GO WITH THE PEOPLE WHO PUT THE BALL IN PLAY? Lachemann's success in Seattle in 1982, which was almost entirely a defensive success (their offense scored only 651 runs in a hitter's park) came from working with power pitchers—Bill Caudill, Jim Beattie, Bannister of course, Bryan Clark. Since Milwaukee's pitching staff, going three or four managers back, has been built out of finesse pitches and nibblers, this is a very sharp contrast, and it almost certainly is going to be an area in which Lachemann is going to make some changes. If I was a young flame thrower, I'd sure like to be in Milwaukee's camp this spring.

DOES HE STAY WITH THE STARTER OR GO TO THE BULLPEN QUICKLY? The Brewers have never had a decent three-man bullpen here; they had nothing, and then they had Rollie Fingers, and then they had Peter Ladd. Lachemann came up with a good team bullpen out of nowhere in Seattle in '82, and he's a safe bet to be trying to repeat that here in '84.

DOES HE LIKE THE FOUR-MAN OR THE FIVE-MAN ROTATION? Kuenn and Rodgers have been using a 4½ or 5-man rotation; Lachemann also used a 5-man staff in Seattle.

DOES HE USE THE ENTIRE STAFF OR DOES HE TRY TO GET FIVE OR SIX PEOPLE TO DO MOST OF THE WORK? We may have covered this, but Lachemann will use the entire staff; the others did not.

HOW LONG WILL HE STAY WITH A STARTER

WHO IS STRUGGLING? Lachemann, a former catcher, has outstanding judgment as to when a pitcher is weakening, and he's a quick hook. Again, this is a strong contrast to Kuenn, who would go with the starter as long as he could.

ARE THERE ANY PARTICULAR TYPES OF PITCHERS OF WHOM HE IS FOND? We'll see; careers aren't long enough to answer this one.

IS THERE ANYTHING UNIQUE ABOUT HIS HANDLING OF THE PITCHERS? Lachemann is arguably the quickest hook in the majors.

WHAT IS HIS STRONGEST POINT AS A MANAGER? Rodgers did an excellent job of reconstructing the Brewer lineup so as to get all the talent he had out there on the field; he deserved more credit for that than he got. Kuenn's only strong point that I can see was that the players like him and respect him. Lachemann is a student of the game, and he has been a successful defensive manager.

IF THERE WERE NO PROFESSIONAL BASEBALL, WHAT WOULD HIS MANAGER PROBABLY BE DOING? Rodgers would be an industry representative for an aluminum-siding company. Lachemann would be directing TV shows, like "Magnum, P.I." and "Hart to Hart." Harvey Kuenn would be running a bait shop.

Cecil COOPER, First Base
Runs Created: 110

	G	AB	Hit	2B	3B	HR	Run	RBI	BB	SO	SB	CS	Avg
8.62 Years		617	190	36	4	23	92	98	39	74	8	5	.308
1983	160	661	203	37	3	30	106	126	37	63	2	1	.307
First Half	74	305	86	19	2	16	45	54	19	30	1	1	.282
Second Half	86	356	117	18	1	14	61	72	18	33	1	0	.329
vs. RHP		403	130	26	3	23	68	83	24	31	1	1	.323
vs. LHP		258	73	11	0	7	38	43	13	32	1	0	.283
Home	80	322	99	15	2	14	53	58	15	30	0	0	.307
Road	80	339	104	22	1	16	53	68	22	33	2	1	.307
Grass	136	562	174	33	2	25	92	105	35	55	1	0	.310
Turf	24	99	29	4	1	5	14	21	2	8	1	1	.293

Paul MOLITOR, Third Base
Runs Created: 88

	G	AB	Hit	2B	3B	HR	Run	RBI	BB	SO	SB	CS	Avg
4.64 Years		664	194	32	8	13	112	61	58	75	41	12	.292
1983	152	608	164	28	6	15	95	47	59	74	41	7	.270
First Half	68	271	71	12	4	6	36	28	25	38	14	3	.262
Second Half	84	337	93	16	2	9	59	19	34	36	27	4	.276
vs. RHP		389	102	18	4	6	56	25	30	52	23	3	.262
vs. LHP		219	62	10	2	9	39	22	29	22	18	4	.283
Home	77	299	77	9	3	9	40	21	32	33	20	2	.258
Road	75	309	87	19	3	6	55	26	27	41	21	5	.282
Grass	129	515	133	21	5	14	76	40	48	69	30	5	.258
Turf	23	93	31	7	1	1	19	7	11	5	11	2	.333

Jim GANTNER, Second Base
Runs Created: 78

	G	AB	Hit	2B	3B	HR	Run	RBI	BB	SO	SB	CS	Avg
4.23 Years		529	148	21	4	6	63	54	36	43	8	7	.279
1983	161	603	170	23	8	11	85	74	38	46	5	6	.282
First Half	75	277	75	8	4	7	37	38	20	22	3	2	.271
Second Half	86	326	95	15	4	4	48	36	18	24	2	4	.291
vs. RHP		393	122	19	2	9	68	52	20	36	4	3	.310
vs. LHP		210	48	4	6	2	17	22	18	10	1	3	.229
Home	80	281	73	6	3	5	37	36	25	20	2	4	.260
Road	81	322	97	17	5	6	48	38	13	26	3	2	.301
Grass	136	505	136	16	5	8	68	61	35	40	4	5	.269
Turf	25	98	34	7	3	3	17	13	3	6	1	1	.347

Robin YOUNT, Shortstop
Runs Created: 115

	G	AB	Hit	2B	3B	HR	Run	RBI	BB	SO	SB	CS	Avg
8.57 Years		633	180	35	8	13	91	74	42	68	15	6	.284
1983	149	578	178	42	10	17	102	80	72	58	12	4	.308
First Half	75	292	92	19	4	11	56	45	41	28	8	2	.315
Second Half	74	286	86	23	6	6	46	35	31	30	4	2	.301
vs. RHP		376	120	24	6	13	68	58	36	37	9	2	.319
vs. LHP		202	58	18	4	4	34	22	36	21	3	2	.287
Home	75	280	89	27	2	6	51	35	35	26	6	3	.318
Road	74	298	89	15	8	11	51	45	37	32	6	1	.299
Grass	127	496	148	37	7	14	90	64	60	50	12	4	.298
Turf	22	82	30	5	3	3	12	16	12	8	0	0	.366

Ben OGLIVIE, Leftfield
Runs Created: 67

	G	AB	Hit	2B	3B	HR	Run	RBI	BB	SO	SB	CS	Avg
8.76 Years		544	148	26	3	24	76	83	51	81	10	7	.272
1983	125	411	115	19	3	13	49	66	60	64	4	6	.280
First Half	64	222	65	14	3	7	33	33	36	30	2	4	.293
Second Half	61	189	50	5	0	6	16	33	24	34	2	2	.265
vs. RHP		247	73	13	1	7	33	35	47	31	4	5	.296
vs. LHP		164	42	6	2	6	16	31	13	33	0	1	.256
Home	58	188	58	7	2	8	27	30	25	34	3	3	.309
Road	67	223	57	12	1	5	22	36	35	30	1	3	.256
Grass	100	324	92	10	2	11	39	57	50	52	3	6	.284
Turf	25	87	23	9	1	2	10	9	10	12	1	0	.264

Rick MANNING, Centerfield
Runs Created: 53

	G	AB	Hit	2B	3B	HR	Run	RBI	BB	SO	SB	CS	Avg
7.23 Years		605	158	22	5	5	75	51	55	73	21	9	.261
1983	158	569	140	20	4	4	60	43	38	62	18	5	.246
First Half	75	291	75	7	1	3	37	20	18	34	13	3	.258
Second Half	83	278	65	13	3	1	23	23	20	28	5	2	.234
vs. RHP		389	100	14	4	3	49	33	30	32	14	2	.257
vs. LHP		180	40	6	0	1	11	10	8	30	4	3	.222
Home	78	273	75	7	1	2	26	20	17	28	8	2	.275
Road	80	296	65	13	3	2	34	23	21	34	10	3	.220
Grass	134	483	123	14	3	3	50	34	32	51	14	5	.255
Turf	24	86	17	6	1	1	10	9	6	11	4	0	.198

Charlie MOORE, Rightfield
Runs Created: 71

	G	AB	Hit	2B	3B	HR	Run	RBI	BB	SO	SB	CS	Avg
6.35 Years		497	133	23	5	5	58	49	43	49	7	4	.267
1983	151	529	150	27	6	2	65	49	55	42	11	4	.284
First Half	71	245	64	15	5	1	37	20	32	22	4	1	.261
Second Half	80	284	86	12	1	1	28	29	23	20	7	3	.303
vs. RHP		310	89	16	4	0	34	33	30	35	8	3	.287
vs. LHP		219	61	11	2	2	31	16	25	7	3	1	.279
Home	76	253	76	13	6	1	27	21	27	19	5	2	.300
Road	75	276	74	14	0	1	38	28	28	13	6	2	.268
Grass	127	441	132	23	6	2	55	41	51	34	9	4	.299
Turf	24	88	18	4	0	0	10	8	4	8	2	0	.205

Ned YOST, Catcher
Runs Created: 15

	G	AB	Hit	2B	3B	HR	Run	RBI	BB	SO	SB	CS	Avg
0.83 Years		422	98	13	5	12	46	47	18	82	5	1	.233
1983	61	196	44	5	1	6	21	28	5	36	1	0	.224
First Half	37	117	27	3	1	5	14	19	4	24	1	0	.231
Second Half	24	79	17	2	0	1	7	9	1	12	0	0	.215
vs. RHP		112	21	3	1	1	8	11	3	24	1	0	.188
vs. LHP		84	23	2	0	5	13	17	2	12	0	0	.274
Home	34	103	25	4	1	2	13	13	3	19	1	0	.243
Road	27	93	19	1	0	4	8	15	2	17	0	0	.204
Grass	58	189	42	5	1	5	20	26	5	35	1	0	.222
Turf	3	7	2	0	0	1	1	2	0	1	0	0	.286

Ted SIMMONS, Designated Hitter
Runs Created: 89

	G	AB	Hit	2B	3B	HR	Run	RBI	BB	SO	SB	CS	Avg
12.06 Years		601	175	34	4	18	77	99	60	48	1	3	.292
1983	153	600	185	39	3	13	76	108	41	51	4	2	.308
First Half	71	280	86	19	1	6	33	45	19	24	3	0	.307
Second Half	82	320	99	20	2	7	43	63	22	27	1	2	.309
vs. RHP		367	110	27	0	10	50	63	26	27	3	2	.300
vs. LHP		233	75	12	3	3	26	45	15	24	1	0	.322
Home	77	295	85	21	2	8	37	54	18	24	3	2	.288
Road	76	305	100	18	1	5	39	54	23	27	1	0	.328
Grass	129	509	157	35	3	11	66	95	36	41	3	2	.308
Turf	24	91	28	4	0	2	10	13	5	10	1	0	.308

Mark BROUHARD, Outfield
Runs Created: 23

	G	AB	Hit	2B	3B	HR	Run	RBI	BB	SO	SB	CS	Avg
1.24 Years		487	129	21	4	15	62	56	26	98	2	6	.265
1983	56	185	51	10	1	7	25	23	9	39	0	4	.276
First Half	11	35	15	4	0	2	6	6	0	4	0	1	.429
Second Half	45	150	36	6	1	5	19	17	9	35	0	3	.240
vs. RHP		88	24	4	1	2	10	8	2	22	0	1	.273
vs. LHP		97	27	6	0	5	15	15	7	17	0	3	.278
Home	35	118	34	5	1	4	15	16	6	20	0	3	.288
Road	21	67	17	5	0	3	10	7	3	19	0	1	.254
Grass	54	177	50	10	1	7	25	23	9	34	0	4	.282
Turf	2	8	1	0	0	0	0	0	0	5	0	0	.125

Mike CALDWELL

Year	(W–L)	GS	Run	Avg	DP	Avg	SB	Avg
1982	(17-13)	34	164	4.82	43	1.26	9	.26
1983	(12-11)	32	159	4.97	35	1.09	13	.41
1977-1983		198	974	4.92	231	1.17	71	.36

	G	IP	W	L	Pct	ER	ERA
1982 Home	21	162.2	11	8	.579	62	3.43
1983 Home	16	125.2	7	4	.571	50	3.58
1982 Road	14	95.1	6	5	.545	50	4.72
1983 Road	16	102.2	5	7	.636	65	5.70
1983 Grass	27	197.2	11	9	.550	89	4.05
1983 Turf	5	30.2	1	2	.333	26	7.63

Don SUTTON

Year	(W–L)	GS	Run	Avg	DP	Avg	SB	Avg
1982	(17- 9)	34	159	4.68	34	1.00	34	1.00
1983	(8-13)	31	131	4.23	16	.52	40	1.29
1976-1983		252	1064	4.22	170	.67	227	.90

	G	IP	W	L	Pct	ER	ERA
1982 Home	20	157.2	10	4	.714	41	
1983 Home	15	109	2	6	.250	48	3.96
1982 Road	14	92	7	5	.583	44	4.30
1983 Road	16	111.1	6	7	.461	52	4.20
1983 Grass	27	190.1	6	11	.353	82	3.88
1983 Turf	4	30	2	2	.500	18	5.40

Moose HAAS

Year	(W–L)	GS	Run	Avg	DP	Avg	SB	Avg
1982	(11-8)	27	148	5.48	27	1.00	18	.67
1983	(13-3)	25	123	4.92	27	1.08	27	1.08
1977-1983		173	811	4.69	175	1.01	136	.79

	G	IP	W	L	Pct	ER	ERA
1982 Home	12	81.2	5	4	.556	37	4.19
1983 Home	13	96.2	8	2	.800	27	2.51
1982 Road	20	111.2	6	4	.600	59	4.76
1983 Road	12	82.1	5	1	.833	38	4.15
1983 Grass	21	153.2	12	3	.800	55	3.22
1983 Turf	4	25.1	1	0	1.000	10	3.55

Bob McCLURE

Year	(W–L)	GS	Run	Avg	DP	Avg	SB	Avg
1982	(12-7)	26	155	5.96	25	.96	12	.46
1983	(9-9)	23	109	4.74	25	1.09	19	.83
1980-1983		54	282	5.22	54	1.00	37	.68

	G	IP	W	L	Pct	ER	ERA
1982 Home	17	86.2	6	4	.600	41	4.26
1983 Home	13	76.2	5	3	.625	34	3.99
1982 Road	17	86	6	3	.667	40	4.19
1983 Road	11	65.1	4	6	.400	37	5.10
1983 Grass	19	110.2	8	5	.615	50	4.07
1983 Turf	5	31.1	1	4	.200	21	6.03

Chuck PORTER

Year	(W–L)	GS	Run	Avg	DP	Avg	SB	Avg
1983	(7-9)	21	103	4.90	19	.90	22	1.05

	G	IP	W	L	Pct	ER	ERA
1983 Home	11	61	3	4	.429	29	4.28
1983 Road	14	73	4	5	.444	38	4.68
1983 Grass	23	127.2	6	9	.400	60	4.23
1983 Turf	2	6.1	1	0	1.000	7	9.95

1983 OTHERS

Pitcher	(W–L)	GS	Run	Avg	DP	Avg	SB	Avg
Candiotti	(4-4)	8	26	3.25	14	1.75	10	1.25
Gibson	(3-4)	7	28	4.00	4	.57	10	1.43
Augustine	(3-3)	7	39	5.57	8	1.14	9	1.29
Cocanower	(2-0)	3	24	8.00	7	2.33	0	.00
Vuckovich	(0-2)	3	11	3.67	3	1.00	5	1.67
Waits	(0-2)	2	11	5.50	3	1.50	2	1.00

MILWAUKEE BREWERS CHART-I
1979 to 1983 RBI ANALYSIS

Cecil COOPER, First Base

	RBI	RBI In Wins	Victory-Important RBI	RBI Importance	Wins Batted In	RBI Per Win
1979	106		44.25	.417		
1980	122	84	45.62	.374	12.75	9.6
1981	60	47	35.28	.588	8.10	7.4
1982	121	96	51.18	.423	13.35	9.1
1983	126	94	63.16	.501	15.13	8.3
Total	535	321	239.49	.448	49.33	8.7

Jim GANTNER, Second Base

	RBI	RBI In Wins	Victory-Important RBI	RBI Importance	Wins Batted In	RBI Per Win
1979	22		12.05	.548		
1980	40	30	12.32	.308	4.84	8.3
1981	33	25	14.81	.449	3.44	9.6
1982	43	32	18.01	.419	4.95	8.7
1983	74	51	35.35	.478	7.61	9.7
Total	212	138	92.54	.437	20.84	9.1

Paul MOLITOR, Third Base

	RBI	RBI In Wins	Victory-Important RBI	RBI Importance	Wins Batted In	RBI Per Win
1979	62		34.37	.554		
1980	37	24	13.55	.366	3.41	10.9
1981	19	16	6.81	.358	2.35	8.1
1982	71	57	32.55	.458	7.93	9.0
1983	47	31	18.16	.386	5.09	9.2
Total	236	128	105.44	.447	18.78	9.3

Robin YOUNT, Shortstop

	RBI	RBI In Wins	Victory-Important RBI	RBI Importance	Wins Batted In	RBI Per Win
1979	51		21.96	.431		
1980	87	63	35.09	.403	9.00	9.7
1981	49	39	25.08	.512	6.17	7.9
1982	114	88	45.32	.398	10.92	10.4
1983	80	58	42.54	.532	10.42	7.7
Total	381	248	169.99	.446	36.51	9.0

Ben OGLIVIE, Leftfield

	RBI	RBI In Wins	Victory-Important RBI	RBI Importance	Wins Batted In	RBI Per Win
1979	81		42.35	.523		
1980	118	96	49.06	.416	15.07	7.8
1981	72	54	32.36	.449	10.47	6.9
1982	102	66	39.34	.386	9.47	10.8
1983	66	51	34.13	.517	8.21	8.0
Total	439	267	197.24	.449	43.22	8.3

Gorman THOMAS, Centerfield

	RBI	RBI In Wins	Victory-Important RBI	RBI Importance	Wins Batted In	RBI Per Win
1979	123		66.89	.544		
1980	105	70	36.80	.350	9.95	10.6
1981	65	46	28.50	.438	7.39	8.8
1982	112	96	50.78	.453	13.03	8.6
1983	18	9	5.13	.285	1.31	13.7
Total	423	221	188.10	.445	31.68	9.5

Charlie MOORE, Rightfield

	RBI	RBI In Wins	Victory-Important RBI	RBI Importance	Wins Batted In	RBI Per Win
1979	38		17.36	.457		
1980	30	24	13.11	.437	2.83	10.6
1981	9	5	4.40	.489	0.72	12.5
1982	45	38	22.84	.508	4.74	9.5
1983	49	37	25.09	.512	5.58	8.8
Total	171	104	82.80	.484	13.87	9.6

Ted SIMMONS, Catcher

	RBI	RBI In Wins	Victory-Important RBI	RBI Importance	Wins Batted In	RBI Per Win
1981	61	52	31.54	.517	8.83	6.9
1982	97	81	42.48	.438	11.30	8.6
1983	108	69	50.97	.472	11.59	9.3
Total	266	202	124.99	.470	31.72	8.4

Don MONEY Inf–DH

	RBI	RBI In Wins	Victory-Important RBI	RBI Importance	Wins Batted In	RBI Per Win
1979	38		22.54	.593		
1980	46	35	15.55	.338	5.28	8.7
1981	14	6	2.70	.193	0.93	15.1
1982	55	40	22.94	.417	5.32	10.3
1983	8	8	6.33	.791	1.27	6.3
Total	161	89	70.06	.435	12.80	9.6

BOSTON RED SOX

I

"In the middle of your batting order you want men that can slug the ball. But you should never have two slow-footed, righthanded sluggers batting one after the other, because the double plays will murder you. If one of them gets on first, the other team will play the next man to hit the ball to the left side of the infield. And when he does, the runner from first base can't get down to second base fast enough to interfere with the pivot man in completing the double play."

Page 186
Casey At the Bat
By Casey Stengel with
Harry T. Porter,
1962

"Boston outfielders Jim Rice and Tony Armas were first and second, respectively, in home runs in the American League with 37 and 36 and hitting into double plays with 30 and 29."

Page 90
Sports Illustrated
October 3, 1983
(Final totals were 39 and 36 HRs and 31 double-play balls each.)

II

Marty Barrett played for Boston in the National League in 1884 (he went 0 for 6 in catching 3 games). Marty Barrett, should he make the team this year, will mark 100 years apart that men with the same name played major league ball in the same city.
—Jim Baker

III. Maybe He's in Indiana

A year ago, in discussing Jim Rice, I quoted some information that was sent to me by an astute and dedicated Red Sox fan named Chuck Waseleski. For some reason, it stuck in my mind that no matter what I did, that name was going to come out in print Waslewski, rather than Waseleski, and I must have checked the manuscript a dozen times to make sure that did not happen. Unfortunately, I was so concerned that I was going to call him Waslewski, rather than Waseleski, that I wound up calling him Gary, rather than Chuck. My apologies.

Anyway, Chuck has taken this affront in stride (I haven't heard from Gary) and has continued to provide me with fascinating and valuable information about those there Boston Red Sox. He makes scoresheets from each and every Red Sox game, and he extracts from those scoresheets information in which he has an interest or I have an interest. A summary of that information:

IV. Red Sox Situational Statistics

Chuck kept track of what each Red Sox player hit:

1) When there were runners in scoring position.
2) In the 7th inning or later when the score was close (Red Sox two behind to one ahead). These at-bats are described on the sheet as "clutch."
3) When both conditions applied.

Generally speaking, most players hit about as well in those situations as at other times. Gary Allenson couldn't buy a hit in the late innings of a close game, but then Gary Allenson isn't exactly Rod Carew in the early innings of a blowout. Dwight Evans, having an off year, did not produce with runners in scoring position; Tony Armas did fairly well in that situation. (He hit .236, but that's 25 points higher than he hit at other times. On the other hand, 19 of Armas' 31 double-play balls were hit when there was a runner in scoring position.) Glen Hoffmann hit very well in the late innings of close games (.313), although he drove in only 3 runs in those situations. Reid Nichols did not hit well with runners in scoring position. Jim Rice did not hit well in the late innings of close games; that is probably the largest item in the chart. If I were to do a significance test of the data on Chart Red Sox-I, there is no doubt among all tendencies that were found, that one would be the most likely to repeat again next year. Dave Stapleton hit very well with runners in scoring position (83% of his RBI were accounted for in that circumstance), but he did not hit in the late innings of close games. Carl Yastrzemski displayed the same tendencies to an even stronger extent, hitting .329 with runners in scoring position, but only .200 in the late innings of close games.

For the team as a whole, the batting average with runners in scoring position was .270, exactly the same as it was when runners were in the lotus position, the missionary position or the bench position. Batting averages drop in the late innings of a close game because of people like Goose Gossage, Bob Stanley and Dan Quisenberry, and they drop a lot with runners in scoring position in the late innings of a close game, because of lots of people like Goose Gossage, Bob Stanley and Dan Quisenberry.

Seventy-four percent of Boston's RBI (514 or 691) came at times when runners were in scoring positions; however, remember that in many of those situations the runner might have scored from first base or home plate on an extra-base hit when another runner was in scoring position. Opportunities with runners in scoring position accounted for 25% of the Red Sox at-bats, 25% of their hits, 25% of their home runs, 26% of their doubles, 29% of their walks, 39% of their double-play balls, and 100% of their sacrifice flies.

BOSTON RED SOX SITUATIONAL STATISTICS

	AB	H	2B	3B	BB	SO	HP	SAC	SF	GIDP	HR	RBI	AVG.
ALLENSON													
Scoring Position	70	16	3	0	3	10	2	1	5	4	1	20	.229
Clutch	27	3	2	0	5	7	0	2	2	0	0	2	.111
Both	3	0	0	0	1	0	0	0	2	0	0	2	.000
ARMAS													
Scoring Position	161	38	9	1	8	35	1	0	8	19	10	70	.236
Clutch	90	21	5	1	4	23	0	0	1	5	6	19	.233
Both	24	8	4	1	2	3	0	0	1	2	1	14	.333
BARRETT													
Scoring Position	11	2	0	0	0	0	0	0	1	1	0	2	.182
Clutch	10	2	0	0	0	0	0	0	1	0	0	2	.200
Both	6	1	0	0	0	0	0	0	1	0	0	2	.167
BOGGS													
Scoring Position	134	49	10	4	20	11	0	0	7	5	0	64	.366
Clutch	81	29	5	1	17	4	0	3	1	0	1	13	.358
Both	19	8	1	1	8	3	0	0	1	0	0	12	.421
EVANS													
Scoring Position	108	23	5	0	19	27	2	0	2	2	5	35	.213
Clutch	58	13	3	1	11	14	0	0	0	1	5	10	.224
Both	14	5	2	0	4	1	0	0	0	1	1	8	.357
GEDMAN													
Scoring Position	47	13	5	0	8	13	1	1	0	1	1	16	.277
Clutch	36	8	2	0	6	7	0	2	0	0	0	0	.222
Both	5	0	0	0	5	1	0	1	0	0	0	0	.000
GRAHAM													
Scoring Position	1	0	0	0	0	0	0	0	0	1	0	1	.000
Clutch	1	0	0	0	0	0	0	0	0	1	0	1	.000
Both	0	0	0	0	0	0	0	0	1	0	0	1	–
GUTIERREZ													
Scoring Position	3	1	0	0	0	0	0	0	0	0	0	0	.333
Clutch	1	1	0	0	0	0	0	0	0	0	0	0	1.000
Both	0	0	0	0	0	0	0	0	0	0	0	0	–
HOFFMAN													
Scoring Position	133	35	6	0	14	23	1	4	2	2	1	35	.263
Clutch	64	20	0	0	2	7	0	5	0	1	0	3	.313
Both	15	4	0	0	0	2	0	1	0	0	0	3	.267
JURAK													
Scoring Position	40	10	4	1	3	6	0	1	2	3	0	16	.250
Clutch	36	8	3	3	2	11	0	1	1	1	0	3	.222
Both	8	1	1	0	1	2	0	0	1	1	0	2	.125
MILLER													
Scoring Position	69	19	0	1	7	8	0	0	1	2	1	20	.275
Clutch	52	15	1	0	3	6	0	1	0	1	1	5	.288
Both	16	5	0	0	0	2	0	0	0	0	0	4	.313
NEWMAN													
Scoring Position	35	5	0	0	2	7	0	0	1	3	0	3	.143
Clutch	15	4	1	0	2	3	0	1	0	0	0	0	.267
Both	4	0	0	0	0	2	0	0	0	0	0	0	.000
NICHOLS													
Scoring Position	56	12	3	1	2	4	2	0	1	2	0	15	.214
Clutch	46	12	6	0	4	5	0	1	0	0	0	2	.260
Both	8	1	0	0	2	0	0	0	0	0	0	2	.125
REMY													
Scoring Position	123	35	3	1	11	6	0	3	3	6	0	41	.285
Clutch	73	19	3	0	4	6	0	4	0	0	0	4	.260
Both	17	3	1	0	2	1	0	1	0	0	0	4	.176
RICE													
Scoring Position	165	50	10	1	19	24	3	0	5	7	10	77	.303
Clutch	85	18	4	0	11	15	0	0	1	1	5	16	.212
Both	22	4	1	0	6	4	0	0	1	0	1	10	.182
STAPLETON													
Scoring Position	141	40	10	1	15	7	0	2	8	6	3	55	.284
Clutch	80	16	3	0	3	5	1	5	1	1	0	3	.200
Both	20	1	1	0	1	1	0	2	1	1	0	2	.050
WALKER													
Scoring Position	1	0	0	0	0	0	0	0	0	0	0	0	.000
Clutch	2	1	0	1	0	0	0	0	0	0	0	0	.500
Both	1	0	0	0	0	0	0	0	0	0	0	0	.000
YASTRZEMSKI													
Scoring Position	82	27	8	0	22	5	0	0	1	3	4	44	.329
Clutch	50	10	6	0	6	3	0	0	0	2	1	2	.200
Both	9	0	0	0	4	2	0	0	0	1	0	1	.000
TEAM													
Scoring Position	1392	376	76	11	153	187	12	12	48	66	36	514	.270
Clutch	807	200	44	7	80	116	1	25	9	13	17	85	.248
Both	190	41	11	2	36	24	0	5	9	6	3	66	.216

V. Stolen Bases by Pitcher

When Mark Clear was pitching for the Red Sox last year (96 innings, the equivalent of 10 ⅔ games), Red Sox opponents attempted to steal 33 bases and were successful 32 times. When Bruce Hurst was pitching (211 innings, 23½ games) they tried to run only 24 times and were successful 15 times. Opponents attempted to steal three times as often when Clear was pitching as when Hurst was pitching; the Red Sox were twelve times as successful in throwing them out when Hurst was pitching as when Clear was pitching.

Other totals of note: Eckersley was surprisingly good (16 of 25 made it when he was on the mound) and Tudor surprisingly poor (24 of 30 stole successfully). Bird was bad (8/9 in 68 innings), Boyd bad (12/15 in 99 innings) and nobody even tries on Stanley (6/8 in 145 innings). (The data sent to me on Ojeda seems to be in error.)

VI. Game-Winning Runs

The "game-winning" run scored in the first two innings of the game in 61 of the Red Sox's 162 games. The Red Sox were 28–33 in those games, about their final clip. The game-winning run scored in the eighth inning or later in 42 games, and the Red Sox were 22–20 in those games, probably in large part because of Stanley.

VII. Home Runs Against the Red Sox

There were 76 home runs hit by Red Sox opponents in Fenway Park last year, 82 hit against them on the road. Opposing righthanded batters increased their production in Fenway from 55 to 59, but home runs by opposing lefthanders dropped from 27 to 17. Of the 17 home runs hit by opposing lefthanders, nine were off of Dennis Eckersley, and only two were off of a lefthander. And remember the Red Sox had three lefthanders who were doing a lot of pitching.

Righthanded pitchers decreased the number of home runs they allowed from 50 on the road to 36 at home; lefthanders increased their home runs allowed from 32 on the road to 40 in Fenway.

Many people, aware of this at least intuitively, have charged Houk with poor judgment in starting three lefthanded pitchers in Fenway Park. I don't feel that the charge is valid; I think it's an extension of a simplistic and misguided view of Fenway Park. The Red Sox staff ERA was 4.31 on the road, 4.38 at home. That's too high, but it's too high in both places, not just in Fenway. Lefthanders on the staff had an ERA of 3.81 on the road, 4.26 in Fenway; righthanders had an ERA of 4.73 on the road, 4.49 in Fenway.

Clearly, the righthanders did have an advantage, the lefthanders a disadvantage. But even more clearly, the lefthanders that Houk had available to him were better pitchers than the righthanders. I can see questioning the management that provided him with this talent; I can even see wondering why the lefthanders started 49 games in Fenway Park and only 46 on the road. But the "percentage" is exactly that: a percentage. The quality is an absolute. Houk did the right thing in using Hurst, Ojeda and Tudor, because they were the best pitchers he had.

There were two problems, in my mind. The pitching staff was not good enough, and the offense, not the defense, was poorly suited to Fenway Park. Fenway helps righthanders for power, lefthanders for average. There was too much righthanded power here, or rather too little of anything else. Red Sox lefthanders hit only 19 home runs all year.

VIII. Home Runs With Men on Base

Jim Rice hit 64% of his home runs with men on base, and averaged 1.72 RBI per home run. Dwight Evans hit only 36% of his home runs with men on, and averaged 1.55 RBI per shot. More data:

| | Runs Resulting | | | | | % With | | HR |
	1	2	3	4	Total	Men On	RBI	Value
Carl Yastrzemski	2	7	1	0	10	80	19	1.90
Dave Stapleton	5	2	3	0	10	50	18	1.80
Jim Rice	14	23	1	1	39	64	67	1.72
Tony Armas	18	13	4	1	36	50	60	1.67
Dwight Evans	14	4	4	0	22	36	34	1.55
Others	16	5	4	0	25	36	38	1.52

IX. Hits Off the Leftfield Wall

The Red Sox in 1983 had 129 hits off the leftfield wall, including 49 home runs hit into the screen. Of the 80 balls that came off the wall (one a game), 66 were doubles and one was a triple. Boggs hit 20 doubles off of that wall, 30% of the team total (no one else had more than eight).

Opponents hit more home runs into the screen than the Red Sox did (54–49) and were virtually even in balls coming off the wall (79–80). However, the Red Sox did derive a clear advantage on those plays, as only 48 of the opponents' 79 batters got a double out of the deal (one also got a triple). That means that whereas only 13 of the Red Sox were stopped at first after hitting the ball off the wall, 30 of their opponents were. This is due, obviously, to Jim Rice's ability to play the wall; Rice saved the Red Sox 17 bases during the year by his ability to play the ball off the wall and hold the opposition to a single. Also, whereas the Red Sox had no one thrown out on a ball off the wall, Rice threw out five runners (three trying to stretch the hit, two others trying to advance) on that play. So Rice probably took about 8 runs—one game—away from Red Sox opponents by his ability to play the leftfield wall. That's a big thing; within the context of the limited defensive assignment of a leftfielder, it's an enormous thing.

X. Scoring in the First Inning

The Red Sox scored in the first inning only 51 times; their opponents did so 59 times. The Red Sox were 30–21 when they did score in the first; their opponents were 39–20 when they scored in the first inning.

XI. Scoring When Leadoff Batter Reached Base

When the Red Sox leadoff man reached base in 1983, the team scored .93 runs per inning. When he did not reach base, they scored .27 runs per inning. When their opponents' leadoff man reached base, their opponents scored .98 runs per inning; when their opponents did not get their leadoff man on, they scored .28 runs per inning.

What's that? Let me go by that again. The Red Sox and their opponents scored three and a half times as often when they got their leadoff man on as when they did not? Wow.

The data: The Red Sox had 1,451 offensive innings in 1983 and had the leadoff man on 501 times. They scored 464 runs in those innings. In the other 950 innings, the Red Sox scored 260 runs.

Let's make a few projections based on that. The Red Sox got their leadoff man on 34.5% of the time. They scored 724 runs. If they had gotten their leadoff man on an extra 50 times (this would have required a leadoff on-base percentage of .380), how many runs would they have been likely to score?

$$551 \times .93 = 512$$
$$900 \times .27 = \underline{243}$$
$$765$$

A big difference. And the data for their opposition is just as big. Considering the two together, teams scored 50% of the time when they got their leadoff men on, 16.8% of the time when they didn't. They averaged 1.91 runs per scoring inning when they did, 1.65 when they didn't.

(I don't know if this knowledge has the impact on you that it did on Waseleski and it did on me. Try an experiment. Call up your nearest baseball fan, right now, and ask him this question: How many more runs will you score in an inning when you have the leadoff man on than you do in an inning when you don't? I'll bet he says 28% or something. The answer is 242%.)

All of this information, again, comes courtesy of Chuck Waseleski. That's C-H-U . . .

Thanks, Chuck.

This is what Wade Boggs's career statistics are going to look like when he retires. Remember, this is where you read it first.

Year	G	AB	Runs	Hits	2B	3B	HR	RBI	Walk	Avg.
1982	104	338	51	118	14	1	5	44	35	.349
1983	153	582	100	210	44	7	5	74	92	.361
1984	156	584	107	209	37	5	7	88	81	.358
1985	159	594	102	224	43	5	8	96	88	.377
1986	157	581	97	208	35	4	11	91	83	.358
1987	153	562	88	186	32	4	9	81	80	.331
1988	152	554	90	197	33	4	9	85	80	.356
1989	149	542	89	201	34	3	9	86	78	.371
1990	147	529	75	164	28	3	7	70	76	.310
1991	145	518	77	174	29	3	8	74	75	.336
1992	142	507	79	186	31	3	8	79	73	.367
1993	140	496	71	166	28	2	7	70	72	.335
1994	138	485	69	162	27	2	6	68	70	.334
1995	84	293	39	93	15	1	3	39	42	.317
1996	132	458	68	163	24	2	9	69	66	.356
1997	114	394	51	119	18	1	6	50	57	.302
1998	107	366	49	119	18	1	6	50	53	.325
1999	114	388	50	124	19	1	6	52	56	.319
	2,446	8,771	1,352	3,023	509	52	129	1,266	1,261	.345

THE MANAGER

NAME: Ralph Houk

AGE: 64

MANAGERS FOR WHOM PLAYED IN MAJORS: Bucky Harris and Casey Stengel.

CHARACTERISTICS AS A PLAYER: Another catcher; did everything fairly well except that he had zero power. In today's game, he'd probably play some, but for a catcher to lack power in the 1947–1954 era was something they just couldn't live with.

MANAGERIAL RECORD:

Team	Year	Par	Wins	Losses	Pct.	+ or −
Yankees	1961	89	109	53	.673	+20
Yankees	1962	97	96	66	.593	− 1
Yankees	1963	95	104	57	.646	+ 9
Yankees	1966	74	66	73	.475	− 8
Yankees	1967	76	72	90	.444	− 4
Yankees	1968	75	83	79	.512	+ 8
Yankees	1969	78	80	81	.497	+ 2
Yankees	1970	82	93	69	.574	+11
Yankees	1971	85	82	80	.506	− 3
Yankees	1972	82	79	76	.510	− 3
Yankees	1973	82	80	82	.494	− 2
Detroit	1974	85	72	90	.444	−13
Detroit	1975	78	57	102	.358	−21
Detroit	1976	70	74	87	.460	+ 4
Detroit	1977	71	74	88	.457	+ 3
Detroit	1978	76	86	76	.531	+10
Boston	1981	57	59	49	.546	+ 2
Boston	1982	84	89	73	.549	+ 5
Boston	1983	86	78	84	.481	− 8
19 Years		1522	1533	1455	.513	+11

WHAT HE BRINGS TO THE BALLCLUB

IS HE AN INTENSE MANAGER OR MORE OF AN EASY-TO-GET-ALONG-WITH TYPE? Maybe I should have made up a third class here: "tough" and "authoritarian" but not really difficult to deal with.

IS HE MORE OF AN EMOTIONAL LEADER OR A DECISION-MAKER? Much more the former.

IS HE MORE OF AN OPTIMIST OR MORE OF A PROBLEM SOLVER? An optimist, a man who will accept certain shortcomings in his players without worrying about them. (Some of you may remember that Art Hill wrote about this with some dissatisfaction in *Don't Let Baseball Die*).

HOW HE USES HIS PERSONNEL

DOES HE FAVOR A SET LINEUP OR A ROTATION SYSTEM? A set lineup. That was the big change between the '60 and '61 Yankees; Casey made a virtue out of being able to play anywhere, and sometimes juggled his lineup just because he seemed to enjoy it. Houk stopped that.

DOES HE LIKE TO PLATOON? No. He platoons 1) to protect a player who has a weakness, as with

Blomberg, or 2) if he just doesn't have anybody for the spot.

DOES HE TRY TO SOLVE HIS PROBLEMS WITH PROVEN PLAYERS OR WITH YOUNGSTERS WHO STILL HAVE SOMETHING TO PROVE? HOW MANY PLAYERS HAS HE MADE REGULARS OUT OF WHO WERE NOT REGULARS BEFORE, AND WHO WERE THEY? Ralph has made a first-time regular out of 30 players: Tom Tresh, Joe Pepitone, Horace Clarke, Roy White, Steve Whitaker, Jake Gibbs, Bill Robinson, Bobby Cox, Andy Kosco, Jerry Kenney, Gene Michael, Bobby Murcer, Thurman Munson, Ron Blomberg (platoon), Ben Oglivie (platoon), Tom Veryzer, Leon Roberts, Ron LeFlore, Dan Meyer, Jason Thompson, Steve Kemp, Lou Whitaker, Alan Trammell, Tim Corcoran (platoon), Lance Parrish, Glenn Hoffman, Dave Stapleton, Gedman and Allenson (platoon), and Wade Boggs. That's a great many players, even for 19 years of managing, and on that basis you have to say that he likes to give the kids a shot. The list of pitchers probably would be almost as long.

DOES HE PREFER TO GO WITH GOOD OFFENSIVE PLAYERS OR DOES HE LIKE THE GLOVE MEN? Again, an easy answer: He'll stay forever with a glove man, waiting for him to hit. From Clete Boyer to Gene Michael to Glenn Hoffman to Dave Stapleton, that's a consistent pattern.

DOES HE LIKE AN OFFENSE BASED ON POWER, SPEED OR HIGH AVERAGES? His most memorable teams have always had power, and his bad teams have always lacked it.

DOES HE USE THE ENTIRE ROSTER OR DOES HE KEEP PEOPLE AROUND SITTING ON THE BENCH? He rides on an 8-man lineup as much as he can.

DOES HE BUILD HIS BENCH AROUND YOUNG PLAYERS WHO CAN STEP INTO A BREACH IF NEED BE OR AROUND VETERAN ROLE-PLAYERS WHO HAVE THEIR OWN FUNCTIONS WITHIN A GAME? Mostly around prospects; Nichols, Barrett, Valdez, Walker and Jurak mixed with a couple of veterans is a typical Houk bench.

GAME MANAGING AND USE OF STRATEGIES

DOES HE GO FOR THE BIG-INNING OFFENSE OR DOES HE LIKE TO USE THE ONE-RUN STRATEGIES? Big inning manager all the way.

DOES HE PINCH-HIT MUCH, AND IF SO WHEN? He pinch-hits very little. He did use Rick Miller 41 times last year, but that's unusual; even John Blanchard didn't see that much work for him, with no DH rule. The most pinch-hitters he's used was with Detroit in '74 when he had a good bench led by Gates Brown.

ANYTHING UNUSUAL ABOUT HIS LINEUP SELECTION? In Houk's first year as a manager, 1961, he had a tremendously successful season leading off Bobby Richardson. Richardson, frankly, was a horrible leadoff man. He rarely got on base and almost never got into scoring position. Leading-off for the 1961 Yankees, playing 162 games and batting 662 times, with 237 home runs coming up behind him, Richardson scored only 80 runs. 80. Eight-zero. Dick Howser scored 28 more runs that year while batting leadoff for the 1961 Kansas City Athletics, who hit 90 home runs and lost 100 games. Plus Richardson used up a zillion outs while he was not scoring runs.

But, of course, these were the 1961 Yankees, and if he had led off with Moose Skowron and batted Richardson cleanup, they were still going to win the pennant.

And ever since then, Houk has been leading off these terrible little second basemen who may be good defensively, but who hit .270, have no power at all and don't walk. It's painful to think how many runs he must have cost his team by this nonsense over the course of the last twenty years. Jerry Remy, the winner of the 1983 Bobby Richardson look-alike contest, had an on-base percentage of .321 (the league average for all players was .330), reached scoring position under his own power only 32 times and scored only 73 runs; still, he is probably an above-average Ralph Houk leadoff man. After Richardson retired, Houk's second baseman (and therefore his leadoff man) was Horace Clarke, a career .256 hitter who walked about as much as Remy does. Horace led the league in at-bats twice and had a career high of 82 runs scored; he was often in the sixties in the sixties in runs scored, and his worst years, for a man playing a key offensive role, are bizarre. He outlasted Houk in New York by only a few games.

Houk went to Detroit, where the incumbent second baseman was Dick McAuliffe, who in his day had been a good leadoff man. McAuliffe was immediately traded, and the new second baseman and (need I add) leadoff man was (you're not going to believe this) a journeyman named Gary Sutherland. Sutherland in 1974 batted 619 times, hit .254, drew 26 walks, reached scoring position under his own power 27 times and scored 60 runs. That was second on the team.

Sutherland lost his leadoff job late that year to the only non-second baseman that Houk has ever used as his regular leadoff man—Ron LeFlore. LeFlore, in his day, was a great leadoff man; in 1978 he hit .297, had an on-base percentage of .363, reached scoring position under his own power 113 times and scored 126 runs. He had to be that good, because if he wasn't Houk would have led off Tito Fuentes. The 1978 Tigers, with a lineup in which no one hit more than

26 home runs and no one hit .300, let alone .361, scored only eight fewer runs than the 1983 Red Sox.

DOES HE USE THE SAC BUNT OFTEN? No, not much.

DOES HE LIKE TO USE THE RUNNING GAME? He doesn't run at all when he has power; he'll run some when the team lacks power.

IN WHAT CIRCUMSTANCES WILL HE ISSUE AN INTENTIONAL WALK? Uses it a normal amount; I'm not sure in what circumstances.

DOES HE HIT AND RUN VERY OFTEN? Kubek says he does; I haven't seen it. His teams ground into a lot of double plays, which usually you won't do if you make good use of the hit and run.

ARE THERE ANY UNIQUE OR IDIOSYNCRATIC STRATEGIES THAT HE PARTICULARLY LIKES? He's a very straightforward manager.

HANDLING THE PITCHING STAFF

DOES HE LIKE POWER PITCHERS OR PREFER TO GO WITH THE PEOPLE WHO PUT THE BALL IN PLAY? Control pitchers. Ralph Terry, Bill Stafford, Mel Stottlemyre, Fritz Peterson, Vern Ruhle, Mark Fidrych, Dave Rozema, Jim Slaton, Jack Billingham—those are the people he's had success with. Probably one major reason he's stayed this long with Eckersly is that Eckersly does throw strikes.

DOES HE STAY WITH THE STARTER OR GO TO THE BULLPEN QUICKLY? He's a quick hook. And he's had some spectacular success with his relievers—Luis Arroyo had a great year for him in 1961, Lindy McDaniel in 1970, Sparky Lyle in 1972, John Hiller in '74 (not his great year, but the year he went 17–14), Stanley in '83. Plus he's had some great "team" bullpens (1982, 1968).

DOES HE LIKE THE FOUR-MAN OR THE FIVE-MAN ROTATION? Like most managers, has switched now to the five-man rotation.

DOES HE USE THE ENTIRE STAFF OR DOES HE TRY TO GET FIVE OR SIX PEOPLE TO DO MOST OF THE WORK? He uses, and has always used, every pitcher that he has.

HOW LONG WILL HE STAY WITH A STARTER WHO IS STRUGGLING? Not long.

ARE THERE ANY PARTICULAR TYPES OF PITCHERS OF WHOM HE IS FOND? He has a taste for groundball pitchers. He's used a lot of the hard-throwing kids who maybe only had two pitches, if they had one that they could throw for a strike when they needed it. He's had an awful lot of left-handed aces, but that might just be coincidence, or coincidence plus all those years in Yankee Stadium.

IS THERE ANYTHING UNIQUE ABOUT HIS HANDLING OF HIS PITCHERS? He's gotten one or two good years out of a lot of young pitchers who were not destined for glory (Downing, Bouton, Stafford, Sheldon, Kline, Fidrych, Rozema, Bahnsen).

WHAT IS HIS STRONGEST POINT AS A MANAGER? Well, he's managed 19 years in the major leagues and has never been fired. His strongest point is probably his ability to command the respect of his players.

IF THERE WERE NO PROFESSIONAL BASEBALL, WHAT WOULD THIS MANAGER PROBABLY BE DOING? Retired Marine Corps general.

Dave STAPLETON, First Base
Runs Created: 56

	G	AB	Hit	2B	3B	HR	Run	RBI	BB	SO	SB	CS	Avg
3.09 Years		610	169	35	3	13	73	71	34	45	2	4	.277
1983	151	542	134	31	1	10	54	66	40	44	1	1	.247
First Half	67	232	49	12	0	3	23	33	15	20	0	0	.211
Second Half	84	310	85	19	1	7	31	33	25	24	1	1	.274
vs. RHP		374	85	21	1	8	40	47	29	30	1	1	.227
vs. LHP		168	49	10	0	2	14	19	11	14	0	0	.292
Home	74	259	65	17	1	5	26	29	24	23	1	0	.251
Road	77	283	69	14	0	5	28	37	16	21	0	1	.244
Grass	126	449	117	26	1	9	48	52	37	39	1	1	.261
Turf	25	93	17	5	0	1	6	14	3	5	0	0	.183

Glenn HOFFMAN, Shortstop
Runs Created: 51

	G	AB	Hit	2B	3B	HR	Run	RBI	BB	SO	SB	CS	Avg
2.99 Years		500	122	24	2	5	58	51	30	70	1	3	.245
1983	143	473	123	24	1	4	56	41	30	76	1	1	.260
First Half	75	245	61	12	1	1	28	20	19	38	1	1	.249
Second Half	68	228	62	12	0	3	28	21	11	38	1	1	.272
vs. RHP		317	81	14	1	3	35	29	22	45	1	1	.256
vs. LHP		156	42	10	0	1	21	12	8	31	0	0	.269
Home	69	223	63	15	0	3	27	26	19	40	0	1	.283
Road	74	250	60	9	1	1	29	15	11	36	1	0	.240
Grass	118	389	98	16	0	4	42	37	27	67	1	1	.252
Turf	25	84	25	8	1	0	14	4	3	9	0	0	.298

Jerry REMY, Second Base
Runs Created: 62

	G	AB	Hit	2B	3B	HR	Run	RBI	BB	SO	SB	CS	Avg
6.94 Years		627	173	20	5	1	86	46	50	57	29	14	.276
1983	146	592	163	16	5	0	73	43	40	35	11	3	.275
First Half	65	273	67	6	3	0	29	25	12	17	5	1	.245
Second Half	81	319	96	10	2	0	44	18	28	18	6	2	.301
vs. RHP		419	109	10	0	0	50	25	29	22	10	3	.260
vs. LHP		173	54	6	5	0	23	18	11	13	1	0	.312
Home	77	316	87	9	2	0	43	19	20	17	6	1	.276
Road	69	277	76	7	3	0	30	24	20	18	5	2	.274
Grass	128	522	150	15	5	0	67	39	33	29	10	2	.287
Turf	18	70	13	1	0	0	6	4	7	6	1	1	.186

Jim RICE, Leftfield
Runs Created: 113

	G	AB	Hit	2B	3B	HR	Run	RBI	BB	SO	SB	CS	Avg
8.23 Years		644	197	30	8	34	100	116	49	117	6	4	.305
1983	155	626	191	34	1	39	90	126	52	102	0	2	.305
First Half	77	309	92	15	1	22	47	58	30	51	0	2	.298
Second Half	78	317	99	19	0	17	43	68	22	51	0	0	.312
vs. RHP		457	135	26	0	29	70	95	32	76	0	1	.295
vs. LHP		169	56	8	1	10	20	31	20	26	0	1	.331
Home	81	329	107	21	0	16	50	62	27	54	0	2	.325
Road	74	297	84	13	1	23	40	64	25	48	0	0	.283
Grass	312	538	161	32	0	29	73	104	43	88	0	2	.299
Turf	23	88	30	2	1	10	17	22	9	14	0	0	.341

Wade BOGGS, Third Base
Runs Created: 130

	G	AB	Hit	2B	3B	HR	Run	RBI	BB	SO	SB	CS	Avg
1.59 Years		580	207	37	5	6	95	74	80	36	3	2	.357
1983	153	582	210	44	7	5	100	74	92	36	3	3	.361
First Half	76	284	101	23	2	0	50	34	45	21	2	1	.356
Second Half	77	298	109	21	5	5	50	40	47	15	1	2	.366
vs. RHP		397	158	36	6	4	82	43	67	14	0	2	.398
vs. LHP		185	52	8	1	1	18	31	25	22	3	1	.281
Home	80	302	120	34	3	2	53	37	53	18	1	2	.397
Road	73	280	90	10	4	3	47	37	39	18	2	1	.321
Grass	130	495	180	40	6	4	81	59	77	31	2	3	.364
Turf	23	87	30	4	1	1	19	15	15	5	1	0	.345

Tony ARMAS, Centerfield
Runs Created: 55

	G	AB	Hit	2B	3B	HR	Run	RBI	BB	SO	SB	CS	Avg
5.20 Years		589	144	21	4	28	66	93	30	141	3	2	.244
1983	145	574	125	23	2	36	77	107	29	131	0	1	.218
First Half	72	281	67	13	1	18	40	48	18	58	0	1	.238
Second Half	73	293	58	10	1	18	37	59	11	73	0	0	.198
vs. RHP		406	85	18	0	27	61	76	17	102	0	1	.209
vs. LHP		168	40	5	2	9	16	31	12	29	0	1	.238
Home	71	273	69	15	2	17	46	64	18	53	0	1	.253
Road	74	301	56	8	0	19	31	43	11	78	0	0	.186
Grass	121	478	100	21	2	26	63	90	25	109	0	1	.209
Turf	24	96	25	2	0	10	14	17	4	22	0	0	.260

Dwight EVANS, Rightfield
Runs Created: 71

	G	AB	Hit	2B	3B	HR	Run	RBI	BB	SO	SB	CS	Avg
9.01 years		542	144	29	5	23	85	74	76	106	5	4	.266
1983	126	470	112	19	4	22	74	58	70	97	3	0	.238
First Half	77	303	70	12	4	15	53	39	48	62	1	0	.231
Second Half	49	167	42	7	0	7	21	19	22	35	2	0	.251
vs. RHP		318	72	12	2	15	58	39	50	76	2	0	.226
vs. LHP		152	40	7	2	7	16	19	20	21	1	0	.263
Home	64	237	55	8	1	12	35	30	34	48	2	0	.232
Road	62	233	57	11	3	10	39	28	36	49	1	0	.245
Grass	108	398	100	17	3	21	65	55	63	76	3	0	.251
Turf	18	72	12	2	1	1	9	3	7	21	0	0	.167

Carl YASTRZEMSKI, Designated Hitter
Runs Created: 55

	G	AB	Hit	2B	3B	HR	Run	RBI	BB	SO	SB	CS	Avg
20.42 Years		587	167	32	3	22	89	90	90	68	8	6	.285
1983	119	380	101	24	0	10	38	56	54	29	0	0	.266
First Half	47	155	50	11	0	2	16	20	23	11	0	0	.323
Second Half	72	225	51	13	0	8	22	36	31	18	0	0	.227
vs. RHP		343	93	23	0	10	38	54	51	23	0	0	.271
vs. LHP		37	8	1	0	0	0	2	3	6	0	0	.216
Home	61	184	46	14	0	6	18	35	31	16	0	0	.250
Road	58	196	55	10	0	4	20	21	23	13	0	0	.281
Grass	101	322	86	21	0	9	32	49	47	25	0	0	.267
Turf	18	58	15	3	0	1	6	7	7	4	0	0	.259

Gary ALLENSON, Catcher
Runs Created: 23

	G	AB	Hit	2B	3B	HR	Run	RBI	BB	SO	SB	CS	Avg
2.27 Years		417	94	20	1	8	45	53	53	74	1	3	.225
1983	84	230	53	11	0	3	19	30	27	43	0	1	.230
First Half	23	69	17	5	0	1	7	13	6	14	0	0	.246
Second Half	61	161	36	6	0	2	12	17	21	29	0	1	.224
vs. RHP		143	28	5	0	2	11	16	11	29	0	1	.196
vs. LHP		87	25	6	0	1	8	14	16	14	0	0	.287
Home	43	117	26	5	0	1	10	12	8	22	0	0	.222
Road	41	113	27	6	0	2	9	18	19	21	0	1	.239
Grass	73	204	48	10	0	3	17	27	19	37	0	0	.235
Turf	11	26	5	1	0	0	2	3	8	6	0	1	.192

Reid NICHOLS, Outfield
Runs Created: 42

	G	AB	Hit	2B	3B	HR	Run	RBI	BB	SO	SB	CS	Avg
1.50 Years		402	113	25	3	9	59	41	30	52	8	7	.280
1983	100	274	78	22	1	6	35	22	26	36	7	5	.285
First Half	46	121	35	8	0	3	18	12	12	15	2	3	.289
Second Half	54	153	43	14	1	3	17	10	14	21	5	2	.281
vs. RHP		127	37	13	1	2	16	15	12	18	6	2	.291
vs. LHP		147	41	9	0	4	19	7	14	18	1	3	.279
Home	50	151	45	18	0	3	21	14	12	20	3	1	.298
Road	50	123	33	4	1	3	14	8	14	16	4	4	.268
Grass	85	239	69	19	0	5	31	18	21	32	6	5	.289
Turf	15	35	9	3	1	1	4	4	5	4	1	0	.257

John TUDOR

Year	(W–L)	GS	Run	Avg	DP	Avg	SB	Avg
1982	(13-10)	30	135	4.50	29	.97	16	.53
1983	(13-12)	34	138	4.06	39	1.15	30	.88
1979-1983		94	415	4.41	99	1.05	58	.62

	G	IP	W	L	Pct	ER	ERA
1982 Home	17	104	7	6	.538	53	4.59
1983 Home	19	131	7	6	.538	20	4.81
1982 Road	15	91.2	6	4	.600	26	2.55
1983 Road	15	111	6	6	.500	12	3.24
1983 Grass	29	206.1	11	10	.524	99	4.32
1983 Turf	5	35.2	2	2	.500	11	2.78

Bruce HURST

Year		GS	Run	Avg	DP	Avg	SB	Avg
1982	(3- 7)	19	86	4.53	25	1.32	9	.47
1983	(12-12)	32	144	4.50	40	1.25	30	.94
1980-1983		63	303	4.81	74	1.17	47	.75

	G	IP	W	L	Pct	ER	ERA
1982 Home	13	55	3	3	.500	36	5.89
1983 Home	17	112.1	6	7	.461	49	3.93
1982 Road	15	62	0	4	.000	39	5.66
1983 Road	16	99	6	5	.545	47	4.27
1983 Grass	29	188.2	11	10	.524	82	3.91
1983 Turf	4	22.2	1	2	.333	14	5.56

Dennis ECKERSLEY

Year	(W–L)	GS	Run	Avg	DP	Avg	SB	Avg
1982	(13-13)	33	124	3.76	26	.79	25	.76
1983	(9-13)	28	106	3.79	13	.46	20	.71
1976-1983		245	1054	4.30	174	.71	257	1.05

	G	IP	W	L	Pct	ER	ERA
1982 Home	19	128.2	8	7	.533	58	4.06
1983 Home	16	104.1	6	7	.461	64	5.52
1982 Road	14	95.2	5	6	.455	36	3.29
1983 Road	12	72	3	6	.333	46	5.75
1983 Grass	23	141.2	7	10	.412	91	5.78
1983 Turf	5	34.2	2	3	.400	19	4.93

Bob OJEDA

Year	(W–L)	GS	Run	Avg	DP	Avg	SB	Avg
1982	(4-6)	14	65	4.64	17	1.21	6	.43
1983	(12-7)	28	141	5.04	28	1.00	25	.89
1980-1983		59	293	4.97	67	1.14	44	.75

	G	IP	W	L	Pct	ER	ERA
1982 Home	10	29	2	1	.667	76	4.97
1983 Home	15	86.1	6	3	.667	44	4.59
1982 Road	12	49.1	2	5	.286	33	6.02
1983 Road	14	87.1	6	4	.600	34	3.50
1983 Grass	26	159	12	6	.667	68	3.85
1983 Turf	3	14.2	0	1	.000	10	6.14

1983 OTHERS

Pitcher	(W–L)	GS	Run	Avg	DP	Avg	SB	Avg
Brown	(6-6)	18	117	6.50	21	1.17	25	1.39
Boyd	(4-8)	13	51	3.92	13	1.00	10	.77
Bird	(1-4)	6	22	3.67	12	2.00	8	1.33
Nipper	(1-1)	2	4	2.00	3	1.50	3	1.50
Johnson	(3-2)	1	1	1.00	0	.00	0	.00

BOSTON RED SOX
RUNS BATTED IN ANALYSIS

Player	RBI	RBI In Wins	Victory- Important RBI	RBI Importance	Wins Batted In	RBI Per Win
Jim Rice	126	90	60.29	.478	16.86	7.5
Tony Armas	107	67	45.96	.430	10.60	10.1
Wade Boggs	74	60	36.36	.491	9.05	8.2
Dwight Evans	58	41	26.79	.462	6.96	8.3
Dave Stapleton	66	36	22.73	.344	5.96	11.1
Jerry Remy	43	32	20.92	.487	4.97	8.7
Glenn Hoffman	41	29	20.34	.496	4.82	8.5
Carl Yastrzemski	54	29	16.56	.307	3.62	14.9
Gary Allenson	30	23	14.29	.476	3.53	8.5
Reid Nichols	22	15	6.86	.312	3.06	7.2

CLEVELAND INDIANS

If the people who run the Cleveland Indians were in charge of foreign policy, I'd enroll in night school and start studying Slavic languages. The Indians have now accomplished something that many would have thought they never could: They've made their past brighter than their future.

What is there to say about an old, bad team with no past? Not much. Let's document the description. Old? Over 50% of the Indians' value in 1983 was in players who were 30 or older. The percentages for the seven teams in the division: New York, 58%; Cleveland, 52%; Milwaukee, 46%; Baltimore, 45%; Boston, 29%; Toronto, 24%; Detroit, 23%. And those players, classified as "past prime" in the talent breakdowns, played like they're past their primes. Hargrove and Harrah and Bake McBride and Gorman Thomas; none of them had good years.

Bad? That's easy; they were 70–92.

No past? They haven't finished within fourteen games of first place in 24 years.

And if any of you think 1984 is going to be any different, I strongly encourage you to think about it some more.

That being said, it becomes increasingly difficult to make a positive comment about the team. Yet odd as it seems, the Cleveland baseball scene sometimes looks pretty good to a Kansas City baseball fan: No pressure, no tension, no hordes of blotto suburbanites trying to figure where their seat was and itching for a chance to let off some steam. Just a few hard-core baseball fans watching the summer ease by. You coud get a ticket anytime and anywhere you wanted. Maybe we just could sit there and tell Gabe Paul jokes. (If Gabe was running a hospital, I'd invest in a mortuary. If I was on a ship and Gabe was the captain, I'd try to make friends with a shark. If Gabe was an investment counselor, I'd open up a pawn shop. If Gabe was selling furnaces, I'd sell smoke detectors.).

I suppose that's like the successful executive who goes to his 20-year class reunion, sees a high school buddy who became a construction worker, and thinks it looks like a good life—no pressure, when 5 o'clock comes the job's over and you go home to the wife and have dinner. Ah, the simple things in life.

Having been poor most of my life, I can assure you that, as long as you have your health, American poverty is not all that wretched; it's more irritating than anything else. But I'm in no hurry to get back to it. And I'm not going to move to Cleveland and root for the Indians, either.

A Seattle radio person by the name of Don Kiehl has spent some hours with a baseball encyclopedia or two, trying to figure out which pitching staff had the most wins left on it. The most he has found was the staff of the 1964 Cleveland Indians, whose pitchers would win 1,107 games between 1964 and 1983. Individual totals:

1.	Tommy John	248
2.	Luis Tiant	227
3.	Sonny Siebert	140
4.	Sam McDowell	135
5.	Mudcat Grant	81
6.	Don McMahon	61
7.	Gary Bell	54
8.	Ted Abernathy	48
9.	Lee Strange	45
10.	Jack Kralick	20
	Tom Kelley	20
	Pedro Ramos	20
13.	Dick Donovan	8

Other teams of note and their totals through 1982: 1912 Philadelphia Athletics, 957; 1971 Cardinals, 940; 1962 Giants, 936; 1950 Yankees, 908; 1969 Mets, 865; 1959 Cardinals, 777; 1960 Orioles, 638. That's his list; I'll try to contribute. The 1892 Cleveland team had 697 from just four pitchers (Cy Young had 475 and Nig Cuppy 162; John Clarkson was on the team but his career was behind him), and the 1949 Cleveland team had 781. The 1919 Boston Red Sox 1,058, and would hold the record had not one of their best young pitchers, Babe Ruth, unwisely decided to become an outfielder. Their staff included Waite Hoyt (237), Herb Pennock (218), Sad Sam Jones (209), Carl Mays (141) and Bullet Joe Bush (118). The 1953 Milwaukee Braves had 995 wins left on their staff, and went over a thousand if you count a couple of kids who were in the army. The '66 Cubs were over 700 (Jenkins, Holtzman, Hands). I can't find a team that beats the '64 Indians, though.

Only one pitcher in the last 30 years has won 20 games in a season while walking more men than he struck out. Who was he?

Variation on an old philosophical question: If a baseball game is played in Cleveland and nobody comes to see it, does it still count in the standings?

Some positive things about the 1983 Indians:
● They outhit the AL West champion White Sox, .265–.262.
● Julio Franco had a season that in any other year would have made him Rookie of the Year.
● They had the second best team on-base percentage in the AL, beaten out only by world champion Baltimore.
● Their hitters had the best strikeout-to-walk ratio in the league. For every time they struck out, they walked .88 times. This was far better than the second-place Yankee mark of 1:.78 and much higher than the league average of 1:.65.
● Only three teams were shut out fewer times.
● They led the league in sacrifice flies.
● Only Yankee and Ranger pitchers gave up fewer homers.
● Only Kansas City and California turned more double plays. (A big improvement over 1982 when they turned the fewest.)
● Their designated hitters were second in the league with 12 game-winning hits. (Yanks led with 13.)
● Only Baltimore DHs walked more.

134

- Only Baltimore DHs drew more intentional walks.
- Their DHs were the only ones to walk more than they struck out.
- They had the second fewest ground into double plays by DHs.
- They were 7–6 against the Orioles. Only Detroit had a better record against the world champs.
- They unloaded Rick Manning.
- They unloaded Rick Waits.
- Mike Hargrove was sixth in the league in on-base percentage.
- Neal Heaton was fourth in shutouts.

- Rick Sutcliffe was fifth in strikeouts, seventh in victories and eighth in innings pitched.
- Their opponents made 141 errors. Only Chicago (153) and Oakland (152) had their opponents make more.
- Hargrove was third in assists by a first baseman.
- Toby Harrah had the best fielding average of any AL third baseman.
- They have given out much less talent from their farm system (86 points AV) than they have gotten in return (113).
- Franco had the third best range factor for AL shortstops and was second in double plays.

—Jim Baker

THE MANAGER

NAME: Pat Corrales

AGE: Yes

MANAGERS FOR WHOM PLAYED IN MAJORS:
Gene Mauch, Red Schoendienst, Dave Bristol, Sparky Anderson and Don Zimmer.

CHARACTERISTICS AS A PLAYER: Another nonhitting catcher, hit .216 with 4 homers in 767 at-bats in the big time.

MANAGERIAL RECORD:

Team	Year	Par	Wins	Losses	Pct.	+ or −
Tex	1978	1	1	0	1.000	0
Tex	1979	87	83	79	.512	− 4
Tex	1980	83	76	85	.472	− 7
Philadelphia	1982	87	89	73	.549	+ 2
Philadelphia	1983	45	43	42	.506	− 2
Cleveland	1983	29	30	32	.484	+ 1
6 Years		333	322	311	.509	−11

WHAT HE BRINGS TO THE BALLCLUB

IS HE AN INTENSE MANAGER OR MORE OF AN EASY-TO-GET-ALONG-WITH TYPE? An intense, emotional manager.

IS HE MORE OF AN EMOTIONAL LEADER OR A DECISION-MAKER? More of an emotional leader; I don't think he's really into strategy.

IS HE MORE OF AN OPTIMIST OR MORE OF A PROBLEM SOLVER? He attacks problems aggressively. When he sees something he doesn't like, he's not one to worry about it tomorrow.

HOW HE USES HIS PERSONNEL

DOES HE FAVOR A SET LINEUP OR A ROTATION SYSTEM? A set lineup. In Texas in '79, seven players played 135 or more games; in 1980, six did. And, of course, in Philadelphia many thought he worked his regulars too hard in 1982.

DOES HE LIKE TO PLATOON? He's platooned a little, but not much.

DOES HE TRY TO SOLVE HIS PROBLEMS WITH PROVEN PLAYERS OR WITH YOUNGSTERS WHO STILL HAVE SOMETHING TO PROVE? HOW MANY PLAYERS HAS HE MADE REGULARS OUT OF WHO WERE NOT REGULARS BEFORE, AND WHO WERE THEY? His confidence in his own talent judgment is very strong. If four years as a manager, he's made a regular out of four players—Pat Putnam, Nelson Norman, Billy Sample and Bo Diaz; he tried to make a regular out of Bob Dernier but it didn't take.

DOES HE PREFER TO GO WITH GOOD OFFENSIVE PLAYERS OR DOES HE LIKE THE GLOVE MEN? Glove men. He did, on the other hand, try to play Pete Rose in right field last year to get a bat into the lineup.

DOES HE LIKE AN OFFENSE BASED ON POWER, SPEED OR HIGH AVERAGES? High averages, I'm guessing. (His 1980 Texas team, which was still a bad team, hit .284.)

DOES HE USE THE ENTIRE ROSTER OR DOES HE KEEP PEOPLE AROUND SITTING ON THE BENCH? He probably makes more in-game lineup changes than any other current manager, so everybody gets in the act.

DOES HE BUILD HIS BENCH AROUND YOUNG PLAYERS WHO CAN STEP INTO A BREACH IF NEED BE OR AROUND VETERAN ROLE-PLAYERS WHO HAVE THEIR OWN FUNCTIONS WITHIN A GAME? A lot of 26-to-30-year-olds with extensive minor league but little major league experience—Ozzie Virgil, George Vukovich, John Ellis, Jim Norris.

GAME MANAGING AND USE OF STRATEGIES

DOES HE GO FOR THE BIG-INNING OFFENSE OR DOES HE LIKE TO USE THE ONE-RUN STRATEGIES? His first major league manager was Gene Mauch, and it shows sometimes.

DOES HE PINCH-HIT MUCH, AND IF SO WHEN? He did not pinch-hit too much in Philadelphia in '82, but then he didn't have any pinch-hitter who was producing to speak of. In Texas in '79 and '80 he used more pinch-hitters than anoyone in the league except Gene Mauch, plus he makes a lot of defensive substitutions.

ANYTHING UNUSUAL ABOUT HIS LINEUP SELECTION? Like Houk, he's had a certain amount of trouble recognizing his leadoff man. In Texas he had Billy Sample, who hits for a good average, walks some and steals bases, and he batted Bump Wills leadoff for two years. (Bump's a lot better leadoff man than Jerry Remy or one of those guys, I hasten to add.) He had all kinds of trouble finding a leadoff man in Philadelphia, (documented in 1983 *Abstract*), and in Cleveland he was using everybody on the roster in that spot (Harrah, Franco, Hargrove, Bannister, Perkins, Rhomberg and Perconte, at least). Will be interesting to see what he decides.

DOES HE USE THE SAC BUNT OFTEN? 10–15% more than average.

DOES HE LIKE TO USE THE RUNNING GAME? He's not a running manager, no.

IN WHAT CIRCUMSTANCES WILL HE ISSUE AN INTENTIONAL WALK? About the same— 15–20% more than average. In what circumstances, I don't know.

DOES HE HIT AND RUN VERY OFTEN? No, not much.

ARE THERE ANY UNIQUE OR IDIOSYNCRATIC STRATEGIES THAT HE PARTICULARLY LIKES? I haven't seen any.

HANDLING THE PITCHING STAFF

DOES HE LIKE POWER PITCHERS OR PREFER TO GO WITH THE PEOPLE WHO PUT THE BALL IN PLAY? He likes power pitchers, and he particularly likes to have some heat coming out of the bullpen. When he was in Texas they traded for Jim Kern; when he was in Philadelphia they traded for Al Holland. That's what you call a pattern. When Kern went bad on him in 1980, he made Denny Darwin his bullpen ace.

His 1980 Texas staff, which was not a good staff, led the league in strikeouts, and his 1982 Philly team, which did not have a great staff, led the majors in strikeouts. Neither was a strikeout staff before he took over.

DOES HE STAY WITH THE STARTER OR GO TO THE BULLPEN QUICKLY? He'd stay a long time with Steve Carlton, but then who wouldn't? Otherwise, he's a bullpen man.

DOES HE LIKE THE FOUR-MAN OR THE FIVE-MAN ROTATION? Mostly he's used a 5-day rotation.

DOES HE USE THE ENTIRE STAFF OR DOES HE TRY TO GET FIVE OR SIX PEOPLE TO DO MOST OF THE WORK? As with the hitters, everybody at least has a role.

ARE THERE ANY PARTICULAR TYPES OF PITCHERS OF WHOM HE IS FOND? I suspect he's quite a believer in the bullpen. He's paid a pretty fair price in talent, in the past, to come up with the relief ace he wanted.

IS THERE ANYTHING UNIQUE ABOUT HIS HANDLING OF HIS PITCHERS? Can't see anything.

WHAT IS HIS STRONGEST POINT AS A MANAGER? Two things: 1) he's very decisive, knows exactly what he's trying to do, and 2) he has an intense desire to win, which can't help but spray off on some of those around him.

IF THERE WERE NO PROFESSIONAL BASEBALL, WHAT WOULD THIS MANAGER PROBABLY BE DOING? Senior guard dog instructor at Adolf's Doberman City.

Mike HARGROVE, First Base
Runs Created: 71

	G	AB	Hit	2B	3B	HR	Run	RBI	BB	SO	SB	CS	Avg
8.80 Years		560	163	27	3	9	80	70	99	55	3	4	.291
1983	134	469	134	21	4	3	57	57	78	40	0	6	.286
First Half	70	258	76	13	2	3	33	31	44	21	0	3	.295
Second Half	64	211	58	8	2	0	24	26	34	19	0	3	.275
vs. RHP		335	98			3		34					.293
vs. LHP		134	36			0		23					.269
Home	65	212	64	9	1	0	23	29	37	17	0	5	.302
Road	69	257	70	12	3	3	34	28	41	23	0	1	.272
Grass	111	379	109	18	4	2	39	46	69	30	0	6	.288
Turf	23	90	25	3	0	1	18	11	9	10	0	0	.278

Mike FISCHLIN, Second Base
Runs Created: 21

	G	AB	Hit	2B	3B	HR	Run	RBI	BB	SO	SB	CS	Avg
1.77 Years		365	81	11	2	1	40	28	38	49	12	5	.223
1983	95	225	47	5	2	2	31	23	26	32	9	2	.209
First Half	25	60	13	1	1	0	12	10	8	9	3	1	.217
Second Half	70	165	34	4	1	2	19	13	18	23	6	1	.206
vs. RHP		151	35			0		14					.232
vs. LHP		74	12			2		9					.162
Home	44	78	19	2	1	2	11	13	9	7	0	0	.244
Road	51	147	28	3	1	0	20	10	17	25	9	2	.190
Grass	73	167	35	4	1	2	24	13	22	20	9	1	.210
Turf	17	58	12	1	1	0	7	10	4	12	0	1	.207

Toby HARRAH, Third Base
Runs Created: 73

	G	AB	Hit	2B	3B	HR	Run	RBI	BB	SO	SB	CS	Avg
11.40 Years		567	152	23	3	16	85	71	84	64	19	7	.267
1983	138	526	140	23	1	9	81	53	75	49	16	10	.266
First Half	54	194	52	6	1	5	29	20	34	15	8	2	.268
Second Half	84	332	88	17	0	4	52	33	41	34	8	8	.265
vs. RHP		362	98			5		34					.271
vs. LHP		164	42			4		19					.256
Home	71	258	69	12	0	7	43	26	43	28	4	8	.267
Road	67	268	71	11	1	2	38	27	32	21	12	2	.265
Grass	122	459	120	20	1	9	72	44	70	42	12	10	.261
Turf	16	67	20	3	0	0	9	9	5	7	4	0	.299

Julio FRANCO, Shortstop
Runs Created: 61

	G	AB	Hit	2B	3B	HR	Run	RBI	BB	SO	SB	CS	Avg
1.02 Years		578	158	25	8	8	70	81	28	53	31	14	.273
1983	149	560	153	24	8	8	68	80	27	50	32	12	.273
First Half	74	280	80	14	4	7	36	49	12	29	13	5	.286
Second Half	75	280	73	10	4	1	32	31	15	21	19	7	.261
vs. RHP		372	93			6		55					.250
vs. LHP		188	60			2		25					.319
Home	79	286	90	13	4	6	42	51	17	21	15	8	.315
Road	70	274	63	11	4	2	26	29	10	29	17	4	.230
Grass	125	464	135	22	6	7	56	73	24	34	25	10	.291
Turf	24	96	18	2	2	1	12	7	3	16	7	2	.188

Pat TABLER, Leftfield
Runs Created: 63

	G	AB	Hit	2B	3B	HR	Run	RBI	BB	SO	SB	CS	Avg
1.14 Years		542	144	26	7	7	67	68	66	96	2	4	.266
1983	124	430	125	23	5	6	56	65	56	63	2	4	.291
First Half	45	146	48	7	3	2	22	28	20	16	0	1	.329
Second Half	79	284	77	16	2	4	34	37	36	47	2	3	.271
vs. RHP		287	81			3		31					.282
vs. LHP		143	44			3		34					.308
Home	64	217	61	11	2	3	26	34	33	26	1	1	.281
Road	60	213	64	12	3	3	30	31	23	37	1	3	.300
Grass	102	352	105	20	3	5	49	51	48	47	1	3	.298
Turf	22	78	20	3	2	1	7	14	8	16	1	1	.256

Gorman THOMAS, Centerfield
Runs Created: 66

	G	AB	Hit	2B	3B	HR	Run	RBI	BB	SO	SB	CS	Avg
7.19 Years		525	121	26	2	30	77	90	73	150	6	6	.231
1983	152	535	112	23	1	22	72	69	80	148	10	4	.209
First Half	72	249	49	11	1	9	34	30	36	76	3	1	.197
Second Half	80	286	63	12	0	13	38	39	44	72	7	3	.220
vs. RHP		258	61			14		38					.236
vs. LHP*		113	21			3		13					.186
Home	77	264	57	11	0	10	39	33	41	65	6	2	.216
Road	75	271	55	12	1	12	33	36	39	83	4	2	.203
Grass	128	447	94	20	0	17	61	57	67	116	9	4	.210
Turf	24	88	18	3	1	5	11	12	13	32	1	0	.205

*PLATOON STATS WITH CLEVELAND ONLY.

George VUKOVICH, Rightfield
Runs Created: 30

	G	AB	Hit	2B	3B	HR	Run	RBI	BB	SO	SB	CS	Avg
2.13 Years		343	90	15	2	5	39	46	30	44	3	6	.261
1983	124	312	77	13	2	3	31	44	24	37	3	4	.247
First Half	58	153	28	8	2	2	19	22	14	20	0	0	.183
Second Half	66	159	49	5	0	1	12	22	10	17	3	4	.308
vs. RHP		250	62			2		33					.248
vs. LHP		62	15			1		11					.242
Home	59	134	38	8	0	3	19	22	17	12	2	3	.284
Road	65	178	39	5	2	0	12	22	7	25	1	1	.219
Grass	103	274	70	13	1	3	29	39	23	31	2	4	.255
Turf	21	38	7	0	1	0	2	5	1	6	1	0	.184

Ron HASSEY, Catcher
Runs Created: 45

	G	AB	Hit	2B	3B	HR	Run	RBI	BB	SO	SB	CS	Avg
3.22 Years		479	131	23	1	8	49	64	56	48	2	2	.273
1983	117	341	92	21	0	6	48	42	38	35	2	2	.270
First Half	53	152	38	7	0	1	18	11	17	14	1	1	.250
Second Half	64	189	54	14	0	5	30	31	21	21	1	1	.286
vs. RHP		264	66			4		32					.250
vs. LHP		77	26			2		10					.338
Home	59	152	41	7	0	4	27	23	25	18	1	2	.270
Road	58	189	51	14	0	2	21	19	13	17	1	0	.270
Grass	98	291	81	18	0	6	43	40	33	32	2	2	.278
Turf	19	50	11	3	0	0	5	2	5	3	0	0	.220

Andre THORNTON, Designated Hitter
Runs Created: 90

	G	AB	Hit	2B	3B	HR	Run	RBI	BB	SO	SB	CS	Avg
6.98 Years		539	139	27	3	26	85	91	95	87	5	4	.259
1983	141	508	143	27	1	17	78	77	87	72	4	2	.281
First Half	70	247	80	16	0	11	45	45	52	29	3	1	.324
Second Half	71	261	63	11	1	6	33	32	35	43	1	1	.241
vs. RHP		323	87			13		50					.269
vs. LHP		185	56			4		27					.303
Home	73	269	69	14	0	6	34	35	37	31	2	0	.257
Road	68	239	74	13	1	11	44	42	50	41	2	2	.310
Grass	117	425	116	24	1	14	64	64	66	58	3	2	.273
Turf	24	83	27	3	0	3	14	13	21	14	1	0	.325

Alan BANNISTER, Utility
Runs Created: 47

	G	AB	Hit	2B	3B	HR	Run	RBI	BB	SO	SB	CS	Avg
5.30 Years		519	140	25	5	3	74	51	48	53	18	7	.270
1983	117	377	100	25	4	5	51	45	31	43	6	6	.265
First Half	55	184	49	14	2	2	26	24	19	16	3	4	.266
Second Half	62	193	51	11	2	3	25	21	12	27	3	2	.264
vs. RHP													
vs. LHP				NOT AVAILABLE									
Home	61	191	50	16	2	2	26	25	14	19	3	2	.262
Road	56	186	50	9	2	3	25	20	17	24	3	4	.269
Grass	103	332	88	22	3	3	40	40	26	38	6	5	.265
Turf	14	45	12	3	1	2	11	5	5	5	0	1	.267

Rick SUTCLIFFE

Year	(W–L)	GS	Run	Avg	DP	Avg	SB	Avg
1982	(14- 8)	27	122	4.52	21	.78	27	1.00
1983	(17-11)	35	172	4.91	33	.94	22	.63
1976-1983		109	523	4.80	91	.83	100	.92

	G	IP	W	L	Pct	ER	ERA
1982 Home	18	116	7	3	.706	39	3.03
1983 Home	17	120	8	5	.615	61	4.58
1982 Road	16	100	7	5	.583	32	2.88
1983 Road	19	123.1	9	6	.600	55	4.01
1983 Grass	29	194	14	8	.636	97	4.50
1983 Turf	7	49.1	3	3	.500	19	3.47

Lary SORENSEN

Year	(W–L)	GS	Run	Avg	DP	Avg	SB	Avg
1982	(10-15)	30	139	4.63	39	1.30	15	.50
1983	(12-11)	34	148	4.35	34	1.00	22	.65
1977-1983		202	917	4.54	222	1.10	85	.42

	G	IP	W	L	Pct	ER	ERA
1982 Home	17	95.1	5	6	.455	61	5.76
1983 Home	20	126.2	6	4	.600	58	4.12
1982 Road	15	94	5	9	.357	57	5.46
1983 Road	16	96	6	7	.461	47	4.41
1983 Grass	30	181	9	10	.474	89	4.43
1983 Turf	6	41.2	3	1	.750	16	3.46

Len BARKER

Year	(W–L)	GS	Run	Avg	DP	Avg	SB	Avg
1982	(15-11)	33	13	4.64	19	.58	26	.79
1983	(8-13)	24	106	4.42	24	1.00	8	.33
1976-1983		147	650	4.42	95	.65	110	.75

	G	IP	W	L	Pct	ER	ERA
1982 Home	17	132	7	6	.538	52	3.55
1983 Home	13	77.1	5	7	.417	49	5.70
1982 Road	16	112.1	8	5	.615	54	4.31
1983 Road	11	72.1	3	6	.333	36	4.48
1983 Grass	20	121	7	12	.368	71	5.28
1983 Turf	4	28.2	1	1	.500	14	4.40

Bert BLYLEVEN

Year	(W–L)	GS	Run	Avg	DP	Avg	SB	Avg
1982	(2- 2)	4	22	5.50	1	.25	7	1.75
1983	(7-10)	24	91	3.79	28	1.17	13	.54
1976-1983		213	843	3.96	198	.93	177	.83

	G	IP	W	L	Pct	ER	ERA
1983 Home	11	67.1	2	4	.333	34	4.54
1983 Road	13	89	5	6	.454	34	3.44
1983 Grass	22	139.1	5	10	.333	67	4.33
1983 Turf	2	17	2	0	1.000	1	.53

1983 OTHERS

Pitcher	(W–L)	GS	Run	Avg	DP	Avg	SB	Avg
Heaton	(11- 7)	16	76	4.75	16	1.00	12	.75
Eichelberger	(4-11)	15	60	4.00	17	1.13	11	.73
Brennan	(2- 2)	5	23	4.60	5	1.00	2	.40
Behenna	(0- 2)	4	13	3.25	6	1.50	5	1.25
Barnes	(1- 1)	2	12	6.00	4	2.00	3	1.50
Jeffcoat	(1- 3)	2	2	1.00	0	.00	0	.00
Anderson	(1- 6)	1	1	1.00	2	2.00	1	1.00

CLEVELAND INDIANS
RUNS BATTED IN ANALYSIS

Player	RBI	RBI In Wins	Victory-Important RBI	RBI Importance	Wins Batted In	RBI Per Win
Julio Franco	80	51	32.23	.403	7.80	10.3
Pat Tabler	65	42	27.21	.419	6.08	10.7
Andre Thornton	77	42	26.17	.340	7.14	10.8
Toby Harrah	53	38	23.16	.437	5.81	9.1
Mike Hargrove	57	32	20.34	.357	4.97	11.5
Gorman Thomas	51	34	18.01	.353	5.02	10.2
George Vukovich	44	27	16.98	.386	3.90	11.3
Alan Bannister	45	26	15.53	.345	4.32	10.4
Ron Hassey	42	19	10.94	.260	2.95	14.2
Mike Fischlin	23	16	10.88	.473	3.06	7.5

AMERICAN LEAGUE WEST
DIVISION SHEET

Chart I

	1st	2nd	vs. RHP	vs. LHP	HOME	ROAD	GRASS	TURF	DAY	NIGHT	TOTAL	PCT.
Chicago	40-37	59-26	62-43	37-20	55-26	44-37	83-55	16-8	33-18	66-45	99-63	.611
Kansas City	37-36	42-47	51-56	28-27	45-36	34-47	26-36	53-47	22-20	56-63	79-83	.488
Texas	44-34	33-51	51-58	26-27	44-37	33-48	68-69	9-16	12-21	65-64	77-85	.475
Oakland	37-43	37-45	50-51	24-37	42-39	32-49	60-76	14-12	23-37	51-51	74-88	.457
Minnesota	33-48	37-44	50-68	20-24	37-44	33-48	24-38	46-54	22-30	48-62	70-92	.432
California	42-36	28-56	42-59	28-33	35-46	35-46	57-78	13-14	17-22	53-70	70-92	.432
Seattle	30-51	30-51	38-61	22-41	30-51	30-51	22-40	38-62	15-24	45-78	60-102	.370

Chart II

COME FROM BEHIND WINS

Team	1	2	3	4	5	6	7	Total	Points
Chicago	29	8	5	2	3			47	130
Kansas City	21	12	4	5				42	119
Oakland	19	13	8	0	0	0	1	41	117
Texas	16	5	2	2	0	0	1	26	73
Minnesota	19	8	5	2				34	92
California	14	11	6	1	0	1		33	97
Seattle	15	8	2	3	1			29	83

BLOWN LEADS

Team	1	2	3	4	5	6	7	Total	Points
Chicago	16	5	5	0	1			27	73
Kansas City	17	8	3	2	0	0	1	31	88
Oakland	18	15	3	6	1			43	129
Texas	25	13	2	1	1			42	108
Minnesota	18	13	4	2	1			38	107
California	20	10	3	3	2	1	1	40	124
Seattle	32	14	3	1	0	1		51	130

Chart III

DEFENSIVE RECORDS

Team	OSB	OCS	OSB%	DPs	OA/SFA	Fielding Avg.	DER	Opposition Runs
Chicago	99	45	.688	158	27/39	.981	.711	650
Kansas City	107	52	.673	178	19/62	.974	.695	767
Texas	100	63	.613	151	27/43	.982	.707	609
Oakland	95	47	.669	157	39/59	.974	.702	782
Minnesota	134	57	.702	170	51/53	.980	.689	822
California	83	61	.576	190	44/50	.977	.681	779
Seattle	135	55	.711	159	70/40	.978	.685	740

Chart IV

OPPOSITION ERRORS

Team	C	1B	2B	3B	SS	LF	CF	RF	P	UN	Total
Chicago	23	14	26	28	28	7	3	7	25	2	153
Kansas City	10	13	13	12	33	8	3	6	16	5	119
Texas	14	16	16	25	32	7	7	6	5	6	134
Oakland	21	11	22	24	26	11	7	10	17	3	152
Minnesota	8	11	21	29	31	11	2	8	11	5	137
California	5	9	20	29	25	7	6	13	11	2	127
Seattle	11	16	19	18	22	4	6	6	10	9	121

Chart V

LATE-INNING BALLCLUBS

Team	Ahead	Tied	Behind	Net Change
Chicago	86-6	5-11	8-46	−4
Kansas City	63-5	11-8	5-69	+3
Texas	68-6	4-12	5-67	−9
Oakland	54-10	13-7	7-71	+3
Minnesota	57-2	12-14	1-76	−3
California	54-10	8-19	8-63	−13
Seattle	50-4	5-13	5-85	−7

As the military has the Aberdeen proving grounds and Thomas Edison had Menlo Park, baseball has the American League West. It is here that new, interesting and often radical theories are tested in real game situations. It is a division of extremes, young and old, rich and poor, new management and very old managements. All, however, are dedicated to scholarly experimentation in their operations. What are some of the experiments being conducted in the AL West?

Oakland and Chicago have baseball's first computers, while Texas employs the first fulltime sabermetrician.

California has done work in the field of physical stress on the aging.

The Twins on the other hand, are testing the effects of a lack of playing experience and major league success.

Seattle is conducting an experiment in what happens to a team in an unsuitable environment —a team that can't hit in a hitter's park.

Kansas City relies on one relief pitcher, forsaking the concept of "starting pitchers."

California, on the other hand, does without a bullpen.

The Twins and Mariners have undertaken various economic experiments for the good of baseball.

It's all for science; we here at the *Baseball Abstract* appreciate the effort.

—Jim Baker

CHICAGO WHITE SOX

I

Having a good farm system does not have very much to do with having a good ballclub.

That unconventional conclusion was first suggested to me in 1979, when I did a postseason study of which organizations had produced the most major league players and the best major league players and found to my surprise that the most productive teams in the majors were not the best teams in the majors, with any consistency. To return the conclusion to the limited but precise language of the original study, the correlation between approximate value produced and team wins was surprisingly low. When first reporting on that study in the 1980 *Baseball Abstract*. I declined to accept the natural and obvious conclusion: that the two things are not closely related. That was an appropriate response to that study at that time. But four years later, having reviewed that conclusion in several different lights, the time has come to accept that the conclusion is true, and to begin to argue for its acceptance.

First of all, let us look again at the study which originally suggested that this was true, that there was little relationship between having a strong farm system and having a strong team. I have repeated the study annually since 1979, and it has repeated its conclusion annually since 1979. I will discuss the 1983 study in detail here, since the details are easiest to keep straight in the most recent year.

We begin by figuring the amount of Approximate Value that has been produced by each major league system. What we are doing here is similar to a simple count of the number of players produced by each system who are now on major league rosters, except that rather than counting everybody at one, we count Cal Ripken at 17 and Dale Murphy at 17, Bob Bonner at zero and Bob Walk at zero, and everybody else at somewhere between zero and 16. There are a few players whom you might have a tough time figuring out which organization to give credit for, so I'll give you the formal definition that we use to decide that:

A player is considered to be "produced by the first organization of which he is a member in which he 1) reaches the major league level or the Triple-A level or 2) is included in a major league transaction, or 3) goes directly onto a major league roster.

Thus LaMarr Hoyt is considered to be a product of the Yankee system because the Yankees included him in a major league trade, and Dave Righetti is considered a Texas product for the same reason. My feeling is that for a player to be included in a major league trade, his skills must have advanced to the point at which he is recognized as being a player of some value to a major league team, and I think in most cases there is little doubt about that. Dave Righetti may have been a couple of years away

from a major league roster at the time the Yankees acquired him, but I remember exactly what the Yankees said at the time the trade was made. They said, "We think we've got another Ron Guidry here." On the other hand, Pedro Guerrero is not considered to be a product of the Cleveland Indian farm system, Luis Salazar is not considered to be a product of the Kansas City Royals and Ron Kittle is considered a home-grown White Sox player.

We list all of the players who are produced by an organization, and we add up their 1983 Approximate Value. The Dodgers, as noted in Section I, have produced the most talent, and they have made good use of that strength.

The Dodgers are a good team, and they have produced the most talent. Fine. But there is no apparent pattern of the best teams having produced the most talent. Case in point: the Boston Red Sox. The Boston Red Sox system produced 227 points of 1983 Approximate Value, a figure that is dwarfed by the Dodgers' 302, but which dwarfs the rest of the American League to an equal extent. The number 2, 3, 4, 5, and 6 totals in the American League are 174, 170, 157, 155, and 155. The Red Sox are at 227.

Now, who are the players who account for that 227 total? To begin with, you've got 80% of the Red Sox' own 1980 roster—Wade Boggs, Jim Rice, all three pitchers who were in double figures in wins, relief ace Bob Stanley and four of the other seven regulars. In addition, you've got Fred Lynn for the Angels (22 HR, 74 RBI, .272 average), Carlton Fisk of the White Sox, Cecil Cooper and Ben Ogilvie of Milwaukee, Ernie Whitt of Toronto (.256, 17 home runs, and 56 RBI in 344 at-bats), and Chuck Rainey, who won 14 games for a not-so-good Cubs team. If you need a third catcher, Bo Diaz of Philly can fill in. That's a lot of talent, and its not "bulk" talent, by any means. The Red Sox produced four of the top eight American League MVP candidates—Rice, Boggs, Carlton Fisk, and Cecil Cooper. It's quality talent, 227 points, all total.

But where did they finish? 78–84.

I gave you the figures for the next five American League teams, but I didn't give you the teams. The number two team in terms of talent produced in 1983 was the California Angels, 174 points. The full list is given in Chart White Sox-I; let me recap the highlights. The Angels' system produced the best shortstop in the National League in Dickie Thon. They produced one of the finest centerfielders in the National League, in Kenny Landreaux of the Dodgers. They produced Jerry Remy of the Red Sox, Julio Cruz of the White Sox, Willie Aikens of KC, Tom Brunansky of Minnesota, Carney Lansford of the A's, Rance Mulliniks of Toronto and their own Daryl Sconiers. They produced a 22-game winner in Richard Dotson. You put that on the field, and it's a lineup that will definitely put some runs on the board.

They finished 70–92.

Third on the list of value produced is the Texas

Rangers. Highlights: Righetti, Bill Madlock, Len Barker, Toby Harrah, Roy Smalley, Jim Clancy, Pat Putnam, George Wright, Billy Sample and Danny Darwin. Full list: Chart White Sox-I. Finish: 77–85.

Fourth comes Kansas City, another losing team. They, too, are on the chart.

Now, which teams produced the least talent among the American League teams. In last place and next-to-last are the two American League expansion teams, Seattle (62) and Toronto (49). Working largely with cast-off players, the Blue Jays finished 89–73.

And next comes the White Sox. The Chicago White Sox in 1983 had the best record of any team in baseball, 99–63. But where does their farm team rank? Twenty-sixth out of 28 teams, with only 95 units of Approximate Value produced. They produced barely over a fourth of their own talent—Baines, Kittle and Barojas are the only prominent members of the team who came from their own system, and Barojas comes with a big asterisk. Nor have they littered the rest of the league with talent; Goose Gossage is the only star of any magnitude that the White Sox have contributed to any other team. A full list is in the chart; you will need to study it briefly to be able to answer in your own mind some questions I will put to you in a moment.

And this has happened before. The Yankees in 1980 were dead last in the American League in talent produced (except for the expansion teams), yet they won 103 games, the most in the majors. Since then they have begun to move upward in talent produced—and down in the standings.

What I am saying is this: If you look at the teams in the American League which have produced talent, and you look at the teams which have won the most games, you will find that they are not the same teams. The Baltimore Orioles' list of talent produced is detailed in the chart; it totals up to 146 points, which is below average. Yet they won 98 games and a world championship.

And in the National League, with the exception of the Dodgers, you find exactly the same thing. The Cincinnati Reds are second in that league in value produced, 217. I shouldn't have to tell you who all those guys are. They finished 74–88. The Cardinals were third in value produced with 212 units (details in chart). They were under .500, at 79–83. The Pirates were fourth; they were a little over .500. They didn't have as good a record as the team which finished last in the NL in talent produced, Houston (85).

A list of the 26 teams, their 1983 produced, and their 1983 win totals is also given, in the chart labeled White Sox-II.

Not to overstate the case, I'm not saying that there is no connection between producing talent and winning ballgames. There is a positive correlation between the two columns. It's weak, but it is positive. Correlated by the Pearson Product/Moment Method, the 1983 correlation is +.12. Since I began doing this study annually in 1979, the correlation has never gone over +.2.

Now, I know that a lot of you are not going to be convinced by a set of numbers that something you have always known to be true, something of which you have been constantly reassured of by every general manager that you have ever heard on a pregame show, is false.

That is as it should be. I didn't believe this study myself the first time I did it. It was not this study, even repeated five times, that convinced me that a strong farm system was not the key to an organization's success.

And the exact measurement—the number, the +.12 correlation—is not of any real consequence. Is it possible that this study in some ways misrepresents the realities, so that a study cast in a different way might show a stronger correlation? It is very possible. A study that focused not on total value, but on who produced the really big seasons, the 14-to-17 point seasons, might yield a somewhat different result. A study based on talent produced within the last decade or within the last seven years might well yield a stronger positive correlation. A study that was based not on any one season but on value produced over a period of years and wins over a period of years might suggest a different conclusion. It is possible that the last five years are an atypical period in baseball history, and that in the time before and the time yet to be seen the correlation is different, the connection would be stronger. If you're uncomfortable with Approximate Value, you could use a different measure and get a slightly different result.

But what the study did was to plant a seed of doubt in my mind. My own experiences and my own observations since that time have nourished that seed, and have brought me eventually to the point that I could no longer find any rational basis for denying what the study was telling me.

Let me challenge you, now, to submit the conclusion for which I argue to the test of your own experiences. Can you deny, having studied the lists of talent produced on page 33, that the Boston Red Sox produced from their farm system an impressive list of 1983 talent, probably the most impressive list of talent of any American League team? Can you deny that the California Angels and the Texas Rangers have produced an amount and quality of talent that is, at the very least, superior to that produced by the Chicago White Sox? Can you deny that the list of talent produced by the Cincinnati Reds, by the St. Louis Cardinals, by the Pittsburgh Pirates is an impressive list? Can you deny that the list of talent produced by the Houston Astros or the Toronto Blue Jays is puny by comparison?

And if you cannot deny that, then can you deny the fundamental conclusion that the teams which have produced the most talent and the teams which have won the most games are not the same teams?

And if they are not the same teams, then on what basis can you assert that the key to having a successful organization is having a strong farm system? What theory can you advance to explain why the farm system is the crucial element of a champion, when you cannot deny the fact that the teams which have produced the most talent are not winning, and teams like the White Sox are winning divisions when they haven't produced much talent? How can that be?

My friend Craig Wright makes a good argument that the farm system is becoming more important every year. He might well be wright. It is certainly worth noting that this study measures the present, and the future might very well be different. Failing to see the future is human; failing to see the present is blindness.

If having a strong farm system isn't the key to the success of an organization, then what is?

It is a common assertion that the farm system represents the "backbone" of an organization. Well perhaps, indeed, that is an apt figure of speech. Because when you think about it, there is an awful lot that goes into having good health other than having a good backbone. A good, strong backbone is nice; yes, no one denies that. But millions of people die of cancer every year whose backbones are in great shape. Your backbone can be in great shape, but if the heart is weak you still won't get any bargains on life insurance. Poor muscle development, rotten teeth, a dose of hemorrhoids that would make a lion wince—there are any number of things that can slow you down when your backbone is fine.

So what is the key to good health? No one thing. To bring together a core of people who want to win and who are willing to pay the price for that; that, I continue to believe, is terrifically important, the heart of a team. If I had to choose between a good heart and a good backbone, I'd choose the heart. Talent judgment, making good decisions about the people who you have and those who are available to you—that is terrifically important, more so than producing talent. A sense of direction and purpose in making those decisions; that is something you will likely not go anywhere without. And a good backbone is nice to have. But it ain't all it's cracked up to be, either.

II

Two final comments about the White Sox.

(1) They're about that far away from being a great team, a truly great team. But to get there, they're going to have to continue to be aggressive about addressing their problems. They can't use the 20-game margin as an excuse to do nothing about the left side of their infield.

They're probably going to have to replace Fisk before too long, and that's not going to be easy, although Skinner looks good. I doubt that LaMarr Hoyt can be effective over a period of years in the kind of shape that he's in; the White Sox lead the league in fat pitchers. Baseball needs super teams, and I'd love for the White Sox to be one, but they're not there yet.

(2) I have a lot of respect for LaRussa, as you can probably tell, and I think he's a man who has respect for knowledge. With that in mind, I sincerely hope that he will consider this for one minute.

Tony, when you get into the playoffs this year, tone down the baserunning a little bit. Aggressive baserunning does not work against a good team; the same baserunning move that is a "positive" percentage move against a bad team is often a "negative" percentage move against a good team. You said going into the playoffs last year that you thought your baserunning might be the difference in the series, and it was. Tony, it sure as hell was. Let's take a look at every instance during that series that either you or the Orioles lost a baserunner other than by a forceout.

GAME ONE
WHITE SOX
7th inning: Vance Law was on third base with one out, McGregor pitching. The pitch bounced away from

Dempsey and Law tried to score, but Dempsey got it and fired to McGregor, Law out 2–1. The White Sox had two walks, a sac bunt, a balk and a double in the inning, but failed to score, entirely because of this play.
8th inning: Runners on first and third, one out. Baines hit ground ball to Murray. Runner tried to score from third and was out, 3–2–5.
ORIOLES: None
RESULT: White Sox won, 2–1.

GAME TWO
WHITE SOX
2nd inning: White Sox had runners on first and second, one out. Two-strike hit-and-run play resulted in strike-'em-out, throw-'em-out double play, Paciorek caught stealing at third.
ORIOLES: None
RESULT: Orioles won, 4–0.

GAME THREE
WHITE SOX: None
ORIOLES:
5th inning: Lowenstein thrown out at third (9–4–2–5) after hitting 2-run double. Ended inning.
RESULT: Orioles won, 11–1.

GAME FOUR
WHITE SOX
1st inning: Fisk doubled off first after Baines hit liner to short; deprived Luzinski of a chance to hit with a runner on.
7th inning: White Sox had runners on first and second, one out. Todd Cruz was charging at third; Julio Cruz swung away and ripped the ball under his glove. Roenicke charged the ball and held the runner at third but the runner off first didn't see that and rounded second too far, resulting in a putout at the plate (7–5–4–2). White Sox had three singles and a balk in the inning but failed to score. It cost them the game.
ORIOLES: None
RESULT: Scoreless tie through nine innings; Orioles won in tenth.

The White Sox lost five runners in the four games; the Orioles lost one. Of the five runners they lost, four were in scoring position before being cut down.

And if you keep talking about your baserunning being the edge in the playoffs, Tony, that's going to keep happening to you. It doesn't always happen, but it happens more often than it ought. It happened to the 1976–78 Royals. The Royals were a better team than those Yankee teams, but they couldn't beat them because they kept farting away baserunners trying to go first to third on infield outs. And you look on back through history—the Brooklyn Dodgers against Casey's Yankees, Ty Cobb's Tigers against the 1907–1908 Cubs, and you'll find that teams that live by the extra base, die by the extra base. In the 1977 play-offs the Royals had more baserunners than the Yankees did, 57–55, and hit three homers to the Yankees' two, but lost six runners on the base paths while the Yankees lost none.

Why does this happen? I wrote down Tony Kubek's

words at the time of the biggest mistake, Dybzinski's trying to go first to third in the 7th inning of Game Four, without first insuring that third base was available for occupancy. "The White Sox," Kubek said, "are a very aggressive baserunning team, and they have probably been going from first to third on that play all year. It's just that Roenicke played the ball very alertly, and then the cutoff man threw behind him."

Precisely. On the nose. You do that all year, and all year it helps you win ball games, and then you do it against the Baltimore Orioles, and it helps them win ball games. Steve Henderson wouldn't have picked that ball up like that. Dave Edler or Manny Castillo or whoever the Mariners would have had at third base; he's not going to fire behind you.

If the ball bounces away from the Seattle Mariners' catcher, he's not going to get to the screen and throw home before Vance Law can score from third. If he does, the pitcher isn't going to be there covering. If you try a two-strike hit-and-run play against the Minnesota Twins, the pitcher is less likely to strike you out, and if he does the catcher is less likely to throw you out.

So you beat the crap out of the Seattle Mariners and the Minnesota Twins. The White Sox in 1983 were 38–13 against the four worst teams in the league, whereas the Orioles were only 29–20. The 1977 Royals were 36–14 against the four worst teams in the league, whereas the Yankees were just 31–20. The 1952 Dodgers were 54–11 against the three worst teams in the National League, enough to win the pennant even though they were under .500 against the rest of the league.

And Tony, please don't tell me that after you've been playing that way all year, you can't afford to change your game plan going into the playoffs. Why the hell can't you? Would you rather lose? You start Jerry Koosman all year, and then you don't start him in the playoffs, do you? You use a different lineup when you're facing Scott McGregor than you do when you're facing Storm Davis, don't you? When you go to Fenway Park, you respond to Fenway Park, don't you? Do you play just the same on artificial turf as you do on grass?

Then why can't you teach a team to run the bases aggressively against Seattle, thus taking advantage of the things that Seattle cannot do, but hold it down a little against Baltimore?

III

Teams which win a pennant by 15 or more games (the Sox won by 20) almost always repeat. A complete list of teams which have done this:

Year	Team	Margin of Victory	Finish In Following Year
1902	Pittsburgh Pirates	27⅓ Games	First
1906	Chicago Cubs	20 Games	First
1907	Chicago Cubs	17 Games	First
1923	New York Yankees	16 Games	Second
1927	New York Yankees	19 Games	First
1929	Philadelphia Athletics	18 Games	First
1936	New York Yankees	19½ Games	First
1939	New York Yankees	17 Games	Third
1941	New York Yankees	17 Games	First
1943	St. Louis Cardinals	18 Games	First
1969	Baltimore Orioles	19 Games	First
1970	Baltimore Orioles	15 Games	First
1971	Oakland A's	16 Games	First
1975	Cincinnati Reds	20 Games	First

Of the four previous post-split teams, all have won not only the division but the league championship in the following year; all except Baltimore in '70 (as repeaters in '71) were world champions in the year following.

The two Yankee teams which failed to repeat both suffered serious all-over-the-roster declines in performance, yet each still failed to win by only two games.

When you're that much better than anybody else, it takes a real team effort not to repeat.

CHART WHITE SOX-I

BOSTON (227)

INFIELD—Wade Boggs (15), Cecil Cooper, Mil (14), Glenn Hoffman (9), Dave Stapleton (6), Ed Jurak (2), Rick Burleson, Cal (2).
OUTFIELD—Jim Rice (16), Fred Lynn, Cal (11), Ben Ogilvie, Mil (8), Dwight Evans (9), Carl Yastrzemski (6), Rick Miller (5), Reid Nichols, (5), Juan Beniquez, Cal (4).
CATCHER—Carlton Fisk, Chi (15), Ernie Whitt, Tor (9), Bo Diaz, Phi (9), Gary Allenson (3), Rich Gedman (3).
PITCHER—Bob Stanley (14), John Tudor (10), Bruce Hurst (8), Peter Ladd, Mil (8), Mike Smithson, Tex (8), Chuck Rainey, Chi (7), Bob Ojeda (6), Luis Aponte (4), Oil Can Boyd (4), John Curtis, Cal (4), Mike Brown (3).

ST. LOUIS (212)

INFIELD—Keith Hernandez (12), Ken Oberkfell (10), Tommy Herr (7), Garry Templeton, SD (7), Bill Stein, Tex (4), Manny Castillo, Sea (2), Kelly Paris, Cin (2), Mike Ramsey, St.L (2), Jeff Poyle (1).
OUTFIELD: Larry Herndon, Det (11), Jose Cruz, Hous (11), Jerry Mumphrey, Hous (9), Leon Durham, Chi (7), Andy Van Slyke (6); Jim Dwyer, Bal (4), Bake McBride, Cle (2), Mike Vail, Cin (1), Tito Landrum, Bal (1).
CATCHER: Ted Simmons, Mil (12), Jody Davis, Chi (12), Terry Kennedy, SD (12), George Bjorkman, Hous (1), Glenn Brummer (1), Marc Hill, Chi (1).
PITCHER: John Denny, Phil (14), Steve Carlton, Phil (12), Jerry Reuss, LA (9), John Stuper (9), Luis DeLeon, SD (9), Mike Torrez, NY (6), Bob Forsch (6), Mike Proly, Chi (4), Danny Cox (2), Victor Cruz, Tex (2), Eric Rasmussen, KC (1).

PITTSBURGH (200)

INFIELD: Dale Berra (11), Luis Salazar, SD (11), Al Oliver, Mon (10), Willie Randolph, NY (7), Vance Law, Chi (7), Richie Hebner (3), Craig Reynolds, Hou (1).
OUTFIELD: Tony Armas, Bos (12), Dave Parker (9), Omar Moreno, NY (7), Richie Zisk, Sea (3), Mitchell Page, Oak (1), Doug Frobel (1).
CATCHER: Tony Pena (14), Milt May (2), Junior Ortiz (1), Steve Nicosia (1).
PITCHERS: Al Holland, Phil (11), Kent Tekulve (11), Rick Honeycutt, Tex/LA (10), Pascual Perez (9), John Candelaria (9), Fred Breining, SF (7), Lee Tunnel (7), Cecilio Guante (6), Bruce Kison, Cal (5), Odell Jones, Texas (5), Jose DeLeon (4), Ed Whitson, SD (4), Gene Garber, Atl (4), Doug Bair, Det (4), Rod Scurry (3).

CALIFORNIA (174)

INFIELD: Dickie Thon, Hous (14), Willie Aikens, KC (10), Jerry Remy, Bos (10), Julio Cruz, Chi (9), Rance Mulliniks, Tor (8), Carney Lansford, Oak (6), Daryl Sconiers (4), Ron Jackson (4), Brian Harper, Pitt (2), Steve Lubratich (2), Jim Anderson, Tex (1), Fat Floyd Rayford, StL (1); Ricky Adams (1), Dick Schofield (1).
OUTFIELD: Ken Landreaux, LA (12), Tom Brunansky, Minn (12), Dave Collins, Tor (7), Jay Johnstone, Chi (2), Bobby Clark (2), Mike Brown (1), Gary Pettis (1), Thad Bosly, Chi (1).
CATCHER: Dave Engle, Minn (7).
PITCHERS: Richard Dotson, Chi (15), Ken Schrom, Minn (9), Sid Monge, SD (6), Tom Burgmeier, Oak (6), Frank Tanana, Tex (5), Mike Witt (4), Mark Clear, Bos (3), Chuck Porter, Mil (3), Steve Brown (2), Andy Hassler, (1), Ricky Steirer (1), Mike Walters, Minn (1).

TEXAS (170)

INFIELD: Bill Madlock, Pitt (12), Roy Smalley, NY (11), Mike Hargrove, Cle (10), Toby Harrah, Cle (9), Pat Putnam, Sea (8), Wayne Tolleson (8), Pete O'Brien (7), Roy Howell, Mil (2), Greg Pryor, KC (1), Mike Richardt (1).
OUTFIELD: George Wright (12), Billy Sample (10), Jeff Burroughs, Oak (5), Larry Biittner (1), Bobby Jones (1).
CATCHERS: Jim Sundberg (6), John Wockenfuss, Det (5), Bobby Johnson (2).
PITCHERS: Dave Righetti, NY (10), Jim Clancy, Tor (9), Ed Lynch, NY (6), Len Whitehouse, Minn (6), John Butcher (6), Danny Darwin (6), Ray Fontenot, NY (5), Walt Terrell, NY (4), Dave Schmidt (4), Len Barker, Cle/Atl (3).

KANSAS CITY (157)

INFIELD: George Brett (12), Frank White (12), U.L. Washington (9), Brad Wellman, SF (2), Onix Concepcion (2), Ken Phelps, Sea (2).
OUTFIELD: Willie Wilson (10), Ruppert Jones, SD (6), Marvell Wynne, Pitt (5), Pat Sheridan (5), Al Cowens (4), Warm Front Davis (2), Daryl Motley (1).
CATCHERS: John Wathan (7), Buck Martinez, Tor (5), Don Slaught (4), Jamie Quirk, StL (1).
PITCHERS: Dan Quisenberry (14), Aurelio Lopez, Det (11), Greg Minton, SF (10), Atlee Hammaker, SF (8), Paul Splittorff (7), Bill Laskey, SF (6), Bob McClure, Mil (5), Renie Martin, SF (3), Dennis Leonard (3), Rich Gale, Cin (1).

BALTIMORE (146)

INFIELD: Cal Ripken (17), Eddie Murray (15), Bobby Grich, Cal (9), Doug DeCinces, Cal (7), Rich Dauer (7), Enos Cabell, Det (7), Bob Bailor, NY (5), Kiko Garcia, Phil (3), Wayne Krenchiki, Det (2).
OUTFIELD: Don Baylor, NY (10), Al Bumbry, (6), John Shelby (5), Lou Piniella, NY (2).
CATCHERS: None
PITCHERS: Mike Boddicker (10), Storm Davis (9), Sammy Stewart (9), Bryn Smith, Mon (8), Mike Flanagan (6), Dennis Martinez (3), Jim Palmer (3), Allan Ramirez (2), Don Hood, KC (2).

HOUSTON (106)

INFIELD: Johnny Ray, Pitt (11), Bill Doran (10), Cliff Johnson, Tor (9), Joe Morgan, Hous (8), Bob Watson, Atl (3), Rusty Staub, NY (2).
OUTFIELD: Terry Puhl (9), Mike Easler, Pitt (7), Greg Gross, Phil (5), Danny Heep, NY (4), Cesar Cedeno, Cin (3), Derrel Thomas, LA (3), Tim Tolman (1), Dave Rajsich, NY (1), Cesar Geronimo, KC (1).
CATCHERS: Alan Knicely, Cin (1), John Mizerock, (1).
PITCHERS: Floyd Bannister, Chi (10), Ken Forsch, Cal (8), Mike Stanton, Sea (5), Dave Smith (4).

CHICAGO WHITE SOX (91)

INFIELD: Bucky Dent, Tex (6), Greg Walker (4), Jorge Orta, Tor (3), Mike Squires (2), Chris Nyman (1).
OUTFIELD: Harold Baines (11), Ron Kittle, (1), Brian Downing, Cal (7), Jerry Hairston (3), Rusty Kuntz, Minn (4).
CATCHERS: None
PITCHERS: Goose Gossage, NY (12), Terry Forster, Atl (7), Britt Burns (6), Salome Barojas (6), Steve Trout, Chi Cubs (5), Juan Agosto (4), Tim Stoddard (3).

TORONTO (49)

INFIELD: None
OUTFIELD: Lloyd Moseby (14), Jesse Barfield (8), George Bell (1).
CATCHERS: None
PITCHERS: Dave Stieb (13), Luis Leal (8), Jim Gott (5).

CHART WHITE SOX II

American League			National League		
Team	Production	Wins	Team	Production	Wins
Boston	227	78	Los Angeles	302	91
California	174	70	Cincinnati	217	74
Texas	170	77	St. Louis	212	79
Kansas City	157	79	Pittsburgh	200	82
Detroit	155	92	Atlanta	182	88
Milwaukee	155	87	Philadelphia	169	90
Oakland	149	74			
Baltimore	146	98	New York	164	68
New York	136	91	Montreal	159	82
Minnesota	129	70	San Francisco	128	79
Cleveland	106	70	San Diego	122	81
Chicago	95	99	Chicago	113	71
Toronto	65	89	Houston	106	85
Seattle	62	62			

THE MANAGER

NAME: Tony LaRussa

AGE: 39

MANAGERS FOR WHOM PLAYED IN MAJORS: Ed Lopat, Bob Kennedy, Hank Bauer, John McNamara, Dick Williams, Luman Harris, Chuck Tanner.

CHARACTERISTICS AS A PLAYER: Another middle infielder who didn't hit; hit good in minors. Was a bonus baby with the A's in 1963, a year before Lachemann was (Kansas City, cradle of managers) and was a member of the awesome 1966 Modesto team in the California League, which contained the nucleus of the 1973 A's. He and Lachemann spent years as minor league teammates.

MANAGERIAL RECORD:

Team	Year	Par	Wins	Losses	Pct.	+ or −
Chi	1979	25	27	27	.500	+ 2
Chi	1980	75	70	90	.438	− 5
Chi	1981	50	54	92	.509	+ 4
Chi	1982	78	87	75	.537	+ 9
Chi	1983	84	99	63	.611	+15
5 Years		312	337	307	.523	+25

WHAT HE BRINGS TO THE BALLCLUB

IS HE AN INTENSE MANAGER OR MORE OF AN EASY-TO-GET-ALONG-WITH TYPE? He's intense.

IS HE MORE OF AN EMOTIONAL LEADER OR A DECISION-MAKER? He's more of a decision-maker; his qualities as a leader of men have been questioned, but he does work, and I for one feel that it's very important to have a hard worker at the head of any organization.

IS HE MORE OF AN OPTIMIST OR MORE OF A PROBLEM SOLVER? He's a problem solver, a man who reacts strongly to perceived weaknesses and tries to take corrective action.

HOW HE USES HIS PERSONNEL

DOES HE FAVOR A SET LINEUP OR A ROTATION SYSTEM? He rotates his personnel quite extensively.

DOES HE LIKE TO PLATOON? Well, I haven't heard him complaining about it.

DOES HE TRY TO SOLVE HIS PROBLEMS WITH PROVEN PLAYERS OR WITH YOUNGSTERS WHO STILL HAVE SOMETHING TO PROVE? HOW MANY PLAYERS HAS HE MADE REGULARS OUT OF WHO WERE NOT REGULARS BEFORE, AND WHO WERE THEY? He has made regulars out of Jim Morrison, Harold Baines, Wayne Nordhagen, Tony Bernazard, Vance Law, Rudy Law (he likes lawyers), Ron Kittle and he made "platoon regulars" out of Greg Walker and

Fletcher/Dybzinski. So clearly, he prefers to get the potential of an unknown rather than the security of a known solution to a problem.

DOES HE PREFER TO GO WITH GOOD OFFENSIVE PLAYERS OR DOES HE LIKE THE GLOVE MEN? He's overlooked a lot of defensive shortcomings. Rudy Law can't throw, Kittle's no fielder, Tom Paciorek's no glove man. On the other hand, the shortstops are not hitters, and Vance Law is surely one of the weakest bats in the league at third.

DOES HE LIKE AN OFFENSE BASED ON POWER, SPEED OR HIGH AVERAGES? It's a power offense with speed at two spots.

DOES HE USE THE ENTIRE ROSTER OR DOES HE KEEP PEOPLE AROUND SITTING ON THE BENCH? If they'd let him carry 30 people, he'd use them all.

DOES HE BUILD HIS BENCH AROUND YOUNG PLAYERS WHO CAN STEP INTO A BREACH IF NEED BE OR AROUND VETERAN ROLE-PLAYERS WHO HAVE THEIR OWN FUNCTIONS WITHIN A GAME? Mostly veteran role-players (Marc Hill, Aurelio Rodriguez, Jerry Hairston.

GAME MANAGING AND USE OF STRATEGIES

DOES HE GO FOR THE BIG-INNING OFFENSE OR DOES HE LIKE TO USE THE ONE-RUN STRATEGIES? He's a big-inning manager, but it's a marginal classification.

DOES HE PINCH-HIT MUCH, AND IF SO WHEN? Hairston led the league in pinch-hitting appearances (78) and Greg Walker was second (42); I guess you could say he'll pinch-hit. Hairston pinch-hits a lot for the shortstops and will pinch-hit leading off an inning. Walker pinch-hits more later in the inning. Also makes a lot of defensive switches.

ANYTHING UNUSUAL ABOUT HIS LINEUP SELECTION? Avoided the temptation to bat Julio Cruz at the top of the order; made a unique, gutty and productive decision to bat Fisk second, for which he deserves all the credit he has received. Too many managers would have intoned "bat control" and batted Cruz or Vance Law second.

DOES HE USE THE SAC BUNT OFTEN? More than you might think in view of the lineup, yes. Dybzinski, Fletcher and Vance Law bunt regularly. Likes to bunt with two men on, nobody out. That's a strong tendency.

DOES HE LIKE TO USE THE RUNNING GAME? Yes, and he uses it effectively. He keeps the base stealers and the singles hitters together in the lineup, as a sort of "side offense" to give the opposition something to think about when they're not beating your brains out.

IN WHAT CIRCUMSTANCES WILL HE ISSUE AN INTENTIONAL WALK? On what I see, there seem to be two essential conditions: 1) that he escapes a big bat, and 2) that he sets up a double play. Platoon advantage doesn't seem to matter much in this decision.

DOES HE HIT AND RUN VERY OFTEN? Very often, yes. Baines is a terrific H & R man; Fisk is good, both Laws are good.

ARE THERE ANY UNIQUE OR IDIOSYNCRATIC STRATEGIES THAT HE PARTICULARLY LIKES? A bunch of them. His defensive positioning is by far the most distinctive in baseball, with the third baseman often drawn in very tight, huge infield and outfield gaps at times with one outfielder frequently deep and another shallow, or infielders playing a batter to pull and outfielders playing him to hit to opposite field. Loves to make one bunt try and then switch to hit and run. He will use the suicide squeeze. Although he's not as flashy about it as a Billy Martin, his strategy is calculated to play on the opposing team's mind, disrupt them. He probably does that as effectively as any manager in the league.

HANDLING THE PITCHING STAFF

DOES HE LIKE POWER PITCHERS OR PREFER TO GO WITH THE PEOPLE WHO PUT THE BALL IN PLAY? The White Sox staff is a power pitcher's staff.

DOES HE STAY WITH THE STARTER OR GO TO THE BULLPEN QUICKLY? About average. He's not a quick hook; he's not Billy Martin, either. I can't prove it, but my impression is that he changes pitchers between innings a lot; he'll let a pitcher finish his mess, and then take him out at the start of the next inning. Had only four games last year in which he allowed a pitcher to start an inning after the pitcher had allowed five runs.

DOES HE LIKE THE FOUR-MAN OR THE FIVE-MAN ROTATION? Again, uses a five-day rotation.

DOES HE USE THE ENTIRE STAFF OR DOES HE TRY TO GET FIVE OR SIX PEOPLE TO DO MOST OF THE WORK? He uses everybody.

ARE THERE ANY PARTICULAR TYPES OF PITCHERS OF WHOM HE IS FOND? His staff is quite diverse—old, young, left, right, power pitchers, ground-ball pitchers. More power pitchers, perhaps, but it's no big thing.

IS THERE ANYTHING UNIQUE ABOUT HIS HANDLING OF HIS PITCHERS? With his starting pitchers he is patient, will give them as long as they need to work out their problems; with the bullpen, he is streaky, will ride a hot hand and demote the guy quickly when he has a bad outing.

WHAT IS HIS STRONGEST POINT AS A MAN-AGER? His inventiveness; his hard-working analytical resourcefulness. He's a beautiful manager to watch.

IF THERE WERE NO PROFESSIONAL BASE-BALL, WHAT WOULD THIS MANAGER PROBABLY BE DOING? What else? He'd be practicing law.

Tom PACIOREK, First Base
Runs Created: 66

	G	AB	Hit	2B	3B	HR	Run	RBI	BB	SO	SB	CS	Avg
6.63 Years		490	140	30	4	11	62	63	30	81	5	0	.286
1983	115	420	129	32	3	9	65	63	25	58	6	1	.307
First Half	54	200	52	14	0	4	24	29	9	28	2	1	.260
Second Half	61	220	77	18	3	5	41	34	16	30	4	0	.350
vs. RHP		226	63	21	1	4	30	42	14	29	2	1	.279
vs. LHP		194	66	11	2	5	35	21	11	29	4	0	.340
Home	53	192	64	15	2	4	39	33	11	28	2	1	.333
Road	62	228	65	17	1	5	26	30	14	30	4	0	.285
Grass	100	362	111	27	3	8	61	55	25	46	4	1	.307
Turf	15	58	18	5	0	1	4	8	0	12	2	0	.310

Vance LAW, Third Base
Runs Created: 49

	G	AB	Hit	2B	3B	HR	Run	RBI	BB	SO	SB	CS	Avg
1.94 Years		468	117	22	5	5	55	53	42	64	5	3	.249
1983	145	408	99	21	5	4	55	42	51	56	3	1	.243
First Half	62	166	38	6	3	3	22	17	16	27	0	1	.229
Second Half	83	242	61	15	2	1	3	25	35	29	3	0	.252
vs. RHP		267	57	12	3	3	28	29	29	42	1	1	.213
vs. LHP		141	42	9	2	1	27	13	22	14	2	0	.298
Home	71	202	49	12	3	1	30	24	32	29	2	0	.243
Road	74	206	50	9	2	3	25	18	19	27	1	1	.243
Grass	123	356	88	20	5	3	49	39	45	49	1	1	.247
Turf	22	52	11	1	0	1	6	3	6	7	2	0	.212

Julio CRUZ, Second Base
Runs Created: 60

	G	AB	Hit	2B	3B	HR	Run	RBI	BB	SO	SB	CS	Avg
5.19 Years		578	141	18	4	3	86	39	69	74	60	13	.244
1983	160	515	130	19	5	3	71	52	49	66	57	12	.252
First Half	77	240	57	11	2	2	36	16	24	28	39	6	.238
Second Half	83	275	73	8	3	1	35	36	25	38	18	6	.265
vs. RHP		329	77	9	4	0	47	27	36	53	41	9	.234
vs. LHP		186	53	10	1	3	24	25	13	13	16	3	.285
Home	82	261	67	10	4	1	34	33	28	38	26	5	.257
Road	78	254	63	9	1	2	37	19	21	28	31	7	.248
Grass	106	347	79	9	4	0	41	31	31	47	25	6	.228
Turf	54	168	51	10	1	3	30	21	18	19	32	6	.304

Scott FLETCHER, Shortstop
Runs Created: 31

	G	AB	Hit	2B	3B	HR	Run	RBI	BB	SO	SB	CS	Avg
0.89 Years		374	86	23	6	3	59	37	39	35	7	1	.229
1983	114	262	62	16	5	3	42	31	29	22	5	1	.237
First Half	50	68	16	6	2	1	15	14	12	4	3	0	.235
Second Half	64	194	46	10	3	2	27	17	17	18	2	1	.237
vs. RHP		175	42	11	4	1	27	21	19	17	2	0	.240
vs. LHP		87	20	5	1	2	15	10	10	5	3	1	.230
Home	51	119	33	9	3	1	22	15	18	9	4	1	.277
Road	63	143	29	7	2	2	20	16	11	13	1	0	.203
Grass	93	216	50	14	4	1	33	24	28	18	5	1	.231
Turf	21	46	12	2	1	2	9	7	1	4	0	0	.261

Ron KITTLE, Leftfield
Runs Created: 81

	G	AB	Hit	2B	3B	HR	Run	RBI	BB	SO	SB	CS	Avg
1.02 Years		539	136	21	3	35	77	105	41	159	8	3	.253
1983	145	520	132	19	3	35	75	100	39	150	8	3	.254
First Half	71	267	71	9	2	18	41	56	9	71	6	0	.266
Second Half	74	253	61	10	1	17	34	44	30	79	2	3	.241
vs. RHP		339	86	10	2	22	48	70	20	98	6	2	.254
vs. LHP		181	46	9	1	13	27	30	19	52	2	1	.254
Home	74	263	71	14	1	18	38	55	25	72	4	2	.270
Road	71	257	61	5	2	17	37	45	14	78	4	1	.237
Grass	123	442	115	17	3	30	61	84	34	129	8	3	.260
Turf	22	78	17	2	0	5	14	16	5	21	0	0	.218

Rudy LAW, Centerfield
Runs Created: 74

	G	AB	Hit	2B	3B	HR	Run	RBI	BB	SO	SB	CS	Avg
2.48 Years		500	143	16	8	3	84	36	36	43	63	15	.285
1983	141	501	142	20	7	3	95	33	42	36	77	12	.283
First Half	60	205	58	7	1	0	37	13	18	14	32	5	.283
Second Half	81	296	84	13	6	3	58	20	24	22	45	7	.284
vs. RHP		410	115	18	3	3	81	31	36	25	68	10	.280
vs. LHP		91	27	2	4	0	14	2	6	11	9	2	.297
Home	69	262	78	12	6	1	54	14	18	21	38	5	.298
Road	72	239	64	8	1	2	41	19	24	15	39	7	.268
Grass	119	423	118	17	7	3	84	28	37	31	64	9	.279
Turf	22	78	24	3	0	0	11	5	5	5	13	3	.308

Harold BAINES, Rightfield
Runs Created: 85

	G	AB	Hit	2B	3B	HR	Run	RBI	BB	SO	SB	CS	Avg
3.33 Years		593	161	29	7	20	79	88	39	86	8	4	.272
1983	156	596	167	33	2	20	76	99	49	85	7	5	.280
First Half	75	288	79	16	2	5	34	41	28	34	5	4	.274
Second Half	81	308	88	17	0	15	42	58	21	51	2	1	.286
vs. RHP		401	122	23	1	17	61	77	44	50	3	3	.304
vs. LHP		195	45	10	1	3	15	22	5	35	4	2	.231
Home	79	284	81	19	1	12	46	54	23	42	4	1	.285
Road	77	312	86	14	1	8	30	45	26	43	3	4	.276
Grass	132	497	134	29	2	15	64	80	42	77	5	2	.270
Turf	24	99	33	4	0	5	12	19	7	8	2	3	.333

Carlton FISK, Catcher
Runs Created: 90

	G	AB	Hit	2B	3B	HR	Run	RBI	BB	SO	SB	CS	Avg
8.93 Years		578	163	29	4	23	92	86	58	87	10	4	.282
1983	138	488	141	26	4	26	85	86	46	88	9	6	.289
First Half	65	212	53	12	3	9	31	30	18	35	4	3	.250
Second Half	73	276	88	14	1	17	54	56	28	53	5	3	.319
vs. RHP		320	92	13	2	18	59	65	26	65	6	2	.288
vs. LHP		168	49	13	2	8	26	21	20	23	3	4	.292
Home	71	245	73	14	1	17	44	52	29	47	3	5	.298
Road	67	243	68	12	3	9	41	34	17	41	6	1	.280
Grass	115	396	114	19	3	22	71	71	43	79	6	5	.288
Turf	23	92	27	7	1	4	14	15	3	9	3	1	.293

Greg LUZINSKI, Designated Hitter
Runs Created: 93

	G	AB	Hit	2B	3B	HR	Run	RBI	BB	SO	SB	CS	Avg
10.47 Years		582	162	32	2	28	80	102	75	135	3	3	.278
1983	144	502	128	26	1	32	73	95	70	117	2	1	.255
First Half	70	235	54	12	0	12	32	39	35	47	1	1	.230
Second Half	74	267	74	14	1	20	41	56	35	70	1	0	.277
vs. RHP		324	82	14	1	19	43	61	43	75	1	0	.253
vs. LHP		178	46	12	0	13	30	34	27	42	1	1	.258
Home	77	273	79	18	1	18	42	53	34	56	1	1	.289
Road	67	229	49	8	0	14	31	42	36	61	1	0	.214
Grass	123	433	113	25	1	25	63	80	53	97	2	1	.261
Turf	21	69	15	1	0	7	10	15	17	20	0	0	.217

Greg WALKER, First Base
Runs Created: 46

	G	AB	Hit	2B	3B	HR	Run	RBI	BB	SO	SB	CS	Avg
0.80 Years		407	113	23	5	15	44	78	38	75	3	1	.278
1983	118	307	83	16	3	10	32	55	28	57	2	1	.270
First Half	54	123	39	11	1	6	18	37	11	28	0	0	.317
Second Half	64	184	44	5	2	4	14	18	17	29	2	1	.239
vs. RHP		261	73	15	2	10	28	51	23	46	2	1	.280
vs. LHP		46	10	1	1	0	4	4	5	11	0	0	.217
Home	51	136	38	5	1	4	17	27	13	29	1	0	.279
Road	67	171	45	11	2	6	15	28	15	28	1	1	.263
Grass	96	246	67	11	3	8	27	43	25	43	1	1	.272
Turf	22	61	16	5	0	2	5	12	3	14	1	0	.262

LaMarr HOYT

Year	(W–L)	GS	Run	Avg	DP	Avg	SB	Avg
1982	(19-15)	32	170	5.31	30	.94	26	.81
1983	(24-10)	36	193	5.36	36	1.00	8	.22
1980-1983		81	414	5.11	78	.96	44	.54

	G	IP	W	L	Pct	ER	ERA
1982 Home	19	122.2	13	3	.813	48	3.52
1983 Home	20	145.1	15	5	.750	52	3.22
1982 Road	20	117	6	12	.333	46	3.54
1983 Road	16	115.1	9	5	.643	54	4.21
1983 Grass	31	221.1	20	9	.690	91	3.70
1983 Turf	5	39.1	4	1	.800	15	3.43

Richard DOTSON

Year	(W–L)	GS	Run	Avg	DP	Avg	SB	Avg
1982	(11-15)	31	128	4.13	28	.90	25	.81
1983	(22- 7)	35	206	5.89	50	1.43	31	.89
1979-1983		127	643	5.06	141	1.11	116	.91

	G	IP	W	L	Pct	ER	ERA
1982 Home	16	97.2	3	9	.250	38	3.50
1983 Home	17	117.1	10	4	.714	43	3.30
1982 Road	18	99	8	6	.571	46	4.18
1983 Road	18	122.2	12	3	.800	43	3.15
1983 Grass	29	196	16	7	.696	78	3.58
1983 Turf	6	44	6	0	1.000	8	1.64

Floyd BANNISTER

Year	(W–L)	GS	Run	Avg	DP	Avg	SB	Avg
1982	(12-13)	35	161	4.60	24	.69	26	.74
1983	(16-10)	34	162	4.76	26	.76	25	.73
1977-1983		190	796	4.19	138	.73	161	.85

	G	IP	W	L	Pct	ER	ERA
1982 Home	17	120	5	8	.385	50	3.75
1983 Home	17	119.1	9	3	.750	41	3.09
1982 Road	18	127	7	5	.583	44	3.12
1983 Road	17	98	7	7	.500	40	3.67
1983 Grass	28	183.2	14	7	.667	61	2.99
1983 Turf	6	33.2	2	3	.400	20	5.35

Britt BURNS

Year	(W–L)	GS	Run	Avg	DP	Avg	SB	Avg
1982	(13- 5)	28	144	5.14	22	.79	14	.50
1983	(10-11)	26	93	3.58	17	.65	17	.65
1978-1983		112	434	3.87	89	.79	73	.65

	G	IP	W	L	Pct	ER	ERA
1982 Home	13	82.2	7	2	.778	43	4.68
1983 Home	13	73.2	4	4	.500	26	3.18
1982 Road	15	86.2	6	3	.667	33	3.43
1983 Road	16	100	6	7	.461	43	3.87
1983 Grass	25	146.2	8	9	.471	56	3.44
1983 Turf	4	27	2	2	.500	13	4.33

Jerry KOOSMAN

Year	(W–L)	GS	Run	Avg	DP	Avg	SB	Avg
1982	(11-7)	19	107	5.63	24	1.26	2	.11
1983	(11-7)	24	119	4.96	18	.75	19	.79
1976-1983		222	908	4.09	194	.87	86	.39

	G	IP	W	L	Pct	ER	ERA
1982 Home	19	79.1	6	4	.600	34	3.86
1983 Home	20	94.1	8	3	.727	49	4.67
1982 Road	23	94	5	3	.625	40	3.83
1983 Road	17	75.1	3	4	.429	41	4.90
1983 Grass	32	148.1	11	6	.647	81	4.90
1983 Turf	5	21	0	1		9	3.86

1983 OTHERS

Pitcher	(W–L)	GS	Run	Avg	DP	Avg	SB	Avg
Lamp	(7-7)	5	18	3.60	9	1.80	1	0.20
Martz	(0-0)	1	4	4.00	1	1.00	0	0.00
Tidrow	(2-4)	1	5	5.00	1	1.00	0	0.00

CHICAGO WHITE SOX
RUNS BATTED IN ANALYSIS

Player	RBI	RBI In Wins	Victory-Important RBI	RBI Importance	Wins Batted In	RBI Per Win
Harold Baines	99	85	53.55	.541	14.42	6.9
Ron Kittle	100	80	51.33	.513	11.82	8.5
Greg Luzinski	95	68	42.11	.443	10.42	9.1
Carlton Fisk	86	67	39.42	.458	10.75	8.0
Tom Paciorek	63	53	32.37	.514	8.47	7.4
Greg Walker	55	45	30.36	.552	6.86	8.0
Julio Cruz	40	34	20.43	.511	6.02	6.6
Vance Law	42	25	16.92	.403	4.39	9.6
Scott Fletcher	31	25	15.98	.515	3.24	9.6
Rudy Law	34	31	15.67	.461	4.30	7.9

KANSAS CITY ROYALS

To this point in his career as a general manager, John Schuerholz has yet to try anything that worked. Schuerholz is a man who likes to use military phrases and figures of speech (at the time of the Pine Tar incident, he said that after their initial shock, "we transferred immediately into our defense mode"). At this moment there can be no doubt that the Royal forces are under heavy siege—driven back by the competition, bombarded unexpectedly by the law. An organization that just two years ago seemed strong enough to command their division for a generation or more now stands on the doorstep of oblivion. How long can the support of the fans hold out? How long can it be until the press corps defects? More players spent the winter in prison than on the award circuit. A return to the top of the division within the next three or four years is all but out of the question. Schuerholz himself, two years ago a rising young star of his profession, must now contemplate the ghosts of Peter Bavasi, Dan O'Brien and John Claiborne. What is it that general managers do after they resign in disgrace?

Let us take a look at the strategy that has brought the Royals to this pass. The essential subject is replacement rates. Suppose that in your house you have a thousand light bulbs, and that for some reason it is important to you to keep all of those light bulbs burning. You have two choices in light bulbs to buy. You can buy Sylvania or GE or something, which costs a little money but which can be expected to last for a couple of years before they go pffft in the night, or you can buy Frank's Famous Light Bulbs, which are cheap but which only last about three months on the average.

Now there is an initial gain involved if you buy Frank's Famous Light Bulbs. And at first, you really don't much notice the difference. You've got a thousand light bulbs; you're used to 42 a month burning out (1,000 divided by 24. Twenty-four months, two years). In the first month, maybe 54 light bulbs will burn out (958 divided by 24, plus 42 divided by three). You won't even notice a thing like that at first.

Then the next month, 65 light bulbs will burn out. In the third month, 77 will go out. Finally, after about twenty months of this, three hundred light bulbs a month are snapping out on you, and you're spending hours a day in which you should be either earning a living or enjoying life, just running around checking light bulbs.

And that's exactly what has happened to the Royals: The bulbs are burning out on them faster than they can replace them. The Royals approach, in the Cedric Tallis era and in the Joe Burke era, was always to try to make a long-term solution—a ten or twelve-year solution—to whatever problem arose. Need a centerfielder? Let's look around and try to find someone who can play the position for several years, like maybe this Amos Otis kid the Mets have. Need a power hitting first baseman? The Astros have this guy named John Mayberry; hasn't hit anything in the majors but he can sure hit in batting practice. Need

a shortstop? The Pirates have one they're not playing, Fred Patek.

Their DH problem was solved eleven years ago by the acquisition of Hal McRae, and has not had to be addressed again since. The third base problem last had to be solved a decade ago, and may not need the treatment for another decade. Their second base problem was put to rest for the time being in 1976. That was the way they attempted to respond to each and every problem, without exception. It didn't always take, but that was always what they tried. They never tried to bring in people who had had their shot in the major leagues. This is the complete list of Kansas City Royals of 1976 who had played regularly with another organization: Fred Patek (sort of), Dave Nelson, Cookie Rojas, Marty Pattin.

That changed dramatically and immediately when John Schuerholz assumed command of this organization. Needing a starting pitcher, he packaged up a bunch of kids who had never done anything in the major leagues —some guy named Atlee Hammaker, a kid second baseman named Brad Wellman—to acquire a proven starter (Vida Blue). When a problem arose in rightfield, he put together another package for the Giants, a grade-B prospect named Bill Laskey and another pitcher, so that the Giants would bestow upon us a proven outfielder named Jerry Martin (who, by the way, the Giants themselves replaced with an unproven outfielder whom they reclaimed from the refuse heap—Jeff Leonard). When Vida Blue failed to plug even one hole on the mound and others began appearing beside him, Schuerholz began buying cheaper and cheaper light bulbs, hauling in Eric Rasmussens and Gaylord Perrys and Steve Renkos, while pitching prospects waited impatiently in the minors. This is the list of 1983 Kansas City Royals who had played regularly for another team: Willie Aikens, Cesar Geronimo, Jerry Martin, Greg Pryor, Leon Roberts, Joe Simpson, Vida Blue, Bill Castro, Don Hood, Gaylord Perry, Eric Rasmussen and Steve Renko.

There is no doubt, absolutely no doubt, that Schuerholz has been unlucky as well as unwise. The moves that he has made were designed to stall fate for one to three years, and instead they've been lasting from zero to one. Vida Blue could easily have gone 19–11 in '82 and 15–9 in '83, and it would all have been different; I'm not saying at all that what Schuerholz has been trying to do could not have worked within the limited framework of his thinking. He was trying to squeeze one or two last pennants out of an old ballclub, and it could have worked. It didn't.

What I am saying is that I have had, for ten years, an almost superstitious respect for the judgment of this organization. I have now entirely lost confidence in them. Why? Because they have cut themselves off from that past. They've cut themselves off from the policies and practices that made them the organization that they were. There are many successful strategies other than the strategy that Cedric Tallis adopted for this organization in 1969; other good teams do things in other ways. But this is my ballclub, and I have lost all confidence in them. I may be a little fanatical, but I think that emotionally I am in the same theater of operations (thought you'd like that, John) as most other Royals fans.

But then, I lose confidence quickly in people who say things like "our mission was to do this" and talk about "campaigns" and "multi-faceted operations." I was in the army. Those people look good on the news, talking about "bringing the unit up to full operational capacity so as to maximize our effectiveness in the advent of a hostile situation." Military jargon exists to disguise the fact that they don't have the foggiest notion of what the hell they're trying to do. The army is run by people whose vision extends as far as the due date on their next report; the officers are largely intelligent men, locked into a command structure that so totally isolates the commanders from the commandees that they have no real concept of how it is that their decisions will impact on other people's lives. An insane fascination with rotating people in and out so as to emphasize that no one is irreplaceable makes it impossible to develop long-term goals or undertake long-term projects; no one will start anything that's going to take three years because no one expects to be where they are three years from today. Better to show progress on paper today than show it in the field in five months.

The pathetic thing about Schuerholz is that he fancies himself a gambler, but a gambler in fact is precisely what he is not. Oh, he's not afraid to make moves; no one in the army is reluctant to change things around. But his whole purpose in making those moves has always been to avoid that awful moment when you have to rest your fate with an "unproven" player. Schuerholz doesn't want to put Ron Johnson in the lineup and find out why he hits .336 at Omaha; he wants to come up with a "proven" player. Somebody like Bruce Bochte.

So what happens in the army? A lack of vision leads to a compulsive need for change, change for the sake of change. All decisions are made according to what things look like on paper. People lose a sense of where they are going and what they are doing, and eventually lose the sense of their own worth. Morale rots; drugs flourish.

I'm not pessimistic about the LONG-TERM future of the Royals. Either Schuerholz will begin to show some results or Kaufmann will fire him. The Royals were dead last in the major leagues in 1983 in young talent on the roster (see Section I, article on where talent comes from), but despite that, and despite all of the unfortunate trades that have been made, giving away people like Marvell Wynne, there remain a lot of young ballplayers in the system who look like they are going to be fun to watch, people like Butch (Warm Front) Davis, John Morris, Danny Jackson, Don Slaught, Onix Concepcion, Pat Sheridan and Frank Wills. As much as I like Amos Otis, I felt better about the organization after he was released. It was the first sign I had seen that Schuerholz realizes that the 1976–1980 team is gone, and that a whole new unit is going to have to be put in its place. Schuerholz isn't dumb; he may be misguided and he's certainly been mislucky, but he's not dumb.

But neither are the people who run the United States Army. And up to now, they've got every reason to be proud of the way that John Schuerholz has run this ballclub.

THE MANAGER

NAME: Dick Howser

AGE: 46 (47 in May)

MANAGERS FOR WHOM PLAYED IN MAJORS: Joe Gordon, Hank Bauer, Ed Lopat, Birdie Tebbetts, George Strickland, Ralph Houk.

CHARACTERISTICS AS A PLAYER: Another middle infielder, but unlike most he was a good offensive shortstop who was not highly regarded defensively. Lost the 1961 American League Rookie of the Year award in one of the strangest award decisions ever, when he scored 108 runs, hit .280, drew 92 walks, was second in the league in stolen bases and scored a higher percentage of his team's runs than anyone in the league except Mantle or Maris. They gave the award to Don Schwall, who started the year in the minor leagues but was called up in time to walk 110 men in 179 innings. Defensively, Howser, a small man, was quick and nimble at short but lacked an outstanding arm.

MANAGERIAL RECORD:

Team	Year	Par	Wins	Losses	Pct.	+ or −
NY	1980	90	103	59	.636	+13
KC	1981	18	20	13	.606	+ 2
KC	1982	85	90	72	.556	+ 5
KC	1983	82	79	83	.488	− 3
4 Years		275	292	227	.563	+17

WHAT HE BRINGS TO THE BALLCLUB

IS HE AN INTENSE MANAGER OR MORE OF AN EASY-TO-GET-ALONG-WITH TYPE? He's an intense man; players that he doesn't think are playing at full speed are going to have some trouble getting along with him.

IS HE MORE OF AN EMOTIONAL LEADER OR A DECISION-MAKER? During the game he tries to keep his emotions in check and his head clear; in that respect, clearly a decision-maker.

IS HE MORE OF AN OPTIMIST OR MORE OF

A PROBLEM SOLVER? A problem solver I think; a man who tries to correct problems rather than trying to live with them.

HOW HE USES HIS PERSONNEL

DOES HE FAVOR A SET LINEUP OR A ROTATION SYSTEM? Well, he has made or has been forced to make quite a few in-season redefinitions of a player's role, such as shifting Otis to right and Wilson to center last year, or moving Guidry to the bullpen for a while in 1980.

DOES HE LIKE TO PLATOON? In Kansas City he has platooned some (Aikens at first last year), but not nearly as much as he did in 1980 with the Yankees.

DOES HE TRY TO SOLVE HIS PROBLEMS WITH PROVEN PLAYERS OR WITH YOUNGSTERS WHO STILL HAVE SOMETHING TO PROVE? HOW MANY PLAYERS HAS HE MADE REGULARS OUT OF WHO WERE NOT REGULARS BEFORE, AND WHO WERE THEY? He made a regular out of Bobby Brown in 1980, although I don't know that that was by choice, and he made Sheridan a regular in KC last year. Mostly he has shown a preference for working with veteran players.

I strongly suspect that some of what I said about John Schuerholz bringing in veterans is actually the work of Dick Howser; at the same time, I don't fault Howser for that. It is a manager's job to try to win baseball games *today* just as in the army it is the first sergeant's job to supervise the day-to-day operation of the company or battery or whatever, or just as it is each player's job to try to win this game today. It is the general's manager job to superimpose the long term interest of the team onto that.

DOES HE PREFER TO GO WITH GOOD OFFENSIVE PLAYERS OR DOES HE LIKE THE GLOVE MEN? Well, Craig Wright says most people manage like they played. He's shown limited patience with people who don't hit.

DOES HE LIKE AN OFFENSE BASED ON POWER, SPEED OR HIGH AVERAGES? He has increased the power in the lineup of each team that he has taken over. An odd thing, which goes against Craig's point, is that although Howser himself was an excellent judge of the strike zone and his one strongest point as a player was his ability to get on base, he has built a KC offense that doesn't get people on base, that walked the absurdly low total of 396 times in 1983.

DOES HE USE THE ENTIRE ROSTER OR DOES HE KEEP PEOPLE AROUND SITTING ON THE BENCH? 25-man team. The 25th man on the KC roster was Joe Simpson, and he got into 91 games.

DOES HE BUILD HIS BENCH AROUND YOUNG PLAYERS WHO CAN STEP INTO A BREACH IF NEED BE OR AROUND VETERAN ROLE-PLAYERS WHO HAVE THEIR OWN FUNCTIONS WITHIN A GAME? Veteran role-players, very much. Leon Roberts, Simpson, Jim Spencer. He has brought up some career minor leaguers and youngsters of medium promise (Dennis Werth, Joe Lefebvre).

GAME MANAGING AND USE OF STRATEGIES

DOES HE GO FOR THE BIG-INNING OFFENSE OR DOES HE LIKE TO USE THE ONE-RUN STRATEGIES? He is a complete, unqualified big-inning manager.

DOES HE PINCH-HIT MUCH, AND IF SO WHEN? Not much at all, no. When he does it's usually in response to an opposition switch from right to lefthanded pitcher, or the other way around. He will make quite a few defensive substitutions.

ANYTHING UNUSUAL ABOUT HIS LINEUP SELECTION? Has inherited well-defined lineups and largely stuck with them. He did have Frank White batting third for a while last year, but I don't kow whether I would describe that as "unusual" or "desperate."

DOES HE USE THE SAC BUNT OFTEN? Dick was involved in an incident with a traffic cop while leaving the stadium one night, replete with charges and counter-charges. Somebody wrote in to the paper and said, "I don't know whether Howser hit that cop, but I know for sure he didn't bunt him over."

It does, indeed, seem like a safe bet. Dick doesn't bunt much to begin with, but in the Royals he has a team that can steal bases with great success, so he has an obvious option if he wants to play for one run. So he doesn't bunt.

DOES HE LIKE TO USE THE RUNNING GAME? Yes; that's what he has the talent to do, and he does it.

IN WHAT CIRCUMSTANCES WILL HE ISSUE AN INTENTIONAL WALK? Whenever it snows in Florida in midseason.

DOES HE HIT AND RUN VERY OFTEN? No, not a lot.

ARE THERE ANY UNIQUE OR IDIOSYNCRATIC STRATEGIES THAT HE PARTICULARLY LIKES? One thing that seems odd for a big-inning manager is that he will bring the infield in early in the game to cut off a play at the plate. Say if he's behind 2–0, third inning, runner on third and one out, he will bring the infield in, thus risking a big inning to cut off the run at the plate. I've no idea what the percentages on the move are, but it seems a little odd for a man who in other respects believes that the games are going to be won by the big inning.

HANDLING THE PITCHING STAFF

DOES HE LIKE POWER PITCHERS OR PREFER TO GO WITH THE PEOPLE WHO PUT THE BALL IN PLAY? His Yankee staff was a power pitcher's staff; the Royals's staff has a conspicuous lack of an effective power pitcher. Can't really answer the question until he has to make some choices among pitching prospects.

DOES HE STAY WITH THE STARTER OR GO TO THE BULLPEN QUICKLY? He's always had Gossage or Quisenberry, so we've never seen him operate in a normal context. He was never too reluctant to get Quiz in the game last year, but I sense that he would like to have one pitcher that he could ask to go nine.

DOES HE LIKE THE FOUR-MAN OR THE FIVE-MAN ROTATION? Five-day rotation.

DOES HE USE THE ENTIRE STAFF OR DOES HE TRY TO GET FIVE OR SIX PEOPLE TO DO MOST OF THE WORK? Entire staff.

ARE THERE ANY PARTICULAR TYPES OF PITCHERS OF WHOM HE IS FOND? I imagine he's pretty fond of Goose Gossage and Dan Quisenberry.

IS THERE ANYTHING UNIQUE ABOUT HIS HANDLING OF HIS PITCHERS? He's been very effective with relief pitchers. You might remember that Goose Gossage in 1980 said that one of the reasons he had such a good year was that there were only two times all year that Howser got him up and then didn't bring him into the game, whereas under Billy he'd throw 200 innings a year in the bullpen.

Howser's gotten good work out of not only his #1 reliever, but also out of his #2 man (Davis in Minnesota, Armstrong in Kansas City).

Also, he doesn't seem to use a lefthanded spot pitcher much, unlike most managers today. He'll rarely bring in a lefthander to get one or two outs.

WHAT IS HIS STRONGEST POINT AS A MANAGER? His intensity, his command of details. He's in a difficult situation in Kansas City, where the fans still have expectations for a winner and the talent just doesn't justify those expectations. I have a lot of respect for him as a manager, but if he can turn them back around, he's Joe McCarthy, Jr.

IF THERE WERE NO PROFESSIONAL BASEBALL, WHAT WOULD THIS MANAGER PROBABLY BE DOING? Acting director of the National Alliance of High School football coaches.

Willie AIKENS, First Base
Runs Created: 78

	G	AB	Hit	2B	3B	HR	Run	RBI	BB	SO	SB	CS	Avg
4.13 Years		542	151	28	0	24	67	93	69	93	1	1	.278
1983	125	410	124	26	1	23	49	72	45	75	0	0	.302
First Half	54	179	60	20	1	6	20	26	20	26	0	0	.335
Second Half	71	231	64	6	0	17	29	46	25	49	0	0	.277
vs. RHP		325	107	22	1	22	44	65	37	53	0	0	.329
vs. LHP		85	17	4	0	1	5	7	8	22	0	0	.200
Home	59	189	60	10	1	11	24	35	21	32	0	0	.317
Road	66	221	64	16	0	12	25	37	24	43	0	0	.290
Grass	49	163	44	9	0	7	16	23	17	36	0	0	.270
Turf	76	247	80	17	1	16	33	49	28	39	0	0	.324

Willie WILSON, Centerfield
Runs Created: 72

	G	AB	Hit	2B	3B	HR	Run	RBI	BB	SO	SB	CS	Avg
5.20 Years		602	184	21	12	3	102	43	29	80	67	13	.305
1983	137	576	159	22	8	2	90	33	33	75	59	8	.276
First Half	74	318	92	14	4	1	53	15	20	36	39	4	.289
Second Half	63	258	67	8	4	1	37	18	13	39	20	4	.260
vs. RHP		394	108	15	3	1	65	20	23	51	52	5	.274
vs. LHP		182	51	7	5	1	25	13	10	24	7	3	.280
Home	66	275	83	13	6	2	49	23	19	33	34	6	.302
Road	71	301	76	9	2	0	41	10	14	42	25	2	.252
Grass	52	217	58	7	1	0	30	9	12	28	16	2	.267
Turf	85	359	101	15	7	2	60	24	21	47	43	6	.281

Frank WHITE, Second Base
Runs Created: 58

	G	AB	Hit	2B	3B	HR	Run	RBI	BB	SO	SB	CS	Avg
8.48 Years		530	137	27	5	8	64	57	24	65	17	7	.258
1983	146	549	143	35	6	11	52	77	20	51	13	5	.260
First Half	72	275	71	17	4	6	28	42	12	27	9	1	.258
Second Half	74	274	72	18	2	5	24	35	8	24	4	4	.263
vs. RHP		372	85	23	2	6	30	52	12	37	9	2	.228
vs. LHP		177	58	12	4	5	22	25	8	14	4	3	.328
Home	76	275	75	21	3	8	29	55	13	21	7	4	.273
Road	70	274	68	14	3	3	23	22	7	30	6	1	.248
Grass	53	209	53	8	3	1	18	12	3	21	3	1	.254
Turf	93	340	90	27	3	10	34	65	17	30	10	4	.265

Amos OTIS, Rightfield
Runs Created: 39

	G	AB	Hit	2B	3B	HR	Run	RBI	BB	SO	SB	CS	Avg
12.09 Years		596	166	31	5	16	90	82	62	82	28	8	.278
1983	98	356	93	16	3	4	35	41	27	63	5	2	.261
First Half	56	205	54	8	2	2	18	18	16	37	4	2	.263
Second Half	42	151	39	8	1	2	17	23	11	26	1	0	.258
vs. RHP		228	53	9	3	2	18	27	14	49	5	1	.232
vs. LHP		128	40	7	0	2	17	14	13	14	0	1	.313
Home	49	172	49	7	2	3	24	24	16	27	4	1	.285
Road	49	184	44	9	1	1	11	17	11	36	1	1	.239
Grass	38	143	32	7	1	1	10	14	7	28	1	0	.224
Turf	60	213	61	9	2	3	25	27	20	35	4	2	.286

George BRETT, Third Base
Runs Created: 100

	G	AB	Hit	2B	3B	HR	Run	RBI	BB	SO	SB	CS	Avg
8.38 Years		633	200	41	12	18	102	95	57	43	16	8	.316
1983	123	464	144	38	2	25	90	93	57	38	0	1	.310
First Half	49	184	67	18	1	14	46	47	29	15	0	1	.364
Second Half	74	280	77	20	1	11	44	46	28	23	0	0	.275
vs. RHP		304	106	30	2	19	63	71	44	17	0	1	.349
vs. LHP		160	38	8	0	6	27	22	13	21	0	0	.238
Home	56	200	63	19	2	7	41	35	28	17	0	0	.315
Road	67	264	81	19	0	18	49	58	29	21	0	1	.307
Grass	56	217	65	17	0	12	37	41	25	16	0	1	.300
Turf	67	247	79	21	2	13	53	52	32	22	0	0	.320

John WATHAN, Catcher
Runs Created: 39

	G	AB	Hit	2B	3B	HR	Run	RBI	BB	SO	SB	CS	Avg
4.34 Years		504	136	17	5	4	64	56	37	50	23	7	.270
1983	128	437	107	18	3	2	49	32	27	57	28	7	.245
First Half	64	219	60	8	3	1	26	19	19	26	17	3	.274
Second Half	64	218	47	10	0	1	23	13	8	31	11	4	.216
vs. RHP		277	70	13	2	2	30	20	20	42	18	5	.254
vs. LHP		161	37	5	1	0	19	12	7	15	10	3	.230
Home	67	231	52	12	1	2	31	15	10	21	15	1	.225
Road	61	206	55	6	2	0	18	17	17	36	13	6	.267
Grass	48	171	48	6	2	0	18	15	11	26	11	5	.281
Turf	80	266	59	12	1	2	31	17	16	31	17	2	.222

U. L. WASHINGTON, Shortstop
Runs Created: 59

	G	AB	Hit	2B	3B	HR	Run	RBI	BB	SO	SB	CS	Avg
4.28 Years		534	137	21	7	6	70	51	50	74	27	10	.256
1983	144	547	129	19	6	5	76	41	48	78	40	7	.236
First Half	72	275	63	12	5	2	34	21	28	36	16	4	.229
Second Half	72	272	66	7	1	3	42	20	20	42	24	3	.243
vs. RHP		354	89	14	4	0	50	22	38	52	33	5	.251
vs. LHP		193	40	5	2	5	26	19	10	26	7	2	.207
Home	71	259	53	8	1	4	34	19	30	39	21	1	.205
Road	73	288	76	12	4	4	42	22	18	39	19	6	.264
Grass	56	221	57	9	4	4	31	20	14	25	11	4	.258
Turf	88	326	72	10	2	1	45	21	34	53	29	3	.221

Hal McRAE, Designated Hitter
Runs Created: 98

	G	AB	Hit	2B	3B	HR	Run	RBI	BB	SO	SB	CS	Avg
10.72 Years		585	171	41	6	15	79	88	51	60	10	6	.292
1983	157	589	183	41	6	12	84	82	50	68	2	3	.311
First Half	73	277	89	24	2	4	45	41	25	29	1	1	.321
Second Half	84	312	94	17	4	8	39	41	25	39	1	2	.301
vs. RHP		398	118	21	4	7	55	51	29	43	1	2	.296
vs. LHP		191	65	20	2	5	29	31	21	25	1	1	.340
Home	78	290	99	24	5	5	47	45	27	29	2	1	.341
Road	79	299	84	17	1	7	37	37	23	39	0	2	.281
Grass	60	227	64	12	1	6	64	30	20	32	0	2	.282
Turf	97	362	119	29	5	6	20	52	30	36	2	1	.329

Pat SHERIDAN, Leftfield
Runs Created: 41

	G	AB	Hit	2B	3B	HR	Run	RBI	BB	SO	SB	CS	Avg
0.67 Years		495	134	18	3	10	64	54	30	95	18	4	.270
1983	109	333	90	12	2	7	43	36	20	64	12	3	.270
First Half	30	82	16	3	0	2	11	8	5	18	0	1	.195
Second Half	79	251	74	9	2	5	32	28	15	46	12	2	.295
vs. RHP		294	82	11	2	7	39	34	17	51	12	2	.279
vs. LHP		39	8	1	0	0	4	2	3	13	0	1	.205
Home	55	168	50	8	1	4	23	21	9	31	4	1	.298
Road	54	165	40	4	1	3	20	15	11	33	8	2	.242
Grass	44	129	28	2	1	3	28	12	10	29	7	2	.217
Turf	65	204	62	10	1	4	15	24	10	35	5	1	.304

Don SLAUGHT, Catcher
Runs Created: 34

	G	AB	Hit	2B	3B	HR	Run	RBI	BB	SO	SB	CS	Avg
0.78 Years		503	152	24	5	4	45	46	26	50	4	1	.302
1983	83	276	86	13	4	0	21	28	11	27	3	1	.312
First Half	31	95	21	3	0	0	3	9			0		.221
Second Half	52	181	65	10	4	0	18	19			3		.359
vs. RHP		159	47	7	2	0	11	16	5	15	2	1	.296
vs. LHP		117	39	6	2	0	10	12	6	12	1	0	.333
Home	38	123	40	7	2	0	15	13	7	7	0	0	.325
Road	45	153	46	6	2	0	6	15	4	20	3	1	.301
Grass	36	118	39	4	2	0	5	10	3	14	2	1	.331
Turf	47	158	47	9	2	0	16	18	8	13	1	0	.297

Larry GURA

Year	(W–L)	GS	Run	Avg	DP	Avg	SB	Avg
1982	(18-22)	37	185	5.00	29	.78	10	.27
1983	(11-18)	31	112	3.61	35	1.13	20	.64
1977-1983		192	893	4.65	176	.92	88	.46

	G	IP	W	L	Pct	ER	ERA
1982 Home	22	152	11	6	.647	64	3.79
1983 Home	15	85	7	5	.583	41	4.34
1982 Road	15	96	7	6	.538	47	4.41
1983 Road	19	115.1	4	13	.235	68	5.31
1983 Grass	14	91.2	4	9	.308	49	4.81
1983 Turf	20	108.2	7	9	.437	60	4.97

Gaylord PERRY

Year	(W–L)	GS	Run	Avg	DP	Avg	SB	Avg
1982	(10-12)	32	128	4.00	32	1.00	18	.56
1983	(7-14)	30	96	3.20	35	1.17	15	.50
1976-1983		252	978	3.88	241	.96	128	.51

	G	IP	W	L	Pct	ER	ERA
1982 Home	16	108.2	5	4	.554	59	4.89
1983 Home	15	85.2	4	7	.364	45	4.75
1982 Road	16	108	5	8	.385	47	3.92
1983 Road	15	100.2	3	7	.300	51	4.58
1983 Grass	12	80.3	3	5	.375	36	4.03
1983 Turf	18	104.4	4	9	.308	60	5.17

Paul SPLITTORFF

Year	(W–L)	GS	Run	Avg	DP	Avg	SB	Avg
1982	(10-10)	28	139	4.96	27	.96	16	.57
1983	(13- 8)	27	120	4.44	34	1.26	17	.63
1976-1983		236	1136	4.81	246	1.04	142	.60

	G	IP	W	L	Pct	ER	ERA
1982 Home	12	68	4	5	.444	32	4.20
1983 Home	15	84.1	6	5	.545	36	3.84
1982 Road	17	94	6	5	.545	41	3.93
1983 Road	12	71.2	7	3	.700	27	3.39
1983 Grass	8	48.1	4	2	.667	17	3.17
1983 Turf	19	107.2	9	6	.600	46	3.85

1983 Others

Pitcher	(W–L)	GS	Run	Avg	DP	Avg	SB	Avg
Renko	(6-11)	17	82	4.82	14	.82	21	1.23
Blue	(0- 5)	14	64	4.57	13	.93	14	1.00
Leonard	(6- 3)	10	33	3.30	10	1.00	6	.60
Creel	(2- 5)	10	39	3.90	9	.90	6	.60
Rasmussen	(3- 6)	9	31	3.44	8	.89	4	.44
Wills	(2- 1)	4	19	4.75	4	1.00	5	1.25
D. Jackson	(1- 1)	3	15	5.00	2	.67	2	.67

Bud BLACK

Year	(W–L)	GS	Run	Avg	DP	Avg	SB	Avg
1982	(4-6)	14	49	3.50	11	.79	10	.71
1983	(10-7)	24	125	5.21	30	1.25	8	.33
1982-1983		38	174	4.58	41	1.08	18	.47

	G	IP	W	L	Pct	ER	ERA
1982 Home	12	45.2	2	1	.667	20	3.94
1983 Home	10	68.2	4	2	.667	30	3.93
1982 Road	10	42.2	2	5	.286	25	5.27
1983 Road	14	92.2	6	5	.545	38	3.69
1983 Grass	11	71.2	4	4	.500	32	4.02
1983 Turf	13	89.2	6	3	.667	36	3.61

KANSAS CITY ROYALS
RUNS BATTED IN ANALYSIS

Player	RBI	RBI In Wins	Victory-Important RBI	RBI Importance	Wins Batted In	RBI Per Win
George Brett	93	59	37.19	.400	9.10	10.2
Willie Aikens	72	52	35.66	.495	9.26	7.8
Frank White	77	54	32.81	.426	9.61	8.0
Hal McRae	82	54	31.73	.387	8.27	9.9
U. L. Washington	41	26	19.14	.467	4.04	10.1
Amos Otis	41	30	16.56	.404	4.21	9.7
Pat Sheridan	36	23	16.20	.450	4.35	8.3
Willie Wilson	33	24	13.94	.422	3.81	8.7
Don Slaught	28	22	12.83	.458	3.91	7.2
John Wathan	32	18	11.20	.350	2.90	11.0

TEXAS RANGERS

I. RUNNING THE BASES

Baserunning is not an "intangible." Running the bases is one of baseball's unmeasured skills, and like all such skills tends to be ignored most of the time, and exaggerated to mythic proportions when it skips into the conversation. We don't really know how many runs result from unusually good or unusually bad baserunning. We don't know how often a good baserunner can go from first to third on a single, and we don't know how many chances he is likely to have to do so. We don't have any real idea how many baserunning mistakes which player will make during the course of a season.

Because we know so few specifics about the subject, we have a limited ability to discuss the issue. And so we don't, for the most part; then, feeling that we have neglected the issue, we attribute enormous significance to it when we do have cause to consider it.

But our ignorance on the subject is not inevitable. Baserunning is perfectly measurable; it can be easily defined and, given properly maintained scoresheets, easily researched. Our lack of knowledge on the subject is attributable entirely to record-keeping decisions that were made a little over a century ago and have never been intelligently or systematically reviewed. We know so much about hitting that we can talk about it forever and measure it with extraordinary precision because a few men, at the beginning of Time, made some very good decisions about how to record and organize information, decisions that are now so natural a part of our thinking about the game that it is difficult even to see that any decision had ever to be made.

For this we applaud them. Their decisions about baserunning and about fielding were much less wise. They failed to address many issues, and drew arbitrary lines where they drew them at all, and time has laid waste to their designs.

II. GOING FIRST TO THIRD

Ignorance that one has inherited from one's grandfather is not venerable or noble ignorance; it is only ignorance. Let us begin to chip away at this granite ignorance, baserunning.

Probably one of the largest elements of baserunning skill is the ability to go from first to third on a single. If it isn't, a lot of people are misrepresenting the subject. Amos Otis, when discussing a list of players from his generation who are still around: Yeah, but I'm the only one who can still go from first to third on a single. Any announcer, when discussing the St. Louis Cardinals or the Oakland Athletics, "They may not have a lot of power on this team, but they'll first-and-third you to death."

Well, how about it? How many times in a season does a player have a chance to go first-to-third on a single? A dozen? A hundred? Two hundred? Does he make it most of the time, or does he stop at second most of the time?

Does he go first-to-third 25% of the time? 45%? 70%? Is there much difference between one player's ability to go first-to-third and another's, or is it mostly dependent on the circumstances, where the hit goes and such like? If the fastest players do it 55% of the time, do the slowest do it 45%, or 35%, or what? How many runs can you pick up by this ability? Who are the best baserunners in this respect, and who are the worst?

All of these questions can be definitively answered for all teams once PROJECT SCORESHEET is completed; for now, we have to deal with them on a catch-as-catch-can basis. Craig Wright sends me the scoresheets from the Ranger games, and thus we have here a chance to study the issue, for one team, for an entire season. I went through those scoresheets for the 1983 season, and recorded every occasion in which one Ranger was on first base, and another Ranger hit a single. There were 327 such occasions, an average of two per game. To have this information is no substitute for complete data, but it goes a long way toward establishing the scale of the ability.

The best players on the Ranger team at going first-to-third on a single, as it turns out, are the two fast outfielders, George Wright and Bill Sample. Each went from first-to-third on a single about 50% of the time. Wright was on first base when a single was hit 38 times, and he went to third 20 times; Sample was on first when a single was hit 33 times and he made it to third 16 times. Neither Wright nor Sample was thrown out trying to go from first-to-third all season, although several other Rangers were. Dave Hostetler, on the other hand, went from first-to-third on a single only one time all year. The complete data for all the Ranger players is given in Chart Ranger-1.

The chart answers the first question: *Does it really make any difference who the baserunner is?* It makes a lot of difference. Some baserunners go first-to-third when a single is hit 50% of the time—others, 10% or less. Assuming that the player is on first when a single is hit about 35 to 40 times in the course of a season, that difference should amount to about 14 to 16 bases a year.

How often does an average runner go from first-to-third when a single is hit? For the team as a whole, runners went from first-to-third on a single 99 times on 327 hits, or 30% of the time. They were thrown out at third base five times—Parrish twice, O'Brien, Tolleson, and Sundberg once each. So only a very good baserunner can go from first-to-third on a single 50% of the time, but the Rangers were successful 95% of the time when they did attempt it. There were also three occasions during the season in which a runner scored from first on a single—Sample did it once, O'Brien once and Tolleson once; Tolleson, however, was thrown out twice trying to score from first on a single.

Who were the best baserunners on the team, looking at this skill? The runners who made it to third subsequently scored 56 times, or 56.6% of the time. Those who stopped at second subsequently scored 92 times, or 41.3% of the time. With this information, we can rate the players as baserunners according to the number of runs they could expect to score from the position they reached. If the player scores from first, that is one full run; if he makes it to third, .566 of a run; if he stops at second, .413 of a run; if he is thrown out at any base, .000 of a run. The ratings for the regulars and near-regulars are given in Chart Ranger-2.

Sample rates as the #1 baserunner on the team, on the basis of this study, followed by Wright, O'Brien and Rivers. Buddy Bell, not exceptionally fast, is still a good baserunner; Bell went from first-to-third on a single hit to right about as often as any player on the team, but rarely tried to go to third on balls hit to left or center. He was never thrown out trying. Tolleson's ranking as a baserunner is hurt, as it should be, by the times he was thrown out trying to do too much, and apart from that he didn't go first-to-third as often as Sample or Wright or Rivers. Bucky Dent and Hostetler rarely went from first-to-third, but were not thrown out trying; Parrish went first-to-third only six times all year and was thrown out twice trying, so he ranks below them. Jim Sundberg, who wasn't all that fast before he caught 1,400 games, brings up the rear.

In most cases, the number of runs the player could have been expected to score and the number that he actually did score are very close to each other; if you rounded the "expectation" off to the nearest integer, it would be within one of the actual number of runs the player scored in these circumstances in all cases except Sample (expectation of 16, scored 20), Wright (expected 19, scored 21) and Bell (expected 18, scored 16). So if you ranked them by actual runs scored following these conditions, rather than expected runs, you'd get about the same thing.

How large are the differences? About four runs a year, top to bottom. Sample is rated at .4999, Sundberg at .4070; there is a difference between the two players of .0929 of a run every time one of them is on first when a single is hit. On the basis of 35 to 40 opportunities a year, that's three or four runs.

How often does the player go from first-to-third on a single to rightfield, as opposed to a single to left or center? I marked the singles as to whether they were infield singles, singles to left, center or rightfield. When the ball was hit to rightfield, the runner went to third over half the time (52/98). The best runners on the team went first-to-third on a single to right about 70% of the time (Sample 9/13, O'Brien 7/9, Wright 12/17, Rivers 4/6, Bell 8/11). Dent, Parrish and Sundberg among them went first-to-third on a single to right eight times in 23 opportunities, or 35%.

When the ball was hit to center, the runner went to third 31% of the time (25/80), with the best runners in this case around 50%. When the ball was hit to left, the runner went to third only 18% of the time (20/114), with only Sample (4/8) and O'Brien (2/6) over 30%, given five or more tries.

There were only two cases all year in which a Texas runner went from first-to-third on an infield single. In both cases, the runner who did that was Billy Sample.

An alternative ranking system would be to list the players according to the number of times that they went first-to-third, but in consideration of where the hits were. Wright went from first-to-third slightly over 50% of the time while Sample was slightly under 50%. But when Wright was on first there were 17 singles to rightfield and only 4 infield singles, whereas when Sample was on first there were 13 singles to right and 7 infield singles. So if you compared the number of actual times going to third base with the number of expected times going to third base in consideration of where the ball was hit, Sample again would edge Wright as the Ranger's best baserunner.

CHART RANGER-1

Player	Oppor	Adv	Percent
Wright	38	20	.526
Rivers	14	7	.500
Sample	33	16	.485
Tolleson	26	11	.423
O'Brien	32	13	.408
Bell	38	15	.395
Stein	19	4	.211
Parrish	37	6	.162
Dent	30	4	.133
Sundberg	19	2	.105
Hostetler	15	1	.067
Dunbar	1	0	.000
Richardt	1	0	.000
Wilkerson	2	0	.000
Jones	2	0	.000
Biitner	4	0	.000
Anderson	5	0	.000
Johnson	11	0	.000

In this chart, "Oppor" stands for opportunities, the number of times the player was on first when a single was hit. "Adv" stands for advanced, the number of times he went to third.

CHART RANGER-II

Player	Exp	Oppor	Rate
Sample	16.50	33	.4999
O'Brien	15.78	32	.4931
Wright	18.74	38	.4931
Rivers	6.85	14	.4891
Bell	17.97	38	.4730
Tolleson	11.30	26	.4347
Dent	12.99	30	.4330
Hostetler	6.34	15	.4228
Parrish	15.36	37	.4151
Sundberg	7.73	19	.4070

On this chart, "Exp" stands for expected runs scored based on position following play. "Oppor" again stands for opportunities, and "Rate" stands for expected runs scored per opportunity.

III. REACHING ON AN ERROR

Going first-to-third is just one baserunning skill. Another unmeasured part of baserunning is the ability to take advantage of a defensive lapse. I have moaned elsewhere in this book about the fact that no records are maintained of how often each batter reaches base on an error.

Well, how about it? *Which Ranger players reached base most often on an opposition error?*

Buddy Bell led, reaching base 13 times on opposition errors. He was followed by: Sample, 12; Parrish, 9; O'Brien, 7; Tolleson, 7; Rivers, 6; Sundberg, 6; Wright, 6; Hostetler, 5; Richardt, 5; Dent, 3; Johnson, 3; Anderson, 2; Stein, 2; Biitner, 2; and Jones, 1.

If you add that up, you get 88. There were 132 errors committed by Ranger opponents in 1983; the other 44 (exactly one-third) did not put a player on base. Not to downgrade "advancement" errors or anything, but errors which put men on base are probably about three times as costly as those which serve only to move a runner along.

Of those errors which did put a runner on, the huge majority occurred on ground balls hit to the infield; a majority occurred on ground balls hit to shortstop or third base. The complete breakdown follows:

Runners Reaching	
Ground balls hit to third	24
Ground balls hit to short	22
Ground balls hit to second	14
Ground balls hit to first	14
Fly balls to center	3
Fly balls to left	3
Fly balls to right	2
Balls hit in air to second	2
Balls hit in air to first	2
Ground balls hit to the mound	2
Total	88

Craig considers all balls ground balls if they do or would hit the ground before landing in the outfield grass, a description that I don't really agree with, and so the "ground ball" total above could be a little misleading; some of those might better be described as "soft liners" or "not-so-soft liners."

A look at who reaches base on an error how often reveals two things: righthanded batters reach base on an error quite a bit more often than lefthanded batters, and fast runners reach base on errors a little bit more often than slow runners. The righthanded batters on the Ranger roster reached base on errors 60 times in 3,422 at-bats, or once every 57 at-bats. The lefthanders and switch-hitters reached 28 times in 2,188 at-bats, or once every 78 at-bats. This is because the righthanded batters pull the ball to the third baseman and the shortstop, who have a) a much more difficult throw to make and b) far less time to recover if a ball handcuffs them. If a batter rips the ball right at the first baseman, and he knocks it and it rolls away from him, he can probably still recover in time to flip the ball to the pitcher covering. If the same thing happens to the third baseman, it's an error. So a right-handed batter who hits .295 probably reaches base as often as a lefthanded batter who hits .300.

I divided the roster arbitrarily into fast runners and slow runners. The fast men were (alphabetically arbitrarily) Capra, Dunbar, Richardt, Rivers, Sample, Tolleson, Wilkerson and Wright; the others were considered slow. The fast men reached on errors 36 times in 2,115 at-bats, or once every 59 at-bats. The slower men were 52/3,495, or one per 67.

IV. BASERUNNING ERRORS

Another thing we need to know is, how many times a year is a runner put out on the base paths? I made another trip through the Ranger scoresheets, and I charged "Baserunning Errors."

A baserunning error occurs whenever a baserunner surrenders a base to which he is entitled, resulting in the loss of a baserunner to his team, but not a caught stealing.

Got that? Basically, it's a baserunning error if you get put out on the basepaths when it's not a forceout, a fielder's choice or a caught stealing. There was only one situation all year that was at all tricky to record, and in that case how it should be recorded is clear. The situation was this: Tolleson was on second when a ground ball was hit to short. Tolleson tried to go to third, and a quick 6–5–4 rundown developed. However, the batter, Billy Sample, tried to go to second on the play, and he too was tagged out. How do you score it?

You can't charge them both with baserunning errors because only one runner is lost. Sample gets the B.E. Tolleson's attempt to go to third cost the Rangers a base, but not a baserunner. Sample attempted to go to second to recover the base, and in the process he lost the runner. So he gets the error.

Later on, I'll throw the pickoffs out of this group and into their own. For now, we'll consider them with the others.

The Rangers lost 48 baserunners during the 1983 season—3 per 10 games. That almost certainly is a lower-than-average total. The circumstances in which those runners were lost are given below:

Thrown out trying to score from second on a single	7 times
Thrown out trying to advance after fly ball	6 times
Batter out at second after throw to another base	6 times
Trying to go first-to-third on a single	5 times
Picked off by pitcher	5 times
Batter out at third after throw home	4 times
Thrown out stretching a hit with no one on base	4 times
Thrown out at home on a double	3 times
Trying to score from first on a single	2 times
Lost track of count and wandered off base	1 time
Trying to score from second on E6	1 time
Doubled off first on D7	1 time
Picked off first after single, throw home	1 time
Trying for third after 2-base E9	1 time
Trying to take second during a rundown	1 time

The runners who were guilty of these infractions are detailed in Chart Ranger-III. Wayne Tolleson was by far the most aggressive runner on the team, surrendering a secure position eleven times. Oddly enough, none of the bit players—Biittner or Johnson or Jones—was put out unnecessarily on the basepaths all year.

One way to use this data—both the number of times reaching base on errors and the number of times being put out on the bases—would be to include it in the player's on-base percentage. The official American League stats list Tolleson with an on-base percentage of .320 and Rivers with .312. In reality, however, Rivers was on base more often than Tolleson was; he reached base more often on errors and was put out on the bases less often. His on-base percentage, adjusted for these things, is .327; Tolleson's is .313.

CHART RANGER - III
ADJUSTED ON-BASE PERCENTAGES

	AB	H	BB	HBP	OBP	SE	BE	AOBP
Pete O'Brien, 1b	524	124	58	1	.314	7	4	.319
Wayne Tolleson, 2b	470	122	40	2	.320	7	11	.313
Buddy Bell, 3b	618	171	50	4	.335	13	7	.344
Bucky Dent, ss	417	99	23	1	.279	3	3	.279
Billy Sample, lf	554	152	44	5	.333	12	5	.345
George Wright, cf	634	175	41	2	.322	6	4	.325
Larry Parrish, rf	555	151	46	3	.331	9	5	.338
Jim Sundberg, c	378	76	35	2	.272	6	2	.282
Dave Hostetler, dh	304	67	42	5	.325	5	4	.328
Mickey Rivers, dh	309	88	11	1	.312	6	1	.327
Bill Stein, inf	232	72	8	0	.333	2	2	.333

Categories are At Bats (AB), Hits (H), Walks (BB), Hit By Pitch (HBP), Official On-Base Percentage (OBP), Safe on Error (SE), Baserunning Errors (BE) and Adjusted On-Base Percentage (AOBP).

This chart would tend to confirm the idea that Sample and Rivers were the best baserunners on the team. Sample's on-base percentage is adjusted upward by .012, Rivers' by .015. O'Brien and Bell again are portrayed as above-average baserunners; Tolleson, again, is making rookie mistakes. Sundberg and Parrish do better this time.

V. CONCLUSIONS

Most of what needs to be known about baserunning could probably be adequately included in the records with the addition of four columns to the league statistics: bases gained, reached on error, baserunning errors and pickoffs. A "base gained" would be credited to a runner whenever he reached a base beyond the routine advancement of a hit, walk, error or HBP. He would be credited with a base gained whenever he moved up on an out, took two bases on a single or three on a double. He would be charged with a baserunning error whenever he attempted to do so and cost his team a runner. Being picked off a base is really a separate thing and should be treated as such, following the principle that unlike occurrences should not be lumped together as long as it is reasonably simple to distinguish among them.

Baserunning has not been totally neglected by the game's statistics. Stolen bases and caught stealing are baserunning statistics; grounding into double plays could be considered such. When a player "legs" an extra base onto a single, he is credited with a double. That is as it should be; it would be artificial and forced to sort out of all doubles those which, in someone's opinion, are doubles of the cleat rather than doubles of the ash. Baserunning is automatically "counted" in that way.

But there have been, at the same time, serious oversights. Outs which result from baserunning mistakes or baserunning decisions that don't work out well are not accounted for, from an offensive standpoint, in any way at all. This is a glaring oversight, and a curious one in view of the meticulous way that everything else that comprises an offense is drawn into a full circle.

There was at one period in the game's history an attempt to include bases gained by baserunners in the records by counting them as stolen bases. Some find this strange; I don't find it strange in the least. It's a perfectly natural grouping.

But the mistake was not in redefining the stolen base to exclude bases gained on hits and outs. The mistake was in carelessly throwing away that part of the old information which did not fit the new definition. We've been doing it wrong for 86 years now. That, to me, is no reason to do it wrong for another 86.

THE MANAGER

NAME: Doug Rader

AGE: 39 (three months older than Ed Kranepool)

MANAGERS FOR WHOM PLAYED IN MAJORS: Grady Hatton, Harry Walker, Leo Durocher, Preston Gomez, Bill Virdon, John McNamara, Alvin Dark, Roy Hartsfield.

CHARACTERISTICS AS A PLAYER: He was a good player, one of the three or four active managers who was a good player. He was the National League's Golden Glove third baseman of his time, and he was a .250 hitter but a .250 hitter who could get on base some and drive in some runs.

MANAGERIAL RECORD

Team	Year	Par	Wins	Losses	Pct.	+ or −
Texas	1983	76	77	85	.475	+1

WHAT HE BRINGS TO THE BALLCLUB

IS HE AN INTENSE MANAGER OR MORE OF AN EASY-TO-GET-ALONG-WITH TYPE? He's an upbeat, positive person; probably would classify him as easy-to-get-along-with.

IS HE MORE OF AN EMOTIONAL LEADER OR A DECISION-MAKER? He's both, an emotional leader and a decision-maker. That's one reason I think he'll be successful over a period of years.

IS HE MORE OF AN OPTIMIST OR MORE OF A PROBLEM SOLVER? I'd say more inclined to address a problem.

HOW HE USES HIS PERSONNEL

DOES HE FAVOR A SET LINEUP OR A ROTATION SYSTEM? He was using a set lineup last year.

DOES HE LIKE TO PLATOON? Only one year; he was platooning only at the DH spot.

DOES HE TRY TO SOLVE HIS PROBLEMS WITH PROVEN PLAYERS OR WITH YOUNGSTERS WHO STILL HAVE SOMETHING TO PROVE? HOW MANY PLAYERS HAS HE MADE REGULARS OUT OF WHO WERE NOT REGULARS BEFORE, AND WHO WERE THEY? Made regulars out of O'Brien and Tolleson, increased playing time for Sample, has traded for Ned Yost for catcher's spot.

DOES HE PREFER TO GO WITH GOOD OFFENSIVE PLAYERS OR DOES HE LIKE THE GLOVE MEN? O'Brien (a glove man) took playing time away from Lamar Johnson; the Rangers's improvement last year was largely a defensive improvement (48 runs offensive improvement, 140 runs defensive improvement).

DOES HE LIKE AN OFFENSE BASED ON

POWER, SPEED, OR HIGH AVERAGES? He's been talking about trying to get more speed in the lineup.

DOES HE USE THE ENTIRE ROSTER OR DOES HE KEEP PEOPLE AROUND SITTING ON THE BENCH? Fourteen Rangers players batted a hundred or more times, which is about average.

DOES HE BUILD HIS BENCH AROUND YOUNG PLAYERS WHO CAN STEP INTO A BREACH IF NEED BE OR AROUND VETERAN ROLE-PLAYERS WHO HAVE THEIR OWN FUNCTIONS WITHIN A GAME? His bench last year was mostly veterans (Stein, Biitner, Rivers. Anderson isn't a kid).

GAME MANAGING AND USE OF STRATEGIES

DOES HE GO FOR THE BIG-INNING OFFENSE OR DOES HE LIKE TO USE THE ONE-RUN STRATEGIES? With this team he really doesn't have big-inning talent, but he didn't use one-run strategies too much.

DOES HE PINCH-HIT MUCH, AND IF SO WHEN? Used 118 pinch-hitters last year (about average).

Since joining the Rangers three years ago, Bill Stein has hit .450, .353 and .333 as a pinch-hitter, totalling 27 hits in 72 tries (.375).

ANYTHING UNUSUAL ABOUT HIS LINEUP SELECTION? No.

DOES HE USE THE SAC BUNT OFTEN? No, he does not.

DOES HE LIKE TO USE THE RUNNING GAME? As mentioned, I think he'd like to do more of it.

Doug was quoted as saying last fall that he thought that Larry Parrish, hitting the ball the way he was hitting it last year, would have hit 35 or 40 home runs in many other parks (Parrish actually did hit 10 home runs at home last year, 16 on the road, so the statement seems reasonable). Because of this, he reportedly said something like, "You can keep the guys who hit home runs; give me the people who can run."

We are so much in the habit of thinking of speed as the alternative to power that it is tempting, when you find out that you can't work with power because of circumstances, to turn to speed. But what I would say is, if you can't get power then you should concentrate on trying to get more people on base. The Rangers were 13th in the league in home runs last year, but they were also 13th in the league in the number of people they had on base. That is definitely an unlucky combination. First, try to get some people who hit for a high average. Next, try to get some people who will take a walk, get on base that way. Then worry about speed. Because speed don't mean a damn thing if you're not on base. If you've got to go back

to the bench after you take your turn at bat, it doesn't matter how fast you get there.

IN WHAT CIRCUMSTANCES WILL HE ISSUE AN INTENTIONAL WALK? The Rangers gave out only 25 intentional walks last year, down from 68 the year before, so that clearly places Rader in the class with Billy Martin and Dick Howser of men who aren't anxious to give anything away.

I went through the Ranger scoresheets and found 23 of those 25 intentional walks; couldn't find the other two. Of those 23:

(a) Ten were issued in the first third of the season, nine in the middle third, four in the final third. Meaning, apparently, that Rader was not growing any fonder of them as the season went on.

(b) Two were issued with nobody out in the inning, nine with one out, 12 with two out. More than half of them, then, did not set up a possible double play.

(c) There were eleven times when the IBB (intentional base on balls) gained a platoon advantage for the Rangers, eleven times when it did not. There was one time (only one time, surprisingly) when it would have gained a platoon advantage but for a response maneuver by the opposing manager. Probably the largest reason why there was only one time when that happened was that Rader hardly ever walked the number six hitter to pitch to the number seven hitter or something, where the opposing manager could respond. Most of his IBB were in the middle of the order; he would walk George Brett to pitch to Hal McRae, or walk Baines to pitch to Luzinski. He wouldn't walk one bad hitter to pitch to another one. The only bad hitter in the league that he walked was Rich Dauer, and he did that twice. Otherwise, it was Upshaw, Baines, Brett, Cooper, Simmons, Parrish, people like that.

(d) Only one IBB was given when there was only a runner on third base. Nine were given with a runner on second, 13 with runners on both second and third.

(e) Making arbitrary decisions about who is a significantly better hitter than who, there were twelve times when the walk was issued to pitch to a significantly worse hitter than the man passed, eleven times when the next man up was substantially as good a hitter as the man walked. There was one time early in the year when he walked Remy to pitch to Wade Boggs, and after the All-Star break he walked Rance Mulliniks to pitch to Lloyd Moseby.

(f) There were only two times all year when he issued walks when he had the lead; in both of these cases, he was putting the potential lead on base. (He got by with it both times.) Eight intentional walks were given with the score tied, thirteen with the Rangers behind.

So, remembering (e) and (f), what he was saying with the intentional walk was that there probably wasn't a lot of difference between being behind 4–1 or being behind 5–1, whereas there was a big difference between being behind 2–1 or 4–1. So if he could set up a double play, plus get a platoon advantage or pitch to a worse hitter, he would take the chance. That makes sense.

(g) Runners coming up after the IBB went just five-for-22 against the Rangers with one walk. But it was a loud 5-for-22. Three of the five hits were doubles and one was a grand-slam home run by Steve Balboni, a fourth-inning shot that broke open a scoreless game. (He had walked Piniella to pitch to Balboni.) So that's a .227 batting average, but a .500 slugging percentage and 11 RBI.

(h) After the intentional walk, the Rangers got out of the inning without another run scoring 16 times. But five times the opponents blew the game open after the intentional walk, scoring four more runs three times, three more runs once and two virtually decisive runs once. Nineteen more runs were scored in 23 innings.

(i) There were five times when the hitter who was walked subsequently scored.

(j) The Rangers won/lost record in games in which an intentional walk was given was 3–18 (there were two games in which they gave two IBB). In view of the fact that they were tied up or ahead at the time of the walk ten of the 23 times, that doesn't seem too good.

(k) Only five of the 23 walks were issued at times when a run would have ended the game.

If we had this kind of data for an entire league, we could "tag" the situations so as to identify the guiding strategies under which the walks were given, examine the results under each strategy, and evaluate empirically the outcome of the various types of situations in which an intentional walk was given. With a sample of 23 intentional walks, obviously, we can't begin to do that. I was just trying to get you to think about it when you go to a game, ask yourself, "What is it that the manager is risking, and what is he gaining? If he is doing it with nobody out in the inning, he is gaining a platoon advantage, he may also be giving Greg Luzinski a chance to put the game away. What is the gamble here?"

I was at a Dodgers/Mets game in Shea last year (August 31) in which Lasorda ordered Valenzuela to walk Jose Oquendo and pitch to get Mike Torrez for the third out in an inning. The game is tied 1-1, bottom of the fourth, Jose Oquendo against Fernando Valenzuela, runner on second. And you're going to walk Jose Oquendo? I was there with another hardcore baseball fan, a SABR member, and he thought it was a good play, but I was just appalled. I thought it was the worst managerial strategem I saw during the 1983 season. My feeling is, any time you're in trouble and you have a chance to get out of it with Jose Oquendo, you better get down on your knees and thank the Lord.

I know it may be tempting to use the pitcher as an escape hatch for any kind of trouble that you're in, but stop and think about it. If Oquendo were to hit a single, which is the worst he's going to do to you, so what? You're one run behind, you've got the pitcher at the plate and a man on first, and you're all but out of it. But if you issue a walk and the pitcher hits a single, as he did, then you've got 1) a runner in scoring position, and 2) the top of the order coming up, and 3) a run in.

In the situation the Dodgers were in, they had two escape hatches—they had Oquendo, and then they had Torrez. By passing up Oquendo, they left themselves with no easy way out of the mess after Torrez singled; Mookie Wilson followed with a home run and the ballgame was over. 5 to 1, just like that.

Lasorda was thinking about one batter—Torrez rather than Oquendo. He should have been thinking about two batters, Torrez and Wilson, rather than Oquendo and Torrez. He was thinking one run, and totally ignoring the possibility of a big inning that was right in front of him. He dodged out of the way of a bicycle and into the path of a truck.

But even if it had been guaranteed to work, it was still a bad play. Because the third thing he wasn't doing was, he wasn't looking at the next inning. If he had gotten Oquendo out, then Torrez would have been leading off the next inning. That is a big item, the difference between Mookie Wilson leading off an inning, and Mike Torrez leading it off. The difference is probably (what?) a third of a run, maybe? Lasorda, apart from the fact that he was making the wrong decision for the inning that he was playing, was just handing the Mets a third of a run in the next inning.

Because he wasn't doing what you and I are doing right now. He wasn't saying, "What am I risking here, and what am I gaining?"

There were only two times among the 23 intentional walks that Rader issued that he risked setting up a subsequent big inning in an attempt to get out of his current mess.

DOES HE HIT AND RUN VERY OFTEN? Quite a bit, yes.

ARE THERE ANY UNIQUE OR IDIOSYNCRATIC STRATEGIES THAT HE PARTICULARLY LIKES? Likes to steal third base or have his runner go to 3rd on a grounder to third.

HANDLING THE PITCHING STAFF

DOES HE LIKE POWER PITCHERS OR PREFER TO GO WITH THE PEOPLE WHO PUT THE BALL IN PLAY? The Rangers are going to power pitchers.

DOES HE STAY WITH THE STARTER OR GO TO THE BULLPEN QUICKLY? He'll go a long time with the starter; he's not anxious to turn the game over to his bullpen.

DOES HE LIKE THE FOUR-MAN OR THE FIVE-MAN ROTATION? Was using five last year.

DOES HE USE THE ENTIRE STAFF OR DOES HE TRY TO GET FIVE OR SIX PEOPLE TO DO MOST OF THE WORK? He was experimenting some in the bullpen, trying to find the right roles for everybody, so they all got some work.

ARE THERE ANY PARTICULAR TYPES OF PITCHERS OF WHOM HE IS FOND? Too soon to tell.

IS THERE ANYTHING UNIQUE ABOUT HIS HANDLING OF HIS PITCHERS? Not yet.

WHAT IS HIS STRONGEST POINT AS A MANAGER? In an article for *Esquire* magazine before the 1983 season, I stepped whimsically into the future and looked back on 1983 from a distance. My summary of the Texas Rangers: Doug Rader began his remarkable managerial career, which would last well into the 21st century, by conjuring a pitching staff out of thin talent. Obviously, nothing that happened here during the year is going to cause me to review that assessment. He did exactly what I had expected him to do. He took advantage of the strengths of the Ranger roster, and visualized a game that they were capable of winning.

A lot was made a year ago of Rader's reputation as a clown when he was younger. Well, Casey Stengel was one of the most famous clowns in baseball history. One of the hardest jobs that a manager has can be to keep the season from getting too long, to keep the pressure from building up. A sense of humor and an ability to enjoy life can be a tremendously valuable weapon in that cause. Wouldn't you rather work for somebody who has a sense of humor than for somebody who doesn't?

So he likes to be center stage. That's great; every good manager likes to be center stage. Earl Weaver liked to be center stage. Leo Durocher liked to be center stage. Whitey Herzog likes to be center stage, and Billy Martin and Tommy Lasorda. Casey Stengel liked to be center stage, and John McGraw. A manager is supposed to be a presence.

Strengths: 1) His respect for knowledge, his desire to learn more and understand more about the game, and 2) his strong ego and positive mental attitude.

IF THERE WERE NO PROFESSIONAL BASEBALL, WHAT WOULD THIS MANAGER PROBABLY BE DOING? Popular country and Western entertainer, singer/comedian, a regular on "Hee Haw."

Pete O'BRIEN, First Base
Runs Created: 58

	G	AB	Hit	2B	3B	HR	Run	RBI	BB	SO	SB	CS	Avg
1.07 Years		550	130	26	6	11	61	61	60	65	6	4	.237
1983	154	524	124	24	5	8	53	53	58	62	5	4	.237
First Half	76	266	63	10	4	3	35	26	31	36	5	1	.237
Second Half	78	258	61	14	1	5	18	27	27	26	0	3	.236
vs. RHP		381	85	17	4	8	42	40	43	36	3	4	.223
vs. LHP		143	39	7	1	0	11	13	15	26	2	0	.273
Home	79	264	69	15	4	4	35	32	34	34	2	1	.261
Road	75	260	55	9	1	4	18	21	24	28	3	3	.212
Grass	130	441	106	21	5	6	47	46	53	56	4	2	.240
Turf	24	83	18	3	0	2	6	7	5	6	1	2	.217

George WRIGHT, Centerfield
Runs Created: 84

	G	AB	Hit	2B	3B	HR	Run	RBI	BB	SO	SB	CS	Avg
1.93 Years		618	167	25	6	15	77	68	37	83	6	7	.270
1983	162	634	175	28	6	18	79	80	41	82	8	7	.276
First Half	78	298	83	15	3	7	40	44	24	48	6	5	.279
Second Half	84	336	92	13	3	11	39	36	17	34	2	2	.274
vs. RHP		424	122	21	4	8	53	48	27	49	7	6	.288
vs. LHP		210	53	7	2	10	26	32	14	33	1	1	.252
Home	81	315	84	16	3	7	40	43	24	43	4	4	.267
Road	81	319	91	12	3	11	39	37	17	39	4	3	.285
Grass	136	537	147	22	5	14	69	74	33	77	7	7	.274
Turf	26	97	28	6	1	4	10	6	8	5	1	0	.289

Wayne TOLLESON, Second Base
Runs Created: 51

	G	AB	Hit	2B	3B	HR	Run	RBI	BB	SO	SB	CS	Avg
1.15 Years		491	117	12	2	3	66	20	40	76	31	10	.238
1983	134	470	122	13	2	3	64	20	40	68	33	10	.260
First Half	64	225	66	10	2	2	36	11	16	41	18	3	.293
Second Half	70	245	56	3	0	1	28	9	24	27	15	7	.229
vs. RHP		309	80	9	1	0	38	8	25	48	25	8	.259
vs. LHP		161	42	4	1	3	26	12	15	20	8	2	.261
Home	70	240	66	6	1	2	32	8	22	44	17	8	.275
Road	64	230	56	7	1	1	32	12	18	24	16	2	.243
Grass	112	385	105	11	1	2	54	18	32	60	26	10	.273
Turf	22	85	17	2	1	1	10	2	8	8	7	0	.200

Larry PARRISH, Rightfield
Runs Created: 82

	G	AB	Hit	2B	3B	HR	Run	RBI	BB	SO	SB	CS	Avg
7.65 Years		576	152	33	4	19	73	78	42	103	3	4	.264
1983	145	555	151	26	4	26	76	88	46	91	0	0	.272
First Half	65	249	72	13	2	13	43	40	27	33	0	0	.289
Second Half	80	306	79	13	2	13	33	48	19	58	0	0	.258
vs. RHP		383	106	19	2	19	50	60	28	62	0	0	.277
vs. LHP		172	45	7	2	7	26	28	18	29	0	0	.262
Home	71	275	81	15	3	10	32	36	26	49	0	0	.295
Road	74	280	70	11	1	16	44	52	20	42	0	0	.250
Grass	124	478	133	23	3	23	67	75	43	78	0	0	.278
Turf	21	77	18	3	1	3	9	13	3	13	0	0	.234

Buddy BELL, Third Base
Runs Created: 78

	G	AB	Hit	2B	3B	HR	Run	RBI	BB	SO	SB	CS	Avg
10.36 Years		616	175	29	4	13	78	74	51	52	4	6	.284
1983	156	618	171	35	3	14	75	66	50	48	3	5	.277
First Half	77	315	90	19	2	10	46	42	29	30	3	3	.286
Second Half	79	303	81	16	1	4	29	24	21	18	0	2	.267
vs. RHP		421	112	22	3	11	49	53	32	33	2	3	.266
vs. LHP		197	59	13	0	3	26	13	18	15	1	2	.299
Home	76	306	92	14	1	8	42	37	26	22	2	3	.301
Road	80	312	79	21	2	6	33	29	24	26	1	2	.253
Grass	130	518	137	24	2	11	63	54	42	44	2	5	.264
Turf	26	100	34	11	1	3	12	12	8	4	1	0	.340

Jim SUNDBERG, Catcher
Runs Created: 26

	G	AB	Hit	2B	3B	HR	Run	RBI	BB	SO	SB	CS	Avg
8.63 Years		515	130	22	3	6	53	65	60	73	2	4	.253
1983	131	378	76	14	0	2	30	28	35	64	0	4	.201
First Half	68	219	46	8	0	1	19	16	15	41	0	2	.210
Second Half	63	159	30	6	0	1	11	12	20	23	0	2	.189
vs. RHP		254	49	7	0	2	20	20	21	47	0	4	.193
vs. LHP		124	27	7	0	0	10	8	14	17	0	0	.218
Home	68	195	45	11	0	0	18	16	18	28	0	1	.231
Road	63	183	31	3	0	2	12	12	17	36	0	3	.169
Grass	111	319	69	13	0	0	27	23	32	49	0	3	.216
Turf	20	59	7	1	0	2	3	5	3	15	0	1	.119

Bucky DENT, Shortstop
Runs Created: 35

	G	AB	Hit	2B	3B	HR	Run	RBI	BB	SO	SB	CS	Avg
8.52 Years		528	130	20	3	5	53	50	38	41	2	3	.247
1983	131	417	99	15	2	2	36	34	23	31	3	7	.237
First Half	75	254	67	11	2	0	24	23	15	18	3	4	.264
Second Half	56	163	32	4	0	2	12	11	8	13	0	3	.196
vs. RHP		282	65	10	0	0	21	24	14	21	0	5	.230
vs. LHP		135	34	5	2	2	15	10	9	10	3	2	.252
Home	73	237	62	10	0	0	17	19	5	15	1	2	.262
Road	58	180	37	5	2	2	19	15	18	16	2	5	.206
Grass	113	364	83	12	1	2	31	30	19	26	2	5	.228
Turf	18	53	16	3	1	0	5	4	4	5	1	2	.302

Dave HOSTETLER, Designated Hitter
Runs Created: 36

	G	AB	Hit	2B	3B	HR	Run	RBI	BB	SO	SB	CS	Avg
1.31 Years		556	128	16	4	26	65	87	64	167	2	3	.229
1983:	94	304	67	9	2	11	31	46	42	103	0	2	.220
First Half	48	167	31	5	2	2	17	20	21	66	0	2	.186
Second Half	46	137	36	4	0	9	14	26	21	37	0	0	.263
vs. RHP		148	26	6	0	4	12	17	19	58	0	1	.176
vs. LHP		156	41	3	2	7	19	29	23	45	0	1	.263
Home	44	147	29	3	2	2	14	19	24	49	0	1	.197
Road	50	157	38	6	0	9	17	27	18	54	0	1	.242
Grass	81	266	56	9	2	9	27	42	36	93	0	1	.211
Turf	13	38	11	0	0	2	4	4	6	10	0	1	.289

Billy SAMPLE, Leftfield
Runs Created: 79

	G	AB	Hit	2B	3B	HR	Run	RBI	BB	SO	SB	CS	Avg
3.36 Years		502	139	27	2	10	78	50	43	44	22	7	.276
1983	147	554	152	28	3	12	80	57	44	46	44	8	.274
First Half	75	289	78	15	1	8	47	37	31	26	25	4	.270
Second Half	72	265	74	13	2	4	33	20	13	20	19	4	.279
vs. RHP		351	98	17	2	9	53	44	29	33	27	2	.279
vs. LHP		203	54	11	1	3	27	13	15	13	17	6	.266
Home	77	294	82	18	3	6	43	39	20	21	18	4	.279
Road	70	260	70	10	0	6	37	18	24	25	26	4	.269
Grass	123	466	131	24	3	11	69	52	35	43	31	7	.281
Turf	24	88	21	4	0	1	11	5	9	3	13	1	.239

Mickey RIVERS, Outfield-Designated Hitter
Runs Created: 35

	G	AB	Hit	2B	3B	HR	Run	RBI	BB	SO	SB	CS	Avg
8.43 Years		631	186	28	8	7	88	55	31	53	31	10	.295
1983	96	309	88	17	0	1	37	20	11	21	9	4	.285
First Half	35	130	32	5	0	0	16	10	4	13	2	2	.246
Second Half	61	179	56	12	0	1	21	10	7	8	7	2	.313
vs. RHP		281	84	16	0	1	36	20	9	19	9	4	.299
vs. LHP		28	4	1	0	0	1	0	2	2	0	0	.143
Home	50	158	43	8	0	0	17	8	4	9	3	3	.272
Road	46	151	45	9	0	1	20	12	7	12	6	1	.298
Grass	82	261	76	13	0	0	31	17	7	16	7	4	.291
Turf	14	48	12	4	0	1	6	3	4	5	2	0	.250

Charlie HOUGH

Year	(W–L)	GS	Run	Avg	DP	Avg	SB	Avg
1982	(16-13)	34	146	4.29	30	.88	26	.76
1983	(15-13)	33	135	4.09	25	.76	21	.64
1979-1983		89	403	4.53	74	.83	69	.77

	G	IP	W	L	Pct	ER	ERA
1982 Home	19	130.1	9	6	.600	55	3.80
1983 Home	20	148.2	10	7	.588	49	2.97
1982 Road	15	97.2	7	7	.500	45	4.15
1983 Road	14	103.1	5	6	.454	40	3.48
1983 Grass	30	218.1	14	10	.583	77	3.17
1983 Turf	4	33.2	1	3	.250	12	3.21

Rick HONEYCUTT

Year	(W–L)	GS	Run	Avg	DP	Avg	SB	Avg
1982	(5-17)	26	88	3.38	35	1.35	11	.42
1983	(14- 8)	25	112	4.48	36	1.35	7	.28
1977-1983		157	611	3.89	191	1.22	71	.45

	G	IP	W	L	Pct	ER	ERA
1982 Home	16	89.2	3	10	.231	53	5.32
1983 Home	10	79	8	2	.800	8	.91
1982 Road	14	74.1	2	7	.222	43	5.21
1983 Road	15	95.2	6	6	.500	39	3.67
1983 Grass	21	146.1	13	6	.684	35	2.15
1983 Turf	4	28.1	1	2	.333	12	3.81

Mike SMITHSON

Year	(W–L)	GS	Run	Avg	DP	Avg	SB	Avg
1982	(3- 4)	8	25	3.13	8	1.00	4	.50
1983	(10-14)	33	132	4.00	30	.91	30	.91
1982-1983		41	157	3.83	38	.93	34	.83

	G	IP	W	L	Pct	ER	ERA
1982 Home	3	19.1	2	1	.667	5	2.33
1983 Home	16	107.1	6	4	.600	52	4.36
1982 Road	5	27.1	1	3	.250	21	6.91
1983 Road	17	116	4	10	.400	45	3.49
1983 Grass	29	197	8	13	.381	88	4.02
1983 Turf	4	26.1	2	1	.667	9	3.08

Frank TANANA

Year	(W–L)	GS	Run	Avg	DP	Avg	SB	Avg
1982	(7-18)	30	99	3.30	27	.90	14	.47
1983	(7- 9)	22	78	3.55	22	1.00	12	.54
1976-1983		221	943	4.27	175	.79	157	.71

	G	IP	W	L	Pct	ER	ERA
1982 Home	15	99.2	2	10	.167	43	3.88
1983 Home	15	86.2	4	5	.444	29	3.01
1982 Road	15	94.2	5	8	.385	48	4.50
1983 Road	14	72.2	6	8	.375	27	3.34
1983 Grass	26	141.1	6	8	.429	53	3.38
1983 Turf	3	18	1	1	.500	3	1.50

Danny DARWIN

Year	(W–L)	GS	Run	Avg	DP	Avg	SB	Avg
1982	(10- 8)	1	2		0		0	
1983	(8-13)	26	102	3.92	14	.54	20	.77
1978-1983		58	262	4.52	39	.67	40	.69

	G	IP	W	L	Pct	ER	ERA
1982 Home	28	46	7	2	.777	15	2.93
1983 Home	14	99	5	6	.454	30	2.73
1982 Road	28	43	3	6	.333	19	3.98
1983 Road	14	84	3	7	.300	41	4.39
1983 Grass	22	145.1	7	8	.467	50	3.10
1983 Turf	6	37.2	1	5	.167	21	5.02

1983 OTHERS

Pitcher	(W–L)	GS	Run	Avg	DP	Avg	SB	Avg
Matlack	(2-4)	9	35	3.89	9	1.00	6	.67
Stewart	(5-2)	8	22	2.75	9	1.13	2	.25
Butcher	(6-6)	6	23	3.83	8	1.33	2	.33
Lachowicz	(0-1)	1	0		0		0	

TEXAS RANGERS
RUNS BATTED IN ANALYSIS

Player	RBI	RBI In Wins	Victory-Important RBI	RBI Importance	Wins Batted In	RBI Per Win
Larry Parrish	88	58	35.95	.409	11.70	7.5
George Wright	80	51	28.29	.354	9.93	8.1
Buddy Bell	66	45	24.29	.368	7.54	8.8
Pete O'Brien	53	31	18.77	.354	6.04	8.8
Billy Sample	57	33	18.17	.319	5.70	10.0
Bucky Dent	34	24	13.19	.388	4.99	6.8
Dave Hostetler	46	19	11.50	.250	3.82	12.0
Jim Sundberg	28	18	9.09	.325	3.17	8.8
Mickey Rivers	20	15	8.85	.443	2.64	7.6
Wayne Tolleson	20	12	4.21	.211	2.11	9.5

OAKLAND A'S

One of the people I interviewed last summer for the job as my assistant was a very nice young man named Paul Izzo. Paul hails from Providence, Rhode Island; he grew up, as it happens, just a few blocks from the boyhood home of Dave Lopes, soon to be designated a shrine. Paul showed me an article in an old *Baseball Digest* which talked about Davey Lopes growing up in an East Providence ghetto. The area in which he grew up is, in fact, not a ghetto at all. It's a very nice, turn-of-the century neighborhood.

I thought about that a lot during the summer, a short essay on the minor irritations and insults of racism in America; a similar essay was what we might call the incident of Eddie Murray's family. David Earl Lopes is sort of black, and everybody knows that black people grow up in ghettos. So Dave Lopes has to live with that.

I am in the same article with the Oakland A's and their blessed computer in more newspaper articles than you can count. I am not complaining; it sells books. Only I haven't quite figured out what I am doing there. My work has nothing to do with computers. I don't know any computer languages and couldn't write the most basic program. I enrolled in a computer science course as a junior. I lasted about three weeks.

But my work, while it has nothing to do with computers, has something to do with numbers, and a lot of people who don't understand the one don't understand the other, either, and so as far as they are concerned, we are all living in the same ghetto.

That having been said, perhaps my thoughts on the future of the computer in baseball would be of as much interest as the next person's. As mentioned, I recently purchased a computer, and am still learning how to use the canned programs that come with it. The main thing that you are struck with in the process of learning about a computer is how totally, incredibly stupid it is. The machine simulates intelligence so well that when you accidentally slip through a crack in its simulations and fall to the floor of its true intelligence, you are awed by the depth of the fall. You give it a series of a hundred or a thousand sensible commands, and it executes each of them in turn, and then you press a wrong key and accidentally give it a command which goes counter to everything that you have been trying to do, and it will execute that command in a millisecond, just as if you had accidently hit the wrong button on your vacuum cleaner at the end of your cleaning, and it had instantly and to your great surprise sprayed the dirt you had collected back into the room. And you feel like, "Jeez, machine, you ought to know I didn't mean that. What do you think I've been doing here for the last hour?" And then you realize that that machine has not the foggiest notion of what you are trying to do, any more than your vacuum cleaner does.

The machine, you see, is nothing; it is utterly, truly, totally nothing. And all of the fascination and the speculation about the computer, about "what *it* is going to do" and "how *it* will change things" in baseball and in other areas is completely misguided, because *it* is not going to do anything and *it* is not going to change anything.

We are going to do things with the computer. *You and I* are going to change the world, and we're going to change baseball, and we're going to use the computer to do it. Machines have no capabilities of their own. Your car cannot drive to Cleveland. What machines do is extend *our* capabilities.

What is unique (exciting, terrifying) about the computer is that it extends our capabilities to such an enormous extent and in so many different areas—in more different areas, I think, than any new invention since the tire iron. The reason for this is that almost everything which can be done on paper can be done easier and faster (some would say better, but I'm not convinced of that yet) on a computer. Since all of our lives revolve to a large extent around literacy, around works on paper and numbers on paper, our lives are in time going to revolve to the same extent around computers. Whether we like it or not.

Some terrible things, unimaginably terrible things, are going to be done with computers in the next thirty years. Do not kid yourself that it's not going to happen; deal frankly with the fact that it is going to happen. Some marvelous, wonderful things are going to be done with computers. I look forward to them. We are going to change our lives, using the computer, far more than we have changed our lives using the automobile, far more than we have changed our lives using the television machine. I have no doubt that that is true, because the computer expands our capabilities, for good or evil, in far more sweeping and comprehensive ways than the automobile, which in truth expands only our ability to move around, or the television, which expands only our ability to observe. I am not afraid on balance. It is only human nature that we are going to see a little more of, blown up larger than life by the new machine.

Before we approach any nearer to that point, I have a recommendation. Computers should be banned from the dugouts. Right now, before any of them are put in there to begin with. BAN them.

Computers aren't going to be bad for baseball; it's not anything like that. But they will, or would, put an unnecessary distance between the fans in the seats and the man in the dugout. Computers do not belong in the dugout for the same reason that bicycles do not belong on the basepaths: They would remove the game from a human level. Let them study their printouts before the game starts.

Some people have expressed to me a concern that what is being done in baseball with the computer is (ahem) not in the best interests of my profession, of sabermetrics. I am speaking here not only of the Oakland experiment, but of the computers that have been hauled into Comiskey, the Kingdome, and a couple of other places. I stress that I do not know any of these people. I have never met them, wouldn't recognize them if I passed them on the streets. I don't share many of their interests. They live in another part of the ghetto.

And from what I hear, I don't *want* to know some of them, either. I gather, frankly, that some of baseball's computer people are world-class oysters, dogmatic fellows who think they know more about baseball than anybody else on the planet, and consequently have no intention of listening to anyone. The concern that has been expressed to me is that some of these people may be doing us more harm than good.

If that's true, it's unfortunate. But I'm not all that concerned, and let me explain why. There is, you see, no such thing as "computer knowledge" or "computer information" or "computer data." Within a few years, everyone will understand that. The essential characteristics of information are that it is true or it is false, it is significant or it is trivial, it is relevant or it is irrelevant. In the early days of the automobile, people would say that they were going to take an "automobile trip." That lasted about ten years; after that, people went back to talking about trips as they had before. They were vacation trips, or they were business trips, or they were trips on personal matters, or they were trips to the coast or they were trips to the mountains. After the novelty wore off people still traveled in automobiles, but they ceased to identify the trip with the machine and returned to identifying it with its purpose. People stopped driving to Cleve-land just to have some place to drive. That's what we're going through now with the computer; twenty years from now, the term "computer information" will sound quaint and silly.

The main thing that is happening in computers now is that they are becoming much easier to use. As computers become easier to use, our dependence on "computer people" becomes smaller and smaller. Computer people are not going to be running baseball in a few years; indeed, computer people are not going to be running anything in a few years except computers. The rise of the computer age is not going to put computer specialists into positions of power any more than the rise of the auto age put auto mechanics and bus drivers into positions of power. Don't worry about it.

I am engaged in a search for understanding. That is my profession. It has nothing to do with computers. Computers are going to have an impact on my life that is similar to the impact that the coming of the automobile age must have had on the life of a professional traveler or adventurer. The car made it easier to get from place to place; the computer will make it easier to deal with information. But knowing how to drive an automobile does not make you an adventurer, and knowing how to run a computer does not make you an analytical student of the game.

THE MANAGER

NAME: Steve Boros

AGE: 47

MANAGERS FOR WHOM PLAYED IN MAJORS: Bill Norman, Bob Scheffing, Bob Kennedy, Fred Hutchinson, Dick Sisler.

CHARACTERISTICS AS A PLAYER: Infielder (basically third baseman); had some power but was inconsistent with the bat.

MANAGERIAL RECORD:

Team	Year	Par	Wins	Losses	Pct.	+ or –
Oak	1983	80	74	88	.457	–6

WHAT HE BRINGS TO THE BALLCLUB

IS HE AN INTENSE MANAGER OR MORE OF AN EASY-TO-GET-ALONG-WITH TYPE? An easy-to-get-along-with type.

IS HE MORE OF AN EMOTIONAL LEADER OR A DECISION-MAKER? A decision-maker. The criticism you hear of him sometimes is that he comes across as a teacher, rather than as a leader. I remember they used to say the same thing about Chuck Noll, though.

IS HE MORE OF AN OPTIMIST OR MORE OF A PROBLEM SOLVER? More of an optimist.

HOW HE USES HIS PERSONNEL

DOES HE FAVOR A SET LINEUP OR A ROTATION SYSTEM? Very extensive rotation of personnel in his first year as a manager.

DOES HE LIKE TO PLATOON? Seems to.

DOES HE TRY TO SOLVE HIS PROBLEMS WITH PROVEN PLAYERS OR WITH YOUNGSTERS WHO STILL HAVE SOMETHING TO PROVE? HOW MANY PLAYERS HAS HE MADE REGULARS OUT OF WHO WERE NOT REGULARS BEFORE, AND AND WHO WERE THEY? He's in a situation where he has so many problems that he tends to look warmly on any possible solution. Made regulars out of Mike Davis and Tony Phillips; increased playing time for Kearney and Hancock. Has imported veterans for other holes.

DOES HE PREFER TO GO WITH GOOD OFFENSIVE PLAYERS OR DOES HE LIKE THE GLOVE MEN? The bent of the organization is probably more defensive at this time.

DOES HE LIKE AN OFFENSE BASED ON POWER, SPEED, OR HIGH AVERAGES? Speed. Loves speed. Minor league teams set base-stealing records. Was first major league coach to take base-running seriously.

DOES HE USE THE ENTIRE ROSTER OR DOES HE KEEP PEOPLE AROUND SITTING ON THE BENCH? Everybody was very much involved last year, to the point of some confusion about who was doing what.

DOES HE BUILD HIS BENCH AROUND YOUNG PLAYERS WHO CAN STEP INTO A BREACH IF NEED BE OR AROUND VETERAN ROLE-PLAYERS WHO HAVE THEIR OWN FUNCTIONS WITHIN A GAME? Too soon to tell.

GAME MANAGING AND USE OF STRATEGIES

DOES HE GO FOR THE BIG-INNING OFFENSE OR DOES HE LIKE TO USE THE ONE-RUN STRATEGIES? Made heavy use of one-run strategies in 1983. The A's invested 151 outs in first-run strategies, highest total in league.

DOES HE PINCH-HIT MUCH, AND IF SO WHEN? Used about an average number. Pinch-hitters hit .296 (34/115) but had no home runs.

ANYTHING UNUSUAL ABOUT HIS LINEUP SELECTION? Yeah, he used Davey Lopes as his cleanup man against lefthanded pitchers sometimes last year, which I though was an odd and gutty move. Lopes has always had a terrific platoon differential, just annihilates lefthanders (slugging percentage last year of .484 against LHP, .386 against RHP). But few managers would try to take advantage of something like that, citing for example the danger that the other side will switch to a righthander during the game and screw up your lineup. A's as a team were terrible against lefthanded pitching (24–37; 50–51 against righthanders).

DOES HE USE THE SAC BUNT OFTEN? More than average.

DOES HE LIKE TO USE THE RUNNING GAME? Oh, does he.

IN WHAT CIRCUMSTANCES WILL HE ISSUE AN INTENTIONAL WALK? About average amount; don't know what circumstances.

DOES HE HIT AND RUN VERY OFTEN? I really don't think so, no.

ARE THERE ANY UNIQUE OR IDIOSYN-CRATIC STRATEGIES THAT HE PARTICU-LARLY LIKES? I saw an article last summer in which Dick Cramer, the man who designed the A's computer package, was quoted as saying that one play that should be tried more often is the attempt to advance from second to third on an infield ground out. He was quoted as saying that that was a play you probably should try even if you were out 95% of the time, because the payoff when you make it is so great compared to the risk. Whether the 95% figure was a careful estimate or included some hyperbole, I don't know.

Anyway, just a week after I read this, there was a Royals game in which Mitchell Page, on second base when Rickey Henderson hit a ground ball to short, immediately lit out for third base. He was out easily, and Denny Matthews immediately delivered a "what on earth was Mitchell Page thinking about?" speech.

But think about it. What's the cost? Rickey Henderson stole second on the next pitch, and the cost in this case was nothing at all; they should have had a runner on second, and they did have a runner on second. Ordinarily, if they make the play to third and you're out, you lose one base.

But what's the gain if they try for the play at third and miss it? Suppose the third baseman, shocked for a second, doesn't get over there. You have gained:

1) a base—second as opposed to third
2) a baserunner—the man on first—and
3) an out.

The baserunner and the out are both a lot bigger items than the base. I don't know if you'd be helping the team if you made it successfully 5% of the time, but I'm sure you'd be helping the team if you made it 20% of the time. Mitchell Page made the right play.

HANDLING THE PITCHING STAFF

DOES HE LIKE POWER PITCHERS OR PRE-FER TO GO WITH THE PEOPLE WHO PUT THE BALL IN PLAY? He'd be happy to have either one, I'm sure.

DOES HE STAY WITH THE STARTER OR GO TO THE BULLPEN QUICKLY? He's pretty quick to go to the pen.

Boros' handling of his pitchers, frankly, is an area that needs a whole lot of work. Early in the year he'd use Burgmeier, who hadn't worked on consecutive days in years, twice in a row, and a lot of other strange stuff. The rash of sore arms late in the year was not unexpected.

DOES HE LIKE THE FOUR-MAN OR THE FIVE-MAN ROTATION? He was trying to keep a five-man rotation together.

DOES HE USE THE ENTIRE STAFF OR DOES HE TRY TO GET FIVE OR SIX PEOPLE TO DO MOST OF THE WORK? Entire staff was involved.

ARE THERE ANY PARTICULAR TYPES OF PITCHERS OF WHOM HE IS FOND? No pattern shown.

IS THERE ANYTHING UNIQUE ABOUT HIS HANDLING OF HIS PITCHERS? Haven't seen it yet.

WHAT IS HIS STRONGEST POINT AS A MAN-AGER? He is an intelligent man, working hard to master all of the things that he needs to know and to teach all of the things that he needs to teach.

IF THERE WERE NO PROFESSIONAL BASE-BALL, WHAT WOULD THIS MANAGER PROBABLY BE DOING? Assistant professor of English literature, University of Michigan; a campus legend, author of three unpublished novels and the short story, "Time Was When a Rose Was a Rose Was a Rose," which was collected along with works by Saul Bellow, Eudora Welty, David Niven and Reverand Leroy in the *New Zealand Anthology of Good Stories By People Who Drive on the Wrong Side of the Road*.

OAKLAND A'S

Player	Record in Lineup	Record Without
Rickey Henderson	61-76	13-12
Davey Lopes	60-70	14-18
Dwayne Murphy	58-67	16-21
Tony Phillips	57-69	17-19
Mike Davis	55-56	19-32
Jeff Burroughs	49-57	25-31
Bill Almon	49-59	25-29
Wayne Gross	43-49	31-39
Mike Heath	41-47	33-41
Bob Kearney	39-49	35-39
Carney Lansford	35-41	39-47
Garry Hancock	28-29	46-59
Don Hill	21-25	53-63
Dan Meyer	20-25	54-63
Kelvin Moore	17-19	57-69
Ricky Peters	17-27	57-61
Mitchell Page	8-11	66-77
Luis Quinones	5- 7	69-81
Marshall Brant	2- 1	72-87
Darryl Cias	1- 3	73-85
David Hudgens	0- 2	74-86

Carney LANSFORD, Third Base
Runs Created: 46

	G	AB	Hit	2B	3B	HR	Run	RBI	BB	SO	SB	CS	Avg
4.56 Years		633	186	32	4	15	95	81	49	84	18	10	.294
1983	80	299	92	16	2	10	43	45	22	33	3	8	.308
First Half	32	124	33	4	0	4	14	21	9	16	1	5	.266
Second Half	48	175	59	12	2	6	29	24	13	17	2	3	.337
vs. RHP		198	68	16	2	6	28	31	12	17	3	6	.343
vs. LHP		101	24	0	0	4	15	14	10	16	0	2	.238
Home	38	133	42	7	0	4	17	18	11	16	1	4	.316
Road	42	166	50	9	2	6	26	27	11	17	2	4	.301
Grass	67	246	73	12	1	7	32	34	19	29	3	7	.297
Turf	13	53	19	4	1	3	11	11	3	4	0	1	.358

Wayne GROSS, First Base
Runs Created: 41

	G	AB	Hit	2B	3B	HR	Run	RBI	BB	SO	SB	CS	Avg
5.39 Years		476	112	20	1	16	54	58	68	70	4	4	.235
1983	137	339	79	18	0	12	34	44	36	52	3	5	.233
First Half	72	204	51	11	0	9	24	30	25	29	2	4	.250
Second Half	65	135	28	7	0	3	10	14	11	23	1	1	.207
vs. RHP		253	63	15	0	11	30	38	29	30	3	3	.249
vs. LHP		86	16	3	0	1	4	6	7	22	0	2	.186
Home	72	157	34	8	0	4	12	20	17	22	2	2	.217
Road	65	182	45	10	0	8	22	24	19	30	1	3	.247
Grass	115	279	61	15	0	9	23	36	32	43	3	4	.219
Turf	22	60	18	3	0	3	11	8	4	9	0	1	.300

Tony PHILLIPS, Shortstop
Runs Created: 48

	G	AB	Hit	2B	3B	HR	Run	RBI	BB	SO	SB	CS	Avg
1.16 Years		425	103	12	4	3	56	37	52	83	16	7	.241
1983	148	412	102	12	3	4	54	35	48	70	16	5	.248
First Half	79	224	50	3	1	2	28	17	27	43	8	3	.223
Second Half	69	188	52	9	2	2	26	18	21	27	8	2	.277
vs. RHP		258	71	11	3	3	42	26	37	40	13	4	.275
vs. LHP		154	31	1	0	1	12	9	11	30	3	1	.201
Home	75	217	56	6	1	1	31	18	25	39	12	2	.258
Road	73	195	46	6	2	3	23	17	23	31	4	3	.236
Grass	125	341	81	8	2	2	43	27	42	61	14	5	.238
Turf	23	71	21	4	1	2	11	8	6	9	2	0	.296

Davey LOPES, Second Base
Runs Created: 76

	G	AB	Hit	2B	3B	HR	Run	RBI	BB	SO	SB	CS	Avg
9.15 Years		605	159	22	5	14	96	54	76	81	51	11	.262
1983	147	494	137	13	4	17	64	67	51	61	22	4	.277
First Half	74	251	73	5	3	9	33	42	20	30	10	3	.291
Second Half	73	243	64	8	1	8	31	25	31	31	12	1	.263
vs. RHP		308	83	8	2	8	37	41	28	42	15	3	.269
vs. LHP		186	54	5	2	9	27	26	23	19	7	1	.290
Home	75	251	72	5	1	10	35	30	32	22	12	2	.287
Road	72	243	65	8	3	7	29	37	19	39	10	2	.267
Grass	124	420	119	12	2	16	53	52	39	46	19	4	.283
Turf	23	74	18	1	2	1	11	15	12	15	3	0	.243

Rickey HENDERSON, Leftfield
Runs Created: 109

	G	AB	Hit	2B	3B	HR	Run	RBI	BB	SO	SB	CS	Avg
4.01 Years		603	175	25	6	9	118	53	108	84	107	30	.291
1983	145	513	150	25	7	9	105	48	103	80	108	19	.292
First Half	73	256	66	17	1	4	48	23	52	53	42	8	.258
Second Half	72	257	84	8	6	5	57	25	51	27	66	11	.327
vs. RHP		320	92	13	4	5	69	35	67	53	69	9	.288
vs. LHP		193	58	12	3	4	36	13	36	27	39	10	.301
Home	72	252	66	10	2	5	44	26	51	44	42	13	.262
Road	73	261	84	15	5	4	61	22	52	36	66	6	.322
Grass	124	443	131	23	5	8	84	43	86	73	89	17	.296
Turf	21	70	19	2	2	1	21	5	17	7	19	2	.271

Dwayne MURPHY, Centerfield
Runs Created: 55

	G	AB	Hit	2B	3B	HR	Run	RBI	BB	SO	SB	CS	Avg
4.49 Years		538	134	16	3	18	79	76	94	113	19	10	.248
1983	130	471	107	17	2	17	55	75	62	105	7	5	.227
First Half	64	223	50	7	0	5	25	32	36	41	5	4	.224
Second Half	66	248	57	10	2	12	30	43	26	64	2	1	.230
vs. RHP		266	69	13	1	14	40	50	44	48	7	2	.259
vs. LHP		205	38	4	1	3	15	25	18	57	0	3	.185
Home	65	232	54	8	0	12	34	38	32	51	3	1	.233
Road	65	239	53	9	2	5	21	37	30	54	4	4	.222
Grass	108	389	93	14	2	15	46	62	51	79	7	4	.239
Turf	22	82	14	3	0	2	9	13	11	26	0	1	.171

Mike DAVIS, Rightfield
Runs Created: 56

	G	AB	Hit	2B	3B	HR	Run	RBI	BB	SO	SB	CS	Avg
1.35 Years		468	128	23	4	7	62	59	28	74	28	13	.273
1983	128	443	122	24	4	8	61	62	27	74	33	14	.275
First Half	71	262	72	15	1	2	36	30	11	38	22	8	.275
Second Half	57	181	50	9	3	6	25	32	16	36	11	6	.276
vs. RHP		309	89	20	1	6	47	50	16	51	21	9	.288
vs. LHP		134	33	4	3	2	14	12	11	23	11	5	.246
Home	61	203	51	12	2	3	28	30	17	28	15	3	.251
Road	67	240	71	12	2	5	33	32	10	46	17	11	.296
Grass	104	342	87	21	2	3	45	46	23	54	25	8	.254
Turf	24	101	35	3	2	5	16	16	4	20	7	6	.347

Bob KEARNEY, Catcher
Runs Created: 31

	G	AB	Hit	2B	3B	HR	Run	RBI	BB	SO	SB	CS	Avg
.82 Years		449	107	17	0	10	49	45	29	73	1	5	.238
1983	108	298	76	11	0	8	33	32	21	50	1	4	.255
First Half	67	200	50	9	0	6	19	22	13	33	1	2	.250
Second Half	41	98	26	2	0	2	14	10	8	17	0	2	.265
vs. RHP		170	39	6	0	6	20	17	10	38	0	3	.229
vs. LHP		128	37	5	0	2	13	15	11	12	1	1	.289
Home	52	153	36	3	0	4	15	15	9	24	0	1	.235
Road	56	145	40	8	0	4	18	17	12	26	1	3	.276
Grass	92	254	63	9	0	5	26	21	16	39	1	2	.248
Turf	16	44	13	2	0	3	7	11	5	11	0	2	.295

Jeff BURROUGHS, Designated Hitter
Runs Created: 51

	G	AB	Hit	2B	3B	HR	Run	RBI	BB	SO	SB	CS	Avg
9.54 Years		553	145	23	2	24	73	89	82	113	2	2	.261
1983	121	401	108	15	1	10	43	56	47	79	0	2	.269
First Half	68	250	70	11	0	5	29	32	25	49	0	2	.280
Second Half	53	151	38	4	1	5	14	24	22	30	0	0	.252
vs. RHP		206	50	6	0	5	17	36	24	49	0	2	.243
vs. LHP		195	58	9	1	5	26	20	23	30	0	0	.297
Home	63	205	51	5	1	3	21	22	31	40	0	2	.249
Road	58	196	57	10	0	7	22	34	16	39	0	0	.291
Grass	104	341	87	12	1	6	33	43	42	68	0	2	.255
Turf	17	60	21	3	0	4	10	13	5	11	0	0	.350

Bill ALMON, Shortstop
Runs Created: 51

	G	AB	Hit	2B	3B	HR	Run	RBI	BB	SO	SB	CS	Avg
5.26 Years		490	127	18	4	3	55	41	33	88	19	8	.260
1983	143	451	120	29	1	4	45	63	26	67	26	8	.266
First Half	68	219	70	16	0	1	28	26	20	30	13	3	.320
Second Half	75	232	50	13	1	3	17	37	6	37	13	5	.216
vs. RHP		231	59	11	0	2	22	33	12	39	16	2	.255
vs. LHP		220	61	18	1	2	23	30	14	28	10	6	.277
Home	69	216	60	15	1	3	20	38	14	25	15	2	.278
Road	74	235	60	14	0	1	25	25	12	42	11	6	.255
Grass	120	374	100	25	1	4	33	56	19	52	21	5	.267
Turf	23	77	20	4	0	0	12	7	7	15	5	3	.260

Chris CODIROLI

Year	(W–L)	GS	Run	Avg	DP	Avg	SB	Avg
1982	(1-2)	3	6	2.00	2	.67	2	.67
1983	(12-12)	31	144	4.65	29	.94	15	.48
1982-1983		34	150	4.41	31	.91	17	.50

	G	IP	W	L	Pct	ER	ERA
1983 Home	17	110.1	7	3	.700	34	.277
1983 Road	20	95.1	5	9	.357	68	6.42
1983 Grass	30	167.1	9	10	.474	81	4.36
1983 Turf	7	38.1	3	2	.600	21	4.93

Steve McCATTY

Year	(W–L)	GS	Run	Avg	DP	Avg	SB	Avg
1982	(6-3)	20	113	5.65	17	.85	15	.75
1983	(6-9)	24	89	3.71	19	.79	17	.71
1977-1983		122	559	4.58	93	.76	98	.80

	G	IP	W	L	Pct	ER	ERA
1982 Home	10	68	5	1	.833	26	3.44
1983 Home	21	87	2	4	.333	43	4.45
1982 Road	11	60.2	1	2	.333	31	4.60
1983 Road	17	80	4	5	.444	31	3.49
1983 Grass	33	139.2	5	7	.417	60	3.87
1983 Turf	5	27.1	1	2	.333	14	4.61

1983 OTHERS

Pitcher	(W–L)	GS	Run	Avg	DP	Avg	SB	Avg
Conroy	(7-10)	18	65	3.56	14	.78	10	.56
Norris	(4- 5)	16	67	4.19	20	1.25	8	.50
Krueger	(7- 6)	16	78	4.88	18	1.13	6	.37
Underwood	(9- 7)	15	68	4.53	18	1.20	5	.33
Heimueller	(3- 5)	14	59	4.21	8	.57	14	1.00
Warren	(5- 3)	9	42	4.67	5	.56	1	.11
Langford	(0- 4)	7	34	4.86	10	1.43	2	.29
Keough	(2- 3)	4	18	4.50	7	1.75	9	2.25
Callahan	(1- 2)	2	12	6.00	1	.50	2	1.00
Young	(0- 1)	2	13	6.50	2	1.00	1	.50
Farmer	(0- 0)	1	8	8.00	3	3.00	2	2.00
Jones	(1- 1)	1	4	4.00	3	3.00	0	.00
Smith	(1- 0)	1	2	2.00	2	2.00	3	3.00
Baker	(3- 3)	1	6	6.00	0	.00	0	.00

OAKLAND ATHLETICS
RUNS BATTED IN ANALYSIS

Player	RBI	RBI In Wins	Victory-Important RBI	RBI Importance	Wins Batted In	RBI Per Win
Dwayne Murphy	75	48	29.09	.388	7.14	10.5
Jeff Burroughs	56	44	28.65	.512	7.02	8.0
Davey Lopes	67	41	24.56	.367	6.65	10.1
Mike Davis	62	34	20.01	.323	5.60	11.1
Bill Almon	63	31	18.81	.299	5.64	11.2
Rickey Henderson	48	31	17.94	.374	5.16	9.3
Tony Phillips	35	22	17.53	.501	3.95	8.9
Bob Kearney	32	25	16.45	.514	4.49	7.1
Carney Lansford	45	26	15.18	.337	4.25	10.6
Wayne Gross	44	23	15.16	.345	4.21	10.5

MINNESOTA TWINS

On June the 15th, 1976, Charles Oscar Finley announced that he had sold three star members of his world championship team for a total of $3,500,000.00. That announcement set into motion a chain of events that led eventually to the establishment of the $400,000 rule, a commissioner's edict prohibiting teams from exchanging more than $400,000 in a player/cash transaction. As baseball now has a new commissioner, I would urge in the strongest possible terms that the policy be reconsidered and abolished in the best interest of baseball.

I have four points to make:

(1) The action was originally taken in the context of a bitter personal battle between Bowie Kuhn and Charlie Finley, and like all things said in the heat of battle needs to be written in stone.

(2) The decision was a key element in the catastrophic series of events that sent baseball salaries skyrocketing in the mid-1970s.

(3) The edict effectively abolished important rights of ownership in baseball, rights that had been exercised to help maintain economic stability, throughout the history of the game, and did so at a time when those rights were most desperately needed by the owners.

(4) The policy, set forth in the interest of the fans, has in fact proven to be in the worst possible interests of the fans that it was designed to protect.

Let us look at those one at a time.

1) *The context of the edict*

Charles O. Finley was an abrasive, frankly obnoxious individual who had been at odds with the power structure of the American League in 1963, thirteen years before the incident, when the league prevented him from moving his team to Louisville. The league attempted unsuccessfully in the mid-sixties to enforce a clause in the league agreement that would have forced Finley to sell the team. He fought a bitter battle with the league in 1967 over his right to move the team to Oakland, during which his actions were widely perceived as threatening baseball's traditional exemption from the anti-trust laws. He embarrassed baseball in 1973 when he attempted to subvert the rules during the World Series by forcing a player to sign a false affidavit that he was injured so that he would be replaced on the roster; Kuhn ordered that the player remain on the roster. Finley publicly referred to Kuhn as the "village idiot."

With this background, at the time that Finley made the sales they were perceived as being something that Charlie was doing with his usual public-be-damned attitude. When Kuhn voided the sales and Finley sued him, the discussion roared for a year about whether or not Kuhn had the *right* to do that. That was the issue in the lawsuit, whether or not Kuhn had the right to take the action that he took. The owners, whose distaste for Finley was as great as Kuhn's, rallied to Kuhn's defense, and supported him in the lawsuit. There was very little discussion about whether the no-sales policy, not even then articulated, was right or wrong; the discussion was whether he could do it. It could be argued that the owners had been looking for a way to get rid of Finley since 1963, and when they saw an opening, took it. It is not my purpose to argue that. It could be argued that Kuhn was responding to Finley's personal vendetta against him, and that the owners at that time did the right thing in supporting Kuhn. That's not the point, either.

The point is that the action was taken and the policy was set in the context of a personal battle that no longer has any meaning, Kuhn and Finley both being gone now. The policy can be and should be looked at with fresh eyes.

2) *The economic impact of the rule*

This decision, in my opinion, did as much as the Messersmith decision itself to catapult baseball salaries upward, and has cost the owners millions and millions of dollars.

How? In several ways. In the absence of this decision, a team that was considering the acquisition of a free agent would have had an important option—to purchase a comparable player from another team. Would a team pay Player X1 $7 million for five years when they could purchase from another team Player X2, who was just as good, for $800,000? Or for $2 million? It seems unlikely. A team needing a first baseman would not have to have that free agent; they would have an option.

Second, many fewer players would have gotten into the free-agent market to begin with if the teams which were losing them could have sold them instead.

In this way, combining these two points, the absence of the $400,000 rule would have placed the owners in a cooperative arrangement, rather than a competitive arrangement, with respect to the players. Thus some portion of the money that was funneled from the owners to the players would have remained with a cycle of the owners, money going from owner to owner rather than from owner to player. And with even a little bit less money going to the players, some fuel would have been removed from the inflationary fire; the rate of growth in salaries might have been 20% per year, instead of 30% per year.

Of course there would still be the Ted Turner, the George Steinbrenner, who was throwing at the player however much money was required to impress him. But it would require then less money to impress him.

In using the term "catastrophic" to describe the economic scenario, I am of course viewing it from the owner's perspective. I do not, in fact, regard it as catastrophic from the standpoint of a fan or from the standpoint of the game as a whole. I've always been on the players' side in economic matters; I work with the agents.

And I have mentioned this idea to two or three agents, and they have always grasped instantly what I meant. Because an agent's a negotiator, and the basic fact of a negotiator's life is that the strength of your position is wholly dependent on one thing and one thing only: how many options you have. What they need to get the salary they want for a free agent is two teams that want him. You can go to your boss and beg and grovel and plead for more money, and it won't mean a thing—but if his competitor offers you a 50% increase in salary, he'll offer a 60% increase.

Kuhn's edict removed from the owners a key option—the only other dollar option that an aggressive owner had. In so doing, he weakened greatly the position of the owners in salary negotiations.

3) *The rights of the owners*
At the time of the lawsuit, Finley claimed that he was merely doing something that owners had done repeatedly throughout the history of the game. Kuhn argued that those situations were different, and that what Finley was doing was unique and uniquely damaging to the fans.

Kuhn was dead wrong about that. It is difficult to imagine how the parallels between Connie Mack's player sales of 1914 and the mid-1930s and Finley's attempted sales of 1976 could have been any stronger or any more perfect. Mack was faced in 1914 with a sudden increase in salary expectations, and with the prospect of losing his star players uncompensated if he did not sell them. From 1933 to 1935, he sold off a formidable list of talent because he could not meet his payroll. How is this different from what Finley was doing?

What Finley was trying to do was exactly what an owner had always done to stay in the card game. The owners reacted to that on a personal level; they said, "We don't want you to stay in the card game. We've been trying to get rid of you for 13 years."

I can see that, but did you also want to get rid of Bill Veeck and Ruly Carpenter and Mrs. Wrigley? Did you want to drive all of the old-line operators out of the game?

What I am saying is, even though it was not often used, the option of selling off players was an essential element in the long-term economic stability of the league. Kuhn removed that option from the members of the league at a time when they most desperately needed it. This contributed mightily to the economic de-stabilization of the game.

In addition to that, selling ballplayers in other situations was something that the owners had always had the right to do, and something which they had done on many other occasions—selling surplus talent, selling front-line talent to support a large farm system, as Branch Rickey did in St. Louis. Kuhn arbitrarily removed that privilege from the owners.

4) *The protection of the fans*
But, of course, he did it for the fans.

Look, suppose that you were the general manager of the Minnesota Twins. Kuhn removed from you two things: the right to buy talent and the right to sell it.

If I were the general manager of a ballclub, the first thing I would want to do would be to try to acquire some more talent. I'd love to be able to go to the Kansas City Royals and say, "Look, if you don't want to play Onix Concepcion, we'd sure like to make you an offer for him."

How does that hurt the fans? Talent that is considered surplus to Kansas City (Concepcion) or Milwaukee (Brouhard) or Boston (Nichols) could be very useful to Minnesota. The Yankees in the 1950s made those kind of sales; at the right price, you could still make them.

But what about going the other way? OK, let's evaluate it. The Twins have (as I write this) a player of very real value in Gary Ward, a player that they could probably sell for a couple of million dollars. Only they can't sell him, and besides that they can't pay him, either. So what do they have to do? They have to get rid of him, but they have to get in return a package of young and unproven players, players who can't command a large salary.

And next year, they'll have to do the same thing with Kent Hrbek, or Gary Gaetti, or Tom Brunansky, or all three and why is this? Because they can't pay them. And why can't they pay them? Because they can't sell Gary Ward for money.

What Kuhn could not have anticipated in 1977 was the coming of arbitration awards that would force a team to pay $300,000 or $700,000 a year to a young player. The Twins are in a position in which they are forced to exchange large sums of money for talent, but they are prohibited from exchanging talent for large sums of money. Does that make any sense?

How does this help the fans of the Minnesota Twins? I defy anybody to give me a semi-cogent, quasi-rational explanation of how the no-sales policy protects the fans of a weak organization. Did it protect the Oakland A's under Finley? Did it protect Seattle when they were in danger of losing Floyd Bannister? Is it protecting the Twins? The no-sales policy in fact contributes to the further destruction of a weak team.

5) *Summary*
The selection of a new commissioner purges the leadership of baseball of their emotional commitment to an established policy. I urge the new commissioner to review that policy in the light of the current needs and goals of organized baseball. I urge him to consider his options, to consider perhaps the option of saying not that we will *prohibit* sales of players, but that we will review them, and retain our option to disallow them if they are damaging to the interest of the game.

I think he would find it difficult to find any logical basis for a continuation of the current policy.

TOPIC: CALVIN GRIFFITH

It has become all too easy to pick on Mr. Calvin Griffith. His flaws are so obvious that to point them out anymore is like digging up a dead horse to beat it. But I come not to damn Mr. Calvin, but to explain him. For too long people have hurled such epitaphs at him as "loser" and "cellar-dweller." But what many don't realize is that if you're not playing the game, you can't lose. And Calvin is not playing the game, at least not the one baseball fans are interested in. In the context of the game he *is* playing, in the parameters of his own little world, he is unequivocally a winner.

If you have ever pitched pennies or played nickel slot machines or penny-ante poker and been successful at it, you know the feeling of winning with nothing at stake. You gambled, you won, and you have nothing to show for it. You take your three dollars and fifteen cents home at the end of the night and say, "Look, I'm ahead of the game. I fought the law and I won." Of course, the big boys are all laughing at you because as they see things, you've done zip. Your experience was not real, at least as far as what it could have been at the baccarat table or playing Russian roulette. But you don't care what they think, because you set your tiny limits and by God you won.

Well that's Mr. Calvin, isn't it? A man who has set for himself the most accessible of goals: stay in the game, eke out a living, hold the line against life's inevitabilities and you'll be OK. And yes, he is succeeding. Each night he goes home to his little apartment and says, "I'm still here."

And that's it.

He is more interested in proving his point than he is in winning ball games. He is saying to the baseball world, "I can maintain a ball club with a tenth the expenditures of anyone else. All you have to do is know where to look for the bargains."

Yes, Ken Schrom was a bargain. And yes, he turned in a very good season—especially for the money. But is he the kind of player with whom the Twins can ride to the pennant? Of course not. Is he the stop-gap until the crew of rookie phenoms arrives in a few years? No. Ken Schrom, I'm afraid, is as good as it gets. He is Calvin's symbol of thriftiness for 1983. Calvin can put Ken Schrom before the other owners and bellow, "Waste not, want not." Schrom is there to prove to the baseball world that for a modicum of relative expense, it is still possible to field a major league franchise. That they win a pennant,

or even contend, is not important. Their very existence is reward enough.

How frustrating it must be to root for this team. In its own way, it has got to be worse than pulling for a team governed by incompetents. Stupid men, bumbling over decisions in an ill-conceived attempt to win, at least offer the promise of excitement, and there's always the chance that they'll stumble into something good, like a pennant. But this—yikes—it's coitus interruptus night after night, year after year.

Calvin had the upper hand on the talent drain in 1983. The Twins have acquired 76 points in AV from other teams while losing only 61. Realize that success in this category is not always accompanied by success on the field. The Dodgers, for instance, have lost 187 points of AV while gaining only 48 from other teams. But in the Griffith schema, this category is all that matters. When his good teams of the late 70's began to wander off, everyone said the talent drain would be his undoing. But here he is in 1983 with 1.25 AV points for every one that he has surrendered. In this baseball age that is antithetical to everything that Mr. Calvin believes in; where evils such as free agency, salary arbitration and long-term contracts lurk to destroy a hard-working, old-fashioned front-office man, he has got that damn talent drain on the run. He set the stakes very low, but he is ahead.

In the cold North he is holding out against all odds, the last bastion of common sense, baseball's final hope for sanity. That there are pennant races and ballgames to be won—well, that's all incidental. Calvin is too busy teaching the rest of us a lesson to be bothered with such trivialities.

—Jim Baker

THE MANAGER

NAME: Billy Gardner

AGE: 56

MANAGERS FOR WHOM PLAYED IN MAJORS: Leo Durocher, Paul Richards, Cookie Lavagetto, Ralph Houk, Pinky Higgins, Johnny Pesky.

CHARACTERISTICS AS A PLAYER: A second baseman who was good enough with the glove to play regularly for five and a half years despite hitting only .237.

MANAGERIAL RECORD:

Team	Year	Par	Wins	Losses	Pct.	+ or −
Minn	1981	36	30	43	.411	− 6
Minn	1982	75	60	102	.370	−15
Minn	1983	68	70	92	.432	+ 2
3 Years		179	160	237	.403	−19

WHAT HE BRINGS TO THE BALLCLUB

IS HE AN INTENSE MANAGER OR MORE OF AN EASY-TO-GET-ALONG-WITH TYPE? I don't know.

IS HE MORE OF AN EMOTIONAL LEADER OR A DECISION-MAKER? I don't know that much about him personally; I would say a decision-maker.

IS HE MORE OF AN OPTIMIST OR MORE OF A PROBLEM SOLVER? More of an optimist, I'd think. He was willing to stay with Engle through some defensive problems early last year, which would be more characteristic of an optimist.

HOW HE USES HIS PERSONNEL

DOES HE FAVOR A SET LINEUP OR A ROTATION SYSTEM? He's using mostly a set lineup with a couple of exceptions, but then he doesn't exactly have a bewildering array of talent options here.

DOES HE LIKE TO PLATOON? Doesn't seem to.

DOES HE TRY TO SOLVE HIS PROBLEMS WITH PROVEN PLAYERS OR WITH YOUNGSTERS WHO STILL HAVE SOMETHING TO PROVE? HOW MANY PLAYERS HAS HE MADE REGULARS OUT OF WHO WERE NOT

REGULARS BEFORE, AND WHO WERE THEY? Has made regulars out of Laudner, Engle, Hrbek, Gaetti, Ron Washington, Brunansky, Bush, Ward and Hatcher. Self-explanatory.

DOES HE PREFER TO GO WITH GOOD OFFENSIVE PLAYERS OR DOES HE LIKE THE GLOVE MEN? Hitters. Odd for a glove man, but a clear pattern.

DOES HE LIKE AN OFFENSE BASED ON POWER, SPEED OR HIGH AVERAGES? Power, I'd say. Definitely not speed.

DOES HE USE THE ENTIRE ROSTER OR DOES HE KEEP PEOPLE AROUND SITTING ON THE BENCH? There are people on his roster who aren't exactly fully involved in the action, but then some of those people probably don't really belong on a major league roster, anyway.

DOES HE BUILD HIS BENCH AROUND YOUNG PLAYERS WHO CAN STEP INTO A BREACH IF NEED BE OR AROUND VETERAN ROLE-PLAYERS WHO HAVE THEIR OWN FUNCTIONS WITHIN A GAME? Has young players; may not have any choice.

GAME MANAGING AND USE OF STRATEGIES

DOES HE GO FOR THE BIG-INNING OFFENSE OR DOES HE LIKE TO USE THE ONE-RUN STRATEGIES? He is the ultimate big-inning manager. He almost never uses the one-run strategies.

DOES HE PINCH-HIT MUCH, AND IF SO WHEN? Hasn't done so much, no.

ANYTHING UNUSUAL ABOUT HIS LINEUP SELECTION? Not noted.

DOES HE USE THE SAC BUNT OFTEN? No; less than any other major league manager.

DOES HE LIKE TO USE THE RUNNING GAME? No.

IN WHAT CIRCUMSTANCES WILL HE ISSUE AN INTENTIONAL WALK? Well, he's behind a lot, and that's when the intentional walk is used most.

DOES HE HIT AND RUN VERY OFTEN? No, not much at all.

ARE THERE ANY UNIQUE OR IDIOSYNCRATIC STRATEGIES THAT HE PARTICULARLY LIKES? Not that I can remember.

HANDLING THE PITCHING STAFF

DOES HE LIKE POWER PITCHERS OR PREFER TO GO WITH THE PEOPLE WHO PUT THE BALL IN PLAY? He's still trying to find his pitchers; we'll be able to answer this better when he does.

DOES HE STAY WITH THE STARTER OR GO TO THE BULLPEN QUICKLY? He will go to the bullpen quickly, even in the early innings of a game.

DOES HE LIKE THE FOUR-MAN OR THE FIVE-MAN ROTATION? Switched to a four-man rotation about the first of July last year, and stayed with it the rest of the way.

DOES HE USE THE ENTIRE STAFF OR DOES HE TRY TO GET FIVE OR SIX PEOPLE TO DO MOST OF THE WORK? Entire staff.

ARE THERE ANY PARTICULAR TYPES OF PITCHERS OF WHOM HE IS FOND? Covered in previous answers.

IS THERE ANYTHING UNIQUE ABOUT HIS HANDLING OF HIS PITCHERS? Ibid.

WHAT IS HIS STRONGEST POINT AS A MANAGER? Well, I think he's got a lot of them. He's done a terrific job of bringing along the kids, Gaetti and Brunansky and others. The thing with Engle last year was amazing; he started the year with no catcher, and he wound up with one of the better catchers in the league. He's a fine offensive manager; the lineup is just a bat or two away from really scaring people. Only question at this point is about his ability to do something with the pitching staff.

IF THERE WERE NO PROFESSIONAL BASEBALL, WHAT WOULD THIS MANAGER PROBABLY BE DOING? Walking around with a fungo bat over his shoulder, wondering what he was supposed to be doing with it.

Kent HRBEK, First Base
Runs Created: 91

	G	AB	Hit	2B	3B	HR	Run	RBI	BB	SO	SB	CS	Avg
1.88 Years		592	175	36	5	24	86	97	62	85	4	4	.295
1983	141	515	153	41	5	16	75	84	57	71	4	6	.297
First Half	64	240	74	23	3	6	39	46	26	38	2	1	.308
Second Half	77	275	79	18	2	10	36	38	31	33	2	5	.287
vs. RHP		371	114	33	4	10	54	55	37	45	4	4	.307
vs. LHP		144	39	8	1	6	21	29	20	26	0	2	.271
Home	75	278	89	14	4	7	42	47	28	37	2	4	.320
Road	66	237	64	17	1	9	33	37	29	34	2	2	.270
Grass	53	190	46	13	0	5	25	23	26	26	2	2	.242
Turf	88	325	107	28	5	11	50	61	31	45	2	4	.329

Tom BRUNANSKY, Centerfield
Runs Created: 72

	G	AB	Hit	2B	3B	HR	Run	RBI	BB	SO	SB	CS	Avg
1.78 Years		582	142	30	3	29	86	75	78	115	2	4	.245
1983	151	542	123	24	5	28	70	82	61	95	2	5	.227
First Half	78	288	58	13	3	11	37	38	32	57	1	3	.201
Second Half	73	254	65	11	2	17	33	44	29	38	1	2	.256
vs. RHP		373	72	13	4	18	44	56	44	73	1	3	.193
vs. LHP		169	51	11	1	10	26	26	17	22	1	2	.302
Home	74	261	61	14	4	8	33	32	36	40	2	4	.234
Road	77	281	62	10	1	20	37	50	25	55	0	1	.221
Grass	58	211	45	6	1	14	29	38	19	39	0	1	.213
Turf	93	331	78	18	4	14	41	44	42	56	2	4	.236

John CASTINO, Second Base
Runs Created: 81

	G	AB	Hit	2B	3B	HR	Run	RBI	BB	SO	SB	CS	Avg
4.06 Years		565	156	21	8	10	71	61	42	73	5	5	.276
1983	142	563	156	30	4	11	83	57	62	54	4	2	.277
First Half	75	304	89	17	2	9	48	35	31	31	2	1	.293
Second Half	67	259	67	13	2	2	35	22	31	23	2	1	.259
vs. RHP		393	100	19	2	8	55	33	45	45	2	2	.254
vs. LHP		170	56	11	2	3	28	24	17	9	2	0	.329
Home	70	270	87	19	4	4	48	33	33	22	3	2	.322
Road	72	293	69	11	0	7	35	24	29	32	1	0	.235
Grass	55	223	50	7	0	6	26	19	25	26	1	0	.224
Turf	87	340	106	23	4	5	57	38	37	28	3	2	.312

Mickey HATCHER, Rightfield
Runs Created: 54

	G	AB	Hit	2B	3B	HR	Run	RBI	BB	SO	SB	CS	Avg
2.34 Years		515	140	24	3	7	52	51	20	42	3	3	.272
1983	106	375	119	15	3	9	50	47	14	19	2	0	.317
First Half	51	167	54	7	3	3	25	21	10	10	2	0	.323
Second Half	55	208	65	8	0	6	25	26	4	9	0	0	.313
vs. RHP		225	74	8	1	4	31	23	9	13	1	0	.329
vs. LHP		150	45	7	2	5	19	24	5	6	1	0	.300
Home	53	189	68	8	2	6	29	31	7	11	2	0	.360
Road	53	186	51	7	1	3	21	16	7	8	0	0	.274
Grass	41	142	42	6	1	1	17	13	6	6	0	0	.296
Turf	65	233	77	9	2	8	33	34	8	13	2	0	.330

Gary GAETTI, Third Base
Runs Created: 74

	G	AB	Hit	2B	3B	HR	Run	RBI	BB	SO	SB	CS	Avg
1.92 Years		582	138	29	4	25	75	86	47	122	4	3	.237
1983	157	584	143	30	3	21	81	78	54	121	7	1	.245
First Half	80	313	78	17	1	10	44	34	29	74	5	0	.249
Second Half	77	271	65	13	2	11	37	44	25	47	2	1	.240
vs. RHP		417	96	22	3	15	51	53	37	93	6	1	.230
vs. LHP		167	47	8	0	6	30	25	17	28	1	0	.281
Home	78	291	70	18	3	7	43	40	27	63	4	0	.241
Road	79	293	73	12	0	14	38	38	27	58	3	1	.249
Grass	60	220	53	9	0	11	31	29	22	43	3	1	.241
Turf	97	364	90	21	3	10	50	49	32	78	4	0	.247

Dave ENGLE, Catcher
Runs Created: 57

	G	AB	Hit	2B	3B	HR	Run	RBI	BB	SO	SB	CS	Avg
1.60 Years		503	137	27	6	11	59	57	32	61	1	1	.272
1983	120	374	114	22	4	8	46	43	28	39	2	1	.305
First Half	61	189	56	13	1	5	21	25	10	23	2	1	.296
Second Half	59	185	58	9	3	3	25	18	18	16	0	0	.314
vs. RHP		227	66	13	1	5	24	26	19	27	2	1	.291
vs. LHP		147	48	9	3	3	22	17	9	12	0	0	.327
Home	57	166	54	13	2	4	20	25	17	15	0	0	.325
Road	63	208	60	9	2	4	26	18	11	24	2	1	.288
Grass	48	158	48	8	1	4	23	13	7	16	2	1	.304
Turf	72	216	66	14	3	4	23	30	21	23	0	0	.306

Ron WASHINGTON, Shortstop
Runs Created: 30

	G	AB	Hit	2B	3B	HR	Run	RBI	BB	SO	SB	CS	Avg
1.58 Years		551	143	17	6	6	56	45	25	92	11	6	.259
1983	99	317	78	7	3	4	28	26	22	50	10	5	.246
First Half	46	150	35	6	1	2	15	15	11	17	4	3	.233
Second Half	53	167	43	1	2	2	13	11	11	33	6	2	.257
vs. RHP		228	56	3	1	4	19	18	18	39	8	2	.246
vs. LHP		89	22	4	2	0	9	8	4	11	2	3	.247
Home	42	129	32	3	1	1	15	9	10	24	5	2	.248
Road	57	188	46	4	2	3	13	17	12	26	5	3	.245
Grass	47	159	39	3	2	3	10	15	7	17	4	2	.245
Turf	52	158	39	4	1	1	18	11	15	33	6	3	.247

Randy BUSH, Designated Hitter
Runs Created: 50

	G	AB	Hit	2B	3B	HR	Run	RBI	BB	SO	SB	CS	Avg
1.10 Years		445	110	27	4	14	51	62	38	71	0	1	.248
1983	124	373	93	24	3	11	43	56	34	51	0	1	.249
First Half	64	196	58	17	2	7	22	39	16	29	0	1	.296
Second Half	60	177	35	7	1	4	21	17	18	22	0	0	.198
vs. RHP		359	91	24	3	11	42	54	34	47	0	1	.253
vs. LHP		14	2	0	0	0	1	2	0	4	0	0	.143
Home	66	192	54	18	2	4	21	36	23	29	0	1	.281
Road	58	181	39	6	1	7	22	20	11	22	0	0	.215
Grass	42	128	26	5	1	2	15	11	9	17	0	0	.203
Turf	82	245	67	19	2	9	28	45	25	34	0	1	.273

Gary WARD, Leftfield
Runs Created: 84

	G	AB	Hit	2B	3B	HR	Run	RBI	BB	SO	SB	CS	Avg
2.57 Years		599	171	31	8	20	84	85	45	101	10	2	.285
1983	157	623	173	34	5	19	76	88	44	98	8	1	.278
First Half	81	336	97	16	3	15	52	52	20	51	2	1	.289
Second Half	76	287	76	18	2	4	24	36	24	47	6	0	.265
vs. RHP		445	119	24	3	8	50	59	33	71	8	1	.267
vs. LHP		178	54	10	2	11	26	29	11	27	0	0	.303
Home	78	314	87	14	5	7	41	50	21	58	1	1	.277
Road	79	309	86	20	0	12	35	38	23	40	7	0	.278
Grass	60	237	68	15	0	11	25	30	14	27	5	0	.287
Turf	97	386	105	19	5	8	51	58	30	71	3	1	.272

Darrell BROWN, Designated Hitter
Runs Created: 26

	G	AB	Hit	2B	3B	HR	Run	RBI	BB	SO	SB	CS	Avg
.71 Years		466	128	8	4	0	65	35	15	44	7	4	.275
1983	91	309	84	6	2	0	40	22	10	28	3	3	.272
First Half	33	104	28	3	0	0	15	12	3	8	0	1	.269
Second Half	58	205	56	3	2	0	25	10	7	20	3	2	.273
vs. RHP		179	47	3	2	0	20	14	7	23	2	1	.263
vs. LHP		130	37	3	0	0	20	8	3	5	1	2	.285
Home	44	141	45	2	1	0	24	12	7	14	3	1	.319
Road	47	168	39	4	1	0	16	10	3	14	0	2	.232
Grass	40	145	31	3	1	0	10	10	3	13	0	2	.214
Turf	51	164	53	3	1	0	30	12	7	15	3	1	.323

Frank VIOLA

Year	(W–L)	GS	Run	Avg	DP	Avg	SB	Avg
1982	(4-10)	22	93	4.33	24	1.09	18	.82
1983	(7-15)	34	154	4.53	33	.97	11	.32
1982-1983		56	247	4.41	57	1.02	29	.52

	G	IP	W	L	Pct	ER	ERA
1982 Home	13	72	1	8	.111	50	6.25
1983 Home	19	123.2	5	9	.357	70	5.09
1982 Road	9	54	3	2	.600	23	3.83
1983 Road	16	86.1	2	6	.250	58	6.05
1983 Grass	11	61.1	1	4	.200	38	5.58
1983 Turf	24	148.2	6	11	.353	90	5.45

Bobby CASTILLO

Year	(W–L)	GS	Run	Avg	DP	Avg	SB	Avg
1982	(13-11)	25	104	4.16	23	.92	13	.52
1983	(8-12)	25	98	3.92	26	1.04	18	.72
1977-1983		52	208	4.00	52	1.00	31	.60

	G	IP	W	L	Pct	ER	ERA
1982 Home	18	112.2	9	3	.750	48	3.83
1983 Home	14	89.2	4	5	.444	44	4.42
1982 Road	22	106	4	8	.333	41	3.58
1983 Road	13	68.2	4	7	.364	40	5.24
1983 Grass	12	64.2	4	7	.364	36	5.01
1983 Turf	15	93.2	4	5	.444	48	4.61

Al WILLIAMS

Year	(W–L)	GS	Run	Avg	DP	Avg	SB	Avg
1982	(9- 7)	26	120	4.26	26	1.00	26	1.00
1983	(11-14)	29	129	4.45	34	1.17	36	1.24
1980-1983		86	398	4.63	99	1.15	86	1.00

	G	IP	W	L	Pct	ER	ERA
1982 Home	15	91.2	7	5	.583	44	4.32
1983 Home	17	75.2	4	6	.400	44	5.23
1982 Road	11	62	2	2	.500	28	4.06
1983 Road	19	117.2	7	8	.467	45	3.44
1983 Grass	21	95	5	8	.385	34	3.22
1983 Turf	15	98.1	6	6	.500	55	5.03

1983 OTHERS

Pitcher	(W–L)	GS	Run	Avg	DP	Avg	SB	Avg
Filson	(4- 1)	8	34	4.25	9	1.13	7	.87
O'Connor	(2- 3)	8	43	5.38	6	.75	11	1.37
Oelkers	(0- 5)	8	33	4.13	10	1.25	8	1.00
Lysander	(5-12)	4	15	3.75	6	1.50	1	.25
Pettibone	(0- 4)	4	9	2.25	7	1.75	4	1.00

Ken SCHROM

Year	(W–L)	GS	Run	Avg	DP	Avg	SB	Avg
1983	(15-8)	28	122	4.36	21	.75	22	.79

	G	IP	W	L	Pct	ER	ERA
1983 Home	17	110.1	7	2	.778	34	2.77
1983 Road	16	86	8	6	.571	47	4.92
1983 Grass	12	62	5	5	.500	37	5.37
1983 Turf	21	134.1	10	3	.769	44	2.95

MINNESOTA TWINS
RUNS BATTED IN ANALYSIS

Player	RBI	RBI In Wins	Victory-Important RBI	RBI Importance	Wins Batted In	RBI Per Win
Kent Hrbek	84	50	36.99	.440	7.97	10.5
Tom Brunansky	82	64	35.51	.433	10.03	8.2
Gary Ward	88	53	33.35	.379	7.68	11.5
Gary Gaetti	78	42	27.90	.358	6.69	11.7
John Castino	57	37	25.99	.456	5.99	9.5
Mickey Hatcher	47	31	21.09	.449	4.25	11.1
Randy Bush	56	30	17.90	.320	4.62	12.1
Dave Engle	43	26	16.50	.384	4.58	9.4
Ron Washington	26	22	13.09	.503	3.49	7.4
Darrell Brown	22	13	6.39	.290	1.58	13.9

CALIFORNIA ANGELS

The most striking thing about the California Angels' roster at this moment is its stunning lack of marketable talent. The Angels in 1983 had the same record as the Minnesota Twins (70–92), but whereas the Twins' roster is loaded with players who are in the early stages of what figures to be good careers, the Angels' roster is glaringly absent of those players, in the class of Kent Hrbek, Gary Gaetti, and Tom Brunansky. They do have lots of players of proven ability but limited future, and several players of promise but unproven ability. They have Dick Schofields and Rick Burleson, Daryl Sconiers and Rod Carew; what they lack are Robin Younts and Kent Hrbeks.

What does that mean for their future? Jim has assumed (see comments on Ellis Valentine) that it dooms them, and he might be right. Obviously, to possess young talent, as Minnesota does, is a desirable thing. Just as obviously, to possess young talent is not a guarantee of a bright future. To lack proven young talent does not guarantee a bleak future.

What is the connection? How strong is it? How many teams are there which overcome a lack of established young talent on hand to embark on a run of successful seasons? Do those teams which are about to begin on a period of dominion over their divisions, such as the 1975 Yankees or Royals or Phillies, generally possess an unusually high number of good young players?

No answers to those questions are going to be produced in this article; they are far beyond the scope of the present study. I will get to them within a few years. But the Angels are an old team and a bad team (the difference between the Angels and the Indians is that whereas the Indians are an old, bad team with no past, the Angels are an old, bad team with a mediocre past) and as such perhaps the most appropriate thing that we can do here would be to establish a context for answering with a little more accuracy that question: What is the future of an old, bad team?

In order to analyze that and related questions, we must first have a way of setting down on paper a representation of something that we can see with our eyes. The method used here is the "Reservoir Estimation Technique," introduced previously in the 1981 and 1982 editions of the *Baseball Abstract*. The Reservoir Estimation Technique attempts to assess the size of each team's pool of talent, by looking at the age and appropriate value of each player. The method was developed by looking at the careers of several hundred players, and asking a long series of questions such as "What is the average remaining Approximate Value of a 25-year-old player with an AV of 12?" From these answers, I developed a formula to predict the normal relationships between Approximate Value, age and remaining Approximate Value. What is the probably worth of Cal Ripken's future? What is the probable worth of Dave Stieb's future? What is the probable worth of Tim Foli's future, or Fred Lynn's, or Ron Jackson's? The Reservoir Estimation Technique attempts to answer these questions.

The formula is certainly quite imperfect; there is no argument about that. There are many things about a player that you can't put on paper, and there are many that you can put on paper that are not considered here. But I believe that it is, at the same time, adequate to the general task at hand, that of assessing the amount of marketable talent on each team. The systems list of the ten American League players with the brightest futures at this moment:

THE AMERICAN LEAGUE'S TEN MOST VALUABLE PIECES OF REAL ESTATE AT THIS MOMENT

Player	1983 Age	1983 Value	Trade Value
1. Cal Ripken	22	17	193
2. Rickey Henderson	24	15	131
3. Robin Yount	27	16	125
4. Lloyd Moseby	23	14	124
5. Wade Boggs	25	15	122
6. Julio Franco	21	11	110
7. Tom Brunansky	22	12	109
8. Eddie Murray	27	15	106
9. Alan Trammell	25	14	106
10. Jim Rice	30	16	103

You'll note that there are no pitchers. There are no pitchers on this list for the same reason that there are no pitchers who get long-term $2 million-a-year contracts: their futures are too dicey. Ten years from now, Cal Ripken and Wade Boggs are very likely to still be among the best players in baseball—but Jack Morris and Dave Stieb are not likely to be among the best pitchers in baseball.

Anyway, Cal Ripken kind of dominates at this moment, as he should. There is probably no doubt about who should be number one on the list at this time. Below that, there is a lot of doubt and a lot of room for argument. But I think there is very little room for doubt that if the whole league were thrown into a pot and the teams were chosen all over again, these ten people would be snarfed up pretty quick. The evaluations are not exactly accurate, but they are substantially accurate. That's all we need for this study.

The next question is, which teams possess the most oung players with the most left in them? We'll deal with nonpitchers first.

NONPITCHERS

Chart Angels-I on page 177 presents information on that issue. The chart gives, in order, 1) the player on each team who is regarded as the most valuable for the future and who is not on the list of the top ten in the league, with his future value in parenthesis, 2) the player who is regarded as the second-most valuable, with his future value in parenthesis, and 3) the total "future value" possessed by all the nonpitchers on the team.

Asterisks indicate that additional players from this team are in the league's top-ten group. Remember, a solid season for a regular player has an Approximate Value of about ten; saying that the Angels have 270 points in "future value" is saying that they probably have about 27 seasons worth of reasonably good playing time left on their major league roster. Lists are based on talent possessed at the end of the 1983 season. OK, go and look at the chart now.

The American League, as you can see, divides neatly into two groups: eight teams which have young talent, six which do not. There is not a lot of difference between the #1 team, Minnesota, and the #8 team, Milwaukee. There is not a lot of difference between #9 and #14. But there is a big division between the two groups.

The Angels, of course, are at the bottom of the bereft group. Their most valuable future commodities are Fred Lynn and Daryl Sconiers; Lynn is a good player but at 32, his best years are probably behind him and how many are ahead is indeterminate, but probably three to six. Daryl Sconiers is young and has ability, but exactly how much is unproven yet. If these players were in the Blue Jays' organization they would rank sixth and seventh on the team in trade value.

The surprise in the rankings is Oakland, which ranks in the positive group. I wouldn't have guessed that.

PITCHERS

The list below gives the ten American League pitchers who would appear at this moment to have the brightest futures, and therefore the most value:

Pitcher	1983 Age	1983 Value	Trade Value
1. Richard Dotson	24	15	92
2. Jack Morris	27	15	74
3. Dan Petry	24	13	70
4. LaMarr Hoyt	28	15	69
5. Storm Davis	21	9	65
6. Dave Stieb	25	13	64
7. Bob Stanley	28	14	59
8. Scott McGregor	29	14	54
9. Dan Quisenberry	30	14	50
10. Dave Righetti	24	10	50
Matt Young	24	10	50

Chart Angels-II is a pitchers variation of Angels-I. You are excused.

Uh huh. There we are again; the Angels are at the bottom. The White Sox are clearly the team that has command of the good young pitchers at this time. Kansas City has virtually nobody of proven value except Quisenberry, but at least they have Quisenberry. Detroit has little behind Morris and Petry, but they do have Morris and Petry. Mike Witt?

The figures for the pitchers probably look a little low, but again, think about what they mean. The "34" for Rick Sutcliffe means he's probably got three, four good years in him; I wouldn't want to bet on his having many more than that. Everybody who was at 50 or higher is on the other chart.

Combining the two charts, this is what you get:

Team	Nonpitchers	Pitching	Total
1. Detroit	578	243	813
2. Toronto	562	247	809
3. Chicago	504	290	794
4. Boston	533	247	780
5. Minnesota	601	177	778
6. Baltimore	503	252	755
7. Oakland	520	232	752
8. Milwaukee	500	151	651
9. Seattle	384	204	588
10. Texas	374	184	558

Team	Nonpitchers	Pitching	Total
11. New York	327	222	549
12. Cleveland	345	143	488
Kansas City*	378	110	488
14. California	270	98	368

*Thanks, John. We could never have done it without you.

Of course, the Angels have players on their roster who could come back and play well. Doug DeCinces's trade value is just 13; that could prove a very erroneous estimate of his future worth. But DeCinces is a 33-year-old third baseman with serious back trouble, so how much can you wager on that? Every team has on it a Rick Burleson or an Ellis Valentine, trying to get back where he was a few years ago. The Royals have Dennis Leonard, the Mariners have Al Cowens. When you put the future of those players up against the future of Alan Trammell, Jack Morris and Lance Parrish, the chart above is what you get.

Although the Angels won a division title in 1982, their measurable talent pool was not a lot larger then than it is now—359 points nonpitching, 156 pitching. On the other hand, just three years ago, after the 1980 season, the Kansas City Royals were drawing from a seemingly limitless pool—919 points (678 nonpitching).

To summarize, the Angels have less visible, projectible talent on their major league roster than any other American League team. A lot less. This is a measurable fact, and a fact that I think no knowledgeable person would dispute.

That is one of the keys to their future, but only one of the keys. The equation of the future has a dizzying number of variables; we must not take too much pride in being able to measure one of them. How large this variable is as opposed to others, we will be in a better position to see in about three years.

CHART ANGELS-I

Rank Team	#1	#2	Team Total
1. Minnesota*	Hrbek (80)	Gaetti (71)	601
2. Detroit*	Whitaker (98)	Parrish (77)	570
3. Toronto*	Upshaw (84)	Barfield (66)	562
Boston**	Hoffman (64)	Armas (54)	533
5. Oakland*	Davis (64)	Phillips (47)	520
6. Chicago	Baines (79)	R. Law (63)	504
7. Baltimore**	Shelby (35)	Roenicke (28)	503
8. Milwaukee*	Gantner (65)	Molitor (63)	500
9. Seattle	D. Henderson (79)	Owen (38)	384
10. Kansas City	Brett (49)	White (49)	378
11. Texas	Wright (89)	O'Brien (45)	374
12. Cleveland*	Tabler (50)	Thomas (26)	345
13. New York	Mattingly (47)	Winfield (45)	327
14. California	Lynn (36)	Sconiers (35)	270

CHART ANGELS-II

Rank Team	#1	#2	Team Total
1. Chicago**	Burns (33)	Bannister (30)	290
2. Baltimore**	Boddicker (44)	Stewart (26)	252
3. Toronto*	Gott (33)	Leal (30)	247
Boston*	Hurst (35)	Boyd (29)	247
5. Detroit**	Berenguer (22)	Rozema (21)	243
6. Oakland	Conroy (38)	Codiroli (35)	232
7. New York*	Guidry (43)	Rawley (34)	222
8. Seattle	VandeBerg (29)	Caudill (27)	204
9. Texas	Stewart (39)	Butcher (24)	184
10. Minnesota	R. Davis (34)	Viola (29)	177
11. Milwaukee	Ladd (30)	Haas (23)	151
12. Cleveland	Heaton (42)	Sutcliffe (34)	143
13. Kansas City*	Black (24)	Armstrong (19)	110
14. California	Witt (33)	Sanchez (23)	98

THE MANAGER

NAME: John (Death House) McNamara

AGE: 51

MANAGERS FOR WHOM PLAYED IN MAJORS: Never played in the majors.

CHARACTERISTICS AS A PLAYER: Another catcher; a really bad one. Had no power and was completely overmatched by Double-A or Triple-A pitching (hit .077, .171 and .226 in three shots at Double-A; .171 and .194 in Triple-A).

MANAGERIAL RECORD:

Team	Year	Par	Wins	Losses	Pct.	+ or −
Oak	1969	7	8	5	.615	+ 1
Oak	1970	84	89	73	.549	+ 5
SD	1974	68	60	102	.370	− 8
SD	1975	67	71	91	.438	+ 4
SD	1976	71	73	89	.451	+ 2
SD	1977	22	20	28	.417	− 2
Cin	1979	87	90	71	.559	+ 3
Cin	1980	88	89	73	.549	+ 1
Cin	1981	58	66	42	.611	+ 8
Cin	1982	50	34	58	.370	−16
Cal	1983	84	70	92	.432	−14
11 Years		686	670	742	.481	−16

WHAT HE BRINGS TO THE BALLCLUB

IS HE AN INTENSE MANAGER OR MORE OF AN EASY-TO-GET-ALONG-WITH TYPE? He's more of an easy-to-get-along-with type.

IS HE MORE OF AN EMOTIONAL LEADER OR A DECISION-MAKER? I guess he would have to be an emotional leader.

IS HE MORE OF AN OPTIMIST OR MORE OF A PROBLEM SOLVER? Clearly, he is not a problem solver. John has made fewer major personnel decisions than any other manager that I know of who has managed for as long as he has. When he took over in Oakland, he played the same basic lineup that Hank Bauer had been playing. Bauer's first baseman and leftfielder had been traded and his catcher had been released, so obviously he had to make moves there, but the moves were not exactly brash: He platooned at catcher and in leftfield and installed at first Don Mincher, an established regular of modest ability who had been obtained in a trade. Bauer had gone 88–74; he went 89–73.

When he took over in San Diego, he used basically the same lineup that Don Zimmer had used the year before to finish 60–102, and he finished 60–102. When he took over in Cincinnati, he used Sparky's lineup except that he replaced Pete Rose, who had gone to Philadelphia, with Ray Knight. Sparky had gone 92-69, he went 90–71. When he took over here, he tried everything to keep Gene Mauch's lineup together. Mauch had gone 93-69, and he went Ker-splat.

HOW HE USES HIS PERSONNEL

DOES HE FAVOR A SET LINEUP OR A ROTATION SYSTEM? A set lineup.

DOES HE LIKE TO PLATOON? He'll platoon a little. If he has a choice between making a decision and platooning, he will platoon.

DOES HE TRY TO SOLVE HIS PROBLEMS WITH PROVEN PLAYERS OR WITH YOUNGSTERS WHO STILL HAVE SOMETHING TO PROVE? HOW MANY PLAYERS HAS HE MADE REGULARS OUT OF WHO WERE NOT REGULARS BEFORE, AND WHO WERE THEY? Proven players all the way. He made a semi-regular out of Mike Ivie, regulars out of Ray Knight, Bill Almon, Gene Richards and Ron Oester.

DOES HE PREFER TO GO WITH GOOD OFFENSIVE PLAYERS OR DOES HE LIKE THE GLOVE MEN? Question is irrelevant to him.

DOES HE LIKE AN OFFENSE BASED ON POWER, SPEED OR HIGH AVERAGES? Mostly high averages, as much as you can tell.

DOES HE USE THE ENTIRE ROSTER OR DOES HE KEEP PEOPLE AROUND SITTING ON THE BENCH? The only way the bench will get involved is injuries. Otherwise he'll have three, four people a year on his team who don't bat a hundred times.

DOES HE BUILD HIS BENCH AROUND YOUNG PLAYERS WHO CAN STEP INTO A BREACH IF NEED BE OR AROUND VETERAN ROLE-PLAYERS WHO HAVE THEIR OWN FUNCTIONS WITHIN A GAME? Veterans. Look at it—Mike O'Berry, Rob Wilfong, Juan Beniquez. A few youngsters mixed in.

GAME MANAGING AND USE OF STRATEGIES

DOES HE GO FOR THE BIG-INNING OFFENSE OR DOES HE LIKE TO USE THE ONE-RUN STRATEGIES? Responds to his talent, but has very clear tendencies as a one-run manager.

DOES HE PINCH-HIT MUCH, AND IF SO WHEN? With San Diego he used quite a few pinch-hitters; otherwise, much less than average.

ANYTHING UNUSUAL ABOUT HIS LINEUP SELECTION? No.

DOES HE USE THE SAC BUNT OFTEN? Yes, he likes the sacrifice, particularly when his team lacks speed. Probably uses it to minimize the double-play danger.

DOES HE LIKE TO USE THE RUNNING GAME? Didn't run much with San Diego, despite good team speed, and doesn't force the running game here. But teams in Oakland and Cincinnati were running teams.

IN WHAT CIRCUMSTANCES WILL HE ISSUE AN INTENTIONAL WALK? How many circumstances are there? He is almost certainly freer with an intentional walk than any other major league manager. The Angels gave 72 free passes last year —highest in the league, three times the totals for KC, Baltimore, Texas and New York. His teams have led the league in IBB many times, and even in Cincinnati, where he was usually ahead, he'd be about the league average.

DOES HE HIT AND RUN VERY OFTEN? Some, yes. More than Mauch did.

ARE THERE ANY UNIQUE OR IDIOSYNCRATIC STRATEGIES THAT HE PARTICULARLY LIKES? Definitely not.

HANDLING THE PITCHING STAFF

DOES HE LIKE POWER PITCHERS OR PREFER TO GO WITH THE PEOPLE WHO PUT THE BALL IN PLAY? Has had the most success with control pitchers. The largest reason for the Padres improvement under him was Randy Jones.

DOES HE STAY WITH THE STARTER OR GO TO THE BULLPEN QUICKLY? With this staff, that's like asking if he's anxious to get to the quicksand. And he's never been quick to remove his starters, even when he did have a bullpen.

DOES HE LIKE THE FOUR-MAN OR THE FIVE-MAN ROTATION? Like most people, has shifted to a five-man rotation in recent years.

DOES HE USE THE ENTIRE STAFF OR DOES HE TRY TO GET FIVE OR SIX PEOPLE TO DO MOST OF THE WORK? Everyone is involved; unlike his handling of the lineup, he does use all of his pitchers.

ARE THERE ANY PARTICULAR TYPES OF PITCHERS OF WHOM HE IS FOND? None noted.

IS THERE ANYTHING UNIQUE ABOUT HIS HANDLING OF HIS PITCHERS? There is nothing unique about his handling of anything.

WHAT IS HIS STRONGEST POINT AS A MANAGER? McNamara's an organization man. He rocks no boats, creates no enemies, tries to cooperate in the plans of the organization. In the hands of an organization that knows what it is trying to do, that's a positive thing.

IF THERE WERE NO PROFESSIONAL BASEBALL, WHAT WOULD THIS MANAGER PROBABLY BE DOING? Working as vice-president of a bank.

Rod CAREW, First Base
Runs Created 78

	G	AB	Hit	2B	3B	HR	Run	RBI	BB	SO	SB	CS	Avg
13.88 Years		615	204	30	8	6	95	68	66	680	25	13	.331
1983	129	472	160	24	2	2	66	44	57	48	6	7	.339
First Half	58	229	92	12	2	2	35	26	24	20	2	4	.402
Second Half	71	243	68	12	0	0	31	18	33	28	4	3	.280
vs. RHP		310	111	19	1	1	47	30	38	29	4	5	.358
vs. LHP		162	49	5	1	1	19	14	19	19	2	2	.302
Home	66	239	74	14	1	1	31	21	29	20	3	4	.310
Road	63	233	86	10	1	1	35	23	28	28	3	3	.369
Grass	108	387	125	21	2	2	56	40	49	38	6	5	.323
Turf	21	85	35	3	0	0	10	4	8	10	0	2	.412

Fred LYNN, Centerfield
Runs Created: 76

	G	AB	Hit	2B	3B	HR	Run	RBI	BB	SO	SB	CS	Avg
7.15 Years		591	176	40	5	24	97	100	75	83	7	5	.298
1983	117	437	119	20	3	22	56	74	55	83	2	2	.272
First Half	62	232	60	10	2	14	34	43	41	48	2	2	.259
Second Half	55	205	59	10	1	8	22	31	14	35	0	0	.288
vs. RHP		279	76	14	2	16	36	44	37	52	2	2	.272
vs. LHP		158	43	6	1	6	20	30	18	31	0	0	.272
Home	61	212	58	8	1	14	30	41	34	43	1	1	.274
Road	56	225	61	12	2	8	26	33	21	40	1	1	.271
Grass	98	366	100	16	2	19	44	61	45	70	2	2	.273
Turf	19	71	19	4	1	3	12	13	10	13	0	0	.268

Bobby GRICH, Second Base
Runs Created: 78

	G	AB	Hit	2B	3B	HR	Run	RBI	BB	SO	SB	CS	Avg
10.19 Years		563	151	27	4	18	84	73	89	106	10	7	.269
1983	120	387	113	17	0	16	65	62	76	62	2	3	.292
First Half	70	226	62	6	0	8	38	33	51	38	1	1	.274
Second half	50	161	51	11	0	8	27	29	25	24	1	2	.317
vs. RHP		232	65	10	0	9	35	29	36	42	1	1	.280
vs. LHP		155	48	7	0	7	30	33	40	20	1	2	.310
Home	56	174	60	7	0	8	36	36	39	27	0	1	.345
Road	64	213	53	10	0	8	29	26	37	35	2	2	.249
Grass	100	324	92	13	0	11	54	49	63	53	2	3	.284
Turf	20	63	21	4	0	5	11	13	13	9	0	0	.333

Juan BENIQUEZ, Rightfield
Runs Created: 40

	G	AB	Hit	2B	3B	HR	Run	RBI	BB	SO	SB	CS	Avg
6.31 Years		512	134	21	4	8	66	48	37	58	16	11	.262
1983	92	315	96	15	0	3	44	34	15	29	4	2	.305
First Half	54	184	50	9	0	2	29	15	9	23	4	1	.272
Second Half	38	131	46	6	0	1	15	19	6	6	0	1	.351
vs. RHP		171	50	8	0	2	22	24	13	25	2	1	.292
vs. LHP		144	46	7	0	1	22	10	2	4	2	1	.319
Home	45	146	43	6	0	1	18	10	6	9	3	1	.295
Road	47	169	53	9	0	2	26	24	9	20	1	1	.314
Grass	80	278	85	12	0	3	37	28	12	23	4	2	.306
Turf	12	37	11	3	0	0	7	6	3	6	0	0	.297

Doug DeCINCES, Third Base
Runs Created: 59

	G	AB	Hit	2B	3B	HR	Run	RBI	BB	SO	SB	CS	Avg
6.83 Years		566	149	33	3	23	76	82	58	87	7	5	.263
1983	95	370	104	19	3	1	49	65	32	56	2	0	.281
First Half	61	240	75	15	3	15	40	46	22	38	2	0	.313
Second Half	34	130	29	4	0	3	9	19	10	18	0	0	.223
vs. RHP		212	60	12	1	12	27	38	14	36	1	0	.283
vs. LHP		158	44	7	2	6	22	27	18	20	1	0	.278
Home	44	171	49	9	2	10	26	33	16	24	2	0	.287
Road	51	199	55	10	1		23	32	16	32	0	0	.276
Grass	79	315	91	15	3	15	45	54	26	48	2	0	.289
Turf	16	55	13	4	0	3	4	11	6	8	0	0	.236

Bob BOONE, Catcher
Runs Created: 44

	G	AB	Hit	2B	3B	HR	Run	RBI	BB	SO	SB	CS	Avg
8.70 Years		532	138	24	2	9	50	65	49	44	3	4	.259
1983	142	468	120	18	0	9	46	52	24	42	4	3	.256
First Half	72	239	60	10	0	3	22	29	11	18	3	1	.251
Second Half	70	229	60	8	0	6	24	23	13	24	1	2	.262
vs. RHP		298	86	15	0	5	31	35	13	32	2	3	.289
vs. LHP		170	34	3	0	4	15	17	11	10	2	0	.200
Home	73	227	60	10	0	6	24	30	14	14	3	2	.264
Road	69	241	60	8	0	3	22	22	10	28	1	1	.249
Grass	118	380	96	15	0	8	38	43	22	33	4	2	.253
Turf	24	88	24	3	0	1	8	9	2	9	0	1	.273

Tim FOLI, Shortstop
Runs Created: 25

	G	AB	Hit	2B	3B	HR	Run	RBI	BB	SO	SB	CS	Avg
9.98 Years		586	147	23	2	3	57	48	26	38	8	6	.251
1983	88	330	83	10	0	2	29	29	5	18	2	3	.252
First Half	65	250	65	7	0	2	25	26	5	14	2	2	.260
Second Half	23	80	18	3	0	0	4	3	0	4	0	1	.225
vs. RHP		174	44	7	0	1	12	17	2	11	0	1	.253
vs. LHP		156	39	3	0	1	17	12	3	7	2	2	.250
Home	44	156	34	4	0	1	9	14	5	12	1	1	.218
Road	44	174	49	6	0	1	20	15	0	6	1	2	.282
Grass	72	270	67	7	0	2	21	27	5	16	2	2	.248
Turf	16	60	16	3	0	0	8	2	0	2	0	1	.267

Reggie JACKSON, Designated Hitter
Runs Created: 41

	G	AB	Hit	2B	3B	HR	Run	RBI	BB	SO	SB	CS	Avg
14.12 Years		575	154	28	3	34	93	102	79	149	15	8	.268
1983	116	397	77	14	1	14	43	49	52	140	0	2	.194
First Half	57	201	43	5	1	12	29	33	38	73	0	2	.214
Second Half	59	196	34	9	0	2	14	16	14	67	0	0	.173
vs. RHP		248	45	5	1	10	28	33	38	85	0	0	.181
vs. LHP		149	32	9	0	4	15	16	14	55	0	2	.215
Home	57	192	37	8	0	7	22	23	26	71	0	0	.193
Road	59	205	40	6	1	7	21	26	26	69	0	2	.195
Grass	98	336	65	11	0	10	35	38	44	117	0	2	.193
Turf	18	61	12	3	1	4	8	11	8	23	0	0	.197

Brian DOWNING, Leftfield
Runs Created: 64

	G	AB	Hit	2B	3B	HR	Run	RBI	BB	SO	SB	CS	Avg
6.96 Years		521	138	23	1	15	76	66	78	73	4	3	.265
1983	113	403	99	15	1	19	68	53	62	59	1	2	.246
First Half	40	139	31	6	0	5	30	15	32	21	1	0	.223
Second Half	73	264	68	9	1	14	38	38	30	38	0	2	.258
vs. RHP		250	54	12	1	9	37	32	32	39	1	1	.216
vs. LHP		153	45	3	0	10	31	21	30	20	0	1	.294
Home	63	229	50	8	0	10	36	27	32	38	1	2	.218
Road	50	174	49	7	1	9	32	26	30	21	0	0	.282
Grass	98	349	83	12	0	16	54	45	50	50	1	2	.238
Turf	15	54	16	3	1	3	14	8	12	9	0	0	.296

Ron JACKSON, Infield
Runs Created: 33

	G	AB	Hit	2B	3B	HR	Run	RBI	BB	SO	SB	CS	Avg
5.44 Years		527	138	30	4	10	65	62	38	57	4	5	.262
1983	102	348	80	16	1	8	41	39	27	33	2	3	.230
First Half	48	160	38	6	1	4	21	22	14	20	0	1	.238
Second Half	54	188	42	10	0	4	20	17	13	13	2	2	.223
vs. RHP		167	37	10	1	2	18	15	15	17	2	2	.222
vs. LHP		181	43	6	0	6	23	24	12	16	0	1	.238
Home	52	169	41	8	0	5	22	19	9	12	0	1	.243
Road	50	179	39	8	1	3	19	20	18	21	2	2	.218
Grass	86	291	69	14	0	7	35	30	20	28	0	3	.237
Turf	16	57	11	2	1	1	6	9	7	5	2	0	.193

Tommy JOHN

Year	(W–L)	GS	Run	Avg	DP	Avg	SB	Avg
1982	(14-12)	33	149	4.51	39	1.18	11	.33
1983	(11-13)	34	143	4.21	53	1.56	7	.21
1976-1983		251	1144	4.56	334	1.33	102	.41

	G	IP	W	L	Pct	ER	ERA
1982 Home	19	125.3	8	7	.533	52	3.73
1983 Home	19	146.1	8	6	.571	43	2.62
1982 Road	18	95.2	6	5	.545	39	3.69
1983 Road	15	88.1	3	7	.300	70	7.13
1983 Grass	30	209.2	10	12	.454	94	4.03
1983 Turf	4	25	1	1	.500	19	6.84

Geoff ZAHN

Year	(W–L)	GS	Run	Avg	DP	Avg	SB	Avg
1982	(18- 8)	34	190	5.59	41	1.21	10	.29
1983	(9-11)	28	120	4.29	31	1.11	7	.25
1977-1983		213	1020	4.79	277	1.30	80	.38

	G	IP	W	L	Pct	ER	ERA
1982 Home	16	116	10	1	.909	37	2.87
1983 Home	13	100	6	3	.667	30	2.70
1982 Road	18	113.1	8	7	.533	58	4.61
1983 Road	16	103	3	8	.273	45	3.93
1983 Grass	25	174.1	8	8	.500	65	3.36
1983 Turf	4	28.2	1	3	.250	10	3.14

Ken FORSCH

Year	(W–L)	GS	Run	Avg	DP	Avg	SB	Avg
1982	(13-11)	35	167	4.77	27	.77	18	.51
1983	(11-12)	31	164	5.29	35	1.13	20	.64
1977-1983		153	675	4.41	145	.95	98	.64

	G	IP	W	L	Pct	ER	ERA
1982 Home	22	128.1	9	6	.600	57	4.00
1983 Home	14	102	5	6	.454	47	4.15
1982 Road	15	99.2	4	5	.444	41	3.70
1983 Road	17	117.1	6	6	.500	52	3.99
1983 Grass	24	165.2	8	11	.421	81	4.40
1983 Turf	7	53.2	3	1	.750	18	3.02

1983 OTHERS

Pitcher	(W–L)	GS	Run	Avg	DP	Avg	SB	Avg
Witt	(7-14)	19	86	4.53	29	1.53	11	.58
Kison	(11- 5)	17	84	4.94	16	.94	9	.53
McLaughlin	(2- 4)	7	37	5.29	6	.86	5	.71
Travers	(0- 3)	7	25	3.57	6	.86	8	1.14
Goltz	(0- 6)	6	26	4.33	5	.83	4	.67
Steirer	(3- 2)	5	27	5.40	4	.80	2	.40
Brown	(2- 3)	4	6	1.50	6	1.50	6	1.50
Curtis	(1- 2)	3	10	3.33	0		2	.67
Sanchez	(10- 8)	1	3	3.00	3	3.00	1	1.00

CALIFORNIA ANGELS
RUNS BATTED IN ANALYSIS

Player	RBI	RBI In Wins	Victory-Important RBI	RBI Importance	Wins Batted In	RBI Per Win
Doug DeCinces	65	43	30.73	.473	6.15	10.6
Bobby Grich	62	40	25.26	.407	5.91	10.5
Bob Boone	52	36	24.67	.474	5.43	9.6
Fred Lynn	74	41	23.02	.311	6.30	11.7
Reggie Jackson	49	30	21.55	.440	5.09	9.6
Juan Beniquez	34	24	18.73	.551	4.18	8.1
Rod Carew	44	30	18.57	.422	4.56	9.6
Brian Downing	53	27	17.17	.324	3.72	14.2
Ron Jackson	39	21	14.25	.365	3.72	10.5
Tim Foli	29	22	12.00	.414	3.58	8.1

SEATTLE MARINERS

Whew! Am I glad O'Brien's gone. Danny O'Brien had been conducting for three years a dastardly campaign to confuse the sportswriters and sports fans of this country, to render them utterly and hopelessly unable to keep straight who his players were. The Mariners had playing for them at the start of 1983 a double-play combination of Cruz and Cruz, Julio Cruz and Todd Cruz. He dispatched both of them in midseason, sending them (suspiciously) to the two teams which were on their way into the playoffs, causing further identification problems for anybody who might have trouble keeping them straight. The two best hitters on the team were two outfielders named Henderson, Dave Henderson and Steve Henderson. In addition to a "Todd" Cruz and a "Julio" Cruz, or "Steve" Henderson and a "Dave" Henderson, he had on his roster in 1983 a "Rod" Allen and a "Jamie" Allen, a "Jamie" Nelson, a "Rickey" Nelson and a "Gene" Nelson. His roster included an inordinate number of people with names like "Moore," "Clark," "Thomas," "Putnam" and "Reynolds" and enough people named Bill, Bob, Jim, Dave and Rickey to staff the reunion shows of "Ozzie and Harriett," "Leave It to Beaver," "Father Knows Best," "My Three Sons," and "Lost in Space."

Further, the *Baseball Abstract* staff of investigative reporters has now uncovered evidence that many of these people were, in fact, not major league baseball players at all, but hired "ringers" or "rhymers," as they are called, imported specifically to confuse the public. An unnamed source has told us that, as recently as August of 1981, eleven members of the 1983 Seattle Mariners were working in the tobacco industry. Investigator Paula Fastwon in Strawberry Hill, North Carolina, found this advertisement in the help-wanted section of the August 17, 1981 edition of the *Strawberry Sunday News*:

Growth-oriented company looking for a few young men to come help us fight forest fires in the Pacific Northwest. We have a lot of spare time to kill, *so only those with some familiarity with American sports jargon need apply.* Prefer applicants to have at least average manual dexterity and foot speed; those forest fires can come at you pretty fast, you know. Contact Dan at P.O. Box 1392, Strawberry Hill.
(Emphasis mine)

Don't think that's suspicious? Well, consider this: 47% of the people who live in Strawberry Hill, North Carolina, are named "Henderson"! Apparently, O'Brien hoped, once he had the rest of the league properly confused, to get seven people on his roster named "Dave Henderson," and then go to the winter meetings and start trading them; promising each opposing general manager that he was getting *that* Dave Henderson. O'Brien planned to keep the real Dave Henderson, release everybody in his system named "Nelson" or "Allen," and make his bid for *The Sporting News* Executive of the Year award. The plan was uncovered by an alert security guard at the Kingdome, Dick Henderson, who contacted Danny Kaye,

who passed the word to George Argyros. O'Brien pleaded for a chance to see his plan through, but was fired after uttering the unforgivable words, "What else did you expect me to do, you moron, you can't make a ballclub out of mousaka."

The Seattle Mariners of 1984 have the potential to be one of the worst major league ballclubs ever. You take a team that finishes 60–102, and you take away from them their leading hitter (Steve Henderson at .294) and a relief pitcher who saved 26 of those 60 wins, and you've got the potential there for a real sad situation. They also have the potential to be not too bad, win maybe 65, 66 games. A collection of young players, rushed to the majors too soon, tends to be volatile; if a couple of them start playing well, others will follow. But a collection of very young players without adequate veteran on-field leadership... well, you can't be optimistic.

Perhaps, rather than making fun of all those Nelsons and Allens and people, I should help you try to figure them out, keep straight who is who. Here are short synopses of the talents and potential of four of the key Seattle Mariners:

(1) Who is Al Chambers? Al Chambers was the first player in the country drafted in 1979, made steady but not speedy progress through the minors. A big lefthanded batter with some speed and some power, draws a lot of walks but may strike out too much. Was drafted when everybody was looking for a new Dave Parker; couldn't be regarded as superstar material at this time.

(2) Who is Ron Roenicke? Gary's younger brother; he's 27 and the Dodgers released him, so he's hardly superstar material, either.

In spite of that, I do like him quite a bit; I think he's probably as good or better than his brother, and he could make a variety of valuable contributions to the Mariners. He could play centerfield but his range isn't great; has a rightfielder's arm (12 assists last year in just 54 outfield games) but they might be reluctant to move Dave Henderson. Good outfielder.

As an offensive player, he'd make one hell of a leadoff man, one of the best in the American League. At Albuquerque in '81, he had a .464 onbase percentage, and his onbase percentage in the NL in 1982 was .400 when he wasn't pinch-hitting (the Dodgers asked him to pinch-hit a lot, and he was no good at it). He is an excellent percentage base stealer. He has some power, which is just another positive for a leadoff man as far as I'm concerned.

The power might make it hard for the Mariners to resist batting him fifth or something, which would be unfortunate. If they will leave him alone, let him bat leadoff in 150 games, I guarantee that he will score 85, 90 runs, even with this team; I think he will score 100 or 110. The whole team only scored 558 last year.

(3) Who is Spike Owen? Also plays in the National League under the name of Jose Oquendo.

(4) Who is Darnell Coles? Darnell Coles is possibly the key to this team, the man who will most decide what kind of a year they have. With Roenicke, Thomas, D. Henderson and Putnam, they should have a reasonably good four-man offense. Owen is not going to hit. But if Chambers and Coles and Perconte come through, the offensive sequences get long enough to do some real damage.

Coles is a third baseman, potentially a good one (he was a shortstop until last year). He hit very well in the majors last year, and he's always hit in the minors. He has some speed and is not an impatient hitter. But he's only 21, and Lord knows whether or not he's ready to help a major league team.

II

There is some cause for hope in the wake of the Mariners's 1983 season. It is a year not without historical precedent. Every other expansion team has experienced a disheartening "setback season" on their way to contention or decency. Within their first ten seasons, every one of the other nine new teams has established a franchise record for wins, or developed an expected level of performance (i.e., 73–78 wins every year), only to go back to day one very suddenly.

That the Mariners reversed their gains of 1982 is not necessarily a sign that their climb out of infancy is over. History shows that all expansion teams but one were able to bounce back immediately from their setback season,

and all but two improved their records beyond those of the season prior to the great slide:

SETBACK SEASONS

Setback year	1962	1968	1967	1967	1974	1975	1976	1977	1981	1983
Expansion team	Cal.	Wash.	Mets	Hou.	KC	Mil.	Mtl.	SD	Tor*	Sea
Decrease of games won	−16	−11	−5	−3	−11	−8	−20	−4	−11	−16
Setback season +1										
Increase in games won	+12	+21	+12	+3	+14	−2	+20	+15	+21	1984

*Strike adjusted

Many of these clubs went on to even greater improvements in the years following Setback +1. The Mets won it all two years later. The Astros had their first .500 season two years later, as did the Blue Jays. Kansas City won three straight division titles starting in the second year after the setback. The exception to these success stories are the Brewers, who returned to an early expansion level of play for three years before turning it around with a 93-win season in Setback year +3.

The Mariners dropped below their first season win total for the third time, something no other expansion team has done. The Senators won fewer games their second and third years, the Royals their second, the Blue Jays their third and the Angels in their eighth, but no team has returned to the womb on three separate occasions (second, fourth and seventh seasons) as have the Mariners.

—J.B.

THE MANAGER

NAME: Del Crandall

AGE: 54

MANAGERS FOR WHOM PLAYED IN MAJORS: Billy Southworth, Charlie Grimm, Fred Haney, Chuck Dressen, Birdie Tebbotts, Bobby Bragan, Alvin Dark, Harry Walker, George Strickland.

CHARACTERISTICS AS A PLAYER: Excellent player; power-hitting catcher, a key member of the outstanding Braves teams in the mid-fifties. Defensive skills above average.

MANAGERIAL RECORD:

Team	Year	Par	Wins	Losses	Pct.	+ or −
Mil	1972	55	54	70	.435	− 1
Mil	1973	73	74	88	.457	+ 1
Mil	1974	74	76	86	.469	+ 2
Mil	1975	77	67	94	.416	−10
Sea	1983	41	34	55	.381	− 7
5 Years		320	305	393	.437	−15

WHAT HE BRINGS TO THE BALLCLUB

IS HE AN INTENSE MANAGER OR MORE OF AN EASY-TO-GET-ALONG-WITH TYPE? I'm hesitant to answer, but I can't recall that he's ever had many run-ins with his players, can't recall any times when he's blown up and said, "I just can't take any more of this." He even managed to get along

with George Scott for three years. On the basis of that, I'd have to say (b).

IS HE MORE OF AN EMOTIONAL LEADER OR A DECISION-MAKER? Some of each.

IS HE MORE OF AN OPTIMIST OR MORE OF A PROBLEM SOLVER? I wouldn't say he's a problem solver.

HOW HE USES HIS PERSONNEL

DOES HE FAVOR A SET LINEUP OR A ROTATION SYSTEM? Not a lot of player rotation.

DOES HE LIKE TO PLATOON? Hasn't done much of it.

DOES HE TRY TO SOLVE HIS PROBLEMS WITH PROVEN PLAYERS OR WITH YOUNGSTERS WHO STILL HAVE SOMETHING TO PROVE? HOW MANY PLAYERS HAS HE MADE REGULARS OUT OF WHO WERE NOT REGULARS BEFORE, AND WHO WERE THEY? Youngsters. Crandall has never received much credit for one of the most surprising and gutty managerial moves of the 1970s: the decision to make a regular out of Robin Yount at the age of 18. At the time a lot of people said he shouldn't be rushing a kid like this, but you have to say it worked. He may have been helped to this decision because he himself was in the majors and playing pretty well when he was 19. Also made first-time regulars out of Mike Ferraro, Joe Lahoud, Pedro Garcia, Tim Johnson, Bob Coluccio, Darrell Porter, Sixto Lozcano and Bill Sharp.

DOES HE PREFER TO GO WITH GOOD OFFENSIVE PLAYERS OR DOES HE LIKE THE GLOVE MEN? Has never gone too long with a one-dimensional glove man.

DOES HE LIKE AN OFFENSE BASED ON POWER, SPEED OR HIGH AVERAGES? Seems to like power. Best Brewer teams had power at seven spots in the lineup.

DOES HE USE THE ENTIRE ROSTER OR DOES HE KEEP PEOPLE AROUND SITTING ON THE BENCH? For a manager who uses a fairly set lineup, he gets everyone in the act.

DOES HE BUILD HIS BENCH AROUND YOUNG PLAYERS WHO CAN STEP INTO A BREACH IF NEED BE OR AROUND VETERAN ROLE-PLAYERS WHO HAVE THEIR OWN FUNCTIONS WITHIN A GAME? Youngsters.

GAME MANAGING AND USE OF STRATEGIES

DOES HE GO FOR THE BIG-INNING OFFENSE OR DOES HE LIKE TO USE THE ONE-RUN STRATEGIES? Not a big-inning manager.

DOES HE PINCH-HIT MUCH, AND IF SO WHEN? Pinch-hits more here than he did in Milwaukee.

ANYTHING UNUSUAL ABOUT HIS LINEUP SELECTION? Well, since you asked . . .

Look, I'm trying very hard to make these analyses a factual and nonjudgmental look at what the manager does. But. There has got to be a point, some point, at which some decisions are clearly and objectively dumb. Del Crandall had Spike Owen batting leadoff last year, and I'm not talking about a few games. I mean 2½, 3 months. What on earth could have been in the man's head? Spike Owen is a .196 hitter, with a .259 on-base percentage. This is the man that you would choose to be the cornerstone of your offense? Man, that is insane. That is a crime against your ballclub. And he had good leadoff material on the ballclub. He had Bernazard, he had Roenicke, he had Steve Henderson. He could have had the leadoff man on 40, 50% more often than he did. Of course their offense looked terrible. Any offense would look terrible with a .196 hitter leading off.

I can make a lot of excuses for managers who do things that I don't agree with or don't understand. But how in the world could anybody justify something like this? He wanted to build up the player's confidence? You don't build up anybody's confidence by asking him to do something that he is not capable

of doing. Do you? What about the psychological consequences of losing games? Would you make excuses for Crandall if he batted Dave Henderson seventh and Orlando Mercado third? What he did was just as damaging as that. Every time he wrote out a lineup card with Spike Owen's name at the top of it, that was an insult to Bernazard, an insult to Roenicke, an assault on the team and an affront to the Seattle fans. I'm trying to be fair, Mr. Crandall, but I just can't turn a blind eye to something like that.

DOES HE USE THE SAC BUNT OFTEN? An above-average amount.

DOES HE LIKE TO USE THE RUNNING GAME? Yes.

IN WHAT CIRCUMSTANCES WILL HE ISSUE AN INTENTIONAL WALK? I don't know.

DOES HE HIT AND RUN VERY OFTEN? Not sure.

ARE THERE ANY UNIQUE OR IDIOSYNCRATIC STRATEGIES THAT HE PARTICULARLY LIKES? Ibid.

HANDLING THE PITCHING STAFF

DOES HE LIKE POWER PITCHERS OR PREFER TO GO WITH THE PEOPLE WHO PUT THE BALL IN PLAY? In his years in Milwaukee, he reconstructed the staff to be less of an aggressive, power pitchers staff and more of a finesse-pitcher's, a nibbler's staff. Since Lachemann's staff here was very much a power pitchers' staff, it will be interesting to see how he reacts to that.

DOES HE STAY WITH THE STARTER OR GO TO THE BULLPEN QUICKLY? He is a manager who likes his starters to do the work—again, just the opposite of Lachemann. So you have to think that this staff is in for a significant rebuilding.

DOES HE LIKE THE FOUR-MAN OR THE FIVE-MAN ROTATION? Used a four-man rotation in Milwaukee, five-man here last year.

DOES HE USE THE ENTIRE STAFF OR DOES HE TRY TO GET FIVE OR SIX PEOPLE TO DO MOST OF THE WORK? He had some pitchers in Milwaukee who were doing almost nothing.

IS THERE ANYTHING UNIQUE ABOUT HIS HANDLING OF HIS PITCHERS? I haven't seen it.

WHAT IS HIS STRONGEST POINT AS A MANAGER? He has a reputation for being able to work with young players, and in some parts his record seems to justify that.

IF THERE WERE NO PROFESSIONAL BASEBALL, WHAT WOULD THIS MANAGER PROBABLY BE DOING? Managing a roller-skating rink.

SEATTLE MARINERS

Player	Record in Lineup	Record Without
Pat Putnam	49-77	11-25
Dave Henderson	49-80	11-22
Steve Henderson	43-71	17-31
Al Cowens	36-57	24-45
Spike Owen	31-48	29-54
Richie Zisk	30-47	30-55
Jamie Allen	29-50	31-52
Tony Bernazard	27-51	33-51
Rickey Nelson	26-41	34-53
Rick Sweet	24-42	36-60
Orlando Mercado	23-36	37-66
Todd Cruz	22-40	38-62
Julio Cruz	21-37	39-65
Manny Castillo	21-25	39-77
Ron Roenicke	21-36	39-66
Jamie Nelson	12-23	48-79
Domingo Ramos	12-22	48-80
John Moses	11-23	49-79
Phil Bradley	9- 9	51-93
Darnell Coles	9-18	51-84
Al Chambers	8-14	52-88
Harold Reynolds	7-10	53-92
Dave Edler	6-13	54-89
Ken Phelps	8-25	52-77
Jim Maler	5-15	55-87
Bud Bulling	1- 1	59-101

Spike OWEN, Shortstop
Runs Created: 23

	G	AB	Hit	2B	3B	HR	Run	RBI	BB	SO	SB	CS	Avg
.49 years		620	122	22	6	4	73	43	49	89	20	12	.196
1983	80	306	60	11	3	2	36	21	24	44	10	6	.196
First Half	8	32	8	2	2	0	9	3	6	7	1	0	.250
Second Half	72	274	52	9	1	2	27	18	18	37	9	7	.190
vs. RHP		193	33	3	0	1	20	12	18	25	9	4	.171
vs. LHP		113	27	8	3	1	16	9	6	19	1	2	.239
Home	43	159	32	7	3	1	21	12	10	21	7	0	.201
Road	37	147	28	4	0	1	15	9	14	23	3	6	.190
Grass	27	106	22	2	0	1	8	7	7	16	3	5	.208
Turf	53	200	38	9	3	1	28	14	17	28	7	1	.190

Steve HENDERSON, Leftfield
Runs Created: 66

	G	AB	Hit	2B	3B	HR	Run	RBI	BB	SO	SB	CS	Avg
4.89 Years		569	161	27	9	11	76	71	64	111	16	11	.283
1983	121	436	128	32	3	10	50	54	44	82	10	14	.294
First Half	73	276	82	20	1	3	29	24	32	51	10	13	.297
Second Half	48	160	46	12	2	7	21	30	12	31	0	1	.288
vs. RHP		236	74	16	3	5	25	27	28	53	6	7	.314
vs. LHP		200	54	16	0	5	25	27	16	29	4	7	.270
Home	60	204	57	13	2	5	20	27	30	41	5	8	.279
Road	61	232	71	19	1	5	30	27	14	41	5	6	.306
Grass	49	184	58	15	1	2	21	19	12	35	4	5	.315
Turf	72	252	70	17	2	8	29	35	32	47	6	9	.278

Pat PUTNAM, First Base
Runs Created: 67

	G	AB	Hit	2B	3B	HR	Run	RBI	BB	SO	SB	CS	Avg
3.70 Years		486	128	24	2	16	57	64	35	60	2	4	.264
1983	144	469	126	23	2	19	58	67	39	57	2	1	.269
First Half	74	238	56	11	1	9	27	29	20	35	0	1	.235
Second Half	70	231	70	12	1	10	31	38	19	22	2	0	.303
vs. RHP		336	102	17	2	17	51	51	32	37	2	1	.304
vs. LHP		133	24	6	0	2	7	16	7	20	0	0	.180
Home	73	240	66	16	0	11	29	42	22	34	2	0	.275
Road	71	229	60	7	2	8	29	25	17	23	0	1	.262
Grass	54	173	43	4	1	3	20	13	14	15	0	1	.249
Turf	90	296	83	19	1	16	38	54	25	42	2	0	.280

Dave HENDERSON, Centerfield
Runs Created: 67

	G	AB	Hit	2B	3B	HR	Run	RBI	BB	SO	SB	CS	Avg
1.85 Years		504	126	24	3	20	62	63	43	99	7	5	.249
1983	137	484	130	24	5	17	50	55	28	93	9	3	.269
First Half	74	273	71	8	3	8	26	25	17	56	5	2	.260
Second Half	63	211	59	16	2	9	24	30	11	37	4	1	.280
vs. RHP		279	75	16	4	11	28	39	15	57	8	1	.269
vs. LHP		205	55	8	1	6	22	16	13	36	1	2	.268
Home	66	239	67	15	3	9	29	24	13	37	3	2	.280
Road	71	245	63	9	2	8	21	31	15	56	6	1	.257
Grass	56	191	47	9	1	5	14	20	12	45	5	1	.246
Turf	81	293	83	15	4	12	36	35	16	48	4	2	.283

Tony BERNAZARD, Second Base
Runs Created: 71

	G	AB	Hit	2B	3B	HR	Run	RBI	BB	SO	SB	CS	Avg
3.00 Years		560	146	27	6	10	82	57	69	101	16	6	.261
1983	139	533	141	34	3	8	65	56	55	97	23	9	.265
First Half	75	289	78	21	2	3	38	29	28	57	10	2	.270
Second Half	6	244	63	13	1	5	27	27	27	40	13	7	.258
vs. RHP		355	90	25	3	7	41	39	32	68	14	4	.254
vs. LHP		178	51	9	0	1	24	17	23	29	9	5	.287
Home	68	247	71	20	0	6	35	30	33	39	13	5	.287
Road	71	286	70	14	3	2	30	26	22	58	10	4	.245
Grass	84	328	83	15	3	4	35	35	28	67	9	5	.253
Turf	55	205	58	19	0	4	30	21	27	30	14	4	.283

Al COWENS, Rightfield
Runs Created: 28

	G	AB	Hit	2B	3B	HR	Run	RBI	BB	SO	SB	CS	Avg
7.99 Years		560	152	26	8	10	73	71	41	63	14	9	.271
1983	110	356	73	19	2	7	39	35	23	38	10	2	.205
First Half	65	220	40	9	2	2	18	16	17	21	7	0	.182
Second Half	45	136	33	10	0	5	21	19	6	17	3	2	.243
vs. RHP		187	36	11	1	3	22	17	13	21	9	1	.193
vs. LHP		169	37	8	1	4	17	18	10	17	1	1	.219
Home	54	164	31	7	0	2	13	11	12	23	7	0	.189
Road	56	192	42	12	2	5	26	24	11	15	3	2	.219
Grass	45	153	32	10	2	5	19	16	9	13	3	2	.209
Turf	65	203	41	9	0	2	20	19	14	25	7	0	.202

Jamie ALLEN, Third Base
Runs Created: 26

	G	AB	Hit	2B	3B	HR	Run	RBI	BB	SO	SB	CS	Avg
.53 Years		514	115	19	0	8	43	40	62	98	11	9	.223
1983	86	273	61	10	0	4	23	21	33	52	6		.223
First Half	50	166	44	5	0	4	16	16	23	24	3	3	.265
Second Half	36	107	17	5	0	0	7	5	10	28	3	2	.159
vs. RHP		146	30	6	0	1	11	8	19	29	4	3	.205
vs. LHP		127	31	4	0	3	12	13	14	23	2	2	.244
Home	43	130	28	5	0	1	10	7	20	23	3	3	.215
Road	43	143	33	4	0	3	13	14	13	29	3	2	.231
Grass	35	117	24	3	0	1	11	11	8	24	2	2	.205
Turf	51	156	37	7	0	1	12	10	25	28	4	3	.237

Rick SWEET, Catcher
Runs Created: 15

	G	AB	Hit	2B	3B	HR	Run	RBI	BB	SO	SB	CS	Avg
1.68 Years		438	102	14	1	4	37	34	36	43	4	4	.234
1983	93	249	55	9	0	1	18	22	13	26	2	2	.221
First Half	48	129	25	4	0	1	6	11	9	11	2	0	.194
Second Half	45	120	30	5	0	0	12	11	4	15	0	2	.250
vs. RHP		224	50	8	0	1	16	21	12	21	2	0	.223
vs. LHP		25	5	1	0	0	2	1	1	5	0	2	.200
Home	43	114	28	5	0	1	10	11	6	12	0	1	.246
Road	50	135	27	4	0	0	8	11	7	14	2	0	.200
Grass	37	93	22	3	0	0	5	9	7	10	2	1	.237
Turf	56	156	33	6	0	1	13	13	6	16	0	1	.212

Richie ZISK, Designated Hitter
Runs Created: 37

	G	AB	Hit	2B	3B	HR	Run	RBI	BB	SO	SB	CS	Avg
8.97 Years		574	165	27	3	23	76	88	59	101	1	2	.287
1983	90	285	69	12	0	12	30	36	30	61	0	0	.242
First Half	57	195	47	9	0	8	19	25	19	44	0	0	.241
Second Half	33	90	22	3	0	4	11	11	11	17	0	0	.244
vs. RHP		144	29	6	0	1	9	8	13	37	0	0	.201
vs. LHP		141	40	6	0	11	21	28	17	24	0	0	.284
Home	42	143	29	4	0	8	15	16	13	28	0	0	.203
Road	48	142	40	8	0	4	15	20	17	33	0	0	.282
Grass	36	110	28	5	0	3	10	12	14	29	0	0	.255
Turf	54	175	41	7	0	9	20	24	16	32	0	0	.234

Rickey NELSON, Outfield
Runs Created: 31

	G	AB	Hit	2B	3B	HR	Run	RBI	BB	SO	SB	CS	Avg
.60 Years		481	122	21	5	8	53	60	28	83	12	7	.254
1983	98	291	74	13	3	5	32	36	17	50	7	4	.254
First Half	43	129	41	7	1	4	17	17	4	17	6	2	.318
Second Half	55	162	33	6	2	1	15	19	13	33	1	2	.204
vs. RHP		250	66	11	3	5	30	35	15	42	5	4	.264
vs. LHP		41	8	2	0	0	2	1	2	8	2	0	.195
Home	49	160	37	9	2	1	15	14	9	25	4	2	.231
Road	49	131	37	4	1	4	17	22	8	25	3	2	.282
Grass	37	96	27	2	0	3	11	16	3	21	3	2	.281
Turf	61	195	47	11	3	2	21	20	14	29	4	2	.241

Matt YOUNG

Year	(W–L)	GS	Run	Avg	DP	Avg	SB	Avg
1983	(11-15)	31	100	3.23	28	.90	25	.81

	G	IP	W	L	Pct	ER	ERA
1983 Home	17	102.1	4	9	.308	37	3.25
1983 Road	16	101.1	7	6	.538	37	3.29
1983 Grass	11	67.1	5	4	.555	27	3.61
1983 Turf	22	136.1	6	11	.352	47	3.10

Jim BEATTIE

Year	(W–L)	GS	Run	Avg	DP	Avg	SB	Avg
1982	(8-12)	26	9	3.81	23	.88	24	.92
1983	(10-15)	29	99	3.41	27	.93	23	.79
1978-1983		128	497	3.88	124	.97	106	.83

	G	IP	W	L	Pct	ER	ERA
1982 Home	14	86.2	4	6	.400	33	3.45
1983 Home	12	83.2	4	6	.400	26	2.80
1982 Road	14	85.2	4	6	.400	31	3.26
1983 Road	18	113	6	9	.400	58	4.62
1983 Grass	15	91	4	9	.308	51	5.04
1983 Turf	15	105.2	6	6	.500	31	2.81

Bob STODDARD

Year	(W–L)	GS	Run	Avg	DP	Avg	SB	Avg
1982	(3- 3)	9	30	3.33	12	1.33	3	.33
1983	(9-17)	23	74	3.22	29	1.26	21	.91
1981-1983		37	126	3.40	46	1.24	29	.78

	G	IP	W	L	Pct	ER	ERA
1982 Home	3	24.1	2	0	1.000	6	2.22
1983 Home	18	85	6	8	.429	45	4.76
1982 Road	6	43	1	3	.250	12	2.51
1983 Road	17	90.2	3	9	.250	41	4.07
1983 Grass	15	80.1	2	9	.182	40	4.48
1983 Turf	20	95.1	7	8	.467	46	4.34

Mike MOORE

Year	(W–L)	GS	Run	Avg	DP	Avg	SB	Avg
1982	(7-14)	27	95	3.52	21	.78	25	.93
1983	(6- 8)	21	82	3.90	16	.76	22	1.05
1982-1983		48	177	3.69	37	.77	47	.98

	G	IP	W	L	Pct	ER	ERA
1982 Home	15	73.1	5	6	.455	42	5.15
1983 Home	10	65	3	3	.500	36	4.98
1982 Road	13	71	2	8	.200	44	5.58
1983 Road	12	63	3	5	.375	31	4.43
1983 Grass	9	50	3	3	.500	19	3.42
1983 Turf	13	78	3	5	.375	48	5.54

1983 OTHERS

Pitcher	(W–L)	GS	Run	Avg	DP	Avg	SB	Avg
Clark	(7-10)	17	62	3.65	20	1.18	21	1.23
Perry	(3-10)	16	45	2.81	17	1.06	7	.44
Abbott	(5- 3)	15	69	4.60	11	.73	9	.60
Nelson	(0- 3)	5	24	4.80	7	1.40	1	.20
Nunez	(0- 4)	5	12	2.40	5	1.00	4	.80

SEATTLE MARINERS
RUNS BATTED IN ANALYSIS

Player	RBI	RBI In Wins	Victory-Important RBI	RBI Importance	Wins Batted In	RBI Per Win
Pat Putnam	67	38	25.11	.375	8.54	7.8
Steve Henderson	54	29	19.72	.365	5.05	10.7
Dave Henderson	55	30	18.59	.338	5.66	9.7
Al Cowens	35	23	17.07	.488	4.30	8.1
Richie Zisk	36	18	13.64	.379	2.99	12.0
Spike Owen	21	13	9.68	.461	1.96	10.7
Rick Sweet	22	14	9.60	.436	2.89	7.6
Tony Bernazard	30	12	8.43	.281	2.56	11.7
Rickey Nelson	36	14	7.83	.218	3.01	12.0
Jamie Allen	21	12	7.11	.339	2.56	8.2

PLAYER RATINGS

I. ANTI

The idea of rating ballplayers is an arrogant bit of nonsense, incurring inherent intellectual costs which can lead, if unchecked, to intellectual bankruptcy. There are many reasons for believing that and a few reasons for rating players even though I believe it, and I wanted to try to explain what those reasons are.

I am very leery of "great statistics," of statistics which consider everything and provide the once and final answer to great baseball questions, questions like "Who was the greatest player ever?" or "Who should have won the MVP award?" or "Who really belongs in the Hall of Fame?" or even, "Who is better, Dawson or Murphy?" It is my considered opinion that we have no business answering these questions by formula.

Great statistics exist about the fringes of all areas of research; meteorology has yielded up a "comfort index," Jimmy Carter in the 1976 campaign introduced to economics a "misery index," and psychology has the best-known great statistic of all, the "Intelligence Quotient," or IQ. I was much impressed by something that a psychology teacher once said to me about IQ testing. Suppose, he said, that we turn the same assumptions to the evaluation of a person's *physical* attributes. We all have parts which are attractive (even beautiful) and parts which are ugly (even grotesque). We have parts which are strong and parts which are weak. We have parts which are healthy and parts which are diseased. We have parts which are quick and parts which are slow, parts functional and non-functional, parts calloused and parts sensitive, parts agile and awkward and most of us, by the middle of life, are missing a piece or two. We are old and young, male and female, scarred and blemished. To sum all of these, and rate them along a linear scale . . . ? To ask each of us to perform (old men and young women,

the crawling and the doddering, the sick and the healthy) 200 or 300 physical tasks and evaluative mechanisms, and to score each just right so as to wind up with a "BQ" (Body Quotient) and say "OK, you're a 104, you're a 117, but you're a 76" would be preposterous. It would be a stupid waste of time.

Well, if it is preposterous for a person's body, it is not a bit less preposterous for his mind. It not only does not contribute to an understanding of a person's abilities, it gets in the way of it. It is not the proper function of a psychologist to go herding people into straight lines and slapping numbers on them. While we are talking about mental capacities, what about the capacity to love and the capacity to hate, the capacity to endure and the willingness to falter, the capacity to overcome obstacles, the capacity to recognize one's own good. Do we not all remember "intelligent" men who can remember their high school Spanish but forget to be kind to those who love them? If Hitler had an IQ of 126, must we say that he "had a good mind," far above average? Where does one draw the line between a refusal to learn and a lack of intelligence? The truth is that we all have parts which are weak, parts healthy and parts diseased, quick and slow and all the others.

And yet, we are stuck with it. Some Frankenstein or Rappaccini invented it in the innocent adolescence of psychology, and try as we might we cannot get rid of the damn thing, because it has become a part of the way that people *think*. It is the first concept that children are given with which to think about what goes on inside their heads, and when they are grown up to be psychologists, they cannot conceive of themselves without their peg, and set out to find more complicated ways of pegging others, when they should be about the task of developing broader, more

realistic ways to think about human mental capacities. (Saul Bellow: *"We have a word for everything except what we really think and feel."*) The one-dimensional measurement of intelligence has given rise to an entire generation of people who have a one-dimensional concept of intelligence, of the one thing on earth which is most clearly not one-dimensional.

Sabermetrics is to baseball as psychology is to human nature, and I wish to perform no such disservice to baseball. The search for great statistics—and any ranking of a player must be done, if it is objective, by a great statistic—is not and cannot be a scientific undertaking. The "comfort index" is not exactly something a meteorologist would use to try to develop a better explanation of where and when tornadoes develop; it is something TV weathermen use to try to explain meteorology to the largest common denominator. A sophomore economics student would get an "F" for coming up with a "misery index"; it's something that a politician uses to enchant a particularly slow voter.

Great statistics have no clear idea of what it is that they are measuring. Some psychologists—the ones who are hung up on IQ testing—would claim that they were an exception, that they search for intelligence with scientific methods. But is it only the *methods* you use which decide whether what you are doing is science? What seems so odd to me is that while the search for intelligence measures progresses unabated, the question of "What is intelligence?" remains unanswered. How can you make a scientific measurement of how much of something somebody has, when you don't even know what it is that they are supposed to have? Can't you see a couple of chemists confronting the same problem:

"Dr. Durler, could you tell me how much derillium is in this alloy?"

"What's derillium?"

"I'm damned if I know, but we need to know how much of it there is in there, anyway."

Psychologists solve this problem by saying that intelligence is the thing that IQ tests measure, which is the scientific equivalent of taking your ball and going home.

I have a copy of a 1920 Spalding Guide which presents an "All-American Team" picked by something called "Total Average." This version of Total Average added together fielding percentage and batting percentage, plus won/lost percentage if you were a pitcher. Great statistics compress together unlike information into a common shape. Inflation percentage points are added in with percentages of people unemployed, degrees of temperature with humidity figures (maybe somebody should find a way to mix together the heat, humidity, wind, unemployment rate, inflation rate, Dow Jones average, price of gold in Zurich . . . call it the "total financial and economic life enjoyment factor"). They can do this because, like IQ, they have no clear idea of exactly what it is that they are measuring.

Great statistics consume information rather than producing it. When a meteorologist measures barometric pressure, humidity, heat, wind or cloud height, he can make sure of that information in many ways. If the barometric pressure is significantly different here than it is 50 miles from here, we can safely say that some air is going to be moving. If it is 37° in

Kansas but 67° in Denver, then it probably is not going to stay 37° in Kansas very long. Similarly, in economics there are unstable combinations of circumstances; if the rate of unemployment is high but the rate of new construction is also high, something has got to happen. If the tax rates are changed, that will change the economy in vaguely predictable ways. In sabermetrics, there are similarly impossible and unstable combinations of occurrences. A team does not hit .250 with little power in a .265 league and win the division. If a team loses a star outfielder to injury, that will change the team's ability to score runs in vaguely predictable ways (we can predict very accurately the impact of the loss; we cannot predict accurately the impact of the adjustments to the loss).

But great statistics are of little use in studying other issues; they consume knowledge but don't yield it. They are not a part of a discussion, they are the end of a discussion. I feel that it is the proper place of sabermetrics not to *answer* questions —not to say for you that A is a better ballplayer than B—but to develop a broad range of tools and measures that you or I or anyone else could use in developing our own answers. Bad sabermetrics attempts to end the discussion by saying that I have studied the issue and this is the answer. Good sabermetrics attempts to contribute to the discussion in such a way as to enable it to move forward on a ground of shared understanding.

Since great statistics attempt to tell you everything that you need to know about the subject in three easy digits, they must define out of existence everything that is not included in their measurement. We do not know how many times each player was thrown out attempting to take an extra base. We do not know how many times each player gave away a base by throwing to the wrong one. We do not know how many hits Ozzie Smith takes away from the opposition, nor how many doubles Dan Ford gives away in the corner. We do not know how many runs Jesse Barfield prevents by keeping runners on third base. We couldn't even guess how many runs Carlton Fisk saves for a team by his ability to call pitches or his ability to spot a problem with the pitcher's delivery. We do not know which or whether players are especially good in the clutch. And this is only the shadow of the monster; our whole ignorance is much larger than we can conceive of.

The work of sabermetrics is not to ignore all of these considerations or to deny them, but to find ways to deal with them. Given enough good sabermetricians, those ways can and will be found. Bad sabermetricians characteristically insist that those things which cannot be measured are not important, that they do not even exist. They run from the monster in terror, and insist that he does not really exist, that there is only That Shadow.

II. PRO

Why do it, then? Why produce a great statistic, when great statistics have so much against them?

Look, I am very well aware that there are many basic, fundamental facets of a baseball team of which I have little knowledge and with which I cannot deal. All scientists, I suspect, have an enormous respect for their own ignorance. We people who create knowledge are not people who understand things. We are people who *don't* understand things, and consequently must figure them out. Freud

couldn't understand why people did things the way they did, so he filled up about a million notebooks trying to puzzle it all out. Betrand Russell wrote that "physics is mathematical not because we know so much about the physical world, but because we know so little; it is only its mathematical properties that we can discover." Einstein couldn't figure out how things were put together, and it bugged the hell out of him.

My work has been described in a lot of ways, and I don't like most of

them, but one that I particularly don't like is being called a baseball expert. I am *not* an expert; I am a student. I dislike making ratings because it puts me in the position of being an expert.

What I am trying to do in this introduction is to step down off that podium. I am not trying to lecture you—I am not trying to lecture anyone—about who is good and who is bad. I have my ideas on the subject, that's all. I offer those ideas because people expect me to do that, and want me to do it. It sells books, and I have to make a living. If this book sells 100,000 copies, I'd guess that 65,000 people would cite Section III as their favorite part of the book. I write books for people to enjoy, you know. The ratings provide an organization and framework for the comments, and I do have things I want to say about the players.

But people should understand that when I say that opinions are bullshit, it is not other people's opinions that I am referring to. I don't value my own opinions, either.

Baseball ratings are not troubled by one of the major problems of other great statistics. That is because a player is on the field for a single, definable purpose: to help his team win baseball games. No one can really say what a good mind is because no one can really say why we are on earth. I might say that we are here to do what we can to relieve suffering and make other people happy, because that answer satisfies me better than any other, but you might say that we are here to glorify God Almighty, and two scientists with blinders on might say, one that we are here to perpetuate our kind, the other that we are here by comsic chance. Maybe we are each here for a different reason; LaMarr Hoyt is

here because God is conducting an experiment on the effects of obesity on control pitchers.

Anyway, if you could really measure all of a player's contributions to victory and defeat, then you would have a legitimate basis for ranking players. Of course, as I was saying, you can't. Besides that, winning a pennant in baseball requires diverse skills, combinations of unlike skills. You need those little guys who get on base; you need the big guys who hit home runs. You need guys who can turn a double play, and people who know the strengths and weaknesses of the opposition hitters. So even if those skills do all acquire their value along the same line, it would be of questionable value to make a linear representation of them.

So I shrug, and I say, "Well, if people want me to do it, I'll do it the best I can. I do not want to approach this in such a way that, like IQ, it becomes a barrier to understanding. I take the various methods that I have developed to measure different things, and I combine them as best I can. I define what is being measured as best I can.

I don't mind doing them, really; I don't mind offering these suggestions, I do regret that they draw a

grossly disproportionate share of comment—that such a minor, inconsequential and irrelevant part of my work comes to stand for my work in the minds of so many people. I sometimes resent that I am prevailed upon to make these ratings, and then people refuse to accept them in the spirit in which they are offered.

Probably these ratings are not as good as the very best, the most careful, the most informed and meticulous subjective judgment. On the other hand, as I have written before, if formulas evaluate players without respect to timing, clutch ability, baserunning judgment, mental lapses, leadership or other such deeper insights, they also evaluate them without regard to favoritism, press clippings, self-promotion, chance viewings too often remembered, or any of the other greater forms of ignorance. It is perhaps not such a bad trade. These ratings still result from opinion, but it is opinions at one remove—not opinions about players, but opinions about the game they play, about what things are important in that game and which are not. I hope that I might be allowed those opinions; they are offered in the spirit of fun.

III. HOW THE RATINGS ARE DERIVED

How the ratings below are arrived at is explained in detail in *Not of Any General Interest*. What I will explain now is that it all boils down to four won/lost records—a 1982 offensive won and lost record, a 1982 defensive won and lost record, a 1983 offensive won and lost record, and a 1983 defensive won and lost record. The parenthetical expression at the beginning of the player comment gives the combined number of wins and losses that the player has produced for his team over the last two years.

The players are rated, from the won/lost record, according to .350 chance. Suppose that a player over the last two years has produced 21

wins for his team and 16 losses. The chance that a .350 team would win 21 or more out of 37 games is .0055. The smaller that figure, the higher the player is rated. If another player had only, let's say, 21 "games" worth of playing time over the last two years, then he would be rated higher than this player if his record was 14–7 (.0031), but lower if it was 13–8 (.0108).

I should have explained better than I did a year ago why I use this way of rating players. Chance frequency is a standard way of assessing the significance of data; if one event would have only a .0055 likelihood of occurring by blind chance and an-

other has a 30% likelihood of occurring by chance, then we say that we have far better evidence that the first event is meaningful—did not occur by chance—than the second event. "Meaningful" in baseball means winning games. What I am asking by this method is: "How likely is it that this man is a .350 ballplayer? How convincing is the evidence to support the proposition that this man is not a .350 ballplayer?"

Why .350, rather than .500? Because a .500 ballplayer in baseball has value. In measuring value, it's not appropriate to choose a method that considers a 2–1 record to be better than an 11–11 record, or even a

10–12 record. A pitcher who goes 11 and 11 has presented far better evidence that he is a major league pitcher than a 2–1 pitcher. An 18–13 pitcher has presented better evidence that he is an excellent major league pitcher than has a 7–2 pitcher.

I use .350 percentage (a year ago I used .400), because that is about where the replacement level is. If you go 7–13, then you're replaceable; you have presented no real evidence that you're better than somebody we can get off the scrap heap.

Rating players on the basis simply of won/lost percentage, while it would result in the same general arrangement of players, would be even worse. Doug DeCinces has performed brilliantly over the last two years, but he did miss half the season with an injury. It is not appropriate to rank him up there with Schmidt, because he hasn't had equal value. The .350 chance method makes that distinction; it rewards durability.

When a player is out of the lineup, he will probably be replaced by somebody around a .350 winning percentage; the more time he misses, the lower he will rank.

The .350 chance works against injury-prone players, and in favor of the durable player, a little more forcefully than the .400 chance that I used a year ago.

One other change of some significance. A year ago, I rated the players according to the chance frequency of their two-year record only. This year, I rated them according to 1982 and '83 combined, or 1983 only, whichever was smaller (whichever resulted in the higher rating). This makes no difference in most cases because the two-year figure will be the smaller figure the great majority of the time. But it does make a difference in a case like Lloyd Moseby, who had a very poor 1982 season but a brilliant 1983 season. The reasoning a year ago was that it took two years of

performance to really see what a player could do. The reasoning this year is yes, but Lloyd Moseby is very clearly not the ballplayer that he was a year ago. His 1983 performance, by itself, offers clear proof that he is not a replacement level player. If a thing is clearly proven in one year, it cannot be less clearly proven in two. Moseby's ranking isn't what it would be if he had had two seasons like the 1983 one; if he has the same season again, he will move up in the rankings. But the 1982 season is cut adrift; it is no longer used to weigh him down. For those players whose rating is based only on the 1983 season, the season's W-L mark is shown at the end of the comment.

The ratings consider an immense variety of information—how many sacrifice bunts the guy has had, what park he plays in . . . just about everything I can measure. That don't make them right, but it does make them hard as hell to figure.

CATCHERS

1. Gary CARTER, Montreal (33–17) Has been the #1 catcher since I started the player ratings and comments section five years ago. And to my mind, it's still an easy choice. Pena is terrific, but he's never had a year when he drove in as many runs as Carter or scored as many runs as Carter, and the Pirates don't cut off the running game quite as well as the Expos do (there were 115 stolen bases in 203 attempts against the Expos last year, 124 in 201 against the Pirates). Kennedy is as good an offensive player as Carter, but there's no comparison defensively. Parrish is close offensively and close defensively, but not quite there either way. Of the four basic elements of the ratings (1982 Offensive, 1982 Defensive, 1983 Offensive, 1983 Defensive), Carter's worst is 1983 offensive (.604).

A year ago (re: Gaylord Perry) I had a comment about why players' careers were getting longer, suggesting that it was primarily an economic phenomenon. This explanation struck a chord, was picked up by the media and ran the gamut from theory to accepted wisdom to cliché in about

three months. Usually when something strikes like that, it's a sign that there is some truth in it; at the same time, you should see that there is another side to it, the Gary Carter side. Before the free-agent era, I don't think there is any way that a player as valuable as Carter would have been worked as hard as he was worked from 1977 to 1982. The Expos a) are paying Gary Carter a great amount of money, and b) do not own his future. In those circumstances, they are inclined to take more chances with Carter's future than they otherwise might. They are risking a future that doesn't belong to them anyway to get their $2 million a year's worth. For this reason and for others, the long-term career implications of baseball's economic restructuring are very, very different than the short-term implications, which are all that we have seen yet.

Carter has now caught 1,144 games in his career; he should have two or three more years before the effects of his workload become serious. No one has ever caught 2000 games in a career; the legs usually go

about 1300 to 1500, and the career might go on in pain for 300 to 400 more. But Jim Sundberg was the #2 rated catcher just two years ago, and he had 1,123 games behind him then. The best thing for Carter's career would be if the Expos could move him to rightfield now, but they can't.

2. Terry KENNEDY, San Diego (30–19) Has there ever been a regular player before who drove in twice as many runs as he scored? I don't know of one. Lombardi in 1939 scored 43 runs and drove in 85; Triandos was once 47 and 88. Those people, however, were probably pinch-run for 30 or 40 times, so the real ratios are more even than that. Kennedy didn't score any runs because the people behind him didn't hit. Among the people batting fifth for the Padres last year were Luis Salazar, Ruppert Jones and Kurt Bevacqua. I didn't figure what they hit as a group but I'll bet it was no better than the Reds' #3 hitters.

The thing about Doug Gwosdz (the Padres always win when he's in the lineup) is getting beyond the stage of a joke. Before last year they were 9–1 with Gwosdz in the lineup, last year 10–3 with a 2.19 ERA. Mostly those were Sunday games; Kennedy sometimes doesn't play the day game following a night game. Gwosdz isn't a major league hitter, but I sure think I'd keep him around until I figured out what was going on there.

Late note—found one. Vic Wertz in 1960 scored 45 runs and drove in 103.

3. Lance PARRISH, Detroit (29–19) Speaking of records with people in the lineup. . . . for the last two or three years I've been keeping track of the Tigers record with and without Parrish in the lineup; in 1981 and '82 they were 40–16 without him, nine games under .500 with him. We started to see the same pattern again early in '83, and I decided to make a real effort to find out why this was happening.

The Tigers in 1983 were 67–56 (.545) with Parrish in the lineup as the starting catcher, 25–14 (.641) without him. They improved in other games no matter who the other catcher was. With John Wockenfuss in the lineup, the gain was *offensive*. Wockenfuss can hit lefthanders about as well as anybody around; his RBI rate in 1983 was nearly the same as Parrish's. Parrish was then available to be the Tigers' DH, and he's no Kirk Gibson; he drove in 22 runs in 27 games as DH. With Wockenfuss as the starting catcher, the Tigers scored 6.15 runs per game, allowed 4.15, and won two-thirds of the time. There was no visible defensive cost; stolen bases by the opposition were up quite a bit, but runs allowed were down a little, from 4.21 with Parrish.

With Bill Fahey in the lineup, the gain was *defensive*. Offense stayed about constant, but runs *allowed* dropped to three per game (2.40 ERA). The strikeout-to-walk ratio improved noticeably to 1.8–1. Fahey was not starting a lot of Jack Morris's games or anything like that; Morris started two of those games and Petry three, but Wilcox started one, Howard Bailey one (4.88 ERA; the game Fahey started was Bailey's only good start), and Pashnick one (5.26 ERA). It is, on the other hand, only eight games.

Two explanations are distinctly inferior to one. We kept track of all kinds of things like the average number of pitchers used, the relationship between expected opposition runs by the runs created formula and actual opposition runs, opposing starting pitchers and in-game patterns of runs allowed, and it doesn't show a thing. The only thing that shows is that they scored more runs with Wockenfuss catching, and allowed fewer with Fahey catching. But anyway, over a three-year period the Tigers are now 170–168 (.503) with Parrish as the starting catcher, and 65–30 (.684) without him. No reasonable, coherent explanation for this has yet been advanced.

Which is not to say that Parrish isn't a great ballplayer. He can't rate number one because of his poor strikeout/walk ratios. His on-base percentage last year was only .320, which is below average, and quite a bit below average for a catcher. The ability to reach base is one of the three most fundamental traits of any player, and it would be very difficult for a player who was below average in that respect to be so outstanding in other respects that he was the best player in baseball at his position. Parrish is close, but he's not quite there.

4. Carlton FISK, Chicago (26–18) I think it would be almost impossible to overstate what Fisk has meant to the White Sox; I could easily see an MVP vote for him in 1983. Fisk might never have another good year (he is 36 and has caught over 1300 major league games), but even if he doesn't the White Sox are likely to go on winning the division. They have a kid catcher, Joel Skinner, who is ready to step in and play. But I don't think the White Sox would have won 99 games a year ago with Joel Skinner catching. Fisk has done a lot to help bring along the young pitching staff, and to help show the team the way to the top. The White Sox will owe him a debt for years after he is no longer playing for them.

5. Tony PENA, Pittsburgh (26–20) Awesome second half of the season (.314, 13 homers, 48 RBI; scored 56 runs). . . . lifetime .300 hitter and now a Gold Glove catcher. . . . Pirates were 80–64 with Pena catching, 4–14 without him in the lineup (4–7 with Nicosia, 0–7 with May, Tenace and Ortiz). The staff ERA was 3.32 with

him, 5.41 without him. . . . lifetime batting average is about 40 points higher against the teams in his own division than it is against the West.

6. Darrell PORTER, St. Louis (22–17) Had a fine year, his best since he gave up drugs. Darrell can help you if he hits .230 because of his other skills, and he hit .262. He had a .365 on-base percentage, hit 15 homers and had the best opposition stolen base rate (.52 per game) in the National League.

Darrell's had one of those Mickey Vernon careers, Rico Carty careers, where if you just took the high points and filled in a normal path between them, you'd have a Hall of Fame career. He had a fine year as a 21-year-old in 1973, had as good a season as I've ever seen anybody have in 1979, won a World Series MVP award in '82 and had a real good year in '83. But there have just been too many gaps in there.

7. Bo DIAZ, Philadelphia (25–22) Didn't come close to repeating his big 1982 year with the bat, but still drove in some runs and played well defensively (defensive won/lost percentage, .60, was third in the league behind Carter and Pena, tied with Yeager). Only major league player ever named "Baudilio."

8. Butch WYNEGAR, New York (15–12) You may not believe this, but the November 1977 issue of the *Baseball Digest* contains an article solemnly entitled: "How the Tigers Missed Out on Drafting Butch Wynegar." The Tigers in 1974 drafted Lance Parrish in the first round and were planning to pick Wynegar in the second until the Twins, drafting two ahead of them, picked him. The Tigers, according to the article, "still cringe when they recall how close they came to claiming the switch-hitting Wynegar." I haven't asked, but I reckon they've given up cringing since then.

9. Rick DEMPSEY, Baltimore (19–18) At Yankee Stadium on the ninth of September, 1983, Rick Dempsey drove in a run with a second-inning single off of Ron Guidry. The Orioles lost the game anyway, 5–3. What is unusual about this is that that was the only time during the 1983 season that Rick Dempsey drove in a run,

193

and the Baltimore Orioles did not win the game. He had 31 other RBIs, all of them contributing to victory, and two more in the World Series, both contributing to wins. . . . if I picked an "All People I Like to Watch" team, he'd be on it. . . . Do you realize that Rick Dempsey played for the Minnesota Twins in the 1960s? He did (a few games in 1969).

10. Ernie WHITT, Toronto (16–15) The Blue Jays were shopping him around this winter, which makes sense. His value is never going to be any higher, and they have a young catcher they like. . . . I don't know which it is, but either the Blue Jays have one hell of a hitting coach, or they're doing something funny with the bats. Whitt never hit as well in the minors as he has the last couple of years, and Buck Martinez has always been a fine defensive catcher but where did he come up with a .452 slugging percentage? Toronto got 27 homers in 565 at-bats out of a grab-bag platoon combination that plays good defense. . . . Martinez much better than Whitt on defense, but Whitt's not bad.

11. Bruce BENEDICT, Atlanta (19–20) Had the best strikeout-to-walk ratio of any National League player, 61 walks and only 24 strikeouts. He's sort of a negative image of Lance Parrish, has no power and his arm is not the strong point of his defensive game, but he does get on base (hit .298) and helps the team in some other ways. (1983 season: 11–9.)

12. Jody DAVIS, Chicago Cubs (21–23) The man who drove in the big runs for the Cubs (39.09 VI-RBI, most on the team; also led in RBI Importance, Wins Batted In and fewest RBI per win). . . . had a very disappointing defensive year, as you know if you watch the cable (I love Harry Carey). Had 21 passed balls and didn't throw well; the 21 PB were the most by a National League catcher since Ted Simmons had 28 in 1975. But he can hit.

13. Ron HASSEY, Cleveland (16–17) Your basic Cleveland Indians half-good ballplayer. Fairly good arm, hits for a decent average, draws some walks, hits a few doubles. In the context of a powerful offense, having to

deal with a Ron Hassey would seem like an additional threat, like Bruce Benedict. In the context of a really bad offense, he would look like Ron Hodges.

If the Indians had some really bad ballplayers who were dragging down the good players, like the Mets do, for example, then there would be some hope in that; all you have to do is replace the bad ballplayers and you improve. But the Indians really don't have *bad* ballplayers. They just don't have *good* ballplayers. What can you do?

14. Dave ENGLE, Minnesota (10–11) Had an impressive 1983 season. He began the year as a 26-year-old outfielder, had never caught in professional ball. He had some problems throwing early in the year, but really put it together and was throwing about as well as any catcher in the league the last couple of months. Then for a bonus, he hit .305 and showed some power. He probably isn't as good as he looked at the end of the year, but he's not Tim Laudner, either. (1983 season: 8–7.)

15. Ron HODGES, New York (12–13) In the same class with Benedict, Hassey; he doesn't throw as well as Hassey, but he's a better offensive player. His offensive strength, like their's, is his ability to get on base; the Mets bat him seventh or eighth, which is the most efficient way to waste that strength. His reputation is horrible, and he's not real good, but mostly what that stems from is that people who play for losers always get hung with the rap of being losers. He's not that bad.

16. Alan ASHBY, Houston (14–16) The Astros had a better record with everybody else starting than Ashby. They were 39-40 with Ashby, 46-37 with other catchers. . . . Then there is the curious case of Luis Pujols, the modern Bill Bergen. Will someone please explain to me why Luis Pujols is in the majors? Since he came up in 1977 he's hit .067, .131, .227, .199 .239, .199 and .195. He's what you might call a proven hitter. In 1982, he led National League catchers in passed balls while playing only 65 games. He has no power. He doesn't throw well—opponents stole 45 bases in the 26 games he started last year.

His strike-zone judgment is one of his weaker points. It's not a question of the positives and negatives not balancing out; there *aren't* any positives. He stays in the majors, apparently, solely on the basis of being willing to try to catch the knuckleball. Astros catchers in 1983:

	G	AB	H	HR	RBI	Avg
Ashby	87	275	63	8	34	.229
Pujols	40	87	17	0	12	.195
Bjorkman	29	75	17	2	14	.227
Mizerock	33	85	13	1	10	.153
Spilman*	42	78	13	1	9	.167

*Spilman caught only 6 games.

In the Astrodome, where runs are scarce, I can easily see sacrificing offense to keep control of the running game. But Astros's opponents stole 182 bases in 235 attempts, plus these people made 26 errors and were charged with 35 passed balls (both figures the highest in the league). Ashby's decent, but he's being platooned with the Charity League.

17. Bob BOONE, California (20–26) Scored only 46 runs, drove in 52 in 142 games. With a .293 on-base percentage, would have to win two Gold Gloves a season to carry his bat, and considering that the Angels had a staff ERA of 4.31, I can't see where he's making an impact, although he's certainly a good defensive catcher. He's the kind of guy they always say would make a good manager, but I'd like him a lot better if he could manage to get on base once in awhile. Good bunter.

18. Bob BRENLY, San Francisco (10–11) The Giants had him figured as a platoon player, but he didn't hit lefthanders (.196), so that's probably out the window. Had excellent .363 on-base percentage against righthanders, but down to .260 against lefties . . . . hit .224 on grass fields and .224 on turf . . . there sure are a lot of teams that need catching help . . . . I always liked Nicosia, but he may have sat on the bench too long.

19. Steve YEAGER, Los Angeles (13–16) With the benching of Cerone and the doubtful status of Scioscia, the departure of Gene Tenace, major league baseball apparently did not have a prominent (regular) Italian catcher in 1983 for the first time since 1931. You ever notice how many great Italian catchers there have been?

Lombardi, Berra, Joe Torre; Campanella's father was Italian. Even when there was nobody great there were always a bunch of guys around like Jim Pagliaroni, Johnny Romano, Chris Cannizaro, John Boccabella, Ray Fosse (I guess Fosse is Italian; I don't know), Joe Garagiola and Gus and Frank Mancuso. All of a sudden they're gone.

20. Jim SUNDBERG, Texas (18–24)
Now with Milwaukee. His value has taken a dramatic plunge, and it probably has some recovery left in it. On the other hand, it's hard to see where he'll give the Brewers anything they couldn't have gotten by putting Charlie Moore back behind home plate, and it's hard to generate much enthusiasm for an organization that regards a burnt out big-name catcher as a solution to a problem.

21. John WATHAN, Kansas City
(16–23) Don Slaught probably has the job. The last catcher to win a batting title was Ernie Lombardi in 1942; Slaught could be the next one. I like Slot a laught. His arm is just so-so, but he's a hustling, hardworking hitter. He fights the pitcher, fouls off pitches until he sees something he can hit; I was very surprised to see that he drew only eleven walks, and I think he'll increase that sharply as he gets older. Wathan's a likable guy, but he'll be more of an asset to the team as a Derrel Thomas-type 5-position utility player than as a regular. He has good speed and can throw and doesn't make concentration mistakes, but that doesn't justify a regular spot for him.

22. Gary ALLENSON, Boston (10–16)
Platoon combination, Allenson and Gedman. Allenson, supposedly a good defensive catcher, had good defensive marks a year ago, not so good in 1983 (although still far better than Gedman). The Red Sox had a 4.34 ERA with Allenson in the lineup (4.67 with Gedman) and allowed .80 stolen bases per game with Allenson (1.35 with Gedman). Newman, always a surprisingly good defensive catcher, seems to have been the best of the three. The Red Sox had a 3.97 ERA with him in the lineup, and allowed only .66 stolen bases per game. Also he fielded .990.

But he didn't hit. I suppose what I should say is that Gedman has to hit a lot to compensate for his glovework, and Allenson has to field a whole lot to make up for his bat . . . Allenson hit only .111 (3 for 27) in the late innings of close games; Gedman hit .222 but drove in no runs in 36 at-bats in the same conditions.

23. Rick SWEET, Seattle (10–16)
Marginals used Sweet (.260 on-base percentage, .269 slugging percentage), Mercado (.259/.298), Nelson (.312/.281) and Bulling (.000/.000). So offensively the best of the lot was Nelson, who hit .219 but did hit one homer in just 96 at-bats, and whose on-base percentage was almost as good as Lance Parrish's. Nelson also runs well . . . Kearney doesn't figure to be much of an improvement.

24. Dann BILARDELLO, Cincinnati
(6–9) I wrote the Yeager comment before he came up, decided to leave it. . . . Bilardello's a better prospect than the guy they had a year ago (Trevino). He drove in 38 runs in less than 300 at-bats. . . . Just 24, and hit with good power and for a good average in the minors. . . . a note in The Baseball Register says that he "led Texas League catchers . . . in stealers caught with 42 in 1982." Hmm . . . Texas league statistical information is apparently ahead of the majors. No surprise. . . . Reds played almost .500 ball with Bilardello in the lineup.

. . . do you suppose his mother calls him Dannnny?

25. Bob KEARNEY, Oakland (7–11)
The rating could be a little higher; there's no appreciable difference between spots 21 and 26 here. . . . played surprisingly well; he never hit as well in the minors as he did last year for Oakland. But Rick Sweet had the same kind of a year in 1982, and nobody offered them any relief aces for him . . . in view of the number of teams which need catching help, it's taken amazingly long for Mike Heath to get a full shot at a regular job. Heath's not great, but he's a .250 hitter with some power, and he can throw. How many teams can match that? (1983: 6–9.)

26. Ned YOST, Milwaukee (5–10)
Now with Texas. Rader feels he can play; it's sure hard to see the evidence for it. He strikes out about 20% of the time; strikeout-to-walk ratio of 7 to 1. Doesn't hit for average, power not impressive, wretched defensive catcher. Hits lefthanders fairly well, but everybody on the Rangers hits lefthanders; he's Steve Yeager with no arm. Sometimes those guys will fool you, but I can't see what he gives the Rangers that they didn't already have in Bobby Johnson—a slow, righthanded power hitter who strikes out a lot. But Johnson's a better defensive catcher.

CATCHERS

Player	Offensive 1982		1983		Defensive 1982		1983		Total	.350 Chance
1. Carter	.733	12-4	.604	10- 6	.67	6-3	.65	6-3	33-17	.000001
2. Kennedy	.697	11-5	.645	10- 5	.56	5-4	.47	4-5	30-19	.00016
3. Parrish	.642	9-5	.540	10- 8	.61	5-3	.63	5-3	29-19	.00028
4. Fisk	.543	8-6	.679	10- 4	.57	5-3	.06	5-3	26-18	.00094
5. Pena	.559	8-6	.575	9- 6	.48	4-4	.61	5-4	26-20	.00229
6. Porter	.554	6-5	.643	8- 5	.53	4-3	.54	4-4	22-17	.00504
7. Diaz	.602	9-6	.416	6- 8	.56	5-4	.60	5-4	25-22	.00798
8. Wynegar	.549	4-4	.694	6- 2	.47	2-3	.53	3-3	15-12	.02292
9. Dempsey	.459	5-5	.376	4- 7	.60	4-4	.66	5-3	19-18	.03000
10. Whitt	.512	4-4	.574	6- 4	.46	3-3	.50	4-4	16-15	.04237
11. Benedict	.328	4-8	.561	7- 5	.55	4-3	.50	4-4	19-20	.17928
12. Davis	.492	6-6	.559	8- 7	.44	4-4	.38	3-6	21-23	.05559
13. Hassey	.474	5-5	.499	5- 5	.47	3-3	.47	3-4	16-17	.07678
14. Engle	.318	2-4	.580	6- 4			.48	2-3	10-11	.11323
15. Hodges	.557	4-3	.522	4- 3	.38	2-3	.35	2-4	12-13	.12542
16. Ashby	.585	6-4	.479	4- 4	.36	3-4	.44	2-3	14-16	.12631
17. Boone	.381	5-9	.320	4-10	.65	6-3	.48	4-5	20-26	.14686
18. Brenly	.593	3-2	.411	4- 5	.35	0-1	.53	3-3	10-11	.16233
19. Yeager	.394	2-4	.304	3- 8	.66	3-2	.60	4-3	13-16	.17928
20. Sundberg	.479	7-7	.204	2-10	.48	4-4	.62	5-3	18-24	.18175
21. Wathan	.488	6-7	.305	4- 9	.47	3-4	.41	2-4	16-23	.26411
22. Allenson	.276	2-6	.318	2- 5	.64	4-2	.38	2-3	10-16	.42691
23. Sweet	.382	3-5	.147	1- 7	.63	3-2	.35	2-3	10-16	.42691
24. Bilardello			.389	4- 5			.46	3-3	6- 9	.43572
25. Kearney	.090	0-2	.398	4- 5	.40	0-1	.44	3-3	7-11	.43572
26. Yost	.564	2-1	.255	2- 4	.35	1-1	.22	1-3	5-10	.64806

FIRST BASE

1. Eddie MURRAY, Baltimore (28–9)
The great one. . . . turned in another good stretch run (9 homers, 25 RBI in 31 games after September 1). . . . hit six homers in 13 games against the #2 team, the Tigers. The White Sox staff gave him trouble all year. . . . surprisingly, doesn't figure to post really awesome career marks. I estimate his chance of hitting 500 career home runs at only 34%, and not growing rapidly. The career projection method discussed in the San Francisco comment also hauls him in with about 450 homers, 2700 hits. And that method, while it has a lot of problems, is most accurate when working with a great player of consistent performance. You can't get much more consistent than Eddie.

2. Cecil COOPER, Milwaukee (28–14)
The only player in the majors who could be described as a currently proven 200-hit man. Boggs and Ripken have just done it once, and Garvey hasn't had 200 since 1980 . . . how do you like these stats for July?

G	AB	R	H	2B	3B	HR	RBI	Avg
27	112	26	41	7	1	10	39	.366

at that rate he'd drive in 234 runs on the year . . .

I think the Brewers' infield of the last two years is clearly the greatest infield of my lifetime. Two members of the group (Cooper and Yount) are probable Hall of Famers, right at their peak, and the other two are better than good ballplayers. Molitor will probably wind up his career with 2000, 2500 hits and some other good totals, and Gantner's a good second baseman with a good bat. I think the AV of the four of them last year was 54, and I doubt that you could find many higher. The Cardinals' all-star infield of '63-'64 isn't even close, nor is the Dodgers' long-time infield. I don't know that I could name a better four-man infield ever.

3. Keith HERNANDEZ, New York Mets (25–12) It doesn't take a Philadelphia lawyer or even an Earl Weaver second baseman to figure out that the Mets are going nowhere until they clear Hookie and Mubie off the top

of the batting order. The logical step, it would seem to me, would be to move Keith Hernandez into the leadoff spot and bat Wally Backman second. Hernandez had the second-best on-base percentage in the National League in 1983; Hernandez reaches base a full 25% more than does Wilson. Although he's not the running threat that Wilson is, he's a smart baserunner who usually has good success when he does attempt to steal. Moving him out of the third slot also moves Strawberry and Foster up in the batting order. Seems a shame to bat your main power sources fourth and fifth when they can be batted third and fourth, and Hernandez is not so great an RBI threat that he'll be missed at number three. Not that an RBI threat could do much threatening given the few times Mets number one and two batters reach base.

There is also another factor to consider, and that is that Hernandez has a reputation for needing some pushing now and again. Many think that is how the Mets were able to get him in the first place. The responsibility of batting leadoff is the kind of challenge he needs. The Mets are a team of many weaknesses. It seems a shame that they would waste one of their few strengths by not using it where it will do the most good.
—Jim Baker

4. Darrell EVANS, San Francisco (22–10) Now with Detroit; gives the Tigers the big lefthanded bat they needed . . . has a unique ability to avoid the double play. In the last five years has grounded into only 38 DPs in 2,463 at-bats (15 per 1,000 at-bats, a lower rate than Tim Raines). The only other power hitter in baseball whose rate is as low (unless you consider Kirk Gibson a power hitter) is Willie Upshaw, and Willie's only had about half as many at-bats.

His odd April/May pattern in 1983:

	AB	H	HR	RBI	Avg
April	60	12	3	7	.200
May	97	41	9	23	.423

is something that he has done before:

	AB	H	HR	RBI	Avg
April 1978	72	14	1	8	.194
May 1978	86	27	3	10	.314
April 1980	73	16	3	7	.219
May 1980	94	29	3	17	.309

He doesn't seem to hit well in cold weather—doesn't hit in April, doesn't hit much in September, never hit as well in Candlestick as he did on the road. He will likely get off to a slow start, and have to deal with the pressure of that.

I still have to like the Tigers' move in signing him. They've got to make an effort to get over the hill; they can't sit and wait. Evans addresses their needs beautifully—a first baseman, a lefthanded power hitter. He is getting old, but if he has a good year in this park it's going to be a *good* year.

5. Jason THOMPSON, Pittsburgh (24–12) Not as consistent as the top three and can't do much damage to a lefthander, but he's right up there. He gets on base as much as Hernandez and has power to match Murray in a good year, plus he's a solid first baseman. The record of pitchers opposing him over the last two years (method for deriving these explained on pages 184-186 of the 1983 *Abstract*):

G	IP	W	L	Pct	H	R	ER	HR	SO	BB	ERA
41	261	9	21	.300	280	195	177	49	235	200	6.10

If he has an off year and Garvey has a good year, as happened in 1983, they're about even as offensive players.

6. George HENDRICK, St. Louis (21–10) Hit over .300 in all breakdowns except the second half the season (.287). . . . hit .352 against lefthanded pitching. . . . has to be one of the most consistent players ever to play the game. He's had eleven straight good years, nothing even resembling a bad one. His lowest average in that span was .258, but that year he hit 24 homers and drove in 86 runs, and his lowest home run total is 16, but that year he hit .300. His .318 average last year was his fourth .300 year but his highest average; his career high in home runs is only 25. . . . if it was my ballclub I'd move Hendrick back to right, put Green in center, Van Slyke at first and leave Oberkfell at third, getting rid of McGee. Then you could lead off Lonnie, bat Van Slyke second and Porter third and Hendrick would drive in 120 runs.

7. Al OLIVER, Montreal (24–15) In addition to the problems with his production outlined in the Expos comment, he was not driving in meaningful runs, for a clearly visible reason: They wouldn't pitch to him in a game situation. With a righthander on the mound they would walk him (he was intentionally passed 17 times) and pitch to Wallach; with a lefthander they'd pitch to Oliver, but he hit only .213 against lefthanders (he usually has a large platoon differential). Result: 31 VI-RBI on the year, and the lowest RBI Importance among the Expo regulars. . . . still has defensive problems at first. . . . should be a platoon player at this point.

8. Kent HRBEK, Minnesota (22–13) Hit .386 and had a .750 slugging percentage in the three American League turf parks away from the Metrodome . . . turns 24 in May; looks like he's headed for the #1 spot among first basemen. He struck out 71 times last year, and I swear I can't understand why. I never see him swing and miss the ball. He must take a lot of 2-strike pitches or something. . . . better than 50/50 chance of winning a batting title in the next few years.

9. Chris CHAMBLISS, Atlanta (21–12) Has absolutely nothing in common with Cecil Cooper except that they are both lefthanded-hitting first basemen, black, bald-headed, were each born in late December (one in 1948, one 1949), are about the same size, each led the leagues they were playing in in hitting in 1970, each once led the American League in fielding percentage with a mark of .997, and have each won Gold Glove awards. Nothing else. Except they have the same initials.

10. Dan DRIESSEN, Cincinnati (20–11) I shouldn't be so hard on him; he's turned in a couple of pretty decent years. . . . grounded into double play frequency over the last five years is just 19 per 1,000 at-bats. . . . me-

dium range power, excellent strike zone judgment. . . . the kind of player, like Ron Hassey, who looks as good as the team he's playing for.

11. Ray KNIGHT, Houston (23–16) Has grounded into 95 double plays in the last five years (36 per 1,000 at-bats; this is the highest frequency in the National League). I'll bet if we had the career home and road breakdowns of all major league players, Ray Knight would have the largest homefield disadvantage. He has never played in a park that didn't cut about 40 points off his average. His home/road breakdowns since he became a regular in 1979:

	HOME			ROAD		
	HR	RBI	Avg	HR	RBI	Avg
1979	4	34	.309	6	45	.326
1980	6	39	.238	8	39	.287
1981	1	11	.254	5	23	.264
1982	0	34	.269	6	36	.318
1983	3	31	.259	6	39	.345

12. Willie UPSHAW, Toronto (23–16) The rating is low because as far as I'm concerned he's had one good year. I wasn't impressed with the '82 season; I definitely am with the '83. He seems to be emerging in the Cecil Cooper mold. Good defense, rarely grounds into double plays. Had a strong finish, hitting .352 with 7 homers, 28 RBI in 28 games after September 1. Has no platoon differential to speak of, but hits a lot better in Toronto than he does on the road (both of those things were also true in 1982). Has led the league in errors twice in a row; the 21 last year were the most by a first baseman since 1977. But he also led the league in starting 3–6–3 double plays.

13. Bill BUCKNER, Chicago Cubs (24–18) Watching his battle for 3000 hits is kind of like watching *Das Boot*; you know they're not going to make it, but you keep waiting and waiting for something to happen. Every year that Buckner makes it through with another 175, 190 hits cuts into the remaining distance further than the last one did. He's about five and a half, six years away now; odds against him are 3–1. . . . never cared much for him as a player, really. Singles hitter, seems like he complains a lot. He's kind of a poor man's Al Oliver.

14. Steve GARVEY, San Diego (20–14) Sure does look strange in a San

Diego uniform. . . . doesn't have Grade A power, grounds into a lot of double plays, never walks, hasn't hit .300 for three years. The record of pitchers opposing him over the last two years:

G	IP	W	L	Pct	H	R	ER	K	BB	ERA
38	240	12	17	.414	290	136	124	125	49	4.65

He would have ranked higher in the past, and he might do things that will help you sell tickets. Personally, I prefer players who do things that will help you win ballgames.

15. Rod CAREW, California (19–13) The move to California probably cost him a couple of batting titles. He hit .369 on the road last year (48 points higher than Wade Boggs), but only .310 in California. . . . still has larger–than-average platoon differential . . . hit .412 in 21 games on artificial turf. . . . highest ranked nonpower-hitting first baseman.

16. Willie AIKENS, Kansas City (17–11) Has grounded into 79 double plays in the last five years (37 per 1,000 at-bats). . . . *Webster's Thesaurus* suggests the following words as possible synonyms or related words for "error:" mistake, inaccuracy, miscalculation, miscomputation, oversight, slip, blooper, blunder, boner, bull, bungle, fluff, lapse, miscue, misstep, rock, slipup, trip, faux pas, bevue, fault, misdoing, misjudgment, stumble, boo-boo, botch, fumble, muff, howler, screamer, impropriety and indecorum. Their list of suggested synonyms for "inept" is even more generous. It includes awkward, bumbling, maladroit, unhandy, wooden, infelicitous, graceless, ill-chosen, unfortunate, unhappy, improper, ill-timed, inappropriate, inapt, unapt, malapropos, undue, unseasonable, unseemly, unsuitable, unadept, undexterous, unfacile, unhandy, unproficient, inefficient, incapable, incompetent, inexpert, unexpert, unskilled, unskillful and unworkmanlike. Just a note to the Toronto press corps: You never know when one of these words might come in handy. You never know when a few minutes spent studying this list now might save you valuable deadline-pressure seconds during the course of the long, long, long season. I particularly like "botch," "howler" and "unfacile." I also like "fluff" and "bevue," although I don't really know how to use them. I'm sure you'll have the opportunity to work them in somewhere, though.

17. Mike (Showtime) HARGROVE, Cleveland (20–16) Has grounded into 78 double plays in the last five years (34 per 1,000 at-bats). . . . another Indians half-good player. With the acquisition of Bernazard they now have seven leadoff men in their lineup, and their cleanup hitter looks like Julio Franco.

18. Tom PACIOREK, Chicago (15–10) Excellent three-man platoon arrangement with Paciorek (.340 against lefthanders), Greg Walker (a more productive season per at-bat than Ron Kittle; drove in 51 runs in 261 AB against righthanders) and Squires for defense (143 games and 153 at-bats would have to be some sort of record if you could define it right). Ranks right up there with Lowenstein/Roenicke and Easler/Lacy as a powerhouse combination. . . . Paciorek is Susie's least favorite player. She doesn't like him because of the way he wears his uniform, his socks, his hair and everything. She says she feels silly disliking a player over stuff like this, but then most of us have equally arbitrary disfavorites, and it's certainly not personal, Tom. Baker and I were trying to figure out who would be the Joe Garagiola of the next generation. We decided on Paciorek. You'll get used to him, honey.

19. Ken GRIFFEY, New York (16–12) Hit .373 on artificial turf. . . . this is some team: They had a first baseman-centerfielder (Griffey), a first baseman-shortstop (Smalley), and a first baseman-rightfielder (Mattingly). None of these ordinary first baseman-leftfielder or first baseman-designated hitter types. . . . has had six .300 seasons.

20. Greg BROCK, Los Angeles (10–8) When Tommy Lasorda plays a hunch, he plays a hunch. Why on earth did he play Brock, in a terrible slump, in the playoffs? John Denny pitched against the Dodgers in Philadelphia on August 28, and the Dodgers pounded him, knocked him out in five and beat him 8–3. The man who did most of the damage was Rick Monday, who went 3-for-3 and drove in three runs in the first two innings of the game, including the game-winning RBI. Now you're playing the same team, facing the same pitcher again a month later for the league championship, and Rick Monday is nowhere to be seen. Does this make any sense to you? (1983 season:10–7.)

21. Wayne GROSS, Oakland (11–10) Now with Baltimore. . . . Bruce Bochte will be the A's first baseman in 1984. We heard a lot in Kansas City about his return to baseball; Schuerholz apparently wanted him. The "noble" way Bochte handled his contract demands was called refreshing by many. I agree. What I want to know is why, since he stated that no team could raise the bid for his services, he chose Oakland over Boston and Kansas City. The reason I ask is, in his past four seasons he has not hit as well in Oakland as in the other two cities:

Bruce Bochte 1979–1982

	G	AB	R	H	2B	3B	HR	RBI	Avg
In Oakland	20	68	7	18	4	1	2	12	.265
In Boston	21	78	14	29	7	0	1	11	.372
In Kansas City	23	91	15	33	8	0	5	20	.363

Actually, "not as well" is kind of an understatement. Bochte's performance on natural surfaces is also nowhere near as good as his turf performance:

1979–1982	G	AB	R	H	2B	3B	HR	RBI	Avg	SA
On Turf	325	1122	158	354	80	4	37	183	.316	.493
On Grass	216	796	82	215	29	6	10	95	.270	.359

The differential is growing, too. His average on the real stuff has dropped steadily over this period. In 1979 it was .297; 1980, .277; 1981, .261; 1982, .239. In 1982, the turf/grass differential in his batting average was .099. In 1984 he'll only play about 25 games on turf, which doesn't bode well for his chances of posting a batting average we usually associate with Bruce Bochte.

But maybe all that isn't important to Bruce. He has chosen to play in a stadium that is not ideally suited for his talents, and is doing so at a "reasonable" salary. Since the choice was entirely his, there has to be a reason. I speculate he was tired of playing for directionless teams with no sense of hope. He saw in Kansas City and Boston two franchises that are moving into periods of decline, and in Oakland a rather progressive ownership that appears to care about the future. Having had enough of the Mariners and their ilk, perhaps he chose to be a part of something positive for a change.—Jim Baker

22. Pat PUTNAM, Seattle (10–10) Still has the enormous platoon differential that I remarked on two years ago, but the Mariners apparently have decided not to worry about it. Crandall moved him out of the middle of the order against lefthanders, which shows good sense. . . . 1984 might be the best year that he ever has.

23. Enos CABELL, Detroit (12–17) It took Joe Falls to do it, but there is finally an award that Enos Cabell could win. It's called the Big Ed Award. According to Mr. Falls, Enos won it this year because he had a very good relationship with the working press. That reminds me of the Monty Python sketch where a mass-murderer is so well-mannered and gracious in the court room that the judge and jury lose all objectivity and begin to like him. He receives a suspended six month sentence and the whole courtroom sings "For He's a Jolly Good Fellow" to him. That's the really nice thing about writing for the *Abstract*—we don't have to sing "For He's a Jolly Good Fellow" to a bad ballplayer because he helped us get some stories.—J.B.

You may not believe this, but Cabell and I have friends in common. I happened to be visiting last fall with some people that Enos had been staying with just a few days before. He apparently has taken my remarks about his abilities in stride, and left an unfriendly but good-natured gesture with an intermediary. Public life is rougher than you think it is; you learn to accept those things.

Everybody tells me that Enos is a hell of a good guy, and you know, you can tell he is. His abilities being what they are, would he be in the major leagues if he wasn't? Tom Reich insists that if the Tigers don't re-sign Enos, it will cost them 10 games next year because they'll lose Enos' steadying influence on some of the other players. I don't deny it; I just don't have any way of knowing about it. I'm an outsider. And I find that the closer I get to becoming an insider, the harder it is for me to tell the truth about players, the harder it is to resist their distortions and misjudgments. So I spray a little acid around, make a few enemies. It helps keep me honest. (1983 season: 7–6.)

24. Pete ROSE, Philadelphia (17–22) Now with Montreal . . . Hit .157 on grass fields last year . . . career batting average in Montreal is .315.

Pete Rose represents something to the American sports journalist, an incarnation of what an athlete in our times is supposed to be and supposed to do. He hustles constantly, is accessible to the media and superficially quotable. He raises the team to the standard of a religion, loves the game, drags his son around with him, chases women and goes out on the town with the rookies, not necessarily in any order. He has gotten everything out of his ability that God put in it, and has done everything that he could on and off the field to help his teams win. In that way, he might make a massive contribution toward removing from the Expos the ballast of self-doubt which has weighed so heavily upon them.

That being said, the affection that

the nation's media still bears for him has become an embarrassment. It's the seventh inning of the final game of the World Series, and Pete Rose is standing innocuously at his position doing nothing and having nothing to do with the game, which his team is losing and he has helped to lose, and Cosell, Michaels and Weaver, who have been talking about Pete Rose since Game 1, Inning 1, Pitch 1, now consume I swear 2½ minutes taking turns summing up their feelings about what it is that makes Pete Rose such a special guy.

Look, fellas, nobody cares. Pete Rose is not and never was a figure of genuine public adulation. We didn't care five years ago, when he was a great player, and we sure as hell don't care now, when he's a terrible player. It was always the *media* that loved him, not the fans. The media is like a schoolboy with a crush on a girl of some beauty but limited grace and charm and intellect, and they go on and on and on about what a wonderful human being she is. We can't stop them, but we stopped listening a long time ago. At least when the World Series is being decided, can't you take off a minute to talk about the World Series?

Pete's selfishness in sacrificing the good of his team to forge on in sub-

mediocrity after his own goals is, in its own way, about what you would expect from a spoiled beauty. It's a sad way to end a distinguished career, but you'll do us both a favor if you'll just pull the plug on it, and let him get his 4,000th hit two years from now in an empty parking garage in a dark corner of the nation, at a far remove from the pennant race.

25. Pete O'BRIEN, Texas (9–11) Good baserunner, terrific glove man at first (probably should have won the Gold Glove), good strike-zone judgment (58 walks, 62 strikeouts). If he can hit .265, .270 with medium-range power, he'll be around for several years, and my guess is that he can do that. But if he's not consistent about it, he's going to be the new Jim Spencer.

26. Dave STAPLETON, Boston (15–22) Did you realize that if you graph Dave Stapleton's career you get a drawing of a ski slope? When the Red Sox got off to a hot start in 1982, Stapleton got a lot of credit for it; everybody said that he had moved over the whole infield. They've been cold for a year and four months now, and Stapleton's still in there. Give me Willie Aikens, any day.

FIRST BASE

	Offensive				Defensive					.350
Player	1982		1983		1982		1983		Total	Chance
1. Murray	.780	12- 3	.767	12- 4	.62	2-1	.56	2-1	28- 9	.000001
2. Cooper	.702	13- 5	.672	12- 6	.59	2-1	.48	1-2	28-14	.00003
3. Hernandez	.670	11- 5	.669	10- 5	.63	2-1	.65	2-1	25-12	.00006
4. Evans	.624	9- 5	.763	11- 4	.62	1-0	.54	1-1	22-10	.00010
5. Thompson	.742	11- 4	.635	10- 5	.52	2-1	.53	2-1	24-12	.00011
6. Hendrick	.617	9- 6	.717	10- 4			.61	1-1	21-10	.00021
7. Oliver	.779	12- 4	.568	10- 7	.34	1-2	.42	1-2	24-15	.00065
8. Hrbek	.667	10- 5	.651	9- 5	.56	2-1	.51	2-1	22-13	.00072
9. Chambliss	.572	9- 6	.671	9- 4	.64	2-1	.64	1-1	21-12	.00075
10. Driessen	.626	9- 6	.670	7- 4	.65	2-1	.61	1-1	20-11	.00077
11. Knight	.619	11- 6	.668	9- 5	.46	1-1	.51	2-1	22-14	.00124
12. Upshaw	.512	9- 8	.693	11- 5	.40	1-2	.53	2-1	23-16	.00190
13. Buckner	.604	11- 7	.542	10- 8	.62	2-1	.63	2-1	24-18	.00275
14. Garvey	.560	10- 8	.640	7- 4	.55	2-1	.45	1-1	20-14	.00386
15. Carew	.580	9- 6	.661	9- 4	.50	1-1	.49	1-1	19-13	.00417
16. Aikens	.600	8- 5	.702	8- 3	.45	1-1	.33	1-1	17-11	.00484
17. Hargrove	.496	8- 9	.571	8- 6	.66	2-1	.68	1-1	20-16	.00920
18. Paciorek	.660	7- 3	.613	7- 5	.47	1-1	.59	1-0	15-10	.00931
19. Griffey	.541	8- 6	.662	8- 4			.43	1-1	16-12	.01361
20. Brock	.191	0- 1	.581	8- 6	.45	0-0	.53	2-1	10- 8	.03833
21. Gross	.489	5- 6	.473	5- 5	.27	0-0	.45	0-1	11-11	.10698
22. Putnam	.388	2- 2	.532	7- 6	.46	0-1	.55	1-1	10-10	.11323
23. Cabell	.318	4-10	.505	6- 5	.42	1-1	.62	1-1	12-17	.12947
24. Rose	.466	9-10	.358	5-10	.54	2-1	.41	1-1	17-22	.16892
25. O'Brien	.614	1- 1	.423	7- 9	.61	0-0	.64	1-1	9-11	.23762
26. Stapleton	.412	7- 9	.348	6-10	.56	1-1	.55	2-1	15-22	.29259

SECOND BASE

1. Lou WHITAKER, Detroit (30–18) One day the whole country is going to wake up and say, "Damn, that Lou Whitaker can play ball." . . . RBI Importance (.510) was the highest among Tiger players; he was only eight behind Parrish in meaningful RBI. . . . has no significant negatives at this point of his career. He hits for average, has good power for a second baseman, has good range and good hands at second, drew 67 walks last year, has speed. Not exceptional on the double play (the Tigers were last in the league in double plays last year) . . . somebody asked me on a Detroit radio station if I would describe Whitaker as the new Frank White. I'd say a comparison to Charlie Gehringer or Rod Carew was more apt. First of all, Frank was never this good. Besides that, Frank isn't really the same type of player. He's flashier on defense, but his offense has a lot of gaps in it. Gehringer was very much the same type of player that Lou is. He had the same broad range of offensive skills, and about the same emphasis on each. Of course, Gehringer had years like this, rather than one. . . . Carew had more O but less D.

2. Bobby GRICH, California (25–14) Another terrific offensive year. It might have been his best year with the bat if it hadn't been for the injury . . . .417 on-base percentage (only Boggs was better) . . . defense began to decline. He turned more double plays in 118 games than Whitaker did in 160, but he also led the league in errors. . . . I still say he's a great player. He's probably the only unrecognized great player at this moment.

3. Joe MORGAN, Philadelphia (23–14) Now with Oakland. . . . Joe Morgan was quoted in *Sports Illustrated* (October 3, 1983, page 24) as saying, "I don't think I've ever had a bad September." I think we've finally found Joe's weakness: the man has no memory. He has probably had more bad Septembers than any other great player in history. Between 1973 and 1979 he hit below his average in September every year, seven straight years. And no, he was not compensating in other areas of the game. Through that span his records were:

	Average on August 31	Average in September	Difference
1973	.291	.283	− 8
1974	.297	.264	− 33
1975	.329	.318	− 11
1976	.335	.250	− 85
1977	.304	.189	−115
1978	.240	.216	− 24
1979	.255	.233	− 22

The .250 average in '76 included only four extra-base hits in 27 games; in 1979 he drove in two runs after August 31, 2 RBI in 86 at-bats. He drove in less than ten runs in the month in '74, '77, '78 and '79. He did have a very good September in '80 (17 RBI) and '82 (16 RBI), but in '81 he had one homer and 4 RBI (91 AB, .242 average) in the month, and even in '82, his average was .297 before September 1 and .260 after. It seems obvious to me that when he was playing 155 games a year, his bat showed it at the end of the season. He became a good September hitter only after he was cut back to about 120 games a year.

Pete Rose, when discussing his favorite subject, Pete Rose, likes to talk about how winners "follow me around." Since Pete has only been on two different ball clubs in his career, that really doesn't make for much following; the only team he has left, the '78 Reds, won the division the next year, while his new Phillies dropped from first to fourth.

No, the man who has a right to boast of such stuff is Pete's two-time teammate, Joe Morgan. I don't think anyone has ever been on so many teams in such a short period of time (four in five years) and had them all be so successful. From 1979 to 1983 he has been on three division winners ('79 Reds, '80 Astros, '83 Phils) and a third-place team that finished only two games out (the '82 Giants). That's four separate franchises, which is pretty damn good and probably unprecedented.

What I like about this chart is its symmetry. Morgan found the Reds in fourth and left them in first. After he was gone they reverted to third. The Astros are a perfect 2–1–2. The Giants were a fifth-place team before Morgan, the same after.

The man Morgan begins 1984 trailing in career home runs by a second baseman, Rogers Hornsby, also spent a portion of his career wandering around the National League with results somewhat similar, but not as spectacular. From 1926 to 1929 Hornsby played with four teams. Two (the '26 Cards and '29 Cubs) were pennant winners, and one, coincidentally, was a third-place Giants team that finished only two games out (1927). The fourth team was the unfortunate '28 Braves, who finished 44½ games out of first. —Jim Baker

4. Bill DORAN, Houston (17–10) Believed to be a different Bill Doran than the one who played briefly with the Indians in 1922. . . . he's about where Thon was a year ago. They are by far the best double-play combination in the National League. Doran is a terrific second baseman, has some power, speed, creates a good many runs in a run-scarce environment. Has some trouble with lefthanders and hasn't learned to make use of his speed as a base stealer yet . . . would have had Whitaker-like stats playing in any other park.

5. Jim GANTNER, Milwaukee (24–19) A lefthanded Gerry Priddy—on the field, that is. To describe some-

		Before Morgan				First Year With Morgan				Last Year With Morgan				After Morgan		
	YR	W	L	Fn	YR	W	L	Fn	YR	W	L	Fn	YR	W	L	Fn
Reds	'71	79	83	4th	'72	95	59	1st	'79	90	71	1st	'80	89	73	3rd
Astros	'79	89	73	2nd	'80	93	70	1st	'80	93	70	1st	'81	61	49	2nd
Giants	'80	75	86	5th	'81	56	55	4th	'82	87	75	3rd	'83	79	83	5th
Phils	'82	89	73	2nd	'83	90	72	1st	'83	90	72	1st	'84			

one as a modern Gerry Priddy off the field would be libelous. Priddy was a con man, but he was a heck of a ballplayer—hit, like Gantner, in the .280 range with some power and could turn the double play. Gantner has inched steadily forward over the last five years . . . hit .347 on turf, only .229 against lefthanded pitching.

6. Johnny RAY, Pittsburgh (26–24) We're entering a very large knot of largely indistinguishable players here, from 6 to 15 (Garcia); the differences among them are not appreciable. Really, from 6 to 19 (Trillo) the differences are not large. If you moved around any of those players it wouldn't change the teams by more than a game a year. Ray hits for a good average, hits a lot of doubles (38 last year), is a good second baseman. Bill Madlock said he was the team's MVP last year; I would say he's as good a candidate as anyone. But there's really no big difference between him and number 15.

7. Tommy HERR, St. Louis (19–15) On-base percentage over .400 before his injury . . . base stealing success has gone down steadily over last few years . . . hit .401 in Busch Stadium last year . . . switch hitter, but a far better hitter against righthanders than left. . . . still think he has the potential to move up.

8. Tony BERNAZARD, Seattle (24–22) Now with Cleveland . . .

The drop in his defensive abilities after the injury—the reason given for the trade—shows up very clearly in his defensive stats. His defensive won/lost percentage dropped from .68 to .49, from nearly the best in the league to a little below average. I still like him as a player, and I think it's a shame that he's going to be stuck with unflattering comparisons with Julio Cruz for the rest of his life. But you've got to start wondering about a 27-year-old player who is playing for his fourth major league team. . . . apparently we're going to find out whether Jack Perconte is as good as I think he is. Crandall managed Perconte in the minors, has him here now and nobody else to play second.

9. Frank WHITE, Kansas City (23–24) Did not win the Gold Glove award, although he may have had his best defensive season. Nobody's complaining; he's won enough of them . . . 100-point platoon differential in '83; last two years has hit .324 and .328 against lefthanders. Can pull a lefthander, too . . . Howser sometimes batted him third, and it seemed to me he was hitting real well in that spot, so I checked. Not as well as I thought (.274 average, .432 slugging) but he did drive in 21 runs in 24 games as a #3 hitter. The Royals were 13–11 in those games . . . here's another one of those "I've lost the notes from the study but I remember what it showed" things. Dick Howser made a comment on a pregame show last year about players who lead the league in fielding percentage winning the Gold Gloves, but he'd take the fielders who got to more balls, made a few more errors on plays the other guys wouldn't reach. So I decided to check and see how often the player who led the league in fielding percentage did win Gold Glove awards, and how often the players who led in range factor won the award.

Comparing ten years worth of Gold Glove awards with ten years of fielding statistics, I found that in the infield it was about even; the player who led in fielding percentage was about as likely to win the award as the player who led in range. There were a couple more "percentage" winners, but just a couple. But in the outfield, it was range factors all the way; among the 60 Gold Glove winners, there were over 20 who had had the highest range factor of any player at their position, whereas there were only two or three who had won the award and also led in fielding percentage. So on balance a player who leads his league in range factor is more likely to win a Gold Glove than a player who leads in fielding percentage.

10. Willie RANDOLPH, New York (21–19) Peaked early, seems to be drifting gradually downward. Still a good leadoff man (scored 73 runs last year in 104 games; Jerry Remy scored 73 in 146 games and had better hitters coming up behind him). . . . the Yankees have had only four regular second basemen since 1959 (Richardson, Clarke, Alomar and Randolph), only ten since 1926 (Lazzerri, Gordon, Stirnweiss, Coleman, Martin, McDougald) . . . If they don't get rid of him soon, he's going to start breaking into the Yankees list of all-time leaders (he's already third in stolen bases). . . . George, with his enormous respect for Yankee tradition, usually doesn't allow that . . .

11. Steve SAX, Los Angeles (26–26) Peter Goldstein says that his research shows that the Dodgers are the only team ever to lead off with two players whose names end in "x". . . . not a great leadoff man. Was caught stealing 30 times last year, the most of any major league player. But he will be a great leadoff man if he improves just a little in three areas: batting, strike-zone judgment and stolen-base percentage. If he hits .280, draws 58 walks and steals 65% of 86 tries, that's just another leadoff man. But if he hits .290, draws 68 walks and steals 75% of 86 tries, that's a whole different story.

12. Glenn HUBBARD, Atlanta (23–22) Looks like a hobbitt. . . . still coming on, drove in 70 runs last year and stopped bunting so much. . . . excellent second baseman. . . . will probably rank in the top five next year if he repeats his 1983 season . . .

13. Ryne SANDBERG, Chicago (23–23) An excellent Gold Glove selection. He deserved it, and he got it.

Probably helped as much as any Cub by Wrigley Field. Has hit .320 and .289 at home in his two seasons in the big time, while hitting .232 and .234 on the road. . . . in the National League list of the ten most valuable properties (see comment on California Angels), he was the surprise. Mostly the list was who you'd expect it to be—Murphy, Dawson, Strawberry, Raines, Pena, Guerrero—but I hadn't really expected Sandberg and Sax to turn up on the list.

14. John CASTINO, Minnesota (19–21) Baker says he wears the second highest socks in baseball, behind Rusty Staub. . . . played a terrific second base last year; I really think it's his position. Reportedly the Twins are going to put Tim Teufel at second base (International League MVP) and move Castino somewhere else, like leftfield or Montreal . . . I'd have to be awfully impressed by Teufel before I started moving this guy. He's the only second baseman I've seen who can run down a pop fly in shallow right as well as Frank White. He doesn't have a shortstop's arm, and I never cared much for him as a third baseman. (1983 season: 13–10.)

15. Damaso GARCIA, Toronto (22–23) Hit .342 on turf, .240 on grass. Three hundred hitter, but never walks, has no power and hurts the team with his mediocre base-stealing efforts (31 steals in 48 tries last year). On-base percentage is just .339, about the same as the other players in this knot (6–15). He's not much of a glove man, and you don't win ball games by hitting singles.

16. Davey LOPES, Oakland (19–21) I had him prematurely written off a year ago; I was never happier to be wrong. I have a longtime affection for Lopes. He played college basketball near me when I was growing up in the mid-sixties, and I felt, in the idiotic way that we fans have, that I had some one-sided personal connection to him. He was always a great percentage player, a multi-dimensional player, could be loosely described as a National League Amos Otis or a lower-class Joe Morgan . . . wonder what he'll be doing now that they have Joe, too? Maybe he'll inherit Bill Almon's job. (1983 Season: 11–9.)

17. Julio CRUZ, Chicago (22–25) Will not file for arbitration in 1984. . . . excellent #9 hitter; I would lead him off against a lefthander. Although he is a switch-hitter, he has one of the largest platoon differentials in baseball.

18. Ron OESTER, Cincinnati (21–25) Subjectively, I like him a lot; I just can't verify statistically the ability that I think he has. Although he looks like a good second baseman, his defensive stats the last two years are very poor, and as a hitter he's just another one of the group. Drove in some runs, but struck out 106 times and grounded into 17 double plays. I have a good feeling about him, but I can't really show cause.

19. Manny TRILLO, Montreal (19–23) Now with San Francisco. . . .

Why is it that the Cubs will give their second-base job to Sandberg, the Dodgers will give their second base job to Sax, the Pirates will give theirs to Ray, and the Astros will give theirs to Doran, but the Expos will not give theirs to Little? Doug Flynn played second base here (Montreal) in 107 games, but he's not a major league player.

20. Juan BONILLA, San Diego (14–17) The latest of Dick Williams's mystery-men second basemen. The mystery is what it is that Williams thinks they do that makes him keep them around.

I can't stand it when people say that if he does the job with the glove it doesn't matter what he hits. *Of course* it matters what he hits. Why on earth wouldn't it matter what he hits. If one player drives in 40 runs and another 70, how can those 30 runs not matter? The difference between a first-place team is maybe 200, 250 runs, offense and defense; maybe sometimes 300 or 350, but not usually. How can 30 runs not matter?

Whenever you hear that when you have one thing, this doesn't matter or that doesn't matter, and you'll hear it 50 times this year, you're listening to baseball games go flying out the window. It all matters. Juan Bonilla hit .237 last year, and it matters, and he grounded into 19 double plays, and that matters, and he has no power, and that matters.

21. Rich DAUER, Baltimore (18–24) Returned to form (.264) in the second half of the year.

22. Brian GILES, New York (11–14) Thought he would hit a little, but he didn't. . . . suspect he may resurface somewhere else and do better. He hit .271 on the road, but only .216 in Shea Stadium. Hit .298 on artificial turf. . . . good glove. . . . I liked him a lot a year ago, and I still think there are teams that he could help.

23. Wayne TOLLESON, Texas (9–13) One of only four American League batting title qualifiers to have an on-base percentage higher than his slugging average:

	Slugging	OB%
Mike Hargrove	.367	.393
Wayne Tolleson	.315	.320
Jerry Remy	.319	.321
Toby Harrah	.365	.365

His bat was a pleasant surprise

to the Rangers, yet even so it is questionable if he could stick at this level . . . hit .293 before the All-Star break, .229 after . . . drove in only 20 runs in 470 at-bats. You can't use too much of that. (1983 season: 9-11.)

24. Jerry REMY, Boston (20–30) Drove in only two runners from first base all year (Rice led the Red Sox with 29) . . . my evaluation of Remy is on record, but nobody is any more likely to believe it if I say it all again, so I won't.

25. Mike FISCHLIN, Cleveland (7–12) Bernazard how has the job.

26. SAN FRANCISCO (VACANT)
Manny Trillo will help the team; he'll probably take 30, 40 runners off base with double plays, and despite his other problems that's got to help. . . . The Giants in '83 were using Kuiper, Wellman and Youngblood at second base, all about equal amounts. The amazing Duane Kuiper had one of the best strikeout-to-walk ratios in the league (13–27); Wellman has a good-glove reputation that doesn't seem justified by his stats. Wellman was a pretty decent hitter in the minors, but nobody seems to think he's going to hit major league pitching.

The Youngblood gamble—the idea of playing a slugging outfielder at second base—is one of the more intriguing managerial maneuvers of 1983. With his strong arm, Youngblood probably was better on the double play than either Wellman or Kuiper, but his defense there in other respects left a lot to be desired. On the other hand, the man can hit. I did not get around to checking, but I would bet that the offensive gain was larger than the defensive cost. I'd bet the Giants had a better record with Youngblood in the lineup at second base then either Wellman or Kuiper. But it's a strange move, even by the standards of the Giants organization. Since the Giants came west, 55 men have played second base for them. The top ten in games played are Tito Fuentes (842), Hal Lanier (419), Chuck Hiller (399), Ron Hunt (357), Daryl Spencer (285), Derrel Thomas (237), Rob Andrews (230), Joe Morgan (207), Bill Madlock (183) and Joey Amalfitano (165). Four other players have been the incumbent second baseman for a season: Danny O'Connell, Dan Blasingame, Marty Perez and Rennie Stennett, and two others have been the most regular in a season when there was no regular, Brad Wellman and Joe Strain. So that's 16 primary second basemen in 26 years; Trillo makes 17 and he can't last more than a year or two.

SECOND BASE

Player	Offensive				Defensive				Total	.350 Chance
	1982		1983		1982		1983			
1. Whitaker	.573	9- 7	.689	12- 5	.69	5-2	.52	4-4	30-18	.00009
2. Grich	.599	9- 6	.720	8- 3	.67	5-2	.53	3-3	25-14	.00020
3. Morgan	.734	10- 3	.637	8- 4	.50	3-3	.39	2-4	23-14	.00068
4. Doran	.505	2- 1	.631	9- 6	.48	0-1	.68	5-3	17-10	.00281
5. Gantner	.507	6- 6	.530	9- 8	.60	4-2	.68	5-3	24-19	.00417
6. Ray	.502	10- 9	.515	8- 8	.48	4-4	.61	4-3	26-24	.01004
7. Herr	.454	7- 8	.668	6- 3	.63	4-2	.50	2-2	19-15	.01016
8. Bernazard	.532	9- 7	.487	8- 8	.68	5-2	.49	3-4	24-22	.01246
9. White	.579	8- 6	.380	6-10	.58	4-3	.73	5-2	23-21	.01389
10. Randolph	.512	8- 8	.529	6- 6	.51	4-3	.64	3-2	21-19	.01728
11. Sax	.527	10- 9	.516	9- 9	.47	3-4	.37	3-5	26-26	.01850
12. Hubbard	.418	7- 9	.512	8- 7	.60	4-3	.67	5-2	23-22	.01915
13. Sandberg	.442	8-11	.461	8-10	.60	1-0	.75	6-2	23-23	.02583
14. Castino	.346	4- 8	.541	9- 7	.46	2-3	.58	4-3	19-21	.02826
15. Garcia	.506	9- 8	.469	7- 8	.56	4-3	.45	3-3	22-23	.03825
16. Lopes	.427	6- 8	.608	9- 5	.43	3-3	.38	2-4	19-21	.05317
17. J. Cruz	.423	7- 9	.409	7- 9	.52	4-3	.65	5-3	22-25	.06324
18. Oester	.436	7- 9	.490	8- 8	.41	2-4	.42	3-5	21-25	.08852
19. Trillo	.383	6-10	.415	5- 8	.65	5-2	.49	3-3	19-23	.11067
20. Bonilla	.476	2- 3	.369	6-11	.52	1-1	.57	4-3	14-17	.15903
21. Dauer	.518	8- 8	.311	4-10	.40	2-4	.44	3-3	18-24	.18175
22. Giles	.420	2- 2	.369	4- 8	.69	1-1	.45	3-4	11-14	.22884
23. Tolleson	.022	0- 2	.414	6- 8	.00	0-0	.48	3-3	9-13	.23762
24. Remy	.381	7-11	.374	6-11	.43	3-5	.46	3-4	20-30	.27356
25. Fischlin	.420	3- 5	.301	2- 5	.23	0-0	.31	1-3	7-12	.51883
26. Wellman	.207	0- 0	.274	2- 4	.26	0-0	.12	0-4	2- 8	.91405

THIRD BASE

1. Mike SCHMIDT, Philadelphia (30–12) Hit between .245 and .263 in all of his breakdowns (.245 first half, .263 second, .255 against righthanders, .252 against lefties, .251 at home, .258 on the road, .250 on grass, .256 on turf). . . . only major league player to hit twice as many homers as anybody else on his team.

Schmidt's talents are narrowing rapidly now. He used to steal 20 to 30 bases a year, but he hasn't done that for years, and he's down now to 7 stolen bases in 15 tries. He hit 34 doubles in 1975 and 31 in '76, but has been in constant decline in that area since, and was down to 16 last year. His triples totals have gone the same way. He hit .286 and .316 in his MVP seasons, but he doesn't seem likely to get back to that level unless he sacrifices some power. He's lost a significant amount of range at third base. From '74 to '77 he had a constant 3.5 chances a game at third base; he slipped steadily, and now handles 3.0 chances per game. He still wins the Golden Glove and probably still deserves it; his defensive won/lost percentage at third was the best in the National League last year, but only

because the league does not have a really good glove man at third, no Buddy Bell or Gary Gaetti.

But his central talents—his strike-zone judgment and his ability to hit the long ball—are as good as ever, maybe better than ever, and on the basis of those he is still the best third baseman in baseball.

2. Wade BOGGS, Boston (23–9) It was reported that Wade Boggs' .349 batting average was a record for an American League rookie appearing in 100 or more games. That is not correct. Taffy Wright hit .350 in 100 games in 1938, and of course Shoeless Joe was a borderline rookie (115 prior AB) when he hit .408 in 1911.

—Bill James

My friend and sometimes fellow sabermetrician Andrew Kennedy reminds us that we can only look up the deeds of Ty Cobb and Honus Wagner in books, or see Ted Williams in film clips, but that we are actually living through Wade Boggs. It is kind of exciting, when you think about it. Nobody in a long time has entered the majors with such author-

ity. According to Bob Davids, Wade's batting average of .357 after two seasons is the highest since Chuck Klein's .359 over 50 years ago. Boggs is the first man to begin his career after World War II to establish at least a chance of cracking the top ten all-time batting average leaders. Rod Carew and George Brett, the other two men who have posted anachronistic batting averages in recent history, did not hit the big time with such authority this early in their careers.

Oddly, his ascent to this juncture has been a slow one. He spent two full years in Double-A, two full years in Triple-A and a good portion of 1982 riding the Red Sox bench. While Yaz was having a notoriously terrible August of '82, driving in five runs for the entire month and batting just .144, Houk had Boggs cooling his .358 batting average in the dugout. Even this season Houk batted the American League on-base percentage champion fifth over 40 games before realizing it might help to get him up in front of the RBI men rather than behind them. . . . Probably one of the best seasons ever without making the All-

Star team.... Platoon differential against LHP was only minus .023 in '82. Fell to − .117 for '83.... Red Sox have only a 1–4 record in his 5 career four-hit games. Has scored only four times on those 20 hits.... I wonder how many times he was on base when Rice or Armas did their double-play routine.... Team averaged 4.98 runs per game with Boggs batting second and only 4.05 with him up fifth. Other averages: Leadoff, 4.28; third, 4.40; and sixth, 4.60. Boston was 2 and 7 when Boggs didn't play, averaging only 2.0 runs per game and never scoring more than three runs.

—Jim Baker

Jim is a Red Sox fan, and it shows there a bit. Boggs is an exciting young player, but not nearly as exciting as Cal Ripken, and I'd say frankly that he reminds me a whole lot more of a young Pete Runnels than a young Ted Williams. How excited can you get about a 25-year-old player who drives in 74 runs? "Nobody in a long time has entered the majors with such authority?" Come on; Ripken's been up for the same two years and I'd say he's been considerably more "authoritative." Boggs is a singles hitter with no speed who has a good swing and a strong ability to take advantage of Fenway Park. It is extremely unlikely that he would have hit .350 if he played in any other park.

But anyway, there are a lot of things that people are wondering about Wade Boggs, and I wanted to try to get some evidence to them. Why didn't he drive in or score more runs? Where's his lifetime batting average going to wind up? What are his chances of hitting .400? Will he develop more score power as he gets older? Let's take a look at those questions:

1) Boggs' low RBI rate is solely and exclusively attributable to the fact that he spent most of the season batting behind people with a limited ability to get on base. Look at the data sent to us by C-H-U-C-K W-A-S-E-L-E-S-K-I; he batted only 134 times with runners in scoring position, while Armas batted 161 times in those situations, Rice 165 times, Stapleton (ecch!) 141 times and even Glenn Hoffman 133 times. His ability to produce runs in that situation was superior to any of those players or anyone else on the team

except Carl Yastrzemski; he just wasn't *in* the situation.

To some degree this may be unavoidable; the man batting behind a .360 hitter is always going to get more at-bats with runners on base than the .360 hitter himself. On the other hand, Boggs did spend an awful lot of the season batting behind a couple of people who didn't get on base much. He started out batting behind Tony Armas, who leaves himself on base less than any other regular player in the league, and spent a good bit of the season batting behind Jerry Remy, whose inability to get on base consistently should prohibit his being used as a leadoff man.

So yes, it was an empty .360, but who emptied it? Check the lineup cards, and I don't think you'll find Wade Boggs' signature on them.

2) Where is Wade Boggs' career batting average going to wind up?

I'd say the .345 estimate given in the Red Sox team comment is probably a little high; .335, .338 might be more realistic. The method probably doesn't reduce batting average as a player ages as much as it should. It can't be assumed that Boggs will play his entire career in Fenway Park, and any move that he makes is going to cut points off his average.

One way to look at the question is to try to find a group of players whose careers have paralleled Boggs' in certain respects, and look at what happened to their career batting averages after their first two years. With that in mind, I asked Jim to find the career batting records of all players who

(a) reached the majors at the age of 24,

(b) batted 250-450 times in their rookie seasons and

(c) played regularly (450 AB) in their second seasons at age 25.

There are 32 qualifying players. Of the 32, only ten wound up their careers with higher career batting averages than their average through the first two years. Of these ten, three actually have not done so; they are still active (Rich Dauer, Darrell Evans and Steve Henderson), and still in danger of winding up with lower batting averages than their first two years. Six of those ten players improved their averages by six points or less. The four who improved their career marks significantly after the first two years

were all players whose early averages were in the range of .250 to .275. Of the seven players in the study who hit .300 over their first two years, all wound up with career averages lower than those two years except one. That one was Lyman Bostock.

The odds strongly favor Boggs' winding up his career with an average lower than .357.

3) What are the chances of Boggs' hitting .400?

To hit .400, Boggs needs to exceed his career average to this point by 43 points, and to exceed his career best to this point by 39 points. Of the 32 players studied, only 4 ever had a season which was 39 points above their career high after two years. Three of those were players whose careers began in the dead-ball era, and reached their peak in the lively-ball era. The fourth was Luke Appling.

Luke Appling was the same type of offensive player that Wade Boggs is—singles and doubles hitter, good batting eye, limited power. If it was possible for Luke Appling to grow from .274 as a 25-year-old sophomore to .388 four years later, it certainly is possible for Wade Boggs to grow from .361 to .400.

But the odds against it are long. Over half the players studied (17 of the 32) never again reached a career high in batting; of the 15 who did, most did so by only a few points. You've got to remember that there is all the difference in the world between the growth potential of a 25-year-old sophomore and a 22-year-old sophomore. One is probably two years away from his peak, the other is probably five years away.

Five of the 32 players would eventually have a season that was 43 points higher than their career average after two years.

4) Will Boggs develop more power as he gets older?

It's always been my feeling—I can't prove it—that a player who hits a lot of doubles as a youngster will eventually turn those into home runs, while a singles hitter who hits 20 doubles a year generally might develop doubles power later, but probably not home-run power. Yastrzemski would be a good example of that, and Brett. Boggs hit 44 doubles, most of them opposite field hits, off the wall. Whether or not he will later be able to lift these onto the screen. . . . who knows?

3. Pedro GUERRERO, Los Angeles (26–13) Power-speed number of 26.8. . . . would win a triple crown if he played in a good hitter's park. . . . they asked him to play third base; he said, "Is that that one over there?" and just kept on hitting. You've got to like that.

4. Paul MOLITOR, Milwaukee (30–18) Brewers may put Randy Ready at third and move Molitor back to the outfield, now that Thomas is not around to pout about it. Aesthetically, I hate to mess up this gorgeous infield, but the move would make sense.

5. Doug DeCINCES, California (25–13) In the same situation as Grich. . . . big strong guy out of the Oriole system, multidimensional offensive and defensive player, fighting a back injury. Better than Molitor when he's healthy, but not as healthy.

6. George BRETT, Kansas City (24–12) Played six games last year in Toronto and had 26 total bases. . . . Jim says he hopes that as time passes, things will get mixed up and historians will remember that the Kansas City Royals of 1983 had a pine tar-sniffing problem. . . . defense at third has really gone to pot now; I was surprised they made the Balboni trade because I thought they would move George to first. . . . Royals last year were 20–18 when he was not in the lineup, and allowed only 4.13 runs per game without him in the lineup, as opposed to 4.92 with him.

7. Buddy BELL, Texas (27–18) Hit under his career average for the first time since 1974. . . . with over 1800 hits already behind him and still playing well at the age of 32, he's a serious 3000-hit candidate, although it will require very good durability . . . hit .340 on artificial turf. I've always wondered whether people who ground into a lot of double plays (as Bell does) hit well on artificial turf. With the grass/turf data on record, I will check once I get time.

8. Toby HARRAH, Cleveland (26–17) One of the six remaining Washington Senators still active in the majors in 1983. Probably will be the last to survive, too. Jim Kaat, who was a member of the previous Senators team, is gone now. Larry Biittner is struggling to stay around; Bill Fahey and Aurelio Rodriquez continued on in utility roles and Jeff Burroughs was, for some reason, the starting DH for the Oakland A's.

Have you ever noticed how we always hear about old Brooklyn Dodger fans, but never really about any other dispossessed followers of transferred franchises? Think about it. I've been to Philadelphia many times and I've never once met a disgruntled A's fan. Randy Lakeman lives near St. Louis and says he rarely comes across any bitter, disenfranchised Brownie rooters. Somebody wrote a novel called *The Man Who Brought The Dodgers Back to Brooklyn* or something like that. I've never seen any book called *The Man Who Brought the Bees Back To Beantown*. There must be some remaining fans of these teams still around, mustn't there be? Or maybe not. That's why they pulled up stakes and left these cities behind, right? Because nobody cared in the first place.—Jim Baker

Somebody sent me a clipping from a paper in which Toby said that he liked to guard the lines more than other third basemen (who mostly guard them late in the game), because he figured that the balls which got by him in the hole, while there might be more of them, would be singles, while the balls down the line would be doubles if he didn't stop them. This comment explains something which has always puzzled me, which is how Toby could have a good range factor as a shortstop, as he did in 1976, but a low range factor as a third baseman, as he did in 1977 and has ever since. Since he is guarding the lines a lot, the number of fair-ball plays that he makes is lower than it otherwise would be—but, as he suggests, the balls that he gets to are more important than the ones getting through.

Toby's range factors, then, are probably not as good an indication of his defensive ability as they would be for another player—and he probably deserves a better defensive won/lost percentage than the method gives him.

The next question is, how do we evaluate the trade-off? Is it a good idea for Toby to guard the lines? Is he saving as many runs on doubles as he is giving up in singles?

The answer is: I don't know. The data to evaluate the trade-off fairly just isn't available. Craig Wright says he doesn't think there are enough balls hit down the line to justify the move, but I will say this: Toby is one of the best percentage baseball players of our time. He has been a superb percentage base stealer. He does all of the things that he needs to do to be a valuable player as a .265, .270 hitter—he takes the walk, hits for power, doesn't make mistakes. He plays hard but in control; he doesn't wipe out his season trying to make a play. His career has shown remarkable growth and development; I would say he's gotten as much out of his ability as any player of our time. I trust his judgment about where he should position himself.

9. Bill MADLOCK, Pittsburgh (23–15) He's the only National League batting champion in the last 40 years to have fewer hits than his team's games played, and he's now done that twice, shoplifting a batting title in 1983 with just 153 hits. . . . also became the first player in 41 years and the second player ever to win a batting championship without hitting a triple. . . . is guaranteed to wind up the season with a batting average higher than what he's hitting at the All-Star break.

10. Bob HORNER, Atlanta (21–14) Here's a trivia question that none of you are going to get unless you live in Arizona. The 1977 Arizona State team had three major league third basemen on their team, Bob Horner, Jamie Allen and Hubie Brooks. (Well, the Mets think he's a major league third baseman.) Who played third for them? Answer: Brandt Humphrey.

At least you got the initials right, eh?

Horner is only 26 (he is about the same age as Ron Kittle), so maybe it is rather early to be drawing any conclusions about his career. It is beginning to look, however, as if he never is going to have That Year. When he came up in 1978 he played 89 games and won the NL Rookie of the Year award, and we all wondered what he would have done if he had had 162 games. Then in 1979 he was injured and played only 121 games, but his production was terrific so we all said, "Wow. Just wait 'til he gets in a full year." It's been six years now and we're still waiting. He has played more than 124 games only once—140 then—has never batted 500 times in a year, and has averaged, for one reason or another, only 110 games a year. Although his career averages per 162 games played are 39 home runs and 113 RBI, he has never hit 39 home runs and never driven in even 100 runs; the 98 in 121 games his second year up is still his career best. It is beginning to look like he is just going to be one of those players who can never stay healthy enough to play a full season.

But wait a minute. *One of* those players? What others are there? What other player can you name, in all of baseball history, who possessed star-quality ability but could never stay healthy enough to play a full season, even once, during his career? Mantle played 88% or more of his team's games 12 times in his 18-year career. Brett has had four full seasons, three seasons of 634 or more at-bats. Fred Lynn has had three seasons of almost fulltime play, four seasons over 500 at-bats. But Horner's injuries are so frequent and so serious that, while of course he might, there is no reasonable expectation that he will ever get through a year without one.

Another funny thing is that most people who are hurt a lot are inconsistent, even when they are brilliant—like Fred Lynn, who next year is likely to hit somewhere between .340 and .220. But Horner is a consistent offensive player; he's just not there for 40 games a year.

The inexhaustible diversity of baseball statistics, derived from the inexhaustible variety of the players and personalities that they represent. After 100 years, after thousands of careers, something new is always appearing in every window.

Bob Horner's Career Records
Projected to 155 games a year

Year	G	AB	R	H	2B	3B	HR	RBI	SB	Avg
1978	155	563	87	150	30	2	40	110	5	.266
1979	155	624	85	196	19	1	42	126	0	.314
1980	155	579	101	155	18	1	44	111	4	.268
1981	155	589	82	163	20	0	29	82	4	.277
1982	155	552	94	144	27	0	35	107	3	.261
1983	155	575	112	174	37	1	30	101	6	.303

Actual career highs: 140 games, 499 at-bats, 85 runs scored, 153 hits. 25 doubles, 1 triple, 35 home runs, 98 RBI, 4 stolen bases.

11. Tim WALLACH, Montreal (25–20) Of the 48 players who homered in their first major league at-bat, Wallach figures to become the best home run hitter in his career. The leader now is Earl Averill with 238; Wallach ought to beat that. . . . stats have paralleled Gary Ward's for the last three years. . . . Still making progress, I think. Didn't have a good year but evened out his K/W ratio a little more, improved at third. . . . with the double-play combination batting seventh and eighth, he's the end of the Expos' offense, which is a bit of a load to put on a young hitter.

12. Ron CEY, Chicago (24–20) Set a career high in extra-base hits, had a super second half of the season . . . a very Cey-like season, leaving little to be cead about him. Has stopped diving for balls, resulting in a sharp decline in his defensive won/lost percentage.

13. Carney LANSFORD, Oakland (17–12) Rating is lowered by the playing time he's missed; one of the good ones when he is in the lineup . . . the last two years has reversed his normal platoon differential, hit righthanders better than lefthanders . . . caught stealing 8 times in 11 tries.

14. Phil GARNER, Houston (22–19) Now 35 and treading water at best. .238 average was the lowest of his career. . . . Third base is not his best position. . . . was second to Pedro in errors.

15. Ken OBERKFELL, St. Louis (20–17) Had the highest RBI Importance on the Cardinals (.501). . . . has developed an immense platoon differential. Last year he hit .317 against righthanders, .196 against lefties; in 1982 it was .331 and .197. . . . I commented a year ago that his on-base percentage had been dropping steadily. Well, he turned that around with considerable force, posting a .373 mark this time . . . defensive won/lost percentage (and therefore overall rating) is unfairly lowered by being used as a defensive substitute. . . . may be fighting Van Slyke for playing time.

16. Graig NETTLES, New York (18–16) Oddly enough, probably the greatest everyday player (nonpitcher) ever whose name begins with an "N." If he was an "M," now, he'd have to battle guys like Medwick, McCovey, Manush, Mize and Mathews just to get to the real competition: Willie Mays, Mickey Mantle, Joe Morgan, Stan Musial. It wouldn't be much of a battle. As an "N," his main competition is some 19th-century third baseman named Bill Nash.

17. Gary GAETTI, Minnesota (21–23) Denny Matthews remarked that the bottom half of the Twins batting order looks like somebody spilled a scrabble board. . . . there probably is no ranking this year that I subjectively disagree with as much as this one. Gaetti's a terrific third baseman, and he hits for power—drives in and scores 80 runs a year. But the evaluation formulas say that, for the position he's playing, the park he's in, the number of outs he uses, that's just not enough. . . . stole 7 bases in 8 attempts last year.

18. Nick ESASKY, Cincinnati (7–5) Has a shot at the major league record for strikeouts in a season, 189. He struck out 99 times in 85 games last year. . . . he's a young Mike Schmidt type, as opposed to being a young Mike Schmidt. He figures to be pretty good, but probably not that good. . . . doesn't have the speed that Schmidt had when he was young, but should hit about 30 homers . . . defense needs work. He led the AL in fielding percentage in '82, but that's a laugh. He fielded .915; the only other third baseman in the league to play 100 games was Tabler, who fielded .906 . . . —Bill James

Johnny Bench finishing out his career as a utility player finally justifying his inclusion on this team:

THE ALL-TIME APPROPRIATELY-NAMED-AT-BIRTH BASEBALL TEAM

Jim Field	1B	Joe Wall	OF
John Strike	2B	Matt Batts	C
Jocko Fields	3B	Fleet Walker	C
Neal Ball	SS	Mike Armstrong	P
Homer Summa	OF	Bob Walk	P
Charlie Spikes	OF	Johnny Bench	Ut
Fielder Jones—Manager			

The trainer, of course, is the Orioles' Ralph Salvon.

Why was Jim Command never made a manager?—Jim Baker

19. Rance MULLINIKS, Toronto (14–15) Beginning to shake off the rust and hit the way he is capable of hitting . . . looks like he may take over the third-base job. He and Iorg hit .275 each in about the same number of tries last year (Iorg had eleven more at-bats, but Mulliniks led Iorg 34–22 in doubles, 10–2 in home runs, 57–13 in walks). In the last two years Mulliniks has hit 59 doubles in less than 700 at-bats. He's a very good platoon player at the least; never did understand why the Angels gave up on him.

20. Luis SALAZAR, San Diego (18–21) Would also be a good platoon player (.259 and .301 against lefthanders the last two years). . . . rarely grounds into double plays (4 last year) . . . and a good defensive third baseman, arguably the best in the NL. But his strikeout and walk totals are unacceptable, and his bat really doesn't justify his being in the lineup. . . . Carmello Martinez probably will get a job, and it might be Salazar's.

21. Vance LAW, Chicago (13–15) Platoon player, shouldn't be playing everyday but was needed. Last two years he's driven in 54 runs in 261 at-bats against lefthanded pitchers, 55 in 506 against righthanders. He has some positives, but I don't think they add up to what you'd like to have at third base.

There sure is a whole lot a shakin' goin' on at third base right now. Three teams started the year with rookie third basemen of substantially identical skills and credentials; all three washed out but three other teams wound up the year breaking in players with can't-miss tags on them. The first three were Lorenzo Gray in Chicago, Howard Johnson in Detroit and Leo Hernandez in Baltimore. All of them, as minor leaguers, hit for average and power (Gray in '82: .358, 16 HR at Edmonton; Johnson: .317, 23 HR at Evansville; Hernandez: .301, 31 HR between Charlotte and Rochester). Johnson may be the brightest prospect, and there are very good reasons to think that he is a major league player, but Sparky gave him 66 at-bats and decided that he just had to get Tom Brookens back in there (Howard was hitting .212 and fielding .851). Gray got 78 at-bats and did nothing, so he got sent out; the Orioles went as long as they could with Hernandez, whose bat was OK

but glove wasn't, and then bailed out.

All of these players remain prospects, but they've had their shot so who knows when they'll get another one.

Anyway, the season ended with three new phenoms in place: Esasky in Cincinnati, Van Slyke in St. Louis, Randy Ready in Milwaukee. Among the six young players, I'd pick 'em Van Slyke, Esasky, Ready, Hernandez, Johnson and Gray, and I like Lorenzo Gray, so there's definitely some young talent there. In addition, there's Darnell Coles in Seattle, who looks pretty good, 1B-3B Carmello Martinez in San Diego and Brook Jacoby trying to run off Toby Harrah in Cleveland. Then, of course, you've got Boggs coming on just a year ago in Boston, Guerrero moving to third base after already being established as one of the best players in the league. So if you're looking around for a third baseman, there's no shortage of candidates.

22. Tom O'MALLEY, San Francisco (12–15) With Trillo being signed, Youngblood may wind up here if the Giants don't trade an outfielder . . . 1000 to 1 against Tom being the first person named "O'Malley" to get in to the Hall of Fame.

23. Hubie BROOKS, New York (15–26) Clint Hurdle was playing third base for Tidewater last year, had a big year. A comparison of Brooks' and Hurdle's major league records in seasonal notation:

	Hurdle	Brooks
Years	2.41	2.46
At-bats	477	603
Hits	130	161
Doubles	30	25
Triples	5	4
Home runs	11	5
Runs	56	55
RBI	71	59
Walks	57	33
Strikeouts	84	100
Stolen bases	0	9
Caught stealing	2	5
Batting average	.272	.267

Clint is also a year younger than Hubie.

Hurdle has had his problems, and he got them the old-fashioned way: He earned them. But he has his act together now, and he is a better player than Hubie by every conceivable yardstick and by the whole yard. The Mets have just been so desperate for a third baseman for so long that they've

lost objectivity, and gone on kidding themselves about Brooks' ability. I expect Hurdle to take the job away if he's given a shot.

24. Tom BROOKENS, Detroit (10–20) Addendum to the Tigers main comment . . .

How many pennants have the Tigers lost at third base? I mean, I know the Tiger fans loved Don Wert, but he wasn't exactly MVP material, and he's somebody you have to look at very closely when you're trying to figure out how the Tigers lost the sixties I didn't mention the 1950s in the Tiger article, but they had a couple of good ballclubs in the late fifties (Bunning, Lary, Foytack and Hoeft on the mound, Kaline, Bolling, Harvey Kuenn and Charlie Maxwell) that were trying to take on the Yankees with Reno Bertoia at third base. In the late thirties they had some damn good second-place teams that had Marv Owen and Don Ross at third base. Owen wasn't bad, but it wasn't Gehringer, Greenberg, Goose Goslin and Al Simmons that were keeping them from winning.

And then let's look a minute at Bob Jones. Bob Jones took the third-base job away from Ozzie Vitt late in the season in 1918. He hit .275, a good average for that time, and although he did not homer in 287 at-bats, he seemed like a small step forward from Vitt.

In 1919, he hit .260 with 1 home run in 439 at-bats. The ball is just starting to jump now; the three Tiger outfielders that year hit .331, .384 and .355. The first baseman hit .320 and the catcher hit .292. The team finished in contention, 8 games out at 80–60.

Well, the Tigers decided, we'd better try somebody else at third base. Platooning was having its very first vogue right at that moment, and so the Tigers decided to platoon Bob Jones with somebody named Babe Pinelli. Babe had a wonderful baseball name, but he didn't hit. He hit .229 and this in 1920, the first year of the lively-ball era, when good *teams* are hitting .300. Jones, platooning with Pinelli, hit .249. No more Babe Pinelli.

And what do they do? They put Bob Jones back at third base on a regular basis. OK, in 1921 he has a decent year. He hits .303, which sounds better than it is until you remember that in 1921 the team as a whole hit .316 and finished sixth. Still, .303—well, it will keep you in the lineup. In 1922, Jones was still in the lineup. He hit .257.

Now this is a third-place team, moving back into contention. Everyone else on the team has hit .267 or higher; the averages of the eight regulars are 1B: .300; 2B: .267; SS: .300; 3B: .257; RF: .356; CF: .401; LF: .327; C: .323. Of the top five reserves, four hit between .308 and .352 and the fifth hit .292.

And remember, this is 1922. There are about nine million third basemen in the minor leagues, all of them for sale at the right price. The farm system hasn't been developed yet. The Tigers are not short of options.

They select their option. They send Bob Jones back to play third base for them in 1923. Harry Heilman hits .403, Cobb hits .340, Manush .334. Every other regular hits .282 or higher. The top three men off the bench hit .321, .315 and .310. Jones hits .250. The Tigers finish second.

And what do they do about this? Believe it or not, they again decide to play another season with Bob Jones at third base. Again, everybody else on the team hits .289 or better. Jones hits .272 with no homers, 2 stolen bases and 20 walks in 393 at-bats. And they miss the pennant by six games.

Finally, in 1925, they decided to give up on the guy. But why did it take them six years?

Who knows? I can't even figure out why they keep playing Tom Brookens now. Maybe it's part of the Tiger tradition; they figure they've been losing pennants at third base for 75 years, so why stop now? Maybe they figure it's bad luck to have a good third baseman. The only time they had a good third baseman, George Kell, the ballclub went bad on them. (Brookens' 1983 season: 5–9.)

25. Jamie ALLEN, Seattle (4–8) Allen

washed out; Coles apparently will get a shot at the job.

26. Todd CRUZ, Baltimore (8–24) The Charlie Moore of the 1983 World Series ("look at that arm").... My friend Bob Costas said during the playoffs that he thought Cruz's batting had been influenced by playing in the Kingdome, where he'd gotten home-run happy and was paying for it with strikeouts. That makes sense, but it doesn't happen to be right. Todd played in Kansas City in his rookie year, and he was exactly the same then—drew three walks in 55 games, hit .203, struck out a lot and hit more MF8s and DF7s in a week than you could have used in a year. Even when he was with Oklahoma City in 1979, he drew 17 walks and struckout 71 times in 121 games.... Strikeout-to-walk ratio, which was 8–1 (96–12) with Seattle in '82 and the same (56–7) in 1983, improved immediately (to 52–15, 3½–1) upon joining the Orioles. But there was a concurrent loss in power.

THIRD BASE

Player	Offensive				Defensive				Total	.350 Chance
	1982		1983		1982		1983			
1. Schmidt	.773	12- 3	.767	12- 4	.52	3-2	.54	3-3	30-12	.000001
2. Boggs	.688	6- 3	.778	12- 3	.73	1-1	.56	3-3	23- 9	.00002
3. Guerrero	.676	11- 5	.773	12- 4	.23	0-1	.39	2-4	26-13	.00006
4. Molitor	.670	13- 6	.578	10- 8	.61	4-2	.60	3-2	30-18	.00009
5. DeCinces	.657	12- 6	.607	7- 4	.72	4-2	.62	2-1	25-13	.00011
6. Brett	.710	11- 4	.762	9- 3	.57	3-2	.37	1-3	24-12	.00011
7. Bell	.657	10- 5	.507	9- 9	.74	4-2	.67	4-2	27-18	.00054
8. Harrah	.717	12- 5	.527	8- 7	.48	3-3	.53	3-2	26-17	.00058
9. Madlock	.715	11- 4	.672	9- 4	.39	2-3	.35	2-3	23-15	.00116
10. Horner	.627	9- 6	.734	8- 3	.42	2-3	.39	2-2	21-14	.00220
11. Wallach	.602	10- 7	.607	10- 6	.45	3-3	.46	3-3	25-20	.00379
12. Cey	.582	9- 7	.605	10- 7	.52	3-2	.30	2-4	24-20	.00616
13. Lansford	.589	8- 6	.627	5- 3	.46	2-2	.51	2-1	17-12	.00791
14. Garner	.586	10- 7	.532	9- 8	.48	0-1	.43	3-3	22-19	.01094
15. Oberkfell	.528	7- 6	.606	8- 6	.57	3-2	.43	2-3	20-17	.01352
16. Nettles	.461	6- 6	.610	8- 5	.47	2-2	.46	2-3	18-16	.02406
17. Gaetti	.431	7- 9	.457	8- 9	.57	3-2	.64	4-2	21-23	.05559
18. Esasky	.000	0- 0	.621	6- 3	.00	0-0	.34	1-2	7- 5	.08463
19. Mulliniks	.416	4- 6	.605	7- 4	.34	1-3	.36	1-3	14-15	.09779
20. Salazar	.410	7- 9	.483	7- 7	.59	3-2	.51	2-2	18-21	.09958
21. V. Law	.464	5- 5	.443	5- 7	.18	0-1	.61	3-2	13-15	.14275
22. O'Malley	.546	4- 4	.465	6- 6	.46	1-2	.29	1-3	12-15	.20240
23. Brooks	.380	5- 9	.349	6-11	.30	2-4	.44	2-3	15-26	.47388
24. Brookens	.291	3- 9	.326	3- 7	.43	2-2	.36	1-3	10-20	.57728
25. J. Allen	.000	0- 0	.292	3- 6	0	0-0	.46	1-2	4- 8	.65335
26. T. Cruz	.271	4-11	.167	2-12	0	0-0	.48	1-2	8-24	.91821

SHORTSTOP

1. Robin YOUNT, Milwaukee (36–16) An easy #1 choice; an obvious #1 choice given the criteria of the evaluation—performance over the last two seasons. Per at-bat, Yount had a better season in '83 than Ripken. Per 1,000 plate appearances:

	Run	Hit	2B	3B	HR	RBI	BB	K	SB	CS	HBP	GIDP
Yount	156	273	64	15	26	123	110	89	18	6	5	15
Ripken	168	293	65	3	37	141	80	135	0	6	0	33

Per at-bat, Yount was getting on base more, getting more extra-base hits; Yount was making 633 outs per 1,000 plate appearances (including double plays and caught stealing), while Ripken was making 676. That's a big difference.

Of course, doing this over the course of 149 games, 653 plate appearances is not quite the same as doing it over 162 games, 721 at-bats; Ripken deserved the MVP award, and would rate #1 if the ratings were based only on one season. But Yount still had a fine 1983 season—42 doubles (forget it's Robin Yount and just think about it a second—42 doubles), 10 triples, 17 homers, .308 average, played a good shortstop. That's quite a season.

2. Dickie THON, Houston (33–17) A fantastic season, just terrific. Offensively, he hit for average (.286), with power (20 homers, 9 triples), speed (34 stolen bases) and walks (54) despite playing in the Astrodome, where runs are hard to come by. He hit 4 home runs in Houston, 16 on the road.... Power/Speed number of 25.2.... plus he was driving in *big* runs. His RBI Importance was .554, one of the highest in the league, and he was producing a win with each 6.4 RBI, which is a tremendous ratio.

Defensively, he should have won the Gold Glove Award. I'm certainly not trying to take anything away from Ozzie; I have been writing for years that Ozzie was the best defensive player in the major leagues at any position. But recognition usually lags a couple of years behind the fact, and Thon passed him by last year: he is now the best defensive shortstop in baseball. His arm is better than Ozzie's; he turns the double play

better. He doesn't match his ability to make the flashy plays—nobody does—but on balance, he'll make more plays. He is the best.

3. Cal RIPKEN, Baltimore (32–19) We are blessed with some shortstops.

...I would have voted for him for the MVP; I'm not knocking him. Would also have voted for him for the Gold Glove, for the same reasons as Thon: His arm is quite a bit better than Trammell's, which is particularly important on the double play ...three years younger than Ron Kittle.... why do I have this feeling that some tragedy is waiting for him? Things seem too perfect, too good, as if someone was setting him up for something.... I have the feeling that the greatest shortstop since Honus Wayner is now active, and I don't even know who it is.

4. Alan TRAMMELL, Detroit (28–22) Hit .417 on artificial turf. Second straight year he's done all his damage after the All-Star break. If he hits all year the way he did the second half of '83, the American League will have its third straight shortstop for an MVP.... Three shortstops in 1983 were among the ten best offensive players in the league. Ranked according to Park-Adjusted offensive won/lost percentage, Yount was fifth, Trammell ninth and Ripken tenth. I wonder if that's ever happened before?

5. Ozzie SMITH, St. Louis (28–23) From 1978 through 1982 he was probably the greatest defensive shortstop ever.

It is an article of faith among baseball traditionalists that a shortstop is a defensive player first and foremost, and that it doesn't matter much what he hits. I did a study of the batting averages of shortstops, to see how common it was for a team to win a division with a .210-hitting shortstop. If a shortstop hits .280, how often does his team win the

division? If he hits .220, how often does his team win the division?

The group studied was all teams from 1969 to 1982, except 1981. There were 322 teams in the group. Of the 36 shortstops who hit .280 or better, 11 (or 31%) played for teams which won their division. Of the 165 shortstops who hit .240 to .279, 29 played for championship teams (or 18%). Of the 107 shortstops who hit .200 to .239, 12 played for championship teams (11%). Of the 14 who hit less than .200, none played for a championship team.

The traditionalist likes to cite Mark Belanger and the Orioles. But Belanger's batting average in the five years that he was the regular shortstop on a division-champion team was .246, not .200. When he hit .210, the Orioles didn't win. When Belanger was benched and Kiko Garcia took the job in 1979, Garcia was ripped as an artistic failure because he hit .247 but didn't field anything like Belanger—but the Orioles won the division. Bill Russell and Frank Taveras played for championship teams; Roger Metzger and Don Kessinger didn't. It takes runs to win ballgames.

6. Rafael RAMIREZ, Atlanta (29–27) Destroys lefthanders (.336 in 1982, .358 in 1983). 76-point platoon differential in 1982, 82 points in 1983. ...probably will set a record for consecutive years leading NL shortstops in errors (he has three already and nobody figures to challenge him). It takes a heck of a player to break a record like that.... good offensive and defensive shortstop.

7. Roy SMALLEY, New York (21–19) All of his breakdowns—first half, second, against righthanded pitching, lefthanded, at home, road, on grass, turf—are in the .270s.... record breaks down as 4–8 on defense, 17–11 on offense. Would be a better shortstop if they'd leave him alone there. Will never match Robertson as a fielder.... will be interesting to see how Andre comes back.... did you realize Andre Robertson was a second baseman in college? Ron Gardenhire was the shortstop.... strange how abilities and perceptions of abilities shift over time.

8. Dale BERRA, Pittsburgh (26–27) Hit .218 with 9 homers the first half of the season, .281 but with only 1 homer the second half. I'd rather have the former; he batted 33 more times after the All-Star break but was down significantly in runs scored and RBI.... the Berras between them now have 2,595 hits in their careers. Does that give you a little respect for the 3000-hit men?

9. Dave CONCEPCION, Cincinnati (24–27) Tied for league lead for grounding into double plays (21, with Al Oliver). I wonder how many short-stops have led the league in GIDPs? Why he batted third in 88 games I haven't a clue. He had his worst season since the Nixon administration. Why did the Reds' Nixon stay with him in the middle of the lineup for so many games? Legends die hard, I suppose. Perhaps the Reds want to keep their link with the past alive by placing the surviving players in highly visible batting positions.—Jim Baker

One thing that this rating system of mine needs is some way to adjust for a "collapse" season, some special rule that covers a 34-year-old player whose batting average drops by 50 points, like Concepcion or Dusty Baker. This rating is too high, but Concepcion was a good player a year ago. Under the 2-year rating system, he probably will come back and hit .250 next year and drop to about 16th in the ratings, and people will say, "How come you rated him 9th a year ago when he had a miserable year, and 16th now when he's had a good year?" And you're right; it doesn't make a lot of sense.

10. U. L. WASHINGTON, Kansas City (22–25) Stole 40 bases in 47 attempts.... grounded into only 3 double plays while hitting second a lot of the year.... reportedly on the market. Onix Concepcion looks good, not great. Concepcion has a Grade A arm and is fast, but has a lot to learn as a hitter.

11. Chris SPEIER, Montreal (19–21) Hit only .189 and didn't play much on grass fields. Little played most of

the time on grass (123 at-bats to 37 for Speier) and hit well there (.301), probably because he is such a good bunter. It's good to see Virdon reacting to individual talents like that, taking advantage of what each player can do.... I'm not sure I agree with it in this case, but it's worth a try.... I still think Speier is a better shortstop than half or two thirds of the regulars in the National League.

12. Larry BOWA, Chicago (21–28) A switch-hitter, but the last two years has hit .297 against left-handed pitchers, only .243 against righthand-ers.... had his best defensive season in years; defensive won/lost percentage aided by ground-ball staff.... the lifetime leaders in games played at shortstop:

1.	Luis Aparicio	2581
2.	Luke Appling	2218
3.	Rabbit Maranville	2154
4.	Bill Dahlen	2132
5.	Bert Campaneris	2097
6.	Tommy Corcoran	2073
7.	Roy McMillan	2028
8.	Larry Bowa	2015
9.	Pee Wee Reese	2014
10.	Roger Pekinpaugh	1983

So Bowa could be in the #3 spot by the end of the year. Concepcion is at least one year off the list (1848); Bill Russell is not close. Yount, with 1359 at age 28, would wind up as the #1 man if he stayed at short for the rest of his career, but I doubt very much that he will.... the Cubs have some young shortstops. Shawon Dunston, the #1 pick in the country in 1982, is doing everything right in the minors—hitting over .300, stealing over 50 bases. Some people say he has the best arm of any shortstop in baseball.... the AAA shortstop was Dave Owen, Spike's brother (and a college teammate of Gardenhire and Andre Robertson), and he looks like he's probably closer to being ready to play in the majors than his brother. (Bowa's 1983 season: 12–12.)

13. Bill RUSSELL, Los Angeles (21–26) Dave Anderson or Alejandro Taveras will probably complete the infield renovation this year; Sax has had a couple of years at second to get ready to run the thing.... did you know that if you chose up 676 All-Star teams by initials, Bill Russell would probably be on the winning team? The Bambino would have to pitch for them as well as bat cleanup,

but he wasn't too bad at either one.... three people with the initials "B.R." are in the Hall of Fame (Brooks Robinson, Babe Ruth, Branch Rickey)... the "J.C." team would be awfully good.

14. Garry TEMPLETON, San Diego (21–27) One more step down the ladder... my description of him four years ago as "the Cedeno of the eighties" now seems to have been too kind.

15. Ivan DeJESUS, Philadelphia (22–30) Wonder if there's any chance that that fellow they arrested in Hawaii is the real Ivan DeJesus and the guy who has been playing for the Phillies is the imposter? If you look at his record you sure don't have any trouble figuring out when the swap was made.

16. Johnny LeMASTER, San Francisco (18–26) World's worst full time leadoff man. It should be a misdemeanor to bat this guy first. Shame on you, Mr. Robinson. Projected to score only 73 runs in 138 games batting in the top spot; the men behind him got him home 80 times, which leads me to believe that if the Giants had even a mediocre ball player batting number one they could have scored many more runs.

Leadoff	W	L	Pct	Team Runs	TR Per Game
LeMaster	66	72	.478	576	4.17
Others	13	11	.542	111	4.63

Actually, the relative success of the "others" is merely coincidental. To be honest, their combined performances did not match Johnny's in any one category. Chili Davis would make a better leadoff man than Le Master, even if he never regains his rookie season form. —Jim Baker

17. Glenn HOFFMAN, Boston (17–32) Probably the most controversial thing that I wrote in the 1983 *Abstract*, to my complete surprise, was a one-line dismissal of Glenn Hoffman as a championship calibre short-stop. In view of his performance over the previous two years, I had not anticipated the withering lack of acceptance that this comment would meet with among the Boston Fans.

Is Hoffman better than I thought he was? Yes, almost certainly; not a lot better, but a little. He's only 25, but what kind of a defense is that? He's 18 days younger than Dickie Thon, six months younger than Alan Trammell, two years older than Cal Ripken, three years older than Julio Franco and three years younger than Robin Yount. He's had 1500 major league at bats and he is, in all likelihood, as good as he is going to be. He's a decent defensive shortstop; he is not and never will be a legitimate Gold Glove candidate. His .260 average represents the sum and substance of his offensive worth.

What I said, actually, was that the Red Sox were not going to win the pennant with Hoffman at short. The Red Sox, I should now add, are not going to win the pennant with *anybody* at short. The Red Sox organization can't make basic talent decisions, and while Wade Boggs and Jim Rice may keep them around .500 for a few years, in the long run they're going to be damn lucky to stay ahead of the Indians. But Hoffman isn't their biggest problem. The Dodgers won the pennant with Bill Russell last year, and at this point in their careers, Hoffman's basically even with Bill Russell. (1983 season: 10–14.)

18. Alfredo GRIFFIN, Toronto (21–33) What are they waiting for? Who is Alfredo Griffin to keep anybody waiting at the AAA level? . . . .290 on-base percentage.

19. Julio FRANCO, Cleveland (11–18) On July 21 Julio was hitting .288 with 7 home runs and 53 RBI. Then it occurred to him that he was a) a rookie, b) a shortstop and c) with the Indians. He still finished with good numbers, though . . . hit only .188 on artificial turf . . . will rate higher next year, but he's not a great offensive performer at this point. The two most important offensive categories are on-base percentage and slugging percentage, and Julio is below average in both . . . I still would not trade Von Hayes to acquire him, even up. (1983 season: 11–16.)

20. Tim FOLI, California (15–24) Now with Yankees . . . Burleson and Schofield will fight for the job. . . . Foli still good defensive player . . .

21. Scott FLETCHER, Chicago (6–11) Shares time with Dybzinski. Be-tween them, they drove in 63 runs and scored 72 in just over 500 at-bats (518) . . . also totaled 16 stolen bases in 21 attempts . . . bet on Fletcher to take the job by the end of the season. He's a better offensive player, three years younger (he is Hoffman's age rather than Yount's), and not that far behind with the glove . . . from this point on, the players are rated on how convincingly they have shown that they are *not* good ballplayers. (Fletcher in 1983: 6–9.)

22. Bucky DENT, Texas (13–25) Led AL shortstops in fielding percentage. . . . Little Curtis Wilkerson probably gets a shot at the job after hitting .312 at Oklahoma City. (Dent in '83: 8–13.)

23. Tony PHILLIPS, Oakland (8–17) The passing of Fred Stanley from the major league scene means that the last of the Seattle Pilots is now gone. Mike Marshall had a brief comeback attempt in the minors in '83, and of course George Brunet is still pitching down in Mexico. Unless somebody buys Brunet, who was old even when he was on the Pilots, it looks like Stanley is the last of the *Ball Four* ballclub to appear in a big league game . . . Phillips was supposed to be a defensive whiz but wasn't; his bat was OK but his glove undid him; Donny Hill now has the job . . . one of the reported reasons for signing Morgan was that he might help with the development of Hill. I'd hope so; Hill took only four walks in 162 plate appearances last year . . . (Phillips in '83: 7–12.)

24. Ron WASHINGTON, Minnesota (12–22) Also Lenny Faedo, Gagne, Jimenez. . . . don't understand the reluctance to give the job to Faedo: he looks like he's obviously the class of the group. . . . must be something that doesn't show up in the records, there.

25. Jose OQUENDO, New York (5–13) There was a genius in my college dorm (we'll call him "X") who can help illustrate a point about glove men. X was, in common parlance, weird. His appearance could be described as "masculine bag lady," and his hygiene was suspect, except on warm days when suspicion turned to conviction; the boy could clear a room. Apart from all this, he claimed to be from another planet, or a time-space continuum . . . well, some place other than earth. His stated purpose at college was, aside from majoring in physics, to study humans in their natural habitat. He would say this in all sincerity to anyone and everyone.

On his way to class or the dining hall he would run full speed and flap his arms as if expecting to take off, or as if he were already flying. Drugs, naturally, were suspected, but once inside the dining hall his real power source was discovered. X ate nothing but desserts and drank nothing but soda. He was 100% sugar-fueled. He had no sense of the social graces, even the low forms of which are practiced in American colleges. He interrupted conversations, made funny noises and would often bolt away from the dinner table in a hailstorm of flying silverware and unfinished pie, cake and ice cream. All attempts to civilize him went for naught.

Our initial impression of X was that his bizarre behavior was legitimate because he was no doubt a physics genius of some note. That he was on a full scholarship further solidified this image. So we gave him a wide berth, looking upon his bizarreness as a necessary evil, something that came with the territory. "You know how a genius can be," we said when he would cause our little group some embarrassment with an outburst of arm-flapping or dervish-like whirling at the dining hall; Einstein, after all, was reported to have been most odd outside his realm of expertise. X's extreme behavior was merely a part of this syndrome.

It was because of X that I developed the "eccentricity quotient" or "EQ." Needless to say, X had a very high EQ, but the higher the IQ, the higher the EQ that is tolerable. A true genius, after all, is too busy thinking about loftier things to be bothered with the mundanities the rest of us trifle over. Things like bathing and walking normally pale in comparison to the importance of the study of the physical universe.

At the beginning of his second freshman semester, we found out that X was on academic probation. Most of his grades were of the failing variety. That we never saw him study we had taken as further proof of superior intelligence, but apparently his strange behavior was carried over into the classroom. His favorite pastime, it seems, was disrupting lectures with a series of the most inane comments and noises. Because of this and his poor academic performance, he was kicked out of the physics program and asked to find a less strenuous discipline.

Then we realized the truth; he wasn't a genius at all. He was nothing like the mad scientist we made him out to be. In other words, his exorbitant EQ was not at all justified by his IQ.

Which brings us back to Jose Oquendo. Like X, Jose is reported to be strong in one field while severely lacking in another. Allegedly he is one hell of a fielder. Obviously, he is one poor excuse for a hitter. What must be asked is how much offense can be sacrificed in the name of defense? Can a team afford to have two pitchers in the batting order? (Look at Oquendo's second-half stats. They're on to him. I can think of ten pitchers I'd send up to pinch-hit for him.) I realize that he's still very young, but I can't see him improving that much. At least not to the point where his range factor won't have to be 7.0 to offset his shortcomings at the plate. Where do you draw the line? At what point does the IQ stop justifying the EQ?—Jim Baker

26. Spike OWEN, Seattle (4–11) Why don't we call this guy "Julio" and rename the other guy "Spike Franco?" It seems like a shame to waste such a good baseball nickname on somebody who is going to be out of the league in two years. Unless, of course, he learns to hit the curve, or the fastball, or the slider, or one of those pitches in there.

SHORTSTOPS

Player	Offensive 1982		1983		Defensive 1982		1983		Total	.350 Chance
1. Yount	.791	13- 4	.746	12- 4	.58	6-4	.55	5-4	36-16	.000001
2. Thon	.691	9- 5	.666	12- 6	.60	5-3	.72	7-3	33-17	.00001
3. Ripken	.589	10- 7	.696	12- 5	.61	4-2	.61	7-4	32-19	.00005
4. Trammell	.480	7- 8	.700	10- 4	.53	6-5	.56	6-4	28-22	.00191
5. Smith	.466	7- 8	.466	7- 9	.77	7-2	.60	7-4	28-23	.00283
6. Ramirez	.456	8-10	.512	9- 8	.59	6-5	.55	6-5	29-27	.00728
7. Smalley	.557	8- 7	.638	8- 5	.36	2-4	.32	2-4	21-19	.01728
8. Berra	.460	7- 9	.468	7- 9	.47	5-5	.59	6-5	26-27	.02444
9. Concepcion	.538	9- 7	.287	5-11	.59	6-4	.50	5-5	24-27	.05060
10. U.L. Washington	.559	7- 6	.394	6-10	.53	4-4	.44	4-6	22-25	.06324
11. Speier	.455	7- 9	.492	4- 4	.52	6-5	.33	2-3	19-21	.06992
12. Bowa	.327	5-10	.448	6- 8	.38	4-6	.59	6-4	21-28	.09423
13. Russell	.545	8- 6	.357	5- 9	.43	4-6	.49	4-5	21-26	.10894
14. Templeton	.400	7-10	.378	5- 9	.51	5-4	.51	4-4	21-27	.13204
15. DeJesus	.388	6-10	.460	7- 8	.46	5-5	.38	4-7	22-30	.16833
16. LeMaster	.416	4- 6	.434	7- 9	.41	4-5	.38	3.6	18-26	.25078
17. Hoffman	.204	3-12	.384	5- 9	.43	4-6	.44	4-6	17-32	.31335
18. Griffin	.252	4-12	.329	5-11	.56	6-5	.46	5-6	21-33	.32014
19. Franco	.334	0- 1	.392	7-10	.31	0-1	.45	5-6	11-18	.33021
20. Foli	.256	4-10	.245	2- 8	.61	6-4	.55	3-2	15-24	.38196
21. Fletcher	.105	0- 1	.419	3- 5	.00	0-1	.39	3-4	6-11	.43572
22. Dent	.170	2- 8	.317	4- 8	.43	3-4	.47	4-5	13-25	.46351
23. Phillips	.281	1- 2	.451	5- 7	.09	0-3	.25	2-5	8-17	.51883
24. R. Washington	.393	5- 8	.318	3- 6	.31	2-4	.34	2-4	12-22	.54995
25. Oquendo			.164	2- 8			.45	4-4	5-13	.81138
26. Owen			.201	2- 8			.49	2-3	4-11	.82730

LEFTFIELD

1. Tim RAINES, Montreal (28–15) Missed becoming the first man to score 20% of his team's runs by only three runs scored. The record for scoring the largest share of your team's runs is held by Kindly Old Burt Shotton of the 1913 St. Louis Browns (I don't think he was "Kindly Old" at the time) who has to be one of the few St. Louis Browns to hold a single season mark of any kind. George Sisler's hit record of 1920 is the only other one to come to mind. Anyway, see the chart at right.

Raines did establish a new NL record, breaking the old one set by Mays in 1964 by a good margin.

All-Time % of Team's Runs Scored

	YEAR	PLAYER	TM	L	RUNS	TEAM RUNS	%TEAM RUNS
1.	1913	Burt Shotton	STL	A	105	528	.1988
2.	1983	TIM RAINES	MTL	N	133	677	.1964
3.	1981	Rickey Henderson	OAK	A	89	458	.1943
4.	1920	Babe Ruth	NY	A	158	838	.1885
5.	1915	Ray Chapman	CLE	A	101	539	.1874
6.	1921	Babe Ruth	NY	A	177	948	.1867
7.	1944	Snuffy Stirnweiss	NY	A	125	674	.1855
8.	1942	Ted Williams	BOS	A	141	761	.1852
9.	1915	Ty Cobb	DET	A	144	778	.1851
10.	1964	Willie Mays	SF	N	121	656	.1844
11.	1972	Bobby Murcer	NY	A	102	557	.1831
12.	1968	Willie Davis	LA	N	86	470	.1830
13.	1928	Babe Ruth	NY	A	163	894	.1823
14.	1919	Babe Ruth	BOS	A	103	565	.1823
15.	1948	Stan Musial	STL	N	135	742	.1819
16.	1951	Stan Musial	STL	N	124	683	.1816
17.	1907	Spike Shannon	NY	N	104	573	.1815
18.	1965	Billy Williams	CHI	N	115	635	.1811
19.	1964	Dick Allen	PHI	N	125	693	.1804
20.	1932	Chuck Klein	PHI	N	152	844	.1801

Raines and Henderson are two of the few leadoff men on this list; Shotton was another. Mostly, they're sluggers.

An interesting thing is that most of the players come from relatively good teams; there don't seem to be too many cases of exploitation of a team's low production. Shotton is the only member of a last-place team on the list, although Chapman's, Davis' and Billy Williams' teams were under .500. —Jim Baker

2. Jim RICE, Boston (27–15)
ALL-WEDDING TEAM: Bob Groom-P; Bake McBride-OF; Jimmy Rice-P; Vida Blue-P; Ossie Chavarria-INF; Sam Rice-OF; Gus Bell-OF; Buddy Bell-3B; Hi Church-OF; Bubba Church-P; Dixie Parsons-C; "Shotgun" Shuba-OF; Mike Vail-OF; John Bliss-C; Bob Usher-OF; Jake Virtue-INF/OF; George McBride-SS. —Jim Baker

Rice has grounded into 106 double plays in the last five years (38 per 1,000 at-bats), 60 in the last two years (50 per 1,000 at-bats). It appears to be just a matter of time until he breaks the single-season record (32), and his 60 over a two-year period is unprecedented.

3. Rickey HENDERSON, Oakland
(26–14) The ratings are mixed up here; Rickey should be #1, Raines #2 and Rice #3. This happens because of a small flaw in the rating system, having to do with rounding the won/lost records into integers. Henderson is listed at 26 wins, 14 losses, but his two-year winning percentage is actually .659, not .650. I'll try to get that problem straightened out by next year. . . .

We are living in the age of the great leadoff men, and I think it's important to appreciate that. I grew up in the sixties, and we had all of those awesome power pitchers—Gibson, Koufax, Drysdale, Maloney, Veale, Sam McDowell. I had no sense of historical perspective, as a child doesn't, and I didn't understand that it hadn't always been this way and wouldn't always be this way. Now they're mostly gone, of course, and I feel like somebody should have told me to appreciate them.

Well, during the next ten years or so, let's appreciate these leadoff

men. Are Rickey Henderson and Tim Raines the two greatest leadoff men ever to play major league baseball? Probably not; we should not declare them that until they reach their prime. There have been great leadoff men before, only not so many of them at the same time.

To repeat the Rickey Henderson comment of a year ago, leadoff men can be evaluated with great accuracy by taking apart their records and figuring out how many times they reach each base, then weighting the bases reached by a uniform chance of scoring from that base once you have possession of it. A leadoff man will score about 35 runs for each 100 times that he is on first base, so you figure how many times he will be on first base (Hits + Walks − Extra-Base Hits − Stolen Base Attempts) and multiply that by .35. A leadoff man will score about 55 runs for each 100 times that he reaches second base on his own power, so you add together his doubles and his stolen bases, and multiply that by .55. He will score about 80 runs for each 100 triples that he hits, so you multiply the triples by .80. A home run is a run scored.

If you make these projections, you will find that the number of runs a leadoff man scores is a highly predictable outcome of his own offensive production; the actual number of runs scored is not likely to deviate significantly from the projection even if the player is exceptionally fast or unusually slow for a leadoff man. The deviation caused by having a good offense or a poor offense coming up behind you might be a little larger, but it's still not normally going to be more than 10%. It was 11% for Rickey in '83; he projected to score 118 runs, but actually scored only 105 due to the lack of an effective middle of the order coming up behind him.

The best and worst leadoff men in the majors in 1983:

Thirty-one runs per 100 outs made . . . well, Lou Brock's best figure ever was 25.7 in 1971 (also the year in which Brock had his career high in runs scored), and his career mark was just 21.8. Rickey also was the best leadoff man in the majors in 1982, and then he was getting in position to score just 26.4 runs per 100 outs. Raines' 28.8 is a terrific figure; Rickey's 30.8 is, while not a record, the sign of a historic year.

One other note . . . Rickey is now 25, and there is now virtually no doubt that he will demolish Lou Brock's career record of 938 stolen bases. He has stolen 427 bases in his career; Brock at the same age had 40. Rickey could hold up a liquor store, shoot the clerk, draw 15-to-life, make parole in eight years and return to the majors in plenty of time to break Brock's record. The only doubt remaining about his stealing 1,000 or 1,200 or 1,800 bases in his career is what I call residual doubt, the anything-can-happen doubt that is always there until it's in the books. But I estimate that he has an 85% chance of stealing 1,000 bases in his career, and a 19% chance of stealing 2,000.

4. Jose CRUZ, Houston (26–15) Had
a remarkable comeback season, probably the best year of his career. His .318 average was the closest that anyone has ever come to winning a batting title in the Astrodome (missed by five points). And with 30 stolen bases, 92 RBI and 65 walks, it was far from a quiet .318. . . . oldest man among NL leaders in batting except for Al Oliver, who is a year older. . . . grounded into only 4 double plays.

5. Dave WINFIELD, New York (25–14) A classic illustration of why it is difficult to evaluate a defensive player by watching him play. Winfield likes to play deep because he gets great publicity when he climbs the wall to rob somebody of a home run. But he plays so deep that he misses many

	Projected Runs	Outs Made	Runs/ 100 Outs
		BEST	
Rickey Henderson	118	382	30.8
Tim Raines	128	446	28.8
Joe Morgan	81	313	26.0
		WORST	
Johnnie LeMaster	75	425	17.5
Omar Moreno	70	437	16.1
Spike Owen	34	252	13.6

more catchable balls in front of him so he can make those three or four spectacular plays a year. . . . he's still an above-average defensive leftfielder, but not by much. . . . grounded into 30 double plays.

6. Lonnie SMITH, St. Louis (24–14) The Cardinals' season was lost in the period when Lonnie was out of the lineup. They were 15–26 in games that he didn't start; if they had just played .500 ball in that period they would have been right in the middle of the race. . . . another outstanding leadoff man; projected to score 86 runs, actually scored 83 in just 130 games. . . . made 15 errors in the outfield. No other NL outfielder was in double figures. . . . his career is basically a continuation of Lou Brock's. There are no significant differences between them as to on-field capabilities and shortcomings.

7. Leon DURHAM, Chicago Cubs (21–11) Didn't repeat his super 1982 season (.312, 22 HR, 28 stolen bases, 90 RBI) but still contributed offensively, slugging .466 with an on-base percentage near .400.

8. Dusty BAKER, Los Angeles (24–15) A rating-system error. Baker was an outstanding player a year ago, but doesn't seem likely to regain that level. He's still good. He has a broad base of offensive skills, which make him a valuable performer even if his Triple-Crown stats aren't much. Last year he drew 72 walks, stole 7 bases in 8 attempts and grounded into only 9 double plays. Of the other 11 NL leftfielders, only four hit as many home runs as Dusty, even though he was having a bad year. . . . Candy Maldonado seems to be the man most likely to move into this job.

9. Gary WARD, Minnesota (25–17) Now with Texas. Stats aren't likely to suffer from the switch in parks (he didn't hit at all well in Minnesota), but there is some question yet about his ability to come back from a beaning in early August. . . . excellent outfielder. He threw out 24 baserunners in 1983, the most by an American League outfielder since 1944 . . . in the last two years has stolen 21 bases in 23 attempts (13/14 in 1982, 8/9 in 1983). . . . strikeout/walk ratio is poor but improving;

grounds into a few too many double plays . . . it sure is hard to figure out why he had such a lackluster minor league career, the way he's played in the majors.

10. Brian DOWNING, California (22–14) Again, an excellent leadoff man (23.4 projected runs per 100 outs). He led the Angels in runs scored (68) despite playing in only 113 games. Per out used he scored more runs than Lou Whitaker, Damaso Garcia, Paul Molitor, Willie Wilson, Billy Sample, Rod Carew, Ryne Sandberg, Mookie Wilson, Steve Sax, Brett Butler, Alan Wiggins or Eddie Milner. Or 90% of the other players in the league. . . . set a record, as you probably know, for consecutive errorless games in the outfield. . . . a clean-up hitter against lefthanders. His slugging percentage against lefthanded pitching has been over .500 each of the last two years, and he hit .386 against lefthanders in 1979. . . . a better hitter than his raw statistics show, because he is not well suited to his home park. Last year he hit only .218 in California, .282 on the road.

11. John LOWENSTEIN, Baltimore (16–8) The platoon combination (Lowenstein and Roenicke) would probably rate about fourth; Lowenstein by himself rates tenth . . . I commented a year ago that Lowenstein had hit .372 against the Western division teams, but .276 against the East. The difference in the calibre of the pitching wouldn't account for anything like that kind of a margin; it just creates a 10, 15 point East/West differential for most players. But last year John hit .382 against the West, but .193 against the East. . . . hit .320 on the road, only .244 in Baltimore. . . . drove in 16 runs in 60 at-bats in September.

12. Larry HERNDON, Detroit (24–17) Last two years has hit .335, .353 against lefthanded pitchers, totaling 20 doubles, 9 triples, and 17 homers in 386 at-bats (.575 slugging percentage). Among them Herndon, Wockenfuss and Parrish provide a valuable service to Whitaker, Evans, et al: They prevent the opposition from throwing too many lefthanders at the team.

13. Ben OGLIVIE, Milwaukee (22–15) Limited playing time in '83 due to a couple of injuries, but had one of his better years when in the lineup. Hit .280 and drew 60 walks in 411 AB for a .377 on-base percentage. Played well afield and hit lefthanders better than he has the last couple of years. He's 34 now, but with his trim frame should last a few years, I would think . . . third-grade riddle for the year: What does Ben Oglivie have in common with Pat Underwood? (knits slaitini sih) You're right, that's terrible . . .

14. Gary MATTHEWS, Philadelphia (21–17) Also hit .400 and slugged .750 in the miniseries in '81. His record in postseason play:

G	AB	R	H	2B	3B	HR	RBI	Avg
14	50	8	18	1	0	5	10	.360

Expect him to return strong in '84 . . .

15. Mike EASLER, Pittsburgh (17–13) Now with Boston. . . . Hit only .224 on grass fields last year, .331 on turf . . . no strong evidence that he can't hit lefthanders; won't have many of them to worry about with the Red Sox, anyway. . . A natural DH and a pretty decent one, but what can you say about an organization that would trade its number one starting pitcher to come up with a designated hitter? Look what the Blue Jays gave up to acquire Mike Easler's brother-in-law a year ago. Easler's brother-in-law is Cliff Johnson, and what the Blue Jays gave up to acquire him is nothing, and he solved their DH problem pretty solid.

16. Jeff LEONARD, San Francisco (16–12) The Giants lead the league in outfield arms—Leonard, Clark, Youngblood and Davis. They can all throw. . . . Leonard's a cleanup hitter against lefthanded pitchers (.323, 11 home runs in 161 at bats) but not a middle-of-the-lineup guy against righthanders. (1983 season: 11–7.)

17. Alan WIGGINS, San Diego (16–12) Hit only two triples. . . . Laid down 16 sacrifice bunts. Wonder why? That would help explain Kennedy's scoring only 47 runs with 98 RBI. Wiggins batted second a lot; if Brown got on and Wiggins bunted, Kennedy would often bat with two out and a man on second. . . . Padres led the league in sacrifice hits. I've got a lot of respect for Dick Williams, but I can't understand bunting with your #2 hitter. I mean, it's not like Wiggins is going to ground into a double play and ruin the inning, is it? If he grounds into a forceout he can steal second. Why bunt him? (1983 season: 11–7.)

18. Billy SAMPLE, Texas (19–16) May be fighting Gary Ward for playing time. Had a decent season, stole 44 bases in 52 attempts. Has some power, excellent speed, good outfielder, draws a few walks, hits for a pretty good average. Just give him about 5% in each area and he'd be an All-Star.

19. Gary REDUS, Cincinnati (12–8) You may remember that I pointed out a couple of years ago that all outstanding hitters reach the majors at an early age. Boggs was 23 when he came up, and that is unusually late; that's the outside. Players who reach the majors at 25 or 26 are not going to become outstanding hitters, period. It's an absolute rule with no known exceptions.

So ordinarily, when you see a 25, 26-year-old rookie, you can place an upper limit on him in your mind and not think too much about it. Those players are usually one-dimensional players, slow moving sluggers or leg men or singles hitters or something. But Redus is the first player I've seen in maybe ten years that I thought had a chance to become an exception to the rule. He came into organized baseball fairly late (21) and made inconsistent progress through the minors, but those things happened in part because the Reds organization was slow in adapting to his defensive abilities and impatient with him as a hitter. But his offensive skills are anything but one-dimensional. He's the kind of player who could hit .300 with 25 homers, draw 100 walks and steal 80 bases. Even hitting .247 last year, he was one of the best leadoff men in the National League, drawing 71 walks, having a power/speed number of 23.7 and scoring 90 runs in 125 games despite playing for a team with the weakest 3–4–5 offense in the league (their RBI leader had 58). With any luck at all, Redus is going to be one of the best of the leftfielder/leadoff men types in the major leagues.

20. George FOSTER, New York (20–21) Figures to be the highest-paid reserve outfielder in baseball by this time next year. There are several reasons for saying that, some of them serious and some of them not. Among the latter, he was the Mets' RBI leader in 1983, and if you look at Mets' history you'll find that they usually get rid of their RBI leader one way or another before a season passes. Dave Kingman, who led them in RBI in '82, was on the bench in '83. Lee Mazzilli, who led them in RBI in '80, was on the bench by the end of '81 and was traded before the '82 season. Richie Hebner, the RBI leader in '79, was immediately traded; Willie Montanez, the leader in '78, was traded in midseason in '79. Kingman led in '76, was traded early in '77; Staub led in 1975 and was gone immediately. This goes way back; from '63 to '67 they traded their RBI leader by the end of the next season four times and benched him the other time.

Apart from that, Foster is now 35, he's not helping the team, and the Mets have some people who are ready to play in the outfield. So salary or no salary, he's got to go.... hit .168 in 47 games on artificial turf.

21. Brett BUTLER, Atlanta (13–17) Now with Cleveland. What he's going to do with Cleveland, I've little idea. Cleveland already has 9 leftfielders and 38 leadoff men on their roster. I suppose he will play centerfield for them, which is probably his natural position. He's a good outfielder and not a bad leadoff man; I'm not knocking him. I just don't understand what he brings to the Indians. There is just no way to get Hargrove, Thornton, Harrah, Tabler, Butler, Perkins and Jocoby all in the lineup.... Komminsk presumably will play left for Atlanta after hitting .334 with 24 homers, 26 stolen bases at Richmond. he's 23, 6′3″; I'd rate him a 70, 80% shot at sticking in the big leagues; 30, 40% chance of being a star.

22. Ron KITTLE, Chicago (10–9) Big improvement in his strike-zone judgment the second half of the season.

Tony Kubek said during the playoffs that a lot of people have been surprised at what a good outfielder Ron Kittle is. How in the world could anyone possibly be surprised by what

a good outfielder Ron Kittle is? What would your expectations for such an outfielder have to be? Saying you're surprised by what a good outfielder Ron Kittle is is like saying you're saying you're surprised at how nimble Willie Aikins is while running the bases. Being surprised by what a good outfielder Ron Kittle is is like being surprised by how good Elizabeth Taylor looks in a bikini. Being surprised by what a good outfielder Ron Kittle is is like being surprised by what a with-it, snappy kind of guy James Watt turned out to be. This ranks right up there with being adrift in a rowboat for two weeks and saying, "Gee, somehow I always thought the Pacific would be bigger than this."

Defensively speaking, Ron Kittle is the worst young outfielder I have seen since Greg Luzinski came up. I don't mean to be unkind or anything, but when they take a guy out in the late innings so that leftfield can be patrolled by Tom Paciorek or Jerry Hairston, you don't exactly figure he's going to be the one who keeps bringing up defense during salary negotiations. He fielded .964 and had the range factor of a three-toed sloth. I'm sure that he made some nice plays from time to time, and I'm sure that Elizabeth Taylor occasionally skips lunch. But she makes up for it over the weekend. (1983 season: 10–8.)

23. Steve HENDERSON, Seattle (12–13) Finished second in the balloting for Seattle's "Henderson of the Year" award . . . how come players named "Steve" are never called "Stevie"? Baseball announcers are so fond of diminutive nicknames that I've heard Rafael Ramirez called "Raffy" on occasion, but what baseball player was ever known as "Stevie." . . . I've got to get off this nickname thing.

24. Pat TABLER, Cleveland (9–9) The reasons why he was traded all those times are a lot clearer now than they were a year ago. He's no infielder and no outfielder (he had 4 assists and ten errors in 88 games in the outfield), has little power and no speed (he had six homers, grounded into 18 double plays and stole only two bases in six attempts). With all that, he can hit, and that's probably going to keep him in the major leagues for quite a few years.

He's a young Lou Piniella. I don't

215

know why this is—I don't even like Lou Piniella—but a lot of young players seem to remind me of him. A year ago I described Broderick Perkins as a black Lou Piniella. Some players remind me of Lou because they have quick wrists and sweet swings. Some remind me of him because they're hot tempered and intense, some because they're good-looking, Italian model #27. Players who get trapped at the AAA level and shuttled around from team to team for three or four years always remind me of Lou, as do high-average hitters with a little power and no defensive position. Tabler qualifies on about six points. He is a more patient hitter than Lou, gets on base more and probably could hit for more power. He can help you . . .

25. Dave COLLINS, Toronto (11–15) Platooned with Bonnell, who has now been traded to Seattle. Bonnell makes his living entirely off of lefthanded pitching. . . .

Ten years ago only three or four major league teams regularly led off with their leftfielder (St. Louis, Brock; Cincinnati, Rose; Atlanta, Garr; the White Sox, Pat Kelly, a sometime leftfielder; others on occasion, of course). The usual leadoff man was a middle infielder (Campaneris, Carew, Patek, Clarke, Aparicio, Grich, Lopes, Bowa, Cash, Hunt) or sometimes a centerfielder, and leftfield was primar-

ily a slot for sluggers (Luzinski, Williams, Stargell, Burroughs, Horton, Wynn). In 1983 eleven major league teams led off primarily with their leftfielders (Mon, StL, Cal, Oak, SD, Tex, Cin, Atl, Sea, Tor, KC). In part this might be just a matter of shifting images. The managers of ten years ago were trying to find an Aparicio or a Wills; now they're trying to find a Lou Brock. In part, there might be a growing realization that the leadoff position is just too important to waste on a .260 hitter. Or, to put it another way, to ask your shortstop to also be a leadoff man is asking the same man to perform a key offensive and a key defensive responsibility. There aren't too many players who have that many skills. It makes more sense to leadoff with an offensive player, and make what use you can of his speed on defense. (Collins' 1983 season: 7–7).

26. Pat SHERIDAN, Kansas City (5–6) The Royals' outfield situation is a mess; Sheridan isn't really a leftfielder, nor for that matter is anybody else on the team, nor is anybody a centerfielder or a rightfielder. Otis opened the season in center, moved to right and was released; Wilson opened in left, moved to center and wound up the year in the hoosegow, and Martin opened the year in right, was hurt, was released and wound up the year in the hoosegow.

We have plenty of outfield prospects. Sheridan opened the year in the minors, was called up and didn't hit, then hit very well for two months, then wound up the year lunging at balls in the dirt. He played all three OF positions some, is a superb outfielder and hit on balance better than expected; had a lot of trouble with lefthanders. Warm Front Davis, who a year ago seemed to be nobody, opened the year at Jacksonville (AA), tore hell out of the league, was promoted to Omaha (AAA), tore hell out of that league, too, and was called to the majors in August. He hit .344 and slugged .508 in 122 at-bats; he has speed and power but no arm. His ability to hit offspeed stuff is questionable but he looks like he might make a good living off of fastballs. Darryl Motley, who apparently was sulking for a year and a half after losing his status as the organization's top hitting prospect, has added some muscle to his little Hal McRae body, and has re-emerged as a good hitting prospect with some speed and very good power, but his arm isn't much, either. Jack Morris, the MVP in the Southern League, is the organization's best outfield prospect since Hurdle. His tools aren't spectacular, but he's a hustler and a hitter, some speed and a good arm. So there's a lot of talent there if Howser can bring it along and figure out what to do with it.

LEFT FIELD

Player	Offensive				Defensive				Total	.350 Chance
	1982		1983		1982		1983			
1. Raines	.601	11-8	.736	13-4	.56	2-1	.60	2-2	28-15	.00006
2. Rice	.656	10-6	.652	12-6	.48	2-2	.61	2-2	27-15	.00010
3. Henderson	.618	11-6	.753	11-4	.52	2-2	.62	2-2	26-14	.00011
4. Cruz	.566	10-7	.766	12-4	.43	2-2	.51	2-2	26-15	.00019
5. Winfield	.695	10-5	.618	11-6	.53	2-1	.55	2-2	25-14	.00020
6. L. Smith	.662	11-6	.689	10-4	.53	1-2	.43	1-2	24-14	.00037
7. Durham	.714	11-4	.694	7-3	.51	2-2	.41	1-2	21-11	.00041
8. Baker	.682	11-5	.620	9-6	.39	2-2	.44	2-2	24-15	.00065
9. Ward	.659	11-5	.509	9-9	.72	3-1	.64	3-1	25-17	.00101
10. Downing	.657	12-6	.600	7-5	.60	2-2	.51	1-1	22-14	.00124
11. Lowenstein	.813	7-2	.720	6-3	.50	2-2	.38	1-2	16- 8	.00156
12. Herndon	.587	10-7	.629	11-6	.58	2-2	.48	1-2	24-17	.00176
13. Oglivie	.548	10-8	.642	8-4	.60	2-2	.61	2-1	22-15	.00205
14. Matthews	.632	11-7	.561	7-6	.38	2-2	.36	1-2	21-17	.00833
15. Easler	.586	8-6	.623	6-4	.41	1-2	.37	1-2	17-13	.01236
16. Leonard	.561	4-4	.635	10-5	.35	1-1	.48	1-2	16-12	.01361
17. Wiggins	.429	3-5	.610	9-6	.48	1-1	.69	2-1	16-12	.01361
18. Sample	.524	6-5	.576	9-7	.45	2-2	.59	2-2	19-16	.01503
19. Redus	.364	1-2	.645	9-5	.38	0-0	.55	2-1	12- 8	.01957
20. Foster	.479	8-8	.474	9-9	.45	1-2	.58	2-2	20-21	.04806
21. Butler	.166	1-7	.549	9-7	.55	1-1	.56	2-2	13-17	.05317
22. Kittle	.480	0-1	.585	9-6	.38	0-0	.36	1-2	10- 9	.05969
23. S. Henderson	.326	3-5	.564	7-5	.45	1-1	.46	1-2	12-13	.11323
24. Tabler	.376	1-2	.561	7-5			.32	1-1	9- 8	.13906
25. Collins	.369	4-7	.463	5-6	.49	0-1	.55	2-1	11-15	.18359
26. Sheridan			.480	4-5			.58	1-1	5- 6	.33169

CENTERFIELD

1. Dale MURPHY, Atlanta (30–15) First player since 1970 (Bobby Bonds) to score 131 runs and not lead the league.... things you notice while going through old *Sporting News*: 1) the mole or beauty mark or whatever it is on his cheek is definitely growing, and 2) if anybody tells you that he was in attendance at Dale Murphy's first major league game, chances are he is lying. The attendance at that game (September 14, 1976) was 970.... there has never been a major league player whose initials were M.V.P.... highest power/speed number in the majors, 32.7.... stole his 30 bases in only 34 attempts.... scored his 131 runs while reaching base 270 times, an exceptional percentage.... I didn't get the study done, but I'd bet that Murphy's batting record the last four years has been better when Horner was out of the lineup than when he was in. Whenever Horner gets hurt, they always say that's going to hurt Murphy, too, but it doesn't ...

Of the eight previous repeat MVPs, none suffered serious declines in performance in the year following. Two maintained their performance at the same level, and six suffered declines in runs created in the range of 12 to 25%. All still had very good seasons, and most could have been MVP candidates in the third year. The only pitcher to win the award twice in a row, Hal Newhouse in '44 and '45, had a better year in '46 than he had in the last war year. Yogi Berra, who won the award while creating 105 runs in '54 and 87 in '55, created 104 in '56. Ernie Banks, who won in '58 and '59 with runs created totals of 139 and 131, dropped by 12% in 1960, to 115. Jimmie Foxx, who was named the MVP for creating 206 runs in 1932 and 181 in 1933, dropped by 13% in 1934, to 158. Joe Morgan in 1977 was 15% off his MVP pace of 1976 (totals 118–123–104). Mickey Mantle in 1958 ws 16% off of his second MVP season in 1957 (175–162–136). The maligned Roger Maris, winner of the MVP award in 1960 before his 61-homer season in 1961, dropped by 25% in 1962 (108–135–101). The 101 runs he created in 1962 are the fewest of the seven hitters on the list. Mike Schmidt created 132 runs in his first MVP season in 1980, 99 in 107 games in '81, which would adjust to 150. He was down to 113 in 1982, which could also be called a 25% decline. So it appears likely that Murphy will create about 107 runs in 1984, which would be an 18% decline.

2. Andre DAWSON, Montreal (30–16) Lost his #1 spot in the rankings despite having his best year.... Murphy rated #15 two years ago.... would rate higher than Murphy if he didn't insist on swinging at 3–1 pitches regardless of where they are. Drew only 26 walks other than the 12 intentional walks.... is not developing as a base stealer.... on the other hand, he had 78 extra-base hits last year, 14 more than Murphy, and if he played in Atlanta his Triple Crown stats would be better than Dale's, and I mean a lot better. In road games over the last two years:

	G	AB	R	H	2B	3B	HR	RBI	Avg
Murphy	163	605	119	157	19	3	31	108	.260
Dawson	162	646	112	206	38	10	36	117	.319

That's a 59-point difference in batting average and a 121-point difference in slugging percentage in neutral parks (.576-.455).... the 78 extra-base hits were the most in the major leagues (Ripken had 76, Rice 74).

3. Fred LYNN, California (21–13) Still has trouble staying in the lineup; still the best in the league when he is in the lineup.

4. Chet LEMON, Detroit (22–15) Such an odd player; talented and productive, plays hard. And he's the captain of baseball's airhead team. Although he is fast he's an awful baserunner. He tried to steal 7 bases last year and ws out all seven times; in the last two years he is 1 for 12. The last time he was over 50% was 1977, when he was 8 for 15. And besides the caught stealing, he must make 20 baserunning errors a year. On the other hand, he is on base a lot, is a patient hitter and always leads the majors in being hit by the pitch (he did again last year, with 20). He hits for power (24 homers last year), is a good center-fielder with a good arm. (Sparky claims he's the best centerfielder in the league, but you know Sparky. He did, however, have the highest defensive winning percentage of any center-fielder in the league.) Other than Dawson and Murphy, the only other centerfielders who have as much power as Chet does are Armas and Gorman Thomas, and they don't have the man's other skills. It's an interesting combination and seriously flawed, but there is no doubt that he is valuable.

5. Ken LANDREAUX, Los Angeles (21–15) One of the keys to the Dodgers' inability to beat lefthanders. Landreaux's a hell of a player, but he's a platoon player. He hits for a good average, has power and speed and plays a decent centerfield. If you take that out of the lineup (and you have to; he can't hit lefties), it makes a dent.

6. Jerry MUMPHREY, Houston (21–15) The Astros did get something out of the Moreno signing: they got Mumphrey. Mumphrey hit .288 last year (his career average), and he does that with doubles and triples power (41 extra-base hits last year in just over 400 at-bats), has speed and is a good judge of the strike zone. He's just an average centerfielder, and if I was doing these ratings on the basis of my opinions, rather than on the basis of verifiable performance, he wouldn't rate this high. But he would still rate a long, long way ahead of Omar Moreno.

7. Lloyd MOSEBY, Toronto (21–19) Gammons was right about him ... Peter started writing in '82 that Moseby was going to make a great leap forward, and he must have picked up something because he sure did.... figures to rate about #3 next year.... For a player to clearly establish one level of ability then abolish it and establish a higher level of ability, is very unusual. On the other hand, it is not nearly as unusual as a fluke year, and even though Moseby put in three years as a .230 hitter and has had only one as a good player, there is little doubt in my mind that he is going to remain at his 1983 level. Fluke seasons, when they occur, don't occur in seven categories of performance, and Moseby in '83 did everything that you can do. He also hit .330 at home and .301 on the road, .286 before the All-Star break and .339 after, .339 on grass and .282 on turf, .293 in day games and .328 at night, .296 against lefthanded pitchers and .326 against right, 304 in April, .304 in May, .288 in June, .319 in July, .351 in August, and .305 in September. He hit .317 or better against every team in his own division (.349 against Baltimore, .333 against Boston, .388 against Cleveland, .380 against Detroit, .317 against Milwaukee, .400 against New York). That's no fluke year . . . could be an MVP one year (1983: 13–7.)

8. Gorman THOMAS, Cleveland (24–22) Will be interesting to see how he does in the Kingdome. If his conditioning hasn't caught up with him, he could hit 50 homers in this park. But he's 33 and he's not exactly Steve Carlton. . . . I'll say this: I'll bet either he hits 35 homers or more, or he hits 15 or less.

9. George WRIGHT, Texas (24–22) Still coming on. . . . as an offensive player, almost identical to Gary Ward (Texas' GW twins) except that he's a switchhitter. They're close in all three extra-base categories, strikeouts and walks, stolen bases, batting average . . . good centerfielder. Now rivals Buddy Bell as the Rangers' best all-around player.

10. Willie WILSON, Kansas City (20–17)

ALL TIME DRUG AND ALCOHOL TEAM

PITCHERS	INFIELDERS
John Boozer	Andy High (3B)
Jim Brewer	Bobby Wine (SS)
Tom Brewer	Mel Roach (2B)
Dave Downs	Johnny Walker (1B)
Ed Head	Mickey Finn (2B–3B)
Herb Hash	Crash Davis (SS)
Ed High	Johnny Lush (1B–P–OF)
Dave Vineyard	
Chief Bender	OUTFIELDERS
Jim Barr	Horace Speed
Ed Wineapple	Jack Daniels
Ralph Winegarner	Coaker Triplett
Larry Sherry	Ernie Lush
	Ed Pabst
CATCHERS	Jimmy Ripple
Jimmie Coker	Gene Rye
Mike Roach	
MANAGER	
Norm Sherry	

—Jim Baker

11. Eddie MILNER, Cincinnati (19–16) Strong improvement; probably as good defensively as any NL centerfielder, and looks like he will hit enough to stay. . . . fielded .990 in over 400 chances. . . . drew 68 walks, swiped 41 bases. The Reds outfield isn't great, but it looks about 40 times better heading into 1984 than it did heading into 1983.

12. Dwayne MURPHY, Oakland (22–20) Reminds me some of Jimmy Wynn; he's bigger and has a better arm, hasn't been as consistent with that bat, but the same basic abilities. Murphy has a battle with some people in the Oakland organization who want him to cut down on his swing; Wynn had the same thing. With his defense, speed, walks and power Murphy can help you if he hits .227, as he did last year. Obviously, he can help you more if he hits .260.

13. Rudy LAW, Chicago (17–14) A sub-par August (.212) kept him from hitting .300 for the second straight year . . . his stolen base total (77) would have attracted a lot of attention five years ago. . . . it was a White Sox record. . . . comparable to Rivers, Bumbry, Bill North at their prime. A whole lot of teams win their divisions with centerfielders who can't throw.

14. Ruppert JONES, San Diego (17–14) Rumor has him returning to the Kingdome. . . . I wouldn't begin to guess what kind of season Ruppert has up his sleeve next, but a return to form would not surprise me if he does go back to Seattle. . . . shouldn't rate this high, but he's better than people think he is. If he can stay healthy and hit .260, he's quite a player. Unfortunately, he can usually manage one or the other during a season, but not both.

15. Mookie WILSON, New York (24–24) Forty-eight players named "Wilson" have played in the major leagues. Among their familiar names are Hack, Tack, Hickie, Artie, Grady, Icehouse, Chink, Fin, Highball, Maxie, Zeke, Mookie, Mutt, Gomer and Squanto. Gomer was called "Tex," "Fin"'s real name was Finis. The player who was called Icehouse Wilson was really named George Peacock Wilson. There was also a Frank Wilson, who was nicknamed

"Squash," and a Charlie Wilson, who was called "Swamp Baby," probably not to his face. One Wilson, Hack, holds the record for runs batted in in a season. Another, Chief, holds the record for triples. A third, Willie, holds the record for at-bats.

16. Tom BRUNANSKY, Minnesota (18–16) A Twins fan wrote me that he looks like the new Bob Allison . . . same basic collection of talents, yes. He's a good one, a real good one. Good arm, power, aggressive baserunner. Hit only 8 home runs in Minnesota last year, 20 on the road (all of the Twins' power hitters hit most of their home runs on the road). . . . has averaged .302 against lefthanders each of the last two years; average against regular people dropped to .195 last year. A valuable property.

17. Chili DAVIS, San Francisco (22–23) I've always thought that if I were in a position to do so, I'd be very reluctant to try to tell players to take more walks, even though I know how valuable walks are, because I'd be afraid it would make the players less aggressive at the plate. Frank Robinson, obviously, knows more about hitting than I do, and he's not reluctant to tell people that at all—he's got everybody on the team taking ball four whenever they can get it. It might have had negative impact on Chili, though; something certainly has. A year ago I was comparing him to a young Andre Dawson. Last year he had a big improvement in his K/W ratio, drawing 55 walks, but was way off his game in every other way. Andre, of course, is a very free swinger with a poor strikeout-to-walk ratio, but he's Andre Dawson; you live with it. Chili has the ability to be one of the very best in the league, and I think he'll overcome the '83 season. . . . did you realize there are two major league players whose last name is Davis and whose first name is a weather condition? Chili and Storm . . .

18. Mel HALL, Chicago (10–8) Hit only .114 (8 for 70) and had no extra-base hits against lefthanded pitching . . . the Cubs have been curiously reluctant to get excited about him, start touting him as a potential star. He sure looks good to me. . . . should be a top ten player next year. (1983 season: 9–6.)

19. Dave HENDERSON, Seattle (17–17) Coming on, but maybe not as fast as was hoped. Strikeout-to-walk ratio (93–28), on-base percentage (.310), runs scored and RBI counts (50 and 55) all negative factors; has power, speed, good throwing arm. These three players—Davis, Hall, and Henderson—are all about the same, young players of great promise but have a ways to go. One of the three is likely to be a superstar, but who knows which. . . . Henderson is the oldest of the three and hasn't really shown a lot, but it can't be that easy to play good baseball with a team like this.

20. Willie McGEE, St. Louis (18–20) Showed some improvement. I still have no use for any of the Omar Moreno type centerfielders.

21. Al BUMBRY, Baltimore (17–19) Last Vietnam veteran around, platoons with Shelby. I'm still far from convinced that Shelby is a major league hitter. He hit .395 in April but .238 the rest of the year, .227 after August 1 and he (Shelby) strikes out nearly 20% of the time, doesn't walk much and doesn't have power. He is fast, though . . .

22. Garry MADDOX, Philadelphia (14–15) Was never much of an offensive player unless he hit over .300; defense is still pretty good but not good enough to carry his bat. Hit .275, but scored only 27 runs in 97 games. . . . pretty much interchangeable with Shelby at this point of his career . . . still effective against lefties (.317 in '83, .316 in '82), and hit .333 on artificial turf.

23. Rick MANNING, Milwaukee (19–26) When the Manning/Thomas trade was made last year, Fred White (Royals announcer) assured us that of course Manning would hit better when he got to Milwaukee and was surrounded by all those good hitters. Kansas City played Milwaukee in August and Manning, who had hit .278 with Cleveland (.270 the year before), was down to about .255, but all the same Fred broke off about 20, 25 games in which Manning had hit .280 something and explained that he had been a .265, .270 hitter when he was

with the Indians, and had been under a lot of pressure when he joined the Brewers, but he was settled in now and guess what? He was hitting better than he ever had in his career, because he had all those good hitters around him.

Isn't that amazing? People are so sure that it is easier to hit with good hitters around you, so convinced that Rick Manning is going to hit better with a good team around him, that even though it doesn't happen—even though it doesn't show the slightest signs of happening—they still see it and still report that it is happening just the same as if it really were. There is no effect there. It doesn't happen. It doesn't exist. Open your eyes; there ain't no little green man there.

I suppose I should try to understand their reasoning, but I just can't fathom what the Brewers were thinking of when they made this trade. Do they really believe that if you have three people in the lineup who can hit home runs, it doesn't matter if you have four? Do they think that if you have six good hitters in the lineup, the seventh one doesn't matter? *Of course* it matters. Why on earth wouldn't it matter? When you score fewer runs, you win fewer ballgames.

That's the Law of Competitive Balance again: Whenever you say that if you have this, that doesn't matter, you're throwing baseball games out

the window. And that's exactly what the Brewers did. They figured they had such a great infield, it didn't matter if their outfielders didn't hit. They figured that since their catcher would drive in 100 runs, it was OK if their centerfielder drove in 40. And so they put two outfielders out there who don't hit, and completely wasted their beautiful infield, neutralized it. They wound up sixth in the league in runs scored. Harry Dalton may be a bright man, but he sure made one stupid move here.

24. Tony ARMAS, Boston (15–23) The ultimate one-dimensional offensive player. Compared to Tony Armas, Dave Kingman looks like Willie Mays. Armas hit 36 homers and drove in 107 runs, and in every other respect he was an absolute offensive zero. He stole no bases, led the league in grounding into double plays, walked only 29 times while striking out 131 times, hit just .218. I thought Kingman in '82 didn't do anything except hit home runs, but Kingman drew twice as many walks (59), stole four bases in four attempts, grounded into only a third as many double plays (11). The really sad thing is that Armas (and now Easler as well) is keeping a good young centerfielder on the bench. Reid Nichols can play. He's not great, but he's a hell of a lot better than Armas. But the Red Sox just won't give him a job . . . Armas

CENTER FIELD

Player	Offensive 1982	1983	Defensive 1982	1983	Total	.350 Chance
1. Da Murphy	.686 12- 5	.778 12- 4	.43 3-3	.49 3-3	30-15	.00002
2. Dawson	.696 12- 5	.690 12- 6	.58 3-2	.53 3-3	30-16	.00003
3. Lynn	.683 9- 4	.659 8- 4	.54 3-2	.49 2-2	21-13	.00131
4. Lemon	.563 7- 6	.595 9- 6	.58 2-2	.66 3-2	22-15	.00205
5. Landreaux	.610 8- 5	.621 9- 5	.49 2-2	.43 2-3	21-15	.00355
6. Mumphrey	.677 9- 4	.616 7- 5	.48 2-3	.50 3-3	21-15	.00355
7. Moseby	.342 5-10	.690 10- 5	.51 3-2	.54 3-2	21-19	.00602
8. Thomas	.620 11- 6	.439 7-10	.51 3-3	.46 3-3	24-22	.01246
9. Wright	.447 7- 9	.545 10- 8	.52 3-3	.57 3-3	24-22	.01246
10. W. Wilson	.633 10- 6	.497 8- 8	.00 0-0	.39 2-3	20-17	.01352
11. Milner	.499 6- 6	.573 9- 6	.54 2-1	.65 3-2	19-16	.01503
12. Dw Murphy	.581 10- 7	.437 7- 8	.63 3-2	.55 3-2	22-20	.01549
13. R. Law	.642 6- 3	.569 8- 6	.26 1-2	.49 2-3	17-14	.01856
14. R. Jones	.647 8- 5	.459 5- 5	.55 2-2	.41 2-2	17-14	.01856
15. M. Wilson	.521 10- 9	.489 9- 9	.51 3-3	.51 3-2	24-24	.02310
16. Brunansky	.636 8- 5	.475 8- 8	.00 0-0	.51 3-2	18-16	.02406
17. C. Davis	.528 10- 9	.428 6- 9	.54 3-3	.50 3-3	22-23	.03825
18. Hall	.377 1- 1	.671 7- 4	.28 0-1	.45 2-2	10- 8	.04219
19. D. Henderson	.505 5- 5	.521 7- 7	.50 3-3	.51 3-2	17-17	.05140
20. McGee	.512 6- 6	.523 9- 8	.25 1-3	.46 2-3	18-20	.07852
21. Bumbry	.420 7- 9	.505 6- 5	.53 3-2	.41 2-2	17-19	.08827
22. Maddox	.524 6- 6	.433 4- 5	.47 2-2	.37 1-3	14-15	.09779
23. Manning	.445 7- 9	.342 6-11	.44 3-3	.56 3-3	19-26	.19396
24. Armas	.453 7- 9	.295 5-13	.00 0-0	.53 2-2	15-23	.33633
25. Moreno	.332 7-13	.363 6-11	.46 3-3	.54 3-2	18-30	.35339
26. Wynne	.000 0- 0	.450 5- 6	.00 0-0	.35 1-3	6- 9	.43572

did play pretty well in centerfield, though.

25. Omar MORENO, New York (18–30) Ecch. Unless Buddy Biancalana happens to make the Royals, Omar Moreno is the worst player in the major leagues. There can be absolutely no excuse for writing his name on a lineup card.

26. Marvell WYNNE, Pittsburgh (6–9) The Pirates were 51–40 with Wynne in centerfield, 21–30 with Mazzilli, 11–8 with Lacy, 1–0 with Orsulak. They scored 4.4 runs a game with Marvell in center and allowed 3.7; with other players out there they scored 3.7 and allowed 4.3

A lot of that probably has nothing to do with Marvell; all the same,

it happened, and he is going to get credit for it. . . . this rating doesn't mean "bad," this rating means "unproven." Like Pat Sheridan in left; we start him out at the bottom and wait to see what happens. 103 games of hitting .243 with 26 RBI does not constitute effective proof that you're a major league player.

RIGHTFIELD

1. Jack CLARK, San Francisco (26–13) Probably would have ranked around #8 if he had these two seasons four years ago, when there were all the outstanding rightfielders around. He's an excellent player, offensively and defensively, has averaged 93 runs scored and 90 RBI a season (per 162 games). . . . The 93 runs a year are the most of any major league rightfielder; the 90 RBI are exceeded only by Dave Parker, Steve Kemp and Darryl Strawberry. . . . Some of his data isn't right. The Giants sent us the breakdowns and we used what they sent us rather than also figuring it. I apologize for the errors; we won't do it again. . . . Clark hit .268 against righthanders, .268 against lefthanders. . . . there are still trade rumors surrounding him. If he gets a chance to play a season in Pittsburgh or some place, you're going to see just how good he is . . .

2. Terry PUHL, Houston (21–15) The situation among rightfielders is this: just four years ago, the major leagues were crawling with top-flight rightfielders; the MVP ballots were full of them. In 1979 Baltimore's regular rightfielder hit .295 with 35 homers and 111 RBI, Milwaukee's hit .321 with 28 homers and 101 RBI, Boston's hit .274 with 21 homers, the Yankees' hit .297 with 29 and 89. Other totals: Cleveland (25 HR, 85 RBI, 34 stolen bases, .275), California (21 HR, 101 RBI, .290), Kansas City (9 HR, 73 RBI, .295), Texas (18 HR, 64 RBI), Pittsburgh (25 HR, 94 RBI, .310), Montreal (21, 82, .276), St. Louis (16, 75, 300), New York Mets (16, 60, .275, 37 doubles), Cincinnati (.316

average), San Fancisco (26, 86, .273), San Diego (34, 118, .308), Atlanta (27, 90, .308). Minnesota's rightfielder hit .293, the White Sox' .280, Seattle's .283, Philadelphia's .280, the Cubs' .289, the Astros' .290. The Dodgers had a reasonably effective combination going with Reggie Smith when he was healthy and Joe Ferguson when he was not.

That is 16 teams getting good to outstanding production out of the rightfielder spot, and seven more who were at least getting some singles out of the spot. The only teams that were really hurting in rightfield were Detroit, Toronto and Oakland.

In two years this changed with dramatic suddenness. They grew old, they got hurt; a half dozen just stopped hitting, two or three were shifted to leftfield and two more to designated hitter. I commented on this in the 1982 *Abstract*, p. 157, re Joe Lefebvre. The teams began to make changes; of the 26 rightfielders rated in the 1982 *Abstract*, only seven were still playing rightfield in the major leagues in 1983. (Dan Ford, Dwight Evans, Harold Baines, Al Cowens, Dave Parker, Claudell Washington, Jack Clark).

Those seven players are basically what we have to choose from in naming the top rightfielders in the major leagues today. We've got seven established players, seven players who were playing regularly two years ago at other positions and have been shifted to rightfield, and a dozen young rightfielders who are trying to establish themselves. The 7 established players have an average rank of 10.6, and range from Jack Clark (#1) to

Al Cowens (#24). The seven transfers have an average rank of 13.6 and range from Terry Puhl (#3) to Juan Beniquez (#25). The 12 young players have an average rank of 15.5, and range from Darryl Strawberry (#6) to George Vukovich (#26). Most of the players who will be the top five rightfielders of the next two or three years are in that latter group. . . . Puhl hit only .165 against lefthanders, .326 against righthanders (.222 vs. LHP in '82, .218 in '81). . . . the seven rightfielders who were playing other positions two years ago are Puhl and Otis (centerfield), Steve Kemp (leftfield), Charlie Moore (catcher), Larry Parrish (third base), Warren Cromartie (first base) and Juan Beniquez (left end) . . . Puhl probably shouldn't play against lefthanders, but is the kind of player who can win games for you in the Astrodome. Hits for average, hits some doubles and triples, gets on base, avoids the double play, plays good defense.

3. Harold BAINES, Chicago (25–20) My favorite opposing player to watch. He is gorgeous, absolutely complete. I've seen him drop down bunts that would melt in your mouth, come up the next time and execute a hit and run that comes straight off the chalkboard. I've seen him hit fastballs out of the yard on a line, and I've seen him get under a high curve and loft it just over the fence. He's 25 now, should be just entering his best years . . . straight second half player . . .

4. Dwight EVANS, Boston (22–17) In-and-out, up-and-down career was down quite a bit last year. Still scored

74 runs in 126 games. . . . hit only .167 on artificial turf. . . . the Red Sox would score a lot more runs if they'd lead off with him. They can't stand the thought of his hitting all those home runs with nobody on, but he's never been an RBI man, anyway.

5. Darryl STRAWBERRY, New York (11–5) Seems likely to be #1 next year. Park-adjusted offensive winning percentage (.699) was the best at his position, one of the best in the league. . . . did you realize that strike-out-to-walk ratio (128 to 47) was the *best* among the Mets' outfielders. Foster was about the same (111 to 38), but Wilson was almost 6 to 1 (103 to 18).

6. Tony GWYNN, San Diego (12–7) Gwynn will probably win a major league batting championship in the next three or four years, at least if the effect of the new hitting background is what Craig Wright and Bill Carr believe it is. He's almost a prototype of a potential batting champion. . . . young lefthanded hitting outfielder, can run. Played regularly the second half of the season and hit .309, with a 25-game streak included. . . . Sixto Lezcano had a combined (SD-Phil) RBI Importance of .653, which I believe is the highest I've ever seen for a player with 40 or more RBI. He was at .656 with San Diego, .618 with Philadelphia. . . . This is the beginning of another "knot" of very comparable players. The players rated from 7 through 18 here are all comparable; you could flip-flop the rankings in that region and they'd be about as accurate. Amos Otis is rated 18th with a contribution of 14 wins, 13 losses, and if he was 15-12 he would rate tenth. There's no really significant difference among these players.

7. Larry PARRISH, Texas (20–17) Not only drove in a lot of runs, but a lot of big runs for Texas. His RBI Importance was the highest among Ranger regulars, and he was producing a win with each 7.5 runs, also the best ratio among Ranger regulars except for Bucky Dent . . . with the acquisition of Gary Ward, the Rangers now have two players who scored 76 runs and drove in 88 . . . defense in right still marginally adequate; may DH in '84.

8. Keith MORELAND, Chicago (19–16) Led the NL in batting against lefthanded pitchers (.385) and concentrated a large share of his power against them, too. . . . I was watching Cub games on TV the last couple of weeks of the season. Harry, Steve and Miles started talking about Keith Moreland's drive to hit .300 with about ten days to go of it; every at-bat, every out, each step along the path to .302 were carefully charted. It reminded me so much of listening to the Kansas City A's finish out the season when I was a kid. The A's had a lot of people who hit .301. The announcers had nothing else to talk about, so they'd start finding out what the players' goals were about the All-Star break, and the rest of the year was consumed in watching them try to reach these. They usually had an exciting battle for the team leadership in wins (in 1961 it was Norm Bass with 11, Bob Shaw with 9, Jim Archer with 9, Jerry Walker with 8. I still remember the day that Bass won his 11th game, clinching the title. Norm Bass was the Steve Trout of his day . . .), plus once in awhile somebody was trying to stay among the league leaders in doubles. I've been watching a good team for the last few years, and had forgotten all about that stuff.

9. Mike MARSHALL, Los Angeles (12–8) A very good offensive player right where he is, almost even with Strawberry, hit .284 with power . . . hit .311 with 10 homers, 43 RBI after the All-Star break. Defense in right-field needs a lot of work.

10. Glenn WILSON, Detroit (15–12) Bat was a disappointment after he hit well in '82 . . . probably the best defensive rightfielder in the American League, and there are worse hitters around . . . hit .295 in night games, just .207 in day games. The only player with a larger edge in night ball was Todd Cruz.

11. Claudell WASHINGTON, Atlanta (20–19) He's half of a good platoon arrangement if the Braves can come up with the other half. Terry Harper doesn't look like the answer . . .

12. Warren CROMARTIE, Montreal (17–15) Now somewhere in Japan. . . . Scored only 37 runs, drove in only 43. . . . what is this guy doing ranked #12? . . . He has adjusted surprisingly well to the rightfield assignment.

13. Steve KEMP, New York (18–17) Didn't adjust as well to Yankee Stadium as I thought he would (.208, 3 homers at home; .272 and 9 on the road), and wilted in the second half. Those two things—a poor home-park performance, a collapse in the second half after a decent first half—are the classic signs of a collapse under the day-in, day-out pressure of being expected to do inhuman things.

The thing that is called "pressure" that means game pressure has really no relationship to the "pressure," the "living pressure," of sustained expectations; a lot of people who can deal with one can't deal with the other. Dave Parker's decline after he got the big contract in Pittsburgh is another example of the same thing, as is George Foster's 1982 season—Foster's first half/second half breakdowns in 1982 are strikingly similar to Kemp's in 1983. Some players go through this after they get a big contract, others after they have their first big year. Everybody keeps watching you, watching you, waiting for you to break loose, and eventually it just wears you down. Most players come back from it.

14. Mike DAVIS, Oakland (11–8) He was the one player whose absence from the lineup seemed to have a negative impact on the A's performance. They were 55–56 with him in the lineup, 19–32 without him. Many of the games without him were the games against lefthanded pitching, but he did bat 134 times against southpaws. . . . hit .347 and slugged .564 on artificial turf.

15. Jesse BARFIELD, Toronto (16–15) Interesting player; obvious strengths and conspicuous weaknesses. Last year he struck out 110 times in 388 at-bats, almost exactly the same strike-out frequency that Bonds had the year he struck out 189 times, and drew only 22 walks. He has terrific home run power, but not much doubles and triples power, which makes him a good but not great RBI man. He would do the team a favor if he would stop trying to steal bases, as he's just wasting runs with a 30% success rate. He has one of the best outfield arms in the American League

—a Clemente type arm, rifle shots, rather than an Ellis Valentine, Dwight Evans type of arm, long-distance artillery. He has huge splits in his record. He hit .288 with 17 home runs after the All-Star break. He hit .304 with great power at home, but hit only .193 without much power on the road (22 HRs in Toronto, 5 on the road). He hit .191 and slugged less than .300 on grass surfaces. He hit .348 in day games, .200 at night; that is the widest day/night difference in the American League. He also hit much better in day games than night games a year ago, so that probably isn't entirely a fluke.

The combination of things—the 5–1 strikeout-to-walk frequency, the big splits in his record, the lessened hitting at night—suggest that there may be a visibility problem, that he hits the ball well when he sees it, but doesn't always see it.

16. Dave PARKER, Pittsburgh (15–14)
Now with Cincinnati. . . .

I wanted to say something about weight clauses. Incentive bonuses in baseball are a negotiating tool, used by both sides to resolve an impasse and put an agreement on the table. To people who are involved in the negotiations, the criticism that so often is directed at them seems puzzling and at times more than a little bit bizarre.

What happens initially is that the player and his agent will make a decision, based on the information that is available at that time, to ask for a certain amount of money—let us say $450,000. The player has just had a good year; he has finished 19th in the voting for the MVP award, third at his position in the voting for the AP post-season All-Star team, and he is beginning to think of himself as one of the better players in the league at his position.

Meanwhile, the owner and his agent, who is called a General Manager, will meet and make a decision about what to offer the player. As they see it, the young man has shown some progress, and he is in the general class now with Chico in Chicago and Abdul in Atlanta and Herman, our own young infielder. Chico is in the second year of a three-year package averaging $265,000 a year, Abdul is unsigned but played last year for $160,000, and Herman is knocking

on the other door asking for $345,000. Owner and GM mull this over, and they come up with what they think is a very fair offer: $275,000 for one year, or $650,000 for two.

A phone call is arranged. Offers are exchanged, and then grimaces. This one ain't going to be easy.

They begin to talk. Reasons are given. Strengths of the ballplayer are pointed out by the agent; weaknesses of the player are pointed out by the GM; weaknesses of the comparable players are pointed out by the agent; strengths of the comparable players are pointed out by the GM; alternative sets of comparable players are introduced by the agent (look at Bob in Boston and Louie in LA); strengths and weaknesses of these comparable players are elucidated ad infinitum. Weeks pass; calls are being made every day.

And as each man talks, he becomes more and more convinced that he is right—convinced that if the case must be sent to an arbitrator, he is going to win it. Irritation grows; positions harden. Eventually an offer is declared Our Final Offer. $310,000; that's it. You're not getting a penny more.

Well, says the agent, this is Our Final Offer: $425,000. Take it or fight.

Silence reigns. A week goes by with no contact. War preparations are begun. Arbitration cases are being written, and that means 16-to-18-hour days for both sides. Another week of this begins to wear on the combatants. Ten days until the arbitration schedule begins. Both agent and GM have other things to do, other contracts to worry about.

But while the positions are not changing, the information bank is. Abdul in Atlanta signs for $350,000 plus $50,000 in soft incentives and $25,000 in star bonuses. The club reaches an agreement with Herman at $325,000. Bob in Boston agrees to a long-term deal that will pay him somewhere between $400,000 and $7 million in the next ten years, rendering him virtually useless as a comparison in an arbitration case. The agent asks the statistician who is working on the case whether or not he can sustain the comparison to Louie in LA; the statistician says I doubt it. The GM looks carefully at Herman's stats, and realizes that he would have a tough time explaining to an arbitra-

tor why he is paying Herman more than he is paying this guy.

Both sides now realize that they cannot defend the positions they have taken, they cannot present a solid arbitration case at the figures given —but, unfortunately, they can't get out of them. Because when they convinced themselves that they were going to win, they also convinced the people whose money it was. The GM has convinced the owner (or the assistant GM has convinced the GM) that $310,000 is a generous offer, a winnable figure in arbitration. The agent has convinced the player that he deserves every bit as much as Bob in Boston, and he's not about to take what Herman got. The owner has got another arbitration case on a pitcher with the same amount of experience, and if he settles this one at $400,000 it's going to hurt him on that one. Neither side can move, and neither side really wants to fight this thing out to the bitter end.

So what can they do? I was not in any way connected with those negotiations, but it certainly is not a coincidence that the precedent-setting weight clause in the Bob Horner contract grew out of a situation in which the two sides of the negotiation had hardened to an unusual extent. Incentives. Bonuses. They serve as a bridge between the solidified positions. The GM finally goes to the owner, and he says, "You know, I wouldn't mind paying this bozo something like what he's asking for if we just didn't have to worry about conditioning. He had a pretty good year last year, but you know he tends to put on weight in the offseason, and I just don't feel like we can count on his having as good a year again."

And the owner says, "I thought we were in a good position on this one?"

And the GM says, "We should have been, but then that moron in Atlanta gave all that money to Abdul, and I'm afraid it's going to kill us. You just never know what an arbitrator is going to listen to."

And the owner says, "Well, maybe we can come up a little if we can get some guarantees—a weight clause, some performance clauses. I don't mind paying him if he has a good year, just as long as we don't wind up paying through the nose for a bad one."

Presto. A contract is agreed to within 24 hours—$310,000, plus $50,000 in incentives based on playing time, plus $40,000 in weight clauses. The war is avoided; the GM doesn't have to go into arbitration and tell the player why he doesn't deserve more. His staff can concentrate on the other case. He doesn't have to explain to Herman why he gave a bigger contract to somebody else. He doesn't really have to back down on his "final" offer, a practice which could kill him in future negotiations if he makes a habit of it. He has gained a measure of control over the player's conditioning program; at least when he thinks about the player's conditioning, he has a reason for optimism. The player is happy; as far as he's concerned it's a $400,000 contract as long as he keeps his weight down. The team has acknowledged that he's a better player than Herman is. He can now go to spring training and concentrate on playing baseball. The agent is happy; he feels that he's done the job for the player —not like that guy who represents Chico in Chicago, who has the guy playing for $265,000. Good feelings emanate all around; an agreement is made to meet in June and talk about a long-term contract.

And then some old plaster brain working for the local paper, who knows as much about negotiating a contract as he does about playing the French horn, will write a column in which he rips you all to shreds—the greedy player and his greedy, greedy agent who expect to receive $40,000 a year for just not getting fat, the stupid owner and his stupid, stupid GM who yield to this kind of blackmail, and I remember Stan Musial used to do jumping jacks all winter just to keep his ankles in shape and nobody had to pay him anything to do it, and isn't the world just going to shit these days when you have to pay an athlete an extra $40,000 just so he won't O.D. on Twinkies and chocolate bars.

Well, friends, Stan Musial was not a typical ballplayer from the 1950s. And if I had a ballclub, just about everybody on it would have a weight clause. Why? If you were managing the Pirates over the last three years, wouldn't you have wished to God that Dave Parker had a weight clause in his contract? Allow me to point out that Dave Parker is not the first fat ballplayer who's ever played the game. He's not going to be the last. Mickey Lolich and Smoky Burgess and Dick Radatz and Ernie Lombardi and Bob Fothergill and Piano Legs Hickman and Wilbert Robinson— as far back in the history of the game as you can see, they've always been there.

Weight clauses are an intelligent attempt to deal with a problem that major league teams have been attempting to deal with from day one. The need for their existence says a mouthful about human nature, but it says not a word about the decade that we are living in.

17. Charlie MOORE, Milwaukee (18–20) Had a decent year with respect to what his abilities are; still drove in only 49 runs as a fulltime player. . . . you can't imagine how much it pains me to rank this guy ahead of Amos. . . . (1983 season: 11–8.)

18. Amos OTIS, Kansas City (14–13) Now with Pittsburgh.

In the years that Amos Otis was in Kansas City you would occasionally, maybe once a year, see a note in the letters section of the paper that went something like this:

> *As I was leaving Royals Stadium after the Royals/White Sox game of June 13, I experienced car trouble and was stranded for 25 terrible minutes in the heat beside I-70 as the postgame traffic rolled by. I was wondering how we would ever get out of there when a car stopped behind me and the driver asked if we needed help. To my amazement, the driver of that car was Amos Otis.*

Amos has been cast by the media as a moody and unapproachable man, and that he is; he is moody, and he is unapproachable. In his last three or four years as a Royal, I can never remember him interviewed on the pregame show. This wasn't because Denny and Fred didn't want to interview him. I tried to interview him myself a time or two and got nowhere much. He might consent to interviews in spring training, but once the season began the evasions began, the "No Interviews" sign went up and came down and went up again. He always said that he didn't like to talk to the press when he was going good and they never wanted to talk to him when he was going bad.

Yet anytime I was in the clubhouse, I always enjoyed watching him talk to the other players. I remember seeing him explaining to John Wathan how he hit Len Barker. "Fastball," he said, swivelling his head to watch the imaginary pitch go by. "Fastball . . . slider . . . fastball." Then he yelled "CHANGE-UP" and his eyes blazed and his hands leaped into action and an enormous smile seized hold of his face.

His Kansas City career came to a sad end when he cleaned out his locker in mid-September with the team on a road trip, denying the fans a last at-bat or a last cheer or a turn and wave goodbye. We all felt a little cheated, and we all felt that Amos had been a little selfish walking out that way, and I think he was. But it would have been out of character for him to do it any other way.

Amos was an intensely private man living an intensely public life. He disdained showmanship—probably he hated showmanship—of any type and to any extent. He could never quite deal with the fact that his business was putting on a show. This is what is called "moodiness" by the media. Yet there was a rare, deep honesty about him that was the defining characteristic of him both as a man and as a ballplayer. He could not stand to do anything for show. He could not charge into walls (and risk his continued existence as a ballplayer) after balls that he could not catch. He could not rouse the fans (and risk his continued existence as a baserunner) with a stirring drive for a base too far. He never in his career stood at home plate and watched a ball clear the fence. McRae and Brett, they did that sort of thing; Otis would sometimes turn away interview requests with a sardonic comment, "Talk to Brett and McRae. They're the team leaders."

It went further than that. Amos could not quite walk down the line when he hit a popup (that, too, would be dishonest), but he could not quite bring himself to run, either. Because it was false, you see? He wouldn't have been running for himself or for the team or for the base; he would have been running for the fans, or for the principle that one always ran.

But what you must also see is that the same honesty which denied Otis the indulgence of flair, the same feeling which required that he keep his kindnesses out of the view of the public, this is what built the wall around Amos. He could not give interviews because he could not recite clichés, and he could not recite clichés because they are false. We're eight and a half behind on September eighth, and somebody asks you if you think we still have a chance to win, and you're supposed to say, "Absolutely. We've got to go out and play hard every day and not be watching the scoreboard." It would have turned Amos's stomach to recite that stuff; it wasn't fair of us to expect him to do it. There is truth in it, but there is falsehood in it, too. Amos could not digest the falsehood to be nourished by the truth. It is a way of putting out your hand and feeling the wall there, and when you reach out and you can't feel a wall there anymore, custom or maybe it really is common sense requires that you pretend that there is still a wall there. If there is no wall, then you have no support, and you will fall.

But Amos could not pretend to feel the wall. He could not mime the wall; he could not put on the show.

And what is running out a pop fly ball to Manny Trillo, but a cliché in action? George and Hal, that was their schtick. Amos was the one that the young black players on the team, U. L. and Willie and Al Cowens, always grew to admire. Amos was the one who picked you up at the airport when you had to come to town in the winter. Amos was the one who led quiet workouts in the offseason, far out of view of the press. (It is to laugh that there were charges late in his career that Otis was not in shape. He was as trim and strong the day he left the Royals as the day that he arrived. Only he was 37 years old.)

And yet, Amos ached for the recognition he denied himself. It bothered Amos that others were regarded as the leaders of the team. And how did they reach that position? By showmanship, disreputable showmanship. It ragged at his heart that players no better than he got far more recognition because they put on the dog. He had a tendency, in his rare mo-

ments of communication with the press, to whine about those things.

Yet even Amos's playing talents were shaped by the need to avoid attracting attention. Amos could have hit 30 home runs (with a lower average) or he could have hit .320 (with less power) or he could have stolen 70 bases (with 25 times caught stealing). He would take a day off in the last week of the season with 93 RBI. If his average was at .301 with a week left, he'd decide to become a power hitter. To give in to those numbers, those attention-getting goals, that was not honest enough for him. His goals were private; you never knew whether he had reached them or not.

Amos could not often bring himself to protest a particular scorer's decision, because that would be admitting that he cared about the show. So instead, he would grumble in a general way about the scorer's treatment of him.

He was a purposefully unburnished silver player. If the public wanted to love him, he would make them do it privately; he would brook no flashy displays of affection. A small man with effeminate cheerleading gestures sat behind home plate wearing the number 26 for three years; Amos, interviewed on the subject, spoke cuttingly about the strange things people would get it in their heads to do. If you reject them first, of course, they have no chance to reject you.

His tender ego and his suffocating, defining honesty made him a lesser ballplayer than he might have been, and a greater ballplayer than he probably should have been. But it was, on the whole, an enjoyable ride; there were quite a few changeups in there among the fastballs. Baseball needs Hal McRaes and George Bretts, but it needs Amos Otises and George Hendrickses, too. It needs people who cannot stand to recite clichés. His ambivalence toward public life was harder for him to live with than it should be for us.

19. Paul HOUSEHOLDER, Cincinnati (13–18) Presumably out of a job. Parker's got to help. (1983 season: 8–7.)

20. Mickey HATCHER, Minnesota (10–11) Hit .317 with some power; needs to stay at this level to rate.

Impatient hitter, rarely walks or strikes out. One of the league's great hustlers. (1983 season: 7–5.)

21. David GREEN, St. Louis (12–12) Like him a lot better than the ratings, but he does have some problems. His strikeout-to-walk ratio is about 3–1, which would be a negative thing if he was a power hitter, and is a large negative thing for a player who has shown neither home-run power nor line-drive power. He's not stealing bases well enough (68%) to help the team, and his outfield play has not been what it probably is going to be. I figure 1984 to be the year he should make a large step forward.

22. Dan FORD, Baltimore (15–17) Jim Dwyer, the other half of the platoon combination, had a fine year; Ford stands to be in for a serious challenge from Tito Landrum . . . he did hit 30 doubles in just over 400 at-bats, with a .280 average. Rating is lowered by poor 1982 season.

23. Von HAYES, Philadelphia (15–18) Hit only .217 in Philadelphia, .327 on the road. So you'd have to think he was pressing, trying to be worth five men. . . . if you look at his career record in seasonal notation, you'd still have to think he's going to be a good ballplayer unless he's got what they call a "lifestyle" problem or something . . .

24. Al COWENS, Seattle (15–18) Had a worse year than a biker in a Clint Eastwood movie.

25. Juan BENIQUEZ, California (10–11) Shares playing time with Reggie, Ellis Valentine, Bobby Clark, Ron Jackson, Mike Brown, Gary Pettis and the Seven Dwarfs on loan from Disneyland . . . The "young" man who reportedly had been promised the job in '83, Bobby Clark, is six months older than Jack Clark. He is also now on Milwaukee.

The Angels' future is self-evident. Their fate has been sealed. No article on the Angels this year failed to mention their injury problems. Excuses are nice, and yes Alibi Ike, I think injuries are a bitch and I wish they wouldn't happen, but damnit, fellas, when you cross Death Valley in a Model T you better be expecting some trouble. Have your Triple A card ready, because sooner or later you're going to need some towing. When you load your lineup with aging and proven injury-plagued players, you've got to expect this sort of thing. Sorry you have to play with a handicap, but you brought it upon yourself.

I could really see this sort of thing if the Angels had (a) a good bench and/or (b) a decent farm system. Unfortunately, they have neither. They have one good young ballplayer, Daryl Sconiers (who plays, just what an old team needs, first base), and one good prospect, Dick Schofield. The bench consists of all manner of known ne'er-do-wells. In 1983 Joe Ferguson and Mike O'Berry both saw duty as the Angels backup catcher. This is a program for disaster to be sure, but one that could be changed for 1984. Well, make that could have been changed. The Angels have resigned everybody in sight, including, gulp, Ellis Valentine.

Think of what the Angels could have done with the money tossed away on this proven underachiever. No, I'm not going to say feed the poor or build hospitals or any of that usual flotsam. On the contrary, I think high salaries are good things, especially when they are justified. It's certainly better for the economy to give an irresponsible ballplayer a million dollars than it is to have the owner keeping it. The irresponsible ballplayer is going to release that million dollars almost immediately, whereas the owner would merely leave it in some tax shelter where it does nobody any good. The irresponsible ballplayer practices conspicuous consumption and injects a great deal of cash flow in the American economy. I think that's how supply side economics is supposed to work.

Anyway, for what they gave to Ellis for several years of guaranteed mediocrity and unfulfilled potential they could have done any number of things to improve the operation of their ball club:

● They could have made life more comfortable for every one of their minor leaguers. It's an interesting experiment, I think. How would they respond later on in their careers? Would it promote better franchise loyalty if you gave them more meal money and a living wage in the early stages of their careers?

● They could afford to lure an intelligent baseball man to take Buzzy Bavasi's place.

● How about bribing every baseball writer in the country to say only nice things about them?

● Gone after a quality relief pitcher so they wouldn't have to lose two out of every three games that are decided after the sixth inning like they did in 1983.

● Hired ten new scouts for several years each.

● Improved their talent wasteland of a farm system.

● Cut ticket prices by $.25 each. Not an earth-shattering reduction, but a nice gesture to some of baseball's most supportive fans.

Of course, Gene Autry could afford to do all of these things anyway. To paraphrase Robin Williams, signing Ellis Valentine to a multiyear contract is God's way of letting you know you have too much money. When your sense of what a dollar is worth is distorted to the point that it seems like chicken-feed to pay this man what most would consider a middle-range to top-end salary, then there is little hope for success. Excess is the soul of waste, and this is one excessive ball team. —Jim Baker

26. George VUKOVICH, Cleveland
(10–16) Hit .182 until August 1, then hit .345 in August and .343 in September to save a spot for himself on a major league roster. Platoon player at best; not even that at the level of 1983 performance.

RIGHTFIELDERS

Player	Offensive 1982		1983		Defensive 1982		1983		Total	.350 Chance
1. Clark	.695	11-5	.665	9-5	.60	3-2	.53	2-2	26-13	.00006
2. Puhl	.549	8-7	.668	9-4	.45	2-2	.51	2-2	21-15	.00355
3. Baines	.589	11-7	.547	9-8	.47	2-3	.52	3-2	25-20	.00379
4. Evans	.616	10-7	.547	8-6	.52	3-2	.59	2-1	22-17	.00504
5. Strawberry			.699	8-4			.54	2-2	11- 5	.00620
6. Gwynn	.597	4-2	.618	5-3	.59	1-1	.64	2-1	12- 7	.01144
7. Parrish	.534	7-6	.598	10-6	.34	1-3	.41	2-2	20-17	.01352
8. Moreland	.469	7-7	.666	10-5	.58	1-1	.37	1-3	19-16	.01503
9. Marshall	.607	2-1	.660	9-4	.36	0-1	.29	1-2	12- 8	.01958
10. Wilson	.562	5-4	.492	7-7			.69	3-1	15-12	.02292
11. Washington	.531	9-8	.545	8-6	.32	1-3	.45	2-2	20-19	.02679
12. Cromartie	.574	9-6	.519	5-5	.57	2-2	.47	1-2	17-15	.02690
13. Kemp	.612	10-7	.455	5-6	.33	1-3	.53	2-1	18-17	.03363
14. Davis	.785	2-0	.504	7-6	.33	0-0	.61	2-2	11- 8	.03469
15. Barfield	.470	6-6	.539	6-5	.48	2-2	.51	2-2	16-15	.04237
16. Parker	.575	4-3	.499	8-8	.38	1-1	.53	2-2	15-14	.04764
17. Moore	.363	5-9	.538	8-7	.62	2-2	.52	3-2	18-20	.05317
18. Otis	.549	8-6	.424	4-6			.64	2-1	14-13	.05362
19. Householde	.284	4-9	.513	6-5	.56	2-2	.63	2-1	13-18	.07534
20. Hatcher	.290	2-6	.567	6-4	.50	1-1	.56	1-1	10-11	.08463
21. Green	.508	3-2	.507	7-6	.49	1-1	.35	1-3	12-12	.09423
22. Ford	.374	5-8	.573	7-5	.48	2-2	.49	1-2	15-17	.11194
23. Hayes	.437	7-9	.478	5-5	.56	2-2	.40	1-2	15-18	.14124
24. Cowens	.560	9-7	.226	2-9	.55	2-2	.52	1-1	15-18	.14124
25. Beniquez	.490	3-3	.512	5-4	.39	1-2	.43	1-2	10-11	.16233
26. Vukovich	.501	5-5	.331	3-6	.34	1-2	.36	1-3	10-16	.42691

DESIGNATED HITTER

1. Andre THORNTON, Cleveland (21–10) Seemed to be on target for his second straight outstanding year, but dropped off late in the year. . . . hit .325 on artificial turf. . . . seventh in the American League in on-base percentage.

2. Hal McRAE, Kansas City (22–11) My comment on Hal McRae a year ago discussed a study which showed that he hit a pitcher much better the second time he was facing him, or the second time in a reasonably brief period of time. The same study for the 1983 season did not confirm this effect. There were 36 pairs of games in which McRae saw the same starting pitcher twice within a period of 17 days. He hit .299 in the first games of the pair (41/137), .291 in the second games (39/134). He did increase his power output somewhat, from one home run and a .416 slugging percentage in the first games, to four homes runs and a .440 slugging percentage in the second. The Royals as a team had 37 such pairs of games, the same 36 plus one set in which McRae did not play in the first game. They were 19-18 the first time they saw those pitchers, and 19-18 the second time. . . . McRae is one of eleven major league players who has hit .300 in each of the past two years . . . he has hit 87 doubles in the past two years, a total exceeded only by Robin Yount. Early in the 1984 season, he will become one of the top 50 players of all time in career doubles. The top 50 end with Luke Appling and Roberto Clemente at 440; Mac has 435.

3. Greg LUZINSKI, Chicago (20–11) His stats the last two years have matched those of the White Sox leftfielders:

1982	G	AB	R	H	HR	RBI	Avg
LF	160	580	91	166	19	98	.286
Bull	159	583	87	170	18	102	.292
1983	G	AB	R	H	HR	RBI	Avg
LF	145	520	75	132	35	100	.254
Bull	144	502	73	128	32	95	.255

The strange thing is, of course, that it's a different player: he had

about the same stats as Steve Kemp in 1982, and about the same as Kittle in 1983 . . . if they could only get Jim Rice from the Red Sox . . .

4. Don BAYLOR, New York (11–7) The key to his first .300 season was lefthanded pitching. The Yankees face a lot of mediocre lefthanded pitchers, and Baylor tore them up (.357 batting, .602 slugging), giving him a good season although he didn't do much against righthanders. I still doubt that he had any real value to the Yankees; as I said a year ago, he just took playing time away from other hitters of equal ability. Yankee designated hitters:

	AB	H	HR	RBI	Avg
1982	625	172	28	109	.275
1983	628	181	24	96	.288

No striking improvement that I can see.

Did you know that Oscar Gamble over the last five years has the third-highest slugging percentage of any player in baseball (.526), behind Schmidt and Brett but ahead of Jim Rice, Eddie Murray or Cecil Cooper? Over that period he is also seventh in the majors in on-base percentage, and has driven in more runs per at-bat than any of those same players—Rice, Murray, Cooper, or Dave Winfield or Reggie. He has also scored more runs per at-bat than any of those players except Eddie Murray, has a higher home run percentage than any of them except Reggie, walks more than any of them and strikes out less than any except Cooper. Over those five years he has grounded into only 20 double plays, a lower DP frequency than any of these players. . . . over the last two years, Oscar has hit .338 against lefthanded pitching (22/65), with a .569 slugging percentage.

5. Ted SIMMONS, Milwaukee (19–13) Unsigned at this writing; everybody seems to think he'll stay in Milwaukee. Not a great offensive player now; slow, has medium range power, doesn't walk a lot and has hit for average only once in the last

three years. He's driven in some runs, though.

6. Ken SINGLETON, Baltimore (19–13) Has grounded into 102 double plays over the last five years; his GIDP rate of 40 per 1000 at-bats is the highest in baseball over the five-year period. . . . hit .400 on artificial turf (see comment on Buddy Bell).

7. Richie ZISK, Seattle (13–9) Retired.

8. Jeff BURROUGHS, Oakland (12–8) He helped the A's. They probably would have been better off making him a fulltime DH, rather than platooning:

	AB	H	HR	RBI	Avg
Burroughs as DH:	395	107	10	56	.271
Other Oakland DHs:	218	48	1	17	.220

I doubt seriously that his platoon differential is that large, plus if he had not been platooning he would have had a better chance to get something going. And, as I've mentioned elsewhere, it was the lefthanders who were beating them. . . . also drove in more meaningful runs than any other A's player. Among the seven A's with 40 or more RBI, he was the only one with an RBI Importance over .400, and he was over .500 (.512) . . . I commented a year ago that he had a good record as a pinch-hitter. Last year he was 5 for 13 as a pinch-hitter (.385), making him 25 for 71 over the last four years (.352) and 32 for 103 lifetime (.311) in that role.

9. Cliff JOHNSON, Toronto (11–7) What would his career record be like if he had played full time? Who knows . . . I decided to play around with it, adding his record together into two-year groups (the "1976" line below represents his combined 1975–76 performance level) and then projecting that into (a) 670 plate appearances or (b) the actual number of at-bats that he had over the two seasons, whichever was less. This is what I get:

Year	G	AB	Run	Hit	2B	3B	HR	RBI	BB	Avg
1972	5	4	0	1	0	0	0	0	2	.250
1973	12	24	6	7	2	0	2	6	3	.292
1974	90	191	32	45	6	1	12	35	34	.236
1975	151	511	78	133	20	2	30	94	79	.260
1976	162	571	76	144	32	3	26	99	94	.252
1977	162	572	78	149	35	2	30	98	100	.260
1978	143	460	66	117	25	1	28	73	73	.254
1979	141	478	68	114	25	1	26	86	64	.238
1980	160	593	89	148	24	1	32	113	77	.249
1981	162	594	86	145	18	1	30	112	76	.244
1982	139	487	59	122	18	0	24	90	54	.251
1983	161	583	73	149	31	1	27	100	87	.256
12	1488	5068	711	1274	236	13	267	906	743	.251

Johnson does not have a particularly large platoon differential, plus he has played most of his career in parks that were very poor for a righthanded power hitter. So I'd say that was a fairly conservative look at what he might have done...

10. Reggie JACKSON, California (15–12) Reggie said an interesting thing about Eddie Murray in the World Series when Eddie was struggling, trying to get untracked. He said that he thought Eddie had the "character" and the "determination" and the "fortitude" to fight his way out of this thing and make his presence felt. You get it? What he's saying is, "I didn't hit all those homers in the World Series play because I happen to be a great athlete. I didn't win two World Series MVP awards because I am strong and have a quick bat and saw a few pitches I could hit and hit them. Oh, no. I did that because I have *character* and *fortitude* and *determination*. I succeeded because I was a better human being than those other people out there on the field."

You hear that stuff every day, although most athletes are smart enough to disguise it a little better. Many athletes truly believe that they are successful at what they do not because God made them strong and fast and agile, but because *they're better people than the rest of us.* And in order to believe that, they must believe that the games themselves are not merely contests of skill and luck, but are tests of *character* and *determination* and *will.* That's where all of the bullshit about clutch ability comes from. Clutch ability is that thing that wells up from inside of you when the game is on the line, that thing that separates the "winners" from the "losers," that thing which *only an*

athlete can possess, and therefore only an athlete can understand.

The problem with that is that when the public is sold enough cow manure in little plastic bottles marked "character" and "attitude," the public is going to stop buying any little plastic bottles marked "character" and "attitude." I had a long conversation with a friend of mine, a highly intelligent and successful attorney, who tried to convince me that such things as "character" and "attitude" and "wanting to play baseball" had nothing to do with winning a pennant, that they didn't even exist. He reminded me about the way that Clemente when he came up and Joe Morgan when he came up and Frank Robinson in his early years got labeled "attitude problems." Then, of course, as soon as Clemente learned to hit a curve ball, he was a great human being, and the "attitude" label went away. Did his "attitude" ever really have anything to do with it?

But *of course* "attitude" is real, and so is "character" and "determination" and "will." Wanting to win a pennant has *everything* to do with winning a pennant. Just as there are people in your school or people in your law firm or people in your Gay Rights activists group who have the ability to be outstanding students or lawyers or Gay Activists but who don't really want to do it, there are people in baseball who have the ability to be outstanding baseball players, but have bad attitudes.

But if athletes keep debasing those qualities by focusing them on ridiculously small moments in a person's life, if they keep using them to explain every dramatic success and every dismal failure, then they're eventually going to convince the public that they don't exist, at all. Every time a favorite player delivers a key

single to bring a win closer, and the announcer delivers a speech about the "courage" and the "determination" and the "guts" that the player has shown, then those words become a little cheaper, and the act that they describe becomes smaller and less significant. Reggie Jackson is an ordinary human being, glib but of average intelligence at best, of character unshining and fortitude unknown, who has hit ten home runs in World Series play, and who is not, on that basis, entitled to the stature of a demi-god.

11. Carl YASTRZEMSKI, Boston (13–11) From *The Sporting News*, October 2, 1976: "With his sights now trained on the 3000-hit mark, 37-year-old Carl Yastrzemski says he hopes to play at least 3 more seasons for the Red Sox. 'I've been with the Red Sox for 16 years and I'd like to remain with the club for another 16,' said Yastrzemski, who passed the 2,500-hit mark earlier this season. 'Realistically, I think I can play at least three more years.'"

12. Kirk GIBSON, Detroit (11–9) Has grounded into only 13 double plays in his career (11 per 1000 at-bats).... I still think he can play. There is some question about how badly he wants to.

13. Dave HOSTETLER, Texas (11–11) Platooned with Mickey Rivers. Craig Wright refuses to give up on him, but he's the only one I know who hasn't. Hoss did hit very well after the All-Star break (9 home runs, 26 RBI in 137 at-bats), and hit well enough against lefthanders to make himself useful. The Rangers figure to destroy lefthanders. Anyway this year (look up LHP stats on Ward, Wright, Bell, Parrish, Yost), it's going to be an upset if they ever see one. They'll beat the Yankees anyway.

The Rangers are putting up a new scoreboard in right field which will cut off the wind and, apparently, increase the number of runs scored in the park. Hostetler is one of the people who might benefit from the change; Parrish and Wright are others.

14. Randy BUSH, Minnesota (7–8) Faded badly in the second half.... will stay in the majors if he can add about 20 points to his average.

DESIGNATED HITTERS

	Offensive 1982		1983		Total	.350 Chance
1. Thornton	.668	11-6	.661	9-5	21-10	.00021
2. McRae	.714	12-5	.646	10-6	22-11	.00021
3. Luzinski	.661	11-5	.660	10-5	20-11	.00077
4. Baylor	.525	9-9	.689	10-5	20-13	.00236
5. Simmons	.554	8-7	.616	10-7	19-13	.00417
6. Singleton	.528	9-8	.641	10-5	19-13	.00417
7. Zisk	.635	9-5	.471	4-4	13- 9	.01796
8. Burroughs	.737	6-2	.509	6-6	12- 8	.01958
9. C. Johnson	.468	3-3	.655	8-4	11- 7	.02123
10. R. Jackson	.693	10-5	.367	4-8	15-12	.02292
11. Yastrzemski	.551	7-6	.539	6-5	13-11	.04225
12. Gibson	.533	4-4	.546	7-5	11- 9	.05317
13. Hostetler	.516	7-6	.449	4-5	11-11	.10698
14. R. Bush	.430	2-2	.503	6-5	7- 8	.24516

PITCHER RATINGS AND COMMENTS

The pitcher ratings method this year is very similar to what was used last year, at least in terms of what goes into the ranking and how that information is evaluated. The same elements, however, have been adapted to bring the pitcher's rankings more into line with the method by which the position players are ranked. The pitchers are ranked, as are the players, by taking a series of steps to express other data first as runs, then as wins and losses, and finally by the chance that a .350 ballclub would post the same number of wins or more in the same number of decisions.

There are two essential things to understand about the rankings:

1. The rankings are based on the last two seasons worth of performance, not just on the 1983 season. Players who had poor 1982 seasons, like Tom Seaver, Scott McGregor, Rick Honeycutt, John Denny and Mike Scott, are not going to rank as well as you might think they would if only the 1983 season were considered. However, unlike the position player rankings, the 1982 and 1983 seasons are not weighted evenly. The 1982 season is 40% of the ranking, the 1983 season 60%.

2. The rankings are based on won/lost records and runs allowed per nine innings. Each of those is 50% of the ranking. The won/lost record is adjusted for the offensive support that the player has received. This, being something that most people pay no attention to, might result in some surprises in the rankings. Fernando Valenzuela, for example, was not winning the number of games that he should have been winning in view of his offensive support last year, and for that reason he does not rank among the very best lefthanders in

the game at this moment. Dennis Eckersley's ERA was unsightly, but in view of the offensive support that he was receiving (in Fenway Park, no less), a 9–13 record isn't bad at all; combined with a good 1982 season (13–13, 3.73 ERA), it results in a surprisingly high ranking for him.

The pitcher rankings are presented this year in chart form. The chart gives the ranking, the "complete won/lost percentage" for the pitcher for the last two seasons, and the number of wins and losses attributed to the pitcher over the last two seasons. Two basic "comments" are offered about each pitcher as in past Abstracts, a brief description of the number of double plays turned in the games the pitcher has started (V Hi is "Very High," meaning lots of double plays turned behind him, and V Lo is something you can probably figure out) and a letter grade assessing his ability to hold base runners, which is based on the number of bases stolen by the opposition in games which the pitcher has started.

When I have a longer comment that I wanted to make about the pitcher, it is referenced in the chart by a number, and the comments are given after the chart.

The exact method by which the pitchers are ranked is explained below. I have to explain it, so that people have a fair chance to examine the method if they choose. But unless you're really interested in sabermetrics, I wouldn't read it.

HOW EXACTLY THE PITCHERS ARE RANKED

The pitchers are ranked according to fifteen pieces of initial information by a series of seventeen formulas. The fifteen pieces of information which go into the ranking are:

A The average number of runs per game in the league that the pitcher was in in 1982.

B The average number of runs per game in the league that the pitcher was in in 1983.

C The number of games that the pitcher started in 1982.

D The number of runs scored by the pitcher's team in the games that he started in 1982.

E The number of games that the pitcher started in 1983.

F The number of runs scored by the pitcher's team in the games that he started in 1983.

G The park adjustment factor the park or parks in which the pitcher has labored.

H The pitcher's 1982 Win Total.

I The pitcher's 1982 Loss Total.

J The pitcher's 1983 Win Total.

K The pitcher's 1983 Loss Total.

L The number of innings that the pitcher pitched in 1982.

M The number of runs that the pitcher allowed in 1982.

N The number of innings that the pitcher pitched in 1983.

O The number of runs that the pitcher allowed in 1983.

The first formula which is applied to this data is (2D + 3F) divided by (2C + 3E). This figures the pitcher's offensive support over the last two seasons—weighting, as always, the 1982 season at 40% and the 1983 season at 60%. The outcome of this formula will be known as "P" in the subsequent formulas.

The second formula adjusts the offensive support for the park in which the pitcher has been pitching. It is easier to win with four runs per game in the Astrodome than it is with four runs a game in Fulton County Stadium. The formula is P divided by G; four runs a game in the Astrodome would become 4.34833 runs a game, and four in Fulton County Stadium would become 3.80753. The outcome of this formula will be known as "Q" in the subsequent formulas.

The third formula states the ratio between the pitcher's wins and his losses. The formula is $(2H+3J)$ divided by $(2I+3K)$. This is an intermediary step toward adjusting the pitcher's won/lost record to a normal level of offensive support. The outcome of this formula will be known as "R" in the subsequent formulas.

The fourth formula finds the square root of R. The reason for doing this is to express the ratio between wins and losses as a ratio between runs scored and runs allowed. If a pitcher is supported by four runs a game and allows three a game, he will probably win about 64% of his decisions; this we know by the Pythagorean formula. Thus if a pitcher is supported by four runs a game and wins 64% of his decisions, then we might say that he is winning with the consistency expected of a pitcher who allowed three runs a game. Three runs a game is what we might call his effective level of runs allowed. If he is actually allowing four runs a game, that will affect the other half of his complete winning percentage, but it won't affect this half. The square root of R represents the ratio between the number of runs scored in support of the pitcher and the effective number of runs allowed. The square root of R will be referred to as figure S in the subsequent formulas.

The fifth formula creates the pitcher's "individual league," the normal amount of run support for a pitcher who has had the number of starts that this pitcher has had in the leagues that he has started in. The formula is $(2(A \text{ times } C)+3(B \text{ times } E))$ divided by $(2C+3E)$. The outcome of this formula will be known as figure T in the subsequent formulas.

The sixth formula adjusts the ratio between the pitcher's run support and runs allowed to a normal (league-average) offensive support

level. The formula is (S times T) divided by Q. This will be known as figure U in the subsequent formulas.

The seventh formula returns this to a winning percentage. The formula is U squared divided by (U squared + one). This completes the process of turning the pitcher's offensive support and won/lost record over the last two years into a single winning percentage. This will be known as figure V in the subsequent formulas. Figure V is one of the two major parts of the pitcher's complete winning percentage.

The eighth formula begins the process of converting the pitcher's runs allowed and innings pitched over the last two years into an equivalent thing—a single won/lost percentage. The first formula is $((2M+30) \text{ times } 9)$ divided by $(2L+3N)$. This just weights the 1982 data at 40% and the 1983 data at 60%, and figures the number of runs allowed per nine innings. This will be known as figure W in the next formula.

The ninth formula adjusts this for the park in which the pitcher works. The formula is W divided by Q, and the outcome is known as figure X in the next formula.

The tenth formula states the ratio between the league average of runs per game and the (park adjusted) number of runs that this pitcher has allowed. The formula is T divided by X, and the outcome will forever be known as Y.

The eleventh formula expresses this ratio as a winning percentage. The formula is Y squared divided by (Y squared + 1). This completes the process of expressing the runs allowed data as a won/lost percentage, and the result will be known as figure Z in the subsequent formulas.

The twelfth formula begins the process of turning the two winning percentages into a number of wins and losses. The formula is $(V+Z)$ divided by 2. This is just the average of the two major winning percentages, the one derived from won/lost data and the one derived from runs allowed data. This will be known as figure a in the subsequent formulas.

The thirteenth formula finds a number of "decisions" to assign the pitcher based on the actual number of decisions that he has had over the last two years. The formula is $(2(H+I)+3(J+K))/2.5$. This just

weights decisions in 1983 more heavily than those in 1982. A pitcher who had 20 decisions in 1982 and 20 in 1983 would be assigned 40 decisions. A pitcher who had 10 decisions in 1982 and 30 in 1983 would have 44 decisions. This will be known as figure b in the subsequent formulas.

The fourteenth formula assigns decisions by one for each nine innings pitched, but otherwise in the same way. The formula is $(2L+3N)$ divided by 22.5. This will be known as figure c in the subsequent formulas.

The fifteenth formula takes the average of the two methods of assigning decisions. The formula is $(b+c)$ divided by 2. This is figure d, the number of decisions assigned to the pitcher in the rankings.

The sixteenth formula finds the number of wins by multiplying the complete winning percentage, known as figure a, by the decisions, known as figure d. This will be known as "Wins."

The seventeenth formula subtracts Wins from decisions (figure d) to find Losses.

The highest winning percentage of any major league pitcher is, surprisingly, by Joe Price of Cincinnati; Price has pitched exceptionally well but not very much, so that he ranks fourth among lefthanders despite his .700 complete winning percentage. The highest winning percentage is by another lefthander, John Candelaria. Candelaria was sixth in the league in ERA and sixth in winning percentage in 1982, and he was fourteenth in ERA and second in winning percentage in 1983. No other National League pitcher was among the league leaders in winning percentage both in '82 and '83; not many were among the list of ERA leaders in both years.

If the rankings of right and left handed pitchers were combined, Dave Stieb of Toronto would be the #1 ranked starting pitcher in the major leagues. His percentage, .634, is a little below Candelaria's or Mario Soto's, but he extends that performance level over far more decisions—61 as compared to 42 for Candelaria, 26 for Joe Price. AL Cy Young Award winner LaMarr Hoyt is the only pitcher who gets identical winning percentage figures from his runs allowed totals and his won/lost marks: both place him at exactly .571. Both Stieb's

ERAs and his won/lost marks are far more impressive than Hoyt's.

But he's not exactly Sandy Koufax. Just for the heck of it, I rounded up all the necessary data for Sandy Koufax and Juan Marichal to rate them based on the 1965 and 1966 seasons. Using these formulas, I figured Koufax's record for the two seasons at 52–20, Marichal's at 48–19. Dave Stieb's 39–22 record would occur for a .350 team by chance about 28,500 times as often as Koufax's 52–20 record. Ranked according to chance frequency for a .350 team, Koufax's record bears about the same relationship to Dave Stieb's that Stieb's does to Mike Moore of Seattle, the 58th ranked righthanded starting pitcher in the major leagues.

RIGHTHANDED STARTING PITCHERS

Rank		Pct.	W-L	DP	Hold	Comments
1.	Dave Stieb	.634	39-22		B+	#8
2.	Steve Rogers	.635	37-22	Low	B+	#9
3.	Mario Soto	.620	36-22	V Lo	B	#3
4.	Richard Dotson	.578	31-22	V Hi	D-	#4
5.	Jack Morris	.570	36-28		B-	
6.	Bob Welch	.587	30-21	Low	A	#27
7.	LaMarr Hoyt	.571	35-27		A-	#15
8.	John Denny	.585	27-19	High	A-	#7
9.	Charlie Hough	.564	31-24	V Lo	C	#5; #25
10.	Rick Sutcliffe	.560	29-22	Low	D+	#1; #6
11.	Nolan Ryan	.565	28-21		C-	#11
12.	Dan Petry	.553	31-25	V Hi	B	#10
13.	Mike Boddicker	.651	18-10	V Lo	D	
14.	Jim Clancy	.555	30-24	Low	A-	
15.	Joe Niekro	.544	32-27	Low	D-	#19
16.	Charlie Lea	.566	27-21	Low	C+	
17.	Pascual Perez	.591	21-14	High	C+	
18.	Jim Beattie	.557	25-19		D	#14
19.	Moose Haas	.586	22-16		D	#1
20.	Phil Niekro	.552	25-20		D+	#1; #5; #18
21.	Ken Schrom	.614	17-11	Low	D+	
22.	Storm Davis	.561	20-15	Low	A-	
23.	Craig McMurtry	.593	17-12	V Hi	B-	
24.	Bill Gullickson	.510	28-26	V Lo	B	#16
25.	Rick Rhoden	.527	27-25		B	
26.	Eric Show	.534	23-20	V Lo	B	#1
27.	Bobby Castillo	.522	22-20		C+	
28.	Luis Leal	.512	26-25	Low	B-	
29.	Lee Tunnell	.583	14-10	V Hi	A-	#28
30.	Bob Stoddard	.534	18-15	V Hi	D	#12
31.	D. Eckersley	.506	23-22	V Lo	D	#1
32.	Joaquin Andujar	.495	25-25		B-	#2; #24
33.	Alejandro Pena	.556	15-12	Low	C+	
34.	Bob Forsch	.501	23-23		B-	#17; Good hitter
35.	John Stuper	.524	20-19	High	B+	
36.	Don Sutton	.486	24-25	V Lo	D	
37.	Milt Wilcox	.507	21-21		A-	
38.	Bill Laskey	.495	21-21		D	
39.	Glenn Abbott	.617	9- 6	Low	C	
40.	Gaylord Perry	.487	21-22		B	#1; Retired
41.	Ken Forsch	.474	23-25		C+	#2
42.	Danny Darwin	.512	18-18	V Lo	D+	
43.	Al Williams	.494	20-21	High	F	
44.	Fergie Jenkins	.482	20-21	High	C	
45.	Randy Smithson	.494	17-17	Low	D	
46.	Mike Krukow	.470	21-23	V Lo	D	#30
47.	Bruce Berenyi	.472	22-25	High	D+	#2; #3; Good hitter
48.	Lary Sorensen	.460	22-25	High	B	
49.	Bert Blyleven	.503	12-11		B	
50.	Fred Breining	.484	19-21	V Lo	C	#22
51.	Dick Ruthven	.461	21-24		D+	
52.	Walt Terrell	.547	11-10		D	
53.	Len Barker	.464	22-26	Low	B	
54.	Ed Whitson	.499	12-12	Low	B-	#21
55.	Steve McCatty	.479	14-15	V Lo	D+	
56.	Neil Allen	.468	16-18	V Hi	B	#2
57.	Chuck Rainey	.471	18-21	V Hi	A-	#1
58.	Mike Moore	.458	15-17	V Lo	D-	#1
59.	Jim Gott	.447	17-21	Low	C-	
60.	Tom Seaver	.440	18-23		D-	#13
61.	Charles Hudson	.467	10-11	V Lo	D-	#26
62.	Frank Pastore	.423	18-24	High	B+	
63.	Ed Lynch	.441	15-20	V Hi	A	#29
64.	Chris Codiroli	.442	13-17		B+	Led AL, Errors
65.	D. Martinez	.413	19-27		D-	
66.	Doyle Alexander	.437	11-14		C+	
67.	Burt Hooton	.431	13-18	V Lo	C+	
68.	Mike Scott	.400	14-20	High	C-	#3; #20
69.	Charlie Puleo	.388	14-21		F	#23
70.	Mike Torrez	.399	18-28		D+	
71.	Chuck Porter	.404	8-11	Low	D	
72.	Marty Bystrom	.380	9-16	Low	D-	

RIGHTHANDED STARTERS

#1 His won/lost record is better than you would expect it to be in view of the number of runs scored in support of him and the number of runs he has allowed (this comment is indexed for any pitcher whose winning % is .060 better than expected with at least 25 decisions over the last two years).

#2 His won/lost record is not as good as you would expect it to be in view of the number of runs scored in sup-port of him and the number of runs he has allowed (this comment is in-dexed in reference to any pitcher whose winning % is .060 worse than expected with at least 25 decisions over the last two seasons).

#3 Would rate higher if the ratings were subjective.

#4 Richard must have been doing something different last year because the number of ground balls that he was getting went way, way up. You can see that in several ways. His double-play support increased from just average to nearly the highest in the league. The number of assists that he was getting increased by about the same ratio—from 1.10 per 9 in-nings pitched to 1.80; he led the league in assists by a pitcher. His home runs allowed dropped from .87 per 9 innings to .76, and he was also the one man most obviously affected by the change at second base . . . received the best offensive support of any major league pitcher, 206 runs in 35 starts.

#5 Some people particularly dislike facing knuckleball pitchers because they feel that not only do they beat you, they mess you up, throw off your timing so that you can't hit the next day. The Cardinals' George Hendrick doesn't play against Phil Niekro because Niekro just fouls him up anyway, and a couple of American League teams felt last year that Charlie Hough had put them into a slump.

Well, what about it? I decided to take a look at what happened to teams in the games *following* a game against a knuckleball pitcher—Phil Niekro or Charlie Hough, in particular. The study suggests that there might possibly be a small or localized effect (by "localized" I mean not general; it might affect one hitter here or there, like Hendrick).

Hough and Niekro started 33 times each in 1983. In the 33 games following an appearance against Charlie Hough, American League teams were 18–14 (one tie); in the 33 games against Niekro, Phil, NL teams lost the first nine times but rallied to finish 13–20. That's 31–34 total; that certainly proves nothing but you wouldn't expect them to be 20–45. The effect, if it exists, can't be all that large. Following Hough, teams hit .261 (290/1113) and scored 4.00 runs per game; following Niekro they hit .237 (259/1093) and scored 3.64 runs per game.

Not all of those appearances followed on the very next day, but if you throw out the games following two or three days later, it doesn't change anything. Following the knuckleballer on the same day or the next day, teams were 25–28–1, and hit .250 (458/1831).

These facts are subject to any number of possible outside influences. Most of the time the team following Niekro is facing another Atlanta pitcher, hence those games are not representative of the entire league as to the number of games facing each pitcher or played in each park, or against each defense.

One way that you can get a sort of control on that without breaking

your jaw on a calculator is to focus on the specific pitchers who were following Niekro or Hough a reasonable number of times, and compare their performance in those situations with their overall level. Pascual Perez followed Niekro nine times and was sensational in those games, going 6–0 with a 1.70 ERA. Most of those games, however, were early in the season when he was pitching very well, so there you are again, another outside influence. Craig McMurtry pitched eight times following Philip, and should be happy that he won't have that opportunity again: He won just once, was 1–2 with a 4.10 ERA. Randy Smithson followed Charlie Hough twelve times; he was 3–4 with a 4.11 ERA, about his normal performance. There is nothing dramatic there, but whereas these three pitchers in these number of starts could have expected to allow about 75 earned runs in 190 innings (3.54 ERA), they actually allowed 72 in 198 (3.27), and whereas they could have expected a won/lost percentage of about .544, they actually finished 10–6 (.625).

Another angle would be to focus only on the games in which 1) the knuckleball pitcher pitched well, and 2) the next game was immediate. Now the "cross-correlation" or "outside influence" concerns become really severe, because how do we know that we're not looking at a bunch of teams that were already not hitting well? We don't, but anyway we do get data. Teams trying to come back after Charlie Hough had pitched a good game against them were 8–10 and hit .220 (128/583); teams following a good outing by Phil Niekro were 7–8 and hit .235.

Issue filed under "further study."

#6 Sutcliffe gave up 44 runs in 49 and a third innings of day baseball in '83. As a power pitcher without real good control, he does fit the prototype of the pitcher who is most effective at night (see article on Power Pitchers and Night Baseball, Section IV). . . . his average start last year lasted two hours, 56 minutes, making him the league's slowest-working pitcher.

#7 Denny led major league pitchers in errors, with eight.

#8 Dave Steib led majors in hit batsmen with 14; Blyleven was second with ten.

#9 The parallels between his career record and Red Ruffing's are strong. Many of you probably know that Ruffing led the league in losses twice before joining the Yankees, but what you may not realize is that it took him six long years after joining the Yankees to get to the 20-win level. He kept winning 15–19 every year, made 20 in 1936 at the age of 32, and didn't get his career won/lost mark over .500 (after a 39–93 start) until his third 20-victory season in 1938.

#10 Led majors in home runs allowed with 37. Not coincidentally, he was just 6–6 in Tiger Stadium, 13–5 on the road.

#11 5.4 years away from 300 wins at his present rate of progress. I'd rate his chances of getting there as good if he wants to do it badly enough. . . . record in the Astrodome the last two years is just 11–12; on the road it's 19–9.

#12 You learn something every day, huh? . . . received the poorest offensive support of any AL pitcher, 3.22 runs per game. The bottom three were Stoddard, Young, and Beattie . . .

#13 Was 2.6 years away from 300 wins two years ago, 3.2 years away a year ago, 3.0 years away now.

#14 I have a copy of a 1963 book by Tex Maule about a fictional character named Jim Beatty who plays for the Yankees.

#15 Has won 28 games the last two years (28–8) in Chicago; away from Comiskey he's 15–17.

#16 18–8 the last two years in Montreal, 11–18 on the road.

#17 17–7 the last two years in Busch Stadium; 8–14 on the road. Was 1–5 and had a 6.39 ERA on grass fields in '83.

#18 Getting released by Atlanta can't hurt him too much. He's 7–8 and has a 4.78 ERA in Atlanta the last two years, whereas he's 21–6 and has a 3.03 ERA on the road.

#19 Had a 5.89 ERA, 3–6 record in 10 starts on grass fields in '83. With Gaylord's retiring, I wouldn't sell short the Niekro brothers' chances of beating his and Jim's career wins total. With 26 last year, the Niekros now have 445 (268 for Phil, 177 for Joe); the Perrys had 529. Eighty-four wins are a lot of ballgames, but either one of the Niekros could get that many more by himself.

#20 His improvement last year was not just the effect of being in the Astrodome. His record in road games improved from 3–10 to 5–1; ERA dropped from 6.88 to 3.94.

#21 6.13 ERA on artificial turf.

#22 2–5 record, 5.73 ERA on artificial turf.

#23 Opponents stole 35 bases in his 24 starts, now have stolen 69 in 49 major league starts . . . . I commented a year ago that he had pitched well when pitching with 3 days rest. Last year he started only once with three days rest. He won the game, giving up 4 hits, 2 runs in six and two-thirds innings.

#24 Started 14 times on 3 days rest, was 3–7 in those games but had respectable 3.89 ERA. In his other games he was 3–9 with a 4.34 mark. . . . had 15 good outings in which he didn't win (April 30, May 23, 27, 31, June 9, 14, 22, July 1, 10, 15, 21, 26, August 27, September 4, 8. A good outing is defined as any start in which a pitcher pitches five or more innings allowing less than four runs per nine innings pitched, or allows three or less runs through the first seven innings). In ten of those starts he pitched seventy-two and a third innings with a 2.24 ERA, but was 0–5; in five other outings he pitched well through seven innings but was hit hard in the eighth or ninth.

#25 Average game last year lasted only 2 hours, 24 minutes, making him the league's fastest-working pitcher.

#26 Received the best offensive support in the National League last year, 5.0 runs per game.

#27 Went 15–12 last year despite dismal offensive support (3.19 runs per game). Won two games 1–0, won six games with three runs or less to work with. . . . toughest pitcher to run on in the National League. It is very rare for a righthanded pitcher to lead the league in fewest OSB per start.

#28 Best double-play support of any National League pitcher.

#29 Second in the NL in both double-play support and fewest OSB per start. . . . he's an extreme of a type, a pitcher who gives up a lot of hits but no walks, no stolen bases, gets ground balls. Effective left-handed pitchers of this type are common—Tommy John, Honeycutt, Zahn, Caldwell, Randy Jones, etc. Effective righthanders in this mold are very rare.

#30 Received the least double-play support of any NL pitcher, just 11 in 31 starts. . . . one of the best hitting pitchers in baseball, arguably the best with Don Robinson's health in question. He hit .254 last year; his lifetime average of .234 doesn't compare to Terry Forster or Renie Martin (.293, 22/75), but he does have close to 400 at-bats, and he'll hit a few doubles a year.

LEFTHANDED STARTERS

		Pct.	W-L	DP	Hold	Comments
1.	John Candelaria	.652	27-15		A	#12
2.	Ron Guidry	.595	32-21	Low	A –	#15
3.	Steve Carlton	.576	37-27	Low	A	
4.	Joe Price	.700	18- 8	V Lo	B	#11
5.	Scott McGregor	.557	30-23		A	#6
6.	Floyd Bannister	.571	29-22	V Lo	C	
7.	John Tudor	.561	28-21	High	B –	#7
8.	L. McWilliams	.580	25-18		A	#1
9.	Jerry Reuss	.548	29-23	High	A	#10
10.	F. Valenzuela	.527	31-27	Low	C+	
11.	Mike Flanagan	.577	22-17	High	A+	#1
12.	A. Hammaker	.575	22-17		B	
13.	Britt Burns	.562	22-17		B	#1
14.	Geoff Zahn	.536	25-21	V Hi	A+	#9
15.	Dave Dravecky	.563	20-15	High	C	
16.	Dave Righetti	.538	24-20		C–	#5
17.	Matt Young	.603	17-12		C	#13
18.	Shane Rawley	.517	25-23		A	#4
19.	Dave LaPoint	.542	20-17		B	#1; #13
20.	Paul Splittorff	.532	20-18	High	B	#14
21.	Tommy John	.492	25-25	V Hi	A+	#8; #16
22.	Jerry Koosman	.514	19-18	Low	B+	#1
23.	Bob Ojeda	.518	16-14	High	C	
24.	Larry Gura	.480	26-28		B+	
25.	Rick Honeycutt	.493	23-24	V Hi	A	#16
26.	Tim Lollar	.492	21-22	V Lo	B	Good Hitter
27.	Bud Black	.517	15-14	High	A	
28.	Frank Tanana	.487	19-20		B	
29.	Mike Caldwell	.468	24-28	High	A+	
30.	Bruce Hurst	.474	18-20	V Hi	C	
31.	Bob McClure	.450	16-20		B	
32.	Steve Trout	.416	16-22	High	B	
33.	Mark Davis	.485	6- 7		A	#3; #13
34.	Frank Viola	.357	14-24		A	
35.	Bob Knepper	.377	15-26	High	D	

LEFTHANDED STARTERS

Comments 1, 2, 3 are the same here as for the righthanded starters.

#4 Record in Yankee Stadium just 10–13 over last two seasons; is 15–1 on the road. Pitched complete game victories in all four starts on artificial turf allowing just four runs.

#5 He's 16–7 over last two years in Yankee Stadium, just 9–11 on the road.

#6 Won all seven of his starts and had 1.21 ERA on artificial turf.

#7 ERA has got to improve on escaping Fenway (4.71 ERA there the last two years, against 2.93 on the road).... pitched well on artificial turf last year, but five starts don't mean much.

#8 Led major league starters in double-play support for the umpteenth time last year. Also the hardest pitcher in baseball to run against.

#9 Virtually a Tommy John clone. I didn't study it, but I'd bet that when a team sees John and Zahn back to back, the second one gets killed. Having them in the same rotation makes them both less effective than they should be.

#10 Hit .282, the highest average of any regular starter.

#11 This rating is as much of a surprise to me as it is to you, but on careful inspection you'd have to say that Price was pitching as well as any starter in baseball before his injury last year. He was 10–5 on July 24 in spite of the fact that they weren't scoring any runs; he was, in fact, the worst-supported pitcher in the major leagues, at 2.90 runs per outing.... only pitcher on this chart to have had an ERA below 3.00 in each of the last two seasons... had 16 good outings in his first 18 starts last year.

#12 Highest-rated head case in the majors.

#13 There are three young lefthanders in the majors that I really like

—Matt Young, Dave LaPoint and Mark Davis. Young throws a fastball that looks like it tails away from a righthanded batter, and he keeps it down and away—down and in to a lefthander—and there's not much you can do with a pitch like that. I also like his delivery; he just looks like a pitcher who could pitch that way for about ten, fifteen years. Davis is a strikeout pitcher who is still in the "spotty" phase of his career, but he had an ERA of 0.86 in his last four starts. He gets knocked out early a lot, because he doesn't really know what to do if he shows up without the good fastball. In my mind he rivals Righetti as the best young power pitcher in baseball, and in the long run I'd a lot rather have him than Atlee Hammaker.

LaPoint I like in a more analytical way—lots of positives, no negatives. He never had a losing season in the minor leagues, and he's now 23–12 in the majors. He strikes out a few people, his control is coming, he's tough to run on and gets good double-play support. All of his pitches are above average.

#14 Can you believe this? Paul Splittorff led the Royals' staff in strikeouts last year with 61. Sixty-one! Milwaukee had four pitchers with more than 61 Ks; every other team in the league had at least five. If Splittorff had had *twice* as many strikeouts as he did (122), the only other staffs in the league he could have led would have been California and Oakland. The Royals' staff has been last in the league in strikeouts for three straight years.

#15 With his 21–9 record in 1983, Ron Guidry has entered into some real fast company. This marked his

seventh consecutive season with a winning percentage over .600. Only ten other pitchers in baseball history have had as many or more. Seven of them are in the Hall of Fame.

One more season over .600 will net Guidry the American League record. Some interesting things about this list: Keefe's streak was accomplished on three different New York teams in three different leagues, 1883–4 in the American Association, 1885–9 in the National League and 1890 in the Players League. Actually, 48% of all the seasons on the list were accomplished on one New York team or another. Reulbach and Brown were Cub teammates for six seasons of their streaks. Their combined record for that period (1906–1911) was 248–96, a .721 winning percentage. After his seventh consecutive 10+ victory season over .600, Whitey Ford's career record stood at 122–51. Guidry is now at the same juncture and his career record is an almost identical 121–50.

#16 With Honeycutt more or less available last summer but looking for big bucks to sign a contract, I got interested in the question of what his career prospects are like from now on. In Los Angeles late last year he was being referred to as the new Dave Goltz, and there may be some reason for that pessimism: He certainly has not proven that he can sustain excellence over a period of years. On the other hand, he was 16–11 last year, and if he can stay around that level... well, you'd like to have him. What are his chances? What is Rick Honeycutt's future?

I started by looking around for parallels—for similar types of pitchers who had big (unexpected) years at about the same point in their careers. By far the best parallel is

Consecutive Seasons Over .600—10 or More Victories

Pitcher	No.	Years	W	L	Pct.
Christy Mathewson	12	1903-1914	302	133	.694
Sam Leever	8	1901-1908	144	58	.713
Three Finger Brown	8	1904-1911	181	77	.702
Kid Nichols	8	1891-1898	249	111	.692
Tim Keefe	8	1883-1890	267	132	.669
Lefty Grove	7	1927-1933	172	53	.764
Ed Reulbach	7	1906-1912	121	47	.720
RON GUIDRY	7	1977-1983	122	50	.709
Whitey Ford	7	1953-1959	112	49	.696
Ed Plank	7	1909-1916	137	62	.688
Ed Lopat	7	1948-1954	109	51	.681

Mike Caldwell in 1978. Like Honeycutt, Caldwell is a lefthanded control-type pitcher. In 1978 he was 29 years old; Honeycutt in 1983 was 29. Over his two previous years Caldwell had compiled a record of 6 wins, 15 losses and a 4.66 ERA. which puts him in the general class of the performance of Honeycutt in 1982 (5 wins, 17 losses, 5.27 ERA). Caldwell's career record before that season was 40 wins, 58 losses; Honeycutt's record going into 1983 was 42 and 64. They were both in the 800s in career innings pitched, both in the low fours in ERA.

Caldwell had the big year then, 22–9, and while he has never repeated it he has remained a quality pitcher, with more wins than losses in every season since that one. It probably is safe to assume that if Honeycutt pitches as well over the next five years as Caldwell has over the last five, the Dodgers won't be unhappy.

I could, of course, name a couple of less encouraging parallels. Ross Grimsley, who is in the same general class as to type of pitcher, had a big year the same year with Montreal (20–11), signed a nice contract and took a dive. Grimsley is not nearly as good a parallel, in that his career before that point is much better than Honeycutt's (in the prior season he had gone 14–10) and, most significantly, he had thrown a lot of innings. He threw 296 innings as a 24-year-old in 1974, and had totaled 1449 through the age of 27 (his big year was at 28).

Caldwell is a great parallel, but of course, what happened to Caldwell is far from being the assigned fate of Rick Honeycutt. I just thought it might be an interesting guide. This led me to the realization that Honeycutt is a member of the Tommy John family of pitchers. The Tommy John family of pitchers have 5 things in common:

(1) They are all lefthanded.
(2) They are control-type pitchers.
(3) They cut off the running game very well.
(4) They receive excellent double-play support.
(5) They allow moderate to low totals of home runs, lower-than-normal totals for a control pitcher.

Their being lefthanded is essential because it maximizes the ability to cut off the running game and the double-play support; there are virtually no righthanders who have the same kind of ratios between opposition stolen bases and double plays that these pitchers have.

This combination of abilities or tendencies enables this family of pitchers to be effective and to win at unusually high levels of hits per game, which then is another defining characteristic of the group. Honeycutt allowed nearly one hit per inning while in the American League last year, and still led the league in ERA.

There really are not that many pitchers who meet all of these criteria; it is a relatively small family. John is the prototype in that he gets the best double-play support of anyone, cuts off the running game the most effectively, allows the fewest home runs and consequently can win while allowing the most hits. Others that I could cite would include Caldwell, Geoff Zahn, Steve Trout, Bill Lee. Grimsley is not a member of the family, as his double-play support was not generally exceptional; a couple of new pitchers on the scene who might be in there are Bud Black and Steve Fontenot. A closely related and much larger family would be the Warren Spahn family, which includes people like Larry Gura, Scott McGregor, John Candelaria, and a lot of less-successful pitchers like Matlack and Tanana. The Spahn group is different in that they are basically spot pitchers or weakness pitchers; they strike out more people, give up more home runs, and don't get the double-play support that the John group does, and for that reason these pitchers, though they have good control and do cut off the running game, cannot win when they allow ten or ten and a half hits per nine innings.

Anyway, the fact that there was another pitcher who went through the same sort of dramatic upsurge who is from this rather small "family" of pitchers becomes, I think, a little more interesting. But there are some other things about the group, and also about the larger group, which strike you. For one thing, a lot of them seem to go through their best years in their thirties or even mid-thirties. John had a record of 95 wins and 96 losses in his twenties, but was terrific (142–75) in his thirties. Zahn was just 6–14 in his twenties, and had his best season at the age of 35. Caldwell we covered before; he was around for a long time before he found himself. Bill Lee is an exception to the rule; he pitched a lot of innings early, had his best years early.

Of the larger group, it would also seem that there were quite a few who had their best years in their thirties. Spahn, of course, and also Gura, Jerry Reuss; an average pitcher, I should remind you, posts only 29% of his career victories after his thirtieth birthday.

But there is one other thing about this group of pitchers which I think it is most important to notice. In 1981 the Texas Rangers were a good team, winning 57 games and losing only 48, and Honeycutt won 11 games and lost 6. In 1982 the Rangers collapsed, finishing with only 64 wins, and Rick Honeycutt led the way, collapsing all the way to 5–17. In 1983 the team came back strongly, and Honeycutt came back the strongest of any pitcher on the staff.

That performance—going from a bad record with a bad team to a good record with a good team—that is very, very typical for a pitcher in the Tommy John family; it is something that you see over and over again in their records, that these guys will pitch .300 or .350 or .400 ball with a .400 team, but will pitch .700 ball with a .580 or .600 team. They are the *most* team-dependent group of pitchers that there are.

The other end of the spectrum might be, perhaps, the Nolan Ryan family of pitchers. Members of the Nolan Ryan family might pitch .550 ball with a bad team and .570 ball with a good team. An ordinary pitcher, if he has a certain quality about him, might tend to stay about 25 points ahead of his team no matter how good or bad the team is. Knuckleball pitchers, like Charlie Hough and Phil Niekro, often seem to be able to go 16–13 with any team no matter how bad it is.

But look at the pitchers in the John family:

Mike Caldwell was with the Brewers when the team jumped from .414 to .574 in 1978; Caldwell jumped from .385 to .710. When the team further improved to .590 in 1979, he went up to .727; when they had an off year in 1980, he had an off year.

Tommy John was 2–9 with a

sixth-place club in 1964; when traded to a good club in '65, he went 14–7. After three straight losing years with the losing White Sox in 1969 to 1971, he was traded to a good club, the Dodgers, and had an awesome 40–15 (.727) record for two and a half years before his injury. John's career record when pitching for losing clubs is just 57–71—but when pitching for good clubs, it's 191–113.

Geoff Zahn was 10–11 with a high ERA for the Angels in 1981, when the Angels were just 51–59, but jumped to 18–8 (.692) in 1982 when the team won the division. When the team went back down last year, he went back to 9–11.

Bill Lee, Steve Trout—they have all had winning years on good teams, but it's been a very rare thing indeed for a member of the family to post a good record with a poor team.

And it makes perfect sense. They're not striking people out; they're just keeping the ball in play. They *need* those double plays. They need to have a catcher who can help keep the runner on first.

So that, to me, is the real key to the issue of whether or not you would make much of an effort to acquire a Rick Honeycutt, or a Steve Trout or any member of the family: Are you going to be able to help him?

What I am thinking is that this might make us look again at Honeycutt's seasons with the Mariners, and possibly to conclude that the way he pitched last year and the way he pitched in 1981 is his real level of ability with a good club, that this is something that he has always been able to do, if he had a good enough team behind him. You should keep in mind that I am generally very

skeptical about control-type pitchers, about their ability to sustain excellence over a period of years.

But one thing that is absolutely clear about this group of pitchers is that they account for a disproportionate share of the .650-to-.740 range seasons—Caldwell's .710 and .727; John's .688, .696, .700, .710, and .813; Zahn's .692 season in 1982; Lee's .654 season in Boston. In a modern pennant race, where divisions are often won by teams that are around twenty games over .500, I just don't think you can overestimate what it means to have a pitcher who is ten over.

Honeycutt might be able to give the Dodgers that kind of season. He has never had a bad year with a good team. He hasn't thrown enough innings to worry about. Anything can happen, but as far as I can see the positives far outweigh the negatives.

RELIEF ACES

I have been promising for the last three or four years to develop some way of rating relief pitchers, and I'd better get to it. The method I have chosen is a broad-based evaluation along a series of scales, largely devoid of theoretical underpinnings. The results, as in other cases, will eventually be stated as a winning percentage, then as a number of wins and losses. The relief aces will be rated according to the chance that a .350 ballclub would post this record. The relief aces, like other pitchers, are rated over the last two seasons, with the 1982 season counting 40% and the 1983 season at 60%.

The relief pitchers are evaluated by eight criteria. Seven of these are taken from their individual records: saves, ERA, hits per nine innings, strikeout-to-walk ratio, walks per nine innings, won/lost percentage, and the percentage of the games in which they appeared that they finished. (GF, or games finished, is an official statistic.) The eighth category is the late-inning record of the team for which the man pitches.

These categories are assigned different weights. The heaviest weight

is given to "saves" and "ERA." There are two 40-point categories; each of them accounts for 20% of the final winning percentage. There are two thirty-point categories—hits allowed per nine innings, and the record of the team in late-inning reversals. (I feel that hits allowed per nine innings is a key measure of relief pitchers, who often enter the game with a runner in scoring position, a runner who will score if a hit is allowed. And losing a lot of games in the late innings, obviously, is not a sign of a team with a good bullpen).

There is one 20-point (10%) criteria, strikeout-to-walk ratio, and there are two 15-point categories, walks per nine innings and winning percentage. The percentage of his games that the pitcher has finished is the smallest (10-point, 5%) consideration.

If you're adding that up, it totals up to 200 possible points. The best relief ace in the majors, Dan Quisenberry, totaled 150 points in 1983; Dave Beard of Oakland totaled 64 points. Quisenberry was also the #1 relief pitcher of the 1982 season, with a total of 132. The 150 points out of a

possible 200 means a winning percentage of .750; 64 out of 200 means a percentage of .320.

The technical explanation of the ratings follows if you want to read it. Remember that the system is set up to evaluate relief *aces*, not relief *pitchers*. A .500 percentage means not that this man is just an average pitcher, but rather that he is about the calibre of relief ace that would be expected of a .500 ballclub. A .350 relief ace is the relief ace that would be typical of a last-place ballclub.

The rating system is primitive, experimental, and should be seen as such. I have seen two other rating schemes for relief pitchers, the free-agent rankings which are done each year at each position, and the system that the Elias Bureau foisted off on *Sports Illustrated* in their season-opening issue in 1982. Compared to those systems, of course, this method is complex, sophisticated, and advanced. When the only way that you know of to evaluate players is by average rank, and you're too lazy even to weight the categories being averaged so as to allow the most important information to have a proportionate impact on the rankings, it's a good sign that you're probably in the wrong line of work. All the same, this system is *not* advanced or sophisticated; it only seems so by comparison to the feeble attempts of the Elias Bureau. I am not displeased with the rankings; no pitcher emerges more than a couple of spots away from where I think that he should be.

TECHNICAL EXPLANATION

There are three terms which we will need to use to explain this ranking system—the base, the mid-point, and the interval. The mid-point is the middle of the range; on the forty-point scale, 20, on the twenty-point scale, 10, etc. On the 15-point scale, 7 is treated as the mid-point.

The "base" is the level of performance at which the player receives that number of points. The "interval" is the distance from the base at which the number of points given changes.

Let's begin with the 40-point scales, saves and ERA. Saves are stated as a percentage of appearances; Goose Gossage's 22 saves in 57 appearances are listed at .39. The base for saves is .31; a reliever who saved games in 31% of his appearances would receive 20 points in this category. The interval is .02; so the Goose is four intervals above the base. He receives 20 + 4, or 24 points in this category. The .31 figure is the cut-off for 20 points; if you are at .30, that's 19 points, and .28 is 18 points. You can't exceed the boundaries of the range; you can't go over 40 or below 0. That's rarely a consideration; there are few maximum or minimum performances in the study. Quisenberry shattered the save record in 1983, but didn't max out on the save chart.

The "base" for saves is the same in both leagues; in most categories it is different in the American and National Leagues. The ERA base is 3.15 in the American League and 2.85 in the National. Jesse Orosco (1.47 ERA) and Steve Howe (1.44 ERA)

received the most points on this 40-point scale, 29 each.

The base for hits per game is 8.4 in the AL and 7.8 in the NL. The interval is 0.3. Peter Ladd of Milwaukee, who allowed only 30 hits in 49.1 innings in 1983, received 23 of the possible 30 points in this category.

For the other 30-point category, the performance of the team in the late innings, we refer to the division sheet, where the chart entitled "Late-Inning Ball Clubs" appears. If the team for which the pitcher works breaks even in the late innings (± 0), the pitcher receives 15 points in this category. Zero is the base. The interval is 1.4 games; since the New York Mets and Baltimore Orioles gained ten games after the seventh inning, Jesse Orosco and Tippy Martinez pick up 22 of the possible 30 points in this category, while Luis Sanchez of California receives only 5.

The 20-point criteria is strikeout-to-walk ratio. Intentional walks are not included when this is figured. The American League base is 2.4, meaning 2.4–1, meaning that a pitcher who strikes out 2.4 times as many as he walks would receive 10 points. The National League base is 2.7, and the interval is 0.2 going down and 0.3 going up (in other words, a National League pitcher has to strike out 2.5 times as many as he walks to receive nine points, 2.7 for ten points, or 3.0 for eleven points).

The base in walks per nine innings is 3.6 in the AL and 3.8 in the NL; you get 7 points at the base and the interval is 0.3.

The base in won/lost percentage is .450; the interval is .075.

In the final category, percentage of games finished, the base is .80 in the American League and .70 in the National. The interval is .04.

Add the pitcher's 8 totals together, and put the figure aside. We'll call it the "W" figure. Once we get decisions figured, we'll use it to figure the pitcher's wins and losses.

Decisions are figured in two different ways, and the average of the

two is used. A relief ace is on the mound at moments when a run allowed will do more than usual to change the outcome of a game. Pete Palmer estimates that runs allowed or prevented by relief aces have about twice the impact on the won/lost column as runs allowed by a starter. Using his estimate, we can figure that a game is decided about once each 4.5 innings that a relief pitcher pitches. This figure, however, is not uniform; a relief pitcher who comes into the game early probably does not have the same per-inning impact as a reliever who pitches only the last inning or two. To adjust for this, we divide the pitcher's innings pitched by (3 plus innings pitched per outing). A pitcher who pitched 40 games, 40 innings would have responsibility for one decision each 4.0 innings, or 10 decisions. A pitcher who pitched 40 games, 80 decisions would be assigned one decision for each 5.0 innings, or 16 decisions. A pitcher who pitched 40 games, 120 innings would have responsibility for one decision for each six innings pitched, or 20 decisions.

The second estimate of decisions is simpler; it counts wins, losses and one-half of saves. Bill Dawley, with six wins, six losses and 14 saves, has responsibility for 19 decisions.

OK, now we have two estimates of "decisions," which we add together into one. Multiply 1982 decisions by the 1982 W figure and divide by 200; you've got 1982 wins. Subtract wins from decisions and you've got losses. Multiply 1982 wins and losses by .8 and 1983 wins and losses by 1.2, and add them together. The winning percentage is figured from this; the wins and losses are rounded off and the .350 chance figured from those.

Simple? Well, no, not exactly. I would like it better if it were simpler. I would like it better if it were supported by clear reasoning, rather than intuitive judgments about the relative importance of various abilities. But I am glad to stand by the rankings that result.

RELIEF ACES
COMMENTS AND RANKINGS

1. Dan QUISENBERRY, Kansas City (42–17) The mind wilts and the imagination sags, confronted with the incontrovertible fact that a group of men entrusted with the responsibility of recognizing the outstanding pitcher in the American League could cite LaMarr Hoyt for that distinction. What on earth could they have been thinking about?

The fact that Dan Quisenberry failed to win the American League Cy Young Award in 1982 is surprising and a little unsettling. In view of the established precedents at that time, he could have been expected to win it. Several relief pitchers have won it in the last decade—Marshall in '74, Lyle in '77, Sutter in '79, Fingers in '81. Quisenberry's 1982 season was well within the performance standards that these pitchers had established for a Cy Young season. Lyle in 1977 pitched in 72 games, 137 innings; Quisenberry in 1982 pitched in 72 games, 137 innings. It is a fortunate coincidence, allowing for easy comparisons. Lyle was touched for 133 hits; Quisenberry for only 126. Lyle gave out 33 walks, Quisenberry only 12. Lyle saved 26 games, Quisenberry 35. Lyle threw ten wild pitches, Quisenberry 1; Lyle hit two batters with pitches, Quisenberry none. Lyle did have a significant advantage in wins against losses (13–5 as opposed to 9–7), and a small advantage in runs allowed (41–43), yet on balance Quisenberry's year is clearly as good as Lyle's.

Lyle was in competition for his award with three pitchers who won twenty games, plus Nolan Ryan (19–16, 2.77 ERA, 341 strikeouts). Yet he won the award. Quisenberry was in competition with absolutely nobody, and they gave the award to nobody. Pete Vuckovich, 18–6 with a 3.34 ERA and 102 walks in 224 innings, would not have drawn a vote in the 1977 competition which Lyle won. The other starters available had far better credentials.

What happened? What happened between 1974, when Mike Marshall could win a Cy Young Award for saving 21 games with a 2.42 ERA, and

1982, when Quisenberry could not win one over inferior competition for saving 35 with a 2.57 ERA? The strange thing is that we live in a time in which the importance of the relief pitcher has grown to Goliathan proportions in the popular press—and yet those same writers, when offered a chance to reward a relief pitcher for an exceptional year without having to deny the award to any starter of merit, chose instead to debase the Cy Young Award, to bestow it upon by far the most unworthy pitcher ever to receive it (Vuckovich shattered almost every imaginable record for mediocrity by a Cy Young winner) rather than to recognize one of those relief pitchers whose importance they constantly extol.

How strange was 1982; how stranger 1983. Dan Quisenberry added a fluttering knuckleball to his arsenal, and his performance took another strong stride forward. His hits per inning dropped sharply, his home runs allowed were cut in half. His phenomenal control was even more phenomenal and his strikeouts edged forward. His ERA dropped to 1.94. He threw no wild pitches, hit no batters and committed no balks. He saved the unimaginable total of 45 ballgames.

That a single Cy Young voter could have put LaMarr Hoyt at the head of his ballot—that even one voter could have scrounged up somewhere a logic or an excuse or a misconception by which to consider Hoyt to have been more valuable than Quisenberry—would have been shocking. Shocking? Appalling, disgusting, or perhaps only ridiculous. That a whole set of voters could have reached that conclusion is bewildering, bizarre beyond description. How could it happen? What on earth could have been going on in their heads? By what reckoning did they guide their votes? Was Quisenberry's season so brilliant that it blinded the voters, so far removed from the ordinary standards by which relief pitchers are judged that they couldn't comprehend what it meant? Dick Stuart once said that he used to hear

baseball people get all excited about some kid who hit 35 homers in AA ball, but when he hit 66 homers one year they couldn't quite take that in, so they just discounted it.

Something was made of the fact that LaMarr Hoyt received no Cy Young votes in 1982, when he won 19 games. That's not strange; hell, he didn't deserve any votes. He also didn't deserve any votes in 1983. If one voter had voted for Hoyt, they'd have laughed at him, made sure he never got a ballot again. There is security in numbers.

Oh, Hoyt didn't have a *bad* year. His 3.66 ERA is easily the worst of any Cy Young winner ever, but he's an above-average pitcher. He won 24 games for one reason, and one reason only: the White Sox scored 193 runs for him. He gave Detroit five runs on April 10th, but he got a "win" for it, and he gave five more to the same team in five innings on August 2 and he got another "win" for it. He gave Oakland six runs on September 6 and was credited with a "win." With that kind of offensive support, a lot of pitchers would win 24 games.

Quisenberry's performance was superior to Hoyt's in every important area. Quisenberry allowed 7.6 hits per nine innings; Hoyt allowed 8.1. Quisenberry allowed 1.94 earned runs and 2.27 total runs per nine innings; Hoyt allowed 3.66 and 3.97. Quisenberry allowed 0.39 home runs per nine innings; Hoyt allowed over twice that, 0.93. Even Hoyt's famous control, his strong point, doesn't match Quisenberry's (Hoyt: 1.07 walks per nine innings; Quisenberry: 0.71).

And as to the impact on the pennant race, how do you have an impact on a 20-game pennant race? Do you realize that if LaMarr Hoyt had pitched .500 ball (17–17) the White Sox would have won the division by only 13 games? If Hoyt had finished 10–24, they'd have won the pennant by only six games? What impact did he have on the pennant race?

When a little time passes, you're going to look back and see just how bizarre this award is. People are going to stare at 1983, and stare at it, and scratch their heads. Quisenberry had a year of historic magnitude, a year that nuked the major performance record in his area of expertise. There can be no conceivable excuse for his failure to win the award.

Other notes on Quisenberry's last two seasons: the league leaders in fewest baserunners allowed per nine innings (minimum: 100 innings):

	1982		1983	
1. Quisenberry	9.07	Quisenberry	8.35
2. Palmer	10.39	Hoyt	9.25
3. R. May	10.53	Boddicker	9.70
4. Armstrong	10.67	T. Martinez	9.84
5. Kison	10.71	Morris	10.51
6. Burgmeier	10.76	Guidry	10.57
7. Spillner	10.88	Berenguer	10.67
8. Stieb	10.97	Stieb	10.68
9. Eckersley	10.97	Lopez	10.69
10. S. Davis	11.05	Haas	10.71

In 1982 the difference between Quisenberry and the #2 man is larger than the difference between the #2 man and the #10 man. In 1983 the difference between Quisenberry and the #3 man is larger than the difference between the #3 man and the #10 man. . .

If Quisenberry had saved only about 20 games a year over the last two years, he would still be the #1 rated reliever because his other statistics are so strong. Among the 16 elements of his rating (8 in 1982, 8 in 1983) all 16 are positive. The weakest element of his rating in 1983 was his record of hits per innings pitched (118 hits in 139 innings). That scores at 17 over 30; everything else is better. His strikeout-to-walk ratio is the best of any reliever in the league, as is his control record and his ERA. One pitcher completed a higher percentage of his team's games.

2. Goose GOSSAGE, New York (30–17) Rumor has him with San Diego. Performance in '82 may not have been as good as his record indicates. One thing I intended to do in '83 but didn't get done was to count the number of baserunners allowed to score by a reliever after he entered the game. Goose had a bunch of them, around 30. He was *winning* games that he should have been *saving*. But that beats hell out of losing them.

3. Steve HOWE, Los Angeles (22–15) His problems have to this point largely obscured his very considerable abilities. He probably has a better combi-

nation of control and stuff than any other major league pitcher. Ignoring intentional walks, his strikeout-to-walk totals the last two years are 49–6 and 52–5, both figures the best in this group. His 18 saves in 46 games are a percentage exceeded by only one National Leaguer, Lee Smith . . . is available for work this summer as an investment counselor. The line forms to the left. . .

4. Al HOLLAND, Philadelphia (24–18) Will rate even higher if he can repeat the '83 season . . . 100 strikeouts and 18 walks in 92 innings.

5. Bob STANLEY, Boston (31–27) This system at this time has no park adjustments. Stanley still comes out alright . . . seems to be edging toward a traditional reliever's role. That makes sense to me. His ability to negate power makes him a valuable

6. Jesse OROSCO, New York (24–22) Rated on 1983 season only, the differences in the 6–11 range are insignificant. Pitchers are so unpredictable. What's Orosco ever done that would suggest he was ready to break loose with a year like this? . . . Mets had excellent three-man bullpen with Sisk and Carlos Diaz. (Orosco's 1983 season: 16–10.)

7. Tippy MARTINEZ, Baltimore (25–21) I thought until last year that he would have been better off as a starter; his most effective minor league stop was the one place he was used that way. Finally seemed to fit the role last year. . .

8. Bruce SUTTER, St. Louis (28–25) Stats are not as bad as they might appear at a glance. He did have a 4.23 ERA and gave up 90 hits in 89 innings, but the 64–16 K/W data suggests that he still has something going for him. Whitey kept going to him last year even when he wasn't getting the job done, which made the entire staff look worse than it was. He'll have to find somebody else if Sutter doesn't show signs of recovery . . . rating here is too high.

9. Peter LADD, Milwaukee (14–9) Saved 25 games while pitching only 49 innings, which must be some sort of record. Finished 91% of the games that he appeared in; hits allowed,

K/W data all excellent. I figure him to emerge as a name in '84. (1983 season: 11–5.)

10. Lee SMITH, Chicago (25–22) Probably should rate higher than Sutter, Ladd. His basic data—1.65 ERA and 29 saves—is super, but the Cubs' poor record in the late innings hurts his ranking quite a bit, and his 6–15 won/lost mark over two seasons doesn't help. Subjectively I would as soon head into the '84 season with him as anyone in the league.

11. Kent TEKULVE, Pittsburgh (26–24) Career in some respects resembles Wilhelm's. Didn't reach the majors until he was 27; didn't stick until he was 29, but has now pitched 657 major league games and shows no signs of stopping . . . 1.64 ERA last year was the best of his career. I still think that a Quisenberry or Tekulve-type pitcher would be just as effective as a starter as he is as a reliever. Well, I don't mean he'd have a 1.64 ERA, but with the control and the ground balls they get, if you kept the infield back they'd virtually never give up a big inning, and I think they'd win an awful lot of 3–2 ballgames.

12. Bill CAUDILL, Seattle (24–23) Now with Oakland. Gossage-type 1982 season, in and out 1983 season. Has been on up-and-down pattern since the low minors, has never put two good years or two bad years together.

13. Jeff REARDON, Montreal (24–24) Had his first off year in 1982; has bullpen help now in Lucas, but it may take him awhile to get back where he was after being overworked the last couple of years . . .

There is something to be learned from the incident of Reardon's wife, which was that Mrs. Reardon, having completed a given amount of charity work, stood up in front of a Montreal crowd and was, her husband not having pitched well of late, greeted with a chorus of boos. This scorched any bonds of kinship Reardon might have felt for the Montreal fandom, and inasmuch as he learned a lesson by it, so might we all.

The lesson is this: public life is rougher than you think it is. It all looks smooth from the outside. Public men make a lot of money, often for not even working very hard, for working at things less distasteful than, say, collecting garbage, working in a steel mill, or selling life insurance. People recognize them on the street and deluge them with get-well cards when they are in the hospital.

Publicity magnifies the good things that come into your life—but it also magnifies the bad things. It is people like me who make it rough, with our caustic comments and our cold analysis. And as I do to Doug Flynn and Enos Cabell and Bucky Dent, other people do to me at times, and others to them, and it doesn't feel so good. The IRS takes a special interest in you if your name is in the papers; they live by promoting the fear that you might always get caught, and they would love to use a Jeff Reardon or a Norman Mailer to advance that fear. Willie Wilson goes directly to jail for an offense that would draw a stern look from a judge if it were you or I, because somebody is using him to prove a point. Strangers will stop you on the street or call on the phone and want something that you can't give them, and if you get famous enough they will actually start shooting at you.

About my small acre of fame I am certainly not complaining, just trying to make you see a little clearer what comes with the title. Willie Wilson's comment, while being led away in handcuffs, was "expletive publicity"; it is not reported whether he made the same remark at the time of signing his $4 million contract. And as to Mrs. Reardon, well, my sister has devoted her entire adult life to working with homeless and destitute people, and she doesn't stand up in front of no crowd and expect them to applaud on Sunday. When you decide to be a public figure, you take what comes. You cannot control it, and you cannot choose it.

14. Aurelio LOPEZ, Detroit (18–17) This guy must have one of the greatest arms that God ever made. He's 35, threw about nine million pitches in the Mexican League before he came to Los Estados Unidos, where he has been working 60 games a year since 1979, and he trains on beans and beer with three side orders of meat, and he can still blow his fastball by good major league hitters.

15. Steve BEDROSIAN (24–27) The Braves have a "group" bullpen, with Bedrosian (19 saves), Forster (13 saves), Garber (9 saves) and others (Camp, Boggs, Brizzolara, Falcone, Moore). They had a great year in '82, with 51 saves, and still led the league in saves in '83 with 48, although that is probably one of the season's more deceptive statistics. The Braves lost nine games in which they held a lead after seven innings, tying Pittsburgh for the most in the league, and had the league's worst record in one-run games. Only Forster had a good ERA.

I'm a little skeptical about group bullpens in principle. Jim Baker has suggested that teams which have great group bullpens in one year, like Atlanta, San Francisco and Seattle in 1982, often tend to have group collapses the next year. We can't prove that, but it does seem that way. Even if it doesn't, I still don't really like group bullpens. For one thing, if you're counting on three or four relief pitchers, then you have to get work for all of them. That means taking the ball away from the starter whenever he gets into trouble, and I don't like that. I think that one of the things that makes Billy Martin so effective is that he makes it very clear that he expects his starters to be able to get out of trouble, even in the sixth or seventh inning. For another thing, if you don't have a bullpen ace, things can get awfully confused sometimes; one pitcher gets into a slump and then another and another, and you don't really know who it is that is supposed to get you out of this.

I like *definition* in a pitching staff; I like a staff with four starters, a relief ace, a middle-inning man, a spot starter/long man, a lefthanded spot reliever, a mop-up man. I like that for a reason that I wrote several years ago: it is easier to find five guys who can pitch than it is nine or ten. When you have a group bullpen, you're going to have your #8 pitcher out there on the mound with the game on the line 30 or 40 times a year. I don't like that. It also means that you have to find 8 or 9 effective pitchers, and I don't like that. Bedrosian has one of the best fastballs in the major leagues, and he has control of it. My inclination would be to try to make a Goose Gossage out of

him, and to leave Garber and Forster and Moore out of it.

16. Frank DiPINO, Houston (11–9) Had a good year after converting to the relief role; was most effective as a starter in the minors. Had 67 strikeouts, 15 walks, allowed only 52 hits in 71 innings. The Astros' bullpen had been weak since Sambito's injury, but DiPino and Dawley ended that.

17. Greg MINTON, San Francisco (25–29) Had a great year in '82, subpar in '83. He had a 3.54 ERA and the worst hits per inning, worst strikeout-to-walk ratio of any listed relief ace. Craig Wright told me a year ago that Minton had been overused in '82 (78 games) and would likely be off form in '83 . . . had a .909 slugging percentage, with six hits including a double and a homer in eleven at-bats.

18. Ron DAVIS, Minnesota (22–25) Finished 61 of the 66 games he was called into (92%), the highest percentage in the majors . . . allowed a hit an inning. He's saved a lot of games, but over the last two years his ERA (3.92) and won/lost mark (8–17) are hardly typical of a quality reliever . . . ERAs the last two years have been 5.03, 4.43 in Minnesota but 3.78, 2.23 on the road. Also had a 4.14 ERA in day games last year, 2.77 at night . . .

19. Gary LUCAS, San Diego (18–23) Now with Montreal . . . hasn't had a hit in two years (0 for 26) . . . If the Padres do sign Gossage, I would assume they would move DeLeon to the starting rotation. He was a starter in the minors.

20. Odell JONES, Texas (8–9) Now 31; led AAA leagues in strikeouts four times . . . looks like he is playing the part of Satchel Paige in a movie. Same gangly, skinny body, big ears sticking out; has one of the best fastballs in the league . . . Won 87 games in the minor leagues. Wonder how many major leaguers have won more? . . . 2.48 ERA in night games.

21. Randy MOFFITT, Toronto (10–13) 1.53 ERA before the All-Star break, 6.11 ERA after . . . the Blue Jays have a minor league pitcher named Colin McLaughlin. I wonder if they'll call him "Co"...

22. Dennis LAMP, Chicago (11–15) Another group bullpen with Barojas, Agosto, Koosman, Hickey, Tidrow. They were second in the league in saves, but if you get into their bullpen you always figure you've got a chance... Barojas probably the best of the lot.

23. Dan SPILLNER, Cleveland (18–27) Reverted to form after fine 1982 season (you know what they say, the sludge always sinks to the bottom)...

had pitched .500 ball or better for six straight years before last year.

24. Bill SCHERRER, Cincinnati (8–11) Pitched well, Cincy has no confidence in him, so he gets no saves; is 26, started the 1982 season in the Florida State League. One of Rapp's main tasks is going to be to find a relief ace. Hume never recovered from working 78 games, 137 innings in 1980.

25. Dave BEARD, Oakland (13–22) Now with Seattle.

26. Luis SANCHEZ, California (14–24) The Angels lost 10 games in which they held a lead after seven innings, a total exceeded only by Toronto (11), and were 8–19 in games that were tied after seven. Sanchez is so-so but they seem to have no confidence in him, and the rest of the bullpen is Curtis (1–2, 3.80 ERA), Hassler (0–5, 5.45), Goltz (0–6, 6.22) and Byron McLaughlin (2–4, 5.17). In view of the alternatives, the reluctance to let Sanchez do the job is difficult to understand.

RELIEF ACES

		1982	1983	Winning %	Wins/ Losses	.350 Chance
1.	Dan Quisenberry	20-10	22- 7	.713	42-17	.00000002
2.	Goose Gossage	14- 8	15- 9	.629	30-17	.00005
3.	Steve Howe	11- 9	11- 6	.606	22-15	.00205
4.	Al Holland	9-10	15- 8	.583	24-18	.00275
5.	Bob Stanley	13-13	17-14	.539	31-27	.00303
6.	Jesse Orosco	7-12	16-10	.521	24-22	(.00516)
7.	Tippy Martinez	11-13	14- 9	.544	25-21	.00556
8.	Bruce Sutter	16-13	12-12	.524	28-25	.00583
9.	Peter Ladd	2- 3	11- 5	.630	14- 9	(.00620)
10.	Lee Smith	9-11	15-11	.530	25-22	.00798
11.	Kent Tekulve	15-14	11-11	.517	26-24	.01004
12.	Bill Caudill	17-10	8-12	.505	24-23	.01714
13.	Jeff Reardon	13-11	11-13	.498	24-24	.02310
14.	Aurelio Lopez	2- 5	13-11	.502	18-17	.03363
15.	Steve Bedrosian	11-12	13-14	.466	24-27	.05060
16.	Frank DiPino		9- 7	.560	11- 9	.05317
17.	Greg Minton	17-11	9-17	.462	25-29	.05700
18.	Ron Davis	9-14	12-12	.463	22-25	.06324
19.	Gary Lucas	8-12	9-12	.434	18-23	.15129
20.	Odell Jones		6- 8	.450	8- 9	.21276
21.	Randy Moffitt	3- 5	6- 7	.437	10-13	.25918
22.	Dennis Lamp		9-13	.420	11-15	.27814
23.	Dan Spillner	16-13	5-13	.408	18-27	.28867
24.	Bill Scherrer		7- 9	.435	8-11	.31185
25.	Dave Beard	10-12	5-10	.378	13-22	.45772
26.	Luis Sanchez	6-10	7-14	.358	14-24	.46613

ESSAYS & ARTICLES

THE WORLD SERIES PREDICTION SYSTEM, REVISITED

In the fall of 1982, I wrote an article for *Inside Sports* magazine detailing the one major analytic discovery that I have never written about in the *Baseball Abstract*. That discovery was that the World Series can be predicted with 70% accuracy, and without recourse to subjective judgments. That is a statement of fact; it can be shown to be true. The method was developed ten years ago. Since that time there have been 34 postseason playoff series (10 World Series, 20 league championship series, 4 Miniseries in 1981). The system has been right 23 times and wrong 11 times. Flipping a coin, your chances of doing that well would be less than one in 30. You can also use the method to make retrospective predictions about all of the postseason series in this century. When you do, you get 83 correct answers and 31 wrong answers. Flipping a coin, you'd wear out your thumb before you did that well. The system works.

Which it will take me another ten years to convince anyone. What happened was, I went on the "Today" show on October 5, 1982 to discuss the World Series prediction system, why it worked and how it worked, and to offer up my predictions for the 1982 playoffs. That's right, California and Atlanta. They met in the real World Series that year, in a cow pasture just south of Chicago; that thing you thought you saw was just a TV show.

No, the system went 0 for 2 on the 1982 playoffs. Logically, of course, a 0 for 2 performance would not convince anyone that a system which had worked 70% of the time for a century does not actually work. The chance that a system which is 70% accurate would miss in two tries is exactly the same as the chance that a .300 hitter would get two hits in two at-bats. That's not exactly an uncommon occurrence, and this is not exactly a logical universe. A week later, nobody was much interested in who the system picked to win the World Series, and a month later *Inside Sports* folded. The entire trip was not a great success.

Why the system did not work well in 1982 is, by the way, extremely easy to see, but we'll get to that later. First of all, I ought to explain what the system is, how it was developed, and why it usually works. I also need to run a couple of charts to allow you to put it to the test, see that it actually does work. Then we'll get back to 1982.

WHAT THE SYSTEM IS

The system is a series of weighted indicators, each of which points to one team or the other as the likely victor in the matchup. They are weighted according to how consistently they point to the right team; shutouts are the most heavily weighted indicator because teams which throw a lot of shutouts have a better record in World Series play than teams which do anything else very well. The full list of rules for the system is given below:

1. Compare the won/lost records of the two teams involved. Award 1 point per half-game difference to the team with the better record.

2. Give 3 points to the team that has scored more runs.

3. Give 14 points to the team that has hit fewer doubles.

4. Give 12 points to the team that has hit more triples.

5. Give 10 points to the team that has hit more home runs.

6. Give 8 points to the team with the lower team batting average.

7. Give 8 points to the team that has committed fewer errors.

8. Give 7 points to the team that has turned more double plays.

9. Give 7 points to the team whose pitchers have walked more men.

10. Give 19 points to the team that has thrown more shutouts.

11. Give 15 points to the team whose ERA is further below the legue ERA.

12. Give 12 points to the team that has been in postseason play more recently. If both last appeared in postseason play in the same year, award the points to the team that was more successful at that time.

13. (League or divisional playoffs only) Give 12 points to the team that led in head-to-head competition during the season.

HOW THE SYSTEM WAS DEVELOPED

The system grew, as did most of my methods, from attempts to figure out whether something that people said was true. That's like Tony LaRussa's statement that he thought the White Sox baserunning would be the difference in the playoffs; people say things like that. I had heard people say that they thought that what was important in a World Series was pitching, heard other people say "front-line pitching," heard other people say relief pitching, strength up the middle, etc.

So I got to wondering, is that true? Do teams which have a lot of power do well in postseason play? Do teams with high averages do well in the World Series? If a team with a good offense but not such a good pitching staff meets a team with a so-so offense but a spectacular pitching staff, does the team with the pitching usually rule? Why can't we answer these questions?

Why not, indeed. What I decided to do was to compare categories of accomplishment. In each World Series, one team has hit more triples than the other team. What is the record of the teams which have hit more triples? What is the record of the teams which have hit for a higher average? What is the record of the teams which have turned more double plays?

I found some surprising things. I found that the teams which had hit for a better average had usually lost the World Series—that is, they had lost it more often than they had won it. Offense as a collective thing didn't seem to mean much; the good offenses had won a few more than they had lost, but not a lot. The power-hitting offenses had done very well; the high-average offenses had

not done well. Teams which hit a lot of doubles had been wiped out with demonic consistency; in every generation, almost in every decade, the teams which had hit more doubles than their opponents had lost around 60% of the time.

I found those things, and I could easily have just filed them away, except. Two things happened to keep the subject alive. Just as the 1982 season was a textbook in why the systems don't always work, the 1974 season was a textbook in why they do. I had found that teams which had high batting averages usually lost the World Series and playoffs, and sure enough, Baltimore (.256) bowed before Oakland (.247), Pittsburgh (.274) lost to the Dodgers (.272), and the Dodgers, with a team batting average 25 points higher despite having no designated hitter to help them, were destroyed by the Oakland A's. And, while you would have a hard time believing it today, the Dodgers were the betting favorite in that Series.

The second thing that happened was, I happened to be working around some people who were baseball fans, and we kept talking about this, saying, "Isn't there some way to make use of this information?" I began to look for some way to formally incorporate in an objective prediction system the knowledge I had gained about what types of teams had done well in the past in World Series play.

After a good many false starts, the system here detailed is the result. You get 19 points for throwing shutouts, because at the time the research was done, teams which had thrown more shutouts were 45–26 (+19) in postseason play.

WHY THE SYSTEM WORKS

I never expected the system to work. I knew that, in retrospect, the system distinguished the winning team from the losing team 70% of the time; I did not expect that it would continue to do so. I had no understanding of *why* it worked, and so it seemed to me to be a compilation of past coincidences, and not truly likely to predict the Series winner with any consistency.

Two things have happened since then. One, the system has continued to work. Murphy's Law has operated; the more attention that has been paid to the predictions, the less they have tended to come true. It didn't work in 1975, when (invigorated by the successes of 1974) I passed out copies of it to all of the baseball fans that I worked

with. This experience was repeated on a national scale in 1982. But it has worked extremely well when it was sitting quietly in my file cabinet, being watched over only by me. Since the "Today" show debacle in 1982 there have been four more postseason series (the 1982 and 1983 World Series, the 1983 playoffs). The system has been right on three of those four series, as you can confirm if you will take the time. That's 3–3 since it's introduction to a national audience; 23–11 since it's invention.

Equally important, I have come a long way toward understanding *why* it works.

Why do teams with high batting averages do poorly in World Series play? A simple reason: it takes them too

246

many hits to score. If they are legitimately a better offensive team than their opponents, then that's another story. Most of the time they're not; everybody who gets into a World Series has got some bats. The higher batting average doesn't indicate the team which has a *better* offense, but the team which has more of a *high-average* offense, as opposed to a power offense.

High-average offenses score by stringing sequences together. To get a three-run inning, it might take them five or six hits. Every one of those hits gets harder to come by. If each one of them becomes 10% more difficult to get, how much more difficult to get are *all five* of them? You've got five chances to stop that inning.

With the three-run home run, on the other hand, you've got only three chances to stop it. As each element of the offense becomes 10% less common, the 5-element offense is damaged much more than the 3-element offense is. That's why good pitchers, as a group, allow a higher percentage of their runs on home runs than do poor pitchers. And in a World Series, you're always facing a good pitcher. So the percentage of runs that score on home runs is consistently higher in a World Series than it is during the season.

The 1983 series are a good illustration of that. There were 27 runs during the World Series—10 of them home runs. In postseason play as a whole there were 73 runs scored, 20 of them by home runs (does not count baserunners who scored on home runs). That's 27% of all the runs. During the season as a whole, only 18% of runs scored on home runs. Did the rate at which home runs were being hit increase? No, it decreased slightly, from 1.57 HR/game to 1.54. But the rate of *other* runs decreased by much more than that, so the home runs attained an added importance. That is exactly what happens.

So, with that knowledge, it makes perfect sense for the high-average teams to do poorly in World Series play. Other interpretations of odd rules might be more speculative, but I am absolutely convinced that teams which hit a lot of doubles during the season are never going to do well in the aftermath because they are aggressive baserunning teams, teams which are exploiting weaknesses that will not be there when the Series starts. Shutouts are important because most shutouts are thrown by front-line starting pitchers, and front-line starters do a much larger share of the pitching in a World Series than they do during the season. Walks are not that important because they are disproportionately influenced by fourth and fifth starters who will spend the World Series in hibernation. The other rules are positive rules; all the system does is weight them according to their historic importance.

WHY DID THE SYSTEM HAVE A BAD YEAR IN 1982?

Well, for one thing, there is luck; I never said it would work 100% of the time. But in exactly the same way as it is not unusual for a .300 hitter to go 2 for 2 but when he does, there is still a reason for it (they threw him a pitch he could hit, he guessed right, they defensed him wrong, etc.), it is not unusual for a system which is 70% accurate to be wrong twice in a row, but when it does there's a reason for it.

And you could see this reason coming from a month off. The chart below gives the earned run averages of the 56 teams which have won their divisions since 1969, subtracted from the league ERA (that is, a 3.00 ERA in a league with a 4.00 ERA is 1.00):

	National		American		
Year	East	West	East	West	Total
1969	.59	.05	.79	.38	1.81
1970	.35	.34	.57	.49	1.76
1971	.16	.14	.47	.41	1.18
1972	.65	.25	.11	.49	1.50
1973	.44	.28	.74	.53	1.99
1974	.13	.65	.35	.67	1.80
1975	.61	.26	-.20	.50	1.17
1976	.40	-.01	.05	.35	.79
1977	.20	.69	.45	.54	1.88
1978	.25	.46	.58	.32	1.61
1979	.32	.15	.96	-.12	1.33
1980	.17	.50	.45	.20	1.32
1981	.19	.48	.76	.36	1.79
1982	.23	-.22	.09	.25	.35
1983	.29	.53	.43	.39	1.64

The system is supposed to measure what happens when *good* pitching staffs and *good* defenses collide. Remember: shortens the offensive sequence, eliminates the value of aggressive baserunning by making it too difficult to exploit the defense? Ordinarily, that's what we're talking about in a World Series or playoff—good offenses against good defenses.

But they ran in a ringer on me. For the first time since God-has-forgotten-when, there was not one team in the postseason round that had that kind of pitching or that kind of defense. They were just a little above average pitching and defense teams, teams which got in by scoring a jillion runs.

So the advantages that should have been negated, weren't. It was possible to take advantage of the California Angel defense, with Reggie in rightfield and an ailing Doug DeCinces at third base. It was possible to put together a long offensive sequence against the Atlanta Braves.

But what could I do? I had chosen in August to go public with the system this fall; I couldn't go on the "Today" show in October and say, "No, I don't think this is the year for it." Those were the cards that the dealer had for me at the moment I decided to get in the game; I had nothing to do but play them.

So it will take forever to convince people, but the system still works. It has been in the public domain for two years now; when it has been there for ten or fifteen, there will be enough evidence about it to make a reasonable evaluation. It may not continue to work 70% of the time, but it is not going to start working 40%, either. I am not afraid to see what happens to it.

FOR YOUR CONVENIENCE

Years when the system works and does not work.

WORLD SERIES

System is right in:	System is wrong in:
1903, 1905, 1907, 1908, 1909	1906
1913, 1916, 1917, 1918, 1919	1910, 1911, 1912, 1914, 1915
1921, 23, 24, 26, 27, 28, 29	1920, 25
1930, 1932, 33, 34, 35, 36, 37, 38, 39	1931
1940, 41, 44, 45, 46, 47, 48, 49	1942, 43
1950, 51, 52, 53, 54, 56, 58, 59	1955, 57
1961, 62, 65, 67, 69	1960, 63, 64, 66, 68
1970, 72, 73, 74, 75, 76, 78	1971, 77, 79
1982, 83	1980, 81

AMERICAN LEAGUE PLAYOFFS

1969	
1970, 71, 72, 73, 74, 76, 77, 78, 79	1975
1981, 83	1980, 82

NATIONAL LEAGUE PLAYOFFS

1969	
1970, 71, 72, 74, 76, 77, 78, 79	1973, 75
1981	1980, 82, 83

System is correct on all four 1981 mini-series.

CAREER RECORDS FOR OUTFIELDERS ASSISTS

The following charts present the career assists records of the principal outfielders on each of the 26 major league teams. I have never seen these records presented anywhere else, and while they may not be a perfect way to measure anything, they are certainly more informative than single-season assists totals, which are the only other throwing records that there are. There are three categories of the record—career outfield games, career outfield assists and career outfield assists per 162 games played. Mostly I am going to let these records speak for themselves (please take the trouble to actually look at them before you decide what they mean), but I did want to make a couple of quick remarks:

1. The one largest problem with single-season assists records is simply time; 162 games is not a large enough sample to really tell much. You have to look at assists records over 400, 500 games before they will tell you much of anything. But if you look at the career charts below, you'll find that the top man on almost every team is somebody who throws very well, and the bottom man on most teams is somebody who doesn't.

2. Totals for centerfielders are usually lower than those for the other fielders, over a period of time. There are many fewer times during a season when a centerfielder is directly challenged to throw somebody out than there are for the corner men. When he catches a fly ball, he is so far away from home plate that there is usually no way he is going to do anything. If he picks up a single in left-center the man isn't going to try to go from first-to-third, and if he picks it up in right-center he hasn't got a chance of stopping him from it. The leftfielders pick up a lot of assists—probably 20, 30% of their assists—from cutoff men on 7-5-4 plays, where one run scores and the other

guy is picked off trying for second. The centerfielder doesn't get those because he throws in to second to begin with. So if you're going to make direct comparisons between a centerfielder's throw-out rates and a leftfielder's, you have to add maybe 30 or 40 percent to the centerfielder.

3. The little fast guys, particularly in leftfield, are always going to throw out a few extra runners because they pick the ball up so quick. It's my guess that there are more times during a season when you stop a runner from going first-to-third by picking the ball up quick than there are when you can stop him by making a good throw. It's probably harder to go from first-to-third on an outfielder who can run than it is on an outfielder who can throw.

4. The notion that assists aren't really that important, because a man who gets a lot of assists might be letting too many baserunners advance, is nonsense. If an outfielder throws out 20 men in a season, like Gary Ward and Tim Raines and Jim Rice did last year, there is no way in hell that he could be allowing enough other runners to advance to negate that. Those 20 assists occur in the context of a couple of hundred possible plays, on most of which the outfielder is powerless to do anything. There just aren't enough plays there to offset the 20 men that he takes off base.

AMERICAN LEAGUE OUTFIELDERS

Baltimore	G	A	A/162
Roenicke	596	40	10.9
Lowenstein	836	50	9.7
Bumbry	1126	61	8.8
Ford	1050	48	7.4

Detroit	G	A	A/162
G. Wilson	223	20	14.5
Lemon	1022	72	11.4
Herndon	928	56	9.8
Gibson	234	8	5.5

New York	G	A	A/162
Winfield	1453	115	12.8
Moreno	1071	73	11.0
Kemp	857	52	9.8

Toronto	G	A	A/162
Barfield	282	33	19.0
Bonnell	734	48	10.6
Moseby	496	30	9.8
Collins	741	37	8.1

Milwaukee	G	A	A/162
Moore	323	28	14.0
Oglivie	1173	88	12.2
Brouhard	135	10	12.0
Manning	1159	63	8.8

Boston	G	A	A/162
Rice	987	89	14.6
Nichols	190	17	14.5
Evans	1378	111	13.0
Armas	797	58	11.8

Cleveland	G	A	A/162
Tabler	88	4	7.4
Thomas	1125	50	7.2
Vukovich	121	3	4.4

Chicago	G	A	A/162
Baines	533	36	10.9
Kittle	144	7	7.9
R. Law	338	13	6.2

Kansas City	G	A	A/162
Otis	1896	121	10.3
W. Wilson	811	49	9.8
Sheridan	100	6	9.7

Texas	G	A	A/162
Parrish	256	23	14.6
Rivers	1222	92	12.2
Wright	310	20	10.5
Sample	478	27	9.2

Oakland	G	A	A/162
M. Davis	154	18	18.9
Murphy	698	51	11.8
R. Henderson	639	38	9.6

Minnesota	G	A	A/162
Ward	399	45	18.3
Brunansky	284	27	15.4
Hatcher	238	16	10.9
D. Brown	94	2	3.4

California	G	A	A/162
Valentine	849	85	16.2
Lynn	1126	83	11.9
Beniquez	897	62	11.2
Downing	353	22	10.1

Seattle	G	A	A/162
D. Henderson	292	32	17.8
R. Nelson	91	10	17.8
S. Henderson	671	59	14.2
Cowens	1218	92	12.2

Philadelphia	G	A	A/162
Lezcano	1069	101	15.3
Matthews	1539	116	12.2
Hayes	255	18	11.4
Maddox	1521	88	9.4
Dernier	235	8	5.5

Pittsburgh	G	A	A/162
Easler	462	33	11.6
Lacy	564	36	10.3
Wynne	102	3	4.8

Montreal	G	A	A/162
Cromartie	774	74	15.5
Raines	356	34	15.5
Dawson	1020	72	11.4

St. Louis	G	A	A/162
L. Smith	430	44	16.6
Green	222	15	10.9
Hendrick	1458	95	10.6
McGee	262	10	6.2

New York	G	A	A/162
Strawberry	117	8	11.1
Foster	1543	100	10.5
M. Wilson	410	21	8.3

Chicago	G	A	A/162
Hall	137	12	14.2
Durham	399	31	12.6
Moreland	241	16	10.8
Woods	320	16	8.1

Los Angeles	G	A	A/162
Baker	1689	102	9.8
Landreaux	721	40	9.0
Marshall	130	3	3.7

Atlanta	G	A	A/162
Washington	1083	79	11.8
Murphy	579	41	11.5
Butler	257	17	10.7

Houston	G	A	A/162
T. Scott	830	52	10.1
Mumphrey	942	55	9.5
J. Cruz	1620	92	9.2
Puhl	844	43	8.3

San Diego	G	A	A/162
Richards	780	73	15.2
Wiggins	177	14	12.8
Gwynn	133	10	12.2
Jones	872	53	9.8

San Francisco	G	A	A/162
Youngblood	521	62	19.3
Clark	941	91	15.7
C. Davis	292	23	12.8
Leonard	438	30	11.1

Cincinnati	G	A	A/162
Redus	140	14	16.2
Householder	276	22	12.9
Milner	250	17	11.0
Cedeno	1555	93	9.7

PROJECT SCORESHEET

This article represents the beginning of an attempt to organize a project to bring together and make available to the public the scoresheets from every major league game that is played during a season. When I began writing about baseball in 1975, I assumed that those scoresheets were available to the press (and thus, ultimately, the public) if you had a reason for wanting them. I have since learned, and relearned and relearned from many attempts to gain access to them, that they are not. The official scoresheets of major league games are the jealously guarded possessions of the bureaus which compile the official statistics. They have not the slightest intention of allowing anyone else to get access to them.

Let us begin by asking what information we might stand to gain from this. Well, to begin with there is all the information about the sequence of play. What does Dale Murphy hit with runners in scoring position? Does Mookie Wilson hit any better when leading off an inning than he does in another situation? Is Tom Seaver more likely to get a strikeout when there is a runner on third and less than two out than he is in another circumstance? How many runners did Dan Quisenberry allow to score after he came in the game? How many runners were out there at the time he came in the game? Does Jim Rice hit as well in the late innings of a close game as he does at other times? Does Eddie Murray tend to let down with a big lead? When there is a runner on first and less than two out and a ground ball is hit to Glenn Hubbard, how many times does he get a double play and how many times does he not get a double? All this and any other information that you can imagine about who does how well in what circumstance, you would be able to figure if you had the scoresheets from the games. You can't figure it now.

Next comes information about players. Suppose you want to know what somebody hits against lefthanded pitchers. If you want to know this now, you are at the mercy of the team, or failing that you are at the mercy of Bill James, who is at the mercy of the team. If they make a mistake, you get the wrong information.

Suppose, however, that you want to know what a player hits against *a particular type* of lefthanded pitcher. Suppose that you believe that Dickie Thon handles the lefthanded power pitcher, the Mark Davis or Larry McWilliams, very well, but has trouble with a lefthanded junkball pitcher. You cannot get that information. It doesn't exist, and nobody in the world is going to figure it for you.

Suppose that you want to keep "books" on the hitter/pitcher matchups. What is Lou Piniella's career batting average against Scott McGregor? How good of a hitter is Mike Schmidt against Bruce Sutter?

That information is not available to you.

Suppose that you want to know exactly how many bases are stolen when Steve Yeager is catching, and exactly how many he throws out. Suppose that you want to know how many errors he commits while in the process of throwing to second.

That information is not available to you.

Suppose that you are a baseball historian, and you are wondering about the exact circumstances of the game in which Al Simmons had his first major league at-bat and his last major league at-bat.

That information is not available to you.

Suppose that you want to know how many of Bob Horner's errors were costly, and how many were just missed popups for the second strike when the next one was strike three.

That information is not available to you.

Suppose that you want to know what Dwayne Murphy hit when Rickey Henderson was on first in a possible-steal situation, and what he hit with the bases empty.

That information is not available to you.

Suppose that you want to know how many times the Cleveland Indians had the potential tying run in scoring position in the late innings and failed to get him in. Suppose you want to know how many times the Baltimore Orioles got a game-winning home run after two were out in the inning.

That information is not available to you.

Suppose that you want to calculate the exact impact of getting a leadoff man on in an inning. To do that you need to find out how many times there were when a team got a leadoff man on in an inning and how many runs they scored when they did, and how many times they didn't and how many runs they scored when they didn't. You need to know some other stuff about where you were in the batting order when these things happened.

None of that information is available to you.

Suppose that you are wondering how many runners go from first-to-third on a single to center when Mickey Rivers is in centerfield, and how many go from first-to-third on a single to center when Andre Dawson is in centerfield.

That information is not available to you.

Suppose that you are designing a table game, and you need to know how often a runner goes first-to-third on a single with one out in an inning, and how often with none out or two out.

That information is not available to you.

Suppose that you are curious about how many times in his career Hal McRae has been thrown out trying for an extra base, and how many times Joe DiMaggio was thrown out trying for an extra base.

That information is not available to you.

Suppose you are wondering what percentage of the time a player is hit by a pitch the next at-bat after he has hit a home run.

That information is not available to you.

Suppose that you are wondering if a given hitter—Pete Rose—hits a pitcher better the second time he sees him in a game, or the third time, or the fourth time.

You can't get the information to figure that.

Suppose that you are trying to study the defensive impact of a player being in or out of the lineup, and to do that you need to isolate "defensive innings"—something that you also need in order to make complete sense of fielding statistics.

But that information is not to be had.

In short, we as analysts of the game, or even not as analysts of the game, but as historians or record-makers or biographers or simply fans, are blocked off from the basic source of information which we need to undertake an incalculable variety of investigative studies. We need accounts; we are given summaries. We need access to an exact record of what happens. We are told that that is for the big boys, not for us measley fans.

I feel this is very wrong. *I want that information*. I want it bad. I also feel, though it is not particularly germane to this article, that the actions of the league constitute a) a conspiracy in restraint of free trade (if I had access to the data, I would sell for about $12 the same information that the Elias Bureau sells for thousands of dollars), and b) an unfair labor practice (the teams don't want to make the information available because they want to have access to better information than the players do when they are negotiating salaries). I have considered a legal challenge on these points, but one of my goals in life is to die without ever being involved in a lawsuit, and anyway lawsuits are expensive even when they are successful and expensive as hell when they are not successful, so, as I said, the questions about the legality of the National League's position are not really germane.

What is germane is that it is wrong. The entire basis of professional sports is the public's interest in what is going on. To deny the public access to information that it cares about is the logical equivalent of locking the stadiums and playing the games in private so that no one will find out what is happening. It is stupid and counterproductive. But baseball has been doing this for fifty years and they're not about to stop unless someone stops them.

And that's what we're going to do. We're going to put together a group of people who want those scoresheets, and we're going to get them.

Perhaps to this point in the article I have focused too much on the negative aspects of having to get the information the hard way. I'm not talking here about building an organization that would compile scoresheets that are

as good as the official scoresheets. In the short term, for next year or the year after, we aim for that, for duplicating the official records but making them available to the public. But in the long term, we are talking about building an information record that is *far better* than what the "officials" of baseball have access to.

Think about it. What information would you like to have about baseball games that is not officially recorded? Information on where the hits go, how many go by Mike Schmidt down the line and how many go by Pedro Guerrero down the line? We can collect that information. Are you curious about what people hit when the first pitch is a ball and what they hit when it is a strike? Want to know who is a good two-strike hitter and who is not? Want to know which pitchers usually work ahead of the batters and which usually work behind the batter? We can keep the data on record. Want to know how many pitches are called strikes against the home team and how many against the road team? We'll find out. Want to keep records of flashy defensive plays? I would strongly encourage the group of people who were doing the work not to try that —but if that's what they want, we can do it. Wondering what the connection is between the number of pitches thrown to a leadoff man and the number of runs scored in an inning? Wondering how many pitches a pitcher throws in a season? The teams have no way of getting that information. We can get it if we want to.

Not to be too grandiose about it, I guess what I am saying is that baseball fans sometimes get very upset about the fact that we are treated as sort of nonentities by baseball officials. When the agreement between players and owners is renegotiated, where are the fans? When the rules are changed, when the playoffs are being lengthened or new scoring rules are adopted, everybody is consulted except the fan. Bowie Kuhn always liked to claim that he represented the interests of the fans, but nobody ever asked me if I wanted to vote for him. When the awards are given out, when the Hall of Fame election time comes, the media is consulted, and the players are consulted and the owners are consulted, but where are the fans?

But what do the fans do? We sit back and holler about the records that are kept. We say that "they" should change this scoring practice and "they" should keep track of that and "they" should consider this a part of the official records. And I've been saying that "they" should make this available to us, and they should. But what about what *we* should do?

I strongly believe that the fans are baseball's rightful owners, and that there is every reason why they should have a voice in how things are done. PROJECT SCORESHEET isn't going to change the way things are very much, but it is something that the fans can do. It is a small way of asserting that we're not waiting for them to do whatever they see fit. It is not impossible that it could lead to other small assertions of the fans' rightful place in the game.

And that's really why I'm doing this the way that I am doing it. PROJECT SCORESHEET is an attempt to build a network of fans to collect those scoresheets, and to construct the necessary administrative framework to get the scoresheets to the public. I'm asking for your help.

What do you have to do? At a minimum, score some

ballgames. Put the scoresheets in an envelope with somebody's name on it.

Send a postcard to Bill James, 945 Kentucky, Lawrence, KS 66097; put your name, address, the team you most follow and PROJECT SCORESHEET on the card. I'll take it from there.

When PROJECT SCORESHEET is in place, all previous measures of performance in baseball will immediately become obsolete, and an entire universe of research options will open up in front of us. With your help, ladies and gentlemen, there is no need for the next generation to be as ignorant as we are.

A FEW WORDS ABOUT THE HOME-FIELD ADVANTAGE

This article addresses a largely technical issue, an issue that we need to deal with in order to use the numbers to understand baseball; it doesn't have much to do with baseball itself. Those of you who are interested in what sabermetrics has to say about baseball, but not interested in sabermetrics per se, are now excused.

Is the home-field advantage usually larger for a good team than for a bad team? The home-field advantage in baseball is 100 points exactly; this we know. The home team wins 55% of all ballgames. But is that a straight-line 100 points, or is it a proportional 10%, or what?

A straight-line 100-point advantage would mean that a .400 baseball team could be expected to play .350 baseball on the road, but .450 at home; a proportional 10% advantage would mean that they could be expected to play .360 baseball on the road and .440 at home. A straight-line 100-point advantage would mean that a .650 baseball team would play .600 on the road, .700 at home; a proportional 10% would mean that they'd be at .585 on the road and .715 at home. Which is it, or what is it?

We need to know the answer to that question in order to make proper adjustments while studying how other factors might alter the home-field advantage.

To study the issue, I took five years worth of team data, 1977 through 1982 except 1981. I sorted the teams into 10-point groups of teams, teams playing .610 to .619 ball, teams playing .430 to .439 ball, etc., and recorded the records at home and on the road of the teams in each group. For example, there were five teams in the study which had won/lost percentages in the .460s. Those five teams had a combined record 203 wins, 201 losses at home (.503), 174 wins, 231 losses on the road (.430).

That done, I combined the 10-point groups into 100-point "regions," a .460–.559 region, a .450–.549 region, a .440–.539 region, etc. Then I figured the records at home, the records on the road and the combined records of all of the regions. This is what I got:

Range	Overall Winning%	Home	Road	Home-Field Advantage
.550-.649	.587	.647	.525	.122
.540-.639	.577	.635	.519	.116
.530-.629	.568	.622	.513	.109
.520-.619	.564	.618	.511	.107
.510-.609	.554	.605	.502	.103
.500-.599	.544	.597	.492	.105
.490-.589	.539	.591	.488	.103
.480-.579	.532	.585	.479	.106
.470-.569	.526	.577	.477	.102
.460-.559	.518	.566	.469	.097

Range	Overall Winning%	Home	Road	Home-Field Advantage
.450-.549	.505	.549	.460	.089
.440-.539	.494	.537	.451	.086
.430-.529	.484	.530	.438	.092
.420-.519	.474	.519	.430	.089
.410-.509	.458	.503	.414	.089
.400-.499	.448	.487	.409	.078
.390-.489	.440	.478	.403	.075
.380-.479	.433	.468	.399	.069
.370-.469	.426	.463	.390	.073
.360-.459	.418	.457	.379	.078
.350-.449	.406	.444	.368	.076
.340-.439	.404	.442	.365	.077
.330-.429	.395	.430	.360	.070
.320-.419	.384	.420	.349	.071

As a glance at the data will quickly tell you, the home-field advantage has the basic elements of a proportional advantage; it clearly is not a straight-line advantage. A .600 team usually has a much larger difference between how well they play at home and how well they play on the road than does a .400 team.

Let us place this information into the context of an issue, in order to see what the difference is. Suppose that a .600 team is playing a .550 team. How often will the .600 team win? The Log5 method tells us that the .600 team will win 55.1% of the time.

Let us now assume that the game is being played at the home park of the .600 team. If we assumed that the home-field advantage was a straight-line advantage, then we would be dealing with a .650 team against a .500 team. The home team would probably win 65.0% of the time. Since we know that is is probably more like a proportional advantage, we are dealing with a .660 team against a .495 team. The home team will probably win about 66.5% of the time.

It is more *like* a proportional advantage; what it is exactly, we still don't know. Neither the straight-line assumption nor the proportional assumption can be perfectly true; there must be cases in which each is false. If you have a team which has a .960 won/lost percentage, it can have neither a proportional nor a direct 100-point home-field advantage. If they had a proportional home-field advantage, that would mean that they played 1.056 ball at home; a straight-line edge would mean 1.010 ball. A .960 ballclub cannot possibly have a 100-point home-field advantage; it must have an advantage that is smaller than that.

Of course, there are no .960 ball teams, but the fact that the method could not work if there were is still important, because it shows that the proportional representation of the home-field edge, while better than a straight-line representation, is still not exactly right. If it couldn't work for a .960 ballclub, you've got to wonder whether it *does* work for a .700 ballclub. In order for the line representing the home-field winning percentage to "bend in" so that it doesn't go over 1.000, it must *begin* to bend in at some point, a point probably short of .700. And there have been .700 ballclubs.

I keep thinking that there must be some very simple theoretical model that will get us out of this, that will explain how it is that the advantage increases up to a point and then stops. That's the basic reason for presenting all of this data, which is not going to be of any interest to 80% of the readers of the book; I keep thinking that if you graph that data, there has got to be some four-element formula which a) describes the line representing the actual data, and b) doesn't create theoretically impossible winning percentages for any team. But I keep turning it over and over in my head, and I just can't hit on it. I know I'll feel stupid when I finally do, because it can't be that difficult. Make Bill James feel stupid; figure it out.

3000-HIT CANDIDATES

According to *The Favorite Toy*, a method introduced in past editions of the *Baseball Abstract*, there are 45 major league players at this moment who have established at least a remote chance of getting 3000 hits in their careers. Three of those players stand out as having established particularly good shots at the mark; the other 42 are underdogs or long shots to one degree or another.

To recap the method very quickly, it assesses a player's chances of reaching a goal by asking three questions: how fast is he approaching the goal, how far away is he and how long does he have? In more precise terms, that means these questions: What level of performance in this category has the player established? What is his present career total? How old is he?

Eddie Murray is 27 years old, he has a career total of 1,175 hits, and he has established a level of performance at 175 (174.75) hits per season. The method considers these factors, and guesses his chances of getting 3000 hits at about 25%, a one-in-four shot.

We can sort the players who have a chance into three groups—young players who have shown promise as players who could post impressive career totals, players in their prime who could get to 3000 if they display unusual durability, and veteran players who have survived until late in their careers without eliminating their chances.

I. PLAYERS OF PROMISE

Eleven of the 45 players are in this group, and at this moment they are awfully hard to sort out one from another. The highest listed shot among players aged 25 or younger is given to Tim Raines of Montreal. Raines, just 23 years old, has had three straight good seasons in the major leagues, establishing a performance level of 175 hits. Without increasing his performance at all, Raines could easily cross 3000 hits before the age of 40. The odds against his doing so are 4–1.

Listed behind Raines, and perhaps belonging ahead of him, is Cal Ripken of Baltimore. The method assesses performance across a three-year period, though weighting their most recent year most heavily, and it doesn't see Ripken as having proven that he can get 200 hits a year, year-in and year-out. If Ripken does get 211 hits again this year, then it will see him that way, and Ripken's chances of getting 3000 hits will vault forward, all the way up to 35%. Until that happens, he's at 16%.

The complete chart of the young ones coming on looks like this:

Player	1983 Age	Established Hit Level	Career Hits	3000 Chance
1. Tim Raines	23	174.92	458	20%
2. Cal Ripken	22	159.42	374	16%
3. Rickey Henderson	24	156.42	703	15%
4. Rafael Ramirez	24	165.58	465	13%
5. Harold Baines	24	158.50	537	12%
6. Alan Trammell	25	147.75	811	11%
7. Steve Sax	23	155.75	388	11%
8. Lloyd Moseby	23	145.33	362	8%
9. Ryne Sanberg	23	140.08	328	4%
10. Wade Boggs	25	157.50	328	3%
11. Kent Hrbek	23	133.83	329	1%

Again, as you can see, established hit level does not mean the best that you've ever done; it means the level of performance that you have clearly established that you can meet. Henderson, Baines and Ramirez rank near the top of this list because they have been around long enough to have an up and a down, and let us get a full look at what they can do.

Wade Boggs has gotten a late start; he's 25, and 2,672 hits away. Toward a goal like 3000 hits, getting off to a good start is terrifically important. One might tend to think that at 210 hits a year he could catch up in a hurry, but the truth is that he *can't* catch up in a hurry at any performance level. If he beats Tim Raines by 30 hits a year, which doesn't figure to be all that easy, it would take him four years just to draw even with Raines in career totals, and then he would still be two years behind him in age. To draw even with Raines at the same age is something he could only do if 1) he gets about 240 hits a year or 2) Raines starts hanging out with the wrong crowd again. If he beats Alan Trammell by 50 hits a year it will take him ten years to catch him. Boggs could conceivably get to 3000 hits in his career, but he faces a long, long uphill battle. There are an awful lot of players who have hit better than .361 and not even come close to 3000 hits.

II. PLAYERS IN THEIR PRIME

The top of this group is, generally speaking, the best players in baseball today. These are proven, high-quality players, yet even so they are men who must, with one exception, display good or even unusual durability if they hope to get to 3000 hits.

The one exception is Robin Yount. Given his unusually early start, Robin has basically a 50–50 shot at 3000 hits, and that figure (49%) seems too conservative. He succeeds in raising his chances pretty much every year; a year ago I had him figured at 46%. He has crossed the halfway point in career hits now, with 1,541, and between now and age 40 he needs only to average 112 a year. That's far from a give-away; 1,459 hits is a lot of hits. If his career begins to go into an eclipse within the next three years, then he probably will not make it. If he stays at full strength until age 30, he's got it barring serious injury. Robin is also the only player in the majors except Pete Rose who has established a chance of getting 4000 hits in his career. That chance figures now, as it did a year ago, at 9%.

Behind him, coming out of a midcareer eclipse, is Jim Rice of Boston at 31%. Rice turned 31 this spring; he needs eight more very good seasons to make it. That's asking a lot, but he's a lot of hitter. With 1,620 hits, he has only a few more than Yount, and he's a couple of years older:

Player	1983 Age	Established Hit Level	Career Hits	3000 Chance
1. Robin Yount	27	184.75	1541	49%
2. Jim Rice	30	186.50	1620	31%
3. Eddie Murray	27	174.75	1175	25%
4. Andre Dawson	28	185.25	1167	23%
5. George Brett	30	154.58	1676	20%
6. Lou Whitaker	26	178.33	832	19%
7. Willie Wilson	27	177.42	956	18%
8. Paul Molitor	26	165.75	899	16%
9. Keith Hernandez	29	166.42	1315	15%
10. Dale Murphy	27	167.75	864	11%

Should Dale Murphy be higher? Probably not, no; he's Yount's age and has a long, long way to go to catch up, and as great as he is he's never been a 200-hit-a-year man or anything close to that. He'd have to maintain his peak hit production until he was 40 to make it. That seems unlikely.

Brett has more hits than Rice and is the same age, but his recurring injuries make it questionable that he can stretch the run out long enough to get 3000 hits.

After the top ten, you get into players who rack up a lot of hits early but then don't develop, or players who don't start having good years until it's too late, or players who would make it if they were good enough to play until they were 40 but probably aren't. These people are real long shots:

11. Claudell Washington	28	142.24	1226	8%
12. Larry Herndon	29	176.92	930	6%
13. Jerry Remy	30	168.33	1200	6%
14. Garry Templeton	27	130.83	1171	6%
15. Jack Clark	27	143.08	969	5%
16. Gary Carter	29	150.83	1190	5%
17. Damaso Garcia	26	157.92	578	5%
18. Pedro Guerrero	27	171.33	532	4%
19. Terry Puhl	26	134.33	918	4%
20. Mookie Wilson	27	169.58	469	2%
21. Terry Kennedy	27	162.08	536	1%
22. Omar Moreno	29	150.67	1051	1%

The odds are reasonably good that one of those players will come out of the pack in his thirties, as Al Oliver did, and make a serious run at the 3000-hit ring. Mostly they will wind up with 1500 or 2500 hits before they retire.

III. THE SURVIVORS

The final dozen players are the ones who have made it into their 30s without being wiped out. This is where the competition begins in earnest. It is the most volatile group of the three; a good year and these players can eat up a third or a fourth of the distance remaining, plus giving themselves the kind of momentum that reduces the distance even more. A bad year here, and the chase can be over; your chances can go from 40% to 0% in one giant step. A year ago, having just led the American League in home runs with 39 and needing only 36 more, Reggie Jackson seemed like a lead-pipe cinch to get 500 career home runs. Now, limping and needing a comeback just to stay in the major leagues, he is anything but a cinch. If you're hitting .299 on the last day of the season, in two hours your chances of hitting .300 are either going to be 100%, or they're going to be 0%. Same thing.

Rod Carew has been the man at the top of the charts since I began figuring this several years ago. His chances

were about 50/50 two years ago; now, he's in command, 97% sure. Al Oliver has been gaining steadily over those years, too, and he's about where Carew was two years ago. He still needs 450 hits, and he's 37. He's got a good shot; if he hits .300 this year he's about got it. but if he hits .260 this year, it's about over. Nobody wants a 38-year-old .260 hitter. So this is the year for Al Oliver.

Player	1983 Age	Established Hit Level	Career Hits	3000 Chance
1. Rod Carew	37	163.42	2832	97%
2. Al Oliver	36	192.50	2546	52%
3. Ted Simmons	33	161.33	2116	27%
4. Bill Buckner	33	187.25	1964	26%
5. Buddy Bell	31	165.00	1813	25%
6. Cecil Cooper	33	203.08	1639	13%
7. Dave Winfield	31	163.33	1568	12%
8. Steve Garvey	34	146.17	2082	7%
9. Chris Chambliss	33	138.00	1931	4%
10. Greg Luzinski	32	145.67	1697	4%
11. Bill Madlock	32	160.58	1557	3%
12. Gary Matthews	32	142.17	1663	1%

Ted Simmons is trying to become the first catcher ever to get to 3000; a year ago he was on the ropes, but he's back in the game now. Cecil Cooper got a late start, and the odds against him are still long. He's got to go on getting 200 hits a year until he's 40. Very few players have ever maintained a steady course of 160 hits a year beyond the age of 35.

Steve Garvey's chances may be rated too low, as the system overreacts to his injury; on the other hand, 918 hits are a lot of hits for a 35-year-old ballplayer. Is Chambliss's chance gone? No, I don't think so; he's already got over 1900 hits. He needs to show unusual durability, keep rolling on right about where he is for seven more years. I think there's about a 1 in 25 shot of that.

For the three groups of players, the expectation would be that about seven of them (Carew and six others) would eventually get to 3000 hits. History suggests that that is a reasonable estimate. Of the players active in 1969, seven subsequently got to 3000 hits, and Rod Carew will make it eight. This method is not inevitably right about who it is that's going to get there or how many are going to get there; that's not the purpose. The idea is to try to help you focus a little better on how the race to 3000 is going, to give you a sense of where each candidate stands with respect to the goal and what he must do to get there. I'm just trying, as always, to see things a little more clearly than other people will take the trouble to see them.

WHAT MAKES A SEASON?

What is it that makes a baseball season a good season or a not-so-good season or a great season? These are matters of personal tastes, not capable of objective analysis, but at the same time, our personal taste is probably a shared one to a large extent, and thus it might be useful to put it down on paper and see what it looks like. What is the one most important thing that makes a season memorable? What's the second most important thing? The third? Briefly:

The seventh most important thing in having a great baseball season: Having a great team to watch. Having a team like the 77-78 Yankees, the 75-76 Reds, the 72-74 A's, the 69-70 Orioles; it adds a lot to a season. A dominant team provides a frame of reference for every other team. It can be studied and examined from many angles, its weak points blown up and examined, its strength by historic standards debated. There is the pleasure of watching a team like that, tinged with the sadness of losing. But when your team does beat one of the great, then you feel like something has happened.

The sixth most important thing: Having something in baseball that is truly new, that can be seen with fresh eyes, watched over and worried over with no distracting backdrop of history. Significant new things come into baseball once or twice a decade, minor things more often. In the last twenty years we've had free agency, the DH Rule, artificial turf, expansion—all of which are good for baseball. Every year there's something—Game-Winning RBI, an Old-Timers All-Star Game or something. The split-season in '81 was new, in terms of human memory. Eagh.

The fifth most important thing, to me, would be the opportunity to see personal accomplishments or quests of some significance. Records broken, milestones reached, seasons of magnitude rung up. Some people might rate this category as high as #2, judging from the hype that surrounds events like Aaron's quest for Ruth's record, Brock's stolen-base record and McLain in '68. But none of it means that much to me. I wouldn't walk across the street to see Pete Rose get his four thousandth hit. I don't cheer for numbers.

The fourth most important thing, to me, is that a season have incidents or controversies provoking genuine public interest. The Tar Wars Game was a classic in this line; the class includes such diverse occurrences as Bob Forsch's first no-hitter and Lenny Randle punching out his manager. These things have a charm in that they occur spontaneously, always completely without warning; they have a right thing to do and a wrong thing to do, and people on both sides of the issue.

The third most important thing, and the other strong part of the 1983 season, is the emergence of new talent, new stars blazing toward impressive but as yet uncertain heights. Probably nothing else is as exciting before the first of September.

We are getting beyond the point of needing explanation. Number 2 is a quality round of postseason games; Number 1 is good pennant races, pennant races that have form and tension and retain a hold on the public imagination; pennant races that leave you, on into January, recounting a September game that could so easily have gone the other way.

Sounds a little mechanical? Well, I don't keep charts to see whether or not I'm enjoying the season. I enjoyed the 1983 season, but it certainly was not a memorable or brilliant season. We have no great teams; we have some that might be forming, which is about as exciting, but none that are great now, no teams which expose the weaknesses of their opponents just by walking onto the field. There was nothing to keep an eye on in 1983 that was totally new, nothing anyway of much significance. The major personal accomplishments of the season were probably Quisenberry's save record and the Carlton/Ryan all-time strikeout duel, but neither of those was exactly Roger Maris against the Bambino.

On four and three, we were in great shape, with the Tar Wars game, Dave Winfield vs. Jonathan Dead Seagull, and the emergence of three players into the "star of stars" class—Boggs, Ripken and Murphy. That comment might seem strange with respect to Murphy, since he was already an MVP. But there's an MVP every year. I wouldn't have thought it necessary, a year ago, to make a point-by-point comparison of him to Willie Mays. Ripken, the youngest MVP, seems to be on a line toward dizzying heights, and Wade Boggs could be the first career .355 hitter since Rogers Hornsby. Probably won't, of course.

But. The postseason play was terrible, the worst in years. With a couple of exceptions, the games were boring, one-thrust victories almost devoid of give and take. And none of the four pennant races amounted to much of anything.

Probably no season since 1962 has hit them all. 1982 was a great season, and it came at a moment when baseball needed a great season. 1983 had its points, and I am grateful for them.

DRUMBEATS

My sister Carol prefers not to read a book, particularly a novel or one of those pop sociology things that come and go, while it is "hot," or indeed for several years after it has *been* hot. She feels, with some reason, that it becomes difficult to see the book itself through the furor surrounding it, and thus that many of the books which enjoy a period of fashion and are praised by otherwise intelligent people will look perfectly silly if you let them set for a year before reading them. And if they are good, then they will seem even better after time, when they have reacquired the ability to surprise.

It must have been in this spirit that I picked up last summer a copy of a 1977 book by Bernard Gittleson. The book was *Biorhythm Sports Forecasting*. Please don't groan and go away; I promise to make this as painless as possible.

Mr. Gittleson's belief, in short, is that our lives are conducted according to a tune composed by three rhythms: a 23-day physical rhythm, a 28-day emotional cycle and a 33-day intellectual rhythm. These little buggers go into motion the day that you are born, and for the rest of your life they weave up and down patterns—one up and two down, then two up and one down—and occasionally they all come together for a thing called a triple high or a triple low. The physical cycle is "positive" for 10 days, "negative" for 11, and spends the remaining two crossing the tracks. Mr. Gittleson also implies strongly, through occasional disclaimers, that if you monitor closely enough who's got the positives and who's got the negatives and whose highs and lows are where, you can make a lot of money by betting on what people will do.

I find the thesis, frankly, to be lacking in immediate credibility. While other elements of the construct might be entirely reasonable, my problem has to do with this notion of an outsider's being able to pinpoint where the rhythms are at a given point in time, given only the birthdate of the subject. Take the physical cycle, for example. Suppose that, on June the 28th, 1987, just as you are entering an "up" physical cycle, you are involved in a car wreck and you lose gallons of blood, and your body is separated from one of its legs. The next morning, surely, is not going to be one of your better days, physically speaking?

Ah, but it will; if you're due for an "up" day, by God, you've got to have an up day. Because if you don't, you're going to screw up your charts for the rest of your life. And if your emotional life comes due for a chipper occasion on the day your wooden leg is delivered and your girlfriend tells you that she never thought she'd be so lucky but she's found a man with two good legs already—well then, you just whistle a happy tune and enjoy the experience.

And these cycles keep *time*, I'm telling you; 23 days, 28 days and 33 days, regular as clockwork. Because if one of you has a cycle that runs 28 days and 15 minutes, then you might as well save the price of Mr. Gittleson's book, because the whole deal is ruined. I mean, these are tenacious bastards; we're all living in a veritable prison, doomed to be on an emotional high every 28 days until we die. Whether we can get out of it then, I'm not sure.

And the truly amazing thing is, you've been doing this all your life, and *you never even noticed*. Every four weeks since you were born, no matter what was happening in your life, you woke up with a smile on your face and had to figure out a reason why it was there, and two weeks later you woke up sullen and morose, and yet somehow this inflexible biological drumbeat has escaped drawing your attention.

Anyway, this book in its day was not exactly obscure; *The Sporting News* gave Mr. Gittleson a big spread, and treated him most respectfully. So let us spend a little time here and examine the merits of his thesis, not on the basis of whether it seems to make any sense (many things which do not make sense are nonetheless true), but on the basis of whether it does tend to predict performance.

I decided to focus for this study on eleven players —eleven outstanding hitters. What I thought I would do is take a look at the days when all three of the cycles were in the same zone—all three positive or all three negative. This, it seems to me, is the very minimum that might be expected from the system: that a player perform somewhat better, on the average, when all of his functions are positive than he does when they are unanimously negative. A player would tend to be triple-positive about one day in eleven, I figured, so if we chose eleven players to study, we should have about a full season's worth of triple-positive performance and a season's worth of triple-negative performance to compare.

The eleven players chosen were Dale Murphy, Andre Dawson, Mike Schmidt, Eddie Murray, Dave Winfield, Lance Parrish, Cecil Cooper, Jim Rice, Greg Luzinski, Robin Yount, and George Brett. I wanted to get a reasonably consistent group of hitters, so I chose the people who figured to be around the league lead in slugging percentage.

Well, you probably guessed the punch line. Some of the players within the study did, indeed, perform much better when on a triple high than when on a triple low.

258

Dale Murphy, for example, was a kind of a triple-MVP when he was on a high, but a fairly ordinary player when his vital fluids were at low ebb:

Dale Murphy	G	AB	R	H	2B	3B	HR	RBI	SB	Avg.
+ + +	18	63	19	25	2	2	5	14	6	.397
– – –	19	81	11	22	2	2	3	13	1	.272

Mike Schmidt hit .273 when he was up, and only .177 when he was down, albeit an extraordinarily loud .177:

Mike Schmidt	G	AB	R	H	2B	3B	HR	RBI	SB	Avg.
+ + +	16	55	9	15	0	0	6	12	0	.273
– – –	18	62	14	11	0	0	6	16	0	.177

Cecil Cooper hit 97 points higher on his good days than on his bad days, Robin Yount 77 points higher, Lance Parrish 50 points higher and Dave Winfield 40 points higher:

	G	AB	R	H	2B	3B	HR	RBI	SB	Avg.
Cooper										
+ + +	12	47	11	18	4	0	3	10	0	.383
– – –	12	56	4	16	5	0	1	5	0	.286
Yount										
+ + +	12	39	6	13	8	0	0	8	0	.333
– – –	11	43	7	11	2	2	2	10	1	.256
Parrish										
+ + +	14	52	12	16	4	1	4	10	0	.308
– – –	17	62	10	16	5	0	2	13	0	.258
Winfield										
+ + +	17	69	9	17	1	0	1	10	1	.290
– – –	18	60	9	15	1	0	4	13	6	.250

And George Brett. All of the players played about the same number of games while upupup as they did while downdowndown except George, who played 20 games in positive cycles and only 7 while in negative cycles because he injured himself twice in the early parts of negative cycles. I am sure that Mr. Gittelson will find some use for this bit of knowledge:

George Brett	G	AB	R	H	2B	3B	HR	RBI	SB	Avg.
+ + +	20	79	14	27	6	0	6	18	0	.342
– – –	7	26	6	6	2	0	1	3	0	.231

And then, of course, the other shoe drops.

Jim Rice, while on his "up" cycles, hit a solid .340. Impressive, but when all of his cycles were telling him he should have stayed in bed he hit

Jim Rice	G	AB	R	H	2B	3B	HR	RBI	SB	Avg.
+ + +	13	50	10	17	5	0	2	11	0	.340
– – –	14	58	7	24	6	0	2	8	0	.414

four-fourteen. Andre Dawson could not recognize his rightful place in the Gittelson scheme of things, at all:

Dawson	G	AB	R	H	2B	3B	HR	RBI	SB	Avg.
+ + +	14	64	6	15	4	1	0	7	3	.234
– – –	14	58	9	22	5	1	2	10	0	.379

When his body, mind and spirit were all in ascendancy, Eddie Murray struggled along at a sub-Murray pace; when they were all against him, his bat didn't seem to mind. In 17 down games, Eddie scored 19 runs, drove in 22, and slugged .708:

Murray	G	AB	R	H	2B	3B	HR	RBI	SB	Avg.
+ + +	17	68	9	17	1	0	1	9	1	.250
– – –	17	65	19	23	4	2	5	22	0	.354

Greg Luzinski's average was higher when he was up, but he hit for far more power when he wasn't:

Luzinski	G	AB	R	H	2B	3B	HR	RBI	SB	Avg.
+ + +	18	61	6	15	4	0	2	8	0	.246
– – –	20	71	14	15	2	0	6	19	1	.211

If you add all the players together, this is what you get:

	G	AB	R	H	2B	3B	HR	RBI	SB	Avg.
+ + +	171	647	110	198	42	8	30	117	11	.306
– – –	167	642	110	181	34	7	34	132	9	.282

The cumulative batting average was higher in the good group than in the bad group, but on balance I scarcely think that this data would convince a skeptic.

A final note. One very strange thing did happen during this study, the sort of thing exactly that *should* happen when you are studying something like biorhythms. Jim Rice was beginning a triple-negative period on July 4. A player has three or four triple-negative periods during a year, and during the study I was always interested to see what would happen at the beginning of each one. The Red Sox were playing the Yankees on July 4. Rice went hitless. So did the Red Sox. Righetti threw a no-hitter.

Andre Dawson had a late-season triple-negative period beginning on September 26. The Expos were playing St. Louis on that day. And Bob Forsch threw a no-hitter.

Later in the week, Greg Luzinski began a triple-negative period. The White Sox were playing in Oakland. And Mike Warren was pitching.

There were three no-hitters in the 1983 season, and all three of them came on days when the big hitter in the opposition lineup was beginning a triple-negative period. And in choosing just eleven big hitters, we got them all in the study.

I only hope that Mr. Gittelson doesn't get wind of this.

POWER PITCHERS AND NIGHT GAMES

If you were a major league manager, and you were reading this book looking for something in it that might give you a tiny edge sometime during the season, this article would be the one thing in the 1984 edition to which you should pay the most careful attention.

A year ago, in analyzing the pitchers who had been most successful in Shea Stadium, I concluded that the evidence suggested that one of the defining characteristics of the park was its less-than-ideal lighting, and that the players best able to take advantage of this were power pitchers. This got me to wondering whether there was a more generalized connection between power pitchers and changing visibility conditions, and in particular, day games as opposed to night games. It is something that you do hear said once in a while—that this pitcher or that pitcher is going to be tough under the lights.

So when I got the American League statistics together in October, I looked through the listings to see whether I could discern any patterns with regard to day/night effectiveness. Tim Conroy of Oakland was 1–5 with a 5.71 ERA in day games, but had a winning record with a 3.34 ERA at night. Aurelio Lopez's ERA at night was less than half what it was in day games. Rick Sutcliffe, one of the better pitchers in the league, had a record in day games that suggested a man looking for an outright release. Floyd Bannister's ERA was 5.10 in day games, 2.61 at night. Dave Righetti was at 4.92 in day games, 2.96 at night. On the other hand, Mike Caldwell was 5–1, 3.83 ERA in day games, but lost 10 of 17 decisions and had 4.91 ERA at night. Scotty McGregor was 5–0 in day games, Mike Flanagan 4–1, Moose Haas 5–1 and Dan Quisenberry had a 0.69 ERA in 19 daylight appearances.

On that basis, one could make a prima facie case that power pitchers are most effective at night, and control pitchers most effective in the daytime. But this raises more questions than it answers. How large is the difference? How many pitchers are there whose records don't jump out at you, but who don't fit the pattern? If the pattern is real, how important is it? Is it consistent enough to be predictable, and thus exploitable?

The question, in short, warranted a systematic study. I decided to analyze the question by sorting American League pitchers into nine (9) "cells" according to their frequencies of strikeouts and walks per inning pitched. The divisions went this way:

- All pitchers who struck out at least .65 men per inning pitched were coded "A."
- Pitchers who struck out .451–.649 men per inning were coded "B."
- Pitchers who struck out .45 batters per inning or less were coded "C."
- Pitchers who walked .41 batters/inning or more were coded "1."
- Pitchers who walked .291–.409 batters/inning were coded "2."
- Pitchers who walked .29 batters/inning or less were coded "3."

A dedicated power pitcher, then—a man who had high ratios of both strikeouts and walks, a Nolan-Ryan-type—was coded "A1." A complete finesse pitcher, a man with low ratios in both categories, like McGregor or Quisenberry, was coded "C3." Like this:

A1	A2	A3
High Strikeouts High Walks	High Strikeouts Medium Walks	High Strikeouts Low Walks

B1	B2	B3
Medium Strikeouts High Walks	Medium Strikeouts Medium Walks	Medium Strikeouts Low Walks

C1	C2	C3
Low Strikeouts High Walks	Low Strikeouts Medium Walks	Low Strikeouts Low Walks

The most effective category of pitchers, not surprisingly, was that coded A3—high strikeout totals, few walks. This was also the smallest cell of the nine. The only Type A3 pitchers who pitched 50 or more innings were Bert Blyleven, Goose Gossage and Jack Morris. The least effective group, also not surprisingly, were in cell C1. The only pitcher among the 28 in this group who could be described as effective was Jim Slaton; others worthy of note included Wayne Gross and Joe Simpson.

The ERA breakdown for the nine cells is given below:

	1	2	3
A	4.52	3.60	3.43
B	4.74	3.98	4.05
C	5.08	4.15	3.70

The ERA breakdowns for the six code elements are as follows:

A	(High Strikeouts):	3.90
B	(Medium Strikeouts):	4.22
C	(Low Strikeouts):	4.07
1	(High Walks):	4.73
2	(Medium Walks):	3.90
3	(Low Walks):	3.75

The first thing that this data shows us is something which we probably already knew, but can see here again: walks are a lot more important than strikeouts. The ERA differences between the pitchers who strike out a lot of people and the pitchers who strike out very few people are small; the ERA differences between the pitchers who walk people and the pitchers who don't are large. It is a substantially accurate synopsis of the data to say that it shows that pitchers who issue a lot of walks have high ERAs, whether they get strikeouts or whether they don't, and pitchers who don't issue a lot of walks have good ERAs, whether they get strikeouts or whether they don't.

The other thing we should note is that the data in cell B3 is aberrant, and it is going to stay that way throughout the study. The cell consists of ten pitchers, two of them twenty-game winners (Guidry and Hoyt) and the others generally ineffective. But you get that in any study, unless you make the thing mammoth.

Anyway, from there on we look at the daytime and nighttime ERAs of the pitchers in each cell. If it is true that darkness favors a power pitcher, then we should find that the differences between the daytime and nighttime ERAs are highest at the top and left of the chart, near cell A1, and the lowest at the bottom and right, near cell C3.

Here's the data. Daytime ERAs are given on top; nighttime ERAs on the bottom.

	1	2	3
A	5.21	4.06	3.92
	4.26	3.40	3.20
B	5.01	3.82	4.78
	4.64	4.04	3.77
C	5.49	4.26	3.73
	4.86	4.10	3.69

Pitchers in all cells but one have better ERAs at night than in day games, showing that the impact of night baseball, which drove ERAs lower and lower and lower from 1938 through 1968, is still with us although it has been contained. But the ERA differential for the control-type pitchers in cell C3 is only four hundredths of a run; in cell C2 only sixteen hundredths. In cell A1 it is almost a full run!

Why the exclamation mark? Because among the percentages that we usually deal with in stat analysis, a run a game is a whale among minnows. Suppose Mike Schmidt is out of the lineup for a game. Mike Schmidt created 110 runs last year while playing in 154 games. While he's out, the guy you can probably replace him with should create about 60 runs in the same number of plate appearances—at least. That's not assuming you put Joe Lefebvre there. The difference—50 runs for 154 games, or .325 run per games—is a big thing, a large percentage. There aren't many percentages that impact on a decision that are that large. Getting a guy in the lineup against a pitcher that he can hit, resting the regular against a pitcher he can't hit—those decisions are made to gain 5/100 or 7/100 of a run most of the time.

What that means becomes clear when you place this information in the context of a decision that needs to be made. It is the middle of the week, and the manager is trying to line up his pitching plans for the weekend. He's got a game Friday night and a game Saturday afternoon. The ace of the staff, a veteran control pitcher, started Sunday and could go on four days on Friday, but there was no game Monday so nobody will be on normal rotation and ready for Saturday's game. Sometime during the homestand he wants to work in a start for the kid just up from the minors, a hard thrower with control problems—an A1 type of pitcher.

Now, a smart manager probably could find 40 variables in there by which to make the decision whether to start the kid on Friday night or Saturday afternoon. He could say, "Well, if I start him on Saturday, the other manager might rest a couple of his regulars [day game after a night game], so the kid might get a little easier lineup to wade through." Or he could say, "If I hold back the ace an extra day, that might delay his next start by a day and wind up costing him a start by the end of the year." Or he could say, "I'd like to match up my ace against his ace, so maybe I'll try to stall and see if he won't announce his pitchers first." Or he might feel that his #1 pitcher is more effective on four days rest than five, or vice versa.

But unless he was an unusual pitcher, it is very unlikely that starting the ace on four days rest instead of five or whatever would significantly alter his performance. But to gain a run on the pitcher's ERA—that's the equivalent of the opposition losing Mike Schmidt for the series. It is unlikely that any of the other differences would be large enough to hold much significance against a full-run difference in the probable effectiveness of the A1-type pitcher. And thus, in that decision, it is very probable that the difference between the power pitcher's effectiveness in the night game as opposed to the day game should be the dominant factor leading to the selection.

And besides the fact that you are cutting a run off the rookie's ERA, you are also, in one sense, using the ace of the staff in his most effective circumstance—the day game. The ERA of the control-type pitcher is not likely to be improved by moving to the day game—but his won/lost percentage is. If he allows about the same number of runs, but in a circumstance in which runs are more plentiful, then he is going to become a more successful pitcher. The ERA of the C3 pitchers was 3.73 in day games and 3.69 at night—but their won/lost percentage was .571 in day games and .541 at night. So you are really helping *both* pitchers by using the power pitcher at night and the control pitcher in the day game.

This leaves at least 3 questions that need to be answered:

(1) Could the study be wrong?
(2) What are the other differences between day games and night games that might help to explain this phenomena?
(3) Is this something that major league managers already know and already make use of, or is it an advantage that has not been utilized in the past?

Let's look at those.

1. *Could the study be wrong? Could it be overstating the advantage?*

Of course. You can always be wrong, even when you are basing a conclusion on three or four studies. One study of one league can be wrong in lots of ways.

But I wouldn't have written this article if I thought there was a large chance of that. The key to the study really is two cells—the A1 cell and the C3 cell. Both are large cells, showing consistent internal results. The A1 cell contains 33 pitchers, who threw over 1900 innings among them. Their won/lost record was 20–32 in day games, 81–77 in night games. The strongest internal influence on the cell is Rick Sutcliffe, whose ERA in day games was 4.45 higher than his ERA in night games. But if you throw out Sutcliffe, the records are 16–29 (.356) in day games and 68–69 (.496) at night. The strongest remaining influence on the cell is Conroy of Oakland. If you eliminate him, the group is 15–24 in the day games (.385) and 62–64 (.492) at night. The next strongest influence on the cell is Aurelio Lopez. But if you throw out Aurelio, the remaining pitchers are 12–21 (.364) in day games and 56–59 (.487) at night. So it's not a matter of two or three pitchers creating the appearance of an effect in the study.

On the other end, the C3 cell, we have 30 pitchers pitching over 3500 innings, 1034 in the day and 2503 at night. A differential should show up in that many innings if it was going to show up.

Further, the data from the rest of the chart suggests the same general conclusions. In the high-strikeout groups which do not have control problems (cells A2 and A3), the ERA differentials are .66 and .72. In the high-walk groups which do not have high strikeout totals, the differentials are .37 and .63. A differential of .95 in cell A1 is entirely consistent.

One thing I really miss by being in a nonacademic area of research is having people to check my work. If sabermetrics was an established science, if we had people employed throughout the country doing this sort of thing and journals in which they could publish their work, then as soon as I published this study, somebody else would try to replicate the results using a different data set (a different league, a different year, a different grouping pattern). I would like very much for that to be done, but I doubt that it will be.

2. *What are the other differences between day games and night games that could help to explain this phenomena?*

The batting average in American League day games in 1983 was .270; in night games it was .264. That difference is small but certainly significant. Ten of the 14 teams hit better in day games than in night games, and three AL teams hit between .289 and .296 in day games.
• The slugging percentage was off more than the batting average, .413 to .396.
• League runs per game were off at night from 4.71 to 4.39.

• Doubles in night games declined by 5%.
• Triples declined by 10%.
• Home runs declined by 9%.

Sacrifice hits, sacrifice flies, hit batsmen, stolen bases, caught stealing, and grounding into double plays all declined, oddly enough, by .01 (not 1%—one occurrence per 100 team games). Errors in night games were up by the same amount.

Most surprisingly, strikeouts did *not* increase in night games; they too declined, from 4.89 per game to 4.81. Walks declined from 3.19 in day games to 3.10 at night. The strikeout-to-walk ratio, thus, was slightly more favorable to the pitcher at night, 1.55–1 as opposed to 1.53–1.

One difference that might contribute to some extent to the power pitcher's decreased effectiveness in the daytime is stamina. There clearly is a difference in this area. Starting pitchers completed 22% of their nighttime starts in the American League, but only 19% in the daytime, and more pitchers per game were used in the daytime (4.98–4.84). The control pitcher, who throws many fewer pitches in a game than a power pitcher, would seem likely to benefit whenever stamina was at issue.

The first few points in this section suggest that either the ball does not travel as well at night as it does in the day, or else there are significantly fewer hard-hit balls in a night game than there are in a day game. Apart from that, one would be hard-pressed to interpret this data in such a way that it sufficiently explains the phenomenon in question.

3. *Are major league managers already making use of this knowledge?*

No, they are not. At least not to any significant degree.

Twenty-nine per cent of American League games in 1983 were day games. The pitchers in group A1 made 29% of their starts in day games, and the pitchers in group C3 made 29% of their starts in day games. There was a small difference in innings pitched—pitchers in group A1 threw only 27% of their innings in the daylight—but that seems most likely to have been a direct result of their decreased effectiveness (they just didn't stay in the game as long).

And that is the potential value of sabermetrics to a major league team. Every major league manager has probably heard the thought expressed that power pitchers are most effective when the lighting is least effective; we've known that since Vander Meer. But without studying the issue from the outside, without stepping back and measuring it, how could he ever know how to evaluate the theory, how much weight to put on it? He can't know that, and so he can't use the knowledge. And I'll tell you for sure, Don Zimmer ain't going to take the time to look up no pitchers in cell C3 and figure out what happens to them. But other things being equal, a manager who has respect for knowledge is going to beat the crap out of a manager who doesn't. And that's why sabermetrics is an inevitable part of baseball's future.

A REACTION FROM CRAIG WRIGHT

I have a subjective conviction that the dominant cause for all the relationships noted is that the poorer visibility attributed to artificial light reduces the amount of time a hitter has to react to a fastball.

The hitter's weakness at night is the fastball. Everyone *looks* faster at night. The fastball is *the* major league pitch, and it is only natural that scoring overall should decline at night. In the daylight the fastball becomes less important because it is less effective, while changing speeds and pitch-types and locations gains importance and relative effectiveness.

This isn't to say there are no other theories that could explain the overall drop in ERAs at night for all pitchers as a group and significantly large drops for power pitchers lacking control. One of my favorites is that homo sapiens are diurnal animals biologically geared to perform better in the day than the night. It is more difficult to perform a complex highly skilled feat such as hitting a baseball at night than it is to perform the relatively easier task of pitching a baseball. And it would be easier to pitch as an A3 pitcher where you just throw as hard as you can and who cares where it goes.

Now do I believe that theory? Hell, no. But I like the creativity.

BIRTHDAY STUDY

The birthday boys did not repeat their glorious showing of 1982:

	G	AB	R	H	2B	3B	HR	RBI	SB	AVG.
1982	89	285	59	96	17	6	12	48	13	.337
1983	100	345	41	87	19	1	5	36	4	.252

The birthday wonder of the past, Phil Garner, went zero for three and made an error as the Astros lost to the Phillies. In fact, teams having a birthday celebrant in their lineups had a combined 47–52 (one tie) record. The best birthday showing was by the second oldest man in the study, Joe Morgan, who celebrated his day with 4 hits, including two homers and a double, four RBI and the game winning hit. The oldest player in the study, Yaz, also had a gamer on his birthday. There were seven game-winning hits in the study. There were also three games in 1983 in which both teams boasted a birthday man. On May 13, the Twins with Lenny Faedo going 3 for 5 with a double and the gamer beat the Angels with Juan Beniquez giving a zero for five showing. On June 15, Lance Parrish was 2 for 4 with a homer as the Tigers downed the Red Sox with Wade Boggs tripling in four at-bats. July 12 saw the Mariners' Bryan Clark throw a strong 7 1/3 innings to beat the Red Sox, whose Tony Armas was going zero for 4.

The 1983 *Abstract* suggested that it might not be a bad idea for gamblers to keep a list of pitcher's birthdays around. Nobody said anything about mortgaging homes to bet on these men, though, and hopefully, nobody did, because birthday pitchers were routinely awful.

W	L	ERA	IP	H	SV
4	11	4.22	91.2	99	2

Starters were the main cause for the high ERA as the breakdown shows:

	W	L	ERA	IP	H	SV
Starters	3	8	4.52	69.2	78	–
Relievers	1	3	3.27	22	21	2

After five wins, Pascual Perez got bombed for his first loss of the season on his birthday. Mike LaCoss, Steve Trout, Dave Rozema, Bob McClure and Bert Blyleven were all roughed up, too, with only Trout lasting into the sixth inning. The Phillies gave Tug McGraw a rare start on his birthday and he was tagged for three runs in three innings.

On the positive side, Floyd Bannister had his first outstanding outing of the year on his birthday. (10 innings, 4 hits, no decision). Pete Filson and Eric Show pitched shutout ball for 7 1/3 and 6 innings respectively before being removed. Tippy Martinez (save), Ben Hayes (win), Jeff Reardon and Joey McLaughlin were superb in relief. Of course, their appearances weren't scheduled.

—Jim Baker

ON BEING A DICK SMITH

If there are any young men named Dick Smith out there who are entertaining notions of a career in the big leagues, some advice: either effect a name change now or plan a reevaluation of your career goals. Dick Smith, you see, is not a name steeped in baseball glory. In fact, the three men who have worn that monicker and played major league baseball have done, well, rather poorly. With history as our guide, we know that a baseball Dick Smith makes the big leagues at age 24, pokes a few singles, and is soon gone from the scene. The record:

THE COMPOSITE DICK SMITH

Career Years	G	AB	H	2B	3B	HR	R	RBI	BB	SO	SB	Avg.
9 years 1951-69	167	356	59	8	4	0	37	18	40	71	9	.166

Not the kind of tradition that I'd want to be born into.

Dick Smiths also seem to have an attraction for bad teams—really bad teams. DS I was a proud member of the legendary '52 Pirates, contributing a .106 batting average to their 42–112 effort. DS II was on both the '63 and '64 Mets. They lost 210 games in his presence. DS III managed to avoid the trap but only by the narrowest of margins. He played for the decent '69 Senators who were bracketed by a miserable '68 team and the doomed club of 1970. DS II managed to hit over .200 twice, but the rest of the Dick Smith seasons were of the sub-.200 variety. Coming off the bench in a pinch, Dick Smiths had 2 hits in 26 tries. Parents, don't play with fate. Do what Mrs. Aikens did and name your boy after somebody good. It certainly can't hurt.

—Jim Baker

SPECIALIST AWARDS

What baseball could use are more awards for specialists. At the present time, only one comes to mind (the Rolaids award for relievers). It's time big business got both feet into rewarding baseball's supporting characters. Think of the possibilities: American Motors, makers of the Jeep Scout, would award the Scout of the Year. A calculator and computer company would be a natural for Most Valuable Team Statistician..Pinch brand scotch can hand out a pinch-hitter plaque. An airline could give a Journeyman of the Season trophy. The combinations are endless.

Scott's Grass Seed would be a natural for the best groundskeeper award, unless a chemical company wanted to bestow one on the keeper of an artificial surface. The gentleman at San Diego would not be in line for this one. Toward the end of the season, Jack Murphy looked as though some kids had built a mini-bike trail in the outfield. Makes you kind of wonder why George Toma remains turf-bound at Royals Stadium. Allegedly baseball's finest groundsman, employing him at a turf park is like having Leonardo da Vinci over to paint your house basic white. The Royals have the best-kept nonplaying area in the game. I suppose they have to pay him to do something.

—Jim Baker

ON SABR AND SABERMETRICS

The Society for American Baseball Research has very little to do with sabermetrics. The two things are not intimately connected. SABR is an organization of some 4600 members at last count, perhaps half or a third of whom are very interested in the analysis of the game and its records, the rest of whom are interested in baseball history, or biographic research, or something else.

The mis-identification of SABR and sabermetrics has been an unfortunate side effect of using the word to describe what I do for a living. There is an unmistakeable need for a term of reference to the work as a whole; no one could write about it very long without sensing that need, a need so strong that John Thorn in *The Hidden Game* was driven to the absurd alternative of describing it as "The New Statistics." I think that some people in SABR think that I have given the public a mistaken idea of who they are and what they are doing, and that's probably true, and resent it. I have no defense, but you must understand that at the time I began using the term, I had no idea that this whole thing would get as large as it has. I thought I was writing to a few hundred people who were interested in the subject, most of them already SABR members; it turned out that the audience was much larger than I thought.

The Society for American Baseball Research, anyway, is a loose association of a few thousand die-hard baseball fans, para-professionals, writers and researchers of various stripes. There are no qualifications for membership other than a desire to memb. There is an annual convention which I attend once in awhile; there are always people there that I enjoy meeting and talking with, although as with any convention you do have to spend half or two-thirds of the weekend trying to find them. There are committees—a committee on the Minor Leagues, a committee on statsanalysis, a committee on ballparks. Some of these committees are well organized and do something; others are not and do not.

The best reason to join SABR is the publications. When you join SABR you automatically receive the annual *Baseball Research Journal*, a compendium of pieces of investigation into all kinds of baseball side topics—I would list some quick topics except that I'm afraid people would think I was trivializing their work—plus the "National Pastime," which is kind of an irregular magazine for baseball nuts, an annual directory which puts you in touch with the other 4,599 people in the organization, an occasional book containing the batting records of great hitting pitchers or minor league stars or something, and a regular newsletter that keeps you up on things being done by the group and its members.

I find it all to be worth the $20 a year, and I think many of you would too. At the same time, one must acknowledge that the organization doesn't have a real clear idea of what it is or where it is going. It is an organization of "researchers," but many or most of its members do no research, and those who do often do things so unlike and unrelated that it would be difficult to find any commonality of interest among us. The organization has been evolving constantly since I joined in 1975. Its' publications have become much more professional. The organization doubles in size every few years, and I expect that it will do so several more times; inevitably, smaller, better-defined side organizations are going to spin out of it.

If you are interested in joining, write to Clifford Kachline, SABR, P.O. Box 1010, Cooperstown, New York, 13326.

LEADING HITTERS AGAINST RIGHTHANDED PITCHING
(Minimum 200 at-bats)
AMERICAN LEAGUE

Player, Team	AB	Run	Hit	2B	3B	HR	RBI	SB	Avg
Boggs, Boston	397	82	158	36	6	4	43	0	.398
Carew, California	310	47	111	19	1	1	30	4	.358
Brett, Kansas City	304	63	106	30	2	19	71	0	.349
Aikens, Kansas City	325	44	107	22	1	22	65	0	.329
Hatcher, Minnesota	225	31	74	8	1	4	23	1	.329
S. Henderson, Seattle	236	25	74	16	3	5	27	6	.314
Hrbek, Minnesota	371	54	114	33	4	10	55	4	.307
Baines, Chicago	401	61	122	23	1	17	77	3	.304
Putnam, Seattle	336	51	102	17	2	17	51	2	.304
Rivers, Texas	281	36	84	16	0	1	20	9	.299

NATIONAL LEAGUE

Player, Team	AB	Run	Hit	2B	3B	HR	RBI	SB	Avg
Lefebvre, Phil	208		71			8	38		.341
Oliver, Montreal	440		147						.334
Herr, St. Louis	225		75			2	26		.333
Gwynn, San Diego	239		79						.331
Puhl, Houston	239		79						.331
J. Cruz, Houston	414		134			12	67		.324
L. Smith, St. Louis	346		112			6	35		.324
Murphy, Atlanta	426		137	16	1	31	100		.322
Hall, Chicago	340		108	23	5	17	51	5	.318
Oberkfell, St. Louis	391		124			3	27		.317

LEADING HITTERS AGAINST LEFTHANDED PITCHING
(Minimum 100 at-bats)
AMERICAN LEAGUE

Player, Team	AB	Run	Hit	2B	3B	HR	RBI	SB	Avg
Baylor, New York	249	39	89	18	2	13	47	7	.357
Bonnell, Toronto	186	24	66	12	2	6	22	4	.355
Herndon, Detroit	201	37	71	12	2	11	43	4	.353
Trammell, Detroit	169	29	58	11	0	3	22	5	.343
McRae, Kansas City	191	29	65	20	2	5	31	3	.340
Paciorek, Chicago	194	35	66	11	2	5	21	4	.340
Cabell, Detroit	171	30	57	9	1	3	16	1	.333
Slaught, Kansas City	117	10	39	6	2	0	12	1	.333
Rice, Boston	169	20	56	8	1	10	31	0	.331
Castino, Minnesota	170	28	56	11	2	3	24	2	.329

NATIONAL LEAGUE

Player, Team	AB	Run	Hit	2B	3B	HR	RBI	SB	Avg
Moreland, Chicago	135	27	52	7	2	7	22		.385
Madlock, Pittsburgh	122		45			6	18		.369
R. Ramirez, Atlanta	159		57	7	2	3	18		.358
Hendrick, St. Louis	162		57			6	74		.352
Garvey, San Diego	100		35						.350
Dawson, Montreal	159		55						.346
Lacy, Pittsburgh	149		50			3	9		.336
Youngblood, San Francisco	144		48	9	1	8	25		.333
Leonard, San Francisco	161		52	5	0	11	30		.323
Thon, Houston	189		61			7	64		.323

LEADING HITTERS ON ARTIFICIAL TURF
(Minimum 75 at-bats)
AMERICAN LEAGUE

Player, Team	G	AB	Run	Hit	2B	3B	HR	RBI	SB	Avg
Trammell, Detroit	23	84	19	35	12	1	3	14	7	.417
Carew, California	21	85	10	35	3	0	0	4	0	.412
Singleton, Baltimore	22	75	12	30	6	0	5	21	0	.400
Yount, Milwaukee	22	82	12	30	5	3	3	16	0	.366
Davis, Kansas City	22	81	11	29	2	6	1	14	2	.358
Gantner, Milwaukee	25	98	17	34	7	3	3	13	1	.347
Davis, Oakland	24	101	16	35	33	2	5	16	6	.347
Boggs, Boston	23	87	19	30	4	1	1	15	1	.345
Garcia, Toronto	85	342	53	117	20	6	1	26	23	.342
Rice, Boston	23	88	17	30	2	1	10	22	0	.341

NATIONAL LEAGUE

Player, Team	G	AB	Run	Hit	2B	3B	HR	RBI	SB	Avg
Herr, St. Louis	109	400	52	128	24	3	14	77	2	.346
Easler, Pittsburgh	81	274	32	93	14	1	6	34	3	.339
Maddox, Philadelphia	70	231	19	77	13	2	2	28	5	.333
Madlock, Pittsburgh	98	357	50	119	18	0	10	59	2	.333
Hendrick, St. Louis	60	211	31	73	8	3	1	24	4	.326
J. Cruz, Houston	113	409	48	130	19	6	9	64	24	.318
Lefebvre, Philadelphia	81	199	29	63	15	8	6	27	3	.317
L. Smith, St. Louis	96	363	60	115	25	5	5	34	36	.317
Landreaux, L.A.	37	134	18	42	9	2	1	22	9	.313
Ramirez, Atlanta	42	170	23	53	4	0	4	12	9	.312

LEADING HITTERS ON NATURAL GRASS
(Minimum 100 at-bats)
AMERICAN LEAGUE

Player, Team	G	AB	Run	Hit	2B	3B	HR	RBI	SB	Avg
Boggs, Boston	130	495	81	180	40	6	4	59	2	.364
Slaught, Kansas City	36	118	5	39	4	2	0	10	2	.331
Carew, California	108	387	56	125	21	2	2	40	6	.323
S. Henderson, Seattle	49	184	21	58	15	1	2	19	4	.315
Paciorek, Chicago	100	362	61	111	27	3	8	55	4	.307
Beniquez, California	80	278	37	85	12	0	3	28	4	.306
Engle, Minnesota	48	158	23	48	8	1	4	13	2	.304
Brett, Kansas City	36	217	37	65	17	0	12	41	0	.300
Lansford, Oakland	67	246	32	73	12	1	7	34	3	.297
Hatcher, Minnesota	41	142	17	42	6	1	1	13	0	.296

NATIONAL LEAGUE

Player, Team	G	AB	Run	Hit	2B	3B	HR	RBI	SB	Avg
Knight, Houston	45	160	18	60	8	1	5	27	0	.375
Dawson, Montreal	42	171	32	58	11	5	9	36	3	.339
L. Smith, St. Louis	34	129	23	43	6	0	3	11	7	.333
Green, St. Louis	36	106	16	35	4	0	3	24	7	.330
Gwynn, San Diego	65	231	26	74	12	2	0	31	5	.320
J. Cruz, Houston	47	185	27	59	9	2	5	28	6	.319
Murphy, Atlanta	119	435	105	136	19	4	30	97	15	.313
Horner, Atlanta	75	292	56	91	21	1	14	47	1	.312
Moreland, Chicago	110	380	56	118	25	2	11	53	0	.311
Hendrick, St. Louis	35	129	21	40	9	0	4	20	2	.310

STARTING PITCHERS RECEIVING BEST OFFENSIVE SUPPORT
(Based on the number of runs scored in games the pitcher has started.)
American League

Pitcher, Team	Starts	Runs	Runs Per Start
Rich Dotson, Chicago	35	206	5.89
Scott McGregor, Baltimore	36	195	5.42
Dan Petry, Detroit	38	205	5.39
LaMarr Hoyt, Chicago	36	193	5.36
Storm Davis, Baltimore	29	154	5.31
Ken Forsch, California	31	164	5.29
Bud Black, Kansas City	24	125	5.21
Mike Flanagan, Baltimore	20	104	5.20
Dave Righetti, New York	31	160	5.16
Luis Leal, Toronto	35	179	5.11

National League

Pitcher, Team	Starts	Runs	Runs Per Start
Charles Hudson, Philadelphia	26	132	5.08
Mark Davis, San Francisco	20	100	5.00
Dick Ruthven, Chicago	32	159	4.97
Fernando Valenzuela, Los Angeles	35	169	4.83
Mike Scott, Houston	24	115	4.79
Craig McMurtry, Atlanta	35	167	4.77
Mike Krukow, San Francisco	31	147	4.74
Bill Gullickson, Montreal	34	158	4.65
John Denny, Philadelphia	36	165	4.58
Burt Hooton, Los Angeles	27	123	4.56

STARTING PITCHERS RECEIVING WORST OFFENSIVE SUPPORT
American League

Pitcher, Team	Starts	Runs	Runs Per Start
Bob Stoddard, Seattle	23	74	3.22
Matt Young, Seattle	31	100	3.23
Jim Beattie, Seattle	29	99	3.41
Frank Tanana, Texas	22	78	3.55
Britt Burns, Chicago	26	93	3.58
Larry Gura, Kansas City	31	112	3.61
Steve McCatty, Oakland	24	89	3.71
Bert Blyleven, Cleveland	24	91	3.79
Dennis Eckersley, Boston	28	106	3.79
Mike Moore, Seattle	21	82	3.90

National League

Pitcher, Team	Starts	Runs	Runs Per Start
Joe Price, Cincinnati	21	60	2.86
Bob Welch, Los Angeles	31	99	3.19
Walt Terrell, New York	20	64	3.20
Mike Torrez, New York	34	113	3.32
Bob Knepper, Houston	29	101	3.48
Atlee Hammaker, San Francisco	23	81	3.52
Mario Soto, Cincinnati	34	122	3.59
Tom Seaver, New York	34	123	3.62
Alejandro Pena, Los Angeles	26	95	3.65
Mike Krukow, San Francisco	31	147	3.72

TOUGHEST STARTING PITCHERS TO RUN ON
(Based on the number of bases stolen by the opposition in this pitcher's starts.)
American League

Pitcher, Team	Starts	OSB	OSB Per Start
Tommy John, California	34	7	.21
LaMarr Hoyt, Chicago	36	8	.22
Geoff Zahn, California	28	7	.25
Shane Rawley, New York	33	9	.27
Rick Honeycutt, Texas	25	7	.28
Milt Wilcox, Detroit	26	8	.31
Frank Viola, Minnesota	34	11	.32
Jim Clancy, Toronto	34	11	.32
Len Barker, Cleveland	24	8	.33
Bud Black, Kansas City	24	8	.33

National League

Pitcher, Team	Starts	OSB	OSB Per Start
Bob Welch, Los Angeles	31	13	.42
Ed Lynch, New York	27	12	.44
Jerry Reuss, Los Angeles	31	15	.48
John Denny, Philadelphia	36	18	.50
Mark Davis, San Francisco	20	10	.50
Dave LaPoint, St. Louis	29	15	.52
Lee Tunnell, Pittsburgh	25	13	.52
Larry McWilliams, Pittsburgh	35	21	.60
Atlee Hammaker, San Francisco	23	14	.61
Frank Pastore, Cincinnati	29	18	.62

EASIEST STARTING PITCHERS TO RUN ON
American League

Pitcher, Team	Starts	OSB	OSB Per Start
Al Williams, Minnesota	29	36	1.24
Mike Moore, Seattle	21	22	1.05
Dennis Martinez, Baltimore	25	25	1.00
Bruce Hurst, Boston	32	30	.94
Mike Smithson, Texas	33	30	.91
Richard Dotson, Chicago	35	31	.89
Bob Ojeda, Boston	28	25	.89
John Tudor, Boston	34	30	.88
Tim Stoddard, Seattle	23	21	.91
Dave Righetti, New York	31	26	.84

National League

Pitcher, Team	Starts	OSB	OSB Per Start
Tom Seaver, New York	34	56	1.65
Charles Puleo, Cincinnati	24	35	1.46
Joe Niekro, Houston	38	51	1.34
Mike Torrez, New York	34	44	1.29
Charles Hudson, Philadelphia	26	33	1.27
Bob Knepper, Houston	29	35	1.21
Mike Krukow, San Francisco	31	37	1.19
Phil Niekro, Atlanta	33	37	1.12
Bill Laskey, San Francisco	25	27	1.08
Mike Scott, Houston	24	26	1.08

BEST DOUBLE-PLAY SUPPORT
American League

Pitcher, Team	Starts	DPs	DPs Per Start
Tommy John, California	34	53	1.56
Rick Honeycutt, Texas	25	36	1.44
Richard Dotson, Chicago	35	50	1.43
Dan Petry, Detroit	38	53	1.39
Paul Splittorff, Kansas City	27	34	1.26
Bob Stoddard, Seattle	23	29	1.26
Bruce Hurst, Boston	32	40	1.25
Bud Black, Kansas City	24	30	1.25
Dave Righetti, New York	31	38	1.23
Bert Blyleven, Cleveland	24	28	1.17

National League

Pitcher, Team	Starts	DPs	DPs Per Start
Lee Tunnell, Pittsburgh	25	35	1.40
Ed Lynch, New York	27	37	1.37
Dave LaPoint, St. Louis	29	37	1.28
Craig McMurtry, Atlanta	35	43	1.23
Chuck Rainey, Chicago	34	41	1.21
Ferguson Jenkins, Chicago	29	34	1.17
Bob Knepper, Houston	29	32	1.10
Pascual Perez, Atlanta	33	36	1.09
Phil Niekro, Atlanta	33	36	1.09
Mike Scott, Houston	24	26	1.08

LEAST DOUBLE-PLAY SUPPORT
American League

Pitcher, Team	Starts	DPs	DPs Per Start
Dennis Eckersley, Boston	28	13	.46
Danny Darwin, Texas	26	14	.54
Britt Burns, Chicago	26	17	.65
Jack Morris, Detroit	37	24	.65
Juan Berenguer, Detroit	19	13	.68
Mike Boddicker, Baltimore	26	19	.73
Ken Schrom, Minnesota	28	21	.75
Jerry Koosman, Chicago	24	18	.75
Charlie Hough, Texas	33	25	.76
Mike Moore, Seattle	21	16	.76

National League

Pitcher, Team	Starts	DPs	DPs Per Start
Mike Krukow, San Francisco	31	11	.35
Mario Soto, Cincinnati	34	17	.50
Fred Breining, San Francisco	32	17	.53
Joe Price, Cincinnati	21	12	.57
Charles Hudson, Philadelphia	26	16	.62
Tim Lollar, San Diego	30	19	.63
Burt Hooton, Los Angeles	27	17	.63
Ed Whitson, San Diego	21	14	.67
Eric Show, San Diego	33	22	.67
Bill Gullickson, Montreal	34	24	.71

SECTION

V

NOT OF ANY GENERAL INTEREST

1. Basic Runs Created Formula:

$$\frac{\text{(Hits + Walks − Caught Stealing)} \times}{\text{(Total Bases + .55 Stolen Bases)}}$$
$$\text{At Bats + Walks}$$

2. Isolated Power is simply slugging percentage minus batting average.

3. Defensive Efficiency Record (DER)

To figure DER, you begin by making two estimates of the number of times that a team's defense has turned a batted ball into an out. The first is:

$$\text{PO − K − DP − 2(TP) − OCS − A (of)}$$

This assumes that a batted ball has been turned into an out every time a putout is recorded unless (1) the putout was strikeout, (2) two or three putouts were recorded on the same play, or (3) a runner has been thrown out on the bases (OCS is Opponent's Caught Stealing and A (of) is outfielder's assists). The second is:

$$\text{BFP − K − H − W − HBP − .71 Errors}$$

This assumes that a batted ball has been turned into an out every time a batter faces the pitcher unless (1) the batter strikes out, (2) he hits safely, (3) he walks, (4) he is hit by the pitch, or (5) he reaches base on an error.

These two estimates are rarely identical, but I've been figuring them for years and I've never yet seen a case where they differed by more than 1%. This exact formula is new, but it's just a small step forward from the one I have been using since 1976; it's basically the same.

We then take the average of the two, whch we call Plays Made (PM). DER is Plays Made divided by Plays Made plus Plays NOT Made:

$$\frac{\text{PM}}{\text{PM + H − HR + .71 Errors}}$$

I should also point out that while the differences derived may look small, they are anything but. DER is similar to the complement of batting average. The effect of having a DER which is .020 below the league average would be very similar to the effect of having a team batting average which is .017 to .018 below league, which is to say that it would wipe you out of a pennant race 99% of the time.

4. The Favorite Toy.

Category = stoves (hits, walks, stolen bases, home runs, whatever)
Need Stoves = Number of stoves needed to reach goal
Years Remaining = A number of years remaining to the player, assigned by his age by the formula: $24 - .6(\text{age})$
Established Stove Level = The number of stoves per years that the player has shown the ability to gather.
Projected Remaining Stoves = Years remaining times established stove level.
Chances of reaching Goal:

$$\frac{\text{Need Stoves − .5(Projected Remaining Stoves)}}{\text{Need Stoves}}$$

With, however, these limitations:

1) A player's chances of continuing to progress toward a goal cannot exceed .97 per year.
2) If a player's offensive won/lost percentage is below .500, his chance of continuing toward a goal cannot exceed .75 per season.

5. Value Approximation Method.

The Value Approximation Method has 13 rules for nonpitchers, 5 for pitchers. These are:

NON-PITCHERS:

1) Award 1 point if the player has played at least 10 games, 2 if 50, 3 if 100 or more, 4 if 130 or more.
2) Award 1 point if the player has hit .250 or more, 2 if .275 or more, 3 if .300 or more . . . 7 if .400 or more.
3) Award 1 point if the player's slugging percentage is above .300, 2 if above .400, 3 if above .500 . . . 6 if above .800.
4) Award 1 point if the player has a HR% (HR/AB) of 2.5 or more, 2 if 5.0 or more, 3 if 7.5 or more, 4 if 10.0 or more.
5) Award 1 point if the player walks 1 time for each 10 official at-bats, 2 if 2 times for each 10 AB, 3 if 3 times for each 10 AB.
6) Award 1 point if the player steals 20 bases, 2 if 50, 8 if 80.
7) Award 1 point if the player drives in 70 runs while slugging less than .400, 1 point if he drives in 100 while slugging less than .500, or 1 if he drives in 130 while slugging less than .600.
8) Award 1 point if the player's primary defensive position is second base, third base or centerfield, 2 if it is shortstop. For

catchers, award 1 point if the player catches 10 games, 2 if he catches 80, 3 if he catches 150.

9) Award 1 point if the player's range factor is above the league average at his position. Catchers and first basemen have no range factors; first basemen get 1 point if they have 100 assists or more.

10) Award 1 point if the player's fielding average is above the league average at his position.

(On points 9 and 10, if you are figuring a player over the course of his career, you will probably wish to establish period norms for range factor and fielding range rather than trying to figure the league average in each separate year.)

11) Award 1 point to a shortstop or second baseman who participates in 90 or more double plays, two for 120 or more double plays and three for 150 or more double plays. Award 1 point to an outfielder who has 12 or more assists plus double plays. Award 1 to a catcher who is better than the league average in opposition stolen-base rate.

12) Award 1 point if the player has 200 hits. Award 1 point if the player leads the league in RBI.

13) Reduce all points awarded on rules 1 through 12 for players who have less than 500 at-bats and less than 550 at-bats plus walks. Reduce by the formula at-bats/500 or (at-bats plus walks)/550, whichever is larger for the player.

When figuring career value approximations, ignore rules 7 through 12. For defensive players, instead assign a verbal description to the player's defensive ability, and read his AV for the season off the chart below:

Position Description	1B	LF	RF	3B	CF	2B	C	SS
Outstanding	2.50	3.00	3.00	3.00	4.00	4.50	5.00	5.00
Excellent	2.30	2.75	2.75	3.00	3.50	4.00	4.50	4.50
Very Good	2.10	2.50	2.75	2.75	3.25	3.50	4.00	4.00
Good	2.00	2.50	2.50	2.75	3.00	3.20	3.50	3.50
Above Average	1.80	2.25	2.50	2.50	3.00	3.00	3.25	3.25
Solid	1.50	2.00	2.25	2.50	2.50	3.00	3.00	3.00
Average	1.25	2.00	2.00	2.25	2.50	2.50	3.00	3.00
Below Average	1.00	1.76	1.75	2.00	2.00	2.25	2.50	2.50
Poor	0.75	1.50	1.50	1.75	1.75	2.00	2.25	2.25
Bad	0.40	1.40	1.25	1.50	1.50	2.00	2.00	2.00
The Worst Ever	0.00	0.50	0.75	1.00	1.00	1.50	2.00	2.00

PITCHERS

1) Award 1 point if the pitcher has pitched in 30 or more games, 2 if 55 or more games, 3 if 80 or more.

2) Award 1 point if the pitcher has pitched 40 innings, 2 if 90 innings, 3 if 140 . . . 7 if 340 innings.

3) Figure for the pitcher his total of 2 (wins plus saves) minus losses. Award 1 point if the total is 6 or more, 2 if 14 or more, 3 if 24, 4 if 36, 5 if 50, 6 if 66, 7 if 84.

4) Award 1 point if the pitcher has won 18 or more games. Award 1 point if the pitcher led the league in ERA. Award 1 point if the pitcher led the league in saves.

5) Subtract the pitcher's ERA from the league ERA, and add 1.00. Multiply this by the number of decisions that the pitcher has had, and divide by 13. (What you are doing here is giving credit for a low ERA. This will result in a negative figure—a subtraction—if the pitcher's ERA is more than one run above league. A pitcher's AV cannot be reduced below zero.)

6. Park Adjustment Factors.

AMERICAN LEAGUE

Baltimore	.992	839	Chicago	1.015	609
Detroit	.996	613	Kansas City	1.013	257
New York	.972	519	Texas	.967	582
Toronto	1.057	897	Oakland	.951	423
Milwaukee	.952	357	California	.988	564
Boston	1.048	102	Minnesota	1.038	616
Cleveland	1.013	793	Seattle	1.042	198

NATIONAL LEAGUE

Los Angeles	.969	519	Philadelphia	1.011	135
Atlanta	1.050	551	Pittsburgh	1.039	515
Houston	.919	893	Montreal	1.017	924
San Diego	.951	808	St. Louis	1.022	646
San Francisco	.970	958	Chicago	1.062	921
Cincinnati	1.008	486	New York	.982	987

Park adjustment factors based on five years' data (1979 to 1983) except in cases where the fences have been tampered with. In those cases, only the data since the moving of the fence is used.

7. Cheap Victory.

A cheap victory, for purposes of discussion, is a game in which the pitcher receives credit for a win despite having a game-ERA higher than 4.00, with the following exceptions:

1) A victory should not be labeled cheap on the basis of runs allowed in the late innings which do not endanger the lead. Ignore any runs allowed from the seventh inning on which do not enable the opposition to pull within four runs or a tie.

2) Before figuring the game-ERA, deduct one run for each run that the pitcher himself has driven in or scored.

8. How the Defensive Ratings are Derived.

As I have explained, each defensive player's DW/L% (defensive won/lost percentage) is based on four considerations which differ from position to position. The maximum point levels are deliberately set at almost impossible levels, since for a player to attain those standards would indicate that he was performing at such a level that he should never lose, which is presumed to be as impossible for a fielder as it is for a hitter or a pitcher. In order to receive the maximum 40 points, a catcher must throw out every base runner who attempts to steal against him; a shortstop, to receive the maximum 20 points for fielding average, would have to field 1.000.

The explanation from that point consists of three charts. Chart I explains what the defensive factors considered are. Chart II sketches out the standards for performance evaluation. Chart III explains how these are combined at each position.

CHART I

WHAT THINGS ARE CONSIDERED

For Catchers: The 40 point consideration is opposition stolen bases per game, divided by league opposition stolen bases per game. The 30 point consideration is the ERA of his staff when he is in the lineup, compared to the league ERA. The 20 point consideration is fielding average. The 10 point consideration is assists per game.

For First Basemen: There are three 30-point considerations —fielding average, assists per game, and estimated 3-6-3 double plays. The estimate of 3-6-3 and 3-6-1 double plays (double plays started by the team's first basemen) is formed by taking the team's double play total and subtracting all double plays involving a second baseman or outfielder, and one-half of the DP involving a pitcher. The 10 point consideration (E 5 & 6) is the number of errors turned by the team's third baseman and shortstop, the theory being that a good first baseman can prevent E 5 & 6 by picking out bad throws.

For Second Basemen: The 40 point consideration is double-play percentage (DP%) which is figured by taking the number of double plays turned by the player, dividing by the number of games played, and dividing that by the number of hits plus walks per game allowed by the team. This adjusts raw double-play rates for number of men on base. The 30 point consideration is range index. Range index—this is new this year; in the past I have used range factors here—is the percentage of the team's plays which the player has made. You figure the player's individual range factor, minus double plays per game (RF - DP/G): we don't want to give overlapping credit for the one skill. This you divide by the team's play opportunities per game, a figure taken from the DER estimates. This in effect adjusts range factor for things like playing for a bad team, which means more balls in play, or playing for a team whose pitchers strike out a lot of people, which means fewer balls in play. The outcome is called range index, and it will be used at all the remaining positions. The 20 point consideration for second basemen is fielding average. The 10 point consideration for all players other than first basemen and catchers if the defensive efficiency record of the team for which the fielder plays.

For Third Basemen: The 40 point consideration is range index. The 30 point consideration is fielding percentage. The 20 point consideration is DP%.

For Shortstops: The 40 point consideration is range index. The 30 point consideration is DP%. The 20 point consideration is fielding percentage.

For Outfielders: The 40 point consideration is range index. The 30 point consideration is fielding percentage. The 20 point consideration is the player's career record of assists per 162 outfield games played.

CHART II

WHAT THE STANDARDS ARE

The standards in this chart are derived from an extensive examination of the fielding records of major league leaders over the last ten years. The middle of each chart represents an average performance over that period; anything above 75% represents an unusual performance. It should be stressed that fielding statistics, like all others, change from decade to decade; these statistics, while they might be useful in evaluating fielders from other eras, were not designed for the purpose and in some cases would yield very misleading results if lifted out of their time.

To save space, each notch of the chart is not detailed; if you want to use it, some interpolation will be required.

CHART III

HOW THESE ARE COMBINED

The player's scores on these four counts are added together and become, with the insertion of a decimal point, his defensive won/lost percentage. These percentages are multiplied by a number of "games" which differs according to the position. Per 162 games played, the defensive games assigned to each position are:

1B	LF	RF	3B	CF	2B	C	SS
3	4	5	6	6	8	10	11

This yields a number of defensive wins and losses. These are added to the offensive wins and losses to obtain the player ratings used in Section III.

9. Reservoir Estimation Technique.

The Reservoir Estimation Technique assesses the "Estimated Remaining Approximate Value" or "Trade Value" of each player based on two things: his age, and his current approximate value. His age is converted into a "Y score" by the formula (24–.6 Age). The Y score and the AV are combined:

$$\frac{(AV - Y)}{190} \quad \frac{(Y + 1) X AV}{13} \quad AV (Y)$$

Trade value for pitchers is reduced by 30% from the outcome of this formula.

DEFENSIVE RATINGS CHARTS
POSITION

Standard	Catcher	First B	2nd B	3rd B	Short	Left & Right	Center
40	0.00		0.1337	0.1357	0.1915	0.1155	0.1292
35	0.25		0.1226	0.1249	0.1740	0.0953	0.1132
30	0.50	1.0000(*2)	0.1111	0.1148	0.1603	0.0855	0.1047
25	0.75	.9980	0.1014	0.1044	0.1493	0.0764	0.0963
20	1.00	.9946	0.0919	0.0961	0.1350	0.0671	0.0880
15	1.25	.9928	0.0850	0.0885	0.1229	0.0602	0.0813
10	1.50	.9896	0.0752	0.0788	0.1146	0.0548	0.0731
5	1.75	.9853	0.0651	0.0687	0.1030	0.0488	0.0646
1	1.95	.9790	0.0054	0.0590	0.0964	0.0424	0.0518
30	−1.50	1.14	0.1765	1.000	0.0760	1.000(*3)	1.000
25	−0.65	0.94	0.1675	.985	0.0642	.998	.996
20	−0.25	0.78	0.1600	.970	0.0575	.990	.991
15	0.00	0.63	0.1530	.955	0.0497	.983	.986
10	0.25	0.46	0.1450	.940	0.0422	.969	.976
5	0.65	0.31	0.1340	.925	0.0348	.954	.965
1	1.33	0.10	0.1050	.909	0.0302	.938	.955

Standard	Catcher	First B	2nd B	3rd B	Short	All OUTFIELDERS Over 400 G	Under 40
30		60					
25		45					
20	1.000(*1)	35	1.000	0.0227	1.000	16.2	22.4
15	.994	26	.990	0.0182	.981	13.2	16.4
10	.986	17	.980	0.0141	.966	10.4	10.6
5	.977	9	.970	0.0104	.950	8.8	7.6
1	.968	3	.955	0.0057	.931	4.7	1.5

Standard	Catcher	First B			All Other Positions		
10	1.02	29			.724		
7	0.70	44			.706		
5	0.52	53			.694		
3	0.34	63			.682		
1	0.05	72			.663		